MOTOCOURSE™

THE WORLD'S LEADING GRAND PRIX & SUPERBIKE ANNUAL

CMG
PUBLISHING

CONTENTS

MOTOCOURSE
2007–2008
is published by:
Crash Media Group Ltd
Number One
The Innovation Centre
Silverstone Circuit
Silverstone
Northants NN12 8GX
United Kingdom
Tel: +44 (0)870 3505044
Fax: +44 (0)870 3505088
Email: info@crash.net
Website:
www.crashmediagroup.com

Printed in Italy by
ALSABA industrie grafiche,
Z.I. Belvedere S. Antonio
53034 Colle Val d'Elsa (SI)
Tel: +39 (0)577 905311
Website: www.alsaba.it

ISBN: 978-1905334-22-3

DISTRIBUTORS

Gardners Books
1 Whittle Drive, Eastbourne,
East Sussex, BN23 6QH
Tel: +44 (0)1323 521555
email: sales@gardners.com

Menoshire Ltd
Unit 13
21 Wadsworth Road
Perivale
Middlesex UB6 7LQ
Telephone: +44 (0)20 8566 7344
Fax: +44 (0)20 8991 2439

NORTH AMERICA
Motorbooks International
PO Box 1
729 Prospect Avenue
Osceola
Wisconsin 54020, USA
Telephone: 1 715 294 3345
Fax: 1 715 294 4448

Dust-jacket: Casey Stoner and Ducati were runaway champions in MotoGP.

Title page: 2007 World Superbike Champion James Toseland on his Ten Kate Honda.

Photographs: Gold & Goose

editor
MICHAEL SCOTT

publisher
BRYN WILLIAMS

text editor
IAN PENBERTHY

art editor
STEVE SMALL

design and production
ROSANNE DAVIS
MIKE WESTON

results and statistics
KAY EDGE

sales promotion
SIMON MOORE

office manager
WENDY SALISBURY

chief photographers
GOLD & GOOSE
David Goldman
Gareth Harford
Mirco Lazzari
Patrik Lundin
Telephone +44 (0)20 8444 2448

MotoGP bike illustrations
ADRIAN DEAN
f1artwork@blueyonder.co.uk

Editor's Acknowledgements

The Editor and staff of MOTOCOURSE wish to thank the following for their assistance in compiling the 2007–2008 edition: Marc Petrier (FIM), Paul Butler and Mike Trimby (IRTA), Henny Ray Abrams, Chuck Aksland, Katie Baines, Jerry Burgess, Peter Clifford, Maria Garcia, Isabelle Lariviere, Iain Mackay, Elisa Pavan, Julian Ryder, Roberta Vallorosi, Debbie van Zon, Steve Westlake, Ian Wheeler and Günther Wiesinger, as well as the riders and technicians quoted in this book, Alpinestars, Marlboro and Repsol hospitality staff, and numerous colleagues and friends.

Photographs published in AUTOCOURSE 2007–2008 have been contributed by:
Chief photographers: Gold & Goose; *Contributing photographers:* 2snap – Graeme Brown, Peter J Fox, Friedemann Kirn; Gavan Caldwell; Clive Challinor, Dave Collister; Martin Gelder; Tom Htnatiw/Flick of The Wrist Photography; Martini Lauricello/Cello; John McKenzie; Dave Purves; Neil Spalding; Hidenobu Takeuchi; Mark Walters; Andrew Wheeler.

MOTOCOURSE
www.motocourse.com

Photograph: Gold & Goose

FOREWORD by CASEY STONER

Winning the championship is a dream come true. A dream I've had for almost as long as I can remember. To see my picture on the cover of **MOTOCOURSE** represents the reality of the achievement. As I said after I became champion in Japan, it proves that if you work hard, then dreams do come true.

And we have worked hard. All of us. My family gave up a lot so that I could start my international career, when we had to leave Australia because I wasn't allowed to race there as a teenager. The first years in Britain and Europe were very tough for all of us.

There have been a few people who believed in me and my talent. This championship is like a prize for them as well. And there've been the critics over the years. I'm glad to have proved them wrong.

People ask me about my motivation. I think you can see that it's very strong. I didn't start the season expecting to win the championship. I just tried to win every race I could, and to get the best finish when it wasn't possible. When I had a big points lead and could have played the percentages, I still kept the same approach.

Even after I became champion, nothing changed. I love riding the motorcycle, and I love racing. When I get on the bike, everything else goes out of my mind.

I owe a lot of thanks to a lot of people. To Ducati, of course – first for believing in me, and secondly for building a brilliant motorcycle. We hardly changed it all year.

And to Bridgestone. At the beginning of the year, their tyres were really good, but they never stopped working at continuing to improve.

And to countless people, in the team and associated with it.

And finally to my wife, Adriana. We married at the end of 2006, and she has been with me every inch of the way through this championship.

Changing of the guard? Valentino Rossi congratulates his nemesis, Casey Stoner, at Catalunya.

Photograph: Graeme Brown/2snap

EDITOR'S INTRODUCTION

DON'T PANIC!

FOR anyone who loves motorcycle racing, 2007 was both a wonderful and a worrying year. The red streak that opened and then dominated the season took everybody by surprise, even the rider. Casey Stoner's rise from 2006's gravel trap to 2007's golden tower was as unexpected as anything, in a year of MotoGP surprises. So too was little specialist manufacturer Ducati's signal defeat of the might of Japan. Both were inspirational...

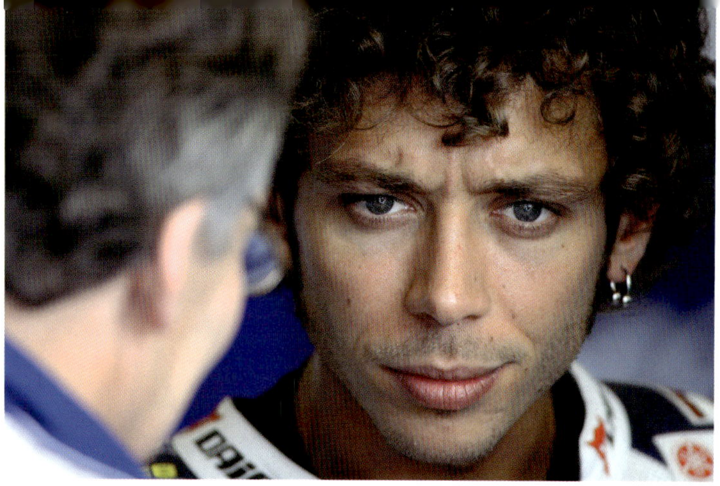

Above: Satellite team men dispute the lower orders: Tech 3 Yamaha and Pramac d'Antin Ducati are at the manufacturers' mercy.

Top left: Rossi, here with crew chief Burgess, remains the star of the show, in spite of his worst season since 1996.

Top right: James Toseland, entering MotoGP in 2008, carries a heavy burden of expectation. The last British champion was Barry Sheene in the 1970s.

Photographs: Gold & Goose

Not all the surprises were as pleasant. Chief among them was that the new 800s were hardly slower than the 990s, probably because of their new electronics, but they were a great deal duller to watch. No power slides, not much wayward braking. And very little overtaking.

As the year wore on and settled into processional racing, the MotoGP establishment reacted with a worrying degree of near panic. It seemed that Dorna didn't feel that MotoGP was strong enough to stand an inevitable spell of adjustment to the new engine size and tyre rules. The radical single-tyre proposal was the symptom, the outcome was for Rossi to blackmail his way on to the newly dominant Bridgestone tyres for 2008.

Given that sponsorships remain slow in coming forward, that the Ilmor team quit after one race and that Team Roberts, the only other true independent, may go too, and looking ahead at what will happen to the fans when Rossi leaves, the worry is understandable. But the affair cut much deeper – to the matter of tampering with the technology to improve the show.

It may be argued that having any technical rules hogties technical advance. If MotoGP really were a true and valuable research tool, the regulations would be much freer. Perhaps a maximum energy allowance, generated and deployed how you will. And, of course, two wheels.

This being so, such restrictive regulations as control tyres, control electronics and even control engine configuration (à la Formula One) are not really radical changes; they simply add detail to the existing restraints. But it was clear from the howls of anguish at the one-tyre proposal that such restrictions would be anathema to most in GP racing.

World racing has a pyramid structure, with MotoGP at the apex. The next tiers are the production-based series – World Superbikes, then national Superbike championships. At this level, many of the restrictions mentioned may be appropriate. World Superbikes already has control tyres, the BSB series is to follow suit in 2008. This not only controls costs, but more importantly, it helps to preserve the show.

The MotoGP show did suffer in 2007, but the pinnacle of the sport is more than only entertainment, and if the need to please the crowd overrules technical development, then we really do need to panic. Racing is also about engineers. It is impossible to imagine that those at Honda in particular, and at Yamaha and Michelin, will repeat the mistakes they made in 2007. Let them get on with it, and let the racing sort itself out.

A final footnote adds a note of gloom, at least for British readers. The 2007 season was the first since the opening World Championship of 1949 was won by Englishman Les Graham that no British rider scored a single point in the premier class. But there is hope as well of future redemption. Englishman James Toseland fully earned his second World Superbike Championship, and in 2008, he joins the Yamaha satellite MotoGP team. He carries a heavy load.

MICHAEL SCOTT
Wimbledon, London
November, 2007

حلبة لوسيل الدولية
LOSAIL INTERNATIONAL CIRCUIT

So Far? Yet So Near

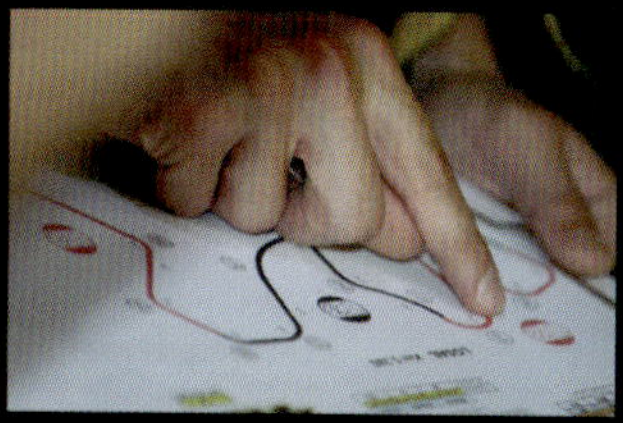

Why chose Losail?

Losail International Circuit is the only circuit in the region with both FIA and FIM homologation licenses.

The state of art circuit inaugurated on October 2004 is fully equipped with the latest facilities and services.

Flood lighting project in progress with the first ever live telecast MotoGP night race scheduled for March 9th 2008.

Friendly & courteous International staff with a professional client oriented approach.

Perfect weather conditions for track activities from October to April, while most of Europe experiences extreme weather.

The circuit is a mere 30 kilometers from Doha International Airport.

The countries flagship carrier, Qatar Airways flies to over 70 destinations worldwide (7 hours flight from London, 6 hours flight from Germany, 10 hours flight from Japan.

Qatar is a perfect tourist destination with world renowned hotel chains such as Ritz Carlton, Intercontinental, Four Seasons, and Marriott etc...

Extremely competitive and attractive hiring rates accompanied with assured exclusivity.

LOSAIL INTERNATIONAL CIRCUIT
Tel + 974 4729 151
Fax + 974 4729 246
info@circuitlosail.com
www.circuitlosail.com
P.O. Box: 4611
Doha, State of Qatar

FIM WORLD CHAMPIONSHIP 2007

TOP TEN RIDERS

The Editor's Choice

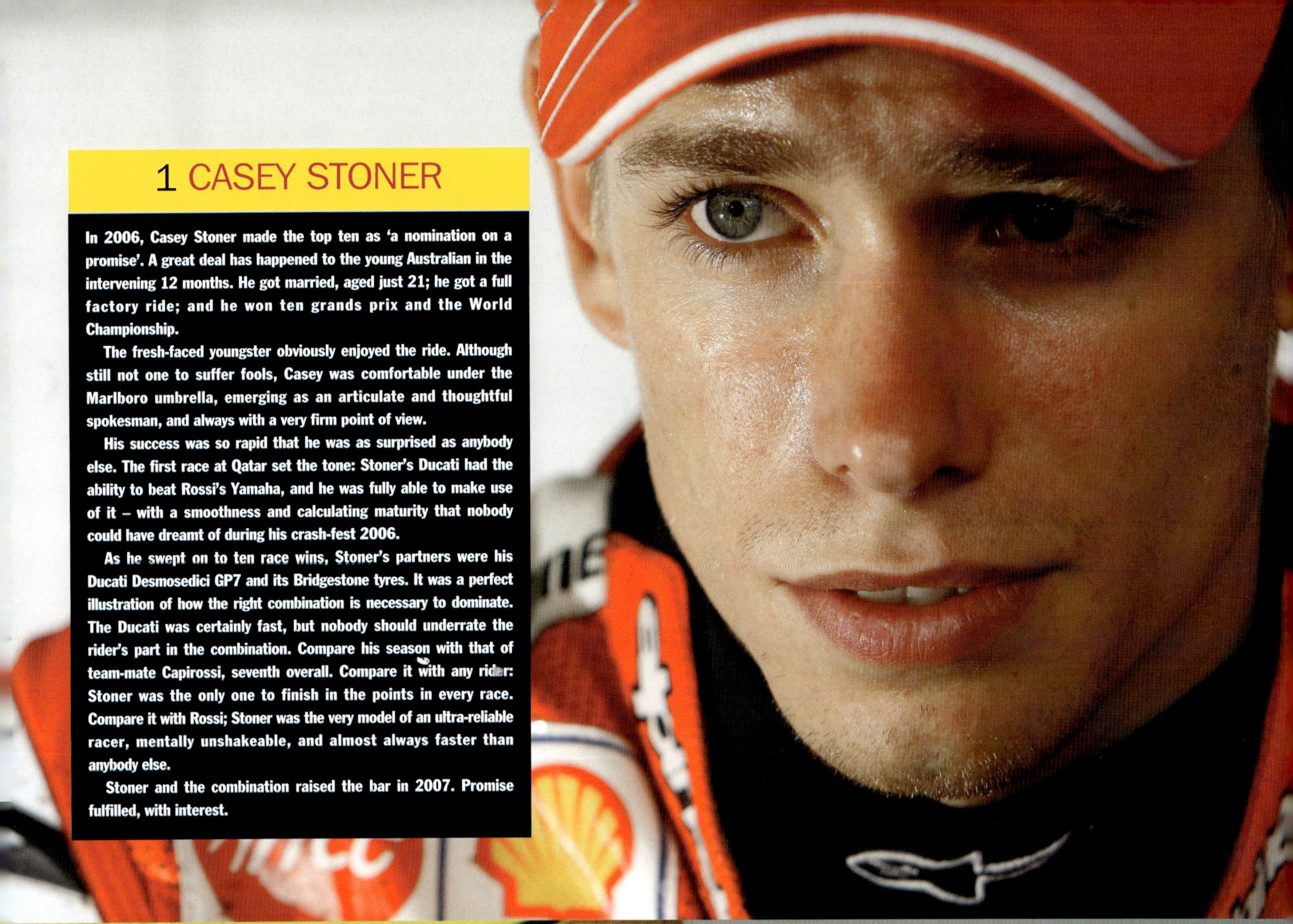

1 CASEY STONER

In 2006, Casey Stoner made the top ten as 'a nomination on a promise'. A great deal has happened to the young Australian in the intervening 12 months. He got married, aged just 21; he got a full factory ride; and he won ten grands prix and the World Championship.

The fresh-faced youngster obviously enjoyed the ride. Although still not one to suffer fools, Casey was comfortable under the Marlboro umbrella, emerging as an articulate and thoughtful spokesman, and always with a very firm point of view.

His success was so rapid that he was as surprised as anybody else. The first race at Qatar set the tone: Stoner's Ducati had the ability to beat Rossi's Yamaha, and he was fully able to make use of it – with a smoothness and calculating maturity that nobody could have dreamt of during his crash-fest 2006.

As he swept on to ten race wins, Stoner's partners were his Ducati Desmosedici GP7 and its Bridgestone tyres. It was a perfect illustration of how the right combination is necessary to dominate. The Ducati was certainly fast, but nobody should underrate the rider's part in the combination. Compare his season with that of team-mate Capirossi, seventh overall. Compare it with any rider: Stoner was the only one to finish in the points in every race. Compare it with Rossi; Stoner was the very model of an ultra-reliable racer, mentally unshakeable, and almost always faster than anybody else.

Stoner and the combination raised the bar in 2007. Promise fulfilled, with interest.

2 VALENTINO ROSSI

Valentino Rossi might have thought things couldn't get much worse after 2006. He was very wrong; 2007 was far and away this gigantic rider's worst year since he first took to GP racing – a lanky, long-haired laughing teenager – in the 125 class in 1996. Since then, he had never finished lower than second in any championship.

It wasn't just the racing. Rossi's whole world was thrown into turmoil mid-summer when the Italian tax authorities swooped. In the coming months, he had to endure taunting by the Italian press, further surprise visits and lurid press leaks by the tax department, and the bitter taste of being thoroughly outclassed in a championship that his many fans regard as his by right.

Rossi bore up well, maintaining his sense of humour, at least in public. By year's end, however, he was fuming about his Yamaha – still seriously down on speed compared with not only the Ducati, but also the Honda and most of the rest – and his Michelin tyres, which too often (and especially at the end of races) were not up to snuff.

And he was still a sublimely brilliant racer, when his machinery and tyres allowed. His win at Mugello was a masterpiece, that at Assen better still. Set those against his headlong crash in Germany and he still comes out well on the credit side.

Rossi may not have long left. One more year of disillusion with Yamaha might prove enough – hence his latest throw of the dice, the switch to Bridgestones for 2008, an anomaly achieved purely through his force of character. As he titled his autobiography: 'What if I had never tried it?'

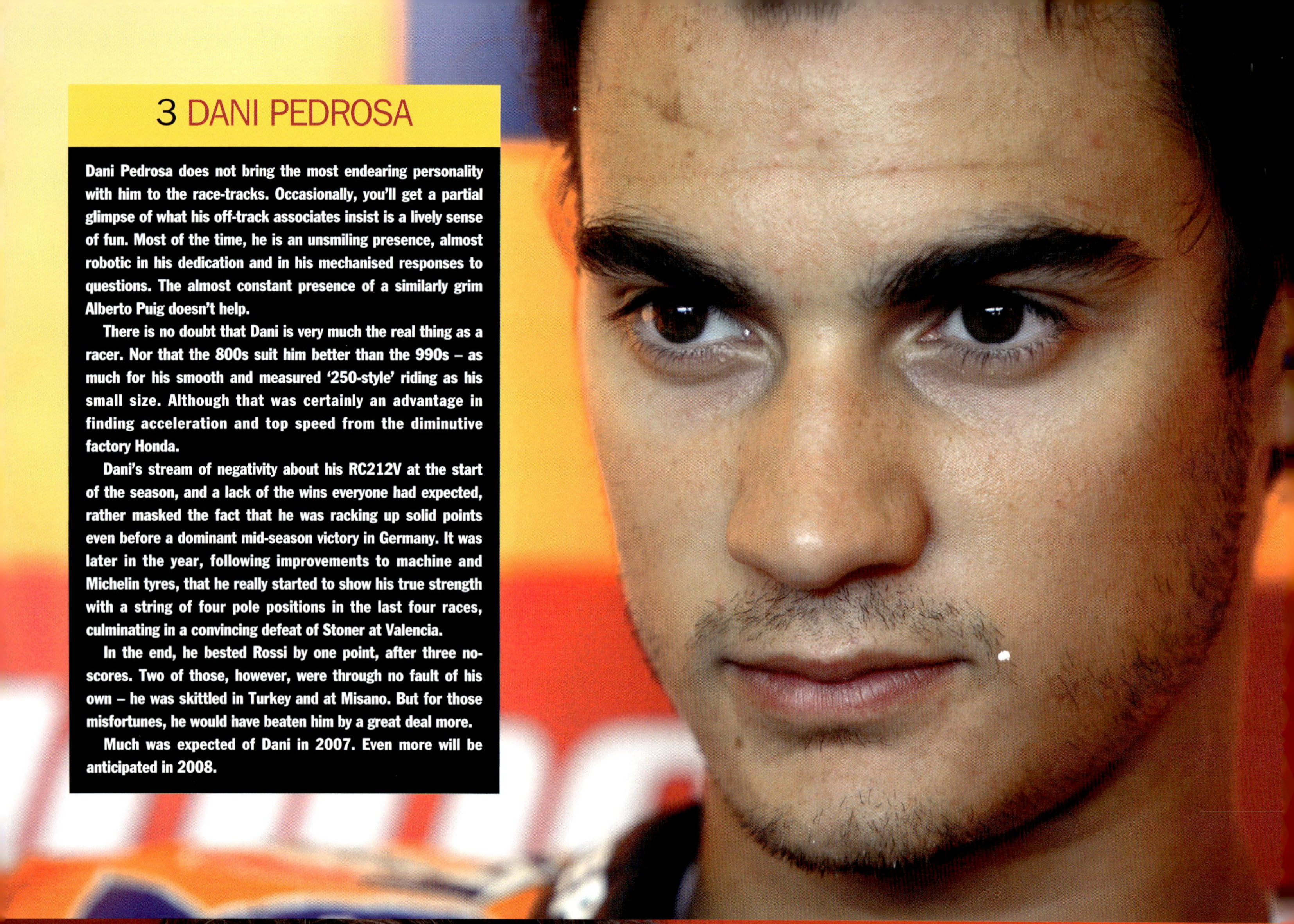

3 DANI PEDROSA

Dani Pedrosa does not bring the most endearing personality with him to the race-tracks. Occasionally, you'll get a partial glimpse of what his off-track associates insist is a lively sense of fun. Most of the time, he is an unsmiling presence, almost robotic in his dedication and in his mechanised responses to questions. The almost constant presence of a similarly grim Alberto Puig doesn't help.

There is no doubt that Dani is very much the real thing as a racer. Nor that the 800s suit him better than the 990s – as much for his smooth and measured '250-style' riding as his small size. Although that was certainly an advantage in finding acceleration and top speed from the diminutive factory Honda.

Dani's stream of negativity about his RC212V at the start of the season, and a lack of the wins everyone had expected, rather masked the fact that he was racking up solid points even before a dominant mid-season victory in Germany. It was later in the year, following improvements to machine and Michelin tyres, that he really started to show his true strength with a string of four pole positions in the last four races, culminating in a convincing defeat of Stoner at Valencia.

In the end, he bested Rossi by one point, after three no-scores. Two of those, however, were through no fault of his own – he was skittled in Turkey and at Misano. But for those misfortunes, he would have beaten him by a great deal more.

Much was expected of Dani in 2007. Even more will be anticipated in 2008.

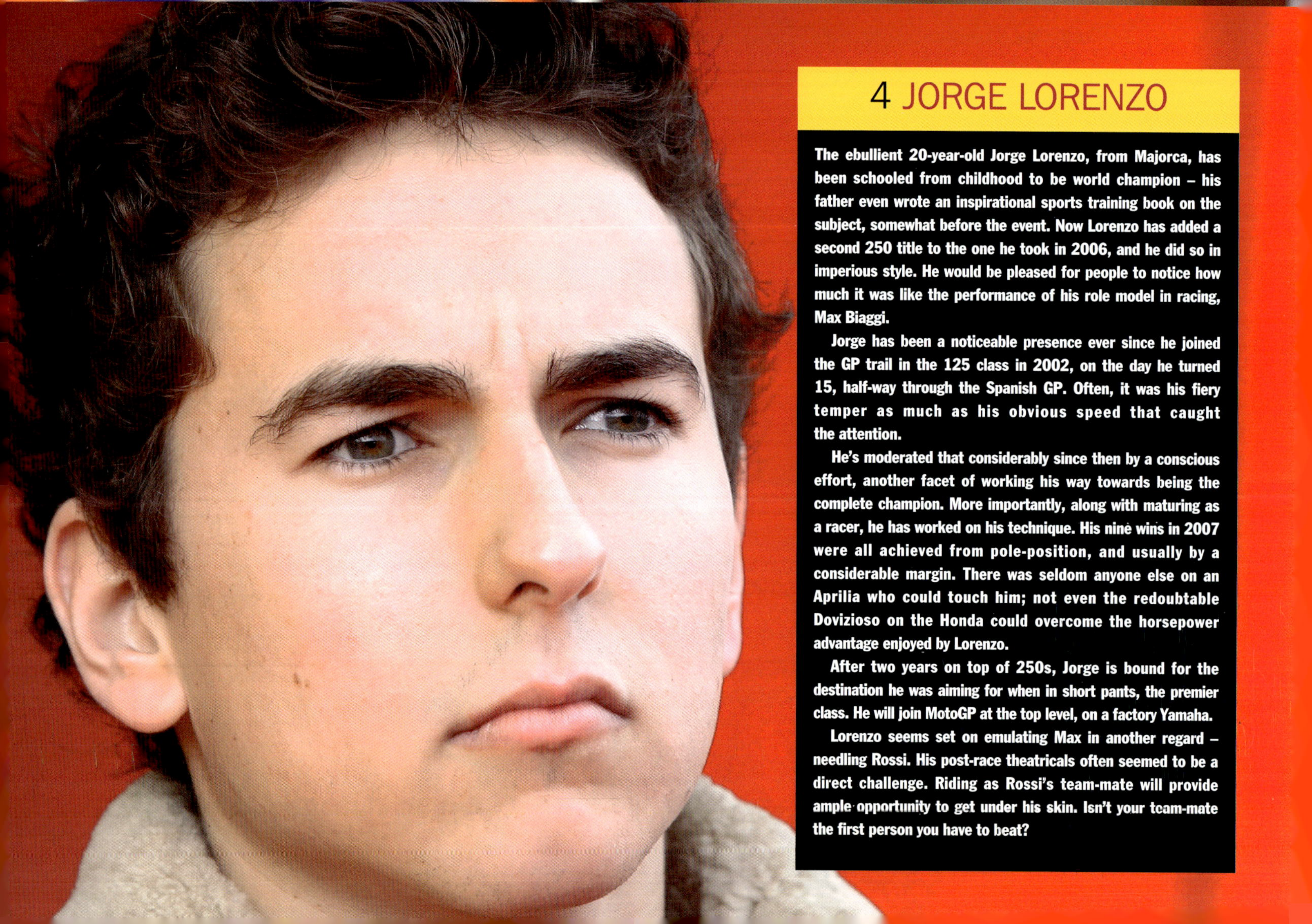

4 JORGE LORENZO

The ebullient 20-year-old Jorge Lorenzo, from Majorca, has been schooled from childhood to be world champion – his father even wrote an inspirational sports training book on the subject, somewhat before the event. Now Lorenzo has added a second 250 title to the one he took in 2006, and he did so in imperious style. He would be pleased for people to notice how much it was like the performance of his role model in racing, Max Biaggi.

Jorge has been a noticeable presence ever since he joined the GP trail in the 125 class in 2002, on the day he turned 15, half-way through the Spanish GP. Often, it was his fiery temper as much as his obvious speed that caught the attention.

He's moderated that considerably since then by a conscious effort, another facet of working his way towards being the complete champion. More importantly, along with maturing as a racer, he has worked on his technique. His nine wins in 2007 were all achieved from pole-position, and usually by a considerable margin. There was seldom anyone else on an Aprilia who could touch him; not even the redoubtable Dovizioso on the Honda could overcome the horsepower advantage enjoyed by Lorenzo.

After two years on top of 250s, Jorge is bound for the destination he was aiming for when in short pants, the premier class. He will join MotoGP at the top level, on a factory Yamaha.

Lorenzo seems set on emulating Max in another regard – needling Rossi. His post-race theatricals often seemed to be a direct challenge. Riding as Rossi's team-mate will provide ample opportunity to get under his skin. Isn't your team-mate the first person you have to beat?

5 JOHN HOPKINS

John Hopkins was probably the most improved rider in the MotoGP class during 2007. Always a conspicuously hard tryer, he had never seemed able to add that touch of polish that would have elevated his performance.

Perhaps his Suzuki was the cause, since it always lacked speed and acceleration, and Hopkins had no option but to ride desperately just to keep up – hard on the brakes and right on the edge of cornering. His aggressive style and lean angles even scraped an elbow now and then. So perhaps it is the bike that made the improvement rather than the rider.

Either way, Hopkins was ready to make the most of it, and his long-awaited career-first podium in China seemed to liberate him still further. The results remained up and down, but the speed and level of effort never slacked, and the rewards came with three more top-three finishes by the end of the year. His lone pursuit of Stoner at Brno was the best race of his life, and fourth overall was a well-earned reward.

Hopkins has had plenty of GP experience, having racked up 96 starts since his debut in 2002. All but one of his years have been with Suzuki, where he has been a loyal team man through a string of bad years. He resisted an approach from Ducati for 2007, which he might have regretted since. Now he must hope his departure to Kawasaki, just as the Suzuki is becoming good again, will be the right move to take him to the next step of challenging for the title.

6 NICKY HAYDEN

The records show that Nicky Hayden's world championship defence was dismal from the start, but he never buckled, and he never stopped working hard and trying hard. His final position would have been better had he not been knocked sideways by other riders in China, the USA and San Marino; and certainly if his engine had not failed while he was lying a strong second in Australia. And he probably would not have fallen in France and England if he had not been pushing desperately to overcome clear weaknesses in the machine.

Honda denied that it had built its smallest-ever MotoGP bike (at least since the tiny first 990 prototype) with Pedrosa in mind, but it certainly had not catered for Hayden, who admitted mid-season that when HRC said as much, 'that pretty much broke my heart.'

One of three racing brothers from Kentucky, Hayden towered over the machine, even as he tried to tuck himself in while searching for the missing top speed. Ever the natural gentleman, he couched his complaints carefully, and his loyalty to Honda never wavered. He was another to resist an approach from Ducati for 2007, but he was under no illusion that HRC will repay his loyalty if he does not come up with strong results in 2008.

Hayden is a rider who relies as much on application as on natural talent; nobody puts more hours and more effort into it. There's a rare intensity to the man. The remarkable thing is how it never spills over to get in the way of the most natural and human personality of them all.

7 CHRIS VERMEULEN

Australian Chris Vermeulen had a patchy year, and in some ways didn't seem to sustain the progress of 2006 – but overall, this was deceptive. He had some weak points, which tended to mask his real strength and depth.

His biggest problem always came in qualifying, and resultant poor grid positions – at 11 of 18 races, he didn't even make the third row. But he has always been a rider who puts genuine progress before flamboyance, and his racing performance was almost always well measured and to the limits of his machine. If only he hadn't always had so many places to make up.

Wet weather is another measure of riding skill, and in this respect, he excelled, taking pole in the wet at Assen, a clear first GP win at Le Mans and a third at Donington Park. His pair of dry-weather second places, in the USA and at Misano, were more important, showing in his second year in the class that he is developing the pace to be fully competitive.

In the end, he was out-pointed by team-mate Hopkins and by Melandri, although sixth was still a respectable finish. But the outwardly relaxed and approachable rider needs to sort out his grid positions to make the most of his obvious talent.

It's tough at the top, and Vermeulen needs to do better still in 2008, otherwise he might start getting a 'nearly-man' reputation.

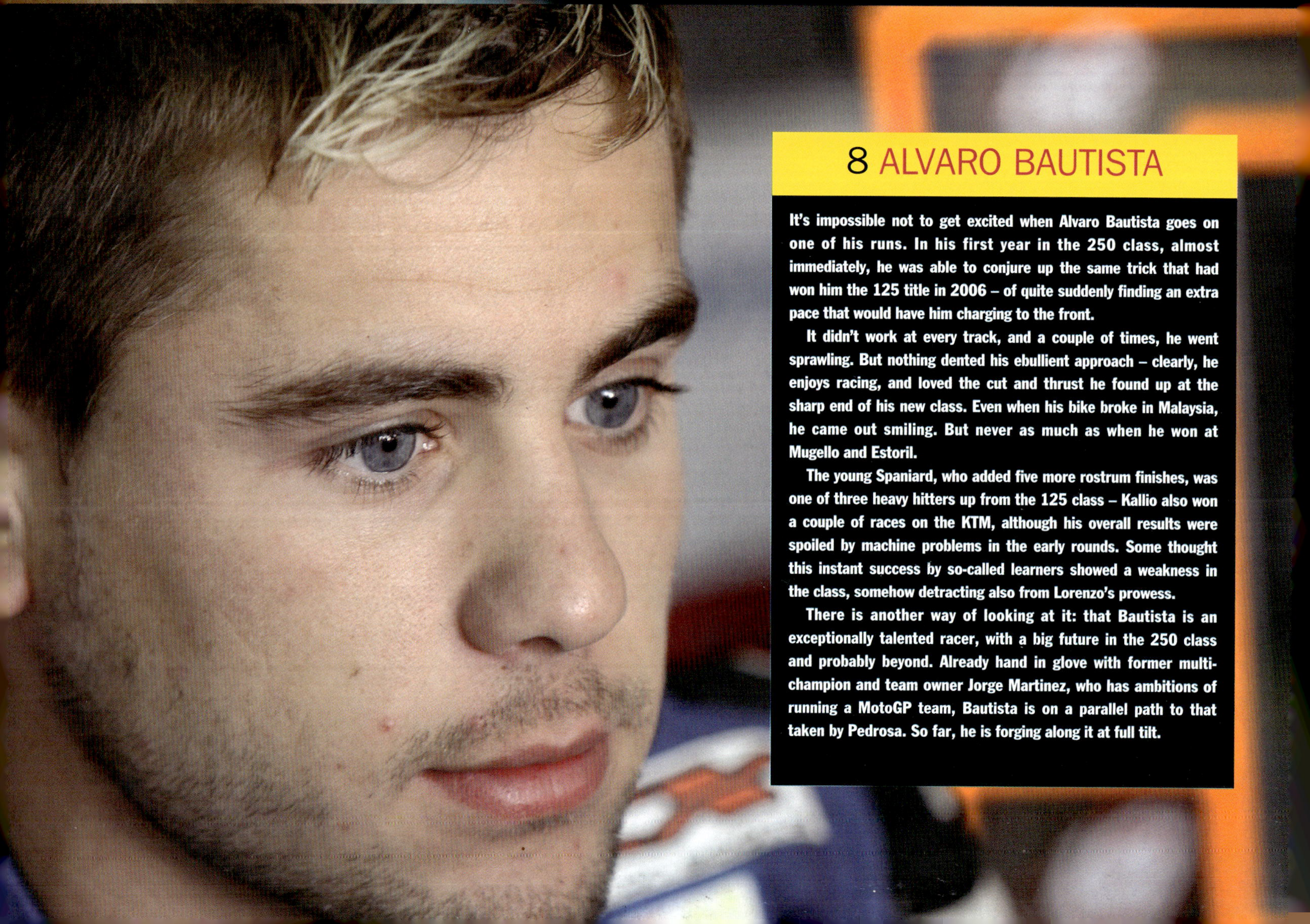

8 ALVARO BAUTISTA

It's impossible not to get excited when Alvaro Bautista goes on one of his runs. In his first year in the 250 class, almost immediately, he was able to conjure up the same trick that had won him the 125 title in 2006 – of quite suddenly finding an extra pace that would have him charging to the front.

It didn't work at every track, and a couple of times, he went sprawling. But nothing dented his ebullient approach – clearly, he enjoys racing, and loved the cut and thrust he found up at the sharp end of his new class. Even when his bike broke in Malaysia, he came out smiling. But never as much as when he won at Mugello and Estoril.

The young Spaniard, who added five more rostrum finishes, was one of three heavy hitters up from the 125 class – Kallio also won a couple of races on the KTM, although his overall results were spoiled by machine problems in the early rounds. Some thought this instant success by so-called learners showed a weakness in the class, somehow detracting also from Lorenzo's prowess.

There is another way of looking at it: that Bautista is an exceptionally talented racer, with a big future in the 250 class and probably beyond. Already hand in glove with former multi-champion and team owner Jorge Martinez, who has ambitions of running a MotoGP team, Bautista is on a parallel path to that taken by Pedrosa. So far, he is forging along it at full tilt.

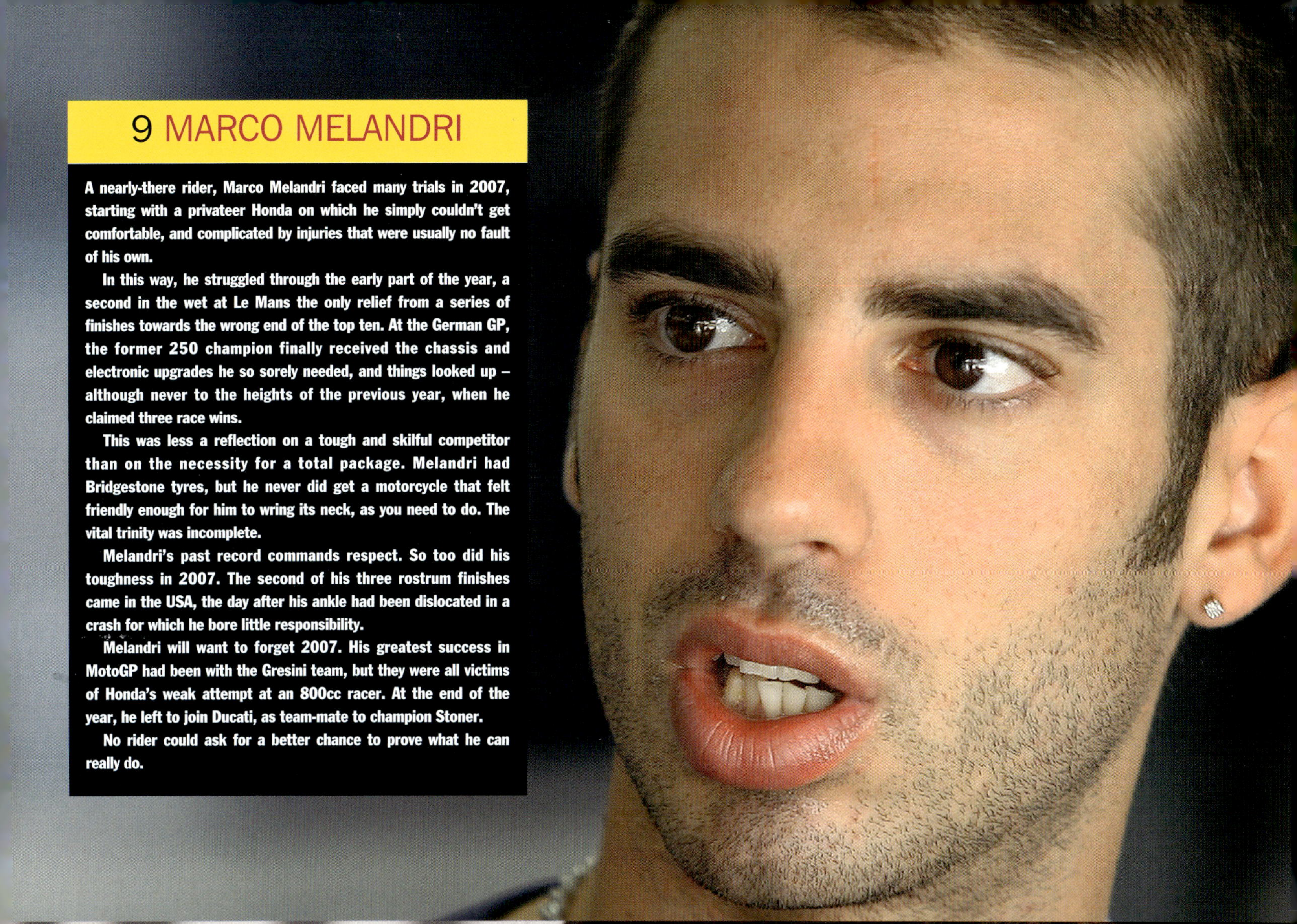

9 MARCO MELANDRI

A nearly-there rider, Marco Melandri faced many trials in 2007, starting with a privateer Honda on which he simply couldn't get comfortable, and complicated by injuries that were usually no fault of his own.

In this way, he struggled through the early part of the year, a second in the wet at Le Mans the only relief from a series of finishes towards the wrong end of the top ten. At the German GP, the former 250 champion finally received the chassis and electronic upgrades he so sorely needed, and things looked up – although never to the heights of the previous year, when he claimed three race wins.

This was less a reflection on a tough and skilful competitor than on the necessity for a total package. Melandri had Bridgestone tyres, but he never did get a motorcycle that felt friendly enough for him to wring its neck, as you need to do. The vital trinity was incomplete.

Melandri's past record commands respect. So too did his toughness in 2007. The second of his three rostrum finishes came in the USA, the day after his ankle had been dislocated in a crash for which he bore little responsibility.

Melandri will want to forget 2007. His greatest success in MotoGP had been with the Gresini team, but they were all victims of Honda's weak attempt at an 800cc racer. At the end of the year, he left to join Ducati, as team-mate to champion Stoner.

No rider could ask for a better chance to prove what he can really do.

10 LORIS CAPIROSSI

The second-oldest rider on the grid, Loris Capirossi had a poor season compared with the previous year, and worst of all was how lacklustre his performance appeared compared with that of his team-mate, Stoner. He suffered greatly throughout the year from this, a psychological disadvantage that made his task all the harder.

Capirossi's biggest problem, it seemed, was with the same motorcycle on which Stoner found it so easy to win. The peaky, edgy nature of the four-pulse 800cc engine, compared with the torquey twin-pulse 990, simply didn't suit his fast-and-loose riding style. Ducati did build him a mid-range special for the Italian GP, and that solved the problem – but at the expense of so much top speed that it wasn't worth further development.

Loris's bad days were highly forgettable, but on his good days, he was like his old self. His victory at Motegi was tactical, it's true, but his other three rostrum finishes – especially second places in Germany and Australia – were achieved with trade-mark vivacity. Clearly, on those days, he still enjoyed racing to the full.

Loris became a father during the year, but this seemed to have little effect on his competitive nature. He will join Suzuki for 2008, for yet another fresh start, and if he really can keep the fire burning as brightly as he promises, in what will be the cheerful veteran's 18th full GP season, he should be fun to watch.

STATE OF RACING

POLITICS AND TYRES

By MICHAEL SCOTT

Above: Teeming with corporate guests and paying fans, the paddock at Barcelona.

Top right: Carmelo Ezpeleta – a swaggering attack on the status quo.

Centre right: Tyre summit group, from left: Dunlop's Jeremy Ferguson, Michelin's Jean-Philippe Weber, Bridgestone's Hiroshi Yamada.

Bottom right: Fixing his Michelin with a steely glare – Rossi at Le Mans.
Photograph: Neil Spalding

THERE once was a time when, as Mike Hailwood famously remarked, tyres were simply 'round and black'. By 2007, they had become a great deal more than that. It was over a question of tyres that the series was held to ransom, by one rider. Such is the power of that rider, Valentino Rossi, that the establishment was turned upside-down. If the strange events of 2007 were not completely at his behest, they were certainly on his behalf.

Use this as an example of the State of Racing, and it is impossible not to find something pitiful. MotoGP has many of the outward trappings of success: ever-greater TV coverage and popularity, record crowds, wider recognition. But there are still holes in the fabric, and it took only a few worrying events to push Dorna's chief, Carmelo Ezpeleta, into drastic action. It looked very much as though he was running scared.

The story unfolded in a year of radical change – only the second such in 59 years of the World Championship, and the second under Dorna's control. The first was in 2002, with the introduction of the 990cc four-stroke MotoGP monsters; the second was 2007's hobbling of the apparently too-powerful new creations with a 20-per-cent cut in cubic capacity.

This was intended to make the class safer by limiting the increase in top speeds. The law of unintended consequence, however, came into effect straight away.

To the surprise of all, the new 800s immediately challenged, and frequently beat, the 990cc lap times. During the year, pole position was faster on five occasions, the lap record broken five times, and most remarkably, the overall race time beaten at seven races.

Top speeds had been curtailed slightly; the lap times came from higher corner speeds, sometimes more than ten per cent faster, the data showed. This came as a surprise to many of the engineers. The bikes had the same minimum weight, after all, and broadly similar chassis design and tyres. The major change was less torque. It was hard to understand, let alone explain, why they actually went faster around the same corners. It also made the safety aspect highly questionable. Most accidents happen in corners, and the new bikes were going around them faster than before.

That was just the start of it. By an unfortunate confluence of circumstances, Dorna departed from one of the golden rules of racing development for the 2007 season. It changed two things at the same time. The second alteration was the new tyre rule. And that took the blame for pretty much everything.

The rule had been a long time in formulation. In 2004, Dorna had first asked the three tyre companies – then-dominant Michelin, 2002 newcomer Bridgestone and the struggling Dunlop – to agree a formula to limit tyre costs. Eventually, they elected to limit tyre numbers: 18 front and 24 rear. Then Michelin pulled out of the agreement, in response to Bridgestone's use of test teams. The proposal was torn up, and the whole of 2005 was spent bickering. In 2006, Ezpeleta set a deadline: decide by the British GP, or we will impose restrictions of our own. At the 11th hour, the companies agreed on the 2007 rules – broadly a modification of their original agreement. This meant an allocation of 31 tyres for the weekend, 14 front and 17 rear, to be selected in advance on Thursday evening.

In the 2006 edition of MOTOCOURSE, we observed in these pages that this removed Michelin's home-territory advantage: that of being able to make special track- and weather-specific tyres after the start of practice, and ship them overnight to tracks in Europe – a facility obviously not available to Japan-based Bridgestone, although Dunlop had done the same in the past. What nobody anticipated was the other advantages that would accrue to Bridgestone.

Ever since 2002, Bridgestone had been obliged to make something like the opposite of track-specific tyres. Having its production facility so far away dictated a quite different approach. Of necessity, tyre development was aimed more towards a broader spectrum of performance, from both rubber compounds and construction. The Japanese manufacturer needed to make tyres that would work well in a wider range of temperatures and conditions. In 2007, it received the pay-off. While Michelin struggled to adapt its basic approach, and the company really did struggle, Bridgestone reaped the benefits of a range of tyres whose windows of performance were often so broad that they overlapped. In this way, tyre choice was much less critical for Bridgestone users, while Michelin's range was

very much hit, or miss by miles.

The tyre rules, or at least Michelin's problem with the rules, took the blame for a series of processional races. This was the case even when Michelin won, as in Germany – that only further proved (ran the argument) that the pre-destination of the tyre performance was resulting in races where riders on rival tyres were unable to battle it out. The sport and especially the spectators were the losers. It was a worrying thought for Dorna, and falling viewer figures mid-season (Spain's expected Pedrosa fever being somewhat in remission) only added impetus.

The riders' viewpoint was even more acute. If being beaten in this way was a new experience for Michelin, whose brand-new director of motorcycle racing, Jean-Philippe Weber, could hardly have chosen a less auspicious time to take up the post, it was worse for the hapless pilots. And while the tyre company could afford to take a longer view, to find a way to regroup and fight back, the riders had their careers to think of. In some cases, notably Rossi's, they did not have much time to play with. He couldn't afford to wait, while Pedrosa couldn't be bothered to. The pair were at the forefront of growing pressure on Yamaha and Honda to switch to Bridgestone for 2008.

Apparently, neither factory had a problem with turning its back on years of success with Michelin, and both approached Bridgestone after the US GP, only to be told no. Bridgestone, already supplying ten riders, did not have the production capacity. Honda and its riders, faced with little choice, eventually came to terms, reassured not only by promises of increased investment by Michelin, but also by improvements towards the end of the season. But Rossi, it transpired, wouldn't take no for an answer. And he had a powerful ally in Dorna's Ezpeleta, well aware of the star potential of probably the most widely recognised rider in the history of the sport.

These were the triggers for his swaggering attack on the status quo.

It came shortly before final qualifying at Motegi. The day before, the tyre companies had presented Dorna with their own proposals – mainly concerning increased testing (ironically, proposals that were adopted, by and large, for the final new rules). Ezpeleta's idea ignored them completely. It was for a single-tyre rule, and he needed a decision from the GP Commission within four weeks, in time for the Grand Prix Commission meeting scheduled for Malaysia.

That put the cat among the pigeons, and then shook the tree as well. This may have been Ezpeleta's only intention, for he was on record from earlier in the year as deploring the notion of control tyres. Asked in Istanbul whether it would not secure closer racing, his reply was plain: 'Of course it would, and with the same bike and the same helmet...and that was called the MoviStar Activa Cup. But this is the World Championship, not a promotion cup. That is why I do not support a single tyre supplier. For me, the ideal is that the championship should be multi-brand in all, because competition serves to better the products.' In the end, he regained that principle, but there was a lot of muddy water to flow under the bridge, and whether it was by accident or design, we cannot know.

Publicly, the tyre companies came up with a modified proposal, increasing the tyre numbers. Meanwhile, meeting rooms were buzzing in Tokyo, Clermont-Ferrand, Brussels and Madrid. The full details will also probably never be known, but when everybody assembled three weeks later in Australia, the heat had gone right out of the discussion. It seemed likely that the proposal would be voted down, thanks (among other things) to a pledge from Michelin to increase investment and redouble its efforts. The only note of disquiet came from rumours concerning Rossi. It seemed he still wasn't happy.

It all blew up again a week later, in Malaysia. Firstly, the Rossi story. Even during race weekend, it seemed, negotiations were in progress. If you can call them negotiations, rather than blackmail. According to Bridgestone, it was more like an ultimatum, delivered by Ezpeleta: give Rossi your tyres, or we will impose the single-tyre rule, with Michelin as the supplier.

Thus, the matter was decided. The planned meeting of IRTA to discuss which way to vote on the tyre proposal was cancelled, when Dorna said that the proposal needed further refinement. No vote was possible. The matter was struck off the agendas of the MSMA meeting and that of the GP Commission. Within the next few days, Dorna publicly announced that the single-tyre proposal had been withdrawn altogether. At Valencia, new 2008 tyre rules were announced: numbers up by nine, with 18 fronts and 22 rears; pre-testing at new or resurfaced circuits; plus the opportunity for each tyre manufacturer to nominate one track off the calendar as a test circuit, although only for four days' use after the race has been held there. And over the following weeks, confirmation came gradually of what everyone already knew: in 2008, Rossi alone of all the Yamahas will be on Bridgestone tyres.

In this way, the fall-out of Ezpeleta's interference in the tyre war adds much spice to the prospects for 2008. Can Bridgestone retain a technical lead that was already under threat at the final race? Has Rossi timed his 'what-if-I'd-never-tried-it' move badly? Will the tyres suit the Yamaha? How will Yamaha deal with having their factory team and pit divided by a 'Berlin wall': Rossi's Bridgestone camp on one side, Lorenzo's Michelins on the other? And will this schism affect the M1's development, itself an urgent matter?

There was one major casualty – Dunlop. After two years of investment, supporting the satellite Yamaha Tech 3 team, the Anglo-Japanese-American company had run out of options. Part of Yamaha's agreement in moving Edwards to Tech 3 had been that the American, a long-serving and valued Michelin tyre tester, would be on the French tyres. Dunlop wanted to continue, and indeed will continue its domination of the 250 and 125 classes, but there was no team available.

Dunlop's progress in two years had been significant, bearing in mind that it had just two riders and had started from a long way behind. By the end of 2007, the yellow bikes – ridden by class rookie Guintoli and fading former Japanese star Makoto Tamada – were becoming increasingly competitive. The yardstick had always been Colin Edwards, as a Yamaha rider on Michelins, and to rule out the Rossi factor. At the final race in Valencia, both Dunlop riders out-qualified Edwards, both being on the second row of the grid, and Guintoli beat him in the race, finishing 11th to Edwards's 13th, while Tamada was just two places down. There was some satisfaction also that 12th place went to Checa, who had abandoned Dunlop to ride a Honda on Michelins.

Below: Stoner stretched everybody's legs, and spaced them out.
Photograph: Gold & Goose

WHATEVER HAPPENED TO CLOSE RACING?

Tyres took the blame, but surely there were many other reasons for a spell of processional races, in sharp contrast to the give-and-take of the last year of the 990s.

One was the nature of the new motorcycles. Dropping the power had sharpened the razor's edge, both in terms of performance and technique. Riders at all levels spoke wistfully of the greater margin of error that the 990 had offered, mainly because of the towering torque available in the mid-range. 'You could make a mistake, then gas it up and make up for it,' as Hayden said.

The 800s had no such margin. Rather, they made fast lap times by super-accurate riding, following the perfect line, keeping the wheels in line, minimising wheelspin. Corner speeds were higher, approach speeds slightly lower, both of which compressed the braking zone. All of these served to make overtaking difficult. Two-wheeled Formula One, said some.

There was a greater culprit than the engine size and the rubber, however. It was the proliferation of electronics that was keeping the wheels so faithfully in line. The same thing would have happened to the 990s. Ultimately, smoother is always faster, no matter what the engine size. And progress is progress. The stop-watch tells us so.

There was another facet, revealed by very close practice times. Far from giving better riders a chance to escape, and in spite of being more exacting, the 800s were easier to ride to the limit. This was another consequence of the electronics, but it flattered to deceive. At times, it may have kept the mid-field closer together, but it didn't make overtaking any easier.

Traction control and its close cousin, anti-wheelie launch control, clearly played as great a part in this secondary development as the smaller engines, if not greater. Once again, what is this if not progress?

Technical advancement is a major reason for factories to go racing. It's a proving ground for their best engineers, and a forcing house for new ideas. And it's all grounded in reality. Unlike cars, motorcycle technology benefits from a very close and direct link between grand prix prototypes and road-going sports machines. Ducati even made a road bike of its Desmosedici, launched at Mugello; and there is much about Yamaha's M1 that will be familiar to riders of the same company's R1.

The benefit of racing goes in the other direction – down to the street bikes. As well as beam chassis, one signal example is the mixed-compound tyre. Developed in grand prix racing, this is now available for the road. Wheelie and traction control are surely headed down the same path. This is what makes racing worthwhile, rather than mere music hall.

It was easy to see, however, that technical progress had changed racing a great deal. Those couple of years of push-and-shove, and rough-and-tumble of the 990s were over. Instead, race order was generally established early in the afternoon, especially up at the front. Without the Formula One joker of pit stops to shuffle it around, it can make a rather austere spectacle.

People started looking for other solutions. Inevitably, these had Luddite overtones – top of the list: ban traction control. To do this would certainly restore the wheelspin and tyre smoke of the early 990s, and hand something back to the riders as well. In short, it would improve the racing. But it would be a first step down a dangerous path. Taking the progress out of grand prix would also take the point out of it. How long would the factories remain interested then?

There was one other culprit, perhaps two – a pair of 21-year-olds, born a month apart. Pedrosa was one, but mainly it was Stoner. His racing technique was formidable, reminiscent of Doohan, and Spencer before him. Blindingly fast from the start, he simply stretched everyone's legs as they tried to chase him. It was this as much as any tyres or electronics that made for processional racing.

The truth is that at the highest level of any motor sport, rough-and-tumble is the exception rather than the rule. The knock-about 990s were an aberration, and they would soon have fallen into line.

FEEDING THE NEED FOR SPEED

Want to be a motorcycle grand prix racer when you grow up? The route became a little easier in 2007 – for the lucky 23. They were culled from more than 1,000 internet applicants to the Red Bull Rookies Cup, launched at the first European GP of the year, at Jerez, and running over eight rounds all the way to the last one at Valencia.

This combination of recruiting drive and promotional series

caught the imagination from the start, although not necessarily in a good way. Many felt a sense of unease at riders as young as 13 (the maximum age is 16) dicing handlebar to handlebar at a world-championship event. What if one were to crash and be badly badly hurt?

Thankfully, that didn't happen in the first year of the series, and the thought ebbed from the front of the mind as highly entertaining racing threw up some notable young talent. Held on Saturday, in strict, almost-military conditions (the mechanics, all with matching tool trolleys, marched out into the pit lane, then lined up inch-perfect along its length), the Rookies Cup became an enjoyable diversion.

And, after all, if they were not racing here, these teenagers from all over the world (all of Europe, Britain and the USA were represented) would be racing somewhere else, where it would be just as easy to crash and get hurt, and where it's a good bet that the safety and medical facilities would fall a long way short of MotoGP standards.

Overseen by Dani Pedrosa's 'Svengali' and general recruiting master, Alberto Puig, as well as long-time racing team boss and two-stroke guru Harald Bartol, the series also employed ex-125 GP winner August Auinger, as a sort of resident uncle to the young riders. This structure kept the parents in the background, while the kids were given identical KTM GP 125s to race on.

A couple of regular stars did emerge. Eventually, the title was a runaway win for French teen Johann Zarco, while others impressed, including spirited young Italian Lorenzo Savadori and English rider Matthew Hoyle, who were second and third overall. Another to catch the eye was a young American, Cameron Beaubier. He finished sixth overall, although, as Bartol pointed out, the range of experience and ability was quite wide at such a young age, and the title results weren't everything, in assessing which riders to keep on in 2008, which to move on to the Dorna Academy, and which to discard.

The significance was in the recruitment potential – the net cast ever younger and ever wider in an initiative driven by Puig, as a natural extension of his earlier Spain-based junior series, which yielded, among others, Dani Pedrosa and Toni Elias. At the same time, Red Bull (for whom the mix of youth and risk is a fine marketing mix) took over backing of the Dorna Academy, which is the next stage for a young rider. And the feed of youngsters from the academy is already well established in the 125 class, Bradley Smith and 2007's new Briton, Danny Webb, being just two examples.

There are other ways into MotoGP. Winning the World Superbike Championship (like Edwards and Bayliss) always helps. James Toseland is the latest to follow this path, also with two SBK titles in his pocket. His immediate predecessor, Chris Vermeulen, adapted to MotoGP quickly enough; we will see how well James accomplishes the same trick, which obviously is not as easy as one might expect.

The hopes of many will ride with him – of all those racers older than 16, who have missed out on joining in the direct-path escalator provided by Dorna and Red Bull, which has been so successful that in 2008, it is set for a secondary series in the United States.

NORIFUMI ABE

7 September, 1975–7 October, 2007

On an October Sunday, a fortnight after the Japanese GP, Norifumi Abe died in hospital, the victim of a futile traffic accident two hours before in Kawasaki City. His scooter had been in collision with a truck, said to have turned illegally. The racing world mourned a favourite member and grand prix winner – and a well-loved pioneer of the Japanese presence in top-level racing.

'Norick', aged 32, won the hearts of many when he burst to attention as a wild-card at his home GP in 1994. Long hair flailing, he had electrified the Suzuka crowd as he disputed the lead with class masters Doohan and Schwantz. Until it ended in a spectacular crash at Turn One with three laps to go.

He so impressed Yamaha and Kenny Roberts that he was drafted into the team mid-year, after Daryl Beattie was injured, and he was retained for the factory team. He repaid Yamaha and cemented his heroic status in Japan by winning at Suzuka in 1996, the first of three GP wins in a grand prix career that lasted until 2004, all with Yamaha. Then Abe spent two years in World Superbikes, and in 2007 made a hugely popular return to racing in Japan, his Yamaha lying third in the All-Japan JSB1000 series.

Norick was widely loved for his ready, if shy, smile and fun-loving nature, as well as for his courageous riding. Partly through the barrier of language, he remained an enigmatic character to Westerners, although he was a national hero at home. He was also a hard-working racer, who pioneered the trend for riders to train on US dirt tracks, having spent a season in California directly after leaving school.

Tributes poured in for the fallen rider, including one from Yamaha President Takashi Kajikawa, who described him as 'an irreplaceable ambassador of motor sports worldwide.'

Above: **Top teen – Red Bull rookie champion Zarco.**

Above left: **No summer holiday for the young ones – Zarco leads the pack.**

Left: **British teenager Bradley Smith, on the podium for the first time, tastes the fruits of success.**

Photographs: Gold & Goose

TECHNICAL REVIEW

TALE OF THE UNEXPECTED

With a new capacity limit, and new restrictions on fuel and tyres, the MotoGP teams faced a steep learning curve in 2007. Neil Spalding explains.

Above: Mixed compounds: tread bands show clearly as Rossi's crew do a quick tyre swap.

Photograph: Neil Spalding

THE 2007 season was a watershed in motorcycle racing. Major regulation changes had been put in place to stimulate the competition. It is fair to say that the result wasn't quite what anybody expected.

The creation of MotoGP for 2002 deliberately omitted the cubic capacity of the competing engines. All that really mattered was that they be noisy, four-stroke and crazily powerful. In that first era, the 990s evolved from being mildly over-powered and under-controlled four-strokes to extremely over-powered and quite well-controlled four-strokes. The 800s were meant to re-establish the levels: with less power, they would be out of shape less often, and theoretically safer.

The new capacity was also sufficiently different to require everybody to design a new motorcycle. From what we have seen, the first-year 800s were making similar horsepower to the first-year 990s, but the vastly improved electronic controls made the bikes seem less out of control.

At the same time as the 20-per-cent capacity cut, two other rule changes occurred. Fuel capacity was further restricted, from the 22 litres of the last 990s to 21 litres, and tyre numbers and choices were severely restricted, an all-new system being devised by the tyre companies themselves. Both turned out to have quite an effect on the season.

In short, the new tyre rule restricted numbers to 31 for the weekend – 14 front and 17 rear (including qualifying tyres) – to be selected on Thursday evening before turning a wheel. Wet-weather tyres were not included. Only Michelin and Bridgestone were affected; Dunlop would have no constraints, until it won two dry-weather GPs.

The background was complex, and the influence on the season profound.

The rule change was an effort to control costs as the competition between main contenders Michelin and Bridgestone became fiercer. With most races in Europe, Michelin's ability to build narrow-focus, race-specific tyres in France on Saturday, in response to data gathered on Friday, had been a successful strategy. Bridgestone, with its factories in Japan, had to make its choices weeks before the race, depending on the best weather and track condition reports available. To compete, it had to bring large numbers of tyres to each race, to be sure of meeting all possible requirements. To counteract Michelin's local advantage, Bridgestone sponsored several test teams, able to run MotoGP bikes at upcoming circuits in the weeks before races. Michelin baulked at the cost of competing on that front, agreeing to the new 31-tyre rule as quid pro quo for the confining of these test teams.

The new restrictions prevented MotoGP bikes from testing at any GP circuit in advance of a race, although you will note that other bikes could do so.

By making a selection on the Thursday, the teams are forced into gambling, firstly on the condition of the circuit, the tarmac surface of which changes according to its use over the previous year; and secondly on the precise weekend weather conditions and track temperature. This rewards a tyre company's research and resulting ability to predict the state of the tarmac.

Restricting the number of tyres rewards the chemists who can come up with rubber compounds that work over the broadest set of conditions, especially with a track that isn't in the condition expected, and with race-day track surface temperatures 10 or 15 degrees different from predictions. Top riders have always had an expectation that if there are only a few 'right' tyres, then they will get them, but those tyres are only right because they are particularly suited to the track and weather conditions. Pre-selection means that such narrow-focus tyres simply don't exist, making the racing theoretically more egalitarian, and the racing and qualifying closer.

Bridgestone won the tyre war resoundingly, but not perhaps for the reasons you would have expected initially. One of Bridgestone's strengths was compounds that worked better over wider temperature ranges and on more varied surfaces that the Michelin equivalents.

Michelin appears to have made a fundamental design error in the early stages of the year, by making a tyre that was very similar to the one that worked for the 990s. The 2006 tyres were designed so that a rider could execute a tight turn mid-corner, then stand the bike up as quickly as possible and fire off a savage burst of acceleration. The carcass that worked in that situation was not stiff enough to deal with the 800s' long sweeping arc through corners, a situation that gets worse as the corners get longer and faster, and the G-forces rise. The more rigid carcass suited to the 800s wasn't available to Michelin runners until around Assen. After that, it was a question of developing broader-based compounds, and experience showed that Michelin could do well where it could reasonably predict the tarmac surface. Where Bridgestone suffered in 2006 whenever there was newly laid tarmac, now Michelin suffered. In the months following Assen, Michelins worked brilliantly at Sachsenring, then failed to perform at the newly surfaced Laguna Seca and Misano.

We shouldn't forget Dunlop, supplying all the tyres in the 125 and 250 classes, and desperate to remain in MotoGP to fight its way back to the top. None of its riders criticises the effectiveness of its front tyre, nor the absolute grip afforded by its rear slicks. The problem is the speed with which the compounds lose their grip during the race, leaving the rider with the choice of going gently and trying to baby the tyre to the finish, or having a few minutes of relative glory, followed by no grip from the rear for the rest of the race. Progress is being made; outings that were painful to watch were followed by occasional sparks of light. It remains to be seen whether Dunlop will even get a chance to finish the job of regaining full competitiveness in the senior class.

By Misano, the rule makers were panicking because of the polarising effect of the tyre war. Bridgestone, or occasionally Michelin, would have superiority at any given track. The FIM, at the behest of the series promoter, Dorna, asked for meetings between the tyre companies involved in MotoGP to see if an enhanced rule would improve the competition. (Unsurprisingly, Bridgestone rejected Michelin's request that the number of tyres be increased to 40, allowing up to three additional-construction rear tyres.) But the FIM's very request had caused a furore. This was open competition. Bridgestone had operated within the rules and comprehensively annihilated its rivals. Michelin's destruction was partially self-inflicted, caused by the initial carcass error plus the difficulty of making compounds that worked in broad temperature ranges and on less specific surface conditions. It is a competition between the French and Bridgestone's entire chemical supply chain. But with development, Michelin might be able to fix its problems quite quickly.

The effect of the fuel rule was just as important, and when the new 800 regulations were announced, most engineers in the paddock agreed that the 21-litre fuel capacity was the real performance limiter. And so it proved to be; the lap times in 2007 were directly comparable with the last few years of the 990s – and it's not unreasonable to assert that lap time is quite closely related to the amount of fuel burned. With one litre less, unless someone had a significant new fuel-saving technology, it was always going to be difficult to employ full power for the whole race.

Competition is almost a cultural thing, some nationalities being more adventurous than others; as a result, they can win more spectacularly, and also fail more spectacularly. Conservative engineers will see a problem and design a solution that takes minimum risks; others like the spin of the dice and make more racy selections. The '07 machines reflected their manufacturers' national stereotypes quite well.

Acknowledgement that the 21-litre capacity was the real limiter of engine performance came from the various designs that rolled on to the grid. Honda and Yamaha designed motors with steel valve springs that were meant to complete the race easily on the fuel. Kawasaki and Suzuki adopted pneumatics, finally releasing themselves from the self-imposed strait-jacket of trying to source ever higher-quality valve-spring material. Ducati stuck with its unique selling point, desmodromic valve gear.

Crucially, all the Japanese engines were designed with fuel consumption in mind; Ducati's was not. The D16-07 was 800cc of 20,000rpm full-power fury. It was up to the race team to come up with strategies to finish the races, but if full power

Below, left: Michelins early season tyres just weren't stiff enough.

Below: Bridgestone's rubber was more capable than the competition over wider track temperatures.

Bottom left: Dunlop's qualifying tyre was a strong point.

Bottom centre: Track temperatures, changing throughout the day, were crucial.

Bottom right: New 21-litre fuel limit didn't seem to slow the Ducati.

Photographs: Gold & Goose

Below right: Ducati's return to 'Screamer' firing intervals meant exhausts for each bank reverted to two-into-one.

Below: Ducati digital dash read to 22,000, but the usual limit was 20,000, and the maximum 20,500.
Photographs: Gold & Goose

Bottom left: Pre-season shot shows vestigial front chassis stopping at the cylinder heads, also the carbon-fibre rear sub-frame.
Photograph: Neil Spalding

Bottom right: Adjustable headstock. Stoner preferred the longest possible wheelbase, for a bike that responded to strong rider inputs.
Photograph: Gold & Goose

was wanted, Ducati Corse technical director Filippo Preziosi's development team made sure it was there for the asking.

Pneumatic valve springs are used for slightly different reasons in MotoGP and Formula One. MotoGP bikes might now be revving to similar levels, but individual cylinder size is much smaller (200cc compared to 300cc), so motorcycle valves are typically smaller and lighter. In simple high-rev terms, we don't need the complexity of pneumatics, but to get the maximum power, combined with the broadest possible power range and the best fuel economy, we do need to open and close the valves very violently.

A plot of a valve's movement looks like a sine curve. It is not merely how high the valve is lifted or how long it is held open that counts; it is the area under the curve that makes the difference. If you can 'square off' the sine curve slightly – accelerating the valves more quickly and shutting them (especially the inlet) slightly earlier, reducing overlap while maintaining the same area under the curve – it is possible to produce the same peak power with better mid-range and slightly better fuel economy. Steel valve springs have a tendency to surge under really violent use, feeding very destructive oscillations into the valve train. The pneumatic system, with its effectively zero-mass spring, doesn't suffer this problem and is an excellent solution.

But MotoGP's technical agenda requires the best possible fuel economy, and desmodromics are starting to appear an even better solution. Current technology means that the 800cc machines use full throttle for about 28 per cent of a given lap; in the days of the 990s, it was only 18 per cent. It seems that at current revs, a desmodromic system can open and close a valve just as violently and effectively as the more common pneumatics. That's fine for the 28 per cent of a lap where the engine is flat out, but the desmo system seems to have an advantage over the other 72 per cent. Road-going desmodromic Ducatis use a small hairspring to assist valve closure; for racing, this is dropped, eliminating even this small source of drag.

A pneumatic spring is simply a canister of gas, and just like squeezing a squash ball, operating it soaks up energy. As a spring rebounds, it does give back some of that energy, but the valve train has to be stiffer to deal with the resulting loads than with a desmo system, and at low-to-medium revs, it is becom-

ing apparent that less energy is required by Ducati's system. In F1, the relative simplicity of the pneumatic valve system wins hands down, but their engines are at full throttle for nearly 70 per cent of each lap, and they have no fuel restrictions. On bikes, where fuel efficiency is critical, desmo is currently the most successful valve operating system; don't be surprised if another factory decides to try it out as a result.

But just because everyone has 21 litres of fuel doesn't mean that they have to use it in the same way. As mentioned, Honda and Yamaha opted for engines that simply wouldn't rev sufficiently to burn more than 21 litres of fuel in the race and that would retain their easily controllable character – a perfectly rational design option. Kawasaki and Suzuki went for more revs and peak power with their pneumatic valves, but risked losing the subtlety of throttle response required for picking up revs accurately in the corners. All four had strategies to ensure that all the fuel carried was used in the race, but always erring on the side of prudence.

Ducati leap-frogged the more conservative Japanese engineers, opting for power over economy, then devising a strategy to get to the finish line. At the first race in Qatar, the Ducati finished with just 300cc in the tank. Just before the race, Rossi's Yamaha engineers had panicked about fuel range and lowered his maximum revs from 18,000 to 17,500, but he finished with over a litre spare. There were similar stories all along the pit lane. On these figures, Ducati legitimately used 3.5 per cent more fuel than the opposition, before one takes into account its efficient valve control system and its complex electronic controls. In later races, the other factories struck back, but it was noticeable that there were several cases of the Ducatis running out of fuel on the cool-down lap.

DUCATI

By 2007 Ducati had paid their dues The manufacturer entered MotoGP in 2003 with an obscenely powerful 990, but four years of constant effort and fine-tuning were needed to get the bike to the point where it could win at any track where its tyres were up to the job. No mean achievement for such a small factory. Better yet, the strategies that took Ducati to this point were exactly the same as those that delivered the championship in 2007.

The 990 needed sophisticated electronics to make it usable; carefully refined tuning of the throttles and as many as three different traction control systems were required. Four years of effort meant that the set-up time for those electronics had been cut to fit the time available at a typical grand prix.

Ducati's initial decision to go for Bridgestone tyres was to pursue a policy of differentiation. Whenever Michelin had a 'bad tyre day', the Bridgestones would be there to pick up the pieces, but by the end of 2006, it was becoming apparent that Bridgestone would soon be capable of much better things.

The new rules gave Ducati the opportunity finally to fully redesign its bike. With the benefit of four years' hard experience, the outcome was always likely to be very competitive.

In some ways, the move to 800cc benefited Ducati most. Its complex engine control electronics could be transferred straight over, and the slightly reduced capacity allowed Ducati to address one of the big disadvantages of its old engine, the length. Shorter cylinder heads, shorter stroke and rotating the 90-degree vee slightly backward all allowed the crankshaft to be moved a few precious millimetres forward for better overall balance. The chassis was redesigned, the steel tubes now terminating at the two cylinder heads, while the rear sub-frame and seat were a much more rigid carbon-fibre structure, attached to the swing-arm pivot and rear cylinder head.

Ducati's critical decision was to go for as much power as possible, reverting to the original 'screamer' or 'four-pulse' engine combustion sequence for the best possible power, then finding a way to limit fuel usage to ensure the bike finished races. This was a three-part system.

Part one was a fuel mapping system that knew where the bike was on the track and ensured that power was available for the straights, but not wasted on the twiddly bits. Part two was a sophisticated fuel-usage monitoring system that allowed the fuel to be leaned off where it would do the least possible damage to performance. From the start, Ducati used all of the fuel in the tank, while initially the opposition was overly conservative.

Part three was a rider who had the aggression and ability to take on Rossi, and also to deal with the specific issues that the Ducati's electronics presented. As good as the Ducati was at maximising its performance within the rules, you have to remember that it was Stoner who had to make it all work on the track, and that wasn't always easy. Just ask yourself, where did the second Ducati finish?

Above: The Ducati engine remained a 90-degree vee, but rolling the vee backwards and moving the centre of gravity upwards and forwards improved weight distribution.
Photograph: Neil Spalding

Above: **Pedrosa's end-of-season bike had little in common with the first one: revised (top of shock to the frame) suspension, finned sump and separate oil radiator were added during the season.**

Right: **This Honda RC212V customer-bike chassis has a different lower cross-member and no shock-absorber top mount – it locates on the swing-arm.**

Below right: **Okada's test mule at Brno used a cast-off Repsol chassis.**

Photographs: Neil Spalding

HONDA

Lets say it early: 2007 wasn't Honda's year. In fact, for a manufacturer of Honda's expertise, it was a disaster. The concept was to build an easy-to-turn, highly-manoeuvrable motorcycle that would easily finish the race within the fuel limit. It might sacrifice a bit of speed on the straights, but it would make up for that in the changes of direction. Since Rossi left, Honda hasn't really had a number-one rider capable of dominating the design direction. With the 800 project, the evidence is that it chose a 'small rider concept' rather than building something to suit its current world champion, Nicky Hayden, with his more power-hungry, back-it-in style.

Honda has never disclosed the precise vee angle, but it looks very close to 75 degrees – good for packaging. It is wide enough for a good intake system between the cylinder heads, yet still allows the crankshaft to be as far forward as necessary for good handling. It does mean that most of the fuel has to be carried under the rider's seat, in line with Honda's philosophy of centralised mass.

The chassis was made of CNC-machined aluminium sections and was narrower than the old 990cc V5 unit, not least because there was one cylinder less at the front of the engine, and the weight was placed in the chassis differently. Honda moved the engine upward and forward, probably to help in the high-corner-speed situations more likely to be seen by the 800s. Moving the weight up would also be the sort of thing you would do to help a lighter rider pitch weight around.

Diving into a corner, the rider applies the brakes and wants the bike to pitch forward to compress the front tyre, increasing the contact patch and grip. Raising the centre of gravity helps this weight transfer, but it looks like Honda went too far. For heavier riders like Checa and Hayden, the bike was a nightmare: as soon as they hit the brakes, it pitched radically forward and then seemed to push the front tyre away.

The riders supposed to be helped by this design were also critical; all of their careers had been on bikes not designed specifically in their favour, so they had developed riding styles to suit. Stiffer springs were tried, but these appeared to load up the chassis more, causing the steering head to deflect and further reducing feel from the front. By the start of the 'fly-aways', Honda had five different chassis designs in the pit lane. At Brno, privateer teams had a massive refit, finally getting chassis similar to the one Pedrosa had been given at the start of the year, the top of the shock absorber being mounted to the frame instead of to the underside of the swing-arm. The factory bikes were several generations ahead. Honda tried everything, even reverting to the style of chassis construction (welded-up stampings) used on the old RC211V, but the bike never really inspired confidence in its riders.

The engine wasn't a lot better, suffering several failures during the year, the most spectacular being Hayden's rear-cylinder-bank detonation as he crossed the finish line in practice at the

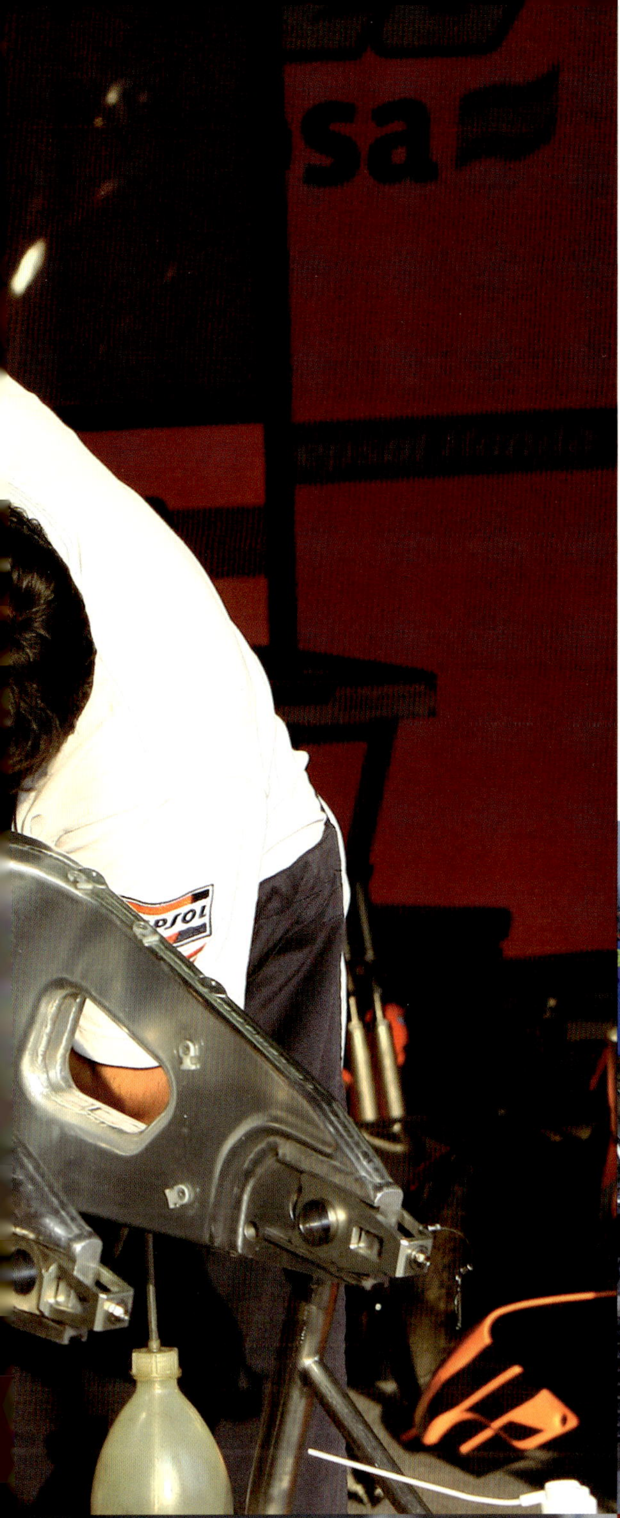

Sachsenring. It's not often in this modern world that bits of engine are sprayed all over the track.

With a conventional four-valve-per-cylinder, gear-driven DOHC layout, the V4 has a front-mounted balance shaft to quell vibration from the narrow vee angle. It is very compact, shorter even than Hayden's 'new generation' RC211V of 2006. At the start of 2007, 17,000 rpm was the engine's limit, but it was around 19,000 by the end. En route, at least nine different exhaust designs were tried, some purely to give Pedrosa the quiet pipe he craved, but most simply attempts at achieving a stable and smooth throttle response. A completely new ECU and engine control system failed initially to deliver the precision and accuracy of throttle response, and fuel consumption necessary. It's difficult to tell from the outside the number of major engine tunes tried, but it's believed to have been at least six, the Repsol bikes quite often running completely different engine set-ups to fit the riders' different styles.

Private teams were given an option to buy an upgrade from the Czech Republic race. By the latter part of the year, the Hondas, especially the Repsol works bikes, could make a good showing, but overall, 2007 is a year Honda will want to forget.

Below: Hayden was given the final versions of the long pipes for Brno.

Photograph: Gold & Goose

Bottom right: The factory test bike at Motegi had the later 'stamped sheet' style of chassis.

Photograph: Neil Spalding

Right: Kawasaki's hollow shell – the gearbox stripped out.

Below right: Mid-session ratio change for West's Kawasaki at Donington.

Bottom: Engine layout more conventional than Yamaha: Kawasaki's crank turns forwards and the cam drive is on the right-hand end.

Photographs: Neil Spalding

KAWASAKI

Kawasaki had a major rethink of the final 990 for its new 800. The chassis looked similar, but the engine was significantly different, sporting pneumatic valve springs and a revised gear drive to the cams.

The basic concept was to prioritise acceleration out of corners, and that it did successfully. Despite several good performances, however, it remained stubbornly behind Suzuki in the results for most of the year. The initial rider line-up of Randy de Puniet and Olivier Jacque was somewhat crash-happy. Once Jacque decided that retirement hurt significantly less, his replacement, Anthony West, proved quite effective, especially in the wet. It is worth noting, however, that while de Puniet had many crashes, most of them seemed to involve losing the front end going into corners, rather as though there was a chassis as well as a rider issue. In Turkey and the Czech Republic, new chassis were tried, and it appeared that without radical geometry changes, some aspects of the frame's flex characteristics were being modified.

The engine is an across-the-frame, four-cylinder, four-valves-per-cylinder, DOHC, irregular-fire four-stroke. Using a combustion sequence that Kawasaki calls BB4-2, it sounds identical to the Yamahas and has similar 90-degree crankshaft throws.

Kawasaki started 800 development quite late, and although a hybrid 990/800 was seen in the hands of test rider Matsudo at Motegi in 2006, the bike wasn't tested in its final form until November 2006, when reliability issues forced a quick rethink. Although coming from behind, Kawasaki managed some significant power increases in the early part of the season, and by the second race, it was on a par with Suzuki. Acceleration and speed were very competitive: by Portugal, the Kawasakis usually only had Ducatis in front of them in the top-speed rankings.

Both Suzuki and Kawasaki tried to obtain additional fuel effi-

ciency by precisely timing the fuel pulse into the engine. To help atomise the fuel and to allow the team to time the introduction of the fuel into the inlet port, the fuel pressure was increased to ten bar, from the more normal (but very low in automotive terms) three bar used by Yamaha to date. Kawasaki was very pleased with the part the improvements to the fuel injection system played during the year, especially as the increase in fuel pressure is one of the variables that can easily affect the very sensitive initial throttle pick-up required for high-speed laps.

Along with the other Bridgestone runners, Kawasaki benefited from the sudden promotion to tyre of choice. However, it looked like the tyres required by the Kawasaki were subtly different to those for the Suzuki and Ducati. It's not certain whether this was a product of the chassis or the in-line engine, but where Ducati and Suzuki would often fit similar tyres over the course of a weekend, it was rare that Kawasaki could do the same. This is not to say that it held Kawasaki back, but less data was available with which to develop subsequent tyres.

In 2007, Kawasaki showed that it was not merely a participant; the new bike allowed Kawasaki to consider itself a contestant. If progress continues at the same rate in 2008, it could be very good for Kawasaki's pairing of West and Hopkins.

SUZUKI

Suzuki stuck its neck out in 2006. It built a 990cc version of its 800cc racer, then spent a year testing it on the GP circuits. While all the main parts of the bike were modified to work in the different environment of 800cc racing, the 2007 Suzuki GSV-R was very similar to the 2006 bike. In the chassis, the main changes were in a more flexible swing-arm and headstock area, improving suppleness for better 'chassis-flex suspension' during the more extended periods the new bikes remained at full lean.

Using pneumatic valve springs, Suzuki developed a 75-degree, four-valves-per-cylinder, DOHC V4 that produced competitive power with a good balance of throttle response and connection. Team manager Paul Denning explained, 'It's all about the rider having the tyre in the palm of his hand; the connection must be very direct. As soon as the 800 engine was put in the 990 chassis last year, the riders said it was better. The engine character is very important, and Suzuki has worked hard to make it very good.'

The experiments in 2006 gave a good start; as soon as Suzuki found the best fuel economy methodology, it started to get podiums. Vermeulen's win at a wet Le Mans clearly had something to do with his riding ability, but he couldn't have done it if the bike hadn't been right. The same applies to Hopkins's podiums; it's not easy getting on to the top three steps, but by Misano, we had two Suzuki riders on the podium.

Over the course of the year, Suzuki used at least two different combustion sequences. At the start of the year, it was a screamer, but revised crankshafts were tested after Le Mans, and by Mugello, two weekends later, the bike sounded very different indeed, both riders preferring the feel and grip coming out of the corners. Suzuki won't confirm it, but there is a good chance that they were using variable-length inlets. Starting to become available on some street bikes, this technology employs a telescoping velocity stack to change the harmonics in the inlet port (just think of a trombone). Typically, inlet lengths are tuned to use harmonics to fill in dips in the torque curve, or enhance top-end power. Having a movable inlet velocity stack gives the engine the best of both worlds. Its very complex to set up, as different fuelling is required for each inlet length.

Above: **Suzuki's first 800 was a natural development of its last 990, almost identical under the fairings. Note the use of an old 2006 fuel tank cover at the front of the airbox to keep prying eyes away from the 200-bar pneumatic valve reservoir there.**

Left: **Prototype for 2008 moved the tank to just above the shock absorber – visible above the main frame beam.**

Photographs: Neil Spalding

Above: Rossi's pneumatic-valve-spring bike at Motegi – yellow blanking piece hides the reservoir. After a smokey blow-up in practice, it wasn't seen again.

Top: Similar to the 990, Yamaha engine has reverse-rotating crank, cam drive behind the block and irregular firing intervals. This is Edwards's bike.
Photographs: Neil Spalding

YAMAHA

Yamaha had had a traumatic 2006 and clearly was in no mood to repeat the experience in 2007. To recap, its slightly modified chassis for 2006 had suffered badly from chatter. New chassis had to be designed, and by the end of August, Yamaha has got on top of the problem. It was no great surprise, then, that the starting point for the 800 project was the final version of the 990 chassis, with a new motor replicating the layout of the 990. Typically, an engine with a shorter stroke would have shorter cylinder barrels; in the Yamaha's case, this would have reduced the height of the cylinder head and changed the engine's centre of gravity. To counteract this, the 800's crankshaft was placed slightly higher.

Yamaha decided to stick with steel valve springs and to build a motor that would finish races within the fuel limit, focusing as ever on ease of handling and control, into and especially out of corners. In testing, the bike looked very quick. Indeed, in the final shake-down tests at Jerez, it was very quick, albeit with a Ducati sitting just behind it. At the first race at Qatar, however, when Ducati revealed the superiority of its fuel-consumption regimen, Yamaha had no answer.

The Yamaha was on pole, but clearly was significantly slower than the Ducati in the top-speed read-outs. Analysis of fuel consumption by the factory technicians immediately prior to the race led to a lowering of the rev limit to 17,500rpm, and it was hoped that victory could be achieved by being fast through the corners. At the time, Yamaha's head of research and development, Masao Furasawa, said that Yamaha would like to show the crowd what its bikes could do and let Valentino Rossi entertain them, but that it would be a lot easier to do with 21.5 litres of fuel than 21. Stoner's Ducati revised everybody's definition of maximum power during the race, and he simply drove past Rossi on the straights at will. Rossi could catch and occasionally overtake him, but he could never pull away. At the end of the race, Stoner's Ducati had about 300cc of fuel left in the tank; Rossi had over a litre. Obviously, some changes were needed.

Yamaha had been flirting with the idea of pneumatic valve springs, and there were many rumours of an arrangement with Meccachrome, the French F1 engine manufacturer, but Yamaha's original plan appeared to have this scheduled for 2008. All engine development went into fast forward, however, with revised steel-valve-spring engines available for Turkey, and a further revision for Mugello. The only way to spot the change from the outside was by the revised exhaust systems and modified sumps, to deal with a different primary-pipe length. Exhaust header-pipe systems are typically shorter for higher revs, and both of these modifications used shorter pipes.

Yamaha was not looking for engine power alone. It also fitted larger 48mm forks to Rossi's bike in the test after Le Mans to improve control under severe braking. From a racing standpoint, the Yamaha was unlikely to beat the Ducati to the end of the main straight, but the plan was to set up Rossi's bike so that he could try to outbrake Stoner if he was anywhere near. Normally, such stout forks would be unacceptably rigid when the bike was leaned right over, and Yamaha designed a deliberately flexible top triple clamp so that the forks could still flex and pivot around the lower triple clamp for grip while leaned over.

Nothing is for free, however, and these forks limited the increase in top speed by acting as air dams. Worse, they reduced the supply of cool air to the radiator, leading almost directly to

Rossi's crash at the German Grand Prix: he couldn't get past de Puniet's Kawasaki for several laps, and the disturbed airflow was sufficient to send the engine temperature soaring. By Brno, Yamaha had reacted with a revised, more slippery fairing. This seemed to add about 3km/h to the bike's top speed, but more importantly may have ducted just a little bit more air through the radiator for additional cooling. This would have increased drag, although it would have been offset to some degree by the cleaner top half.

Immediately after the Brno race, Rossi gave an engine equipped with pneumatic valve springs its testing debut. He didn't sound very enthusiastic, but clearly was in the mood to use it at Misano. All other things being equal, a pneumatic-valve engine should have a little less drag on the cams, the spring effectively being progressive, and it should be possible to redesign the cams to get the same peak horsepower while using slightly less fuel by shutting the valves more aggressively. We simply don't know whether Yamaha had managed at that stage to make these modifications, as the engine self-destructed after five laps. Yamaha went to a lot of trouble to say that the problem wasn't the pneumatic valve system; it appears that the failure was more probably a seized big-end. It is worth noting, though, that one of the easiest ways of destroying a big-end is to flatten the bearing by stopping the piston from going up on the previous revolution – pretty much the sort of failure you would expect if the valves hadn't got out of the way in time.

By Portugal, two weeks later, the new engine was working well and clearly being revved nearly to 19,000rpm on the main straight, quite an increase in the five months since Qatar.

Yamaha started the year with its normal three-bar fuel-injection system, which was perfectly sound for the lower-revving engines. Most of the other teams using pneumatic-valve recovery systems employed around ten bar, but the higher pressure is one of the more sensitive settings for low-throttle-opening fuelling, critical while feeling for grip coming out of a corner. There may well be additional economy to be had by timing the fuel pulse into a specific period while the inlet valve is open, but careful development is needed so that the incredibly important initial crack of the throttle is just as subtle and effective as it was on the previous system.

TEAM ROBERTS

Fresh from a resurgent 2006, Kenny Roberts's team had Honda power again for 2007. And after years of fighting for good tyres, the team had retained its Michelin contract. That's just about where the good news ended.

Rapid chassis development during 2006 meant that the team had a new understanding of the required flex levels for good control in the corners, while retaining the bike's composure when the rider heaved on the bars for a fast change of direction. Fundamentally re-engineered for the new shorter V4 800cc Honda, the new chassis was designed to resist twist, with part of its structure placed down towards the engine mounts. Two different chassis were used, the second having a repositioned motor.

Despite avoiding the overly restrictive standard Honda exhaust design – Team Roberts always had long two-into-one pipes for each cylinder bank – the standard Honda customer engine simply never produced enough power. It wasn't just the lack of power, it was the way it delivered what it had. Strong initial punch out of the corners, rather pointless if your tyres aren't gripping, followed by a very anaemic top end simply destroyed the bike's competitiveness. Revised engine specifications were available from Honda from Brno onward, but the results showed that Team Roberts was unwilling to pay for them.

ILMOR

Renowned car race engineer Mario Illien built an extremely compact 70-degree V4 with a dry sump, pneumatic valve springs and a unique (for a motorcycle) single gear train for both cylinder banks. Electronics were by McLaren.

Very fast in a straight line, the bike was also very difficult to ride, while the team steadfastly defended the decision to develop electronics to control throttle response at the critical initial opening while fully leaned. By the end of testing in 2007, the heavier high-inertia crankshaft brought some improvement, but the smooth control necessary to maximise the limited grip remained elusive.

Why should such a respected engineer pursue the goal of lowest-possible crankshaft inertia when building a MotoGP bike? One factor must be the inevitable gyroscopic effects that the crankshaft has on handling; another the effect on acceleration when the bike is fully vertical. If Illien had managed to develop electronics to soften the initial pick-up, he might have found two valuable advantages.

After one race, the team withdrew. Development continued quietly, and it would be a shame, especially given the current size of the grid, if the team was unable to continue this interesting experiment.

Above and left: Team Roberts had a harrowing 2007, its Honda engine and Michelin tyres simply not being competitive. Over the year, the team tried two chassis, the second (above) having revised weight distribution.

Photographs: Neil Spalding

Above: Ilmor shows airbox intake filters, tortuous double two-into-one exhausts and Suter-built chassis.

Photograph: Neil Spalding

TECHNICAL ESSAY

WHY SMALLER IS FASTER

From their inception, the 800s challenged and often beat the lap times of the significantly more powerful 990s. How so? Kevin Cameron explains…

Main photograph: From left to right, the class of 2007. New season, new rules and new bikes for all.
Photograph: Gold & Goose

DON'T ask why the FIM has chopped MotoGP engine displacement from 990cc to 800 – politics are beyond the scope of this text. But if even part of the object was to reduce average lap speeds, it has failed. The new 800s are uniformly quicker around the circuits, and the beginnings of this development were clear even at the first official test, held at Valencia after the 2006 Spanish GP. What we want to know is how 20 per cent less engine can equal quicker lap times?

How does a motorcycle achieve a quick lap time? Because bikes have little rubber on the ground in comparison to cars, traditionally they have emphasised hard acceleration and braking rather than cornering speed. This was particularly true of the two-stroke 500 GP bikes. The faster they went to make up for slowing so much for corners, the more aerodynamic drag they had to overcome at the far end of the straight, and the more brake they had to carry to achieve the necessary deceleration. Their lap times began to stagnate when their performance became a self-defeating exercise, in which the engine's power was used primarily to keep the brake discs glowing red hot.

Now a thought experiment: imagine another type of machine, one with a constant velocity. Instead of accelerating and braking violently, it maintains a steady speed equal to the winner's average. This is quite impossible, but it offers a new *direction*, even if the goal is unattainable. By raising cornering speeds, we reduce the need to accelerate and brake, which are tyre destroying activities. By lowering speeds on the straights somewhat, losses to aero drag are reduced (fuel consumption rises as the cube of speed). The ideal, from almost every point of view, is a bike that trades top speed to gain cornering speed.

The drop from 990cc to 800 is a small step towards this ideal. With less displacement, the new 800s accelerate less rapidly, but with less tyre distress from extreme acceleration, they retain higher edge grip (grip at full lean angle) and corner faster. This conserves tyre properties, which is what Nicky Hayden observed after the Valencia 800 test – the tyres last longer and work better on the 800.

Is this progress simply a matter of having exactly the right engine displacement? This is a very old idea – mathematician Gordon Blair was asked to determine this optimum in 1973 and, as I recall, suggested that it might be just a little over 350cc. But there are too many variables at work here for that – tyres evolve so fast that mid-season chassis updates are necessary to keep up with them.

Just as tyres compel changes in chassis dimensions, they also direct riding style. When I first picked up tyre irons, Dunlop's 'Triangular' racing tyre was picking up where Avon's 'Green Dot' had left off. Wheel rims were about 2 inches wide, and riders were sure that if they put on too big a tyre, it would cut

their top speed. With a limited area of fairly hard rubber under them, racers had little choice but to commit to a corner line that was the arc of the largest possible inscribed circle. Combined turning and accelerating was a risky business.

When 100hp Suzuki and Kawasaki two-strokes tore up the best available tyres at Daytona in 1972, Dunlop responded with its very wide, round-profile rear with almost a slick tread, mounted on a 3-inch rim. Goodyear spent the next year preparing its reply, which appeared in 1974 as the first full slick. Slicks, spreading loads and forces over a larger area of softer rubber, presented riders with the enhanced ability to combine turning with acceleration. European race tracks were changing too – away from 'natural' road circuits with long straights to 'scratcher's' courses requiring constant manoeuvring.

Kenny Roberts and others soon found that big two-strokes could corner quicker by abandoning the old circular line. These riders got most of the turning done early and on a smaller, slower radius, then reserved the rest of the corner as a drag strip. The result was a higher corner exit speed than if the rider had tiptoed around the classic constant-radius line.

Two-stroke acceleration made the front wheel almost irrelevant, so steering moved from the front wheel to the rear, and from handlebar angle to throttle angle. Initially, Goodyear's heat-tolerant (160°C!) rubber compounds were ideal for this, but steering with tyre spin calls for a compromise combination of grip and abuse tolerance.

Rubber distress rose to crisis level through the early 1980s, but Michelin's introduction of semi-radial construction 're-set' tyre temperatures to a more livable level. Soft, yet strong, rubber compounds capable of delivering very high grip appeared, and there was a brief era of high-side crashes during 1989–90. This was ended by a combination of engine torque controls and moderation of the quest for ultimate grip at the expense of built-in warning that the tyre was nearing its peak.

In the 1990s, higher grip became the goal again, as rubber compounds originally developed for wet weather were made to survive in the dry, on thinner, cooler-running and more stable tyre constructions. During this era, Michelins had the reputation of lacking edge grip – possibly as the price paid for an adequate ability to handle combined turning/accelerating loads during mid-lean corner exit.

Left: Bridgestones were the kings. Note wear pattern change across the tyre shoulder.

Photograph: Gold & Goose

Now came the era of falling engine torque as a result of the reduction, and then the complete banishment of tetraethyl lead as an anti-knock agent in petrol. With less violence from the engine, grippier rubber compounds could survive longer on such machines. This, in turn, influenced riding. When I asked the just-retired Mick Doohan why I no longer saw much 'point-and-shoot' cornering, he replied that it was faster to ride a no-lead 500 more like a 250 as long as edge grip permitted. Once peak properties had faded later in the race, it was quicker and safer to revert to the point-and-shoot style.

Above right: **Double 250 champion Jorge Lorenzo is one more to graduate to MotoGP in 2008.**
Photograph: Gold & Goose

Below: **Kenny Roberts in action in the 1970s. Back then, point-and-squirt was the fastest way.**
Photograph: Crashpa archive

Bottom: **Nicky Hayden had to adapt his dirt-track style to match changing needs. Contrast his lean angle with that of Roberts (below).**
Photograph: Gold & Goose

The coming of the four-stroke 990 MotoGP formula had a two-pronged influence on tyre design. The new engines had a great deal of power and acceleration, but because they were four-strokes with sophisticated controls, their power could be applied very smoothly from zero. Pure power was useless, as Aprilia discovered. In the 500cc era, tyres had always needed abuse resistance first and edge grip second, but they could never provide enough of either. Abuse resistance made throttle steering practicable, while edge grip could raise cornering speed – at least during the early laps of races. With MotoGP wheelspin under control, the breadth of the compromise between these two was reduced. That opened new avenues for development.

A microcosm of this evolution occurred in the career of Nicky Hayden. His early training was dirt-track racing, and his style in AMA road racing applied dirt-track lessons. When he arrived on the GP scene, this no longer worked, and he failed to go straight to the podium as several previous US champions with dirt experience had done. One observer said, 'He just lays it into the corner and starts burnin' the tyre.' It didn't work – his tires faded early, and he was riding too hard for mid-field positions. Tyre fade sometimes put him on the ground. Two years ago, he redirected his style. By keeping the tyres in line more of the time, he dipped less deeply into their abuse tolerance, thereby retaining high grip for longer.

Since the late 1990s, this tyre led change in riding style has been intensified by the altered techniques of new riders. From the Kenny Roberts era to the peak of Mick Doohan's career, riders were often men with either dirt-track or large Superbike experience, or both. After that, as later 500s were moderated by torque controls and no-lead fuel, more riders were able to enter the top class from 250GP, bringing with them that class's tyre and energy conserving, high-corner-speed riding style.

There are always exceptions to trends, and Valentino Rossi was one. Upon riding a 500 for the first time, he immediately understood that the steep torque onset of the large two-stroke would require a riding style different from the 250. Yet as conditions for tyres moderated in the last 500 seasons, it became possible (not yet necessarily optimal) to do more with cornering speed than had been done before, and this is where Mick Doohan's remark is relevant.

Three years ago, Jeremy Burgess articulated the strategy now so clearly being implemented by the teams – the picking of new riders from the graduates of 125 and 250 racing. He said at that time that the teams would make this choice because such riders, having to fend off a cloud of peers on every lap, learned hand-to-hand skills that are less common in national and World Superbike. This meant that nearly every new rider would arrive with a high-corner-speed riding style.

This never had worked before, as it was an adage of the 500 two-stroke era that a 250 style was both slower and more dangerous than the established point-and-shoot method. Slower because exit speed on to the straight was reduced, and more dangerous because of the longer time spent at high lean angle, completely dependent upon always fading edge grip. The on-again, off-again results of 250 stylist Luca Cadalora in 500GP were constantly cited as proof of this.

But it works today, and we have seen one after another 250 champion burst open the doors of MotoGP and step straight on to the podium. This is because the current highly civilised motorcycles have smooth power curves that originate at zero – not the comparatively explosive throttle-up of the 500s, which forced riders to lift the machine well off the edges of its tyres before applying throttle. With the current smooth power, a rider can begin to feed it in at high lean angle without fear that the exhaust pipe's mighty song will strike up, cause torque to spike and knock the tyre loose. Early power application plus high edge grip are the new recipe for higher corner exit speed.

When does evolution become revolution? Throughout the 990 formula, there was steady design progress, as shown by the continual fall in lap times. Yet as engineers play with variables, their minds must run in two tracks at the same time. The first seeks to make the present motorcycle more reliable or faster on Sunday or next week. This is incremental. The second begins to see how emerging trends might be better exploited, if only there were time for the necessary testing. The first class of tweaks keeps the small improvements coming throughout the season. The second may have to be reserved for discussions (usually held at the end of the season) of more basic design changes. Therefore, I suspect that engineers have in hand some ideas for testing at a major design change – such as the switch from 990 to 800cc.

For example, has the development of lateral flex, as a kind of 'sideways suspension' for use at high angles of lean, been a smooth process? Or has enough been learned about it that at least some designers would try a larger leap forward in an all-new motorcycle? Novelties might be applied in a new design that begins afresh, which might not be tried as add-ons to an existing design.

Valve lift limits engine development. If a given engine employs inverted-bucket tappets, increasing the lift requires larger-diameter tappets, but at some point the limits of the cylinder head design are reached. Further changes to the head may be blocked by the presence of other necessary parts or functions. A change in basic design is a good time at which to apply full remedies in place of serial palliatives. A change in formula is the natural point at which to make such leaps.

For a much older argument, consider the 1980-era belief that a 100hp 250 could win 500 GPs. On some circuits, 500 and 250 lap times were tantalisingly close. Add a bit more

power to a 250, and it might become unbeatable.

After disappointment with the four-stroke NR500, Honda slid its chips to the 100hp 250 idea in the form of the NS-3 two-stroke triple. Even observers who should have known better were reporting this machine in 1982–3 as having 'unbeatable reed-valve acceleration'. In fact, the early version made only 108hp and achieved what it did, not by mysteriously out-accelerating its 135–150hp four-cylinder competition, but by *higher cornering speed*. The rear tyre on Spencer's NS-3 experienced a very different duty cycle from those of the four-cylinder competition. As the less-powerful engine abused the tyre less, it retained more of its edge grip, yielding a bonus in higher cornering speed.

Honda engineers, curious during the 1990s about other ways to win races, measured corner speeds of 125s, 250s and 500s. They found that 125s had the highest apex speeds – 10–15 per cent faster than 500s – with 250s only a little slower. Why the difference? High-power 500s not only worked their back tyres very hard, but also were configured front-heavy for their role as 'dragsters with some limited cornering ability'. This forward weight bias, combined with the forward weight shift during braking, limited the corner entry speeds of 500s to what the small front tyre could tolerate. The smaller bikes, with more nearly equal front and rear tyre sections, did not overwork their fronts nearly as much, so they could enter turns and corner at higher G forces.

What are we waiting for? Make bigger front tyres! By reducing the specific loading of the rubber, larger-section fronts are better able to tolerate higher corner entry speeds, but front tyre width has grown only very slowly. The reason for this is that front tyre 'feel' is essential to the rider's sense of well-being, without which nothing is possible. Larger front tyres have been made and tested in all eras, and impatient riders have even tried rear tyres on the front. Making such larger front tyres feel right – so that they give all the essential signals – has been a slow process, but the current move toward 16-inch fronts continues a long evolution.

Honda put this corner-speed revelation together with the FIM's weight break for 500 twins in another experiment, the NSR500V2 twin. It showed occasional promise, but as a strategy, it failed. As soon as its edge grip faded, it became just an underpowered 500. If such a machine did not get away first at the start, the difference between its corner line and acceleration, and those of a four-cylinder made passing unlikely. Advancing beyond this would require new technology – either a motorcycle that abused its tyres significantly less, or a tyre technology that significantly enhanced edge grip by not having to be abuse tolerant.

MotoGP's new 'electronic' four-strokes have eased life for tyres in two stages – 990 and 800cc. Younger riders arrive with corner speed as the centre of their riding style. Tyre design has responded with a fresh compromise, slanted more towards edge grip than abuse tolerance. Now great precision takes the place of 'backin' 'er in and comin' out sideways'.

Main photograph: Drawing black lines. Traction control keeps wheelspin under control, but clearly doesn't stop it completely, as Stoner follows Pedrosa.
Photograph: Gold & Goose

Photograph: Gold & Goose

WORLD CHAMPION PROFILE

THE WIZARD FROM OZ

Once thought of as talented, but crash-happy, Casey Stoner confounded his critics in 2007 with a display of mature, blindingly-fast racemanship. Michael Scott examines the meteoric rise of the self-assured and determined MotoGP World Champion.

Right: First race in England: 14-year-old Stoner made a race-winning debut in the Aprilia Cup.
Photograph: Clive Challinor Motorsport Photography

Centre right: Stoner gave KTM its first GP victory in 2004.

Below: Casey's second GP season, 2003, was on an LCR 125 Aprilia.
Photographs: Gold & Goose

Above: Just seventeen and far from home – Casey in thoughtful mood.

Above centre: Lucio Cecchinello was both rider and team manager. He congratulates his protégé after his first win at Valencia in 2003.

Above right: Stoner leads Pedrosa in the 2004 Istanbul 250 GP, en route to his fifth win of the year.
Photographs: Gold & Goose

THE transformation of Casey Stoner – from rough diamond to priceless gem in the space of one northern winter – has been phenomenal. From crash-happy kid to reliable 100-per-cent finisher; from brusque loner to polished public performer. From crazy racer to mature maestro.

The figure at the centre of the fuss has remained the same throughout, although perhaps nowadays is more outwardly calm. Clean-cut features and a slight, but muscular, frame are surmounted by piercing green eyes. Ask a silly question, or even veer slightly towards one of several sensitive points (like the top speed of his Ducati), and they will turn on you at once, while he issues an articulate rebuttal of any suggestions that may not yet even have been made.

We have seen this type before in motorcycle racing – prickly, quick to rouse, opinionated and totally dedicated. Often as not, it speaks with an Australian accent and from the rostrum. And in recent years, it has had one or maybe a whole lot more world championships in its pocket.

Stoner, who won his first title at 21, fits the mould in spite of his relative youth. Of his two predecessors – Australia's first 500 champion, Wayne Gardner, and the subsequent Five-Timer, Mick Doohan – Stoner nominates Doohan as his role model, although he shows many of the traits of the former as well. But Stoner had a spat with Gardner during the previous season, when the original Digger criticised his fast-growing reputation as a crasher. He's not likely to forget in a hurry. Stoner is a rider who uses resentment to add to his speed. This can be confirmed by many riders who have felt his scorn, after having had the temerity to be even remotely in his way.

There are many similarities, but one big difference. The two before were both famous hell-raisers, at least at some stage of their careers. Stoner, already married at 21 (to willowy compatriot Adriana, whom he met at Phillip Island a couple of years ago), has been a teetotal total racer since 14. His idea of a good night out is to stay in; his favourite food, 'anything my wife cooks' (told this later, Adriana laughingly demurred, 'I can hardly cook anything.'); his favoured recreation, the austere sport of bow hunting. No time for hell-raising. It's like that when your whole life is devoted to a single goal.

There are other differences, including that Stoner has outperformed both of his predecessors. Doohan took one win in his second season, and Gardner never won ten in a year. Stoner did that in his second year in MotoGP. Then again, the trio reflect different eras. Twenty years ago, riders came into GPs from other racing disciplines, both Doohan and Gardner via production-based series for big four-strokes, leading towards 500cc two-strokes. Nowadays, the approved route, the one followed by Casey, is the other way around: start young on two-stroke 125s in Spain, then work your way up via 250s to today's 800cc four-strokes. Oh, and it helps if you can hitch a ride with Alberto Puig along the way.

Not that Stoner's was in any way a gilded path. The elements of a rags-to-riches struggle are quite authentic.

From the old coal-mining town of Kurri Kurri, in the Hunter Valley, about 40km inland from Newcastle, Casey began racing when he was four, in the booming and productive Australian east-coast dirt-track scene. Gardner and Doohan were also graduates; West and Vermeulen two more. The racing lessons learned there mirror those of US dirt-track: how to steer with the rear, how to ride elbow-to-elbow, and above all, how to be adaptable, riding five different motorcycles a day, on surfaces that can change from race to race.

Like his predecessors and two MotoGP contemporaries, Stoner excelled. He won the first of 41 national titles at six, adding another 70 state crowns. Five classes a day, 37 races a weekend – once he took 32 wins; the same weekend, he secured all five championships.

His opinion of his potential was forged right there as an early teenager, a self-belief so strong that it has propelled him fast-forward ever since. It brought him, the way he tells it, straight into conflict with the Australian racing authorities. Aged 14, his career clear in front of him, Casey wanted to go road-racing, on a proper 125. In Australia, he needed to be 16. Simple enough, it seems, but not the way he sees it. 'For unknown reasons,' he now says, hinting at some dark conspiracy, 'I wasn't allowed to race in Australia.'

If you're that determined, and if your family believe in you as strongly as you yourself, there is no choice. Sell up, risk all and go somewhere where the boy can race. That was England.

The year 2000 was tough for them all, with few luxuries beyond what the teenager needed for the tracks. The repayment was a British Aprilia Cup victory at his first attempt at road-racing. And also a couple of rides in the Spanish championship, where Alberto Puig spotted him. 'I could see Casey was talented and very determined,' he said later.

This was a big asset. At the time, Puig was building an influential career in the recruitment business, as well as nurturing Dani Pedrosa, among other promising youngsters. Casey was on the fast track, and in 2001, he contested both Spanish and British 125 championships, finishing as runner-up in each. He also made his GP debut with two wild-card rides (backed, thanks to Puig, by the Spanish MoviStar team), in England and Australia, where now he was old enough. He gained his first points at Phillip Island, his first-ever race there, with 12th in the 125 class.

Another 125 rider, Lucio Cecchinello, who had finished fifth, intended expanding his LCR team, and he was impressed. Casey rode a 250 for the first time in 2002 for LCR, gaining a

Left: Portugal 2004: Stoner was getting used to winning.

Below left: Stoner's first year in MotoGP was impressive, but strewn with debris.

Right: His second, on the Ducati, was masterful.

Photographs: Gold & Goose

Above: Some honeymoon – new wife Adriana was by Stoner's side throughout his campaign.

Top: Impressive faith in his electronics, tyres and talent – Casey won by miles at Laguna Seca.

Photographs: Gold & Goose

best of fifth and several other strong top-ten finishes. The next year, LCR switched him to the 125 class, where he took four podiums – and a first win, at Valencia. This was another turning point in his own mind, and in general as well. Casey did crash rather a lot, but boy was he fast. As Cecchinello said at the time, 'Casey is the future.'

A first factory ride beckoned, however, and Stoner spent 2004 on the orange KTM. He gave the Austrian marque its first win. Then it was straight back to LCR on a factory Aprilia 250. And this was the real thing. In a torrid season, the teenage Australian pushed eventual champion Dani Pedrosa to the end. Stoner took five wins and five more rostrums, but while his speed was dramatic, his tendency to push and push until the crash remained a weakness. Pedrosa took a second successive title and moved straight on to the factory Honda team in MotoGP. Stoner would follow directly, and revenge would come in just two years.

Cecchinello had his own plans for further expansion, moving to the MotoGP class with his favoured rider, on a lease-bike Honda, on Michelins. This fulfilled a lifelong ambition for Stoner – in all but one respect. 'I used to watch my heroes, Rainey and Doohan and Schwantz, and I'd really like to be riding the same bikes as them.' But he was too late; the 500 two-strokes were long gone.

Stoner's debut season was remarkable, for all sorts of reasons. At round two, Qatar, he arrived late, jet-lagged and sick – and he secured pole position. When he dropped back from the battle up front, Rossi had the temerity to opine that it had been because of his inexperience on worn tyres. This really got to Stoner, and he brought it up again at every opportunity, the first of which came after the very next race, at Istanbul. This time, he'd come within inches of winning, after a battle with Melandri and Pedrosa had seen the latter crash out on the last lap. After the race, he said his loss of pace at Qatar had been mainly because he was still ill: in Turkey, his fastest lap had been the second to last. 'Sliding doesn't worry me,' he said.

It was his best result of a year that had been distinguished by a huge number of crashes – he was equal to de Puniet with a total of 17. Seven non-finishes, mostly because of crashing, meant that he made little impression on the championship.

There was a pattern to the crashes. Almost invariably, he would lose the front wheel. As invariably, he would almost always be near the front, or pushing for the front row. Looking back early in 2007, when he was already surging ahead on points, he admitted to me that he had been over-riding the bike, quickly modifying his reply to say, 'probably riding too much for the machine or too much for what setting we arrived with. And also I think we have a better grade of tyres now. You know, the Michelin riders are all saying they had their special tyres flown in last year. I never had this. I was probably trying to keep up, with tyres that I suppose weren't special enough.'

It was a high-risk strategy, but it worked: 'It obviously opened up the right people's eyes to what I could do and what I could be. And Ducati were obviously confident enough in me to take me on.'

In retrospect, Ducati's decision seems visionary; in fact, it was driven by circumstances. The manufacturer had been turned down by Hopkins, Hayden and Melandri. Taking a chance on Stoner, however, has paid the biggest dividends. Ducati built a bike with a big turn of speed and a set of electronics, Casey meshed with the bike immediately, in spite of missing the early pre-season tests for a shoulder operation, to quieten down an old injury. And to get married, of course.

For Stoner, it was a transformation. The crash-happy kid was gone; in his place, a mature and blindingly fast competitor, who would win when he could, take the points when he couldn't. In 2007, there was not one non-finish, and there were ten resounding wins among 18 perfectly judged races. It began with Qatar, where clearly he was able not only to dominate Rossi on the straights, but also to control him in the corners.

An extraordinary season of calm domination unfolds through these pages.

Asked to explain this profound change, Stoner insists, 'I'm no different to last year. I'm surrounded by some great people now, which makes things a lot easier. Things are more organised ... I basically know what I've got to do each day. Don't have things just thrown in there willy-nilly. And ... it's just the

fact that I'm finally on a decent bike, decent tyres and don't have to worry about the small things.

'I'm happy sort of no matter what result I get. I know the team are happy no matter, because they know I've put in 100 per cent, and that's made things a lot more comfortable for me.

'Also being on a competitive bike. Last year, in practices, we were doing great ... running up front, first in a lot of sessions, fastest on race tyres. I'd get to the race, and the bike wouldn't feel the same. It never felt like it did in practice. This year, whatever we do in practice, it feels like it in the race, and this is when I can do what I want. It's the good feeling with the bike ... and not losing the front when I get off the brakes any more.'

There was no easy way to explain his new maturity. Except perhaps to note that in spite of the smart team uniform, the dutiful timekeeping, and attendance to press and sponsor briefings and such-like, and the carefully worded public pronouncements, Stoner is still very much his own man. Fans have complained about the speed at which he rides his paddock scooter among them, his brusque dislike of impromptu autograph sessions. He even was booed on stage at Donington Park's charity Day of Champions, which surprised him somewhat. 'I didn't expect to be absolutely loved here, but I didn't expect to be booed. I think it's because everybody in England, myself included in the past, were that disappointed when Rossi isn't winning they basically want to hate his competitors. Maybe it's another Sete or Biaggi thing. I'm not really sure what to think of it, but I'm not going to let it worry me,' he said.

Acknowledging thus the stature of his chief rival, it is remarkable how Stoner remained steadfast under pressure, in individual races and over the course of the season. Although he still railed against other riders in the pits during practice, it was only in Japan that his hostility spilled out openly on track, after a close encounter with a cruising Checa. For the rest of the year, the anger was kept in check, although not the growing scorn for those defeated Michelin riders who began complaining about the new tyre rules. Why, he wondered, was it unfair now, when it hadn't been when the favoured few had their special tyres flown in? 'I think it's much fairer now,' he repeated throughout the year.

Stoner had everything on his side in 2007. The Ducati was the fastest bike and handled well enough; the Bridgestones were usually the best tyres. The rider absolutely made the most of the package, quite brilliantly, completely overshadowing his experienced team-mate, Capirossi. More importantly, he had the anticipated protagonists of the season, Rossi and Pedrosa, on the ropes from the first race. And he never let up, even when he had a big points lead to protect. Stoner is a rider you never see going slowly, even on an out-lap in practice.

Nothwithstanding the foregoing, ultimately this is what defines Stoner – his riding. Full on, beautifully measured and, for the present, pretty much unbeatable: 'Once you get out on the track, everything leaves you. I love riding the bike.' You can tell he means it.

His riding, and his determination. Resentment and the need to prove his critics wrong have been powerful tools: 'There's been a lot of people in my life that believed in me, and a lot of people that didn't. It's nice that I can give the people that believed in me a gift, which is this world championship. And to prove to the people that didn't believe in me we can do it. It proves that if you never give up, anything can happen.'

Stoner's never been one for giving up, an ominous fact for his rivals. It seems unlikely that his first world championship will be his last.

CENTENARY CELEBRATION

By MAC McDIARMID

Above: **Agostini and his euphonious MV Agusta were among TT legends on hand.**
Photograph: Gavan Caldwell Photography

Right: **George Cohen restored the Norton that won the first TT, and rode it in the recreation. It didn't skip a beat.**
Photograph: Dave Collister/www.photocycles.com

Below: **Dieter Braun (Yamaha) was just one of many world champions lapping it up.**
Photograph: Dave Purves

THEY came to witness. They came in greater numbers, and for longer, than for any other TT, the first arriving a week before even practice began. Seventy-odd thousand came to be part of history, for nowhere reeks of motorcycle racing's story quite like the Isle of Man.

It was a fortnight of memories laced with modern deeds. The racing was as riveting and record-strewn as the Island has witnessed for years.

The first of a host of events to mark the centenary was a re-enactment of the first TT over the St John's course. Although scheduled to begin precisely 100 years to the minute after that first race, delays in clearing the roads meant that Geoff Duke flagged away the first riders 50 minutes late. Unlike that first race, held on a grey, chilly day, blue skies greeted the riders. The crowd, too – many in period costume – was thousands stronger than it had been first time around.

A star-studded line-up included Mick Grant, Sammy Miller and Nick Jefferies, most wearing dodgy period headgear and beatific grins. First away in a haze of oil mist was the Peugeot-Norton twin on which Rem Fowler took twin-cylinder honours back in '07, ridden by George Cohen, the man who restored it after the National Motorcycle Museum fire of 2003. Alongside was the Vindec twin on which Billy Wells initially pushed Fowler and singles winner Charlie Collier so hard before placing second, ridden by its owner, 69-year-old Chris Wells.

No doubt, Cohen was hoping to experience fewer incidents than Fowler, who endured two crashes and a puncture, and rode through the flames of another rider's catastrophe. He lost eight minutes on lap two, set the fastest lap of the race (42.91mph) on lap six, lost another eight minutes on lap seven, and briefly wandered away from his bike in despair before finally emerging victorious, if somewhat singed, after ten laps and 158 miles.

Single-speed and belt-driven it may be, but this time the old warhorse ran perfectly. 'By the end of the Cronk-y-Voddy,' recalled Cohen, 'I'd got the air and throttle levers set to optimum and it was flying. I looked behind and was surprised to see nobody there. Only Guy Martin, on a '38 Speed Twin, overtook me. We got back so quick, they were still flagging bikes away and had to hold us up. The best thing I've ever done.'

'An amazing spectacle, wonderful atmosphere,' agreed Mick Grant. 'They should do it every year.'

The same feel-good factor embellished much of the fortnight.

Even the weather, during a summer that largely spurned the British Isles, was kind for the most part. There was the usual wall-to-wall action – motocross, sprints, trials, beach racing and stunt shows. The great and the good of racing history paraded, signed autographs, swapped old tales. Douglas's 'Party on the Prom' was bigger than ever. Peel hosted gigs such as the Island had never seen, including Madness (fittingly, on Mad Sunday), Deacon Blue and what was left of The Who. Above all, there were bikes and bikers galore. Not for nothing is this known as 'Bikers' Island'.

The racing, as you can read elsewhere, lived up to all expectations, in that particular way that places it a generation and a thousand miles from mainstream short-circuit action. Once, it was Castrol 'R' that wafted like a pungent ribbon around the Mountain Course. As the clock ticked down to the start of the opening race, Braddan churchyard lazed under a fragrant aroma of Women's Institute home baking, steaming tea and bacon butties. Across the road, the smell of wild garlic hazed the ancient grandstand under the dappled shade of trees already old when the first TT was held. In the background, Radio TT's cosy chatter – the TT has had its own radio station for 42 years – counted down to the Superbike TT. For most road race fans, this is as close to paradise – and as distant from the Lauzitsring – as it gets.

Left: A Honda of the 1960s: the Island was a vital showcase and proving ground for the nascent Japanese industry.
Photograph: Dave Purves

Right: Everything was authentic for the Centenary TT recreation, except the weather.

Beow right: TT super-hero Carl Fogarty with veteran commentator Murray Walker.
Photographs: Dave Collister/www.photocycles.com

Below, far right: Cork crash-hats and roll-ups were all part of the atmosphere.

Below left: Yamaha World Superbike rider Nori Haga was a wide-eyed TT visitor.

Below: Mick Grant relives days of smoky glory on the Kawasaki.
Photographs: Gavan Caldwell Photography

Below right: Sidecars are very much part of the TT story.
Photograph: Dave Purves

Bottom: A galaxy of stars past and present join Agostini on the hallowed tarmac.
Photograph: Dave Collister/www.photocycles.com

JOHN McGUINNESS – LIKEABLE LEGEND

Above: Honda suspension bottoming as he threads the line for a 130 mph lap, McGuinness lifts head and shoulders to miss the wall at Barregarrow Bottom.

Photograph: Dave Collister/www.photocycles.com

WHEN John McGuinness was 14 years old, he told TT legend Joey Dunlop that one day he would share the Isle of Man TT podium with him, and in 1997, he did just that. Since then, the laid-back Northerner has become the third most successful rider at the TT, behind all-time greats Mike Hailwood and Joey Dunlop. By 2007, with 25 podiums, 13 wins and a 130mph lap record, McGuinness had gained TT legend status and a well-deserved place in the history books for his personal success around the unforgiving 37.73-mile TT track.

His two-wheeled journey started quite innocently when his dad, John McGuinness Senior, put him on a bike to keep him out from under his feet while he got on with running the family bike shop, McGuinness Motorcycles. 'My dad just put me on a bike when I was three or three-and-a-half. Never looked back, I don't really know anything else. I've never been into cricket or football or tennis. I've got no interest in anything whatsoever apart from bikes – pretty sad isn't it?' he quipped.

Most riders gain their first experience of racing in schoolboy motocross, and the same applied to McGuinness, but he also spent a lot of time attending events where his dad was racing. Once he was old enough for a road bike, that was it – he was off. 'I got a 125 TZR, and I just used to ride round like I was going to be world champion. I had a KLS Kawasaki when I passed my test, and I was flying round the roads like a lunatic, and my dad just said, "You're on the track boy." So I had a bit of a dip in the ocean on the racing front. The first meeting I did was the last meeting of the championship at Aintree; it was just a club championship. That was the back end of 1990, and that was my first road race,' he said. That event set him on his merry way.

The idea of racing at the TT was planted in his mind at the age of 11, when he went across to support his dad racing at Jurby. TT practice started the same week, and that was McGuinness's first taste of the event. As he explained, 'When I first saw it, I was like, "Wow, check that out! I fancy a bit of that," and at the time, it just fascinated me. I logged it in my brain for years and years. I used to sneak across to the Island on my BMX; we lived at Heysham, so it was alright. The four-

Profile by LOUISE CAIN

hour ferry crossing was no drama, just sit on it, go watch a bit, and then I'd come back and do a few days at school, and then bunk off and go back on the ferry – it was perfect.'

McGuinness started racing in pure road events in the early 1990s, entering the events that he could afford, and it wasn't until Paul Bird gave him a break in 1996 that the TT became a real option. 'I remember speaking to Mick Lofthouse and Lee Pullan about the Isle of Man. Mick was like "Do it, you'll be alright." I'd been doing the North West for a few years, and Scarborough and stuff. I said to Birdy, "Should I do it?" and he said we could go and if we didn't like it, we could go home.'

The TT is a tough event – it has its drawbacks and its ghosts, as McGuinness found out in his first year there. 'I went across as a newcomer; I only had a 250, I had no other bikes. Me and DJ were a pair of window lickers with orange jackets on. It was a shitty week as well, to be honest; practice week didn't go too well. It was good for experience, but it was tough as well, as I shared the same room as Mick Lofthouse, and he got killed in practice on Friday. So that is what makes you a hard-nosed bastard,' he said.

Despite the tough initiation, he returned and stood on the podium on his second time there, along with Joey Dunlop, as he had predicted. 'I was just a little kid about 14, and I went up and said, "I'll stand on the podium with you one day," and Joey being Joey just looked at me as if to say, "Who is this little freak," and off I went. I actually did it 11 years later; it was 1997, and I was on the Aprilia. Joey won it from Ian Lougher from me, so I did actually stand on the podium with him. I did the fastest lap of the race that day as well, and I just reminded him on the podium. I don't think he remembered,' he smiled at the memory.

One question that always comes to mind where pure road racing is concerned is why go back when you know how great the consequences are? McGuinness can't explain it: 'I don't know, I didn't know any different, I wanted to do it. You just blank it out don't you? Mick would have wanted us to carry on, all the boys we have lost would have wanted us to carry on wouldn't they? They wouldn't want us to stop. It's the only way to think about it. It is something I want to do, I don't know any different. There is nothing like doing a perfect lap round the Isle of Man, it is the best thing in the world.'

The perfect lap of the TT, like anything perfect, doesn't exist. There are just levels of improvement and honing. McGuinness agrees: 'I don't think there is a perfect lap. Conditions have got to be good, your bike has got to be good, you've got to be confident; you've got to have good tyres. The package has got to be right and [with] years of experience…you can get near enough a perfect lap. There is no secret to it, you just need to concentrate so hard and make sure you hit all the apexes, brake as late as you can, where you can make up time and scratch a bit. Nowadays, you have to scratch a bit. There is time to be made up everywhere on the course. It is just looking for that perfect lap, but it is hard to get one. But when you do get one, and you get the lap record, it is pretty special.'

Ahead of the Centenary, McGuinness had to listen to all the hype. 'I try not to think about it too much to be honest. It's Centenary TT, everybody is excited, everybody is like "This is going to happen and that is going to happen, going to smash the lap record," and all this. All I'm going to do is go to the TT. I'm probably the best prepared I've been for the TT than I've ever been for any other TT. I'm fitter, stronger and healthier; my bikes are probably better and very competitive. I've made it good and competitive over the last few years, just with the experience we've had, I know how to get the best out of my bikes. The walls and trees aren't any softer just because it is 100 years old. I'm just going to take it like I do every other year: turn up, keep me gob shut, and try and do my talking on the track.'

Of course, winning at the Centenary was something he wanted to achieve. He went on to say, 'It would be nice to add to my tally of wins, I'd love to. It would be great to win the Centenary; I'll not see another Centenary unless I get to 135, which would be a miracle. It'll be special; I'd love to win some more,

Above. **Say a little prayer? A quiet moment before taking on the Mountain Circuit.**

Below: **Hats off to the Centenary TT winner.**

Photographs: Gavan Caldwell Photography

Below: **The fascination of that ribbon of road – McGuinness in the Superbike race.**
Photograph: Dave Collister/www.photocycles.com

but you don't know what is going to happen. You need a bit of luck on your side. I'm going to get there and try and do the business, and have fun. That is what it is all about.'

All eyes were on McGuinness from the start of the year, but he did his level best not to let the attention get to him. 'I'm going to try and not put myself under that much pressure, just shut me visor; there is nobody on the bike with me, it is all down to me on the day,' he said. 'If I have a couple of good pit stops and everything keeps going, fingers crossed, we should not be too far away. Just have to see what happens. As long as the sun shines and we are all safe, it will be mega. I'm sure it will be. I'm looking forward to it. Everybody wants a piece of you, don't they? It'll be alright. I can deal with it.'

On Friday 8th June, during the Pokerstars Senior Race, the perfect lap occurred. 'It was probably near as damn it the perfect lap. It is so difficult to get a perfect lap, and obviously I was slowing down for the pits. If I had been on a flying lap, it probably would have whipped another three or four seconds off it. To be fair, it was clean, it was quick; I didn't really miss any apexes, I just felt in control if you like. Maybe it could have been three, four, five seconds quicker, but not much quicker. It felt fast enough!' he joked with relief.

'When you are on the bike, you are concentrating really hard. You don't think to yourself, "I want to do 130." That wasn't really what I wanted to do. I wanted to win the race more than anything, but to be fair, I felt like I was sitting in front of a firing squad all week. "You will do a 130-mile-an-hour lap or you will be shot," you know? It was nice to have done it. I came into the pits and they mentioned it, and the crowd sort of were cheering, so I thought, "Maybe I've done the 130." It was really appreciated by everyone around the track, especially at Quarter Bridge and Bradden Bridge,' continued McGuinness. 'You could actually hear them over the noise of the engine, which I've never heard before ever. It is just something that will stick in my memory for the rest of my life. From Ginger Hall to Ramsey, I was not breathing very well and I was gripping on to the old bike, and I got to the Mountain and I relaxed, took a tear-off off and thought, "Lets do it." I had a mega run on the Mountain and the pit stop, and that seemed to win the race.'

When you are at the top of your game, at peak fitness and with the best team in the paddock achieving what you want to, where do you go next? That is the question McGuinness has been asking himself. He even mentioned retiring at the post-Senior press conference. Since he has had time to think about things, retirement doesn't appear to be an option.

'I don't want to retire. Don't get me wrong, I don't know if it is the right thing to say, but after the race, I thought, "I've nothing left to prove, I've got 25 podiums and 13 wins, 11 years of racing round there. I've never dreamed of that. Ten year ago, I'd have laughed at them. On the flip side, I'm probably riding the best I've ever ridden round there. Probably the fittest I've been in five or six years, and there is no substitute for experience. I'm fit and healthy, and wanting to do it, so why not do it?' he asked. The TT race bug is still there. 'I still want to race round there, I love the place. If I retire, I'll put my thumbs up to the organisers: "Thanks very much." I'd like to help some of the other kids come through. I still want to ride round there, in a nutshell,' he concluded.

The TT is addictive, and McGuinness is hooked like all other TT riders. Giving it up won't be easy, and there is no doubt that, provided the package is right, he will be back in 2008 to hone his perfect lap.

FIRST IS WINNING - SECOND IS NOWHERE
LE OF MAN TT RACES 2008 / MAY 24 - JUNE 7/ NEW 8 RACE PROGRAMME / VISIT WW.IOMTT.COM FOR DETAILS

Photograph: Gold & Goose

TEAM-BY-TEAM

MOTOGP REVIEW

2007 Teams and Riders

MATTHEW BIRT

MotoGP Bike Illustrations

ADRIAN DEAN

GAS
ADVANCE
Alice
Marlboro

Photographs: Gold & Goose

CASEY STONER

Born: 16 October, 1985 – Kurri-Kurri, Australia
GP Starts: 95 (34 MotoGP, 31 250cc, 30 125cc)
GP Wins: 17 (10 MotoGP, 5 250cc, 2 125cc)
World Championships: 1 (MotoGP)

LORIS CAPIROSSI

Born: 4 April, 1973 – Bologna, Italy
GP Starts: 266 (155 MotoGP/500cc, 84 250cc, 27 125cc)
GP Wins: 29 (7 MotoGP, 2 500cc, 12 250cc, 8 125cc)
World Championships: 3 (1 250cc, 2 125cc)

DUCATI DESMOSEDICI GP7

ENGINE

Type: 800cc 90-degree V4, 360-degree crank, DOHC, four valves per cylinder, desmodromic valve gear
Power: Around 225bhp
Ancillaries: Magneti Marelli electronics, NGK sparking plugs, full electronic ride by wire
Lubrication: Shell Advance
Transmission: Gear primary drive, multi-plate dry slipper clutch, six-speed constant-mesh-cassette-type gearbox, Regina chain

CHASSIS

Type: Multi-tube adjustable steel trellis, aluminium swing-arm
Weight: 148kg
Dimensions: N/a
Fuel: 21 litres, Shell
Suspension: Öhlins TTx20 42mm forks front; TTx36 shock with linkage rear
Wheels: Marchesini 16.5in front; 16/16.5in rear
Tyres: Bridgestone
Brakes: Brembo carbon 320mm front; steel 200mm rear

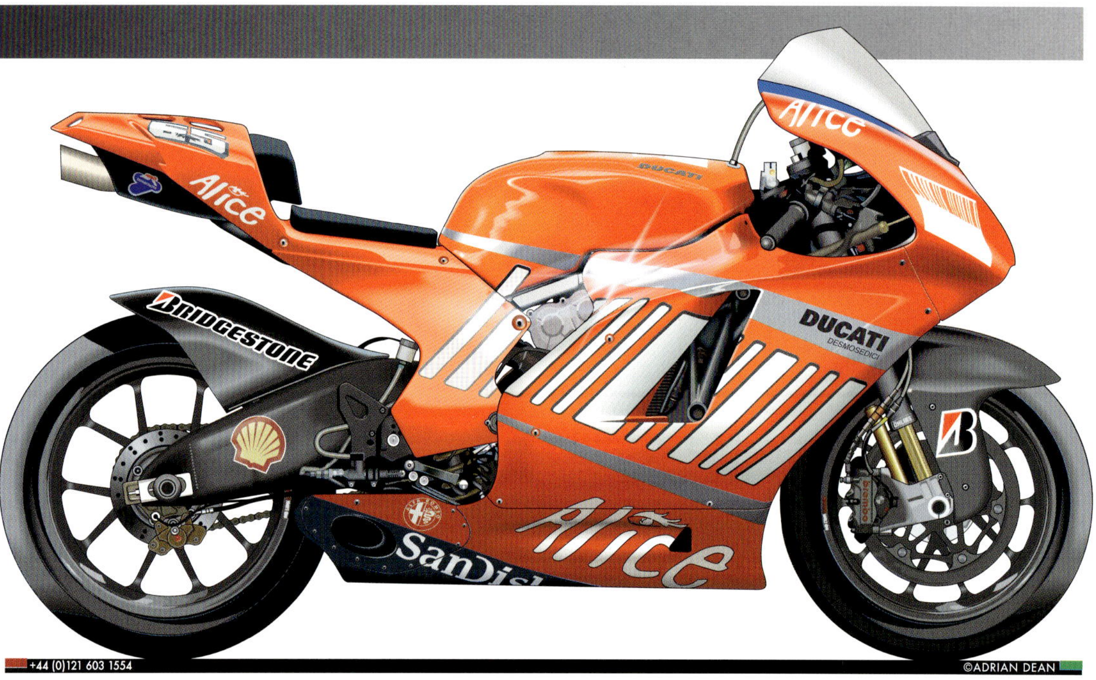

Sponsors & Technical Suppliers
- Alice
- Shell Advance
- Bridgestone
- Sandisk
- Alfa Romeo
- AMD
- Bosch
- Magneti Marelli
- NGK
- Regina Chains
- SKF
- Termignoni
- USAG

TEAM STAFF

Claudio DOMENICALI: Managing Director
Livio SUPPO: Project Manager
Christhian PUPULIN: Technical Co-ordinator
Dario RAIMONDI: Team Manager

DUCATI'S fifth year in MotoGP was laden with unrivalled success, as the Bologna factory heaped humiliation on its Japanese rivals. Such one-sided domination was normally associated with Honda, and more recently Yamaha, but Ducati's supremacy at times bordered on embarrassing for its shell-shocked Far Eastern opposition.

The domination was across the board, as a transformed Casey Stoner took the individual glory, while Ducati won the teams' and manufacturers' titles at a canter

It was evident that Ducati had had the engineering expertise and the tyres (Bridgestone) in previous years, but in gifted Stoner, the final piece of the jigsaw fell into place. Such was his startling form that even Valentino Rossi conceded that the world championship was over as a meaningful contest barely after the half-way stage.

Ducati's success was built on the foundations laid in previous years. Filippo Preziosi remained a pivotal figure behind-the-scenes as technical director, and his ethos remained unchanged. While the Japanese factories seemed preoccupied in worrying about drivability and manoeuvrability in the corners on the new-generation 800s, Ducati continued its philosophy of building a missile for the straights, then worried about handling and fuel consumption.

Alan Jenkins continued his prominent role in charge of aerodynamics, while Livio Suppo remained as project manager. The season's events vindicated Suppo's vision in 2005, when he had persuaded Ducati to ditch Michelin for Bridgestone; he was also the man who snaffled Stoner for a bargain. Both were gambles that paid off handsomely.

Claudio Domenicali continued as Ducati Corse boss, while at senior level, Federico Minoli stood down as Ducati president in May. He was replaced by Gabriele Del Torchio, who was a much less public presence than his predecessor.

Ducati also remained in the blood-red colours of Marlboro, the last survivor of the once-prolific cigarette-brand sponsors, apart from Fortuna in the 250 class, and the longest-standing major team sponsor by far. The bikes could only run fully branded in two races, Qatar and Shanghai; new Europe-wide legislation meant that at first Marlboro's vast, ex-Ferrari hospitality unit was a no-smoking area, until some way was found to circumvent this oxymoron.

Preziosi's new 800cc GP7 was still a beast that only Stoner could master fully, and the Australian rightfully took most of the plaudits. Universally criticised for being crash-happy in 2007, Stoner rejoiced in silencing the loudest dissenters by ending the season with ten victories on his way to inflicting the heaviest defeat of Rossi's illustrious career. In an accident-strewn 125 and 250 career, Stoner had won just seven times in four years; now he won eight times in the opening 13 races, including merciless thrashings in Istanbul, Donington Park, Laguna Seca, Brno and

Misano. Not a bad return for a rider who had been fourth choice on Ducati's wish-list at the end of 2006.

Stoner inherited the bulk of luckless Sete Gibernau's crew from 2006, although the position of race engineer was left vacant when Juan Martinez departed with the Spaniard. Astutely, Ducati signed Cristian Gabarrini from its satellite team, and he would prove a key weapon in Stoner's armoury. He knew what Stoner demanded and liked, and how to channel his occasional volatile temperament into a positive, having worked as an engine-data technician when Stoner rode for Lucio Cecchinello's Aprilia squad in 2003. In a new environment, Stoner immediately found a familiar face he could trust to help his transition.

His reputation as a crasher evaporated completely, as he finished all 18 races, the worst result being sixth in Japan, which ironically secured a first world championship for the rider, Ducati and Bridgestone. By the time Stoner annihilated the field in Turkey, Ducati had moved to secure him on a long-term contract. An option to keep him for 2008 was invoked way ahead of deadline at round seven in Barcelona; less than six weeks later, he had agreed a 2009 contract with an option for 2010.

Stoner's phenomenal success was countered by the wildly contrasting fortunes of Ducati stalwart Loris Capirossi. His crew remained the same as in 2006, with Christian Pupulin at the helm as race engineer. He was also the team's technical co-ordinator. But while Capirossi's team was familiar, his performances weren't. The GP7, which Stoner had clicked with from the start, was almost alien in the hands of the veteran Italian. He scored only three podiums, but bowed out with some of his pride intact when he collected a third straight win at the Twin Ring Motegi in the first-ever, wet-to-dry flag-to-flag race.

Capirossi had to fight allegations that he'd lost his motivation and that retirement beckoned, especially after the birth of his first child, a son called Riccardo, early in the season. At times, he rounded on Ducati. Some of his comments flew close to the wind, and by mid-season, a previously harmonious relationship had become strained. One outburst followed the signing of Marco Melandri after Laguna Seca, in a deal that had been brokered some nine months beforehand. Ducati offered Capirossi a lifeline by proposing a 'three-man' factory team, on the understanding that he would make way for Melandri and switch to the satellite D'Antin outfit.

Capirossi expressed no desire to move nor even remain with Ducati, and he had signed for Suzuki by Brno, having being hotly pursued by Kawasaki. In an expression of goodwill to its first winner on a Ducati, Marlboro made the team's hospitality unit available for him to make the announcement. *MB*

Above: From riders at the sharp end to catering staff in the kitchen, it takes this to make a winning team.
Photograph: Peter J Fox/2snap

Left: Stoner was fast, reliable and devastating.

Below left: Plenty to celebrate – Suppo and Bridgestone's Yamada.

Bottom: Capirossi left with pride intact.
Photographs: Gold & Goose

CASEY STONER PIT CREW

Cristian GABARRINI: Race Engineer
Bruno LEONI: Chief Mechanic
Mechanics
Roberto CLERICI Andrea BRUNETTI
Giorgio CASTURA Lorenzo GAGNI
Gabriele CONTI: Electronics Engineer

LORIS CAPIROSSI PIT CREW

Christhian PUPULIN: Race Engineer
Massimo BRACCONI: Chief Mechanic
Mechanics
Davide MANFREDI Massimo MIRANO
Mark ELDER Luciano BERTAGNA
Marco FRIGERIO: Telemetry

Photographs: Gold & Goose

26

DANI PEDROSA

Born: **29 September, 1985 – Sabadell, Spain**
GP Starts: **113** (35 MotoGP, 32 250cc, 46 125cc)
GP Wins: **27** (4 MotoGP, 15 250cc, 8 125cc)
World Championships: **4** (3 250cc, 1 125cc)

1

NICKY HAYDEN

Born: **30 July, 1981 – Owensboro, USA**
GP Starts: **73** (MotoGP)
GP wins: **3** (MotoGP)
World Championships: **1** (MotoGP)

HONDA RC212V

ENGINE

Type: **800cc 75-degree V4, 360-degree crank, DOHC, four valves per cylinder**
Power: **More than 210ps**
Ancillaries: **HRC electronics, ride-by-wire throttle and fuel-injection system, NGK sparking plugs**
Lubrication: **Repsol**
Transmission: **Gear primary drive, multi-plate dry slipper clutch, six-speed constant-mesh cassette-type gearbox, RK chain**

CHASSIS

Type: **Fabricated aluminium twin-beam**
Weight: **148kg**
Dimensions: **Length 2,050mm; wheelbase 1,440mm; height 1,130mm; width 645mm**
Fuel: **21 litres, Repsol**
Suspension: **Showa 47mm forks front; gas shock with linkage rear**
Wheels: **Enkei 16in front; 16/16.5-inch rear**
Tyres: **Michelin**
Brakes: **Brembo carbon 314mm front; HRC steel 218mm rear (Hayden 255mm rear)**

Sponsors & Technical Suppliers
- Michelin
- Brembo
- NGK
- RK
- Showa
- Showa-Denko
- Snap-on
- DST
- MIVV

TEAM STAFF

Masumi HAMANE: HRC President
Kosuke YASUTAKE: Managing Director
Makoto TANAKA: Team Manager
Roger VAN DER BORGHT: Co-ordinator
Cedric LAPRAEL: Spare Parts Controller
Chris HERRING: Sporting Manager
Norihisa MATSUURA: HRC Engineer

RESTORED as world champion in 2006, Honda's factory team found itself back in the doldrums in 2007. The Japanese superpower contributed to its own downfall with a new 800cc machine that fell well below expectations. Two victories and nine podiums were a paltry return in a new era for MotoGP that everybody had feared would be an HRC walk-over.

It was a widespread belief that Honda had manipulated the capacity reduction from 990 to 800cc. Most feared a repeat of the early 990cc era, when Honda had reigned supreme. The reality was a huge wake-up call for the manufacturer.

Defending champion Nicky Hayden suffered more than most, as Honda grossly underestimated the performance required in the 800 class. The chassis had a confidence draining shortage of feel from the front end, and the early-season V4 motor was sluggish in acceleration and top speed.

Honda was under fire from all quarters from the opening day of testing in Valencia. New project leader Takanori Okuma took over the stewardship from Kyoichi Yoshii. As well as an ear-bashing from his riders, he faced a barrage of questions from the press about accusations that the bike had been specifically engineered and designed to suit the diminutive Pedrosa. Hayden might have been world champion, but it seemed the development responsibility would be Pedrosa's.

Pedrosa remained under the constant gaze of mentor and manager Alberto Puig, while Mike Leitner continued as his crew chief. He won once in impressive, but mind numbingly boring, fashion in Germany – his win was by the biggest margin in ten years. That ended a 12-month victory drought and sparked a rare sign of emotion on the podium. He won again in Valencia, for his first premier-class victory in Spain.

Two of his three non-finishes were caused by French Kawasaki riders. Olivier Jacque wiped him out on lap one in Turkey; Randy de Puniet did likewise in Misano.

As the year wore on, Pedrosa played hardball in negotiating an extension to his contract, and his signing wasn't confirmed until the Japanese GP in September. Rumour was rife that he had been stalling while he waited to see whether his demands for Bridgestone tyres had been met, and that he also wanted cast-iron assurances that Honda planned a major overhaul of the RC212V in '08.

Earlier in the season, Honda had also been sweating on a decision by Repsol, title sponsor for a 13th season." The theory was that Repsol management would wait on Pedrosa's future before extending its contract, their millions and Pedrosa's signature being intrinsically linked. Repsol re-signed in July for another two years, and in truth, Pedrosa was going nowhere. By the time he agreed to stay, every other top factory vacancy had been filled.

Hayden was in the first of a new two-season contract with

Above: The might of Honda's official factory team.

Left: Dani Pedrosa had a hard year with a good finish.

Below: Michelin's Jean-Philippe Weber joins the group around Pedrosa's machine.

Photographs: Gold & Goose

DANI PEDROSA PIT CREW

Alberto PUIG: Crew Chief
Mike LEITNER: Chief Mechanic
Mechanics
Jordi PRADES Mark BARNETT
Christophe LEONCE Masashi OGO
John EYRE: Tyres
Jose Manuel ALLENDE: Telemetry
Manuel OLIVENCIA: Showa
Toshihiko SAWADA: HRC Engineer

NICKY HAYDEN PIT CREW

Pete BENSON: Chief Mechanic
Mechanics
Mark LLOYD Craig BURTON
Koji KAMINAKABEPPU David GUITTEREZ
Yuji KIKUCHI: Tyres
Ramon AURÍN: Telemetry
Takeshi ARAI: Showa
Tetsuo KINOE: HRC Engineer

Right: New HRC president Masumi Hamane wielded a sharp axe.

Below, from left: Team manager Makoto Tanaka; Repsol remained a loyal sponsor; MD Satoru Horiike (on left, with RC212V project leader Takanori Okuma) did not last the year.

Bottom: Nicky Hayden lacked the machinery to defend his 2006 title.
Photographs: Gold & Goose

HRC and again working with Kiwi crew chief Pete Benson. He would be forced to concede, though, that he had contemplated what might have been, since his refusal to switch to Ducati paved the way for Casey Stoner.

The hugely likeable American had a title defence to forget, but throughout, for the most part, he remained supportive of Honda in the face of all the problems. He refused to publicly slaughter HRC, and when he did show signs of frustration, it was always done in a dignified and carefully worded way.

By the time Assen came around, Hayden had scored a best of just seventh in the opening eight races. Pedrosa had received new parts earlier, and once the Kentucky rider got hold of them, his fortunes soared. He scored three podiums in four races in Holland, Germany and the Czech Republic, but they were his only three visits.

Like Pedrosa, Hayden has pushed hard for a switch to Bridgestone, but at the last race, the team confirmed that it would remain on Michelin tyres for 2008.

Aside from the problems on the track, it was a year of upheaval at HRC. Suguru Kanazawa's reign as president ended on April 1, when he took over the running of Honda's car production plant in Swindon, while also becoming vice-president of Honda Europe.

Installed as his successor was Masumi Hamane, who made his first public appearance at the Sachsenring. One of his first presidential engagements in the paddock was to witness Hayden's motor blow itself into dozens of pieces on the start/finish straight in practice.

Hamane gave himself time before exerting his power, and his first major decision was a surprising one. HRC Managing Director Satoru Horiike was relieved of his duties, as was General Manager Tsutomo Ishii. Honda had not only taken flak for poor results in 2007, but also there was derision for the way the controversial 'friendly fire' incident in Estoril the previous season had been handled.

After that calamitous day, when Pedrosa sideswiped title hopeful Hayden, the title 'Team' became spurious. A team in name and appearance, but it operated more like two separate entities, with Hayden admitting that he and Pedrosa barely spoke at all. However, Team Manager Makoto Tanaka escaped Hamane's falling axe.

HRC introduced Horiike's successor in Malaysia, where Kosuke Yasutake was on a meet-and-greet mission among the teams, officials and media.

MB

TISSOT
SWISS WATCHES SINCE 1853
motoGP
TISSOT
SWISS WATCHES SINCE 1853
OFFICIAL TIMEKEEPER
More
than a watch
Tissot. Innovators by Tradition
TISSOT
1853
METEO
THERMO
ALTIMETER
ALARM
CHRONO
COMPASS
SWISS MADE
T-TOUCH

Photographs: Gold & Goose

CHRIS VERMEULEN

Born: **19 June, 1982 – Brisbane, Australia**

GP Starts: **37** (MotoGP)

GP Wins: **1** (MotoGP)

JOHN HOPKINS

Born: **22 May, 1983 – Ramona, USA**

GP Starts: **96** (MotoGP/500cc)

SUZUKI GSV-R

ENGINE

Type: **800cc 75-degree V4, 360-degree crank (180-degree 'long bang' from Mugello on), DOHC, four valves per cylinder, pneumatic valve return gear**

Power: **Around 210bhp**

Ancillaries: **Mitsubishi electronics, NGK sparking plugs, electronic ride by wire**

Lubrication: **Motul**

Transmission: **Gear primary drive, multi-plate dry slipper clutch, six-speed constant-mesh-cassette-type gearbox, RK chain**

CHASSIS

Type: **Fabricated aluminium twin-beam**

Weight: **148kg**

Dimensions: **Length 2,600mm; wheelbase 1,450mm; height 1,150mm; width 660mm**

Fuel: **21 litres, Elf**

Suspension: **Öhlins TTx20 42mm forks front; TTx36 shock with linkage rear**

Wheels: **JB Magtan 16.5in front; 16/16.5in rear**

Tyres: **Bridgestone**

Brakes: **Brembo carbon 305 or 314mm front; steel rear**

+44 (0)121 603 1554 © ADRIAN DEAN

Sponsors & Technical Suppliers
- Bridgestone
- Motul
- Mitsubishi
- Yoshimura
- Kokusan Denki
- Toyo Radiator
- MAG Tools
- RK Chain
- DID
- NGK
- AFAM
- 2D
- Puig Racing Screens
- Dread

TEAM STAFF

Fumihiro OOHNISHI: Group Leader
Paul DENNING: Team Manager
Howard PLUMPTON: Operations Manager
Shinichi SAHARA: Technical Manager
Keiichiro FUKUZAWA: Engine Development
Tetsuya SASAKI: Chassis Development
Davide MARELLI: ECU Control Assistance
Tex GEISSLER: Data Analysis
Richard FRANCIS: Sub-assemblies
Russell JORDAN: Parts and Logistics
Dean MILLIER: Team Physio
Tim WALPOLE: Press Officer

IT was perhaps no surprise that Suzuki re-emerged as a major player in MotoGP in 2007. The superstitious members of the paddock noted that Suzuki's premier-class success came in seven-year cycles – Kevin Schwantz winning the 500cc crown in 1993, and Kenny Roberts Junior in 2000.

Suzuki didn't win the title in 2007, but it did return to winning ways, the Hamamatsu factory claiming its first-ever four-stroke victory, after Chris Vermeulen successfully splashed his way to glory at Le Mans. It was an early reward for a highly promising winter testing campaign, which had seen the British-based squad out of the blocks quickly for the new 800cc era. Much of that was owed to group leader Fumihiro Ohnishi and technical manager Shinichi Sahara, who had set to work early, testing 800 concepts on the final 990cc GSV-R V4 in 2006.

Early evidence that Suzuki would feature more prominently came at the fourth race in Shanghai, where John Hopkins ended his own personal quest for a podium with third place. By the end of the year, further proof of Suzuki's resurgence had come in the World Championship team battle, Hopkins and Vermeulen having out-scored Valentino Rossi's Fiat Yamaha factory effort, and ended up only one point shy of Repsol Honda.

In attempting to re-establish itself as a leading force in MotoGP, Suzuki's squad was pretty much man-for-man identical to 2006. Again, the team was under the guidance of Paul Denning, who had stepped up from successfully managing Suzuki's British Superbike team in 2005. Rizla remained title sponsor, after following Denning from BSB in 2006. A new contract was agreed in Brno for Rizla to stay for a third season in 2008.

Hopkins continued to work under his trusted crew chief Stuart Shenton, while Vermeulen's bond with Tom O'Kane only grew stronger in their second season together.

As in his debut season, Vermeulen's results stood out more than those of Hopkins, at least earlier in the year. This was largely down to his stunning Le Mans success, but he scored three other podiums, including distant second places to compatriot Casey Stoner at Laguna Seca and Misano.

His other podium came in rapidly changing conditions at a dull Donington Park, and by the end of the season, he was still finding it hard to shake off his reputation for being lightning fast only in the rain or on tracks where he flourished in World Superbikes. As well as his wet victory at Le Mans, he claimed pole position in the rain in Assen.

Regardless, a top-six championship finish underlined his progression; his only non-finish was in Assen, where he was the innocent victim of a rash and grossly miscalculated overtaking move by de Puniet. His future was secured when he signed a two-year extension to his contract, a deal that was announced immediately after his rostrum in America.

Hopkins's long-awaited podium breakthrough in Shanghai was followed with further rostrum visits in Brno, Misano and Va-

KOUSUKE AKIYOSHI

Born: 12 January, 1975 – Kurume, Japan

GP Starts: 2 (MotoGP)

Above: Rizla team rolled out in the pits.

Left: Hopkins gets it over in his last year with Suzuki.

Below left: Manager Denning takes advice from the experienced Stuart Shenton.

Below: Vermeulen only had one non-finish all year.

Photographs: Gold & Goose

NOBUATSU AOKI

Born: 31 August, 1971 – Sumaga, Japan

GP Starts: 167 (110 MotoGP/500cc, 57 250cc)

GP Wins: 1 (250cc)

CHRIS VERMEULEN PIT CREW

Tom O'KANE: Chief Mechanic
Simon WESTWOOD: Crew Leader
Mechanics
Tsutomo MATSUGANO Ray HUGHES
Mark FLEMING (assistant)
Renato PENNACCHIO: Telemetry

JOHN HOPKINS PIT CREW

Stuart SHENTON: Chief Mechanic
Ian GILPIN: Crew Leader
Mechanics
George DZIEDZIC Jeffrey OH
Jez WILSON (assistant)
Gary McLAREN: Telemetry

lencia, but a maiden victory remained elusive. Having spent all but one of his six MotoGP campaigns with Suzuki, Hopkins sought a change of scenery and agreed an early deal to switch to Kawasaki's factory squad. The move sparked friction between the Japanese factories, but Suzuki pounced on Loris Capirossi. A deal for the Italian was concluded at Germany's Sachsenring and announced in Brno after the summer break.

Suzuki stole a march on its rivals in Sepang, where test rider Nobuatsu Aoki finished 13th on a prototype of the 2008 GSV-R. The bike ran a modified chassis and swing-arm, new exposed exhaust system and the repackaging of components for mass centralisation, but it was minus the new 2008 motor.

Test rider Kousuke Akiyoshi also figured. He was 17th in his first European race in Jerez, and was running seventh, in front of Hopkins and Vermeulen, in Japan when a mechanical failure ruled him out with just three laps remaining.

There were also incessant rumours about Suzuki's future racing plans in 2007, centred on the ambitions of past and present paddock protagonists. Suzuki was locked in negotiations with former 80 and 125 world champion, and high-profile 125 and 250 team boss, Jorge Martinez about the lease of a third bike for 2008. Martinez had the finances and infrastructure in place, and crucially, it seemed, the support of Suzuki legend Schwantz, who was being touted as team manager. Japanese management, though, was reluctant to commit to anything more than at present, for fear of jeopardising the performance of the factory team.

The issue was clouded further when it became apparent that Schwantz had been actively seeking funding for his own project, possibly for American Superbike champion Ben Spies, or at least to invest in the factory team. As in 2006, rumours abounded that he would replace Denning, but in the end it was just talk.

Suzuki might have been reserved in expanding its involvement for 2008, but as a compromise to Martinez and to prevent him from taking his money and team to a rival, Suzuki agreed to supply the Spaniard with two bikes in 2009. Another way of cementing a future deal is likely to be Martinez running a third GSV-R in selected races during 2008, most likely with Spies on board.

MB

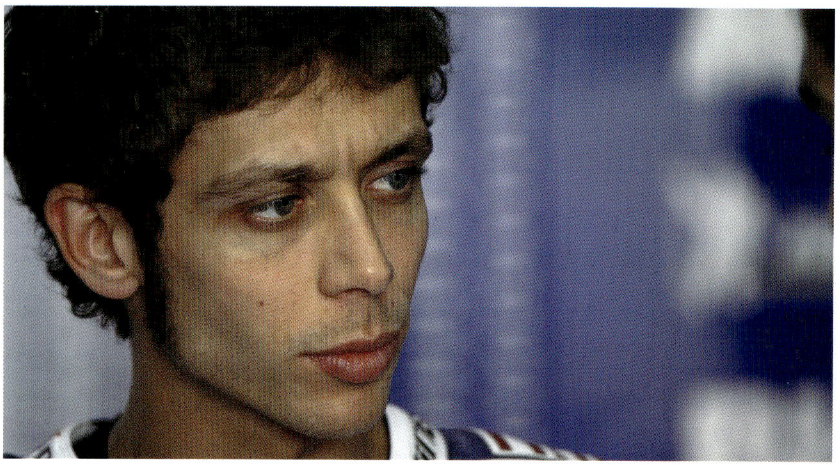

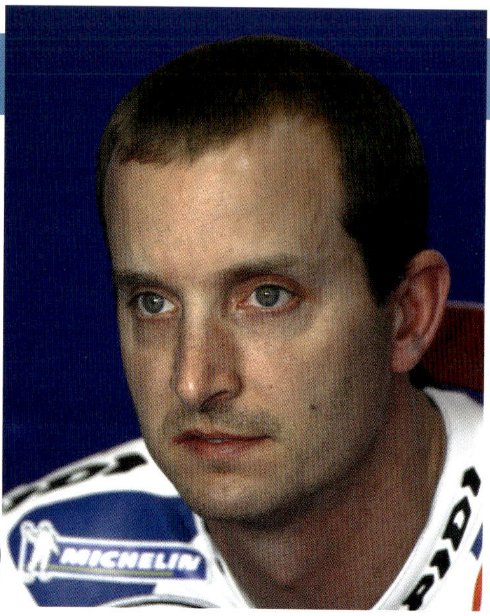

Photographs: Gold & Goose

46

VALENTINO ROSSI

Born: 16 February, 1979 – Urbino, Italy

GP Starts: 192 (132 MotoGP/500cc, 30 250cc, 30 125cc)

GP Wins: 88 (49 MotoGP, 13 500cc, 14 250cc, 12 125cc)

World Championships: 7 (5 MotoGP/500cc, 1 250cc, 1 125cc)

5

COLIN EDWARDS

Born: 27 February, 1974 – Houston, Texas

GP Starts: 84 (MotoGP)

World Championships: 2 (World Superbike)

YAMAHA M1

ENGINE

Type: 800cc across-the-frame in-line four, irregular firing intervals, DOHC, four valves per cylinder, steel valve springs initially

Power: Around 210bhp

Ancillaries: Magneti Marelli electronics, NGK sparking plugs, full electronic ride-by-wire

Lubrication: Motul

Transmission: Gear primary drive with direction-reversing balance shaft, multi-plate dry slipper clutch, six-speed constant-mesh cassette-type gearbox, DID chain

CHASSIS

Type: Fabricated aluminium twin-beam

Weight: 148kg

Fuel: 21 litres

Suspension: Öhlins TTxTR25 42mm forks front (Rossi 48mm forks Mugello onwards; Edwards TTx20 'customer' forks); TTxTR44 shock with linkage rear

Wheels: Marchesini 16in front; 16/16.5in rear

Tyres: Michelin

Brakes: Brembo carbon 320mm front; Yamaha steel rear

Sponsors & Technical Suppliers
- Wudy
- Acer
- Motul
- Michelin
- Blauer
- Termignoni
- Alpinestars
- DID
- NGK
- Magneti Marelli
- Beta
- Brembo
- 2D
- Öhlins

TEAM STAFF

Lin JARVIS: Managing Director, Yamaha Motor Racing
Masao FURUSAWA: Executive Officer, Yamaha Engineering Operations
Masahiko NAKAJIMA: MotoGP Group Leader
Kouichi TSUJI: Project Leader
Davide BRIVIO: Team Director

IF Valentino Rossi and Yamaha's factory team thought 2006 had been tough, nothing could have prepared them for the turmoil both and on off the track in 2007.

The mission to win back the title had started with renewed vigour, helped in the main by the shock early announcement on 1 February that Rossi had extended his contract. The new deal saw him commit to the end of 2008. That was followed four weeks later by the much anticipated confirmation that car giant Fiat would be Yamaha's title sponsor for the two years. Not only was it a boost for Yamaha, but also for the general gloomy economic climate in MotoGP: Fiat was the first major new sponsor to invest since Konica Minolta's arrival in 2005.

Fiat's marketing strategy was to use the huge exposure generated by Rossi to promote specific brands, and at selected races he ran in one-off livery: for the new Cinquecento in the Netherlands, and promoting Abarth in Australia. He was still the biggest star on the grid, but after the morale crushing, last-round defeat by Nicky Hayden in 2006, Rossi's golden run of five successive MotoGP world titles had been ended.

Continuity at least came off the track, with Lin Jarvis continuing as managing director of Yamaha Motor Racing. Davide Brivio, who had been influential in prising Rossi away from Honda at the end of 2003, was team director, while the Japanese hierarchy remained the same. Masao Furusawa was again the most senior figure, in the new role of Executive Officer Yamaha Engineering Operations. Former YZR-M1 project leader Masahiko Nakajima was Yamaha MotoGP group leader, with Shigeto Kitigawa senior manager of the Technical Development Division. For the second successive season, Kouichi Tsuji was YZR-M1 project leader.

Rossi's crew remained identical too, with Jerry Burgess again a key component of Yamaha's bid to start the 800cc era as champion.

In truth, Rossi and Yamaha had a season to forget; the most abiding memories came off rather than on the track. Rossi had his worst premier-class campaign since his debut season in 2000, collecting only four wins, although his brilliant surge from 11th in Assen was one of the most impressive rides of the year.

After his crash in Germany, he conceded that his title hopes were over. Losing clocked up some uncomfortable 'firsts'. He had never before failed to be champion two years in a row. His demotion to third after retirement from the final round was the first time since his rookie year of 1996 that he had finished lower than second in any world championship class.

Not even Rossi's talents could mask a two-fold technical disadvantage against a Ducati on Bridgestone tyres in the hands of a rampant Casey Stoner. Rossi's Yamaha was embarrassingly slow, and by the end of the season, his patience had snapped. He issued an unequivocal threat to re-

tire or join another team unless Yamaha engineers gave him a competitive and reliable bike for 2008.

He also became an outspoken critic of the once all-conquering Michelin tyres. Rossi was anonymous in Laguna Seca and Brno, and his mind was made up. He wanted Bridgestones, which resulted in a controversial and ugly political battle. He faced allegations of manipulating a deal with Dorna boss Carmelo Ezpeleta. After all, it was Ezpeleta whose pressure eventually secured a Bridgestone deal, after Yamaha had initially been knocked back in August.

Bridgestone agreed to supply on 24 October, and this delighted Rossi on two fronts. Double world 250 champion Jorge Lorenzo had already been recruited by Yamaha in 2006, the Japanese factory seeking young talent to fill the void when Rossi does quit. The swoop left Rossi disenchanted, as he had no desire to share the garage with the fiery Spaniard, and he campaigned tirelessly to keep Colin Edwards as his team-mate. Yamaha refused to budge, despite rumours that they might appease Rossi by running a fifth bike in a separate team for Lorenzo.

Rossi's Bridgestone deal, though, ensured that he would need to have little or no contact with Lorenzo in 2008. With Lorenzo on Michelin tyres, there would be a dividing wall in the pit. The solution, largely on Bridgestone's and Michelin's demands to protect their intellectual property, will see Rossi and Lorenzo operate out of two separate boxes, although both in Fiat colours.

The restructure saw Nakajima appointed team director, with team manager Brivio responsible for only Rossi's squad. Edwards's crew chief, Daniele Romagnoli, was appointed manager of Lorenzo's team, with Ramon Forcada signed from LCR Honda to act as crew chief.

On top of all that, Rossi had the distraction of a multi-million-euro tax-evasion charge hanging over his head since the August summer break. The headline grabbing issue remained unresolved at the end of the season, but did see Rossi sever all connection with his egotistical personal manager, Gibo Badioli and his management company, Great White London.

At the same time as news of the tax probe broke, GWL was also under scrutiny. Fiat Yamaha team co-ordinator Marc Canela had been installed as Chief Executive earlier in the year, but without the knowledge of Yamaha management. It was an obvious conflict of interest, and Canela walked before he was pushed.

Lorenzo's arrival ended Edwards's three-year tenure in the factory team. Third in the second race in Jerez, and second and pole position at Donington Park were the rare highlights of a forgettable season. The Texan will ride for Yamaha's satellite Tech 3 team in '08, planning after that to close his career in AMS Superbikes. *MB*

Above: The team and factory staff line up at Mugello.

Left, clockwise from left top: MD Lin Jarvis, executive officer Masao Furusawa, key crew chief Jerry Burgess and team director Davide Brivio.

Bottom: Rossi in action.

Photographs: Gold & Goose

COLIN EDWARDS PIT CREW

Daniele ROMAGNOLI: Crew Chief
Mechanics
Walter CRIPPA Javier ULLATE
Valentino NEGRI
Roberto BRIVIO (assistant/logistics)
Youichi NAKAYAMA: Yamaha Engineer
Carlo LUZZI: Telemetry

VALENTINO ROSSI PIT CREW

Jeremy BURGESS: Crew Chief
Mechanics
Bernard ANSIAU Alex BRIGGS
Brent STEPHENS
Gary COLEMAN (assistant/logistics)
Hiroya ATSUMI: Yamaha Engineer
Matteo FLAGMINI: Telemetry

Photographs: Gold & Goose

TONI ELIAS

Born: 26 March, 1983 – Manresa, Spain

GP Starts: 127 (44 MotoGP, 48 250cc, 35 125cc)

GP Wins: 10 (1 MotoGP, 7 250cc, 2 125cc)

MARCO MELANDRI

Born: 7 August, 1982 – Ravenna, Italy

GP Starts: 155 (79 MotoGP, 47 250cc, 29 125cc)

GP Wins: 22 (5 MotoGP, 10 250cc, 7 125cc)

World Championships: 1 (250cc)

GRESINI HONDA RC212V

ENGINE

Type: 800cc 75-degree V4, 360-degree crank, DOHC, four valves per cylinder

Power: Around 210ps

Ancillaries: HRC electronics and ride-by-wire throttle and fuel-injection system, NGK sparking plugs

Lubrication: Castrol

Transmission: Gear primary drive, multi-plate dry slipper clutch, six-speed constant-mesh-cassette-type gearbox, RK chain

CHASSIS

Type: Fabricated aluminium twin-beam

Weight: 148kg

Dimensions: Length 2,050mm; wheelbase 1,440mm; height 1,130mm; width 645mm

Fuel: 21 litres

Suspension: Showa 47mm forks front; gas shock with linkage rear

Wheels: Enkei 16.5in front; 16/16.5in rear

Tyres: Bridgestone

Brakes: Brembo carbon 314mm front; HRC steel 218mm rear

+44 (0)121 603 1554 ©ADRIAN DEAN

Sponsors & Technical Suppliers
- Hannspree
- Castrol
- Bridgestone
- San Carlo
- Agos
- Valsir
- Morellato
- Manpower
- Polini
- Domino
- Berner
- Leo Vince
- Milwaukee

TEAM STAFF

Fausto GRESINI: Chairman & Managing Director

Carlo MERLINI: Commercial & Marketing Director

Fabrizio CECCHINI: Technical Director

ONCE a shining example of how a satellite squad can seriously rival the big-budget factory teams, Gresini Honda saw its fortunes plummet alarmingly in 2007, in what proved to be a year of major under-achievement.

The evidence was overwhelming. Between 2003 and 2005, Sete Gibernau and Marco Melandri had been significant threats to Valentino Rossi's relentless domination in MotoGP. During that period, Gresini riders had easily outperformed and embarrassed their counterparts in Honda's official factory team. Despite Nicky Hayden's 2006 title success, Melandri won more races than any other Honda rider that year, just as the Italian had done in the previous season.

Results in 2007 never came close to replicating that former glory, however, and for the first time since 2002, a Gresini rider failed to win a premier-class race. By the end of the season, the double 125 world champion was facing another major off-track battle. The words 'sponsorship' and 'crisis' cropped up more and more to describe the Rimini-based squad, but as always, Gresini managed to ease any fears that his team was close to folding.

For 2007, Gresini had his third sponsor in as many years. At the end of 2005, he had lost Telefónica MoviStar and gained Fortuna. After Melandri's dogged title fight in '06, the Altadis owned brand walked. In 2007, backing was from Hannspree, in a Honda dual-sponsorship project that also saw it back the Ten Kate Honda World Superbike and Supersport teams. However, the fresh investment wasn't enough to secure naming rights to the team. Hannspree had gained huge exposure in World Superbikes, thanks to James Toseland's second world title, and also Kenan Sofuoglu's Supersport title. Hannspree duly signed a deal to be title sponsor of World Superbikes in 2008. That deal saw it withdraw from Gresini's squad.

At least on the track, Gresini appeared to have stability. He'd retained Melandri as number-one rider, and the former 250 world champion was again with crew chief Antonio Jimenez, with whom he had joined in mid-2006, after his previously successful relationship with Fabrizio Cecchini had faded. Cecchini remained the team's technical director, which also encompassed being crew chief to Toni Elias.

Unsurprisingly, optimism burgeoned during early winter testing. Melandri had been successful in convincing Gresini to ditch Michelin tyres for Bridgestones, while everybody expected Honda's first RC212V to be a world-beater. Melandri had also been buoyed by assurances, during the late collapse of a Ducati deal, that he would receive official factory-rider status, akin to the level of support for the Repsol duo. HRC had problems of its own, however, and the support, when it came, was too little and too late.

Melandri was only ever on the fringe of being in serious

MICHEL FABRIZIO

Born: 17 September, 1984 – Rome, Italy
GP Starts: 27 (11 MotoGP, 16 125cc)

Above: Team principal and former champion Fausto Gresini.

Above left: Full-time rider Toni Elias was injured mid-season, being replaced by Fabrizio (centre left, number 84) and veteran Duhamel (left).

Bottom: Marco Melandri – on the fringe of HRC largesse.

Photographs: Gold & Goose

MIGUEL DUHAMEL

Born: 26 May, 1968 – Montreal, Canada
GP Starts: 14 (1 MotoGP, 13 500cc)

MARCO MELANDRI PIT CREW

Antonio JIMINEZ: Chief Mechanic
Mechanics
Andrea BONASSOLI Pedro CALVET
Alberto PRESUTTI
Jonny DONELLI (assistant)
Diego GUBELLINI: Telemetry

TONY ELIAS PIT CREW

Fabrizio CECCHINI: Chief Mechanic
Mechanics
Ryoichi MORI Simone ALESSANDRINI
Ivan BRANDI
Renzo PINI (assistant)
Francesco FAVA: Telemetry

contention, however, and largely was overlooked by HRC. Eight times, he was a top-six finisher, and he failed to score points only once, when a nerve problem left him with such severe mobility issues that he withdrew from Brno. That problem was a legacy of a massive crash after a tangle with Kurtis Roberts at Laguna Seca. Ironically, despite being battered and bruised, Laguna saw him claim one of only three podiums. His others were second places in the sodden French GP and the sweaty Malaysian race, yet he still secured fifth in the overall standings.

Melandri was one of the most outspoken critics of Honda's new 800, as not even the superiority of Bridgestone tyres could mask its deficiencies. Throughout the early part of the season, though, he held a carefully guarded secret. A clause in his 2006 contract with Gresini had prevented him from moving to Ducati, but as early as November, he had penned a performance-related pre-contract agreement with the Bologna factory. The incentive was clear: be in the top six in the standings after Laguna Seca, and a Ducati deal was his. Kawasaki sat in the wings waiting to pounce, but third place in America sealed the deal, and the official announcement was made minutes after the race.

Elias, too, experienced another arduous campaign, the highlights being a brilliant second in Istanbul, and third at the Twin Ring Motegi. The lowest point came at his jinxed Assen. In the corresponding weekend in 2006, he had cracked a bone in his shoulder and missed two races. This time, it was worse and the diagnosis bleaker. He suffered a spiral fracture of his left femur in opening free practice, but heroically came back to ride less than two months later in Brno.

In Germany, his seat went to favoured Gresini replacement Michel Fabrizio, who claimed tenth. In America, after Neil Hodgson has politely declined, Elias's substitute was Canadian veteran Miguel DuHamel, whose last taste of the big time had come against the likes of Wayne Rainey, Mick Doohan and Kevin Schwantz. DuHamel retired after ten laps.

Gresini signed perennial 125 and 250 crasher Alex de Angelis immediately after the Estoril GP, and he confirmed Shinya Nakano as second rider in the build-up to the season's conclusion in Valencia. This was at the behest of HRC management, who pledged to give their compatriot one more chance.

Prior to that, he had launched an audacious bid to lure Max Biaggi back into the fold. However, the move was dead and buried before it gathered any serious momentum. The wounds of a stormy relationship at Repsol Honda in 2005 had clearly not healed, HRC blocking a potential swoop, despite publicly denying that it had the right to veto rider selection by a satellite team. Suzuki's World Superbike team had just released Biaggi, but his reputation for being a phenomenal rider, yet flawed character, preceded him. *MB*

19

14

13

Photographs: Gold & Goose

RANDY DE PUNIET

Born: 14 February, 1981 – Maisons Lafitte, France

GP Starts: 148 (35 MotoGP, 80 250cc, 33 125cc)

GP Wins: 5 (250cc)

OLIVIER JACQUE

Born: 29 August, 1973 – Villerupt, France

GP Starts: 136 (56 MotoGP/500cc, 80 250cc)

GP Wins: 7 (250cc)

World Championships: 1 (250cc)

ANTHONY WEST

Born: 17 July, 1981 – Maryborough, Australia

GP Starts: 118 (25 MotoGP/500cc, 92 250cc, 1 125cc)

GP Wins: 1 (250cc)

KAWASAKI ZX-RR

ENGINE

Type: **800cc across-the-frame in-line four, irregular firing intervals, DOHC, four valves per cylinder, pneumatic valve springs**

Power: **Around 215bhp**

Ancillaries: **Magneti Marelli electronics, NGK sparking plugs, electronic ride by wire**

Lubrication: **Elf**

Transmission: **Gear primary drive, multi-plate dry slipper clutch, six-speed constant-mesh-cassette-type gearbox, EK chain**

CHASSIS

Type: **Fabricated aluminium twin-beam**

Weight: **148kg**

Dimensions: **Length, height and width n/a; wheelbase 1,420mm (adjustable)**

Fuel: **21 litres, Elf**

Suspension: **Öhlins TTx20 42mm forks front; TTx36 shock with linkage rear**

Wheels: **JB Magtan 16.5in front; 16/16.5in rear**

Tyres: **Bridgestone**

Brakes: **Brembo carbon 320mm front; steel rear**

Sponsors & Technical Suppliers
- Elf
- Bridgestone
- Akrapovic
- FCC
- Touch 4
- G-Shock
- Magneti Marelli
- AFAM
- EK Chains
- NGK
- 2D
- Beta
- Rex

TEAM STAFF

Ichiro YODA: Racing Director
Michael BARTHOLEMY: Competition Manager
Naoya KANEKO: Technical Manager
Danilo CASONATO: EFI Engineer
Andrea DOSOLI: EFI Technician
Marcel DUINKER: Suspension Engineer
Dario RAIMONDI: Team Co-ordinator
Ian WHEELER: Marketing & Communications

FREE from the bitter in-fighting and power struggles that had cast a shadow over the factory team in 2006, Kawasaki embarked on a fresh start in 2007. The acrimonious split from former team manager Harald Eckl had been resolved without the arbitration that had seemed inevitable, and Kawasaki was looking forward with renewed impetus.

Eckl's departure had allowed the Japanese company to regain some control over its own racing destiny; the result was the creation of a new subsidiary of KHI. Kawasaki Motors Racing was born to oversee the running of the MotoGP team.

Managing director was Yoshio Kawamura, while Kiyoaki Maeda was KHI senior manager of the MotoGP department.

In the new order, operations manager Michael Bartholemy was promoted to the newly created role of competitions manager. In effect, that made him the team manager, the Belgian overseeing key decisions in conjunction with Ichiro Yoda (technical director).

The winter was chaotic and hectic. The new ZX-RR 800 was weeks behind schedule, and when it was rolled out in late November, it was hopelessly unreliable. Development on the track ran in tandem with a rebuilding process off track. Eckl's KMGP company had owned the race trucks and hospitality unit, so Kawasaki had to source a large chunk of the team's infrastructure from scratch. In turning over a new leaf, the team quit its base in Germany and relocated to one in Holland.

Although he was technical director, Yoda's influence was as strong as ever, as he operated more like a general manager, the trusted Naoya Kaneko continuing as technical manager. MotoGP project leader and chief designer of the new ZX-RR, Yoshimoto Matsuda, was also a key member of the squad.

The turmoil within the team and delays with its new 800 led to Kawasaki being turned down by Casey Stoner, Alex Barros and Carlos Checa at the end of 2006. With options fading fast, test and development rider Olivier Jacque was given a shock chance to resurrect a career that had ended in 2004.

It was a situation that Bartholemy and Yoda didn't want to repeat, so during the season, Kawasaki embarked on one of the most aggressive recruitment drives ever seen. The ZX-RR had ducked under the radar in testing, but arguably it was the most improved bike in 2007, and the performance breakthrough grabbed the attention of several top riders. As early as the third race, Kawasaki was being linked with a host of big names, John Hopkins, Marco Melandri and Loris Capirossi being the leading contenders.

Hopkins landed himself a two-year contract shortly after the Dutch TT in Assen, sparking rumours of a hugh sponsorship deal with American energy drink Monster as a result. Monster already sponsored Kawasaki's American Superbike and Supersport efforts, as well as Supercross and Motocross factory

11 87 95

FONSI NIETO

Born: **2 December, 1978 – Madrid, Spain**

GP Starts: **100** (1 MotoGP, 95 250cc, 4 125cc)

GP Wins: **5** (250cc)

AKIRA YANAGAWA

Born: **15 July, 1971 – Kageshima, Japan**

GP Starts: **4** (MotoGP)

ROGER LEE HAYDEN

Born: **30 May, 1983 – Owensboro, USA**

GP Starts: **1** (MotoGP)

Below: **New managing director Yoshio Kawamura.**

Below centre: **Ichiro Yoda guided the green bikes forward.**

Bottom: **Belgian Michael Bartholemy was effectively team manager.**

Below left: **The team photo was taken at the Italian GP, Olivier Jacque's final race.**

Photographs: Gold & Goose

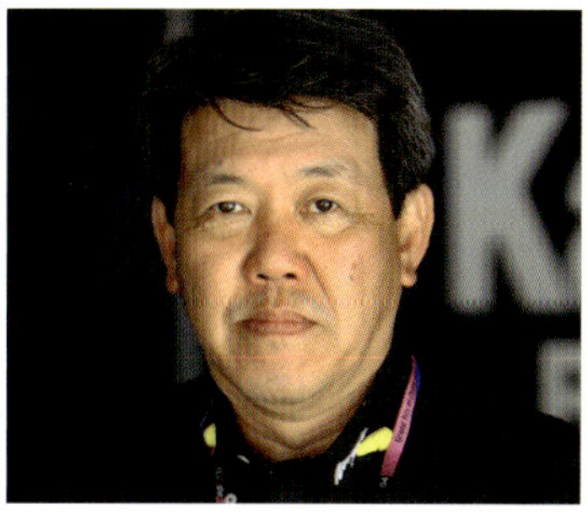

teams. A permanent move is expected in 2009, with some presence likely throughout 2008.

While Hopkins was successfully poached from under the nose of Suzuki, in a move that blew the rider market open earlier than ever, it was unclear at that stage whether he would have one or two team-mates in 2008. Kawasaki pondered long and hard over whether to field a third bike in 2008, which for a while left them debating about rehiring Randy de Puniet and adding Anthony West. By Misano, the third-bike option was abandoned until 2009.

Australian West had finally got his long-overdue shot at the big-time after Jacque's disastrous and injury-hit return. The last in a long line of crashes and resulting injury in Catalunya convinced Jacque to return to his testing role, a move fully supported by Kawasaki's management. West had started the season in the Sicilia Aprilia 250 squad, but quit after a torrid spell. Initially, he'd replaced Kevin Curtain in Yamaha Germany's World Supersport squad, and had impressed with brilliant wins at Silverstone and Misano, which earned him a full-time R6 deal. Then Kawasaki offered him a test ride in Barcelona, after Jacque had crashed again in what proved to be the final straw for the Frenchman, who announced his retirement from racing at Donington Park.

West was duly installed as his replacement for the British GP, but only after he'd paid a 50,000 Euros buy-out fee to Yamaha. By Misano, he'd done enough to convince Kawasaki that he was worth retaining, although his form dipped once he'd secured a permanent seat. He scored bests of seventh in America and Japan, but ended the season last in Valencia. That had followed the embarrassing blunder in Sepang, where he had started from a 250 grid slot.

Frenchman de Puniet made his big breakthrough in 2007. His first podium came with second in the flag-to-flag Japanese GP, and he was always a prominent figure in qualifying, claiming nine top-six grid positions. He was as error-prone as ever, though, and ended the season with 12 crashes, which for the second successive season gave him the unenviable distinction of leading crasher. And he did little to dispel his reputation for being a hot-head. At Assen, he wiped out Chris Vermeulen and, at the first turn in Misano, took Dani Pedrosa and Nicky Hayden into the gravel with him after another rash moment of over-exuberance.

Jacque's disastrous return gave Kawasaki World Superbike rider Fonsi Nieto a replacement ride at Le Mans, after the Frenchman's first injury. Briton Neil Hodgson had also been linked with the ride. The Spaniard was 11th.

Roger Lee Hayden, younger brother of world champion Nicky, got his first taste of MotoGP at Laguna Seca as a wild-card, and he impressed with tenth place. Japanese veteran Akira Yanagawa contested Twin Ring Motegi, finishing 17th. *MB*

OLIVIER JACQUE/ANTHONY WEST PIT CREW

Fiorenzo FANALI: Chief Mechanic

Mechanics

Benoit LEFEBVRE Florian FERRACCI

Jason CORNEY Robert KLEINHERENBRINK

Gerold BUCHER: Telemetry

RANDY DE PUNIET PIT CREW

Christophe BOURGUIGNON: Chief Mechanic

Mechanics

Timothy PALMER Emanuel BUCHNER

Jerome GALLAND Daniel PETAK

Emmanuel ROLIN: Telemetry

Photographs: Gold & Goose

4

ALEX BARROS

Born: **18 October, 1970 – Sao Paulo, Brazil**

GP Starts: **276** (245 MotoGP/500cc, 14 250cc, 17 80cc)

GP Wins: **7** (3 MotoGP, 4 500cc)

66

ALEX HOFMANN

Born: **25 May, 1980 – Mindelheim, Germany**

GP Starts: **106** (64 MotoGP, 41 250cc, 1 125cc)

D'ANTIN DUCATI DESMOSEDICI GP7

ENGINE

Type: **800cc 90-degree V4, 360-degree crank, DOHC, four valves per cylinder, desmodromic valve gear**

Power: **Around 225bhp at 19,500rpm**

Ancillaries: **Magneti Marelli electronics, NGK sparking plugs, full electronic ride by wire**

Transmission: **Gear primary drive, multi-plate dry slipper clutch, six-speed constant-mesh-cassette-type gearbox, Regina chain**

CHASSIS

Type: **Multi-tube adjustable steel trellis, aluminium swing-arm**

Weight: **148kg**

Dimensions: **N/a**

Fuel: **21 litres, Agip**

Suspension: **Öhlins TTx20 42mm forks front; TTx36 shock with linkage rear**

Wheels: **Marchesini 16.5in front; 16/16.5in rear**

Tyres: **Bridgestone**

Brakes: **Brembo carbon 320mm front; steel 200mm rear**

Sponsors & Technical Suppliers

- Calidona
- Gaviota Simbac
- Agip
- Bridgestone
- Motocard
- Condor
- Dada.net
- Regina
- AFAM
- Rex

TEAM STAFF

Luis D'ANTIN: Chairman & Managing Director
Alberto CARRERO: Team Co-ordinator
Felix RODRIGUEZ: Technical Co-ordinator
Manuel CAZEAUX: Ducati Electronics Engineer
Jose CONTRERAS: Electronics Engineer
Liam SHUBERT: Logistics

THE Madrid-based Pramac d'Antin team started 2007 as Ducati's satellite squad for a fourth successive season, and in its healthiest state for a number of years.

Much to the relief of team manager Luis d'Antin, his Pramac backed squad had ended a tense relationship with Dunlop to run on Bridgestone tyres – the same as Ducati's factory team riders Casey Stoner and Loris Capirossi.

Significantly, d'Antin would also benefit from an increased desire from the Bologna factory to see its satellite team's fortunes prosper. Differences between the factory GP7 machines and those leased to d'Antin would be minimal, if any. This was a big shift in Ducati strategy, as previously d'Antin had relied on upgraded, year-old hand-me-downs from the factory squad.

With the switch to Bridgestone rubber, d'Antin's team, formed in 1997, could claim to be more closely associated with its factory supplier than any of the other five independent teams on the grid. Underlying the closer relationship, Ducati had two full-time engineers in the garage, but the pay-off was the desire to have more of a say in rider selection.

The quest to unearth and then nurture another gem like Stoner, ready for the factory team, would be one of the more pressing tasks for d'Antin, although for 2007, he fielded one of the most experienced line-ups. Alex Hofmann was retained, but he failed to see out the entire season after a personal melt-down in Estoril. In addition, Brazilian veteran Alex Barros was rescued from his sojourn in World Superbikes to extend his remarkable record of premier-class appearances to 245. Barros worked with crew chief Fabiano Sterlacchini, while Hofmann was under the guidance of Emanuele Martinelli.

While the team's stock rose considerably off the track, the season was disappointing in many respects and served to add further credence to the performance of Stoner. Barros claimed a solitary podium with third in Mugello, which came shortly after an impressive fourth in Turkey. After that, though, he was just a peripheral figure, fifth in Phillip Island being his best result in a tough second half of the season.

German Hofmann had a season to forget. His best-ever finish was fifth at a saturated Le Mans, but too often he was at the back end of the top ten. The catalyst to his sudden departure came in Laguna Seca, where circuit novice Sylvain Guintoli slammed into him at the top of the famous Corkscrew. He suffered grotesque injuries to his left hand that initially cast doubt on his ability to ride again.

He'd ridden heroically in Misano to claim 11th, but the sympathy was replaced by scorn in Portugal, where he retired early in the race. Inexplicably, he cited a lack of motivation for his withdrawal; hours after the race, he was sacked. Hofmann threatened rather meekly to take legal action to claim his seat back, but the damage was done, and he was not seen again.

Hofmann's misfortune – whether self-inflicted or not – gave a

22 57 72

Photographs: Gold & Goose

IVAN SILVA

Born: 12 June, 1982 – Barcelona, Spain

GP Starts: 8 (4 MotoGP, 4 250cc)

CHAZ DAVIES

Born: 10 February, 1987 – Knighton, Great Britain

GP Starts: 73 (3 MotoGP, 55 250cc, 15 125cc)

SHINICHI ITO

Born: 7 December, 1966 – Miyagi, Japan

GP Starts: 66 (MotoGP/500cc)

Below: Barros's top-three at Mugello gave good cause for celebration.

Bottom right: Chaz Davies was a favoured substitute.

Bottom left: Ex-racer Luis d'Antin.

Photographs: Gold & Goose

surprise MotoGP chance to Briton Chaz Davies. He had quit 250 GPs at the end of 2006, exhausted and frustrated at trying to secure half-decent machinery with no success. While trying to resurrect his career in America, he inadvertently found the door to GPs ajar again, 16th place as a last-minute replacement for Hofmann at Laguna Seca thrusting him back into the limelight.

Spaniard Ivan Silva replaced Hofmann in Brno, but was thoroughly unconvincing, and although officially he was the team's nominated replacement rider, Davies was called upon for the last three races. He had been asked to ride in Japan too, but a serious infection in his left elbow ruled him out. Bridgestone test rider Shinichi Ito replaced Hofmann at the Twin Ring Motegi and finished 15th.

Davies failed to score a point and didn't figure in d'Antin's 2008 plans. Initially, Ducati had been keen to get him to replace veteran Shinichi Ito as Bridgestone test rider. Uncertainty surrounding the one-make tyre issue clouded the matter, however, and Davies didn't want to quit racing full time.

D'Antin briefly flirted with the idea of another deal with Max Biaggi. In 2006, however, not even Biaggi's close confidant and Pramac CEO Paolo Campinoti could resolve their differences, and neither particularly wanted to cover old ground.

James Toseland and Hiroshi Aoyama were considered, along with Alex de Angelis and Andrea Dovizioso. Eventually, Spaniard Toni Elias was signed, shortly after the penultimate round in Malaysia, to partner Sylvain Guintoli.

Pramac was more than just title sponsor, as it continued to co-own the d'Antin effort. In a deal announced at the final race in Valencia, the team clinched a title sponsorship deal for 2008 and 2009 with Italian telecommunications giant Alice, long-term co-sponsor of Ducati's factory team. The new squad will simply be called the Alice Team. *MB*

ALEX BARROS PIT CREW

Fabiano STERLACCHINI: Track Engineer
Marco BALEIRON: Chief Mechanic
Mechanics
Franciso LOPEZ Paul RUIZ
Thomas LANTES
Sergio VERBENA: Telemetry

ALEX HOFMANN PIT CREW

Emanuele MARTINELLI: Track Engineer
Martin ZABALA: Chief Mechanic
Mechanics
Michele ANDREINI David LOPEZ CACHEDA
Alejandro TEJEDO
Andrea OLEARI: Telemetry

Photographs: Gold & Goose

MAKOTO TAMADA

Born: **4 November, 1976 – Ehime, Japan**

GP Starts: **82** (81 MotoGP, 1 250cc)

GP Wins: **2** (MotoGP)

SYLVAIN GUINTOLI

Born: **24 June, 1982 – Montelimar, France**

GP Starts: **99** (19 MotoGP/500cc, 80 250cc)

TECH 3 YAMAHA M1

ENGINE

Type: **800cc across-the-frame in-line four, irregular firing intervals, DOHC, four valves per cylinder, initially steel valve springs**

Power: **Around 210bhp**

Ancillaries: **Magnetic Marelli electronics, NGK sparking plugs, full electronic ride by wire**

Lubrication: **Motul**

Transmission: **Gear primary drive, multi-plate dry slipper clutch, six-speed constant-mesh cassette-type gearbox, DID chain**

CHASSIS

Type: **Fabricated aluminium twin-beam**

Weight: **148+kg**

Dimensions: **Length 2,050mm; wheelbase 1,440mm; height 1,140mm, width 645mm**

Fuel: **21 litres**

Suspension: **Öhlins TTxTR25 42mm forks front; TTxTR44 shock with linkage rear**

Wheels: **Marchesini 16/16.5in front; 16/16.5in rear**

Tyres: **Dunlop**

Brakes: **Brembo carbon 320mm front, Yamaha steel rear**

Sponsors & Technical Suppliers

Wudy
AMV
Magneti Marelli
Alpinestars
NEC
Brembo
NGK
DID
2D
E-max
Rex
Shilton

TEAM STAFF

Hervé PONCHARAL: Team Manager
Gérard VALLEE: Team Co-ordinator
Eric REBMANN: Parts Manager
Olivier BOUTRON: Fuel/Tyres

THE France-based Tech 3 started its started its seventh campaign as Yamaha's solitary satellite team, thanks largely to the continued investment of Dunlop, which had saved Hervé Poncharal's squad from collapse in 2006. Dunlop had grasped the opportunity to finally put its tyres on top-line competitive machinery, but the project had suffered a blow when Carlos Checa left at the 11th hour to join LCR Honda. Checa's Michelin and Bridgestone knowledge, coupled with years of experience, had made him a crucial element of the Tech 3 and Dunlop partnership.

Team and tyre manufacturer had desperately wanted continuity to help drive development forward. Once again, Dunlop committed heavy investment in resources and development, not only to keep Tech 3 afloat, but also to convince other teams that it was a tyre brand worthy of consideration. The loss of Checa took both them back to square one.

His replacement was Makoto Tamada. The Japanese rider had plenty of experience, but had floundered so horrendously on Michelin tyres that his selection was based more on the lack of any other candidates than his technical ability.

On the other side of the garage was MotoGP's only rookie, Sylvain Guintoli, who would need time to learn the intricacies of riding a MotoGP bike fast, let alone to play a key role in the tyre development process.

Tamada fought gamely enough under the guidance of experienced crew chief Guy Coulon, but his best finish was eighth in the searing Laguna Seca heat. And a career that once appeared laden with gold petered out when he departed MotoGP at the end of the season.

In essence, the occasional flashes of brilliance were Dunlop's primary issue. In certain conditions, the tyres performed above expectation, like in the perilous damp at Twin Ring Motegi, where Guintoli produced a brilliant performance to finish fourth. The French rider also grabbed some personal glory in his home race at Le Mans, where he led briefly in the wet before crashing and remounting to finish ninth.

Guintoli, who worked with crew chief Gary Reynders, showed that he more than merited a place among the sport's elite, and he only failed to finish in one race. However, the seasoned 250 campaigner had made an inauspicious start to his Yamaha career. He broke a collarbone tyre testing on the 990cc YZR-M1 at Paul Ricard before Christmas, then he crashed twice in two days on his first serious test at Sepang in January. Yamaha management banned him from riding on the final day, but the rebuke seemed to galvanise him.

Dunlop's fate had been sealed as early as round five, under the grey and gloomy skies of Le Mans. Poncharal and Yamaha had agreed that they would continue for 2008. By signing up so early, Poncharal had time to show riders that he had secured bikes already, but more significantly, he had the time to attract

Left: Guintoli proved a quick learner.

Centre left: Engine swap for the satellite-team M1.

Below: Tamada leads his team-mate.

Below centre: In Dunlop's yellow, team men scan the pit monitors.
Photographs: Gold & Goose

Bottom: Tamada and team manager Hervé Poncheral.
Photograph: Peter J Fox/2snap

fresh investment. Because Dunlop was to be axed.

The agreement with Yamaha had come with several stipulations, one being that the team switch to Michelin or Bridgestone. In Yamaha's eyes, Dunlop had made progress, but nowhere near sufficient to see two of their machines on the Anglo/Japanese rubber for a third successive season. Even with a third of the season remaining, Dunlop boss Jeremy Ferguson had an air of resignation about 2008 premier-class prospects.

Tyres had been a major stumbling block in Poncharal attracting riders, and talk of a Michelin or Bridgestone deal suddenly made Tech 3 an appealing career prospect. Poncharal had brief discussions with Bridgestone, many weeks before the general clamour for the Japanese tyres from the factory Honda and Yamaha teams.

That caused rumours to emerge of an all-American dream team, with Edwards and Hopkins backed by energy drink Monster, a personal sponsor of the latter. These gathered momentum when CEO Mark Hall attended the Italian GP.

It proved only partially correct. At Brno, Edwards confirmed that his three-year tenure as Valentino Rossi's factory team-mate was over. Yamaha softened the blow for the Texan by moving him over to Tech 3, with assurances that he would not be stripped of his factory rider status.

A major coup for Poncharal was the capture of another double World Superbike champion in James Toseland. Both Honda and Ducati had courted the British rider, but Poncharal was a former team-mate of Toseland's personal manager, Roger Burnett, which helped discussions move on at a rapid rate. Talks started as early as Jerez, and became serious in Donington Park as Toseland began to discover that his MotoGP options at Honda were diminishing rapidly.

In the end, he had no option at all, with Honda asking him to remain in World Superbikes. Toseland's confidence had already swung massively in favour of Tech 3 and, like Chris Vermeulen at the end of 2005, he shirked Honda's option, agreeing a deal during the August summer break.

Guintoli, meanwhile, had signed a pre-contract agreement with the d'Antin Ducati squad in Brno, which was confirmed officially by the Spaniard in Estoril.

MB

MAKOTO TAMADA PIT CREW

Guy COULON: Crew Chief
Mechanics
Benoît BRUNEAU Alexandre DUPONT
Julien LAJUNIE
Nicolas GOYON: Telemetry

SYLVAIN GUINTOLI PIT CREW

Gary REYNDERS: Crew Chief
Mechanics
Jerômé PONCHARAL Josian RUSTIQUE
Laurent DUCLOYER
Andrew GRIFFITH: Telemetry

HONDA LCR

Below: Independent team owner Lucio Cecchinello.

This page, far right: Checa and crew chief Ramon Forcada confer with Showa and HRC technicians.

Photographs: Gold & Goose

CARLOS CHECA

Born: 15 October, 1972 – Sant Fruitos, Spain

GP Starts: 220 (192 MotoGP/500cc, 27 250cc, 1 125cc)

GP Wins: 2 (500cc)

Photographs: Gold & Goose

LCR HONDA RC212V

ENGINE

Type: 800cc 75-degree V4, 360-degree crank, DOHC, four valves per cylinder

Power: More than 210ps

Ancillaries: HRC electronics, ride-by-wire throttle and fuel-injection system, Denso sparking plugs

Transmission: Gear primary drive, multi-plate dry slipper clutch, six-speed constant-mesh cassette-type gearbox, RK chain

CHASSIS

Type: Fabricated aluminium twin-beam

Weight: 148kg

Dimensions: Length 2,050mm; wheelbase 1,440mm; height 1,130mm; width 645mm

Fuel: 21 litres

Suspension: Showa 47mm forks front; gas shock with linkage rear

Wheels: Enkei 16in front; 16.5/16in rear

Tyres: Michelin

Brakes: Brembo carbon 314mm front; HRC steel 218mm rear

CARLOS CHECA PIT CREW

Ramon FORCADA: Crew Chief
Mechanics
Joan CASAS Casanovas XAVIER
Roberto GUIDI Chris RICHARDSON
Manolo ZAFFERANI: Telemetry
Yoshimi NAKAIS: HRC engineer

Sponsors & Technical Suppliers
Michelin
Lee
Denso
Givi
Deca
Eurobet

TEAM STAFF

Lucio CECCHINELLO: Team Principal
Oscar HARO: Sponsorship & PR
Elisa PAVAN: Logistics & Press Relations

THE late departure of Casey Stoner saw the LCR Honda squad embark on its second MotoGP campaign with experienced Spaniard Carlos Checa on the satellite machine.

Born out of the remnants of the Sito Pons squad at the end of 2005, the team was run by highly respected former 125 GP winner Lucio Cecchinello. In the absence of a title sponsor again, the Italian continued to operate the team under his own LCR banner out of Monaco. Online betting firm Eurobet figured prominently, extending a partnership into a seventh year with selected 'title sponsor' deals in three of its key markets.

Checa had become something of a nomad in MotoGP, LCR being his third team in as many years. He had knocked back an approach by Kawasaki's factory squad to join LCR, as the prospect of a Honda on Michelin tyres was too good to resist.

Hopes were high as Checa joined forces with vastly experienced crew chief Ramon Forcada. Before nurturing highly rated Casey Stoner in 2006, he had won acclaim for his work with Alex Barros, John Kocinski and Alex Criville.

Checa, though, was completely at odds with the RC212V, which he dwarfed and fiercely criticised. Not even a rigorous winter training regime, which saw him slim down considerably, could help him adapt, and his reputation for being a prolific crasher was restored, as too often he pushed over the limit in a bid to improve a hopeless situation.

He scored points in just three of the opening eight races, and only twice placed in the top six, in Jerez and Misano. A major issue with the RC212V was a vague feeling from the front end, which seemed to handicap Checa more than most.

Some sort of salvation came in the prestigious Suzuka eight-hour endurance race. Checa claimed pole and finished an impressive second on a factory FireBlade Superbike, which he had liked at once. His mind was made up; his future lay in World Superbikes. Honda was impressed by his display and canvassed for his inclusion in its World Superbike plans for 2008. Weeks later, after a career spanning 220 races in GPs, Checa landed a coveted slot with the Ten Kate Honda squad, but only after branding the RC212V the worst bike he'd ever raced.

Cecchinello eyed Andrea Dovizioso and Alex de Angelis; even double American Superbike champion Ben Spies was mooted. Shortly after Brno, though, he opted for a trusted ally in Frenchman Randy de Puniet, who had raced for Cecchinello on an Aprilia 250 in 2003 and 2004, claiming four victories.

A significant loss for LCR was the departure of Forcada, lured to Yamaha's factory team to spearhead 250 maestro Jorge Lorenzo's rookie campaign. His replacement was to be Christophe Bourguignon, poached from Kawasaki's factory team.

The team also negotiated a switch to Öhlins suspension, despite Honda owning Showa. Hamish Jamieson, former factory Suzuki and Kawasaki crew chief, was in negotiation about a return to MotoGP with LCR as suspension technician. *MB*

KONICA MINOLTA HONDA

Photographs: Gold & Goose

SHINYA NAKANO

Born: **10 October, 1977 – Chiba, Japan**

GP Starts: **149** (115 MotoGP/500cc, 34 250cc)

GP Wins: **6** (250cc)

Below: **Shinya Nakano never felt happy on the Honda.**

This page, far left: **The small, but dedicated, Konica Minolta crew.**

Photographs: Gold & Goose

KONICA MINOLTA HONDA RC212V

+44 (0)121 603 1554 ©ADRIAN DEAN

ENGINE

Type: **800cc 75-degree V4, 360-degree crank, DOHC, four valves per cylinder**

Power: **Around 210ps**

Ancillaries: **HRC electronics and ride-by-wire throttle and fuel-injection system, NGK sparking plugs**

Transmission: **Gear primary drive, multi-plate dry slipper clutch, six-speed constant-mesh-cassette-type gearbox, DID chain**

CHASSIS

Type: **Fabricated aluminium twin-beam**

Weight: **148kg**

Dimensions: **Length 2,050mm; wheelbase 1,440mm; height 1,130mm; width 645mm**

Fuel: **21 litres**

Suspension: **Showa 47mm forks front; gas shock with linkage rear**

Wheels: **Enkei 16in front; 16.5in rear**

Tyres: **Michelin**

Brakes: **Brembo carbon 314mm front; HRC steel 218mm rear**

EVERY team, apart from Ducati's factory effort, could be said to have had a tough season in 2007. But such an assessment applied all too well to the dismal fortunes of the Konica Minolta-backed Japan Italy Racing (JiR) squad.

Gianluca Montiron, the driving force behind the JiR project, had won a stay of execution from Konica Minolta for 2007, but the results he desperately needed to prolong the partnership never materialised. At the end of another season that had fallen woefully short of expectations, the ambitious JiR collaboration was in tatters, in its current guise at least. A lack of results and, more significantly, a dearth of exposure saw Konica Minolta quit, having received a minimal return on a hefty investment.

The decision was hardly a shock, as Konica management had threatened to pull the plug after two disastrous years with Makoto Tamada in 2005 and 2006.

The Japanese influence on the team remained as strong as ever, Shinya Nakano having been prised away from Kawasaki's factory team after a moderately successful three-year-stint aboard the ZX-RR.

Nakano's arrival failed to spark a dramatic revival in fortunes, although Honda was largely culpable. Like so many other riders on the new RC212V, Nakano struggled to make any sort of impression. Moreover, the satellite teams were severely restricted when it came to improving their dire predicament, as HRC attention was focused on its factory team more than ever before.

As with Tamada, technical director Giulio Bernadelle and crew chief Hirano Yutaka couldn't get Nakano to meld successfully with the Honda/Michelin package. His best results were three tenth places, two of them in the opening two rounds, and he was always locked in a battle for the minor places.

Rumblings about the team's future first surfaced in early June. Andrea Dovizioso's Kopron Scot 250 team confirmed that it had submitted a formal proposal to HRC to move to MotoGP in 2008. Dovizioso's 250 Honda boss, Cirano Mularoni, was reported to have had the Italian under contract for 2008, and to be reluctant to surrender his involvement with the former 125 world champion. He set about graduating to MotoGP with the British-based Italian.

Refusing to waver from its position of fielding a maximum of six complete machines (excluding the Team Roberts engine-lease contract), Honda suggested that Kopron Scot open negotiations with an existing satellite team.

Weakened by the withdrawal of Konica Minolta, Montiron agreed to a merger after protracted negotiations, the new operation to be called JiR Scot. Dovizioso will be the rider, with Montiron team director and Mularoni team manager. Kopron will remain as an associate sponsor. Scot Construction's continued investment under the leadership of president Giovanni Torri ensured that it retained naming rights. A major additional sponsor was due to be announced in January 2008. *MB*

SHINYA NAKANO PIT CREW

Yutaka HIRANO: Head Technician

Mechanics

Luigi DALLIA Marco Antonio BONESSO

Marco ROSA GASTALDO Filippo BRUNETTI

Alessandro LA BARBA Telemetry

Sponsors & Technical Suppliers

- HRC
- Michelin
- Varese 2008
- Mapei
- Whirlpool
- Gannelli
- DID
- Beta
- Adige
- Rex

TEAM STAFF

Gianluca MONTIRON: Managing Director & Team Manager

Giulio BERNARDELLE: Technical Director

Elisabetta COSTA: Marketing & Communications Officer

10

80

Photographs: Gold & Goose

KENNY ROBERTS Jnr

Born: 25 July, 1973 – Mountain View, USA

GP Starts: 185 (167 MotoGP/500cc, 18 250cc)

GP Wins: 8 (500cc)

World Championships: 1 (500cc)

KURTIS ROBERTS

Born: 17 November, 1978 – Mountain View, USA

GP Starts: 34 (23 MotoGP, 11 250cc)

ROBERTS KR212V

ENGINE

Type: 800cc, 75-degree V4, 360-degree crank, DOHC, four valves per cylinder

Power: More than 210ps

Ancillaries: HRC electronics, ride-by-wire throttle and fuel-injection system

Transmission: Gear primary drive, multi-plate dry slipper clutch, six-speed constant-mesh cassette-type gearbox, Regina chain

CHASSIS

Type: Fabricated aluminium twin-beam

Weight: 148kg

Dimensions: N/a

Fuel: 21 litres

Suspension: Öhlins TTx20 42mm forks; TTx36 shock with linkage rear

Wheels: Marchesini 16in front; 16/16.5in rear

Tyres: Michelin

Brakes: Nissin carbon front; steel rear

+44 (0)121 603 1554

©ADRIAN DEAN

Sponsors & Technical Suppliers

- Motorpoint
- Alpinestars
- Michelin
- Top 1 Oil
- KR Tuned
- K&N
- 2D
- Hotbodies Racing
- WRP
- AFAM
- Nissin
- Garmin
- Regina Chains

KENNY ROBERTS Jnr/KURTIS ROBERTS PIT CREW

Tom JOJIC: Race Engineer

Mechanics

Craig CUMMINGS Carl GILES

James LEONARD Fred KELLO

Brian HARDEN Telemetry

Phil CRIPPS: Spares

Dave ELLIS: Transport

Stuart McNALLY: Transport

TEAM STAFF

Kenny ROBERTS: Team Principal

Chuck AKSLAND: Team Manager

Warren WILLING: Technical Consultant

Charlie MOODY: Operations Manager

OPTIMISM ran high at Team Roberts after its first year of collaboration with Honda had sparked a dramatic upturn in fortunes for both the Banbury-based squad and rider Kenny Roberts Junior. The 2000 World Champion had returned to prominence in 2006, and he started 2007 with the hope of mounting his first serious world-title threat since 2000.

Kenny Roberts remained the team's figurehead, but as its fortunes took a nosedive, so did his interest. Long-serving team manager Chuck Aksland was left to oversee affairs. Warren Willing's widely respected engineering skills were retained, while Tom Jojic continued as crew chief.

As with so many independents, Team Roberts had relied heavily on Dorna subsidies to remain on the grid. That didn't appear sufficient at the start of the season, and before racing had begun, Roberts was indicating that his team would fold. British car supermarket Motorpoint got on board shortly before the first race, but Roberts said it was only a stay of execution.

By the second race, he'd clinched another sponsorship deal. American merchandise company F1 Max-X and MGM's Las Vegas Treasure Island Hotel and Casino signed up, and some of the off-track concerns were put on hold.

On the track, a plan to launch a genuine title tilt was effectively over before a wheel had been turned in anger. The new 800cc RC212V motor was found to be well below expectations. The team's engineers built the chassis, exhausts and bodywork, but couldn't improve the dire performance of the V4 motor.

Above: Kurtis at Laguna – a struggle at home.
Photograph: Gold & Goose

Right: Kenny Roberts, lone independent GP constructor.
Photograph: Peter J Fox/2snap

Below left: Team KR stalwarts, Chuck Aksland (left) and Warren Willing.

Below far left: Last-minute backing brought classic privateer livery, and a stay of execution.
Photographs: Gold & Goose

The season hadn't reached the half-way stage when Roberts Junior went into self-imposed exile. In seven races, he had finished in the points only twice.

Youngest of the Roberts racing dynasty – Kurtis – was drafted in at Mugello. HRC had given the team permission to run two riders for a limited time, engine mileage being a serious restricting factor in fielding a two-rider effort for the rest of the year.

Kurtis remained after his brother left, but had an even more torrid time, although achieving better results.

A relationship that was growing increasingly fragile was further complicated by events leading up to the British GP. Emerging British Superbike rider Jonathan Rea had been given permission to wild-card at Donington Park, but at the last-minute, his ride was vetoed from Japan.

The relationship was doomed once Honda rejected Roberts's request for a two-rider lease deal for 2008. He let an end-of-September deadline expire, then entered negotiations with anybody willing to listen. Kawasaki, Suzuki and Yamaha, however, were all reluctant to expand beyond their current effort.

Only Ducati remained. The Bologna bosses had appeared genuinely interested at Laguna Seca, but with no firm plans put on the table by Roberts, they preferred to sit tight until he came up with a more concrete proposal.

By the end of the season, Roberts was pinning his hopes on being part of a three-pronged American motorsport project, bankrolled by famous Las Vegas hotel the MGM Grand. Ducati continued to remain interested, but at the season's finale, Roberts was still waiting on confirmation from investors. *MB*

ILMOR

FOUR-WHEEL luminary Mario Illien's MotoGP venture had two weaknesses. Firstly, the engine lacked the finesse of control needed on two wheels. Secondly, the rivers of sponsorship he knew from car racing simply didn't exist.

The first might have been solved, electronically or mechanically – Ilmor was experimenting with heavier crankshafts. The second proved crippling.

Australian Andrew Pitt and veteran Jeremy McWilliams joined the England-based team. The first-ever 800 had made a thoroughly underwhelming debut at the end of the previous season, but the high-tech pneumatic-valve-spring V4 had plenty of horsepower, and had been refined and developed over the winter.

Pre-season tests proved it had lost none of its abrupt manners, pitching McWilliams off, a broken femur the worst of several injuries.

He was back for Qatar, but did not race after another bruising crash in practice; Pitt did not finish. It was the last time the bike was seen, though Pitt tested later in the season.

The reason, announced Illien glumly, was financial, and many saw the hand of part-owner Roger Penske in the sudden decision to withdraw. 'We came to the conclusion that we had not sufficient backing for the season,' said Illien. 'We haven't given up. We want to come back if we can find backing.' So far, he has not.

Above left: Jeremy McWilliams was wounded in action.

Above right: Australian Andrew Pitt had just one race.

Above centre: Origami Ilmor was fast, but needed development.

Top: Mario Illien: 'We haven't given up.'
Photographs: Gold & Goose

2007 MOTOGP TEAMS' CHAMPIONSHIP

	TEAM	POINTS
1	DUCATI MARLBORO TEAM	533
2	REPSOL HONDA TEAM	369
3	RIZLA SUZUKI MOTOGP	368
4	FIAT YAMAHA TEAM	365
5	HONDA GRESINI	297
6	PRAMAC D'ANTIN	181
7	KAWASAKI RACING TEAM	176
8	DUNLOP YAMAHA TECH 3	88
9	HONDA LCR	65
10	KONICA MINOLTA HONDA	47
11	TEAM ROBERTS	14

2007 MOTOGP CONSTRUCTORS' CHAMPIONSHIP

	CONSTRUCTOR	POINTS
1	DUCATI	394
2	HONDA	313
3	YAMAHA	283
4	SUZUKI	241
5	KAWASAKI	144
6	KR212V	14

250cc: A SHOT IN THE ARM

jorge lorenzo

andrea dovisioso

THE 250 class, dying slowly on its feet, was given a reviving shot by an influx of talent from 125s. Bright stars from the same source in 2006, Jorge Lorenzo and Andrea Dovizioso, were joined by reigning champion Alvaro Bautista, former champion Thomas Luthi and close challenger Mikka Kallio. They came in at the top, Bautista and Kallio winning two races apiece. But they could change the focus: once again, it was concentrated on defending champion Lorenzo and 2007 close challenger Dovizioso.

The national make-up reflected the duel: six riders from Spain and six from Italy. The next-best-represented was Japan with four riders, and then one each from the Czech Republic, Finland, France, Hungary, Britain, Switzerland, Thailand, Germany and (for the first few races) Australia. Great Britain got a second representative when Dan Linfoot, a frequent wild card last season, took over the seat suddenly vacated by Anthony West, but he had been replaced himself by the end of the season – plans for the promising rider to join mid-season with a proposed new team foundered after encountering sponsorship problems.

The oldest rider in the class was 33-year-old Roberto Locatelli. He was also the most experienced, with a total of 192 GP starts, of which 94 had been in the 125 class. Only Alex de Angelis came close, with a total of 130, 65 each in the two classes. Obviously, he had started younger, being just 23. The youngest was late-season replacement Federico Sandi, at 18, undercutting Aleix Espargaro by less than two weeks.

Machine-wise, the dominance of Aprilia again underlined the continuing lack of interest by Japanese factories. There were 15 of the Italian machines, ranging from factory missiles to privateer veterans, plus two Gilera clones. Honda fielded a rather half-hearted half-dozen, among them four RS250-W kitted machines.

KTM continued with its two-rider team, a full factory-backed effort.

APRILIA/GILERA

The centrepiece of Aprilia's handful of fully factory-backed machines was the lone Fortuna of Lorenzo (20 at the end of the season, from Majorca). The team was down to one rider, save for several impressive wild-card rides from fellow Spaniard Alex Debon (31).

Two more were allocated to Jorge 'Aspar' Martinez, who had added an extra rider to his highly professional team, sponsored by Master Mapfre. It was a second year for San Marino rider Alex de Angelis (23), and a promotion from the 125 team for favoured protégé and Spanish compatriot Alvaro Bautista (22).

Factory support came also for the Emmi-Caffe Latte Aprilia of Thomas Luthi (21, from Switzerland); and for Lorenzo's former team-mate, fellow Spaniard Hector Barbera (20), although not for his Team Toth team-mate, the Hungarian Imre Toth (22).

The remaining Italian V-twins were spread among a range of private teams of sundry levels.

Blusens Aprilia Germany fielded still-promising Spaniard Aleix Espargaro (18), while the other (non-Germany) side of the pit started with 23-year-old Arturo Tizon, until a falling-out saw him replaced by rookie Efren Vazquez (21). Both were from Spain.

The colourful Italian Campetella Racing retained luckless Japanese rider Taro Sekiguchi (31), alongside another ex-125 rider, Italian Fabrizio Lai, too old to stay down at 28. Kiefer-Bos-Sotin Racing was back with two riders again, German Dirk Heidolf (31) and Italian Alex Baldolini (22).

Frenchman Jules Cluzel (19) was in the one-rider Angaia Team; Czech rider Karel Abram (17) was with the Cardion AB squad; and a series of riders were in Team Sicilia, starting with Anthony West (26), then Briton Dan Linfoot (19) and finally, for the last three races, Italian Federico Sandi (18), poached from the 125 class.

The Metis Gilera team was run in close conjunction with the Aprilia factory, taken over in 2006 by the Piaggio group, which owns the Gilera name. It had a strong pair of Italian riders: veteran Roberto Locatelli (33) was paired with Marco Simoncelli (20).

HONDA

The main HRC team, although as much by association as hands-on involvement, was backed by Repsol. It fielded the 22-year-old younger Aoyama brother, Shuhei, for a second year, and another rising youngster fresh from 125s, the Spaniard Julian Simon (20), who had a feisty rookie season.

Technically, there was little to distinguish their machines from the Kopron Team Scot Hondas of Italian Andrea Dovizioso (21) and Japan's Yuki Takahashi (23).

There were just two privateer Hondas: one for well-supported Thai rookie Ratthapark Wilairot (19); the other for Ulsterman rookie Eugene Laverty (21), who made a brave step directly into the world championship under the care of Lucio Cecchinello's LCR Racing.

KTM

Sponsored by Red Bull, KTM retained the services of Hiro Aoyama (26) and brought in its leading 125 rider, Mika Kallio (24), to replace the disappointing Manuel Poggiali, who left GP racing. Again, the team was in the hands of long-respected two-stroke guru Harald Bartol.

hector barbera

thomas luthi

roberto locatelli

alex de angelis

alex debon

hiroshi aoyama

mika kallio

alvaro bautista

shuhei aoyama

fabrizio lai

dan linfoot

yuki takahahi

julian simon

marco simoncelli

eugene laverty

gabor talmacsi

hector faubel

sandro cortese

lukas pesek

mattia pasini

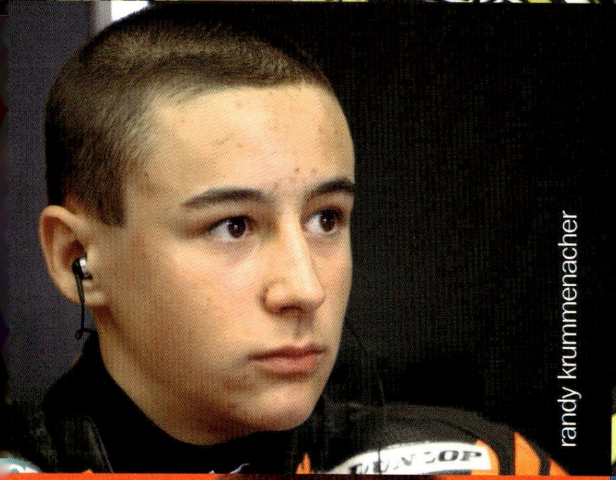
randy krummenacher

pol espargaro

simone corsi

bradley smith

pablo nieto

esteve rabat

tomoyoshi koyama

sergio gadea

joan olive

michael ranseder

125cc: TALENT ON TAP

THE smallest class was thriving, any void left by the departure of the top two in 2006's championship and a number of other bright sparks being easily filled. Entry lists were full, with a supply of talented youngsters readily on stream from the Dorna Academy, itself now fed by the new Red Bull Rookies Cup.

Italians dominated in terms of numbers, with ten riders to seven Spaniards. Dorna's policy of favouring riders from beyond the Latin axis – especially Britain and Germany – showed, no less than 12 nations being represented on the grid. There were two each from Britain, Germany, Switzerland and France; and single spies from Austria, the Czech Republic, the Netherlands, Romania, the USA and Hungary.

In sharp contrast to a decade ago, there was only one Japanese rider.

Again, Aprilia supplied most of the machines (18). In addition, there were four Derbis, seven Hondas and three KTMs. By and large, the machines were at similar levels, although the new-generation Aprilias for the senior teams were altogether different from the old ones, with a skew-driven rotary inlet valve and, at the start of the season, a high-level exhaust. These changed during the year, acquiring a central air intake in the nose and low-level exhausts; they rivalled the KTMs as the only factory machines. Between them, they won almost all of the races.

Riders' ages at the final race spanned more than decade. Oldest and most experienced was Pablo Nieto (27), with 142 starts, all in the 250 class. Gabor Talmacsi (26) had 113; Joan Olive also had racked up 113 starts, but 32 of them had been in the 250 class. The youngest at Valencia was Japanese wild-card Takaaki Nakagami, entered by the Red Bull Academy, in his first GP and just 15.

APRILIA

The high ground was occupied by the core of Jorge Martinez's Bancaja Aspar team, highly professional, well supported and presented, and quite formidable compared with the lowliest one-rider privateer teams. He had three choice riders too. The Spanish pair, Hector Faubel (24 at the end of the season) and Sergio Gadea (22) had been third and fifth in 2006, and had stayed with the team. The third place went to roaming Hungarian Gabor Talmacsi (from Budapest), dropped by KTM at the end of 2005. One of them would win the championship – in some ways, it was the wrong one.

Mattia Pasini (22, from Italy) had left Aspar's team for new sponsor Polaris World in a second high-profile team, with experienced Spaniard Joan Olive (22) as his team-mate. And there was one other three-rider team – the Italian Multimedia Racing squad, with Raffaele de Rosa (20) and Simone Grotzkyj (19), both from Italy, joined by Swiss rookie Dominique Aegerter (17).

Skilled Racing Aprilia fielded the frequently impressive Italian Simone Corsi (20), along with Federico Sandi (18), replaced for the last three races by famous-named Italian 16-year-old Ferruccio Lamborghini. Another strong two-rider team was Blusens Aprilia, with Spaniard Pablo Nieto (27) and German Stefan Bradl (17, son of Helmut), in his first full season.

Italy provided riders for the other pair of two-rider Aprilia teams – Team Sicilia fielded Lorenzo Zanetti (20) and Roberto Tamburini (16), and WTR No Alcol had Stefano Bianco (22) and Andrea Iannone (18).

There was a pair of one-rider teams. The established Campetella team, now backed by Belson, ran Spaniard Pol Espargaro (16, and younger brother of 250 rider Aleix). In his first full season, he made an impression and scored a rostrum finish. The second was the Emmi-Caffe Latte squad, replacing Luthi with 17-year-old German Sandro Cortese.

DERBI

Aprilia-clone Derbis found a new sponsor in Valsir Seedorf, backed by Dutch footballer Clarence Seedorf. The former Derbi Racing team retained the same two riders, the experienced Czech Lukas Pesek (21), who would win his first race, and Spaniard Nicolas Terol (19). Private bikes were leased to Ajo Motorsport, for Michael Ranseder (Austria, 21) and Romanian rookie Robert Muresan (16).

HONDA

Honda's numbers dropped by just one, in spite of a lack of conspicuous enthusiasm from the factory, with seven riders on the sole Japanese make on the grid. Both British riders rode RS125s.

The top team was the Repsol-sponsored two-rider squad, where 16-year-old Oxfordshire racer Bradley Smith was in a second year under the patronage of Alberto Puig. He would make the rostrum for the first time, and was joined by 18-year-old Spaniard Esteve Rabat, who did the same thing, in his first full season.

Second English rider Danny Webb (16), a Dorna Academy graduate, was in his first year, riding alongside Dutch 17-year-old Joey Litjens in the De Graaf team, run by former 125 racer Ari Molenaar. The diminutive Kentish racer scored a best of 13th, in Japan.

Kopron Team Scot also fielded two riders: the experienced French former GP winner Mike di Meglio (19) and 17-year-old Italian Dino Lombardi.

The final Honda rider was Alex Masbou (20), riding in his third year for the French FFM team.

KTM

All orange, and backed by the coveted Red Bull millions, the Austrian manufacturer's team mixed strength with experience in the quest to replace the previous year's riders, Mika Kallio And Julian Simon.

In his third year and recruited from the defunct Malaguti team, 24-year-old Japanese Tomoyoshi Koyama repaid the compliment with a win and five more rostrum places.

Swiss rider Randy Krummenacher (17) was in his first year, but also made the rostrum; ex-dirt-tracker Steve Bonsey (17), from California and a protégé of Kenny Roberts, found his first GP year rather harder.

GRANDS PRIX 2007

Photograph: Gold & Goose

Alice
BRIDGESTONE
Alice

Main photograph: Rossi pushed Stoner to the limit; the youngster took it on the chin, and gave it back.

Inset below: Stoner hadn't expected to win quite so soon. He would get used to it.

Insets bottom: The unique atmosphere of the Qatar GP.

Photographs: Gold & Goose

FIM WORLD CHAMPIONSHIP • ROUND 1

QATAR GP

LOSAIL CIRCUIT

46
Marlboro
27
Marlboro
Marlboro
SanDisk

Above: Rossi's new Fiat Yamahas had their door handles blown off.

Photograph: Gold & Goose

MORE than ever, Qatar was modern MotoGP at its best – and worst. The new 800 era, after only the third significant engine rules change in 59 years, began in splendid isolation, divorced from its location and remote from its surroundings, at the Losail stadium deep in Ozymandias country. Sport and venue, each existing by itself, and for itself. That included the massive tented studio erected for a post-race extravaganza by TVE (Spain's national network), where former-champion Criville hosted a show that went on late into the night. TVE was committed to this scale of coverage for the full season – another big terrestrial TV coup for Dorna. Now it was up to Dani Pedrosa to provide some audience satisfaction.

With the Yamahas now dressed as Fiats (luckily without door handles, for they would have been blown right off), the only camels to be seen were by the long road out through the desert from Doha. Like most of the local inhabitants, they remained utterly indifferent.

A full pre-season of testing had already answered many questions about the new-generation 800s. Often, they were at least as fast as the 990s, and sometimes faster, at least on a single lap. They were making time in corner entry and, to an extent, mid-corner, and the riders enjoyed them. Results from those tests had shown the Suzukis to be surprisingly perky, but when Rossi narrowly squeaked Pedrosa for the sports car at the official Jerez tests, it looked like business as usual. The best rider was on a bike that was good enough; while surely Honda would keep tradition alive by greeting a new mechanical formula with the most powerful engine. Qatar, Stoner and the new Desmosedici were to turn all that upside-down.

There were more things also to learn – about the effect of all the new rules in race conditions. Some riders predicted that the more wieldy steering of the smaller bikes would allow a variety of corner lines; that they'd be running in two or three abreast. This would turn out to be wide of the mark. And would the 'minibikes' be faster over a full 25 or 30 laps? In this case, very much so, although other tracks would be different. In spite of the long straight, they qualified faster than the 990s, smashed the lap record and slashed an astonishing 20 seconds off the race time – almost a second a lap. This despite a loss of 10 km/h, compared with the best ever previous speed.

And, just as importantly, what about the new tyre rules? Limited to a pre-selected set of 31 – 14 front and 17 rear, and including two qualifying tyres (the almost universal selection), plus one front qualifier for the Michelin runners – riders were stepping into the unknown. Only up to a point, however, since they had tested here only four weeks before and had a good idea of the range of rubber required. As many opined, everyone would have to wait until Istanbul, a track without pre-season testing or data for the 800s, before they could really feel the impact of the tyre rules.

All the same, they made a huge difference all weekend, starting with an unaccustomed workload for the tyre staff, who were kept busy coding and registering the chosen tyres. First time out, it took Bridgestone (suppliers this year of ten riders) fully four hours to get it all sorted, a process that would be refined with time.

In practice, advance knowledge did allow riders to narrow the choice, but limited supply still hampered the ability to keep ex-

perimenting (or, indeed, just playing) with changes and set-ups, and riders were making longer runs on the same tyre. Then came the final flurry, all the more exaggerated because of the availability of just two qualifiers apiece. Three-and-a-half minutes before the end of the hour, the track was almost empty as everybody came in to change tyres; then there was almost a traffic jam.

Times tumbled, and the names on the qualifying list shifted up and down like a stock-market screen, the Michelin-shod Yamahas pushing through in the end.

In spite of the intensity of the compressed testing season – this opening round being two weeks earlier than previously – everybody was in good condition. Everybody, that is, except John Hopkins, bravely riding with his right wrist far too painful for him to shake hands, and Jeremy McWilliams, limping in for another comeback after a heavy Jerez testing crash before Christmas that led to skew surgery on a broken femur, from which he had still not fully recuperated. His Ilmor (he was teamed with Andrew Pitt) was powerful, but still a handful, as last year, with over-enthusiastic throttle response; the riders were asking for a heavier crankshaft to tame the beast somewhat. Then McWilliams crashed heavily again on the second day of practice, luckily doing no further damage to his leg, but he knocked himself about badly enough to be out of the race. Considering what was to come for the team, this might have been considered an omen.

The Ilmor was quite fast, however, once it got going down the longish straight, placing seventh overall at 313.0 km/h. The Ducatis were showing the way yet again, Stoner at 324.7, Capirossi at 323.5, then the satellite bikes of Hofmann and Barros. The fastest Honda was Pedrosa's, some way behind at 317.9, Hopkins's Suzuki next. Rossi's Yamaha was way down, only 14th fastest at just 309.9.

Here was a real omen, with a solid copper bottom. Here was conclusive proof that, for once, Honda did not have the edge on engines. In fact, it was already trying to make up lost ground – a new exhaust for Pedrosa with slightly longer tail-pipes (reportedly for noise comfort rather than performance), and a rather slap-happy add-on fairing extension for Hayden, an attempt to give the bulkier rider a chance to get out of the wind.

But where had Ducati found this boost in power, reckoned to be at least 10bhp? It would be a talking point for weeks to come, rumours of cheating only being laid to rest when the bike was stripped for the scrutineers after round four. Was it aerodynamic? Or because the springless desmodromic valves inherently put less load (albeit transient load) on the valve gear? Or because they'd found somewhere to hide extra fuel? Or had the others just been too conservative in their expectations and their need to keep fuel consumption under control? The coming races would prove that whatever the advantage, it ran deep.

Above: **Edwards (top) was gleeful to start the new era on the front row; Hayden and crew chief Benson were already scratching their heads.**

Below left: **Every tyre had an identity and a bar code; scrutineers recorded their every movement.**

Bottom left: **Old soldier McWilliams had a painful start to a very short season.**

Photographs: Gold & Goose

Top: The 800s started out as if they liked close racing: Stoner and Rossi are pursued in the early laps by Pedrosa, Elias, Hopkins and Edwards.

Above: Hopkins hounded Pedrosa to the end.

Above right: Elias communes with a fan.

Below: De Puniet's season got off to a crashing start.

Photographs: Gold & Goose

MOTOGP RACE – 22 laps

With less than half a minute to go, Stoner put his Ducati on pole, repeating his feat of last year. Twenty seconds later, Rossi flashed over the line, five-thousandths faster. He looked at his dashboard: 'I was faster by zero point zero zero zero zero,' he grinned afterwards. Following victory at the official IRTA tests, it filled him with confidence, and he continued to enthuse about his new 800 Yamaha, how much fun it was to ride, and how well it handled. It was pole number 46.

Rossi was backed up by a jubilant Edwards on the far side or row one; Elias narrowly led row two from Pedrosa and Hopkins. Bridgestone was strong on race tyres, but Michelin was still better for qualifying, for Capirossi (in seventh) couldn't find a qualifier to finish a lap.

Rossi led the charge of the light(er) brigade, from Stoner, Elias, Pedrosa and Edwards, as they came out of the last corner for the first time. Then came the defining moment. Stoner wound open the throttle, and the Ducati powered past to lead first time over the line.

Rossi fought back through the back twists, Stoner did it again on lap two. And on lap five. Until as the half-way point approached, Rossi settled into stalking mode, showing a wheel now and then to make sure Stoner knew he was there.

Elias dropped back quickly, and for the rest of the race, but Pedrosa was harrying and nosing ahead of Rossi in the early stages, and performing similar feats of late braking at the end of the straight; Melandri and Hopkins also closed up. At the end of lap five, the leading pack was five strong, with Capirossi pushing through from a muddled start in eighth to take Melandri's place next time around, after the younger rider lost touch with a front-end slide. Then Capirossi did the same, succumbing and sliding to earth at the final turn.

Soon afterwards, Pedrosa nearly suffered the same fate, which let Hopkins by for one lap, while the two leaders escaped ahead. Now it was just Stoner and Rossi.

At first, Rossi had hoped that relentless pressure might force the previously crash-prone Stoner into another indiscretion. A vain hope, for the Ducati was circulating at lap-record pace with apparent ease, while Rossi's bitter-end braking to regain ground lost on the straight made the eyes water.

With four circuits left, Rossi dived inside early on the lap, trying to gain enough of a lead on the back section to keep him in front down the straight. Again, Stoner had enough in reserve. He stayed close, then drove straight past once more.

By the time they started lap 21, Rossi had (in his own words) 'shown the white flag'. He had nothing left with which to challenge. Unaware, Stoner saved his best to the end, setting a final new record on his last lap. He became the youngest ever Australian GP winner, and the only one to win a race in all three current classes.

Pedrosa had immediately got ahead of Hopkins again, but the Suzuki rider had pushed him to the finish. They were less than ten seconds adrift.

Edwards had lost touch with the leading group, as had Melandri, his front-tyre grip problems worsening as the American's started to improve a little. The Yamaha was ahead on lap nine, with a gap of better than a second and five laps to go. But Melandri had enough up his sleeve to charge him down and regain fifth by more than a second.

Hayden had finished lap one in ninth, behind Capirossi, but he fell back among Nakano and Vermeulen; de Puniet and Checa were there as well, until they crashed out on consecutive laps, Checa about to attack Hayden. Vermeulen tried next on lap ten, the Suzuki pulling embarrassingly away from the Number One Honda, then he got past Elias as well.

Elias was behind Hayden also when a run over the Astroturf dropped him way back, but the American was coming under pressure from Barros, who was moving through steadily. This was spur enough for Hayden's last two laps to be his fastest, putting him back ahead of the Brazilian and just one-tenth behind Vermeulen again, but lacking the horsepower for his final attack from the last corner to succeed.

Nakano followed along by three seconds, Hofmann moving through to 11th, then Jacque, Roberts and Elias covered by just four-hundredths of a second. A frustrated Roberts was almost speechless, his Honda the slowest of the privateer machines.

Guintoli was comfortably clear of team-mate Tamada in his first MotoGP race. Pitt had retired the second Ilmor after circulating steadily some five seconds off the pace, right at the back.

250cc RACE – 20 laps

The heat in an otherwise stagnating class was provided by an influx of blazing talent from 125s, including reigning champion Bautista. Current 250 champ Lorenzo demonstrated from the start that he would take some dislodging, claiming pole by better than three tenths from Barbera, and heading an Aprilia clean sweep. De Angelis was next, then Bautista.

Row two had more of the same: new boys Luthi and Kallio topping and tailing it, sandwiching Hiro Aoyama and Dovizioso, on the top Honda.

Luthi took the first glory, shooting through from row two to lead the first half-lap. Lorenzo was ahead by the end of it, however, and he stayed there to the end – not without having to concentrate.

Kallio was with them, but lost touch quickly as Barbera and Dovizioso joined on. Luthi stayed with the fast guys, and so might Bautista, had he not slid off on lap three. Shortly afterwards, Aoyama crashed his KTM while lying eighth.

Barbera took over the pursuit on lap four, but soon Lorenzo began eking out his advantage, gaining a little every time until the gap peaked at almost three seconds on lap 17. Only then did he ease his relentless pace, to win by 1.2 seconds.

Barbera chased on doggedly, while Dovizioso faced a familiar problem – his Honda was down on speed compared with the Aprilias. Luthi re-passed him just after half-distance. De Angelis had been storming through from eighth, breaking the lap record as he charged up to join the battle. He followed Luthi past the Honda, got ahead of the Swiss rider two laps later, then took him with him as he closed on Barbera.

With six laps to go, the San Marino rider swept convincingly past for second, while Barbera had his hands full keeping Luthi at bay. He succeeded by three-tenths.

Dovizioso had faded away by ten seconds at the end, and he finished alone. So too did evergreen Locatelli, making his Gilera debut. They were spaced out more or less all the way, the Hondas of Takahashi and Simon next, then Simoncelli...and so on. Anthony West was 13th and dismayed by the performance of a bike that, in theory, should have been close to the front: 'The only good thing is, I got some laps.'

The closest finish was right at the back, where rookie Eugene Laverty snitched 17th from Imre Toth by a tenth.

Kallio was in a secure seventh when his engine stopped, forcing him to park; Abraham crashed out, while Tizon and Sekiguchi pitted.

125cc RACE – 19 laps

The sponsors names and fairing colours had changed, but the season began with a familiar taste, the Aspar Aprilias setting the pace. It was Talmacsi from Faubel in practice, the other way around at the end of the race, after a piece of poetic justice. In 2005, Talmacsi had snitched the race from KTM team-mate Mika Kallio, costing him the title and losing the Hungarian his job. This time, Faubel did it to Talmacsi, with a carbon-copy move out of the slipstream.

Faubel led away, third Aspar rider, Gadea, starting fast, but fading as quickly to retirement. Pasini was third on lap one, but soon his misfiring Aprilia was disappearing backwards, all the way to the back. He regained enough momentum to move up a few places, before retiring from a dismal 23rd with four laps left. It was the start of a remarkable run of bad luck.

Talmacsi was second by lap three. Soon he was closing a gap to Faubel, which he had been stretching out towards two seconds. On lap ten, Talmacsi set a new record; three laps later, he was in the lead.

The game of stalk-and-pounce went from there to the end. Faubel led again on laps 16 and 17, the start of the last. Talmacsi attacked as expected – but it was too soon, and Faubel was able to regain composure and plan his own final move. Talmacsi was powerless to prevent a classic drafting slingshot over the line.

The battle for third had lasted the whole race, Pesek having the upper hand for most of the time, and also when it mattered, by quarter of a second. Corsi had been alone in fifth, but Koyama put the pressure on in the closing laps and finished right on his tail.

Spaniards Espargaro, Rabat and Nieto were almost side by side over the line, then came Masbou, followed by Olive heading a gang of five for 11th, Smith taking 12th by inches.

Below: Lorenzo got his title defence off to an imperious start.

Bottom right: 125 winner Faubel (left) and Talmacsi would be fighting for supremacy all year long.

Photographs: Gold & Goose

Commercialbank GRAND PRIX OF QATAR

10 MARCH 2007 • FIM WORLD CHAMPIONSHIP ROUND 1

LOSAIL INTERNATIONAL CIRCUIT

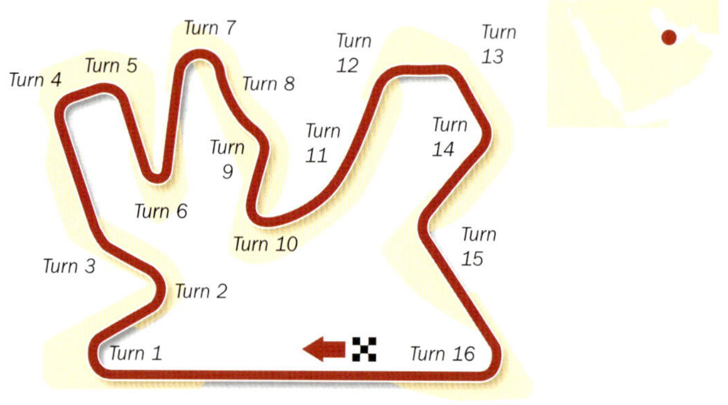

Circuit 5.380km /3.343 miles

MotoGP

RACE: 22 laps, 73.546 miles/118.360km • Weather: Dry • Air 29°C • Humidity 11% • Track 45°C

Pos.	Rider	Nat.	No.	Entrant	Machine	Tyres	Laps	Time & Speed (mph/km/h)
1	Casey Stoner	AUS	27	Ducati Marlboro Team	Ducati	B	22	43m 02.788s 102.511mph/ 164.975km/h
2	Valentino Rossi	ITA	46	Fiat Yamaha Team	Yamaha	M	22	43m 05.626s
3	Dani Pedrosa	SPA	26	Repsol Honda Team	Honda	M	22	43m 11.318s
4	John Hopkins	USA	21	Rizla Suzuki MotoGP	Suzuki	B	22	43m 11.859s
5	Marco Melandri	ITA	33	Honda Gresini	Honda	B	22	43m 20.221s
6	Colin Edwards	USA	5	Fiat Yamaha Team	Yamaha	M	22	43m 21.435s
7	Chris Vermeulen	AUS	71	Rizla Suzuki MotoGP	Suzuki	B	22	43m 25.704s
8	Nicky Hayden	USA	1	Repsol Honda Team	Honda	M	22	43m 25.845s
9	Alex Barros	BRA	4	Pramac d'Antin	Ducati	B	22	43m 28.749s
10	Shinya Nakano	JPN	56	Konica Minolta Honda	Honda	M	22	43m 31.244s
11	Alex Hofmann	GER	66	Pramac d'Antin	Ducati	B	22	43m 37.817s
12	Olivier Jacque	FRA	19	Kawasaki Racing Team	Kawasaki	B	22	43m 45.736s
13	Kenny Roberts Jnr	USA	10	Team Roberts	KR212V	M	22	43m 45.765s
14	Toni Elias	SPA	24	Honda Gresini	Honda	B	22	43m 45.777s
15	Sylvain Guintoli	FRA	50	Dunlop Yamaha Tech 3	Yamaha	D	22	43m 54.427s
16	Makoto Tamada	JPN	6	Dunlop Yamaha Tech 3	Yamaha	D	22	44m 00.641s
	Andrew Pitt	AUS	88	Ilmor GP	Ilmor GP	M	15	30m 31.099s
	Carlos Checa	SPA	7	Honda LCR	Honda	M	8	15m 53.958s
	Randy de Puniet	FRA	14	Kawasaki Racing Team	Kawasaki	B	7	13m 56.908s
	Loris Capirossi	ITA	65	Ducati Marlboro Team	Ducati	B	6	11m 53.279s
	Jeremy McWilliams	GBR	99	Ilmor GP	Ilmor GP	M		DNS

Fastest lap: Casey Stoner, on lap 22, 1m 56.528s, 103.277mph/166.208km/h (record).

Lap record: Valentino Rossi, ITA (Yamaha), 1m 57.305s, 102.593mph/165.108km/h (2006).

Event best maximum speed: Casey Stoner, 201.8mph/324.7km/h (qualifying practice).

Grid order	1	2	3	4	5	6	7	8	9	10	11	12	13	14	15	16	17	18	19	20	21	22	•
46 ROSSI	27	27	27	27	27	27	27	27	27	27	27	27	27	27	27	27	27	27	27	27	27	27	1
27 STONER	46	26	46	46	46	46	46	26	46	46	46	46	46	46	46	46	46	46	46	46	46	46	2
5 EDWARDS	26	46	26	26	26	26	26	46	26	26	21	26	26	26	26	26	26	26	26	26	26	26	3
24 ELIAS	24	24	33	33	33	21	21	21	21	21	26	21	21	21	21	21	21	21	21	21	21	21	4
26 PEDROSA	33	33	21	21	21	65	33	33	5	5	5	5	5	5	5	5	5	5	33	33	33	33	5
21 HOPKINS	21	21	65	65	65	33	5	5	33	33	33	33	33	33	33	33	33	33	5	5	5	5	6
65 CAPIROSSI	5	5	24	5	5	5	24	24	24	24	24	24	71	71	71	71	71	71	71	71	71	71	7
14 de PUNIET	65	65	5	24	24	24	1	1	1	71	71	71	24	24	1	1	1	4	4	1	1	1	8
1 HAYDEN	1	1	1	1	1	1	7	7	71	1	1	1	1	1	24	24	4	1	1	4	4	4	9
33 MELANDRI	56	56	14	14	14	14	71	71	56	56	56	56	56	56	56	56	56	56	56	56	56	56	10
56 NAKANO	14	14	71	71	71	7	14	56	4	4	4	4	4	4	4	4	66	66	66	66	66	66	11
7 CHECA	7	7	56	7	7	71	56	4	66	66	66	66	66	66	66	66	24	24	24	24	24	19	12
71 VERMEULEN	71	71	7	56	56	56	4	66	19	19	19	19	10	10	10	19	10	10	10	19	19	10	13
19 JACQUE	50	6	6	19	19	4	19	19	10	10	10	10	19	19	19	10	19	19	19	10	10	24	14
4 BARROS	6	50	19	6	6	19	66	10	50	50	50	50	50	50	50	50	50	50	50	50	50	50	15
50 GUINTOLI	19	19	4	4	4	6	10	6	6	6	6	6	6	6	6	6	6	6	6	6	6	6	
66 HOFMANN	4	4	50	50	50	66	6	50	88	88	88	88	88	88	88								
10 ROBERTS Jnr	10	66	66	66	66	10	50	88															
6 TAMADA	66	10	10	10	10	50	88																
99 McWILLIAMS*	88	88	88	88	88	88																	
88 PITT																							

FASTEST RACE LAPS

	Rider	Lap	Time
1	Stoner	22	1m 56.528s
2	Rossi	17	1m 56.717s
3	Hopkins	9	1m 56.939s
4	Pedrosa	9	1m 56.951s
5	Capirossi	5	1m 57.234s
6	Edwards	8	1m 57.238s
7	Barros	19	1m 57.290s
8	Melandri	3	1m 57.297s
9	Checa	6	1m 57.406s
10	Hayden	22	1m 57.468s
11	Elias	7	1m 57.581s
12	Vermeulen	14	1m 57.621s
13	de Puniet	4	1m 57.710s
14	Nakano	11	1m 57.815s
15	Hofmann	16	1m 57.897s
16	Roberts Jnr	12	1m 58.365s
17	Jacque	19	1m 58.388s
18	Tamada	2	1m 58.828s
19	Guintoli	9	1m 58.972s
20	Pitt	2	2m 00.990s

QUALIFYING

9 March 2007

Weather: Dry

Air: 27°C Humidity: 14%

Track: 47°C

Pos.	Rider	Time
1	Rossi	1m 55.002s
2	Stoner	1m 55.007s
3	Edwards	1m 55.233s
4	Elias	1m 55.358s
5	Pedrosa	1m 55.361s
6	Hopkins	1m 55.833s
7	Capirossi	1m 55.851s
8	de Puniet	1m 55.933s
9	Hayden	1m 56.041s
10	Melandri	1m 56.222s
11	Nakano	1m 56.306s
12	Checa	1m 56.609s
13	Vermeulen	1m 56.639s
14	Jacque	1m 56.754s
15	Barros	1m 56.814s
16	Guintoli	1m 57.257s
17	Hofmann	1m 57.274s
18	Roberts Jnr	1m 57.495s
19	Tamada	1m 58.024s
20	McWilliams	1m 59.606s
21	Pitt	1m 59.725s

RIDER STANDINGS

After 1 Round

1	Casey Stoner	25
2	Valentino Rossi	20
3	Dani Pedrosa	16
4	John Hopkins	13
5	Marco Melandri	11
6	Colin Edwards	10
7	Chris Vermeulen	9
8	Nicky Hayden	8
9	Alex Barros	7
10	Shinya Nakano	6
11	Alex Hofmann	5
12	Olivier Jacque	4
13	Kenny Roberts Jnr	3
14	Toni Elias	2
15	Sylvain Guintoli	1

TEAM STANDINGS

After 1 Round

1	Fiat Yamaha Team	30
2	Ducati Marlboro Team	25
3	Repsol Honda Team	24
4	Rizla Suzuki MotoGP	22
5	Honda Gresini	13
6	Pramac d'Antin	12
7	Konica Minolta Honda	6
8	Kawasaki Racing Team	4
9	Team Roberts	3
10	Dunlop Yamaha Tech 3	1

CONSTRUCTOR STANDINGS

After 1 Round

Ducati	25
Yamaha	20
Honda	16
Suzuki	13
Kawasaki	4
KR212V	3

statistics

motoGP | TISSOT SWISS WATCHES SINCE 1853 | OFFICIAL TIMEKEEPER

250cc

20 laps, 66.860 miles/107.600km

Pos.	Rider (Nat.)	No.	Machine	Laps	Time & speed
1	Jorge Lorenzo (SPA)	1	Aprilia	20	40m 23.753s 99.306mph/ 159.818km/h
2	Alex de Angelis (RSM)	3	Aprilia	20	40m 24.977s
3	Hector Barbera (SPA)	80	Aprilia	20	40m 26.664s
4	Thomas Luthi (SWI)	12	Aprilia	20	40m 26.987s
5	Andrea Dovizioso (ITA)	34	Honda	20	40m 36.451s
6	Roberto Locatelli (ITA)	15	Gilera	20	40m 45.321s
7	Yuki Takahashi (JPN)	55	Honda	20	40m 55.293s
8	Julian Simon (SPA)	60	Honda	20	41m 04.220s
9	Marco Simoncelli (ITA)	58	Gilera	20	41m 09.945s
10	Shuhei Aoyama (JPN)	73	Honda	20	41m 22.431s
11	Aleix Espargaro (SPA)	41	Aprilia	20	41m 26.515s
12	Fabrizio Lai (ITA)	32	Aprilia	20	41m 31.468s
13	Anthony West (AUS)	14	Aprilia	20	41m 34.375s
14	Ratthapark Wilairot (THA)	8	Honda	20	41m 35.347s
15	Dirk Heidolf (GER)	28	Aprilia	20	41m 36.252s
16	Jules Cluzel (FRA)	16	Aprilia	20	41m 47.504s
17	Alex Baldolini (ITA)	25	Aprilia	20	41m 56.896s
18	Eugene Laverty (IRL)	50	Honda	20	42m 02.211s
19	Imre Toth (HUN)	10	Aprilia	20	42m 02.301s
	Mika Kallio (FIN)	36	KTM	18	DNF
	Arturo Tizon (SPA)	9	Aprilia	14	DNF
	Taro Sekiguchi (JPN)	44	Aprilia	10	DNF
	Karel Abraham (CZE)	17	Aprilia	7	DNF
	Alvaro Bautista (SPA)	19	Aprilia	2	DNF
	Hiroshi Aoyama (JPN)	4	KTM	2	DNF

Fastest lap: de Angelis, 2m 00.121s, 100.188mph/161.237km/h (record).

Previous lap record: Alex de Angelis, RSM (Aprilia), 2m 03.015s, 97.831mph/157.444km/h (2004).

Event best maximum speed: Barbera, 169.2mph/272.3km/h (qualifying practice no. 2).

Qualifying: 1 Lorenzo, 1m 59.432s; 2 Barbera, 1m 59.782s; 3 de Angelis, 1m 59.871s; 4 Bautista, 2m 00.127s; 5 Luthi, 2m 00.316s; 6 H. Aoyama, 2m 00.700s; 7 Dovizioso, 2m 00.702s; 8 Kallio, 2m 00.721s; 9 Takahashi, 2m 00.801s; 10 Simon, 2m 01.087s; 11 Locatelli, 2m 01.216s; 12 Simoncelli, 2m 01.368s; 13 S. Aoyama, 2m 01.554s; 14 Lai, 2m 01.614s; 15 Tizon, 2m 02.504s; 16 Espargaro, 2m 02.525s; 17 West, 2m 02.733s; 18 Heidolf, 2m 02.954s; 19 Toth, 2m 02.962s; 20 Baldolini, 2m 02.968s; 21 Abraham, 2m 03.228s; 22 Wilairot, 2m 03.326s; 23 Cluzel, 2m 03.911s; 24 Laverty, 2m 04.411s; 25 Sekiguchi, 2m 04.878s.

Fastest race laps: 1 de Angelis, 2m 00.121s; 2 Luthi, 2m 00.258s; 3 Lorenzo, 2m 00.289s; 4 Barbera, 2m 00.485s; 5 Dovizioso, 2m 00.702s; 6 Locatelli, 2m 01.332s; 7 Kallio, 2m 01.456s; 8 Simon, 2m 01.488s; 9 Takahashi, 2m 01.515s; 10 Bautista, 2m 02.369s; 11 H. Aoyama, 2m 02.371s; 12 Simoncelli, 2m 02.443s; 13 Espargaro, 2m 02.663s; 14 S. Aoyama, 2m 02.681s; 15 Heidolf, 2m 03.288s; 16 West, 2m 03.557s; 17 Wilairot, 2m 03.570s; 18 Cluzel, 2m 03.706s; 19 Lai, 2m 03.736s; 20 Abraham, 2m 04.049s; 21 Baldolini, 2m 04.115s; 22 Toth, 2m 04.300s; 23 Tizon, 2m 04.302s; 24 Sekiguchi, 2m 04.622s; 25 Laverty, 2m 04.929s.

World Championship: 1 Lorenzo, 25; 2 de Angelis, 20; 3 Barbera, 16; 4 Luthi, 13; 5 Dovizioso, 11; 6 Locatelli, 10; 7 Takahashi, 9; 8 Simon, 8; 9 Simoncelli, 7; 10 S. Aoyama, 6; 11 Espargaro, 5; 12 Lai, 4; 13 West, 3; 14 Wilairot, 2; 15 Heidolf, 1.

125cc

18 laps, 60.174 miles/96.840km

Pos.	Rider (Nat.)	No.	Machine	Laps	Time & speed
1	Hector Faubel (SPA)	55	Aprilia	18	38m 12.029s 94.512mph/ 152.102km/h
2	Gabor Talmacsi (HUN)	14	Aprilia	18	38m 12.102s
3	Lukas Pesek (CZE)	52	Derbi	18	38m 29.528s
4	Raffaele de Rosa (ITA)	35	Aprilia	18	38m 29.783s
5	Simone Corsi (ITA)	24	Aprilia	18	38m 37.671s
6	Tomoyoshi Koyama (JPN)	71	KTM	18	38m 37.906s
7	Pol Espargaro (SPA)	44	Aprilia	18	38m 40.466s
8	Esteve Rabat (SPA)	12	Honda	18	38m 40.556s
9	Pablo Nieto (SPA)	22	Aprilia	18	38m 40.737s
10	Alexis Masbou (FRA)	7	Honda	18	38m 45.698s
11	Joan Olive (SPA)	6	Aprilia	18	38m 52.694s
12	Bradley Smith (GBR)	38	Honda	18	38m 52.708s
13	Michael Ranseder (AUT)	60	Derbi	18	38m 52.944s
14	Mike di Meglio (FRA)	63	Honda	18	38m 53.700s
15	Andrea Iannone (ITA)	29	Aprilia	18	38m 53.793s
16	Nicolas Terol (SPA)	18	Derbi	18	39m 00.672s
17	Sandro Cortese (GER)	11	Aprilia	18	39m 00.685s
18	Lorenzo Zanetti (ITA)	8	Aprilia	18	39m 00.887s
19	Randy Krummenacher (SWI)	34	KTM	18	39m 15.189s
20	Dominique Aegerter (SWI)	77	Aprilia	18	39m 35.103s
21	Joey Litjens (NED)	37	Honda	18	39m 35.176s
22	Steve Bonsey (USA)	51	KTM	18	39m 43.550s
23	Roberto Tamburini (ITA)	20	Aprilia	18	40m 11.181s
24	Hugo van den Berg (NED)	56	Aprilia	18	40m 12.069s
	Daniel Webb (GBR)	99	Honda	16	DNF
	Mattia Pasini (ITA)	75	Aprilia	15	DNF
	Stefano Bianco (ITA)	27	Aprilia	14	DNF
	Sergio Gadea (SPA)	33	Aprilia	12	DNF
	Simone Grotzkyj (ITA)	53	Aprilia	7	DNF
	Federico Sandi (ITA)	15	Aprilia	4	DNF
	Robert Muresan (ROU)	95	Derbi	3	DNF

Fastest lap: Talmacsi, 2m 06.267s, 95.312mph/153.389km/h (record).

Previous lap record: Alvaro Bautista, SPA (Aprilia), 2m 08.591s, 93.589mph/150.617km/h (2006).

Event best maximum speed: Koyama, 142.9mph/230.0km/h (qualifying practice no. 2).

Qualifying: 1 Talmacsi, 2m 06.011s; 2 Faubel, 2m 06.091s; 3 Pasini, 2m 06.135s; 4 Pesek, 2m 06.767s; 5 de Rosa, 2m 07.130s; 6 Gadea, 2m 07.139s; 7 Koyama, 2m 07.207s; 8 Rabat, 2m 07.275s; 9 Smith, 2m 07.348s; 10 Corsi, 2m 07.525s; 11 Nieto, 2m 07.865s; 12 Espargaro, 2m 07.987s; 13 Ranseder, 2m 07.992s; 14 Iannone, 2m 08.048s; 15 Masbou, 2m 08.081s; 16 Bianco, 2m 08.236s; 17 Krummenacher, 2m 08.294s; 18 di Meglio, 2m 08.360s; 19 Terol, 2m 08.419s; 20 Olive, 2m 08.552s; 21 Cortese, 2m 08.662s; 22 Sandi, 2m 08.753s; 23 Grotzkyj, 2m 08.873s; 24 Muresan, 2m 09.903s; 25 Litjens, 2m 10.112s; 26 Webb, 2m 10.238s; 27 Aegerter, 2m 10.324s; 28 Zanetti, 2m 10.388s; 29 Bonsey, 2m 10.614s; 30 Tamburini, 2m 12.387s; 31 van den Berg, 2m 14.125s.

Fastest race laps: 1 Talmacsi, 2m 06.267s; 2 Faubel, 2m 06.369s; 3 Pasini, 2m 06.528s; 4 de Rosa, 2m 07.298s; 5 Pesek, 2m 07.424s; 6 Espargaro, 2m 07.445s; 7 Gadea, 2m 07.447s; 8 Koyama, 2m 07.661s; 9 Rabat, 2m 07.811s; 10 Corsi, 2m 07.910s; 11 Bianco, 2m 07.916s; 12 Masbou, 2m 08.005s; 13 Nieto, 2m 08.062s; 14 Smith, 2m 08.194s; 15 Olive, 2m 08.212s; 16 Iannone, 2m 08.471s; 17 Ranseder, 2m 08.583s; 18 Terol, 2m 08.611s; 19 di Meglio, 2m 08.660s; 20 Cortese, 2m 08.681s; 21 Zanetti, 2m 08.704s; 22 Sandi, 2m 08.951s; 23 Grotzkyj, 2m 09.699s; 24 Krummenacher, 2m 09.741s; 25 Litjens, 2m 10.290s; 26 Aegerter, 2m 10.434s; 27 Bonsey, 2m 10.625s; 28 Webb, 2m 11.165s; 29 Muresan, 2m 11.897s; 30 van den Berg, 2m 12.460s; 31 Tamburini, 2m 12.734s.

World Championship: 1 Faubel, 25; 2 Talmacsi, 20; 3 Pesek, 16; 4 de Rosa, 13; 5 Corsi, 11; 6 Koyama, 10; 7 Espargaro, 9; 8 Rabat, 8; 9 Nieto, 7; 10 Masbou, 6; 11 Olive, 5; 12 Smith, 4; 13 Ranseder, 3; 14 di Meglio, 2; 15 Iannone, 1.

FIAT
YAMAHA
MOTUL
DAINESE
46
FIAT
YAMAHA
MOTUL

Winners celebrate: Rossi (main picture) is clearly relieved and delighted as he side-saddles for the crowd; his nine-pins charade (right) was more contrived than his win. Lorenzo (far right) whips up his home fans before planting his black 'Lorenzo's Land' flag of conquest.
Photographs: Gold & Goose

Meanwhile, Talmacsi (bottom) is just jubilant.
Photograph: Peter J Fox/2snap

FIM WORLD CHAMPIONSHIP • ROUND 2

SPANISHGP JEREZ

THOSE seeking omens could find plenty at Jerez. Happily, they all turned out to be wrong. There was, for instance, a clear signpost back to Business As Usual, in the way that Rossi won quite easily, and took the championship lead. Not for long, as we would see…

Another harbinger was the nature of the race – some called it the first two-wheeled Formula One GP – and what that meant for the future of the new 800cc class. Up front, it was processional, perfect corner lines and no sliding giving the lie to hopes that the sweeter handling 800s would make passing easier. As in F1, the tussle came mid-field, where at least nobody needed pit-stop strategy to be able to make a move. But even there the passes were relatively few. Consider the case of Hopkins, who took the best part of 14 laps before he could find a way past Hayden. 'It looked like I was following him, but I was trying really hard,' he said. He started pulling away immediately, although he rather spoiled it by falling off before finishing another lap, blaming a rogue gust of wind under his fairing while at one of his elbow-scrapingly high lean angles. And consider the case of Stoner, who was mugged so badly in the first part of the race that he had dropped from fourth to ninth by half-distance. Later, he complained of 'a few dodgy passing manoeuvres', adding, 'Some riders were overly aggressive…people outbraking themselves and pushing me wide, others pushing in to make me pick it up again. Like in the 125 class, where you get blocked by someone, and then eight other riders get past.' Leaving aside that it is the other riders' job to try to pass him, he had a point. With the corner lines having to be drawn so accurately, as with F1 cars, often overtaking can only be accomplished with brutal clumsiness.

There had hardly been time for the out-powered Japanese manufacturers to lick their wounds before setting up shop again at Jerez, another track with very recent testing to help at least with tyre choice – and enough corners to redress the horsepower balance somewhat. In other words, Rossi territory.

Qatar post-mortems were still under way, and questions were being asked about how much fuel Rossi had left at the end of the desert race. 'Some,' he said. 'Too much,' said crew chief Jerry Burgess. All engines had adjustment built in: one might use a fuel-greedy setting for qualifying, and something more economical for the race, in the same way (although not to the same degree) that one used qualifying tyres. In these circumstances, liberating a few more revs was about all they could do while awaiting more serious hardware from the factory. It wasn't only consumption, continued Burgess. The whole strategy might need a rethink, sacrificing some of the sweet cornering and feel to bias tuning more towards top-end performance.

In any case, the speed difference was much less pronounced here, because of much lower speeds. Barros was fastest all weekend at 280.2km/h, followed closely by Stoner and Pedrosa. Rossi was only 12th fastest, slower than all three Suzukis, including Japanese wild card Akiyoshi, but at 274.6 there wasn't much in it.

Jerez is notoriously unpredictable for grip; for some reason, qualifying times were almost a full second slower than at preseason tests four weekends before. Pedrosa blamed the circuit, Rossi himself. 'The bigger difference is because in February we had four qualifying tyres, and today just two. It is quite difficult to find the limit.'

Again, apparently, Hayden had been left out to dry, a revised-stiffness chassis leaving him still fighting the Honda for feel, while Pedrosa had power-up pipes that Nicky would have to wait months for. 'I want to be not so aggressive. Hard is not the way to ride this thing. The main issue is I lose the front, and that knocks my confidence, and you have to work back up. It doesn't want to steer in the fast corners.' It would become a familiar song, with Melandri taking counterpoint, and other Honda riders joining the chorus.

Melandri, of course, was on Bridgestones, so the problem afflicted both brands. The tyre war was focused now as much on qualifying as on the race; Bridgestone had followed Michelin's lead in bringing front qualifiers (although not the 16-inch fronts), but waited until after the race to test them, before shelving them.

A complex new rule had been introduced, allowing riders to practise starts from the grid. At Qatar, it had been a free-for-all after morning practice. Now an extra five minutes had been added before the start of race-morning warm-up, and riders were allowed out early to form up and start three at a time, before pitting again.

But the talk was more about money than racing, setting the scene for the hastily arranged forthcoming Dorna 'Sponsorship Summit' in Barcelona in the break before the next GP in four weeks' time. The crisis had grown since Qatar. In the intervening two weeks, one team had disappeared and a second was threatening to do the same.

Ilmor was the absentee, although at the time, Mario Illien was still describing it as 'a postponement' while expressing dismay at the different financial climate of MotoGP compared to car racing. Kenny Roberts had threatened to quit before the end of the year, unless he could find some support by then. But he'd been in bike racing long enough (and also was still optimistic enough) to discern a change in the general climate, with increasing interest and 'plenty of tyre-kickers'. As it happened, some money did roll in that very weekend, Las Vegas high-roller money, from MGM's Treasure Island Hotel and Casino, arranged by expanding management group F1 MAX-X, with more on the way. The threat to quit theseries had had evaporated by Sunday.

The loss of tobacco sponsorship was keenly felt, and there was something symbolic outside the double staircase of the proud, new, four-vehicle mansion of the last bastion, Marlboro – furtive smokers, nico-loading before popping back inside for some more fine cuisine. Current interpretation of Spain's new legislation meant no smoking inside. At least the multi-wheeled marvel got there, and was very welcome. The new Fiat Yamaha palace wasn't ready at all, and they were reduced to a very downbeat tent; HRC's own unit was simply too long and too heavy to be legal on Spanish roads. Last year, nobody seemed to notice, however, and they would find a way around it in time for Catalunya.

The meeting saw the first really horrible crash and injury of the season, in the 250 class. The victim was the evergreen, former 125 World Champion Roberto Locatelli, on Saturday morning. As he ran out of the penultimate double rights on to the short penultimate straight, a suspected mechanical failure caused his Gilera to turn left abruptly and run head-on into the trackside barrier. The 32-year-old suffered severe facial injuries, including a broken jaw (doctors later counted 16 fractures), as well as a compound fracture to his ankle. He was taken by ambulance to intensive care in Cadiz, where he was put into an induced coma. Amazingly, Loca was back for the French GP, just eight weeks later, having missed only three races.

MOTOGP RACE – 27 laps

Qualifying was slower than testing, but much closer – you needed a magnifying glass. In the past, there had been 15 within the same second, but never before the top ten all within 0.352s. Mere hundredths made all the difference.

Roberts made a brief flourish, fastest on Friday morning, then Checa took over, fastest on the long race-tyre runs. On qualifiers, it was played out between Pedrosa and Rossi, the former getting the upper hand. Checa was again strong, bumping an on-form Edwards to row two; Stoner was top Bridgestone runner, in fifth.

Pedrosa led away, Rossi drafting him down the back straight to dive underneath into Dry Sack hairpin. The Italian had a clear track all the way to the chequered flag.

Pedrosa kept him honest, never more than 0.75s behind, and often closer. But he was on the limit and clipping dust on one inside apex, while Rossi was quite in command. There was never any question of a challenge – just two riders in close formation. After half-distance, Rossi's authority and the better balance of his machine showed, as he held on to steady lap times while Pedrosa slipped away by two- or three-tenths a lap. On the 14th, it was over a second; on lap 20, more than three.

It was, Rossi explained, an important victory. The faster up-

Above: All safely through – Pedrosa leads the brawl out of the first corner, from Rossi, Checa, Edwards, Stoner and the rest.
Photograph: Gold & Goose

Centre, top to bottom: Spanish TVE's portable studio; the increasingly opulent paddock; Marlboro's new palace – no smoking, for this race only.
Photographs: Gold & Goose

Botttom left: 'Calling me a what?' Rossi and Pedrosa make friends at a press conference.
Photograph: Peter J Fox/2snap

Top: **Back on the front row for the first time in years, Checa is congratulated by Cecchinello (centre) and team.**
Photograph: Friedemann Kirn/2snap

Opposite, top right: **Simoncelli holds a message of support for his injured team-mate, Locatelli.**

Opposite, top right: **125 winner Talmacsi and Pesek, locked in combat.**

Bottom right: **Bautista heads Dovizioso, Barbera, Lorenzo and de Angelis mid-way through a fine old-fashioned 250 race.**
Photographs: Gold & Goose

coming tracks would not offer such opportunities. They were prophetic words.

Edwards struggled in vain to stay with them, but was losing little by little. By half-distance, he was still less than two seconds behind Pedrosa, and he would get closer again in the coming laps. But he was never a threat, and would have to fight to protect his first podium since China early in 2006.

Hayden was fourth at the end of lap one, with Stoner, Checa, Hopkins, Melandri and Elias all brawling like mad behind him. It was now that Stoner found himself trampled backwards.

Hopkins was the first to barge through, but all he could do was shadow Hayden, until his ill-fated pass under brakes on 16. Elias followed him straight past, and both moved away rapidly, aiming at a gap of less than four seconds on Edwards. Then Hopkins was gone, sliding off before the back straight, but getting straight back on board.

Elias chased down Edwards steadily, whittling the gap from almost four seconds to some 1.6s over the remaining laps. Stoner was on an even more impressive charge.

Melandri and Checa had been disputing the right to attack Hayden, but Melandri had been punishing his front tyre under braking to make up for a speed deficit, and now he was losing time. Stoner was ahead on lap 17, past Checa also directly, and he led the Spaniard past the flagging World Champion.

The red Ducati was flying, lap times tumbling, and he closed steadily on Elias, although he hung back from the risk of an all-out attack. He knew it was all too late, and while he really shouldn't have allowed himself to be mugged early in the race, he had stayed cool, made the most of things and shown a fine turn of speed. 'We minimised the damage today,' he said.

Checa made good his practice promise, another three seconds away, with Hayden and Melandri trailing in. 'Right now, the bike's just not working for me,' said Hayden.

Roberts had been the early leader of a mid-field battle until Barros took over on lap nine. Vermeulen was with them and pushing on, Nakano, de Puniet and Capirossi close behind. With three laps to go, Roberts suddenly slowed. A false neutral and an unexpected jump into second gear mid-corner gave him a big fright, and he slacked off, fearing more problems.

Vermeulen displaced Barros with two laps to go, holding him and the pack at bay. Over the line, Nakano also got past the Brazilian, from Capirossi and de Puniet, ninth to 13th being covered by less than two seconds.

Tamada narrowly won a Dunlop battle for the last points from already impressive rookie team-mate Guintoli; Roberts coasted over the line 16th to park by the pit wall. Suzuki wild card Akioshi, Jacque and Hopkins followed along. Hofmann had been disqualified after stretching his chain off the start line, then stopping to change to his spare bike. This is only allowed if the race is designated 'Wet'.

250cc RACE – 26 laps

Lorenzo's 20th pole was by a narrow margin over Barbera and the Repsol Hondas, Bautista raising eyebrows by leading row two. The 250 riders were heading for a titanic flag-to-flag struggle – just like the good old days.

Lorenzo got the jump, but by the end of the lap, both Dovizioso and Barbera were ahead. Bautista was a second behind, de Angelis chasing hard, and the pair closed up rapidly. By lap eight, Bautista was with the leaders, and next time around, the rookie started to attack, up to second on lap ten, and in the lead two laps later.

By half-distance, the leading five were still covered by just over a second, de Angelis hanging on grimly while the other four passed and repassed, running into corners two and three abreast. It couldn't last, and on lap 15, a distraught Barbera slid off.

Over the last ten laps, de Angelis was outpaced, but the outcome between the other three was anybody's guess. Dovizioso had been the most frequent leader over the line, but they'd all had a turn or two. Lorenzo got it again on lap 22, and with superhuman effort not only held on, but also started the last lap with an advantage of almost a second. It was barely enough, the other two crawling all over him on the run past the flag – all three crossed the line within half a second. Astonishingly, it was Bautista in second, Dovizioso outfumbled and glum.

At first, the pursuit was led by Shuhei Aoyama, but by half-distance, Simon, wild card Debon, and the KTMs of brother Hiro and Kallio were ahead of him. Simon was headed for the gravel trap, then Hiro Aoyama and Debon pulled clear, also swapping back and forth, Debon ahead at the flag.

With two laps to go, Kallio pitted with another mechanical failure. This left Shuhei Aoyama alone in seventh. Takahashi had lost touch with this group, alone also in eighth – just like West in ninth, and Heidolf in tenth. It may have been lively up front, but there was little depth.

Lai pulled through to 11th after a ride-through penalty for a jumped start, narrowly ahead of Wilairot and Baldolini; Laverty took two points for 14th.

Simoncelli crashed on lap one, wild cards Barragan and Molina directly afterwards; Luthi lasted six more laps, being ahead of Kallio when he slid off.

Two in a row for Lorenzo, and a big gold star for Bautista.

125cc RACE – 23 laps

Pasini took pole ahead of Talmacsi, but his personal gremlins were still very much on duty. Engine trouble again, this time on the sighting lap, so he was able to switch to his spare and re-gain his place on the grid. But he was flustered now and it didn't feel right. On only the second lap, he crashed after an over-enthusiastic entry to Dry Sack, taking the unfortunate Bradley Smith with him. They were disputing eighth at the time.

Talmacsi led away, almost a second in front at the end of lap one, the rest piling up behind Espargaro, through from the second row.

Talmacsi gained more ground as the pack shuffled, Pesek pushing through to second on lap two and taking off in pursuit of the Hungarian. Shortly afterwards, Corsi crashed out of third. Faubel inherited the spot, but was even farther behind.

Talmacsi stretched his lead to almost two seconds before half-distance, but Pesek's tyres were getting better, and by lap 14, he had closed right up. The Derbi shadowed the Aprilia to the end, nosing alongside now and then. The final attack came on the last run through the Angel Nieto curve towards the end of the lap. Pesek led through the next rights and on the last gallop to the hairpin. But he was over-ambitious and too late on the brakes, running just wide enough for Talmacsi to tuck into his draft and edge ahead over the line. Just as had happened to him in Qatar.

Faubel stayed third, making little impression. Fourth saw a big fight, still five-strong at the mid-point. At the end, Espargaro managed to outfox Gadea, with Nieto two seconds adrift.

Cortese was seventh, narrowly ahead of Olive and Ranseder; US rookie Steve Bonsey was 13th, in the World Championship points in only his fourth road-race. Smith remounted for a distant and disappointing last. Rabat, Sandi, Koyama and Masbou all joined the crash list.

GRAND PREMIO bwin.com DE ESPANA

25 MARCH 2007 • FIM WORLD CHAMPIONSHIP ROUND 2

CIRCUITO DE JEREZ

Circuit 4.423km / 2.748 miles

MotoGP

RACE: 27 laps, 74.196 miles/119.421km • Weather: Dry • Air 19°C • Humidity 20% • Track 31°C

Pos.	Rider	Nat.	No.	Entrant	Machine	Tyres	Laps	Time & speed (mph/km/h)
1	Valentino Rossi	ITA	46	Fiat Yamaha Team	Yamaha	M	27	45m 53.340s 97.023mph/ 156.143km/h
2	Dani Pedrosa	SPA	26	Repsol Honda Team	Honda	M	27	45m 54.586s
3	Colin Edwards	USA	5	Fiat Yamaha Team	Yamaha	M	27	45m 56.041s
4	Toni Elias	SPA	24	Honda Gresini	Honda	B	27	45m 57.691s
5	Casey Stoner	AUS	27	Ducati Marlboro Team	Ducati	B	27	45m 58.333s
6	Carlos Checa	SPA	7	Honda LCR	Honda	M	27	46m 03.340s
7	Nicky Hayden	USA	1	Repsol Honda Team	Honda	M	27	46m 07.486s
8	Marco Melandri	ITA	33	Honda Gresini	Honda	B	27	46m 13.309s
9	Chris Vermeulen	AUS	71	Rizla Suzuki MotoGP	Suzuki	B	27	46m 18.126s
10	Shinya Nakano	JPN	56	Konica Minolta Honda	Honda	M	27	46m 18.295s
11	Alex Barros	BRA	4	Pramac d'Antin	Ducati	B	27	46m 18.348s
12	Loris Capirossi	ITA	65	Ducati Marlboro Team	Ducati	B	27	46m 19.192s
13	Randy de Puniet	FRA	14	Kawasaki Racing Team	Kawasaki	B	27	46m 19.785s
14	Makoto Tamada	JPN	6	Dunlop Yamaha Tech 3	Yamaha	D	27	46m 29.993s
15	Sylvain Guintoli	FRA	50	Dunlop Yamaha Tech 3	Yamaha	D	27	46m 30.084s
16	Kenny Roberts Jnr	USA	10	Team Roberts	KR212V	M	27	46m 42.251s
17	Kousuke Akiyoshi	JPN	64	Rizla Suzuki MotoGP	Suzuki	B	27	46m 44.124s
18	Olivier Jacque	FRA	19	Kawasaki Racing Team	Kawasaki	B	27	46m 54.241s
19	John Hopkins	USA	21	Rizla Suzuki MotoGP	Suzuki	B	27	46m 56.711s
	Alex Hofmann	GER	66	Pramac d'Antin	Ducati	B		EXC

Fastest lap: Valentino Rossi, on lap 5, 1m 40.905s, 98.052mph/157.799km/h.

Lap record: Valentino Rossi, ITA (Yamaha), 1m 40.596s, 98.353mph/158.284km/h (2005).

Event best maximum speed: Alex Barros, 174.1mph/280.2km/h (free practice no. 2).

Grid order		1	2	3	4	5	6	7	8	9	10	11	12	13	14	15	16	17	18	19	20	21	22	23	24	25	26	27	•
26	PEDROSA	46	46	46	46	46	46	46	46	46	46	46	46	46	46	46	46	46	46	46	46	46	46	46	46	46	46	46	1
46	ROSSI	26	26	26	26	26	26	26	26	26	26	26	26	26	26	26	26	26	26	26	26	26	26	26	26	26	26	26	2
7	CHECA	5	5	5	5	5	5	5	5	5	5	5	5	5	5	5	5	5	5	5	5	5	5	5	5	5	5	5	3
5	EDWARDS	1	1	1	1	1	1	1	1	1	1	1	1	1	1	1	21	24	24	24	24	24	24	24	24	24	24	24	4
27	STONER	27	27	21	21	21	21	21	21	21	21	21	21	21	21	21	24	1	1	1	27	27	27	27	27	27	27	27	5
21	HOPKINS	7	7	27	7	33	33	33	33	33	33	33	24	24	24	24	1	7	27	27	1	1	7	7	7	7	7	7	6
56	NAKANO	21	21	7	33	7	7	7	7	7	7	24	33	33	7	7	7	27	7	7	7	7	1	1	1	1	1	1	7
24	ELIAS	33	33	33	27	27	27	27	27	27	27	7	7	7	33	33	33	33	33	33	33	33	33	33	33	33	33	33	8
33	MELANDRI	24	24	24	24	24	24	24	24	24	24	27	27	27	27	27	27	4	4	4	4	4	4	4	4	4	71	71	9
10	ROBERTS Jnr	56	10	10	10	10	10	10	4	4	4	4	4	4	4	4	4	10	10	10	71	71	71	71	71	71	4	56	10
1	HAYDEN	10	56	56	56	56	4	4	10	10	10	10	10	10	10	10	10	71	71	71	10	10	10	10	56	56	56	4	11
14	de PUNIET	4	4	4	4	4	56	56	14	14	14	14	14	14	71	71	71	56	56	56	56	56	56	56	14	14	14	65	12
4	BARROS	14	14	14	14	14	14	14	56	56	56	56	71	71	14	14	56	14	14	14	14	14	14	14	65	65	65	14	13
71	VERMEULEN	71	65	65	65	65	65	65	65	65	71	71	56	56	56	56	14	65	65	65	65	65	65	65	10	10	6	6	14
65	CAPIROSSI	65	71	71	71	71	71	71	71	71	65	65	65	65	65	65	65	50	50	50	50	50	50	50	50	6	50	50	15
19	JACQUE	19	19	19	19	19	19	19	50	50	50	50	50	50	50	50	50	6	6	6	6	6	6	6	6	50	10	10	
6	TAMADA	64	50	50	50	50	50	50	19	19	19	6	6	6	6	6	6	64	64	64	64	64	64	64	64	64	64	64	
66	HOFMANN	50	64	64	64	64	64	64	64	6	6	19	64	64	64	64	64	19	19	19	19	19	19	19	19	19	19	19	
64	AKIYOSHI	6	6	6	6	6	6	6	6	64	64	64	19	19	19	19	19	21	21	21	21	21	21	21	21	21	21	21	
50	GUINTOLI	66	66	66	66																								

FASTEST RACE LAPS

	Rider	Lap	Time
1	Rossi	5	1m 40.905s
2	Hopkins	3	1m 40.938s
3	Pedrosa	5	1m 41.014s
4	Edwards	5	1m 41.174s
5	Melandri	3	1m 41.303s
6	Elias	3	1m 41.395s
7	Checa	3	1m 41.421s
8	Hayden	3	1m 41.441s
9	Stoner	7	1m 41.443s
10	Barros	3	1m 41.812s
11	Capirossi	5	1m 41.876s
12	Hofmann	4	1m 41.904s
13	de Puniet	5	1m 41.967s
14	Roberts Jnr	3	1m 42.024s
15	Nakano	5	1m 42.024s
16	Vermeulen	7	1m 42.037s
17	Guintoli	4	1m 42.291s
18	Jacque	4	1m 42.327s
19	Tamada	3	1m 42.456s
20	Akiyoshi	4	1m 42.555s

QUALIFYING

24 March 2007
Weather: Dry
Air: 24°C Humidity: 13%
Track: 40°C

Pos.	Rider	Time
1	Pedrosa	1m 39.402s
2	Rossi	1m 39.453s
3	Checa	1m 39.460s
4	Edwards	1m 39.486s
5	Stoner	1m 39.524s
6	Hopkins	1m 39.625s
7	Nakano	1m 39.632s
8	Elias	1m 39.660s
9	Melandri	1m 39.722s
10	Roberts Jnr	1m 39.727s
11	Hayden	1m 39.834s
12	de Puniet	1m 39.883s
13	Barros	1m 40.196s
14	Vermeulen	1m 40.328s
15	Capirossi	1m 40.391s
16	Jacque	1m 40.405s
17	Tamada	1m 40.617s
18	Hofmann	1m 40.710s
19	Akiyoshi	1m 41.202s
20	Guintoli	1m 41.219s

statistics

MotoGP | TISSOT OFFICIAL TIMEKEEPER

250cc

26 laps, 71.448 miles/114.998km

Pos.	Rider (Nat.)	No.	Machine	Laps	Time & speed
1	Jorge Lorenzo (SPA)	1	Aprilia	26	45m 35.846s 94.027mph/ 151.321km/h
2	Alvaro Bautista (SPA)	19	Aprilia	26	45m 36.064s
3	Andrea Dovizioso (ITA)	34	Honda	26	45m 36.324s
4	Alex de Angelis (RSM)	3	Aprilia	26	45m 44.002s
5	Alex Debon (SPA)	6	Aprilia	26	45m 50.593s
6	Hiroshi Aoyama (JPN)	4	KTM	26	45m 50.891s
7	Shuhei Aoyama (JPN)	73	Honda	26	45m 53.764s
8	Yuki Takahashi (JPN)	55	Honda	26	46m 04.284s
9	Anthony West (AUS)	14	Aprilia	26	46m 15.281s
10	Dirk Heidolf (GER)	28	Aprilia	26	46m 38.535s
11	Fabrizio Lai (ITA)	32	Aprilia	26	46m 42.659s
12	Ratthapark Wilairot (THA)	8	Honda	26	46m 43.012s
13	Alex Baldolini (ITA)	25	Aprilia	26	46m 43.217s
14	Eugene Laverty (IRL)	50	Honda	26	46m 47.639s
15	Karel Abraham (CZE)	17	Aprilia	26	46m 49.744s
16	Jules Cluzel (FRA)	16	Aprilia	26	47m 08.530s
17	Taro Sekiguchi (JPN)	44	Aprilia	26	47m 08.887s
18	Imre Toth (HUN)	10	Aprilia	25	45m 47.622s
	Mika Kallio (FIN)	36	KTM	18	DNF
	Hector Barbera (SPA)	80	Aprilia	15	DNF
	Julian Simon (SPA)	60	Honda	12	DNF
	Aleix Espargaro (SPA)	41	Aprilia	10	DNF
	Arturo Tizon (SPA)	9	Aprilia	9	DNF
	Thomas Luthi (SWI)	12	Aprilia	6	DNF
	Alvaro Molina (SPA)	31	Aprilia	2	DNF
	Santiago Barragan (SPA)	53	Honda	0	DNF
	Marco Simoncelli (ITA)	58	Gilera	0	DNF

Fastest lap: de Angelis, 1m 44.295s, 94.865mph/152.670km/h (record).

Previous lap record: Daijiro Kato, JPN (Honda), 1m 44.444s, 94.729mph/ 152.42km/h (2001).

Event best maximum speed: Bautista, 153.3mph/246.7km/h (free practice no. 1).

Qualifying: 1 Lorenzo, 1m 43.099s; 2 Barbera, 1m 43.383s; 3 Simon, 1m 43.707s; 4 Dovizioso, 1m 43.764s; 5 Bautista, 1m 43.955s; 6 Simoncelli, 1m 44.096s; 7 S. Aoyama, 1m 44.174s; 8 Debon, 1m 44.185s; 9 Luthi, 1m 44.200s; 10 Kallio, 1m 44.221s; 11 Lai, 1m 44.329s; 12 de Angelis, 1m 44.358s; 13 H. Aoyama, 1m 44.469s; 14 Takahashi, 1m 44.994s; 15 West, 1m 45.307s; 16 Espargaro, 1m 45.589s; 17 Heidolf, 1m 45.621s; 18 Wilairot, 1m 45.876s; 19 Molina, 1m 45.934s; 20 Toth, 1m 46.268s; 21 Abraham, 1m 46.542s; 22 Baldolini, 1m 47.030s; 23 Sekiguchi, 1m 47.239s; 24 Laverty, 1m 47.280s; 25 Cluzel, 1m 47.362s; 26 Tizon, 1m 47.545s; 27 Barragan, 1m 48.683s.

Fastest race laps: 1 de Angelis, 1m 44.295s; 2 Bautista, 1m 44.399s; 3 Lorenzo, 1m 44.473s; 4 Barbera, 1m 44.532s; 5 Debon, 1m 44.576s; 6 Dovizioso, 1m 44.595s; 7 Simon, 1m 44.604s; 8 H. Aoyama, 1m 44.638s; 9 S. Aoyama, 1m 44.772s; 10 Luthi, 1m 44.820s; 11 Kallio, 1m 45.062s; 12 Takahashi, 1m 45.121s; 13 West, 1m 45.159s; 14 Lai, 1m 45.995s; 15 Wilairot, 1m 46.445s; 16 Laverty, 1m 46.515s; 17 Espargaro, 1m 46.538s; 18 Heidolf, 1m 46.578s; 19 Baldolini, 1m 46.706s; 20 Abraham, 1m 46.847s; 21 Sekiguchi, 1m 47.332s; 22 Cluzel, 1m 47.784s; 23 Molina, 1m 47.940s; 24 Toth, 1m 47.963s; 25 Tizon, 1m 48.492s.

World Championship: 1 Lorenzo, 50; 2 de Angelis, 33; 3 Dovizioso, 27; 4 Bautista, 20; 5 Takahashi, 17; 6 Barbera, 16; 7 S. Aoyama, 15; 8 Luthi, 13; 9 Debon, 11; 10 H. Aoyama and Locatelli, 10; 12 West, 10; 13 Lai, 9; 14 Simon, 8; 15 Simoncelli, 7; 16 Heidolf, 7; 17 Wilairot, 6; 18 Espargaro, 5; 19 Baldolini, 3; 20 Laverty, 2; 21 Abraham, 1.

125cc

23 laps, 63.204 miles/101.729km

Pos.	Rider (Nat.)	No.	Machine	Laps	Time & speed
1	Gabor Talmacsi (HUN)	14	Aprilia	23	41m 52.149s 90.584mph/ 145.781km/h
2	Lukas Pesek (CZE)	52	Derbi	23	41m 52.163s
3	Hector Faubel (SPA)	55	Aprilia	23	41m 57.869s
4	Pol Espargaro (SPA)	44	Aprilia	23	41m 58.638s
5	Sergio Gadea (SPA)	33	Aprilia	23	41m 59.016s
6	Pablo Nieto (SPA)	22	Aprilia	23	42m 01.368s
7	Sandro Cortese (GER)	11	Aprilia	23	42m 11.227s
8	Joan Olive (SPA)	6	Aprilia	23	42m 11.282s
9	Michael Ranseder (AUT)	60	Derbi	23	42m 11.813s
10	Lorenzo Zanetti (ITA)	8	Aprilia	23	42m 20.583s
11	Stefano Bianco (ITA)	27	Aprilia	23	42m 20.964s
12	Andrea Iannone (ITA)	29	Aprilia	23	42m 20.965s
13	Steve Bonsey (USA)	51	KTM	23	42m 35.848s
14	Nicolas Terol (SPA)	18	Derbi	23	42m 38.585s
15	Simone Grotzkyj (ITA)	53	Aprilia	23	42m 40.230s
16	Pere Tutusaus (SPA)	30	Aprilia	23	42m 40.728s
17	Randy Krummenacher (SWI)	34	KTM	23	42m 43.402s
18	Robert Muresan (ROU)	95	Derbi	23	42m 44.309s
19	Dominique Aegerter (SWI)	77	Aprilia	23	43m 03.974s
20	Hugo van den Berg (NED)	56	Aprilia	23	43m 05.283s
21	Joey Litjens (NED)	37	Honda	23	43m 12.438s
22	Ivan Maestro (SPA)	76	Aprilia	23	43m 15.901s
23	Dino Lombardi (ITA)	13	Honda	23	43m 21.037s
24	Daniel Saez (SPA)	78	Aprilia	23	43m 23.825s
25	Roberto Tamburini (ITA)	20	Aprilia	23	43m 37.325s
26	Bradley Smith (GBR)	38	Honda	23	43m 37.357s
	Tomoyoshi Koyama (JPN)	71	KTM	19	DNF
	Federico Sandi (ITA)	15	Aprilia	19	DNF
	Daniel Webb (GBR)	99	Honda	16	DNF
	Alexis Masbou (FRA)	7	Honda	11	DNF
	Raffaele de Rosa (ITA)	35	Aprilia	3	DNF
	Simone Corsi (ITA)	24	Aprilia	2	DNF
	Mattia Pasini (ITA)	75	Aprilia	1	DNF
	Esteve Rabat (SPA)	12	Honda	0	DNF
	Mike di Meglio (FRA)	63	Honda		DNS

Fastest lap: Talmacsi, 1m 47.976s, 91.755mph/147.666km/h.

Lap record: Lukas Pesek, CZE (Derbi), 1m 47.404s, 92.119mph/ 148.251km/h (2006).

Event best maximum speed: Koyama, 132.4mph/213.0km/h (qualifying practice no. 2).

Qualifying: 1 Pasini, 1m 47.245s; 2 Talmacsi, 1m 47.483s; 3 Pesek, 1m 47.485s; 4 Gadea, 1m 47.670s; 5 Faubel, 1m 47.727s; 6 Koyama, 1m 47.791s; 7 Espargaro, 1m 48.030s; 8 Corsi, 1m 48.115s; 9 Nieto, 1m 48.153s; 10 Cortese, 1m 48.435s; 11 Smith, 1m 48.499s; 12 de Rosa, 1m 48.642s; 13 Ranseder, 1m 48.831s; 14 Olive, 1m 48.943s; 15 Iannone, 1m 49.007s; 16 Masbou, 1m 49.056s; 17 Zanetti, 1m 49.316s; 18 Tutusaus, 1m 49.375s; 19 Rabat, 1m 49.460s; 20 di Meglio, 1m 49.607s; 21 Sandi, 1m 49.793s; 22 Bianco, 1m 49.914s; 23 Terol, 1m 50.026s; 24 Krummenacher, 1m 50.269s; 25 Grotzkyj, 1m 50.367s; 26 Bonsey, 1m 50.396s; 27 van den Berg, 1m 50.724s; 28 Maestro, 1m 50.894s; 29 Muresan, 1m 50.905s; 30 Webb, 1m 51.046s; 31 Litjens, 1m 51.220s; 32 Lombardi, 1m 51.230s; 33 Aegerter, 1m 51.349s; 34 Saez, 1m 51.871s; 35 Tamburini, 1m 52.243s.

Fastest race laps: 1 Talmacsi, 1m 47.976s; 2 Pesek, 1m 47.991s; 3 Corsi, 1m 47.997s; 4 Faubel, 1m 48.207s; 5 Nieto, 1m 48.400s; 6 Gadea, 1m 48.517s; 7 Ranseder, 1m 48.537s; 8 Koyama, 1m 48.553s; 9 Espargaro, 1m 48.643s; 10 Cortese, 1m 48.918s; 11 Zanetti, 1m 48.937s; 12 Olive, 1m 49.010s; 13 Sandi, 1m 49.081s; 14 Bianco, 1m 49.144s; 15 Masbou, 1m 49.238s; 16 Iannone, 1m 49.493s; 17 Smith, 1m 49.739s; 18 Bonsey, 1m 49.819s; 19 Grotzkyj, 1m 49.827s; 20 Tutusaus, 1m 49.866s; 21 Terol, 1m 50.014s; 22 Muresan, 1m 50.312s; 23 Krummenacher, 1m 50.507s; 24 de Rosa, 1m 50.631s; 25 Webb, 1m 50.709s; 26 van den Berg, 1m 51.088s; 27 Aegerter, 1m 51.225s; 28 Saez, 1m 51.235s; 29 Maestro, 1m 51.239s; 30 Litjens, 1m 51.285s; 31 Lombardi, 1m 51.771s; 32 Tamburini, 1m 52.296s; 33 Pasini, 1m 58.371s.

World Championship: 1 Talmacsi, 45; 2 Faubel, 41; 3 Pesek, 36; 4 Espargaro, 22; 5 Nieto, 17; 6 de Rosa, 13; 7 Olive, 13; 8 Corsi and Gadea, 11; 10 Koyama, 10; 11 Ranseder, 10; 12 Cortese, 9; 13 Rabat, 8; 14 Masbou and Zanetti, 6; 16 Bianco, 5; 17 Iannone, 5; 18 Smith, 4; 19 Bonsey, 3; 20 di Meglio and Terol, 2; 22 Grotzkyj, 1.

RIDER STANDINGS

After 2 Rounds

1	Valentino Rossi	45
2	Casey Stoner	36
3	Dani Pedrosa	36
4	Colin Edwards	26
5	Marco Melandri	19
6	Nicky Hayden	17
7	Chris Vermeulen	16
8	Toni Elias	15
9	John Hopkins	13
10	Alex Barros	12
11	Shinya Nakano	12
12	Carlos Checa	10
13	Alex Hofmann	5
14	Loris Capirossi	4
15	Olivier Jacque	4
16	Randy de Puniet	3
17	Kenny Roberts Jnr	3
18	Makoto Tamada	2
19	Sylvain Guintoli	2

TEAM STANDINGS

After 2 Rounds

1	Fiat Yamaha Team	71
2	Repsol Honda Team	53
3	Ducati Marlboro Team	40
4	Honda Gresini	34
5	Rizla Suzuki MotoGP	29
6	Pramac d'Antin	17
7	Konica Minolta Honda	12
8	Honda LCR	10
9	Kawasaki Racing Team	7
10	Dunlop Yamaha Tech 3	4
11	Team Roberts	3

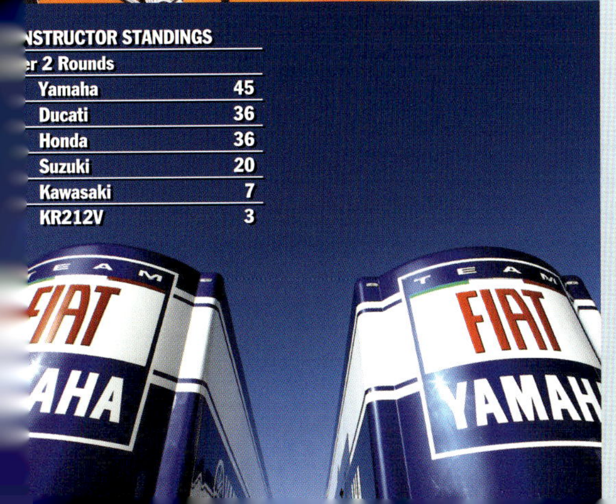

NSTRUCTOR STANDINGS

er 2 Rounds

Yamaha	45
Ducati	36
Honda	36
Suzuki	20
Kawasaki	7
KR212V	3

Team chief Livio Suppo (to left of Capirossi) leads the Ducati chorus after their double rostrum.
Photograph: Gold & Goose

FIM WORLD CHAMPIONSHIP • ROUND 3

TURKISHGP

ISTANBUL

ALL fears of predictability were overturned at Istanbul, in another fine demonstration of the sort of racing a really well-designed race-track can produce. This made it all the sadder that the third race at the still spanking-new Istanbul Park would be the last in the current series. Like the two previous events, it was highly memorable.

Rossi had expected difficulty at this fast track, but nobody could have expected the way it would be decided by tyres – in more than one way. It was the first track where the new tyre rules bit home, there had been no previous testing, and for Bridgestone not much previous success either. Any perceived disadvantage lasted no longer than the first practice, Bridgestone and Michelin being mixed up together at the front. Michelin took back some ground on its front-and-rear qualifier combination to control the front row. But its race was a disaster, Bridgestone taking a tenth GP victory, and not just a clean sweep of the rostrum, but the next three places as well.

Circumstances were very much against Michelin. It had lost two out of three front-row qualifiers even before they'd finished a lap. At the entrance to the final, very tight left-right-left triple corkscrew that ends the lap, which is approached at top speed, Jacque, sucked in by the draft and unsighted in the traffic, missed his braking point. He clobbered Edwards from behind and ricocheted into Pedrosa. Vermeulen was also brought down, but the Suzuki was cushioned by Pedrosa's Honda as it slid across the hard-paved run-off, and he was able to remount. His ride back through was fine, garnering fastest lap on his way from last to 11th.

We would never know what the other two might have done, especially Pedrosa. Michelin still had Rossi, but the ace was in a hole, having run off while leading at 185 mph on the fastest corner of the year, before being thoroughly mugged by Elias. Then it got worse, and he was dropping back rapidly, his rear tyre shaking and sliding, an invisible fault in its construction causing almost terminal vibration.

Rossi made light of his run on to the dirt, but not of his encounter with Elias. It had been a tough move, Elias forcing inside into the triple-turns so that Rossi had to lift, but surely no tougher than many in Rossi's career, most notably when he stole the lead from Gibernau on the last corner at Jerez in 2005. That was different, said Valentino. 'I only go inside – I did not change my line.' But he had the good grace to laugh. A few minutes earlier, he had been generous in his criticism of Elias, even using the D-word – 'Dangerous'. Others thought of the R-word – 'Rattled'. It hadn't been Elias who had lost Rossi the race, but Stoner who had won it, and very convincingly too.

The Honda lament went on. Hayden – fresh from a few days training with Fast Freddie at Spencer's Las Vegas facility – was one race behind Pedrosa in getting a new chassis. He liked it for its 'better rear contact feel and better feedback', but the main problem remained at the front. Both he and Melandri tried variations of 2006 forks, with little success. Nicky wore a red Virginia Tech logo on his helmet, 'to show support for the families' of more than 30 victims of a deranged gunman the preceding week.

Surprisingly, in spite of having no long straights, Istanbul Park was the first track where the 800s were slower than the 990s. Rossi's pole was more than half a second off Gibernau's 2005 pole of 1m 52.334s (it was wet in 2006); Vermeulen's fastest lap of the race was more than a second off Elias's 2006 record.

Less speed did make the fast, blind and daunting Turn 11 a little less so, although it was still no place for the faint-hearted. The 990s had run through in fifth, except for the occasional hero – like 2006 winner, Melandri. Now Rossi at least was using sixth as a matter of course. 'The speed in the middle of the corner is more or less the same, but we arrive a little bit slower,' he said after qualifying. 'Anyway, it remains a good corner and still very fast. I'm not flat-out, but very close. It is difficult for the brain to say, "Don't roll off a little bit."' Perhaps he recalled his words when he ran wide and on to the grass there early in the race, losing the lead and a few more of his nine lives. Team-mate Edwards had already 'lost the front a couple of times on the first day – and it's back to the pits for a change of underwear after that.'

Not a change of tyres, however, most of the time. With no data, the forecasters had to spread their range of choices wider, leaving most riders short of spare examples of the 'right' tyre. If they had one. Rossi, on race eve: 'I have two options. I don't have a perfect tyre, but with this new rule, I think this is normal.' He had pioneered yet another new technique to exploit qualifying. Usually the master of waiting until the very end to set a fastest lap, this time he was too late. A mistake? No. He'd al-

ready got pole, then fitted a race tyre, going out only to practice a start. 'If you do that on a used qualifying tyre, you don't get such a good result,' he explained.

The loss of Istanbul Park to MotoGP was generally mourned, but the three-year Dorna contract had not been renewed, said the circuit builders and operators (a consortium of local government and commercial interests), because of poor crowds and a lack of meaningful sponsorship. In fact, they claimed a respectable 40,052 this year, but the die was cast. At the same time, by coincidence, Bernie Ecclestone was on hand, to sign his own new deal – a lease until 2021 at US $3-million per annum. (The track had cost 120-million Euros to build.) Would he save the bike GP? 'That depends an awful lot on Dorna,' he told a packed press conference. 'But I am a big motorcycle supporter – I think motorcycle racing is super, super, super. We will do whatever we can to help.' Including teaching Dorna a good lesson in how to tie up contracts nice and tight.

In previous years, post-race testing had been arranged among the teams – one would rent the circuit, and share track time and cost with the others. This year, Dorna had taken it over. But although it had booked Istanbul Park for two days, at an expected fee of less than US $20,000, the contract hadn't actually been signed. And, as of now, the track had a new operator, Ecclestone, and a new fee structure – a whacking $5,000 per day for each rider. Suzuki, for one, was planning to add test rider Nobu Aoki to its strength, sending its costs for two days rocketing from $2,000 or $3,000 to $30,000. In spite of a chorus of protest from the teams, and plaintive requests from Dorna, it seemed that Ecclestone wouldn't budge. Yamaha was the first to crumble, saying it would test no matter what the cost. But mass bankruptcy was avoided with a late-Saturday concession. Instead of a fee per rider, the circuit was let for a flat fee of 50,000 Euros.

MOTOGP RACE – 22 laps

As first practice dried up, Stoner took control, staying on top until the qualifiers came out. By then, Rossi and Pedrosa had closed up among the Bridgestones, and on qualifiers, the Michelin runners took control, Yamahas side by side, then Pedrosa, Stoner being condemned to head row two from Capirossi and a slightly happier Hayden.

The two Yamahas led away, Rossi in front, Stoner and Capirossi chasing as they swung through the complex corners and plunged down the hill again. And then, 'I try too much, and I go wide,' Rossi explained. Easily said, but it was a wild, heart-in-the-mouth ride across the grass at the fastest corner of the year. He rejoined behind Hopkins and Elias, in fifth, all lucky to miss the shambles as Jacque speared into the pack jumbling into the triple corkscrew at the end of the lap.

They all stayed close, Rossi getting ahead of Elias on lap five in a shuffle through the triple bends. Something similar next time around saw Hopkins come off badly, losing out to both Rossi and Elias.

Melandri had worked his way past and away from Hayden to join the leaders, although Nicky, Barros and de Puniet were not far away.

Stoner's lead had stretched to just short of two seconds by lap nine, then it got even better. He explained, 'I tried to slow the pace just to make sure everything was safe. The lap times actually dropped from trying to go slower.'

On the same lap, both Rossi and Elias got ahead of Capirossi, but there was no chance for the multi-champion to start work on catching the Ducati, because on the very next lap, Elias came slithering past on the inside under brakes, firmly seizing second.

Rossi lost a full second in their encounter and would never

Above: **Elias's wild braking style clashes with Rossi's corner entry. The move was controversial, and decisive.**

Centre top left: **De Puniet, whose season was starting to pick up.**

Centre left: **Bernie Ecclestone taught Dorna a good lesson.**

Photographs: Gold & Goose

Far left: **The Yamahas lead, briefly, Valentino Rossi (left) on the faster line. Both Ducatis are away well, the Hondas aiming for the same bit of track, Olivier Jacque (19) looming dangerously.**

Photograph: Peter J. Fox/2snap

Top: Lap one: Vermeulen runs to recover his bike, cushioned from damage by Pedrosa's Honda.

Above: Barros, here chased by Melandri, would miss the rostrum by inches.

Above right: Bridgestone tyres at rest, after dominating the race.

Opposite, top right: Dovizioso makes a major save, with Lorenzo and half-hidden Bautista ready to take advantage.

Opposite, centre: Victory was sweet for 'Dovi', and third for Bautista.

Opposite, bottom: Corsi's 125 lead over Faubel, Koyama and de Rosa did not last long.

Photographs: Gold & Goose

get it back. Instead, on lap 14, he was another full second slower, and it would get worse as he slipped away, soon among the next gang and losing place after place. At the end, he was powerless to resist de Puniet, and finally Hofmann, with two laps to go. Afterwards, he broke the taboo and spoke harshly of Michelin: 'We are very upset, because we give the maximum, together with Yamaha. The engineers work a lot to bring me some new parts. It is bad to lose and destroy all the work of the weekend for a tyre. So Michelin have to work like us and have to give heart like us.'

Stoner kept drawing away from Elias, being able to slow over the line for his second win, still more than six seconds clear.

The battle for third was intense. When Rossi slowed, Hopkins was ahead of Melandri, Capirossi, Barros and Hayden, all passing in less time than it takes to read their names. They ran on to the final lap with Capirossi heading Barros, Melandri, Hayden and Hopkins, the last rostrum spot very much up for grabs.

Barros seemed the final victor, as he got the best drive out of the fast right and swept past a wobbling Capirossi towards the final triple corner set. Capirossi made one more effort, braking as late as you can imagine to regain the advantage, and held on for his first rostrum of the year. Without telling anyone, he'd been riding with a broken left finger, caused by a trials-bike training tumble. 'I'm back!' he said. 'Twenty days ago, I had the best moment in my life when our first child was born, and now I'm enjoying riding again.' (The child was a son – Riccardo.)

Barros was a frustrating three-hundredths away, Melandri right behind, then Hopkins, who had passed Hayden on the exit from the last corners, after the Honda rider's failed final bid. 'It was a real dogfight,' said Hopkins.

Hayden said, 'With four or five laps to go, I was thinking I was going to be able to steal a podium.' But deteriorating front grip meant that his final lunge through the fast corner ended in a major moment: 'I barely stayed on.'

De Puniet was only four seconds down for a career-best eighth; Hofmann was closing at the end, then came Rossi. Vermeulen was more than seven seconds adrift, after storming through from the first-lap crash. His last victim had been Checa, then came Nakano, struggling with his Honda. Tamada was less than a second ahead of rookie Guintoli in the Dunlop battle for the final points; Roberts was another 30 seconds away, after battling all race with his own problem Michelin. 'It felt like it was flat,' he explained.

250cc RACE – 20 laps

The action in the 250 class was mainly at the sharp end, and it brought an upset in both practice and the race, Dovizioso being able to use the sweeter handling of his Honda to get ahead of the dominant Lorenzo in both. He took fastest lap as well, although not a record.

The Italian's pole was by less than a tenth ahead of the Spaniard, Bautista and de Angelis filling the front row; Simoncelli led the second from Luthi, Kallio and Simon.

Dovizioso had a lead of 1.7s at the end of lap one, from Bautista, Lorenzo, Luthi, de Angelis and Kallio on the sole KTM – Hiro Aoyama had fallen on the warm-up lap, swapped bikes, then crashed again on lap one. He remounted, only to pit later.

Bautista closed impressively to lead on lap four, the pair pulling away together. On lap eight, they were some 1.5s clear of Lorenzo, de Angelis and Luthi. Lorenzo often gets faster later, and by half-distance, he was closing again, de Angelis with him, Luthi losing ground.

Dovizioso led again at the mid-point for two laps, then ran wide out of Turn 11, falling back into the hands of Lorenzo and triggering an intensification of the struggle. Next time into last corners, Lorenzo passed his rival; both muddled past Bautista as well, who briefly seemed to lose touch and come under pressure from de Angelis. Then, with two laps left, he escaped and closed again, slipping past Dovizioso into second, the three of them inches apart. Barring crashes, it was clear that the result would be determined last time through the final left-right-left.

It was a major barging match, and the places changed at each of the three apexes. But it was Dovizioso ahead over the line by inches, Lorenzo second, Bautista third – the rookie's second rostrum in a row.

By now, de Angelis, complaining of an over-hard choice of tyres, had fallen back by almost five seconds, but was safe in fourth; likewise, Luthi in fifth. Former KTM team-mates Kallio and Simon had been battling all race long, the older rider finally prevailing on the final lap.

The race behind was muddled and depleted. Barbera picked his way through to a lone and distant eighth, after finishing lap one 20th; Simoncelli fell and remounted on lap eight, pulling through some way behind and taking ninth off Lai by inches in the final corners.

Lai had Espargaro, Abraham and Heidolf on his tail. Espargaro's 11th came in spite of a ride-through penalty for a jumped start. Shuhei Aoyama had the same, but finished half a minute away.

West had a dramatic afternoon with a second engine seizure of the weekend in Turn 11, but he had managed to save the almost inevitable crash on both occasions. He'd finished lap one ninth. Takahashi, Cluzel and Tizon also retired; Sekiguchi and Toth joined the crash list.

125cc RACE – 19 laps

Pasini dominated 125 practice, taking pole by almost a quarter of a second ahead of Faubel, Corsi and Talmacsi, all on Aprilias. But his bad luck was not over yet. He seized an early lead and was scrapping over the position on lap four when a third consecutive engine failure – electronics again – saw him rolling to a stop by the track. He did restart, only to retire in frustration on the final lap, having reached no higher than 17th.

Corsi led away, but was displaced first by Pasini and then Faubel. The latter and Corsi were doing most of the leading in a shifting and shuffling pack of seven, four or five abreast into the last tight turns. Olive had picked his way through from a slow start and went to the front on lap 14. He even seemed set to escape, until Corsi closed on him. Faubel was a close third, but ran wide and let them escape. Corsi's attack saw him regain the lead over the line, another race decided by inches.

The group in pursuit was slowing one another down, while Bradley Smith – beginning to show growing strength – as well as Zanetti were closing up steadily. With three laps to go, they were with them, Smith starting the final lap sixth.

It was a tough environment for the teenager, who was shuffled back two places in the final brawl, finishing places being decided again by inches. Koyama headed de Rosa, Talmacsi, Pesek and Zanetti.

Ninth to 16th was another mêlée, covered by just over five seconds; Faubel dropped to tenth, behind Iannone. Bonsey, Cortese and Masbou crashed out, the American rejoining to take 25th.

GRAND PRIX OF TURKEY

22 APRIL 2007 • FIM WORLD CHAMPIONSHIP ROUND 3

ISTANBUL OTODROM

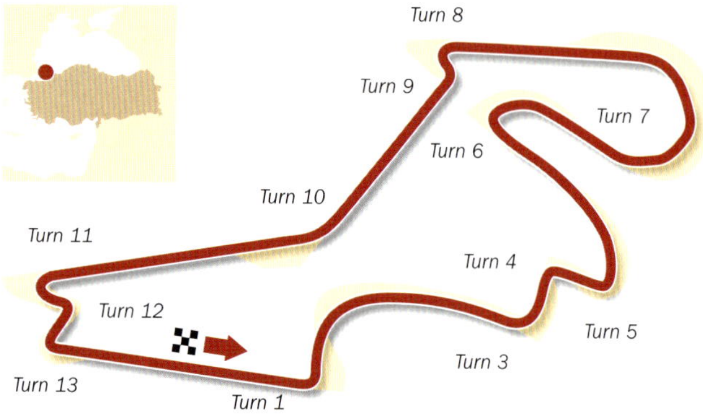

Circuit 5.340km /3.318 miles

MotoGP

RACE: 22 laps, 72.996 miles/117.480km • Weather: Dry • Air 23°C • Humidity 13% • Track 38°C

Pos.	Rider	Nat.	No.	Entrant	Machine	Tyres	Laps	Time & speed (mph/km/h)
1	Casey Stoner	AUS	27	Ducati Marlboro Team	Ducati	B	22	42m 02.850s 104.165mph/ 167.638km/h
2	Toni Elias	SPA	24	Honda Gresini	Honda	B	22	42m 09.057s
3	Loris Capirossi	ITA	65	Ducati Marlboro Team	Ducati	B	22	42m 10.952s
4	Alex Barros	BRA	4	Pramac d'Antin	Ducati	B	22	42m 10.985s
5	Marco Melandri	ITA	33	Honda Gresini	Honda	B	22	42m 11.139s
6	John Hopkins	USA	21	Rizla Suzuki MotoGP	Suzuki	B	22	42m 13.036s
7	Nicky Hayden	USA	1	Repsol Honda Team	Honda	M	22	42m 13.089s
8	Randy de Puniet	FRA	14	Kawasaki Racing Team	Kawasaki	B	22	42m 17.584s
9	Alex Hofmann	GER	66	Pramac d'Antin	Ducati	B	22	42m 18.892s
10	Valentino Rossi	ITA	46	Fiat Yamaha Team	Yamaha	M	22	42m 21.849s
11	Chris Vermeulen	AUS	71	Rizla Suzuki MotoGP	Suzuki	B	22	42m 29.099s
12	Carlos Checa	SPA	7	Honda LCR	Honda	M	22	42m 32.396s
13	Shinya Nakano	JPN	56	Konica Minolta Honda	Honda	M	22	42m 39.772s
14	Makoto Tamada	JPN	6	Dunlop Yamaha Tech 3	Yamaha	D	22	42m 41.390s
15	Sylvain Guintoli	FRA	50	Dunlop Yamaha Tech 3	Yamaha	D	22	42m 42.187s
16	Kenny Roberts Jnr	USA	10	Team Roberts	KR212V	M	22	43m 12.186s
	Olivier Jacque	FRA	19	Kawasaki Racing Team	Kawasaki	B	0	
	Dani Pedrosa	SPA	26	Repsol Honda Team	Honda	M	0	
	Colin Edwards	USA	5	Fiat Yamaha Team	Yamaha	M	0	

Fastest lap: Chris Vermeulen, on lap 21, 1m 54.026s, 104.759mph/168.593km/h.

Lap record: Toni Elias, SPA (Honda),1m 52.877s, 105.825mph/170.309km/h (2006).

Event best maximum speed: Casey Stoner, 187.2mph/301.2km/h (free practice no. 3).

Grid order	1	2	3	4	5	6	7	8	9	10	11	12	13	14	15	16	17	18	19	20	21	22	•
46 ROSSI	27	27	27	27	27	27	27	27	27	27	27	27	27	27	27	27	27	27	27	27	27	27	1
5 EDWARDS	65	65	65	65	65	65	65	65	46	24	24	24	24	24	24	24	24	24	24	24	24	24	2
26 PEDROSA	21	21	21	21	21	46	46	46	24	46	46	46	46	46	21	65	65	65	65	65	65	65	3
27 STONER	24	24	24	24	46	24	24	24	65	65	65	65	21	21	33	21	21	33	33	4	4	4	4
65 CAPIROSSI	46	46	46	46	24	21	21	21	21	21	21	21	33	33	65	33	33	4	4	33	33	33	5
1 HAYDEN	1	1	1	33	33	33	33	33	33	33	33	33	65	65	46	4	4	1	1	1	1	21	6
21 HOPKINS	33	33	33	1	1	1	1	1	1	1	1	1	4	4	4	1	1	21	21	21	21	1	7
14 de PUNIET	4	14	4	4	4	4	4	4	4	4	4	4	1	1	1	46	46	46	46	14	14	14	8
71 VERMEULEN	14	4	14	14	14	14	14	14	14	14	14	14	14	14	14	14	14	14	14	46	66	66	9
24 ELIAS	66	66	66	66	66	66	66	66	66	66	66	66	66	66	66	66	66	66	66	66	46	46	10
19 JACQUE	7	7	6	7	7	7	7	7	7	7	7	7	7	7	7	7	7	7	7	71	71	71	11
56 NAKANO	6	6	7	6	6	6	6	6	6	6	6	6	6	6	6	71	71	71	71	7	7	7	12
4 BARROS	56	56	56	56	56	56	56	56	56	56	56	56	56	56	71	56	56	56	56	56	56	56	13
33 MELANDRI	10	10	50	50	50	50	50	50	50	50	50	50	50	50	56	6	6	6	6	6	6	6	14
6 TAMADA	50	50	10	10	10	10	10	10	71	71	71	71	71	71	50	50	50	50	50	50	50	50	15
7 CHECA	71	71	71	71	71	71	71	71	10	10	10	10	10	10	10	10	10	10	10	10	10	10	
66 HOFMANN																							
10 ROBERTS Jnr																							
50 GUINTOLI																							

FASTEST RACE LAPS

	Rider	Lap	Time
1	Vermeulen	21	1m 54.026s
2	Rossi	4	1m 54.066s
3	Stoner	15	1m 54.210s
4	Elias	8	1m 54.224s
5	Barros	19	1m 54.244s
6	Hopkins	21	1m 54.268s
7	Melandri	5	1m 54.391s
8	Hayden	10	1m 54.396s
9	Capirossi	18	1m 54.461s
10	de Puniet	4	1m 54.530s
11	Hofmann	18	1m 54.820s
12	Checa	19	1m 55.043s
13	Nakano	17	1m 55.266s
14	Tamada	3	1m 55.428s
15	Guintoli	8	1m 55.663s
16	Roberts Jnr	17	1m 56.953s

QUALIFYING

21 April 2007

Weather: Dry

Air: 20°C Humidity: 14%

Track: 34°C

Pos.	Rider	Time
1	Rossi	1m 52.795s
2	Edwards	1m 52.944s
3	Pedrosa	1m 52.971s
4	Stoner	1m 53.375s
5	Capirossi	1m 53.559s
6	Hayden	1m 53.613s
7	Hopkins	1m 53.637s
8	de Puniet	1m 53.706s
9	Vermeulen	1m 53.771s
10	Elias	1m 53.835s
11	Jacque	1m 53.847s
12	Nakano	1m 53.988s
13	Barros	1m 54.082s
14	Melandri	1m 54.143s
15	Tamada	1m 54.206s
16	Checa	1m 54.221s
17	Hofmann	1m 54.421s
18	Roberts Jnr	1m 54.527s
19	Guintoli	1m 54.845s

statistics

250cc

20 laps, 66.360 miles/106.800km

Pos.	Rider (Nat.)	No.	Machine	Laps	Time & speed
1	Andrea Dovizioso (ITA)	34	Honda	20	39m 31.153s 100.754mph/ 162.148km/h
2	Jorge Lorenzo (SPA)	1	Aprilia	20	39m 31.256s
3	Alvaro Bautista (SPA)	19	Aprilia	20	39m 31.471s
4	Alex de Angelis (RSM)	3	Aprilia	20	39m 36.047s
5	Thomas Luthi (SWI)	12	Aprilia	20	39m 50.908s
6	Mika Kallio (FIN)	36	KTM	20	39m 54.099s
7	Julian Simon (SPA)	60	Honda	20	39m 54.436s
8	Hector Barbera (SPA)	80	Aprilia	20	40m 18.831s
9	Marco Simoncelli (ITA)	58	Gilera	20	40m 29.635s
10	Fabrizio Lai (ITA)	32	Aprilia	20	40m 29.887s
11	Aleix Espargaro (SPA)	41	Aprilia	20	40m 39.741s
12	Karel Abraham (CZE)	17	Aprilia	20	40m 40.185s
13	Dirk Heidolf (GER)	28	Aprilia	20	40m 41.158s
14	Alex Baldolini (ITA)	25	Aprilia	20	40m 45.662s
15	Ratthapark Wilairot (THA)	8	Honda	20	40m 48.885s
16	Shuhei Aoyama (JPN)	73	Honda	20	40m 59.622s
17	Eugene Laverty (IRL)	50	Honda	20	41m 20.981s
	Imre Toth (HUN)	10	Aprilia	8	DNF
	Arturo Tizon (SPA)	9	Aprilia	8	DNF
	Jules Cluzel (FRA)	16	Aprilia	6	DNF
	Hiroshi Aoyama (JPN)	4	KTM	4	DNF
	Taro Sekiguchi (JPN)	44	Aprilia	2	DNF
	Anthony West (AUS)	14	Aprilia	1	DNF
	Yuki Takahashi (JPN)	55	Honda	1	DNF

Fastest lap: Dovizioso, 1m 57.815s, 101.390mph/163.171km/h.

Lap record: Dani Pedrosa, SPA (Honda), 1m 57.595s, 101.579mph/163.476km/h (2005).

Event best maximum speed: Bautista, 167.8mph/270.1km/h (race).

Qualifying: 1 Dovizioso, 1m 57.473s; 2 Lorenzo, 1m 57.550s; 3 Bautista, 1m 58.405s; 4 de Angelis, 1m 58.481s; 5 Simoncelli, 1m 58.572s; 6 Luthi, 1m 58.581s; 7 Kallio, 1m 58.588s; 8 Simon, 1m 58.649s; 9 H. Aoyama, 1m 58.676s; 10 Barbera, 1m 58.817s; 11 Takahashi, 1m 58.906s; 12 S. Aoyama, 1m 59.125s; 13 West, 1m 59.494s; 14 Lai, 1m 59.798s; 15 Espargaro, 1m 59.889s; 16 Cluzel, 2m 00.572s; 17 Wilairot, 2m 01.073s; 18 Baldolini, 2m 01.214s; 19 Heidolf, 2m 01.302s; 20 Tizon, 2m 01.328s; 21 Laverty, 2m 01.388s; 22 Toth, 2m 01.455s; 23 Sekiguchi, 2m 01.506s; 24 Abraham, 2m 02.083s.

Fastest race laps: 1 Dovizioso, 1m 57.815s; 2 Lorenzo, 1m 57.870s; 3 Bautista, 1m 57.930s; 4 de Angelis, 1m 57.972s; 5 Luthi, 1m 58.774s; 6 Kallio, 1m 59.067s; 7 Simon, 1m 59.100s; 8 Simoncelli, 1m 59.580s; 9 Barbera, 1m 59.867s; 10 Lai, 2m 00.044s; 11 S. Aoyama, 2m 00.104s; 12 Espargaro, 2m 00.234s; 13 Heidolf, 2m 00.803s; 14 Wilairot, 2m 00.937s; 15 Abraham, 2m 01.198s; 16 Baldolini, 2m 01.230s; 17 Laverty, 2m 02.024s; 18 Tizon, 2m 02.383s; 19 Toth, 2m 02.475s; 20 Cluzel, 2m 02.788s; 21 H. Aoyama, 2m 03.176s; 22 West, 2m 04.279s; 23 Sekiguchi, 2m 04.740s.

World Championship: 1 Lorenzo, 70; 2 Dovizioso, 52; 3 de Angelis, 46; 4 Bautista, 36; 5 Barbera, 24; 6 Luthi, 24; 7 Simon and Takahashi, 17; 9 S. Aoyama, 15; 10 Lai, 15; 11 Simoncelli, 14; 12 Debon, 11; 13 H. Aoyama, Kallio and Locatelli, 10; 16 West, 10; 17 Heidolf, 10; 18 Espargaro, 10; 19 Wilairot, 7; 20 Abraham, 5; 21 Baldolini, 5; 22 Laverty, 2.

125cc

19 laps, 63.042 miles/101.460km

Pos.	Rider (Nat.)	No.	Machine	Laps	Time & speed
1	Simone Corsi (ITA)	24	Aprilia	19	40m 03.557s 94.426mph/ 151.964km/h
2	Joan Olive (SPA)	6	Aprilia	19	40m 03.655s
3	Tomoyoshi Koyama (JPN)	71	KTM	19	40m 05.500s
4	Raffaele de Rosa (ITA)	35	Aprilia	19	40m 05.748s
5	Gabor Talmacsi (HUN)	14	Aprilia	19	40m 06.203s
6	Lukas Pesek (CZE)	52	Derbi	19	40m 06.496s
7	Lorenzo Zanetti (ITA)	8	Aprilia	19	40m 06.676s
8	Bradley Smith (GBR)	38	Honda	19	40m 06.677s
9	Andrea Iannone (ITA)	29	Aprilia	19	40m 13.910s
10	Hector Faubel (SPA)	55	Aprilia	10	40m 14.399s
11	Pol Espargaro (SPA)	44	Aprilia	19	40m 18.003s
12	Michael Ranseder (AUT)	60	Derbi	19	40m 18.978s
13	Pablo Nieto (SPA)	22	Aprilia	19	40m 19.222s
14	Esteve Rabat (SPA)	12	Honda	19	40m 19.427s
15	Randy Krummenacher (SWI)	34	KTM	19	40m 19.531s
16	Nicolas Terol (SPA)	18	Derbi	19	40m 19.693s
17	Stefano Bianco (ITA)	27	Aprilia	19	40m 27.760s
18	Roberto Tamburini (ITA)	20	Aprilia	19	40m 37.225s
19	Federico Sandi (ITA)	15	Aprilia	19	40m 38.088s
20	Joey Litjens (NED)	37	Honda	19	40m 49.172s
21	Kevin Coghlan (GBR)	54	Honda	19	40m 49.187s
22	Robert Muresan (ROU)	95	Derbi	19	40m 49.719s
23	Daniel Webb (GBR)	99	Honda	19	40m 53.409s
24	Dominique Aegerter (SWI)	77	Aprilia	19	40m 55.539s
25	Steve Bonsey (USA)	51	KTM	19	41m 14.809s
26	Hugo van den Berg (NED)	56	Aprilia	19	41m 59.253s
27	Tobias Siegert (GER)	41	Aprilia	18	40m 14.717s
	Mattia Pasini (ITA)	75	Aprilia	18	DNF
	Alen Gyorfi (HUN)	40	Aprilia	17	DNF
	Sergio Gadea (SPA)	33	Aprilia	17	DNF
	Simone Grotzkyj (ITA)	53	Aprilia	13	DNF
	Alexis Masbou (FRA)	7	Honda	11	DNF
	Dino Lombardi (ITA)	13	Honda	9	DNF
	Sandro Cortese (GER)	11	Aprilia	6	DNF
	Nikolett Kovacs (HUN)	39	Honda		DNQ

Fastest lap: de Rosa, 2m 05.217s, 95.396mph/153.525km/h.

Lap record: Joan Olive, SPA (Aprilia), 2m 03.825s, 96.468mph/155.251km/h (2006).

Event best maximum speed: de Rosa, 143.0mph/230.1km/h (race).

Qualifying: 1 Pasini, 2m 04.722s; 2 Faubel, 2m 04.951s; 3 Corsi, 2m 05.299s; 4 Talmacsi, 2m 05.372s; 5 Pesek, 2m 05.386s; 6 Koyama, 2m 05.434s; 7 Olive, 2m 05.748s; 8 Ranseder, 2m 06.051s; 9 Terol, 2m 06.189s; 10 Cortese, 2m 06.209s; 11 de Rosa, 2m 06.267s; 12 Nieto, 2m 06.400s; 13 Smith, 2m 06.408s; 14 Zanetti, 2m 06.464s; 15 Gadea, 2m 06.726s; 16 Krummenacher, 2m 06.732s; 17 Iannone, 2m 06.885s; 18 Espargaro, 2m 06.974s; 19 Masbou, 2m 07.238s; 20 Tamburini, 2m 07.382s; 21 Rabat, 2m 07.464s; 22 Bianco, 2m 07.553s; 23 Sandi, 2m 07.703s; 24 Litjens, 2m 07.754s; 25 Bonsey, 2m 07.838s; 26 Grotzkyj, 2m 08.002s; 27 Coghlan, 2m 08.311s; 28 Muresan, 2m 08.836s; 29 Aegerter, 2m 08.954s; 30 Webb, 2m 09.131s; 31 van den Berg, 2m 09.632s; 32 Lombardi, 2m 09.647s; 33 Gyorfi, 2m 11.384s; 34 Siegert, 2m 12.956s; 35 Kovacs, 2m 17.221s.

Fastest race laps: 1 de Rosa, 2m 05.217s; 2 Pasini, 2m 05.239s; 3 Koyama, 2m 05.276s; 4 Olive, 2m 05.359s; 5 Corsi, 2m 05.375s; 6 Faubel, 2m 05.448s; 7 Talmacsi, 2m 05.474s; 8 Pesek, 2m 05.608s; 9 Iannone, 2m 05.692s; 10 Zanetti, 2m 05.946s; 11 Smith, 2m 06.003s; 12 Rabat, 2m 06.316s; 13 Masbou, 2m 06.339s; 14 Ranseder, 2m 06.427s; 15 Krummenacher, 2m 06.429s; 16 Espargaro, 2m 06.434s; 17 Nieto, 2m 06.453s; 18 Bianco, 2m 06.489s; 19 Terol, 2m 06.745s; 20 Cortese, 2m 06.998s; 21 Gadea, 2m 07.288s; 22 Tamburini, 2m 07.310s; 23 Grotzkyj, 2m 07.412s; 24 Sandi, 2m 07.550s; 25 Litjens, 2m 07.869s; 26 Bonsey, 2m 07.911s; 27 Muresan, 2m 07.925s; 28 Webb, 2m 07.997s; 29 Coghlan, 2m 08.125s; 30 Aegerter, 2m 08.348s; 31 Lombardi, 2m 09.206s; 32 Gyorfi, 2m 09.625s; 33 van den Berg, 2m 11.409s; 34 Siegert, 2m 12.458s.

World Championship: 1 Talmacsi, 56; 2 Faubel, 47; 3 Pesek, 46; 4 Corsi, 36; 5 Olive, 33; 6 Espargaro, 27; 7 Koyama, 26; 8 de Rosa, 26; 9 Nieto, 20; 10 Zanetti, 15; 11 Ranseder, 14; 12 Smith, 12; 13 Iannone, 12; 14 Gadea, 11; 15 Rabat, 10; 16 Cortese, 9; 17 Masbou, 6; 18 Bianco, 5; 19 Bonsey, 3; 20 di Meglio and Terol, 2; 22 Grotzkyj and Krummenacher, 1.

RIDER STANDINGS
After 3 Rounds

1	Casey Stoner	61
2	Valentino Rossi	51
3	Dani Pedrosa	36
4	Toni Elias	35
5	Marco Melandri	30
6	Colin Edwards	26
7	Nicky Hayden	26
8	Alex Barros	25
9	John Hopkins	23
10	Chris Vermeulen	21
11	Loris Capirossi	20
12	Shinya Nakano	15
13	Carlos Checa	14
14	Alex Hofmann	12
15	Randy de Puniet	11
16	Olivier Jacque	4
17	Makoto Tamada	4
18	Kenny Roberts Jnr	3
19	Sylvain Guintoli	3

TEAM STANDINGS
After 3 Rounds

1	Ducati Marlboro Team	81
2	Fiat Yamaha Team	77
3	Honda Gresini	65
4	Repsol Honda Team	62
5	Rizla Suzuki MotoGP	44
6	Pramac d'Antin	37
7	Kawasaki Racing Team	15
8	Konica Minolta Honda	15
9	Honda LCR	14
10	Dunlop Yamaha Tech 3	7
11	Team Roberts	3

CONSTRUCTOR STANDINGS
After 3 Rounds

1	Ducati	61
2	Honda	56
3	Yamaha	51
4	Suzuki	30
5	Kawasaki	15
6	KR212V	3

FIM WORLD CHAMPIONSHIP • ROUND 4

CHINESE GP

SHANGHAI

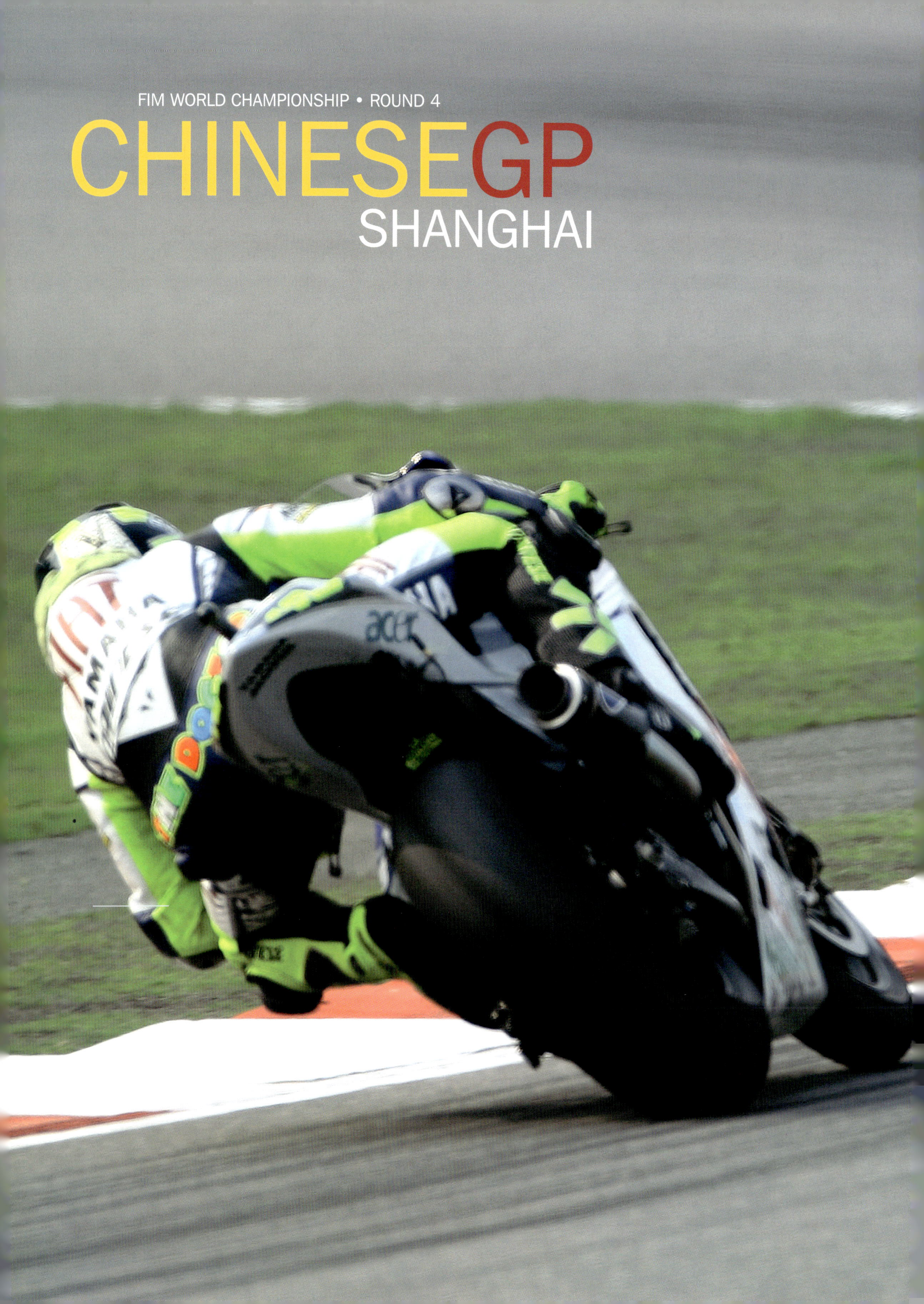

Stoner leads, Rossi chases. Once again, though, the older rider had to raise the white flag.
Photograph: Gold & Goose

Above: Elbow-scraping Hopkins finally made the rostrum, in his 82nd GP start.

Centre right: Men under pressure – HRC's Satoru Horiike (above) and Michelin's Jean-Philippe Weber.

Far right, above: Pedrosa, Alberto Puig at his shoulder, has his race face on.

Bottom right: Hayden and Barros regain the track while Checa rides past – all put off by Elias's first-corner crash.

Photographs: Gold & Goose

THE admission from the managing director of HRC was frank. It had, said Satoru Horiike, aimed too low for the new 800cc class. 'It is sure that our job was not enough,' he continued. 'Our target was maybe wrong.' HRC engineers had concentrated more on engine characteristics than top speed. They had been working since to make up the deficit, and already had more horsepower, thanks to changes to valve timing and the exhaust. But it was still insufficient, said Horiike, pointing to a deficit of some 10km/h down Shanghai's long straight. 'We improved a little, but I think some riders did not notice.' This was fair comment: the grumble of complaint about acceleration was still growing; and while the Hondas at least outpaced the Yamahas, the other continuing lament, about a lack of front-end confidence, meant that Shanghai's long, long corners were punishing the Honda riders just as badly.

China's long, long straight underlined the point that had been made so firmly at Qatar, and not only for Honda. The Ducati speed advantage may have been cut back a little, but it was still good enough for the right rider to be pretty much unbeatable. Stoner was that man, and again anxious to dispel any notion that he was winning races only because of speed. 'I mean, for sure we're not going to have too big a problem passing people at this track, but we still need to get it around the rest of the circuit,' he said. And he had a point, for the rest of the lap is a dizzying series of long corners, some of them very slow indeed.

Official top-speed figures are revealing, but are best taken from qualifying rather than the race, because the latter are influenced more by slipstreaming. And in spite of Rossi's insistence that they had 'closed the gap', the numbers proved that it was only in percentage terms. That was before the race, anyway. Afterwards, he was franker. 'I have never raced against a bike that was so much faster,' he said.

At Qatar, Stoner had topped out at 324.7km/h, about 7km/h faster than Pedrosa's top Honda, and almost 15km/h faster than Rossi's Yamaha. Here, Barros was fastest at 332.5km/h, Stoner 3km/h slower, and Pedrosa within 5 km/h, but Rossi was more than 16km/h down. Again, Kawasaki and Suzuki were ahead of Yamaha. Come the race, and the value of this speed was plain to see, every time down the straight. But of the Ducati riders, only Stoner was in a position to make the most of it.

Frank admissions were forthcoming also from Michelin, after investigating Rossi's tyre. There had been no delamination, said new boss Jean-Philippe Weber. But the carcase had been too soft, had deformed without internal damage and 'the tyre was not round any more.' Ironically enough, Michelin had had a stiffer carcase at Turkey and had tested it successfully the next day, but, as Weber ruefully explained, 'it had not been in the race tyre allocation'. Under pressure from riders (Edwards would suffer a rear tyre problem in the race that would leave him in

fear of his life, even at enforced cruising speeds), from circumstances and from Bridgestone, Weber had taken over the Director of Motorcycle Racing job at the worst possible time.

Elias ended the weekend in even more trouble. Rossi had softened his stance, declining to be drawn into further criticism of the overtaking move he had dubbed 'dangerous', waving his hand airily and saying, 'Yes, but you know is racing. In a very hard race like Turkey…can happen.' But Stoner had hard words after shaking his fist in practice, saying, 'I think every session in the last two races, he either got in my road or stuck on my ass end. You know, there's 5.2 ks of track. Get his own piece, because I'm sick of him following me all the time.' In the race, things went seriously wrong at the very first corner, a first-gear right. Elias overshot, hitting Hayden's back tyre hard enough to fall and sending the champion ricocheting off; Barros was forced to brake to a stop. The incident also disrupted a lot of other riders, including Checa. Later, Elias complained that Hayden had braked early, but the American had another idea: 'It's about the tightest corner on the whole calendar, so a guy does need to brake for it, so…sorry.'

Two incidents in practice ended in injury. In final qualifying, Capirossi and Vermeulen had taken conflicting lines into a tight right and collided. Each blamed the other for the loss of any chance of a decent starting position, but Vermeulen had lost a lot of skin off his toes and would race in some pain the next day. Much more serious was Olivier Jacque's crash at the end of the lap. The tumble was simple enough, but somehow his right arm became caught up in the bike in such a way that the inside of his forearm was terribly gashed at a point where the leathers are relieved by a panel of stretch fabric. It required immediate surgery, performed by Clinica Mobile doctors at Shanghai's Huashan hospital.

There was a fond farewell to the Marlboro racing livery for the rest of the year. Along with Qatar, this was only one of two GPs where the factory Ducatis could run in full fag-packet colours. One good reason, of course, for keeping this event on the calendar, but letting Istanbul Park go. And for the putative replacement of the Turkish round with a race in India. This event is far from popular with participants or, apparently, the potentially huge fan base of China's biggest city: Shanghai's population is thought to top 20 million. The magnificent facility – towering grandstands and a water-village in the back to house teams and riders – has seating for 100,000. This year's 28,400-strong crowd was dwarfed. In spite of increased pre-race publicity, and the rather surprising fact that Rossi had been voted the fifth most popular international sportsman in China, this was down on last year's 32,000. Thanks to tobacco, at least the short-term future of the event was assured.

MOTOGP RACE – 22 laps

Given his top-speed deficit, Rossi needed to perform magic at Shanghai. The first example came with an ethereal lap on his front and rear qualifying tyres. Fastest ever on a motorcycle, he was six-tenths inside Pedrosa's 990cc pole of 2006 and, more importantly, almost a full second faster than next-best Hopkins, who had earlier led from Stoner on race tyres in the free sessions. He tried for more miracles in the race, but the gods proved capable of only so much.

Edwards completed row one; Stoner led the second from Pedrosa and Melandri. The Australian's chances of a better qualifying lap were scuppered when his number-one bike stopped on track with an engine glitch. He lost time and had to switch to his spare.

Hopkins got the jump into the first corner, while a little way behind, all hell broke loose. Elias went out, while Hayden and Barros, among others, were very much incommoded. Neither actually fell, but Hayden's rear mudguard was smashed and jammed between wheel and chassis; Barros came to a complete stop before backing and filling in the gravel, finishing the lap 40 seconds in arrears.

Up front, Rossi took over immediately, with Stoner up to second at the end of the back straight; he followed the Yamaha around the rest of the lap. First time past the pits, he blew by, with Melandri following.

Stoner created a little gap while the two Italians bickered behind him, until Rossi finally disposed of Melandri on lap five and set about closing on Stoner again. Only to see him disappear down the back straight with a stark speed superiority.

Rossi didn't give up, exploiting all his cornering prowess and some quite extraordinary late braking to stay close, and to at-

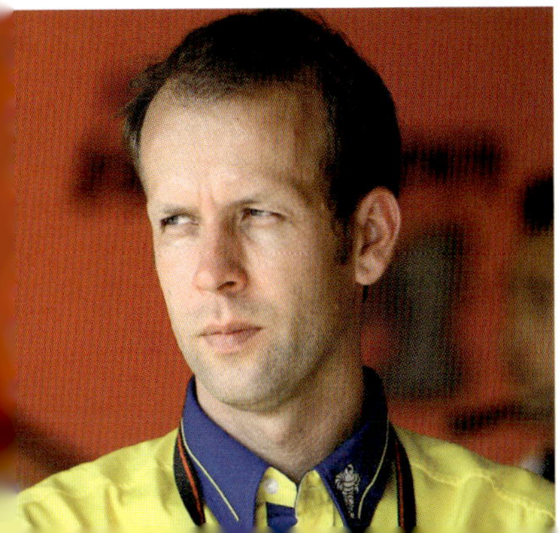

Above: **Drinking deeply, Hopkins had been promising himself podium bubbly for a long time.**

Top: **Elias, doubled over in pain and remorse after triggering another first-corner disaster.**

Main photograph: **View down the front straight shows tight corners immediately following.**

Photographs: Gold & Goose

tack again in the left-hander before the long right on to the back straight. Where the same thing happened again.

Twice more Rossi would get ahead, but with the same result, and Stoner led over the line on every lap. On lap 16, it was over. Rossi pushed alongside again, chased Stoner down the straight, then grabbed a short-lived lead under brakes from the hairpin – from more than 200mph down to little more than 30. Too late, as he hit a bump and ran wide. He lost more than two seconds and also second place – to Hopkins. It had been a good fight.

The Suzuki rider had displaced Melandri on lap seven and remained a close observer. Close enough to strike when Rossi slipped. But he couldn't hold off the Yamaha for more than two laps, and although he followed closely, the thought of his first podium was enough to persuade him to choose safety. For the last lap, he said later, he had thought all the way of his late father, Roy. 'This one is for him,' he said, overjoyed to have stood on the podium after a long, long wait.

Pedrosa had settled in fourth on lap nine and had a lonely ride from there on, his pace just not quite fast enough. Like all the Hondas behind, he was victimised not only by the speed deficit, but also by a lack of front-end feel and fidelity on the long corners. He'd displaced Melandri, whose Bridgestone-shod Honda added chatter to the problems, and who had a similar race, with a comfortable nine-second cushion at the end over a battle for sixth.

This was between qualifying antagonists Vermeulen and Capirossi, and de Puniet. It raged right to the finish after the first two caught and passed de Puniet on lap 20. The Frenchman was still attacking Vermeulen to the final bend, pulling almost alongside."

Hofmann was just a second behind, while Checa was alone in tenth, having passed Edwards on lap 16. This was the final stage of a long decline for the American, who had been fifth on lap one, and seventh next time around. He'd been talked into a tyre choice, even though he hadn't liked it in practice, and it hadn't worked. 'We had a serious wear problem on the right side, as in there wasn't any rubber left,' he explained baldly.

He did stay far enough ahead of Hayden, who had battled on a damaged bike and had been more than a little disheartened, admitting later that he could have gone faster. Behind him came Guintoli and fellow lap-one victim Barros, then Roberts, complaining of the twin ills of poor turning ability and a lack of acceleration – enough to spoil anybody's race.

Tamada and Nakano had knocked each other down on the fourth lap.

250cc RACE – 21 laps

Jorge Lorenzo, 20 on the Friday, celebrated with his third pole of the season on Saturday, then again on Sunday with his third win in four races. But he had to work for it, after spoiling his own party with a blunder on lap one, which had dropped him to sixth by the end of it. It took until lap seven before he was in the lead and pulling clear convincingly to win by almost four seconds, allowing him to plant his 'Lorenzo's Land' victory flag in the gravel.

The biggest battle was for second, between Bautista and Dovizioso. The former had come through from a slow start; the latter had been riding like a demon to overcome his relative shortage of speed, and had managed to draft the faster Aprilia down the final straight. Bautista got back ahead on the run to the final corner, then slammed on the brakes right in Dovizioso's path. They collided, and the Italian was forced on to the rumble strip, spoiling his exit. 'I think the overtake of Bautista is too hard, and a little bit worrying,' he complained, before his English failed him. 'No problem, no crash, but we are at the limit for crash. I think it's too hard.'

Kallio had led the first lap, but soon fell down the order as Dovizioso took over. The Honda rider dropped to third, behind de Angelis, on lap seven, when Lorenzo blew by both of them. Barbera was fourth, having got ahead of Simon and Kallio. Bautista, slowed in a first-lap muddle to end it down in 11th, was cutting through steadily. He was seventh by lap five, where he lodged for a while, sizing up the group.

On lap 11, Bautista was past all three of them, while ahead,

Dovizioso had taken back second from de Angelis. The gap to fourth was 3.3 seconds, but Bautista was lapping almost as fast as Lorenzo, and he took only four laps to catch up, moving cleanly by. His next target was Dovizioso, a little over two seconds ahead.

That took him another four laps to close down; now there were three to go, with Bautista getting ahead on the penultimate lap, heading for their last-lap showdown, the Spaniard pleading innocence of any wrongdoing.

De Angelis was still just 1.5 seconds down in fourth; four seconds away, Kallio snitched fifth from Barbera under brakes at the end of the back straight, with Simon seventh.

Luthi was alone, 20 seconds down, having been kept busy fending off Shuhei Aoyama in the early laps, until the Honda rider crashed out on the ninth. Brother Hiro had been with them, along with Simoncelli, but the KTM rider dropped back for a lonely ninth after Simoncelli fell just in front of him, with eight laps left.

Lai got tenth, from Espargaro and Wilairot, both still battling to the end; West was 13th, after falling and remounting.

Left: Lorenzo's podium prancing was becoming more practised.

Below: Dovisioso leads class rookie Bautista, but he would be out-fumbled at the finish.

Photographs: Gold & Goose

125cc RACE – 19 laps

Pasini had painted a black cat on his helmet to reverse his bad luck, and at least he finished. Again, he was as fast as anyone, on pole and leading more laps of a torrid race than any other rider. But by the end, he was tenth, losing ground at the back of a gang covered by an astonishing 3.4 seconds.

His season so far had been disastrous: at Qatar, a mechanic's error had led to a blocked fuel breather; at Jerez, the disc valve spindle had failed; at Istanbul, after he'd remounted a slipping chain, his engine had seized. Here, his only complaint was fading power at the finish.

He'd led the first lap by more than a second and stayed there for the next seven, but by then with company, Talmacsi the most obtrusive of a six-strong chase group. When the Hungarian took over for two laps, Corsi, Koyama and de Rosa were on his tail, while less than two seconds behind, Gadea and Rabat were at the head of another group and closing.

Now Faubel led over the line for two laps, then Pasini for two more, but changes of position were constant in a battling gang of ten. Then Pasini slowed again, losing ground to the finish. Young Esteve Rabat was ahead over the line for the next two laps, with team-mate Smith only narrowly adrift in 11th, a broiling mass between them. Next it was Gadea's turn to lead.

Pesek led on to the final lap, and the Prague rider held on manfully for his first win, under constant attack. 'In my country, motorcycle sport is not much esteemed. With this victory, I hope something will change,' he said.

Faubel was second, Rabat an excellent career-best third, holding his own in tough company, from Talmacsi, Corsi, Gadea, Ranseder, Smith, Espargaro and Pasini, all across the line faster than you could name them.

Koyama had been with the front gang too, but his KTM did not make the finish.

Above and left: First Czech GP winner Lukas Pesek, on the Derbi and on the rostrum.

Photographs: Gold & Goose

SINOPEC GREAT WALL LUBRICANTS GP OF CHINA

6 MAY 2007 • FIM WORLD CHAMPIONSHIP ROUND 4

SHANGHAI INTERNATIONAL

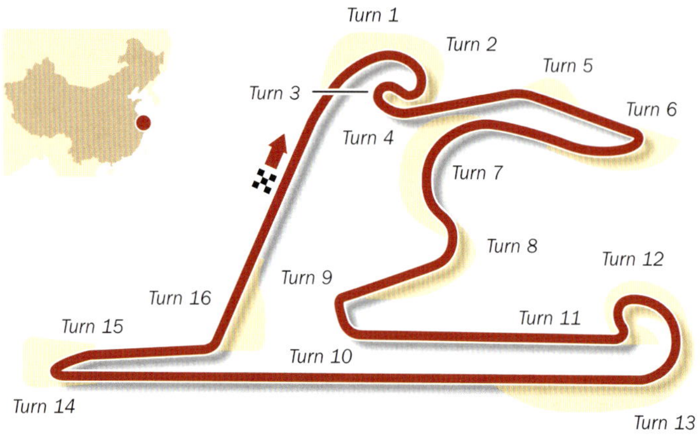

Circuit 5.281km / 3.300 miles

MotoGP

RACE: 22 laps, 72.182 miles/116.182km • Weather: Dry • Air 23°C • Humidity 21% • Track 32°C

Pos.	Rider	Nat.	No.	Entrant	Machine	Tyres	Laps	Time & speed (mph/km/h)
1	Casey Stoner	AUS	27	Ducati Marlboro Team	Ducati	B	22	44m 12.891s 97.965mph/ 157.660km/h
2	Valentino Rossi	ITA	46	Fiat Yamaha Team	Yamaha	M	22	44m 15.927s
3	John Hopkins	USA	21	Rizla Suzuki MotoGP	Suzuki	B	22	44m 19.554s
4	Dani Pedrosa	SPA	26	Repsol Honda Team	Honda	M	22	44m 26.981s
5	Marco Melandri	ITA	33	Honda Gresini	Honda	B	22	44m 30.167s
6	Loris Capirossi	ITA	65	Ducati Marlboro Team	Ducati	B	22	44m 39.147s
7	Chris Vermeulen	AUS	71	Rizla Suzuki MotoGP	Suzuki	B	22	44m 39.482s
8	Randy de Puniet	FRA	14	Kawasaki Racing Team	Kawasaki	B	22	44m 39.916s
9	Alex Hofmann	GER	66	Pramac d'Antin	Ducati	B	22	44m 40.999s
10	Carlos Checa	SPA	7	Honda LCR	Honda	M	22	44m 45.848s
11	Colin Edwards	USA	5	Fiat Yamaha Team	Yamaha	M	22	44m 47.944s
12	Nicky Hayden	USA	1	Repsol Honda Team	Honda	M	22	44m 50.218s
13	Sylvain Guintoli	FRA	50	Dunlop Yamaha Tech 3	Yamaha	D	22	45m 03.596s
14	Alex Barros	BRA	4	Pramac d'Antin	Ducati	B	22	45m 08.155s
15	Kenny Roberts Jnr	USA	10	Team Roberts	KR212V	M	22	45m 10.627s
	Shinya Nakano	JPN	56	Konica Minolta Honda	Honda	M	3	6m 11.246s
	Makoto Tamada	JPN	6	Dunlop Yamaha Tech 3	Yamaha	D	3	6m 11.956s
	Toni Elias	SPA	24	Honda Gresini	Honda	B	0	

Fastest lap: Casey Stoner, on lap 15, 1m 59.857s, 98.561mph/158.61km/h.

Lap record: Dani Pedrosa, SPA (Honda), 1m 59.318s, 99.006mph/159.335km/h (2006).

Event best maximum speed: Casey Stoner, 209.5mph/337.2km/h (warm up).

Grid order	1	2	3	4	5	6	7	8	9	10	11	12	13	14	15	16	17	18	19	20	21	22	•
46 ROSSI	46	27	27	27	27	27	27	27	27	27	27	27	27	27	27	27	27	27	27	27	27	27	1
21 HOPKINS	27	33	33	33	46	46	46	46	46	46	46	46	46	46	46	21	21	46	46	46	46	46	2
5 EDWARDS	21	46	46	46	33	33	21	21	21	21	21	21	21	21	21	46	46	21	21	21	21	21	3
27 STONER	33	21	21	21	21	21	33	33	26	26	26	26	26	26	26	26	26	26	26	26	26	26	4
26 PEDROSA	5	26	26	26	26	26	26	26	33	33	33	33	33	33	33	33	33	33	33	33	33	33	5
33 MELANDRI	26	14	14	14	14	14	14	14	14	14	14	14	14	14	14	14	14	14	14	14	65	65	6
14 de PUNIET	14	5	5	65	65	65	65	65	65	65	65	65	65	65	65	65	65	65	65	65	71	71	7
4 BARROS	65	65	65	5	5	5	5	5	5	5	5	71	71	71	71	71	71	71	71	71	14	14	8
1 HAYDEN	56	56	71	71	71	71	71	71	71	71	71	5	66	66	66	66	66	66	66	66	66	66	9
56 NAKANO	71	71	56	7	66	66	66	66	66	66	66	66	5	5	5	7	7	7	7	7	7	7	10
66 HOFMANN	6	6	6	66	7	7	7	7	7	7	7	7	7	7	7	5	5	5	5	5	5	5	11
24 ELIAS	10	7	7	10	1	1	1	1	1	1	1	1	1	1	1	1	1	1	1	1	1	1	12
7 CHECA	7	66	66	1	50	50	50	50	50	50	50	50	50	50	50	50	50	50	50	50	50	50	13
65 CAPIROSSI	66	10	10	50	10	10	10	10	10	10	10	10	10	10	10	10	10	10	10	10	4	4	14
71 VERMEULEN	50	50	50	4	4	4	4	4	4	4	4	4	4	4	4	4	4	4	4	4	10	10	15
10 ROBERTS Jnr	1	1	1																				
50 GUINTOLI	4	4	4																				
6 TAMADA																							

FASTEST RACE LAPS

	Rider	Lap	Time
1	Stoner	15	1m 59.857s
2	Rossi	15	1m 59.884s
3	Hopkins	8	2m 00.065s
4	Barros	17	2m 00.383s
5	Pedrosa	6	2m 00.523s
6	Melandri	3	2m 00.715s
7	de Puniet	3	2m 00.781s
8	Capirossi	5	2m 00.946s
9	Hofmann	6	2m 01.040s
10	Vermeulen	8	2m 01.177s
11	Checa	9	2m 01.360s
12	Edwards	7	2m 01.405s
13	Hayden	18	2m 01.525s
14	Tamada	3	2m 01.588s
15	Guintoli	7	2m 01.865s
16	Nakano	2	2m 02.032s
17	Roberts Jnr	3	2m 02.452s

QUALIFYING

5 May 2007
Weather: Dry
Air: 24°C Humidity: 43%
Track: 29°C

Pos.	Rider	Time
1	Rossi	1m 58.424s
2	Hopkins	1m 59.315s
3	Edwards	1m 59.406s
4	Stoner	1m 59.516s
5	Pedrosa	1m 59.602s
6	Melandri	1m 59.863s
7	de Puniet	1m 59.985s
8	Barros	2m 00.052s
9	Hayden	2m 00.087s
10	Nakano	2m 00.157s
11	Hofmann	2m 00.175s
12	Elias	2m 00.205s
13	Checa	2m 00.319s
14	Capirossi	2m 00.369s
15	Vermeulen	2m 00.680s
16	Roberts Jnr	2m 00.763s
17	Guintoli	2m 01.157s
18	Tamada	2m 01.178s

statistics

MotoGP | TISSOT SWISS WATCHES SINCE 1853 | OFFICIAL TIMEKEEPER

250cc

21 laps, 68.901 miles/110.901km

Pos.	Rider (Nat.)	No.	Machine	Laps	Time & speed
1	Jorge Lorenzo (SPA)	1	Aprilia	21	44m 17.095s 93.364mph/ 150.255km/h
2	Alvaro Bautista (SPA)	19	Aprilia	21	44m 20.999s
3	Andrea Dovizioso (ITA)	34	Honda	21	44m 22.126s
4	Alex de Angelis (RSM)	3	Aprilia	21	44m 23.655s
5	Mika Kallio (FIN)	36	KTM	21	44m 27.343s
6	Hector Barbera (SPA)	80	Aprilia	21	44m 27.597s
7	Julian Simon (SPA)	60	Honda	21	44m 27.927s
8	Thomas Luthi (SWI)	12	Aprilia	21	44m 47.579s
9	Hiroshi Aoyama (JPN)	4	KTM	21	44m 49.990s
10	Fabrizio Lai (ITA)	32	Aprilia	21	45m 08.072s
11	Aleix Espargaro (SPA)	41	Aprilia	21	45m 08.794s
12	Ratthapark Wilairot (THA)	8	Honda	21	45m 10.131s
13	Anthony West (AUS)	14	Aprilia	21	45m 18.758s
14	Taro Sekiguchi (JPN)	44	Aprilia	21	45m 31.698s
15	Arturo Tizon (SPA)	9	Aprilia	21	45m 31.849s
16	Jules Cluzel (FRA)	16	Aprilia	21	45m 56.985s
17	Eugene Laverty (IRL)	50	Honda	21	46m 04.100s
18	Imre Toth (HUN)	10	Aprilia	21	46m 07.611s
19	Jin Xiao (CHN)	63	Yamaha	20	44m 30.852s
	Marco Simoncelli (ITA)	58	Gilera	13	DNF
	Alex Baldolini (ITA)	25	Aprilia	12	DNF
	Karel Abraham (CZE)	17	Aprilia	10	DNF
	Shuhei Aoyama (JPN)	73	Honda	8	DNF
	Dirk Heidolf (GER)	28	Aprilia	2	DNF
	Yuki Takahashi (JPN)	55	Honda		DNS
	Shi Zhao Huang (CHN)	62	Yamaha		DNS

Fastest lap: Lorenzo, 2m 05.738s, 93.951mph/151.200km/h (record).

Previous lap record: Andrea Dovizioso, ITA (Honda), 2m 06.865s, 93.116mph/149.856km/h (2006).

Event best maximum speed: Bautista, 178.0mph/286.5km/h (race).

Qualifying: 1 Lorenzo, 2m 04.543s; 2 Barbera, 2m 05.285s; 3 Kallio, 2m 05.416s; 4 Simon, 2m 05.587s; 5 Dovizioso, 2m 05.595s; 6 Bautista, 2m 05.650s; 7 Luthi, 2m 05.718s; 8 de Angelis, 2m 05.938s; 9 S. Aoyama, 2m 06.489s; 10 Simoncelli, 2m 06.778s; 11 H. Aoyama, 2m 06.914s; 12 Lai, 2m 07.037s; 13 West, 2m 07.711s; 14 Heidolf, 2m 07.772s; 15 Espargaro, 2m 07.792s; 16 Wilairot, 2m 07.892s; 17 Takahashi, 2m 08.262s; 18 Baldolini, 2m 08.527s; 19 Toth, 2m 08.575s; 20 Cluzel, 2m 08.589s; 21 Abraham, 2m 08.637s; 22 Laverty, 2m 08.713s; 23 Sekiguchi, 2m 09.106s; 24 Tizon, 2m 09.274s; 25 Huang, 2m 11.571s; 26 Xiao, 2m 12.202s.

Fastest race laps: 1 Lorenzo, 2m 05.738s; 2 Bautista, 2m 05.875s; 3 de Angelis, 2m 06.042s; 4 Luthi, 2m 06.051s; 5 Barbera, 2m 06.117s; 6 S. Aoyama, 2m 06.196s; 7 Dovizioso, 2m 06.204s; 8 Simon, 2m 06.361s; 9 Kallio, 2m 06.432s; 10 H. Aoyama, 2m 07.268s; 11 Simoncelli, 2m 07.483s; 12 Wilairot, 2m 07.916s; 13 Lai, 2m 08.077s; 14 West, 2m 08.095s; 15 Espargaro, 2m 08.200s; 16 Abraham, 2m 08.882s; 17 Sekiguchi, 2m 08.984s; 18 Cluzel, 2m 09.051s; 19 Tizon, 2m 09.349s; 20 Baldolini, 2m 09.380s; 21 Laverty, 2m 10.581s; 22 Toth, 2m 10.647s; 23 Xiao, 2m 11.871s; 24 Heidolf, 2m 16.231s.

World Championship: 1 Lorenzo, 95; 2 Dovizioso, 68; 3 de Angelis, 59; 4 Bautista, 56; 5 Barbera, 34; 6 Luthi, 32; 7 Simon, 26; 8 Kallio, 21; 9 Lai, 21; 10 H. Aoyama, 17; 11 Takahashi, 17; 12 S. Aoyama, 15; 13 Espargaro, 15; 14 Simoncelli, 14; 15 West, 13; 16 Debon, 11; 17 Wilairot, 11; 18 Locatelli, 10; 19 Heidolf, 10; 20 Abraham, 5; 21 Baldolini, 5; 22 Laverty and Sekiguchi, 2; 24 Tizon, 1.

125cc

19 laps, 62.339 miles/100.339km

Pos.	Rider (Nat.)	No.	Machine	Laps	Time & speed
1	Lukas Pesek (CZE)	52	Derbi	19	42m 25.923s 88.161mph/ 141.881km/h
2	Hector Faubel (SPA)	55	Aprilia	19	42m 26.110s
3	Esteve Rabat (SPA)	12	Honda	19	42m 26.404s
4	Gabor Talmacsi (HUN)	14	Aprilia	19	42m 26.705s
5	Simone Corsi (ITA)	24	Aprilia	19	42m 27.063s
6	Sergio Gadea (SPA)	33	Aprilia	19	42m 27.114s
7	Michael Ranseder (AUT)	60	Derbi	19	42m 28.298s
8	Bradley Smith (GBR)	38	Honda	19	42m 28.323s
9	Pol Espargaro (SPA)	44	Aprilia	19	42m 28.640s
10	Mattia Pasini (ITA)	75	Aprilia	19	42m 29.346s
11	Andrea Iannone (ITA)	29	Aprilia	19	42m 34.283s
12	Raffaele de Rosa (ITA)	35	Aprilia	19	42m 34.563s
13	Alexis Masbou (FRA)	7	Honda	19	42m 38.603s
14	Mike di Meglio (FRA)	63	Honda	19	42m 42.594s
15	Lorenzo Zanetti (ITA)	8	Aprilia	19	42m 42.700s
16	Pablo Nieto (SPA)	22	Aprilia	19	42m 50.367s
17	Simone Grotzkyj (ITA)	53	Aprilia	19	42m 53.260s
18	Sandro Cortese (GER)	11	Aprilia	19	42m 58.847s
19	Joan Olive (SPA)	6	Aprilia	19	43m 00.952s
20	Roberto Tamburini (ITA)	20	Aprilia	19	43m 02.806s
21	Dominique Aegerter (SWI)	77	Aprilia	19	43m 12.007s
22	Joey Litjens (NED)	37	Honda	19	43m 12.379s
23	Daniel Webb (GBR)	99	Honda	19	43m 14.054s
24	Dino Lombardi (ITA)	13	Honda	19	43m 34.906s
25	Hugo van den Berg (NED)	56	Aprilia	19	43m 35.637s
26	Robert Muresan (ROU)	95	Derbi	19	44m 16.340s
27	Randy Krummenacher (SWI)	34	KTM	18	42m 46.905s
	Tomoyoshi Koyama (JPN)	71	KTM	18	DNF
	Federico Sandi (ITA)	15	Aprilia	9	DNF
	Stefano Bianco (ITA)	27	Aprilia	8	DNF
	Nicolas Terol (SPA)	18	Derbi	1	DNF
	Steve Bonsey (USA)	51	KTM	1	DNF

Fastest lap: Pesek, 2m 12.420s, 89.210mph/143.570km/h.

Lap record: Alvaro Bautista, SPA (Aprilia), 2m 12.131s, 89.405mph/143.884km/h (2006).

Event best maximum speed: Faubel, 151.6mph/243.9km/h (race).

Qualifying: 1 Pasini, 2m 11.946s; 2 Faubel, 2m 12.284s; 3 Pesek, 2m 12.384s; 4 Talmacsi, 2m 12.433s; 5 Smith, 2m 12.547s; 6 Gadea, 2m 12.774s; 7 Corsi, 2m 12.841s; 8 Koyama, 2m 12.987s; 9 Ranseder, 2m 13.093s; 10 Cortese, 2m 13.526s; 11 de Rosa, 2m 13.581s; 12 Rabat, 2m 13.599s; 13 Nieto, 2m 13.686s; 14 Olive, 2m 13.817s; 15 Iannone, 2m 13.866s; 16 Terol, 2m 13.868s; 17 Tamburini, 2m 13.872s; 18 Espargaro, 2m 13.880s; 19 Sandi, 2m 13.923s; 20 Bianco, 2m 13.977s; 21 Zanetti, 2m 14.006s; 22 Masbou, 2m 14.130s; 23 di Meglio, 2m 14.226s; 24 Krummenacher, 2m 14.498s; 25 Grotzkyj, 2m 14.522s; 26 Muresan, 2m 15.008s; 27 Bonsey, 2m 15.060s; 28 Aegerter, 2m 15.512s; 29 Litjens, 2m 15.685s; 30 Webb, 2m 15.908s; 31 Lombardi, 2m 15.974s; 32 van den Berg, 2m 17.111s.

Fastest race laps: 1 Pesek, 2m 12.420s; 2 Ranseder, 2m 12.509s; 3 Gadea, 2m 12.594s; 4 Talmacsi, 2m 12.699s; 5 Masbou, 2m 12.749s; 6 Faubel, 2m 12.826s; 7 Rabat, 2m 12.878s; 8 de Rosa, 2m 12.928s; 9 Corsi, 2m 13.196s; 10 Espargaro, 2m 13.282s; 11 Bianco, 2m 13.336s; 12 Pasini, 2m 13.351s; 13 Smith, 2m 13.366s; 14 Iannone, 2m 13.399s; 15 Koyama, 2m 13.464s; 16 Zanetti, 2m 13.833s; 17 di Meglio, 2m 13.968s; 18 Cortese, 2m 14.143s; 19 Grotzkyj, 2m 14.199s; 20 Nieto, 2m 14.367s; 21 Krummenacher, 2m 14.628s; 22 Olive, 2m 14.748s; 23 Tamburini, 2m 15.015s; 24 Aegerter, 2m 15.065s; 25 Webb, 2m 15.201s; 26 Litjens, 2m 15.255s; 27 Sandi, 2m 15.610s; 28 Muresan, 2m 15.689s; 29 van den Berg, 2m 15.988s; 30 Lombardi, 2m 16.272s; 31 Terol, 2m 23.279s; 32 Bonsey, 2m 23.313s.

World Championship: 1 Pesek, 71; 2 Talmacsi, 69; 3 Faubel, 67; 4 Corsi, 47; 5 Espargaro, 34; 6 Olive, 33; 7 de Rosa, 30; 8 Koyama, 26; 9 Rabat, 26; 10 Ranseder, 23; 11 Gadea, 21; 12 Nieto, 20; 13 Smith, 20; 14 Iannone, 17; 15 Zanetti, 16; 16 Cortese, 9; 17 Masbou, 9; 18 Pasini, 6; 19 Bianco, 5; 20 di Meglio, 4; 21 Bonsey, 3; 22 Terol, 2; 23 Grotzkyj and Krummenacher, 1.

RIDER STANDINGS

After 4 Rounds

1	Casey Stoner	86
2	Valentino Rossi	71
3	Dani Pedrosa	49
4	Marco Melandri	41
5	John Hopkins	39
6	Toni Elias	35
7	Colin Edwards	31
8	Loris Capirossi	30
9	Nicky Hayden	30
10	Chris Vermeulen	30
11	Alex Barros	27
12	Carlos Checa	20
13	Randy de Puniet	19
14	Alex Hofmann	19
15	Shinya Nakano	15
16	Sylvain Guintoli	6
17	Olivier Jacque	4
18	Kenny Roberts Jnr	4
19	Makoto Tamada	4

TEAM STANDINGS

After 4 Rounds

1	Ducati Marlboro Team	116
2	Fiat Yamaha Team	102
3	Repsol Honda Team	79
4	Honda Gresini	76
5	Rizla Suzuki MotoGP	69
6	Pramac d'Antin	46
7	Kawasaki Racing Team	23
8	Honda LCR	20
9	Konica Minolta Honda	15
10	Dunlop Yamaha Tech 3	10
11	Team Roberts	4

CONSTRUCTOR STANDINGS

After 4 Rounds

1	Ducati	86
2	Yamaha	71
3	Honda	69
4	Suzuki	46
5	Kawasaki	23
6	KR212V	4

FIM WORLD CHAMPIONSHIP • ROUND 5

FRENCHGP
LE MANS

Main photograph: Master of treacherous weather conditions, Vermeulen pulls away from Melandri.

Left: The Australian celebrated Suzuki's first-ever four-stroke GP win.

Photographs: Gold & Goose

Above: **Heroic at home, Guintoli leads a cautious Stoner. Caution would pay dividends.**

Centre right: **Locatelli consults Dr Costa, before withdrawing from the race.**

Centre, below right: **Nakano's lacklustre year continued with the Japanese rider crashing out.**

Opposite, top: **Tamada watches as Elias demonstrates the tricky surface.**

Opposite, below left: **Rossi and Michelin – if only he hadn't listened.**

Opposite, below right: **Kenny Roberts Jr. and IRTA's Mike Trimby in discussion on the grid.**

Photographs: Gold & Goose

LE MANS gave its usual dour welcome to the start of the first intense phase of the European season – seven races over ten weekends, culminating in the USA before the summer break. But it's impossible to escape history at this venue, with its unique place in motor sport. It came with the rain on race-day morning – the news that Jack Findlay, aged 71, had lost a long battle with illness during the previous night.

Findlay was unique, an Australian who, after a long career, had settled in France with his French wife, Dominique, taking for a while the role of MotoGP technical director. Always fiercely independent, Jack was the Prince of Privateers, the most successful of that breed who made the backbone of the Continental Circus – running often on a shoe-string and a whiff of racing fuel from one event to the next.

History didn't fail him, although there was a bit of a twist.

Among many accomplishments, Findlay had ridden the first two-stroke to win a premier-class GP – the 500cc Ulster GP at Dundrod in 1971, on an air-cooled, twin-cylinder racer based on the Suzuki T500 Titan road bike. Although Jack had factory help, it was (he would later recall) of the most grudging kind; they demanded the special pistons back directly after the race. Now at Le Mans, a most accomplished piece of determined and carefully measured riding by a new Australian, Chris Vermeulen, brought not only his first win, but also Suzuki's first four-stroke grand prix win. Sadly, nobody in the modern Suzuki GP team seemed to notice.

The return to a track where top speeds are low and straights short was always going to be interesting. Compared with the interminable run down the Shanghai kilometre, where Stoner's Ducati had reached 337.2 km/h, the fastest speed of the weekend was the same rider's 288.5 km/h, with Rossi (ninth fastest) less than 8 km/h down. Stoner remained the man to beat, adding weight to his repeated insistence that the Ducati also turned and put the power down well; in the final gallops, it was Edwards who did beat him, claiming (rather surprisingly) his first pole.

Rossi was ahead in the race, but then it rained, and everything was different, for the second-ever bike-change race – the first had been in Australia in 2006. The result was decided not on dry practice times, but on bravery, skill and composure. And by tyres. Also, to cut a long story short, guesswork on tyres. The home player, Michelin, got it about as wrong as it could, while Bridgestone's broader-spectrum wet tyres claimed not only a first wet-weather win, but another clean sweep of the rostrum.

Vermeulen was the principal beneficiary, but not before two other riders had rewarded their 74,200 compatriots who were suffering the weather trackside. De Puniet and Guintoli each demonstrated an excess of bravery and skill, but an insufficiency of composure. The former (on Bridgestones) lost a most impressive lead with a certain sense of inevitability when he slid off on the increasingly treacherous surface. The latter, a class rookie on Dunlops, had also led and was second to de Puniet when, with the same inevitability, he also fell. Stoner, for his part, rode with consistency and (that word again) maturity to a handy 16 points.

If Michelin believed it had an inside track on the weather, it was mistaken. It thought the rain, which was obviously coming as the start drew closer, would ease off, and recommended a harder-compound tyre for better endurance on a drying track. Some riders were in trouble from the start: Edwards in reverse gear from pole position with a bike he found almost unridable; Hayden falling off after a spirited attempt to reverse his ill for-

tune so far; Rossi a dispirited sixth, after the last five laps had been 'the most difficult of my career'.

Tyres were at the forefront no matter what the conditions, with Rossi heading a demand presented to the Safety Commission to revise the new tyre rules. This was refused. Asked why his mind had changed so completely, he explained that at tracks where there had been no testing, it was all too much of a lottery. This made it unfair, he believed. Stoner felt the opposite, his point of view inflamed when Edwards spoke about the Michelin 'magic tyre' that it used to be able to ship in on Saturday night, tailor-made for the race. It was much fairer now that Michelin couldn't do that any more, asserted the championship leader, rather more reasonably than his doubly thwarted rival.

It was a landmark race for Dani Pedrosa, who became the youngest rider to notch up 100 starts. He had already deposed Hailwood as the youngest to win in 125, 250 and MotoGP; Marco Melandri as the youngest 250 champion; and Rossi as the youngest rider to win three titles.

There was a significant change in the paddock, with the introduction of pass swiping, F1-style. The scrappy, two-piece paddock at Le Mans was not the most convenient place to try out this step towards greater 'professionalism'. It would get worse at Catalunya, where timing and race officials, press and so on were swiped and unswiped even to go to the lavatory – a rather too assiduous record of their movements, thought some.

Jacque was a regretful non-starter at his home GP, still recuperating from the horrible gash to his arm. His place was taken by Fonsi Nieto, who embarked on his MotoGP career almost immediately with a wild ride across the gravel trap after missing his braking for Turn One. He redeemed himself, however, by finishing with good points on a day when many regulars didn't see the finish line.

Among them was Kenny Roberts, but not because his gamble (starting on wet tyres, although the track was still dry) did not pay off. Instead, his V4 Honda engine let go in a big way on the final lap, leaving a bag full of bits and pieces for the team to return to HRC. It was not the first or the last Honda to blow up during a year that already had become the manufacturer's worst since 1982.

Locatelli made a heroic return to the 250 class, a mere eight weeks after his horrendous and life-threatening smash at Jerez, and two weeks before his already implausible predicted return for Mugello. He qualified in last position. Although he ran in morning warm-up, he elected to withdraw from the race.

MOTOGP RACE – 28 laps

Edwards crashed heavily on Saturday morning, and bounced: 'Usually I don't.' Emboldened, he took a career-first pole, depriving Stoner, and was three-tenths faster than 2006's 990 time. Checa was third, while Rossi pushed to fourth, still hunting for set-up. Hopkins, alongside, had been fastest (from Elias) on race tyres.

The sky was lowering, and although it was still dry on the grid as Stoner led away up the hill from Hopkins and Rossi, rain was already spotting out on the back straight. It would become steadily heavier.

Rossi charged to the front and by lap three had almost two seconds on Barros, now ahead of Stoner, with plenty of shuffling. The track was extremely slippery in places and getting worse, and the best riders in the world were hard pressed to find the right balance between bravery and discretion.

Above: Fonsi Nieto made a one-race GP return, taking the place of Jacque, and scored points.

Top: Vive la France! De Puniet takes an early lead from Guintoli on a half-dry track. Rossi and Barros follow.

Photographs: Gold & Goose

The French pair chose the former. Guintoli had been 11th on the grid and seventh on lap one, leading de Puniet rapidly forwards. On lap seven, both went steaming past Rossi on the fast esses at the end of the back straight – an extraordinary sight – and now the rookie was leading his home grand prix.

The pair had swapped next time around, with Pedrosa and Hopkins also ahead of Rossi, who was pursued by a close pack led by Melandri from Stoner, Barros, Capirossi, Tamada and Hayden. Checa had fallen after being jostled off line in the middle of this gang; Elias, far behind, fell alone soon after.

Now Guintoli proved how tricky the surface had become with a graceful high-side, running straight back to rejoin. De Puniet had pulled almost two seconds on Hopkins as he led for two laps, but next time around, the ninth, he too was down. He was 'just about to pit to change tyres.'

Hofmann and Nieto had already done so; on lap nine, Capirossi, Tamada, Hayden, Barros, Nakano and Vermeulen called in, and at the end of lap ten, the rest of them followed suit. The spacing and the much wider pit lane prevented any of the near misses of Phillip Island in 2006, the only other bike-change race so far.

The value of flag-to-flag was clear at the end of lap 11, with everyone back on track on wet tyres and racing hard, and no doubt as to who was in front of whom. Suzukis were first and second, Vermeulen setting the pace as the track became increasingly treacherous.

Hopkins was less than comfortable, and Melandri took over the position almost at once as the second Suzuki started to drop back. The latter steadily cut back a two-second gap to Vermeulen and was challenging by lap 17. Vermeulen was steadfast, but Melandri was struggling, because 'my legs are too short'. Without the usual wet-weather double layer of knee sliders, he was having trouble getting his knee down as it got wetter, and he settled for second.

Stoner had chased Rossi from the 14th lap and was ahead three laps later, after the Italian ran wide at the end of the back straight – a clear sign of growing trouble; he soon lost touch.

By two-thirds distance, Hayden was closing, and he also passed easily on lap 23. Over the next two, he tried hard to escape – until destiny took over at top speed at the end of the back straight: 'I was in for a long ride. As soon as I hit the brakes, the front just folded.'

Pedrosa, on softer tyres, might have caught him. He'd passed Hofmann and then led the German past the slowing Rossi, all on the same lap. He finished a lone fourth, Hofmann a safe, best-ever fifth.

Rossi saved sixth, comfortably clear of Hopkins, who was well ahead of Capirossi, the last rider on the same lap. The Italian's 'wet' bike turned out to have a programming fault, and he'd dropped back rapidly after the change.

Tamada, Guintoli and Nieto were one lap down, but scored good points in a depleted field; Edwards was the only other finisher, three laps away. His rear tyre problems had started in the dry, with the wheel locking up so much off-throttle that he went from pole at the start to second-last by the end of the lap. He pitted after three laps, thinking to gamble early on a wet tyre – but it was too soon. He pitted again by the end for a cut slick.

Kenny Roberts had been ahead; he'd gambled by starting on wet tyres. But the rain came too late. Then on the final lap, his Honda motor blew up in a big way, robbing him of any chance of points.

Nakano crashed out after the change of tyres, while a fading Barros did the same right at the end.

250cc RACE – 26 laps

Lorenzo broke new ground with his post-race celebration – a doppelganger in helmet and leathers ran from the trackside to join in planting his 'Lorenzo's Land' flag. He'd earned it. He had broken bones in his foot with a huge high-side in practice, but had come back for his fourth pole in five races, followed by a fraught and close win.

The rain still held off as Lorenzo got the jump into the first chicane, heading Bautista, Luthi and Barbera. Luthi was fifth one lap later, but retired with his motor tightening after a trip across the gravel. Then Bautista, lying second, had a big front-wheel slide, running into the gravel and rejoining 19th.

After seven laps, Dovizioso and de Angelis were challenging Lorenzo, while Barbera and Simon were dropping away. Then Dovizioso took the lead for the first time, on lap eight, with de Angelis also passing Lorenzo two laps later. They were all over one another, and on lap 15, Dovizioso and Lorenzo collided on the straight, gifting a lead of more than a second to de Angelis.

It didn't last, Lorenzo dealing with Dovizioso two laps later,

Left: Privateer Anthony West (14) disputes sixth with Kallio (36) and Simoncelli.

Below left: Two Lorenzos for the price of one: the 250 winner's celebrations were becoming more elaborate – to upstage Rossi perhaps?

Below: Gadea heads Pasini, while Pesek and Smith (hidden) close up.

Photographs: Gold & Goose

then gaining strength and drawing steadily up on de Angelis to surge into the lead into Museum. Dovizioso took two more laps to get past the Aprilia, and was almost a second behind with four laps to go. It took until the very last corners for him to catch up for a last-ditch attack. Lorenzo staved him off by less than two-tenths; de Angelis settled for a safe third.

Barbera and Simon were together almost the whole race, the younger rider ahead across the line just once. They finished some three seconds down.

Kallio and Simoncelli had been disputing sixth, until West arrived, after finishing lap one in 12th. Soon he was past both of them, but Kallio dropped back after colliding with the Australian and taking a lump out of his rear tyre.

Over and over for the next eight laps, Simoncelli would power ahead, and West would outbrake him. But when Kallio caught up again, with Shuhei Aoyama in tow, the privateer was overwhelmed and, with shot tyres, he dropped from sixth to ninth on lap 14, then lost another place to Bautista, through from the back, with four laps left. Fresh from a first-attempt rostrum in World Supersports the weekend before, West stormed out of the pits after telling a TV cameraman, 'I want a factory bike and better mechanics, or I'm leaving.' Prophetic words.

Simoncelli held on from Kallio; Bautista had also passed Aoyama by the end. West retained tenth, while this time Wilairot narrowly beat Lai, leaving Baldolini, Sekiguchi and Laverty to scrap over the final points.

Hiro Aoyama retired; Abraham and Cluzel had a coming-together; while Espargaro took a tumble, but remounted. Locatelli did not start.

125cc RACE – 24 laps

Pasini was on pole for a fourth race in succession, with Bradley Smith a career-best second. Pasini charged away yet again, the sun shining brightly for the first race, his lead almost two seconds after two laps.

Koyama had held up the pursuit. On lap three, Gadea got by and gradually closed the gap. Then Smith and Pesek also got past, over a second adrift.

At half-distance, they were closing up. Gadea pushed past Pasini and waved him in behind so the pair could escape. Pasini wouldn't play ball, however, and moved ahead again; soon all four were together.

Gadea led for the first time on lap 17, but they stayed locked together until, with four laps to go, Pasini's jinx struck again. As at Jerez, it was the rotary valve spindle, and he slowed suddenly mid-corner to park the bike forlornly against the pit wall. Gadea went on.

Immediately, Pesek managed to get ahead of Smith, after the Briton found a false neutral as he was avoiding the slowing Pasini. He tried to get back on the Derbi, but eventually settled for his own first rostrum, the first by a British rider since Robin Milton in 1989. Pesek harried Gadea to the end.

Talmacsi finally led Olive over the line by three-tenths for fourth, the latter through from the back of a gang of six. Faubel, Cortese, Corsi and di Meglio made up the rest of it. Koyama had fallen back to a lone tenth.

Bonsey was one of four to crash, the others being Iannone, Zanetti and de Rosa; the last two remounted.

Above: Bradley Smith beams after gaining his first rostrum.

Photograph: Gold & Goose

ALICE GRAND PRIX DE FRANCE

20 MAY 2007 • FIM WORLD CHAMPIONSHIP ROUND 5

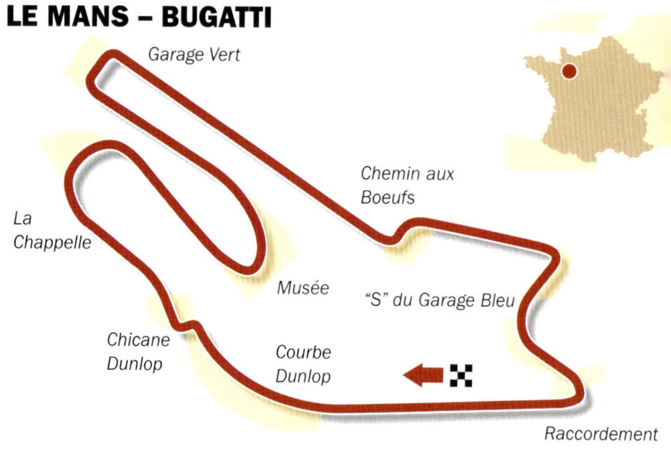

Circuit 4.272km /2.655 miles

MotoGP

RACE: 28 laps, 72.716 miles/117.040km • Weather: Dry • Air 13°C • Humidity 73% • Track 16°C

Pos.	Rider	Nat.	No.	Entrant	Machine	Tyres	Laps	Time & speed (mph/km/h)
1	Chris Vermeulen	AUS	71	Rizla Suzuki MotoGP	Suzuki	B	28	50m 58.713s 85.595mph/ 137.752km/h
2	Marco Melandri	ITA	33	Honda Gresini	Honda	B	28	51m 11.312s
3	Casey Stoner	AUS	27	Ducati Marlboro Team	Ducati	B	28	51m 26.060s
4	Dani Pedrosa	SPA	26	Repsol Honda Team	Honda	M	28	51m 36.041s
5	Alex Hofmann	GER	66	Pramac d'Antin	Ducati	B	28	51m 47.879s
6	Valentino Rossi	ITA	46	Fiat Yamaha Team	Yamaha	M	28	51m 52.276s
7	John Hopkins	USA	21	Rizla Suzuki MotoGP	Suzuki	B	28	51m 59.786s
8	Loris Capirossi	ITA	65	Ducati Marlboro Team	Ducati	B	28	52m 19.954s
9	Makoto Tamada	JPN	6	Dunlop Yamaha Tech 3	Yamaha	D	27	51m 34.842s
10	Sylvain Guintoli	FRA	50	Dunlop Yamaha Tech 3	Yamaha	D	27	51m 40.165s
11	Fonsi Nieto	SPA	11	Kawasaki Racing Team	Kawasaki	B	27	51m 50.572s
12	Colin Edwards	USA	5	Fiat Yamaha Team	Yamaha	M	25	51m 06.769s
	Alex Barros	BRA	4	Pramac d'Antin	Ducati	B	27	50m 05.770s
	Kenny Roberts Jnr	USA	10	Team Roberts	KR212V	M	26	50m 16.009s
	Nicky Hayden	USA	1	Repsol Honda Team	Honda	M	25	45m 50.382s
	Shinya Nakano	JPN	56	Konica Minolta Honda	Honda	M	20	36m 48.570s
	Randy de Puniet	FRA	14	Kawasaki Racing Team	Kawasaki	B	8	13m 35.554s
	Toni Elias	SPA	24	Honda Gresini	Honda	B	7	12m 00.579s
	Carlos Checa	SPA	7	Honda LCR	Honda	M	6	10m 15.683s

Fastest lap: John Hopkins, on lap 5, 1m 38.678s, 94.756mph/152.495km/h.

Lap record: Valentino Rossi, ITA (Yamaha), 1m 35.087s, 98.335mph/158.255km/h (2006).

Event best maximum speed: Casey Stoner, 179.3mph/288.5km/h (qualifying practice).

FASTEST RACE LAPS

	Rider	Lap	Time
1	Hopkins	5	1m 38.678s
2	Capirossi	5	1m 38.678s
3	Pedrosa	5	1m 38.744s
4	Guintoli	6	1m 38.825s
5	Tamada	5	1m 38.915s
6	Elias	7	1m 39.288s
7	Vermeulen	6	1m 39.477s
8	Hayden	5	1m 39.485s
9	de Puniet	5	1m 39.522s
10	Stoner	5	1m 39.537s
11	Checa	5	1m 39.866s
12	Barros	5	1m 39.970s
13	Nakano	6	1m 40.004s
14	Melandri	4	1m 40.050s
15	Hofmann	6	1m 40.161s
16	Rossi	5	1m 40.273s
17	Nieto	4	1m 43.681s
18	Edwards	2	1m 48.875s
19	Roberts Jnr	4	1m 51.967s

QUALIFYING

19 May 2007
Weather: Dry
Air: 22°C Humidity: 16%
Track: 32°C

Pos.	Rider	Time
1	Edwards	1m 33.616s
2	Stoner	1m 33.710s
3	Checa	1m 33.859s
4	Rossi	1m 33.875s
5	Hopkins	1m 34.102s
6	Elias	1m 34.125s
7	Hayden	1m 34.247s
8	de Puniet	1m 34.318s
9	Melandri	1m 34.360s
10	Pedrosa	1m 34.412s
11	Guintoli	1m 34.507s
12	Vermeulen	1m 34.574s
13	Barros	1m 34.817s
14	Nakano	1m 34.834s
15	Capirossi	1m 34.903s
16	Tamada	1m 35.346s
17	Hofmann	1m 35.578s
18	Roberts Jnr	1m 35.681s
19	Nieto	1m 36.312s

Grid order	1	2	3	4	5	6	7	8	9	10	11	12	13	14	15	16	17	18	19	20	21	22	23	24	25	26	27	28	•
5 EDWARDS	46	46	46	46	46	50	14	14	21	33	71	71	71	71	71	71	71	71	71	71	71	71	71	71	71	71	71	71	1
27 STONER	27	27	4	14	14	14	50	21	26	21	21	33	33	33	33	33	33	33	33	33	33	33	33	33	33	33	33	33	2
7 CHECA	7	4	27	4	50	46	26	26	33	26	33	21	46	46	46	46	27	27	27	27	27	27	27	27	27	27	27	27	3
46 ROSSI	4	50	14	50	4	4	21	33	46	27	26	46	21	27	27	27	46	46	46	46	46	46	1	1	1	26	26	26	4
21 HOPKINS	24	7	50	33	27	26	46	46	65	46	46	26	27	1	1	1	1	1	1	1	1	1	46	46	26	66	66	66	5
24 ELIAS	33	33	33	27	26	27	33	4	27	71	1	1	26	66	66	66	66	66	66	66	66	66	66	66	66	46	46	46	6
1 HAYDEN	50	14	7	7	33	7	27	65	1	1	27	27	1	26	26	26	26	26	26	26	26	26	26	26	46	21	21	21	7
14 de PUNIET	21	24	1	26	7	33	4	27	71	65	65	66	66	21	21	21	21	21	21	21	21	21	21	21	21	4	4	65	8
33 MELANDRI	1	1	65	65	65	21	65	1	4	66	66	4	4	4	4	4	4	4	4	4	4	4	4	4	4	65	65		9
26 PEDROSA	14	65	26	21	21	65	6	6	6	4	4	65	65	65	65	65	65	65	65	65	65	65	65	65	65	6	6		10
50 GUINTOLI	65	21	21	1	1	6	1	71	56	6	56	56	56	56	56	56	56	56	56	56	6	6	6	6	6	50	50		11
71 VERMEULEN	66	66	24	6	6	1	71	66	66	56	6	6	6	6	6	6	6	6	6	6	11	11	11	11	11	11	11		12
4 BARROS	71	6	6	24	71	71	24	56	50	50	50	11	11	11	11	11	11	11	11	11	50	50	50	50	50	10			13
56 NAKANO	6	71	66	71	24	24	66	50	11	11	11	50	50	50	50	50	50	50	50	50	10	10	10	10	10				14
65 CAPIROSSI	26	26	71	66	56	56	56	11	10	10	10	10	10	10	10	10	10	10	10	10	5	5	5	5	5				15
6 TAMADA	56	56	56	56	66	66	11	10	5	5	5	5	5	5	5	5	5	5	5	5									
66 HOFMANN	11	11	11	11	11	11	10	5																					
10 ROBERTS Jnr	5	5	5	10	10	10	5																						
11 NIETO	10	10	10	5	5	5																							

statistics

250cc

26 laps, 67.522 miles/108.680km

Pos.	Rider (Nat.)	No.	Machine	Laps	Time & speed
1	Jorge Lorenzo (SPA)	1	Aprilia	26	43m 12.237s 93.784mph/ 150.930km/h
2	Andrea Dovizioso (ITA)	34	Honda	26	43m 12.393s
3	Alex de Angelis (RSM)	3	Aprilia	26	43m 14.970s
4	Hector Barbera (SPA)	80	Aprilia	26	43m 18.208s
5	Julian Simon (SPA)	60	Honda	26	43m 18.348s
6	Marco Simoncelli (ITA)	58	Gilera	26	43m 34.990s
7	Mika Kallio (FIN)	36	KTM	26	43m 35.376s
8	Alvaro Bautista (SPA)	19	Aprilia	26	43m 39.653s
9	Shuhei Aoyama (JPN)	73	Honda	26	43m 41.152s
10	Anthony West (AUS)	14	Aprilia	26	43m 46.187s
11	Ratthapark Wilairot (THA)	8	Honda	26	44m 10.137s
12	Fabrizio Lai (ITA)	32	Aprilia	26	44m 10.248s
13	Alex Baldolini (ITA)	25	Aprilia	26	44m 18.488s
14	Taro Sekiguchi (JPN)	44	Aprilia	26	44m 18.957s
15	Eugene Laverty (IRL)	50	Honda	26	44m 19.886s
16	Dirk Heidolf (GER)	28	Aprilia	26	44m 27.074s
17	Arturo Tizon (SPA)	9	Aprilia	26	44m 43.692s
18	Aleix Espargaro (SPA)	41	Aprilia	26	44m 51.938s
	Imre Toth (HUN)	10	Aprilia	15	DNF
	Hiroshi Aoyama (JPN)	4	KTM	12	DNF
	Jules Cluzel (FRA)	16	Aprilia	5	DNF
	Karel Abraham (CZE)	17	Aprilia	5	DNF
	Thomas Luthi (SWI)	12	Aprilia	2	DNF
	Roberto Locatelli (ITA)	15	Gilera		DNS

Fastest lap: Dovizioso, 1m 38.566s, 94.864mph/152.669km/h (record).

Previous lap record: Hiroshi Aoyama, JPN (KTM), 1m 39.964s, 93.537mph/150.534km/h (2006).

Event best maximum speed: Barbera, 159.1mph/256.0km/h (free practice no. 2).

Qualifying: 1 Lorenzo, 1m 37.934s; 2 Simon, 1m 38.463s; 3 Barbera, 1m 38.610s; 4 Luthi, 1m 38.772s; 5 Bautista, 1m 38.820s; 6 de Angelis, 1m 38.826s; 7 Simoncelli, 1m 38.888s; 8 Dovizioso, 1m 38.890s; 9 Kallio, 1m 38.982s; 10 H. Aoyama, 1m 39.200s; 11 West, 1m 39.217s; 12 S. Aoyama, 1m 39.256s; 13 Lai, 1m 39.741s; 14 Espargaro, 1m 39.884s; 15 Cluzel, 1m 40.359s; 16 Heidolf, 1m 40.488s; 17 Abraham, 1m 40.515s; 18 Sekiguchi, 1m 40.591s; 19 Laverty, 1m 40.630s; 20 Wilairot, 1m 40.716s; 21 Toth, 1m 41.338s; 22 Baldolini, 1m 41.422s; 23 Tizon, 1m 41.432s; 24 Locatelli, 1m 41.719s.

Fastest race laps: 1 Dovizioso, 1m 38.566s; 2 Lorenzo, 1m 38.801s; 3 de Angelis, 1m 38.913s; 4 Barbera, 1m 39.382s; 5 Simon, 1m 39.310s; 6 Bautista, 1m 39.383s; 7 Kallio, 1m 39.583s; 8 Simoncelli, 1m 39.596s; 9 West, 1m 39.784s; 10 S. Aoyama, 1m 39.881s; 11 H. Aoyama, 1m 40.001s; 12 Luthi, 1m 40.747s; 13 Wilairot, 1m 40.885s; 14 Lai, 1m 40.938s; 15 Heidolf, 1m 41.045s; 16 Espargaro, 1m 41.088s; 17 Sekiguchi, 1m 41.531s; 18 Baldolini, 1m 41.538s; 19 Cluzel, 1m 41.609s; 20 Laverty, 1m 41.612s; 21 Abraham, 1m 41.952s; 22 Tizon, 1m 42.092s; 23 Toth, 1m 42.112s.

World Championship: 1 Lorenzo, 120; 2 Dovizioso, 88; 3 de Angelis, 75; 4 Bautista, 64; 5 Barbera, 47; 6 Simon, 37; 7 Luthi, 32; 8 Kallio, 30; 9 Lai, 25; 10 Simoncelli, 24; 11 S. Aoyama, 22; 12 West, 19; 13 H. Aoyama, 17; 14 Takahashi, 17; 15 Wilairot, 16; 16 Espargaro, 15; 17 Debon, 11; 18 Locatelli, 10; 19 Heidolf, 10; 20 Baldolini, 8; 21 Abraham, 5; 22 Sekiguchi, 4; 23 Laverty, 3; 24 Tizon, 1.

125cc

24 laps, 62.328 miles/100.320km

Pos.	Rider (Nat.)	No.	Machine	Laps	Time & speed
1	Sergio Gadea (SPA)	33	Aprilia	24	41m 50.112s 89.402mph/ 143.878km/h
2	Lukas Pesek (CZE)	52	Derbi	24	41m 50.590s
3	Bradley Smith (GBR)	38	Honda	24	41m 53.075s
4	Gabor Talmacsi (HUN)	14	Aprilia	24	42m 03.628s
5	Joan Olive (SPA)	6	Aprilia	24	42m 03.957s
6	Hector Faubel (SPA)	55	Aprilia	24	42m 05.210s
7	Sandro Cortese (GER)	11	Aprilia	24	42m 05.715s
8	Simone Corsi (ITA)	24	Aprilia	24	42m 05.776s
9	Mike di Meglio (FRA)	63	Honda	24	42m 05.889s
10	Tomoyoshi Koyama (JPN)	71	KTM	24	42m 09.220s
11	Pol Espargaro (SPA)	44	Aprilia	24	42m 14.032s
12	Alexis Masbou (FRA)	7	Honda	24	42m 14.322s
13	Randy Krummenacher (SWI)	34	KTM	24	42m 19.629s
14	Michael Ranseder (AUT)	60	Derbi	24	42m 19.813s
15	Pablo Nieto (SPA)	22	Aprilia	24	42m 25.048s
16	Lorenzo Zanetti (ITA)	8	Aprilia	24	42m 35.236s
17	Stefano Bianco (ITA)	27	Aprilia	24	42m 35.420s
18	Simone Grotzkyj (ITA)	53	Aprilia	24	42m 36.254s
19	Nicolas Terol (SPA)	18	Derbi	24	42m 36.462s
20	Dominique Aegerter (SWI)	77	Aprilia	24	42m 50.937s
21	Dino Lombardi (ITA)	13	Honda	24	42m 51.060s
22	Roberto Tamburini (ITA)	20	Aprilia	24	42m 59.813s
23	Robert Muresan (ROU)	95	Derbi	24	43m 00.213s
24	Hugo van den Berg (NED)	56	Aprilia	24	43m 00.407s
25	Joey Litjens (NED)	37	Honda	24	43m 00.583s
26	Federico Sandi (ITA)	15	Aprilia	24	43m 06.608s
27	Daniel Webb (GBR)	99	Honda	24	43m 11.934s
28	Romain Maitre (FRA)	46	Honda	23	42m 41.782s
29	Steven Le Coquen (FRA)	47	Honda	23	43m 12.025s
	Mattia Pasini (ITA)	75	Aprilia	19	DNF
	Raffaele de Rosa (ITA)	35	Aprilia	15	DNF
	Andrea Iannone (ITA)	29	Aprilia	14	DNF
	Julien Cartron (FRA)	48	Honda	11	DNF
	Steve Bonsey (USA)	51	KTM	3	DNF
	Gwen Le Badezet (FRA)	49	Honda		DNQ

Fastest lap: Pesek, 1m 43.859s, 90.029mph/144.888km/h (record).

Prevous lap record: Sergio Gadea, SPA (Aprilia), 1m 44.637s, 89.360mph/143.811km/h (2006).

Event best maximum speed: Koyama, 137.1mph/220.7km/h (qualifying practice no. 2).

Qualifying: 1 Pasini, 1m 43.111s; 2 Smith, 1m 43.569s; 3 Koyama, 1m 43.664s; 4 Faubel, 1m 43.745s; 5 Pesek, 1m 43.773s; 6 Gadea, 1m 43.774s; 7 Iannone, 1m 43.999s; 8 Talmacsi, 1m 44.191s; 9 Ranseder, 1m 44.191s; 10 di Meglio, 1m 44.192s; 11 Masbou, 1m 44.267s; 12 de Rosa, 1m 44.305s; 13 Corsi, 1m 44.518s; 14 Cortese, 1m 44.558s; 15 Krummenacher, 1m 44.668s; 16 Zanetti, 1m 44.680s; 17 Nieto, 1m 44.958s; 18 Olive, 1m 44.968s; 19 Espargaro, 1m 45.193s; 20 Bianco, 1m 45.280s; 21 Grotzkyj, 1m 45.310s; 22 Terol, 1m 45.729s; 23 Lombardi, 1m 45.909s; 24 Muresan, 1m 46.095s; 25 Aegerter, 1m 46.139s; 26 Tamburini, 1m 46.272s; 27 Bonsey, 1m 46.520s; 28 van den Berg, 1m 46.676s; 29 Litjens, 1m 46.724s; 30 Sandi, 1m 46.984s; 31 Webb, 1m 47.001s; 32 Maitre, 1m 49.031s; 33 Cartron, 1m 49.354s; 34 Le Coquen, 1m 50.116s; 35 Le Badezet, 1m 50.616s.

Fastest race laps: 1 Pesek, 1m 43.859s; 2 Gadea, 1m 43.990s; 3 Pasini, 1m 44.010s; 4 Smith, 1m 44.013s; 5 Nieto, 1m 44.089s; 6 Cortese, 1m 44.207s; 7 Olive, 1m 44.223s; 8 Masbou, 1m 44.238s; 9 Corsi, 1m 44.241s; 10 Iannone, 1m 44.254s; 11 Faubel, 1m 44.297s; 12 Talmacsi, 1m 44.325s; 13 de Rosa, 1m 44.364s; 14 di Meglio, 1m 44.493s; 15 Koyama, 1m 44.511s; 16 Espargaro, 1m 44.660s; 17 Krummenacher, 1m 44.792s; 18 Ranseder, 1m 44.810s; 19 Zanetti, 1m 45.115s; 20 Bianco, 1m 45.491s; 21 Grotzkyj, 1m 45.654s; 22 Terol, 1m 45.731s; 23 Aegerter, 1m 45.948s; 24 Lombardi, 1m 46.253s; 25 Tamburini, 1m 46.441s; 26 Muresan, 1m 46.546s; 27 van den Berg, 1m 46.692s; 28 Litjens, 1m 46.702s; 29 Sandi, 1m 46.875s; 30 Webb, 1m 47.047s; 31 Bonsey, 1m 47.177s; 32 Cartron, 1m 49.583s; 33 Maitre, 1m 49.717s; 34 Le Coquen, 1m 51.197s.

World Championship: 1 Pesek, 91; 2 Talmacsi, 82; 3 Faubel, 77; 4 Corsi, 55; 5 Gadea, 46; 6 Olive, 44; 7 Espargaro, 39; 8 Smith, 36; 9 Koyama, 32; 10 de Rosa, 30; 11 Rabat, 26; 12 Ranseder, 25; 13 Nieto, 21; 14 Cortese, 18; 15 Iannone, 17; 16 Zanetti, 16; 17 Masbou, 13; 18 di Meglio, 11; 19 Pasini, 6; 20 Bianco, 5; 21 Krummenacher, 4; 22 Bonsey, 3; 23 Terol, 2; 24 Grotzkyj, 1.

RIDER STANDINGS

After 5 Rounds

1	Casey Stoner	102
2	Valentino Rossi	81
3	Dani Pedrosa	62
4	Marco Melandri	61
5	Chris Vermeulen	55
6	John Hopkins	48
7	Loris Capirossi	38
8	Toni Elias	35
9	Colin Edwards	35
10	Alex Hofmann	30
11	Nicky Hayden	30
12	Alex Barros	27
13	Carlos Checa	20
14	Randy de Puniet	19
15	Shinya Nakano	15
16	Sylvain Guintoli	12
17	Makoto Tamada	11
18	Fonsi Nieto	5
19	Olivier Jacque	4
20	Kenny Roberts Jnr	4

TEAM STANDINGS

After 5 Rounds

1	Ducati Marlboro Team	140
2	Fiat Yamaha Team	116
3	Rizla Suzuki MotoGP	103
4	Honda Gresini	96
5	Repsol Honda Team	92
6	Pramac d'Antin	57
7	Kawasaki Racing Team	28
8	Dunlop Yamaha Tech 3	23
9	Honda LCR	20
10	Konica Minolta Honda	15
11	Team Roberts	4

CONSTRUCTOR STANDINGS

After 5 Rounds

1	Ducati	102
2	Honda	89
3	Yamaha	81
4	Suzuki	71
5	Kawasaki	28
6	KR212V	4

Right: Renaissance Man! Valentino Rossi was magnificent for his sixth straight Mugello win.
Photograph: Gold & Goose

Main photograph: A security policeman, his role forgotten, joins the track invasion for Number 46.
Photographs: Friedemann Kirn/2snap

Below: Guido the Bulldog had a special message for Rossi's one-off helmet.
Photograph: Gold & Goose

Bottom: The special item went into the crowd afterwards.
Photograph: Peter J Fox/2snap

FIM WORLD CHAMPIONSHIP • ROUND 6

ITALIANGP
MUGELLO

46
CEA
46
FIAT
YAMAHA
46
FIAT
TRACK

Above: Barros's private Ducati is ahead of Capirossi's factory bike. He would pass Stoner too, en route to the rostrum.

Above centre right: Severe mountain weather struck the circuit in the shadow of the Apennines.

Centre right: Ducati's block-booking broke up a sea of yellow.

Photographs: Gold & Goose

Bottom right: Olivier Jacque, talking to crew chief Fiorenzo Fanali, missed the front row by thousandths. This would be his final race.

Photograph: Peter J Fox/2snap

TOWERING genius is Rossi's trademark, and that is what drove the capacity crowd (all but one large, Ducati-dedicated grandstand) into frenzies of delight with his sixth successive win at Italy's magnificent grand prix circuit. The quality of his riding was obvious as he made his way from eighth on the first lap to dominate, his speed on the fast swoops and climbs, and the complex Esses worth more than anything the Ducati riders, or anybody else, could do in a straight line. It was a milestone, as he returned to absolute top form. And, for a while, it looked like it might have been a turning point as well. He cut Stoner's lead back to just nine points.

The foundations of the genius were laid over the preceding two days of foul weather, and began with a far-from-clever high-speed crash in the wet, losing the front at Scarperia, one of several downhill entries. His mood was unshakeable; he viewed it as entirely positive – because until then on that lap, he'd been fastest. There was no better way to lay the ghosts of Le Mans and to understand that Bridgestone is not unbeatable in the wet, although he did say he wished he'd used that soft rear the fortnight before. But what about falling off? These things happen. 'I braked a little bit too aggressive, and I touched a place with a little bit more water. I lost the front,' he explained.

What he and his experienced crew had also managed during weather-hit practice was to get the Yamaha settled, making the most of the chassis and tyres while others complained about being short of time. The long straight favoured the Ducatis, but the gap was only 6km/h between Stoner (323.3km/h) and eighth-fastest Rossi. Although, as the latter observed, this year's Ducati was reaching its top speed faster, whereas last year it had only told at the far end of the straight.

When it mattered, however, set-up proved more important than speed.

The weather gradually improved for a dry race day, but was atrocious through two days of practice, hail adding to lashing rain and violent winds on Friday to delay MotoGP practice by ten minutes. There were still rivers across the track, and Roberts was the only one to go out for almost half an hour. One advantage was unrestricted tyre numbers for wets, allowing him to test other areas where his under-performing hybrid Honda was urgently lacking development. This was a growing theme for the hard-pressed independent team, for whom the new tyre rule and consequent restricted dry laps compounded the problem of having only one rider. That was solved now and for the next race by adding Kurtis Roberts to strength, if only to confirm the impressions that his elder brother was bringing back to the pits. They had one bike each, and another problem – a limited mileage allocation for the year from Honda, based on engine service life. 'Last year, we used five engines,' said Kenny Senior. 'We asked for engines for this year for two riders, but Honda said no.' Plus, he added, after Kurtis's comments echoed those of Kenny Junior, "'We need a new chassis. We started designing it this morning. We've missed the target completely with this one.'

At the other end of the Honda hierarchy, there was more evidence of efforts to help their factory men – but which one? Another set of new exhausts turned out to be only for Pedrosa; Hayden had to wait. 'Not enough of them showed,' he said. The pipes are even longer megaphones than before, that on the left flattened into a tall, obtuse-angle triangle, and looking very rough and ready compared with HRC's usual showroom finish.

There was lots of new material all round. Ducati had made some special stuff for Capirossi – altered engine mapping, ride-by-wire response and cam timing, acknowledging his different style from the more successful Stoner, and aimed at making the bike more ridable and less peaky. Suzuki had new-spec engines, with a somewhat different exhaust note. Rossi alone had new 'tree-trunk' large-diameter forks mounted in an interesting top triple-clamp. Instead of the usual plain block of alloy, this was heavily relieved and even cut away in the fore-and-aft plane, the intention being to restore side-to-side flex lost in stiffening the fork legs while improving fore-and-aft stiffness overall. Dunlop, meanwhile, had followed Michelin in a return to a 16-inch front tyre, the bigger contact patch trading heavier low-speed steering against better high-speed direction change.

Hayden found a strange aspect of the growing electronic controls, which are not always as brainy as they might be. In the wet, he needed more traction control in the corners, but he was getting it on the straight instead – the softer-construction

tyres were growing so much with centrifugal fling at high speed that the difference between front and rear-wheel speeds was going beyond the range of the control unit, which was cutting back power just as he was tucking behind his (revised again) fairing to go for top speed.

The traditional lunacy of the event may have been muted by the weather and by even stricter than ever police controls, including a ban on liquor sales around the track on race eve. But again the crowds proved quite beyond control, reinforced fencing notwithstanding, after Valentino had given them the victory they craved. The invasion began on the penultimate lap, and the further back you finished, the more people you had running on to the track ahead of you, all looking the other way. No incidents this time, but only narrowly avoided. Hayden was one who had to brake hard over the line; Roberts, a long way behind, had seen it building up the lap before and trickled over the finish line, then U-turned straight back to his pit.

The ebullience was infectious, spilling over on to the main straight afterwards with a megaphone-exhaust Vespa 'Ape' three-wheeler in yellow just part of the pantomime presided over by Valentino on the balcony, playing to the crowd. It's hard not to enjoy it, but the danger and menace are all too obvious.

MOTOGP RACE – 23 laps

Timing meant everything when rain came, went and came again in qualifying, the track not only never dry, but also different lap by lap. Stoner claimed his and Bridgestone's first pole of the year early on, and was joined on the front row by Vermeulen and Rossi. Valentino had only just made it; he had displaced wet specialist Jacque by thousandths after the Kawasaki rider had set a flier on intermediate tyres.

Pedrosa, fastest in the free practices, was eighth; Hayden 13th, complaining of a lack of acceleration as well as continuing front-end problems, which were exacerbated on the many downhill corners. Edwards was even more at sea, down in 16th.

It was dry and occasionally even sunny as Stoner led away, almost a second clear at the end of lap one, from Vermeulen, Capirossi, Barros and a threatening Melandri. Rossi was seventh after dumping the clutch on the line and having to back off to control a wheelie, and he lost another place to Hopkins on lap two. 'It took two or three laps to find my rhythm,' he said.

The size of the front pack and the frequent overtaking were reminiscent of 125 racing – a full 800cc dogfight. Vermeulen began dropping back from the start, blaming lack of track knowledge as well as poor set-up; Capirossi was pushing Stoner, and was ahead at the start of lap four to lead his home GP. Then Melandri was also past Stoner, and Pedrosa was pushing hard. Rossi was up to fifth, from Hopkins, Vermeulen, Barros and Elias, all still in a huge mêlée. After Capirossi had a pair of scary front-wheel slides on lap six, he dropped from first to sixth. Stoner regained the lead, only to be displaced for four laps by Pedrosa, taking fastest lap (short of Biaggi's two-year-old 990 record).

Now Rossi was up to third, and on lap seven he cut inside Stoner into the second fast chicane; two laps later, he did the same thing to take the lead from Pedrosa. He was never headed again, but far from lonely as half-distance approached. By now, Hopkins and Barros had tagged on to make a pack of five. But Stoner also had imperfect set-up and, at the end of lap 12, was more than a second adrift on Rossi and Pedrosa. The Honda rider kept chasing, but Rossi was relentless and gradually edged further ahead. By lap 19, he was over a second away and unbeatable for a sixth time in a row at Mugello.

Stoner had his hands full with Hopkins and Barros as he lost touch. For a second race, he showed maturity, where a year before he had crashed spectacularly through trying too hard. 'I pushed 100 per cent, but not 110 per cent, because it wasn't possible to do more with the bike today,' he said. But his hopes of a rostrum were dashed by the satellite-team Ducati of Barros. With four laps to go, the veteran Brazilian had disposed of Hopkins and started to press the factory Ducati, drafting past

and outbraking him at the start of the 21st lap. He managed to hold him over the rest of the race, and by inches over the line. 'I hope Ducati will still help us,' he said later. Sixteen points put him in exclusive company, with a total of 2,007 premier-class points. Only Doohan and Rossi had amassed more than 2,000.

Melandri had suffered a return of his queasy handling problems and dropped back. 'I was flying over the first few laps, then the bike was skipping around,' he said. At half-distance, he and Elias were going back and forth, Elias finally prevailing on lap 14 to close on Capirossi for another to-and-fro battle. Capirossi led on to the final lap, but Elias got a better run to the line to prevail by four-tenths. Vermeulen had settled into a battle with Hayden and Hofmann, but broke free by the finish; on the last lap, he got ahead of Melandri too.

An increasingly disgruntled Hayden managed to hold Hofmann narrowly at bay over the line. Edwards was three seconds back after a downbeat weekend: 'I guess it's my bogey track,' he said. Nakano continued his lacklustre year, almost ten seconds down; Guintoli led team-mate Tamada and Jacque over the line in a battle for the last points. Roberts was miles behind.

De Puniet had crashed heavily on lap two, picking up yet more damage; Checa also fell, before half-distance, while lying 14th. Kurtis Roberts retired early, after discovering that a gamble on settings had not paid off. 'We made a plan not to waste mileage on the motor if it didn't work. We need to save that stuff,' he said.

250cc RACE – 21 laps

Practice and qualifying was even more disrupted by rain, Bautista claiming a first 250 pole in an early window of opportunity. Dovizioso and Shuhei Aoyama made a Honda pair, then Luthi was on the far end; de Angelis headed row two from Barbera and West, back after all for another race. Eight riders failed to qualify as the track conditions deteriorated, led by Lorenzo. All were allowed to start because of the exceptional conditions.

Luthi led away on a dry track, but Bautista drafted past on the straight at the end of the lap, with Dovizioso and de Angelis behind. Lorenzo was on a mission, charging through from 20th on the grid to eighth by the end of lap one. At the end of the straight, he collided with Kallio, and then again at the other end of the same lap, on the exit of the last corner. This time, the KTM's exhaust was broken off, and Kallio parked the bike against the pit wall, shaking his fist.

Barbera was also coming through fast, leap-frogging Lorenzo as both passed Luthi on lap five to take fourth, then third ahead of Dovizioso next time around, directly passing de Angelis and shadowing Bautista for two laps before taking the lead. Luthi and Simon were close in sixth and seventh, the rest more than five seconds behind.

Bautista and Barbera exchanged the lead until, just after half-distance, the latter had to put his foot down to save a slide, dropping from first to fifth and out of touch.

Now Lorenzo led for the first time and upped the pace, the two other Aprilias going with him, but Dovizioso was unable to compensate for his lack of straight-line speed.

With four laps left, Bautista was leading once more, de Angelis crawling all over him and Lorenzo poised, pouncing again to lead as they started the last lap and an epic battle. De Angelis took over into the first Esses, and half-way through Bautista followed suit, hitting Lorenzo and pushing him out on to the Astroturf and down.

The survivors disputed every inch of the final lap, running into the last corner side by side. Bautista had the better exit line, and his first 250 victory came by less than a tenth.

Dovizioso was not out of the woods, Barbera catching up again to battle for the last three laps, prevailing by a tenth over the line.

Twenty seconds behind, there had been a four-strong battle for fifth, Luthi managing to prevail narrowly over Shuhei Aoyama and his team-mate, Simon. Hiro Aoyama had lost touch in the closing stages when his engine lost power.

Lorenzo remounted to save eighth, well clear of Simoncelli. West fought hard to prevail over Takahashi, Espargaro, Lai, Baldolini and Sekiguchi, all six across the line in under a second.

Remarkably, only Lorenzo crashed; Wilairot pitted at the end of lap one, while wild card Menghi went out on the last.

125cc RACE – 20 laps

Faubel took his first pole on a drenched track, with di Meglio and Talmacsi next, the front row completed by Lombardi. His previous best qualifying was 23rd. Again, eight failed to qualify; again, all were allowed to start.

The first race of the day, like the remainder, was quite dry and a vintage Mugello 125 epic, with a nine-strong gang still disputing the lead as they started the final lap. From the first, they'd been changing places at every corner, running in three and four abreast.

Koyama was first off the line, but Talmacsi was in front at the end of the first lap; then it was Pasini for the next three. It hardly mattered, given that nobody ever led by more than a few feet. First Talmacsi and then Faubel had a go at sprinting away up front, but the track doesn't lend itself to escape. At half-distance, the first ten were still glued together.

Pesek lost touch, then Iannone crashed out, but Pesek was back when they started the last lap. Faubel was in front, first to ninth covered by 0.835s – all of them with a chance of winning.

Pesek and de Rosa ruled each other out, colliding and falling in the final corner. This split the pack somewhat as Gadea led the slipstreaming group on the long run to the finish line. Just before they got there, Faubel burst out of the slipstream with perfect timing to win by inches, Gadea, Corsi and Talmacsi virtually alongside. A second or so away, Koyama, Pasini and Cortese were as close, with Smith only another second down.

Left: Wide track, first corner – the 250s fan out. Luthi leads Bautista in the centre, with the Aoyama brothers behind, the returned Locatelli (15) between them, Kallio (36) on the outside. Note also Dovizioso (34), ahead of de Angelis (3) on the left; Simon (60) behind them; Barbera (80) on the far side.

Below: Bautista can hardly believe his first 250 win.

Below, centre left: Dovizioso, with special blue bike and leathers, had to be happy with fourth.

Below: The 125 Express. Faubel heads Pasini in the leading pack. They were still this close on the last lap.

Photographs: Gold & Goose

GRAN PREMIO D'ITALIA ALICE

3 JUNE 2007 • FIM WORLD CHAMPIONSHIP ROUND 6

AUTODROMO INTERNAZIONALE DEL MUGELLO

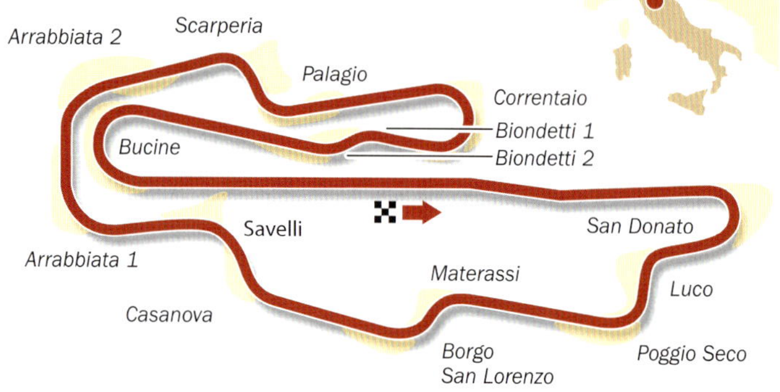

Circuit 5.245km / 3.259 miles

MotoGP

RACE: 23 laps, 74.957 miles/120.635km • Weather: Dry • Air 24°C • Humidity 20% • Track 29°C

Pos.	Rider	Nat.	No.	Entrant	Machine	Tyres	Laps	Time & speed (mph/km/h)
1	Valentino Rossi	ITA	46	Fiat Yamaha Team	Yamaha	M	23	42m 42.385s 105.313mph/ 169.485km/h
2	Dani Pedrosa	SPA	26	Repsol Honda Team	Honda	M	23	42m 45.459s
3	Alex Barros	BRA	4	Pramac d'Antin	Ducati	B	23	42m 48.341s
4	Casey Stoner	AUS	27	Ducati Marlboro Team	Ducati	B	23	42m 48.397s
5	John Hopkins	USA	21	Rizla Suzuki MotoGP	Suzuki	B	23	42m 55.629s
6	Toni Elias	SPA	24	Honda Gresini	Honda	B	23	43m 01.640s
7	Loris Capirossi	ITA	65	Ducati Marlboro Team	Ducati	B	23	43m 02.031s
8	Chris Vermeulen	AUS	71	Rizla Suzuki MotoGP	Suzuki	B	23	43m 05.195s
9	Marco Melandri	ITA	33	Honda Gresini	Honda	B	23	43m 05.222s
10	Nicky Hayden	USA	1	Repsol Honda Team	Honda	M	23	43m 06.798s
11	Alex Hofmann	GER	66	Pramac d'Antin	Ducati	B	23	43m 07.166s
12	Colin Edwards	USA	5	Fiat Yamaha Team	Yamaha	M	23	43m 10.386s
13	Shinya Nakano	JPN	56	Konica Minolta Honda	Honda	M	23	43m 19.118s
14	Sylvain Guintoli	FRA	50	Dunlop Yamaha Tech 3	Yamaha	D	23	43m 27.483s
15	Makoto Tamada	JPN	6	Dunlop Yamaha Tech 3	Yamaha	D	23	43m 27.530s
16	Olivier Jacque	FRA	19	Kawasaki Racing Team	Kawasaki	B	23	43m 27.602s
17	Kenny Roberts Jnr	USA	10	Team Roberts	KR212V	M	23	44m 09.607s
	Carlos Checa	SPA	7	Honda LCR	Honda	M	9	16m 59.065s
	Kurtis Roberts	USA	80	Team Roberts	KR212V	M	3	6m 00.621s
	Randy de Puniet	FRA	14	Kawasaki Racing Team	Kawasaki	B	1	2m 00.523s

Fastest lap: Dani Pedrosa, on lap 3, 1m 50.357s, 106.316mph/171.099km/h.

Lap record: Max Biaggi, ITA (Honda), 1m 50.117s, 106.548mph/171.472km/h (2005).

Event best maximum speed: Casey Stoner, 200.9mph/323.3km/h (free practice no. 3).

FASTEST RACE LAPS

	Rider	Lap	Time
1	Pedrosa	3	1m 50.357s
2	Capirossi	2	1m 50.482s
3	Rossi	4	1m 50.504s
4	Hopkins	2	1m 50.524s
5	Melandri	3	1m 50.637s
6	Elias	2	1m 50.764s
7	Stoner	8	1m 50.807s
8	Barros	7	1m 50.853s
9	Vermeulen	3	1m 51.125s
10	Hayden	3	1m 51.153s
11	Tamada	2	1m 51.495s
12	Checa	7	1m 51.500s
13	Hofmann	3	1m 51.553s
14	Edwards	3	1m 51.615s
15	Nakano	3	1m 51.676s
16	Jacque	3	1m 51.721s
17	Guintoli	7	1m 52.236s
18	Roberts Jnr	8	1m 53.735s
19	Roberts	2	1m 57.409s
20	de Puniet	1	2m 00.523s

QUALIFYING

2 June 2007

Weather: Wet

Air: 19°C Humidity: 40%

Track: 22°C

Pos.	Rider	Time
1	Stoner	2m 00.359s
2	Vermeulen	2m 01.381s
3	Rossi	2m 01.695s
4	Jacque	2m 01.709s
5	Capirossi	2m 01.797s
6	Melandri	2m 02.001s
7	de Puniet	2m 02.443s
8	Pedrosa	2m 02.776s
9	Hopkins	2m 02.932s
10	Barros	2m 03.025s
11	Hofmann	2m 03.920s
12	Nakano	2m 04.185s
13	Hayden	2m 04.353s
14	Checa	2m 04.971s
15	Elias	2m 05.592s
16	Edwards	2m 06.254s
17	Guintoli	2m 06.426s
18	Roberts Jnr	2m 06.660s
19	Roberts	2m 07.571s
20	Tamada	2m 09.080s

Grid order	1	2	3	4	5	6	7	8	9	10	11	12	13	14	15	16	17	18	19	20	21	22	23	•
27 STONER	27	27	27	65	65	26	26	26	46	46	46	46	46	46	46	46	46	46	46	46	46	46	46	1
71 VERMEULEN	65	65	65	27	27	27	46	46	26	26	26	26	26	26	26	26	26	26	26	26	26	26	26	2
46 ROSSI	71	33	33	33	33	46	27	27	27	27	27	27	27	27	27	27	27	27	27	27	4	4	4	3
19 JACQUE	33	71	26	26	26	33	33	21	21	21	21	21	21	21	21	21	4	4	4	4	27	27	27	4
65 CAPIROSSI	4	26	71	21	46	21	21	4	4	4	4	4	4	4	4	4	21	21	21	21	21	21	21	5
33 MELANDRI	26	21	21	46	21	65	4	33	33	65	65	65	65	65	65	65	65	65	24	65	65	65	24	6
14 de PUNIET	46	4	46	71	71	4	65	65	65	33	33	24	33	24	24	24	24	24	65	24	24	24	65	7
26 PEDROSA	21	46	4	4	4	71	71	24	24	24	24	33	24	33	33	33	33	33	33	33	33	33	71	8
21 HOPKINS	1	24	24	24	24	24	24	71	71	1	1	1	1	1	1	71	1	1	71	71	71	71	33	9
4 BARROS	24	1	1	1	1	1	1	1	1	71	71	71	71	71	71	1	71	71	1	1	1	1	1	10
66 HOFMANN	66	66	66	66	66	66	66	66	66	66	66	66	66	66	66	66	66	66	66	66	66	66	66	11
56 NAKANO	19	19	19	56	56	56	56	56	56	56	56	5	5	5	5	5	5	5	5	5	5	5	5	12
1 HAYDEN	56	56	56	5	19	19	5	5	5	5	5	56	56	56	56	56	56	56	56	56	56	56	56	13
7 CHECA	14	5	5	19	5	5	19	7	7	6	6	6	6	6	6	6	6	6	50	50	50	50	50	14
24 ELIAS	5	7	7	6	7	7	7	19	19	19	19	19	19	19	19	19	19	50	6	6	6	6	6	15
5 EDWARDS	50	50	6	7	6	6	6	6	6	50	50	50	50	50	50	50	50	19	19	19	19	19	19	
50 GUINTOLI	7	6	50	50	50	50	50	50	50	10	10	10	10	10	10	10	10	10	10	10	10	10	10	
10 ROBERTS Jnr	6	10	10	10	10	10	10	10	10															
80 ROBERTS	10	80	80																					
6 TAMADA	80																							

statistics

250cc

21 laps, 68.439 miles/110.145km

Pos.	Rider (Nat.)	No.	Machine	Laps	Time & speed
1	Alvaro Bautista (SPA)	19	Aprilia	21	40m 18.605s 101.871mph/ 163.946km/h
2	Alex de Angelis (RSM)	3	Aprilia	21	40m 18.692s
3	Hector Barbera (SPA)	80	Aprilia	21	40m 26.270s
4	Andrea Dovizioso (ITA)	34	Honda	21	40m 26.356s
5	Thomas Luthi (SWI)	12	Aprilia	21	40m 45.872s
6	Shuhei Aoyama (JPN)	73	Honda	21	40m 46.127s
7	Julian Simon (SPA)	60	Honda	21	40m 46.379s
8	Jorge Lorenzo (SPA)	1	Aprilia	21	40m 50.843s
9	Marco Simoncelli (ITA)	58	Gilera	21	41m 10.060s
10	Anthony West (AUS)	14	Aprilia	21	41m 22.913s
11	Yuki Takahashi (JPN)	55	Honda	21	41m 22.923s
12	Aleix Espargaro (SPA)	41	Aprilia	21	41m 23.067s
13	Fabrizio Lai (ITA)	32	Aprilia	21	41m 23.161s
14	Alex Baldolini (ITA)	25	Aprilia	21	41m 23.175s
15	Taro Sekiguchi (JPN)	44	Aprilia	21	41m 23.767s
16	Karel Abraham (CZE)	17	Aprilia	21	41m 29.188s
17	Dirk Heidolf (GER)	28	Aprilia	21	41m 29.192s
18	Roberto Locatelli (ITA)	15	Gilera	21	41m 39.255s
19	Jules Cluzel (FRA)	16	Aprilia	21	41m 39.526s
20	Eugene Laverty (IRL)	50	Honda	21	41m 39.887s
21	Hiroshi Aoyama (JPN)	4	KTM	21	42m 05.381s
22	Imre Toth (HUN)	10	Aprilia	21	42m 13.570s
23	Arturo Tizon (SPA)	9	Aprilia	20	40m 27.567s
24	Thomas Tallevi (ITA)	65	Yamaha	20	41m 15.068s
	Omar Menghi (ITA)	64	Aprilia	19	DNF
	Mika Kallio (FIN)	36	KTM	2	DNF
	Ratthapark Wilairot (THA)	8	Honda	0	DNF

Fastest lap: Barbera, 1m 54.061s, 102.863mph/165.542km/h (record).

Previous lap record: Alex de Angelis, RSM (Aprilia), 1m 54.332s, 102.619mph/165.150km/h (2005).

Event best maximum speed: Barbera, 170.8mph/274.9km/h (free practice no. 1).

Qualifying: 1 Bautista, 1m 57.435s; 2 Dovizioso, 1m 57.923s; 3 S. Aoyama, 1m 58.874s; 4 Luthi, 1m 58.971s; 5 de Angelis, 1m 59.107s; 6 Barbera, 1m 59.449s; 7 H. Aoyama, 1m 59.455s; 8 Kallio, 1m 59.792s; 9 West, 2m 00.022s; 10 Simon, 2m 00.237s; 11 Toth, 2m 00.417s; 12 Baldolini, 2m 00.813s; 13 Simoncelli, 2m 00.876s; 14 Abraham, 2m 01.529s; 15 Locatelli, 2m 01.985s; 16 Heidolf, 2m 02.175s; 17 Menghi, 2m 04.693s; 18 Cluzel, 2m 05.061s; 19 Wilairot, 2m 05.511s; 20 Lorenzo, 2m 07.987s; 21 Laverty, 2m 09.297s; 22 Espargaro, 2m 10.810s; 23 Tizon, 2m 11.127s; 24 Lai, 2m 11.161s; 25 Tallevi, 2m 12.495s; 26 Sekiguchi, 2m 14.749s; 27 Takahashi, 2m 24.976s.

Fastest race laps: 1 Barbera, 1m 54.061s; 2 Lorenzo, 1m 54.204s; 3 de Angelis, 1m 54.264s; 4 Bautista, 1m 54.317s; 5 Dovizioso, 1m 54.530s; 6 Luthi, 1m 55.150s; 7 Simon, 1m 55.229s; 8 S. Aoyama, 1m 55.479s; 9 H. Aoyama, 1m 55.489s; 10 Simoncelli, 1m 56.194s; 11 Heidolf, 1m 56.614s; 12 Abraham, 1m 56.626s; 13 Baldolini, 1m 56.833s; 14 Sekiguchi, 1m 56.881s; 15 Takahashi, 1m 56.904s; 16 Lai, 1m 57.052s; 17 Espargaro, 1m 57.055s; 18 West, 1m 57.099s; 19 Locatelli, 1m 57.200s; 20 Laverty, 1m 57.897s; 21 Cluzel, 1m 57.922s; 22 Toth, 1m 58.896s; 23 Menghi, 1m 59.541s; 24 Tizon, 1m 59.609s; 25 Tallevi, 2m 02.046s; 26 Kallio, 2m 02.077s.

World Championship: 1 Lorenzo, 128; 2 Dovizioso, 101; 3 de Angelis, 95; 4 Bautista, 89; 5 Barbera, 63; 6 Simon, 46; 7 Luthi, 43; 8 S. Aoyama, 32; 9 Simoncelli, 31; 10 Kallio, 30; 11 Lai, 28; 12 West, 25; 13 Takahashi, 22; 14 Espargaro, 19; 15 H. Aoyama, 17; 16 Wilairot, 16; 17 Debon, 11; 18 Locatelli, 10; 19 Heidolf, 10; 20 Baldolini, 10; 21 Abraham, 5; 22 Sekiguchi, 5; 23 Laverty, 3; 24 Tizon, 1.

125cc

20 laps, 65.180 miles/104.900km

Pos.	Rider (Nat.)	No.	Machine	Laps	Time & speed
1	Hector Faubel (SPA)	55	Aprilia	20	40m 14.164s 97.199mph/ 156.426km/h
2	Sergio Gadea (SPA)	33	Aprilia	20	40m 14.184s
3	Simone Corsi (ITA)	24	Aprilia	20	40m 14.230s
4	Gabor Talmacsi (HUN)	14	Aprilia	20	40m 14.298s
5	Tomoyoshi Koyama (JPN)	71	KTM	20	40m 15.826s
6	Mattia Pasini (ITA)	75	Aprilia	20	40m 15.855s
7	Sandro Cortese (GER)	11	Aprilia	20	40m 15.977s
8	Bradley Smith (GBR)	38	Honda	20	40m 17.123s
9	Pol Espargaro (SPA)	44	Aprilia	20	40m 31.659s
10	Lorenzo Zanetti (ITA)	8	Aprilia	20	40m 32.441s
11	Michael Ranseder (AUT)	60	Derbi	20	40m 38.019s
12	Nicolas Terol (SPA)	18	Derbi	20	40m 47.083s
13	Randy Krummenacher (SWI)	34	KTM	20	40m 50.424s
14	Raffaele de Rosa (ITA)	35	Aprilia	20	40m 52.363s
15	Dominique Aegerter (SWI)	77	Aprilia	20	41m 19.218s
16	Joey Litjens (NED)	37	Honda	20	41m 19.270s
17	Simone Sancioni (ITA)	42	Aprilia	20	41m 19.559s
18	Federico Sandi (ITA)	15	Aprilia	20	41m 19.812s
19	Robert Muresan (ROU)	95	Derbi	20	41m 19.864s
20	Steve Bonsey (USA)	51	KTM	20	41m 39.581s
21	Daniel Webb (GBR)	99	Honda	20	41m 39.759s
22	Simone Grotzkyj (ITA)	53	Aprilia	20	41m 59.463s
23	Hugo van den Berg (NED)	56	Aprilia	20	42m 01.071s
24	Roberto Tamburini (ITA)	20	Aprilia	19	40m 25.516s
	Lukas Pesek (CZE)	52	Derbi	19	DNF
	Stefano Bianco (ITA)	27	Aprilia	17	DNF
	Andrea Iannone (ITA)	29	Aprilia	16	DNF
	Pablo Nieto (SPA)	22	Aprilia	10	DNF
	Alexis Masbou (FRA)	7	Honda	7	DNF
	Roberto Lacalendola (ITA)	87	Aprilia	7	DNF
	Mike di Meglio (FRA)	63	Honda	3	DNF
	Joan Olive (SPA)	6	Aprilia	3	DNF
	Dino Lombardi (ITA)	13	Honda	0	DNF
	Tobias Siegert (GER)	41	Aprilia		DNS

Fastest lap: Gadea, 1m 58.636s, 98.897mph/159.159km/h (record).

Previous lap record: Mattia Pasini, ITA (Aprilia), 1m 58.677s, 98.863mph/159.104 km/h (2006).

Event best maximum speed: Gadea, 143.0mph/230.1km/h (race).

Qualifying: 1 Faubel, 2m 15.309s; 2 di Meglio, 2m 16.053s; 3 Talmacsi, 2m 18.750s; 4 Lombardi, 2m 18.829s; 5 Koyama, 2m 19.118s; 6 de Rosa, 2m 19.132s; 7 Iannone, 2m 19.136s; 8 Pesek, 2m 19.780s; 9 Pasini, 2m 19.810s; 10 Olive, 2m 20.090s; 11 Smith, 2m 20.352s; 12 Masbou, 2m 20.504s; 13 Muresan, 2m 20.897s; 14 Corsi, 2m 21.008s; 15 Cortese, 2m 21.143s; 16 Ranseder, 2m 21.833s; 17 Zanetti, 2m 22.268s; 18 Litjens, 2m 22.421s; 19 Krummenacher, 2m 22.469s; 20 Gadea, 2m 22.529s; 21 Terol, 2m 22.699s; 22 Espargaro, 2m 23.354s; 23 Lacalendola, 2m 23.809s; 24 Aegerter, 2m 23.962s; 25 Nieto, 2m 24.187s; 26 Sancioni, 2m 24.391s; 27 Sandi, 2m 25.253s; 28 Grotzkyj, 2m 25.461s; 29 Webb, 2m 25.674s; 30 Bianco, 2m 26.154s; 31 Tamburini, 2m 26.175s; 32 Bonsey, 2m 26.582s; 33 Siegert, 2m 29.687s; 34 van den Berg, 2m 33.106s.

Fastest race laps: 1 Gadea, 1m 58.636s; 2 Cortese, 1m 58.962s; 3 Koyama, 1m 59.007s; 4 Pasini, 1m 59.073s; 5 de Rosa, 1m 59.076s; 6 Iannone, 1m 59.122s; 7 Corsi, 1m 59.157s; 8 Pesek, 1m 59.197s; 9 Faubel, 1m 59.409s; 10 Talmacsi, 1m 59.484s; 11 di Meglio, 1m 59.665s; 12 Smith, 1m 59.835s; 13 Ranseder, 2m 00.058s; 14 Zanetti, 2m 00.169s; 15 Espargaro, 2m 00.188s; 16 Masbou, 2m 00.237s; 17 Nieto, 2m 00.566s; 18 Terol, 2m 00.763s; 19 Olive, 2m 00.765s; 20 Krummenacher, 2m 01.389s; 21 Sancioni, 2m 01.971s; 22 van den Berg, 2m 02.199s; 23 Muresan, 2m 02.259s; 24 Litjens, 2m 02.380s; 25 Bianco, 2m 02.415s; 26 Aegerter, 2m 02.543s; 27 Sandi, 2m 02.556s; 28 Grotzkyj, 2m 02.738s; 29 Tamburini, 2m 02.911s; 30 Webb, 2m 03.434s; 31 Bonsey, 2m 03.499s; 32 Lacalendola, 2m 03.707s.

World Championship: 1 Faubel, 102; 2 Talmacsi, 95; 3 Pesek, 91; 4 Corsi, 71; 5 Gadea, 66; 6 Espargaro, 46; 7 Olive, 44; 8 Smith, 44; 9 Koyama, 43; 10 de Rosa, 32; 11 Ranseder, 30; 12 Cortese, 27; 13 Rabat, 26; 14 Zanetti, 22; 15 Nieto, 21; 16 Iannone, 17; 17 Pasini, 16; 18 Masbou, 13; 19 di Meglio, 11; 20 Krummenacher, 7; 21 Terol, 6; 22 Bianco, 5; 23 Bonsey, 3; 24 Aegerter and Grotzkyj, 1.

RIDER STANDINGS
After 6 Rounds

1	Casey Stoner	115
2	Valentino Rossi	106
3	Dani Pedrosa	82
4	Marco Melandri	63
5	Chris Vermeulen	63
6	John Hopkins	59
7	Loris Capirossi	47
8	Toni Elias	45
9	Alex Barros	43
10	Colin Edwards	39
11	Nicky Hayden	36
12	Alex Hofmann	35
13	Carlos Checa	20
14	Randy de Puniet	19
15	Shinya Nakano	18
16	Sylvain Guintoli	14
17	Makoto Tamada	12
18	Fonsi Nieto	5
19	Olivier Jacque	4
20	Kenny Roberts Jnr	4

TEAM STANDINGS
After 6 Rounds

1	Ducati Marlboro Team	162
2	Fiat Yamaha Team	145
3	Rizla Suzuki MotoGP	122
4	Repsol Honda Team	118
5	Honda Gresini	113
6	Pramac d'Antin	78
7	Kawasaki Racing Team	28
8	Dunlop Yamaha Tech 3	26
9	Honda LCR	20
10	Konica Minolta Honda	18
11	Team Roberts	4

CONSTRUCTOR STANDINGS
After 6 Rounds

1	Ducati	118
2	Honda	109
3	Yamaha	106
4	Suzuki	82
5	Kawasaki	28
6	KR212V	4

FIM WORLD CHAMPIONSHIP • ROUND 7

CATALUNYANGP

BARCELONA

Rossi tried everything, but leader Stoner had it under control. Pedrosa could only follow and watch.
Photograph: Gold & Goose

Above: **Injured and limping, de Puniet had his best ever race.**

Below: **Glum World Champion Hayden had to wait until Monday for some relief.**

Photographs: Gold & Goose

THE Catalunyan GP, the first back-to-back race of the year, didn't quite undo the feeling that Mugello had been a turning point in Rossi's favour, but in retrospect this was not the case. Thus it was another key moment. Everything went perfectly again for Rossi – but this time, he was beaten. The Ducati, on another long straight, had a very clear 12km/h speed advantage, although less than in China: 'At least it didn't take my paint off,' said Rossi. But Stoner used it only as part of his weaponry. He was only in a position to do so because he and the bike were so good around the rest of the track.

The racing between Stoner and Rossi was almost desperate, with a number of overtaking moves; the finish whisker-close, with Pedrosa right there too. Oddly, there was an undercurrent of disquiet after the race. True, it had been exciting, but compared with the 990s, something had been missing.

It seems churlish to complain after 112,600 fans had been treated to such a spectacle. The fighting had been intense, the outcome close, the overtaking moves frequent, Rossi's attack determined and creative, and Stoner's resistance perfectly measured; the first three were over the line in less than four-tenths. tenths. But it was all a bit plastic. Too many of the moves were tit-for-tat – overtake on the way in, get passed on the exit, the rest a matter of braking or acceleration.

This is a matter of technical progress; the closer everyone gets to the fine line, the harder it is for a rider to exploit any difference to his advantage. The 800s may have accelerated this process with the reduction in power, but in truth it was unstoppable. No demonstration of this progress in racing could have been clearer than that laid on by Jorge Lorenzo. In 'maybe the fastest lap of my life', the 250 champion blazed around a scorching Catalunya circuit at an average speed of 161.917km/h to claim his fifth pole of the year. His time was almost half a second faster than the previous best two-stroke lap, and that had been set on a Honda NRS500 by Valentino Rossi just six years before.

Lorenzo raised the bar in showmanship as well, rivalling the amateur dramatics developed by Rossi with his post-victory pantomime: two helmet-and-leathers doppelgangers playing guitars while Lorenzo sang to the crowd in rock-star style. The younger generation was putting pressure on the master in all kinds of ways.

The background was much as for the previous race: Honda still coming up with bits and pieces, this time a chassis for Dani, while Nicky would have to wait until after the race to test it (he had the new pipes). This would prove pivotal for the so-far hapless defending champion. Not that the chassis solved his problems, but two days of typically hard work, still circulating and testing long after everyone else had packed up, offered an improvement along with some better settings. And an important mental step: from now on, he would stop chasing his own tail trying to find a machine balance that didn't exist. He would concentrate on riding it hard instead.

Testing over the following two days was important for another team and rider as well: Kawasaki and Anthony West. But not before the other two Kawasaki riders had also had career changing experiences.

De Puniet was still nursing a strapped-up collar-bone injury sustained in France, and the left knee he had whacked at Mugello was grossly swollen, such that he required special leathers with an extra 10cm for the joint. He proceeded to ride better than ever before. Rossi denied him pole by the merest whisker; in the race, he survived a mid-chicane ramming by Elias right on the injured limb to claim a career-best fifth. Heroic, painful and exhausting. He was in no condition to test the next day.

Nor was team-mate Jacque. Yet another fall on Saturday put him out of the race. Some heart-to-heart conversation with team boss Ichiro Yoda led to a decision the following week, and the former 250 World Champion announced his retirement at the next round in England. He would remain as official tester.

With a roster of tyres and other things to test, Kawasaki solved the problem by inviting West, who had ridden his last 250 race for Team Sicilia the day before and had signed to join the Yamaha 600 World Supersport squad after race wins at Silverstone and Misano. It was not an invitation he could resist, and he proceeded to impress the team by reeling off increas-

ingly fast laps, ending up in touch with Jacque's Friday time, and bringing back to the pits useful comments and analysis. Within a few days, West would be buying himself out of the Yamaha deal and having his helmet painted green. A MotoGP chance at last for this underrated rider.

Kawasaki was also at the centre of a growing brew of rumours as the Silly Season got off to a record early start. Various notions, more or less fanciful, had been floating around at Mugello, and now at least one of them became a reality, Stoner and Ducati extending their one-year deal into 2008. The buzz suggested that Capirossi would soon move to Kawasaki, unless it were Melandri. Untrue; the former would sign for Suzuki during the summer break, and Melandri would take his place at Ducati. Another rumour concerned a proposed second Suzuki team, to be headed by Kevin Schwantz, under the Jorge Martinez/Aspar umbrella with backing from Suzuki Spain. Aspar's sporting manager, Gino Borsoi, was already talking about riders, de Angelis and Dovizioso both being on his list, but it would turn out to be somewhat premature. Dunlop was fighting off rumours that it would be left high and dry, with its Tech 3 team planning a switch to Michelins in 2008.

Memories of 2006's horrendous first-turn pile-up remained fresh: it is a tight corner approached at very high speed. Rossi hoped to help avoid a repetition. 'All the riders should put their hand on their heart, and brake half a metre earlier rather than half a metre later,' he said. Thankfully, they all did.

MOTOGP RACE – 25 laps

Stoner led from de Puniet and Pedrosa in free practice, but on qualifiers it all went Rossi's way. Long straight notwithstanding, his fourth pole lap of the year beat his own 990 time by less than a tenth. In the process, he narrowly eclipsed the heroic de Puniet, while Pedrosa was third, also limping from a heavy Friday spill.

Stoner led the second row from an on-form Hopkins, who

Left, from top: Tamada and crew chief Guy Coulon wonder what to do next; Jacque is stretchered away and out of racing; Vermeulen, under his own scrutiny.

Below: Capirossi – disastrous qualifying, fighting race.

Bottom: You can see the new exhausts, but not the new chassis on Pedrosa's improving factory Honda.

Photographs: Gold & Goose

Above: **Barcelona's architect, Gaudi, provided the inspiration for Toni Elias's surrealist paint job.**

Top: **Kurtis Roberts stayed on to develop the underpowered Honda hybrid after older brother Kenny Junior had quit.**

Photographs: Gold & Goose

might have been faster had not a breakdown forced a switch to his second bike.

Stoner flew off the line, but Pedrosa took over into the first corner, Hopkins following and de Puniet behind Rossi. By the time they crossed the finish line, Elias was ahead of the Kawasaki. Then the progress of the race was defined, as Stoner powered comfortably past Pedrosa to take over before they reached the first corner again.

Two laps later, Rossi dived underneath Hopkins, who had lost a second on the leaders, and they carried on in this order. Pedrosa couldn't attack Stoner, but he wasn't losing ground, and it took Rossi until lap 11 before he was close enough to take over second. Hopkins had also closed, setting fastest lap as he moved up to make it four. As the race wore on, he found himself struggling on the corner exits, and with eight to go, he had dropped more than two seconds behind.

At the same time, Rossi took the lead, sneaking past into the third corner, only for Stoner to do the same to him on the following lap. Rossi's next move was up the inside on to the main straight; Stoner had surged ahead again by the end of it. Rossi found a new place on the run to the downhill hairpin, half-way through the lap; Stoner got ahead again on the way out. Then Rossi started to attack under braking at the end of the straight.

It was tooth and nail alright, but there was a certain inevitability when, on lap 24, Stoner firmly used a combination of speed and precise late braking to make sure Rossi couldn't hold him off at the first corner. And this time, once in front, Stoner made sure to stay there, playing to his strength on the straight and making himself as unassailable on the corners. Again, it was Rossi's turn to experience being dominated, and another finely judged exploitation of his advantages by Stoner.

Pedrosa was a close spectator, but was right on his limit and powerless to become involved. He was still as close as ever over the line.

Hopkins was almost eight seconds adrift, the strongest of the rest, and all on his own.

De Puniet had dropped back by some six seconds by half-distance, but got back ahead of Gaudi-liveried local hero Elias. The two had battled back and forth, the Spaniard running into de Puniet at one point. Then his Honda blew up on lap 15, another indication of the V4's fragility; he was the only retirement.

Capirossi had been making his way through steadily from 17th on the grid: 'My worst Saturday ever.' By half-distance, he was ahead of Melandri and closing on Elias, and then de Puniet, particularly in the last two laps. De Puniet was kept well informed, however, and overcame his own fears that he might not last the race. He held off the Ducati by under two seconds.

Capirossi himself came under attack from Vermeulen, who had been gaining strength and speed after a slow start. He finished just a tenth behind, after nosing ahead on the final lap, only to lose it again on sheer speed.

Melandri had struggled from the start, succumbing in turn to Capirossi, Vermeulen and finally, on the last lap, to Barros. Behind them, Edwards prevailed in a desultory battle for tenth. He'd been dropping back, complaining of zero rear grip, from the early stages. Hayden had been ahead, but his tyre problems were more severe – a vibration from the rear that became progressively worse. His last lap was his slowest of the race by some two seconds. 'I was just trying to stay upright,' he said.

Hofmann, Tamada and Nakano trailed in for the rest of the points; the remainder were all spaced out. At the back, Kenny Roberts got going at the end, passing not only brother Kurtis, but also Checa, a big disappointment to the Spanish fans.

250cc RACE – 23 laps

Lorenzo's extraordinary pole lap gave him an advantage of almost a second over former team-mate Barbera, with Dovizioso and wild card Debon alongside, Luthi heading row two from de Angelis, all separated by mere tenths.

The champion took off, gaining just under half a second on the first lap, ahead of Dovizioso, Luthi, Kallio, Debon and de Angelis. But he wasn't getting away, and by the third, Dovizioso had closed right up, the rest with him; already de Angelis was past Debon, who would soon lose touch.

De Angelis carried on moving forward. He passed Kallio on lap five, and then the KTM rider started to drop away from the group. Four laps later, he finally found a way past Luthi for third, losing a second in the process. Now he put his head down to chase the leaders, setting a new record on lap 12 and closing on lap 14. He got past Dovizioso next time around, but by now Lorenzo was warming up for his familiar closing-laps gallop and had a second in hand. He kept building on that, to win by better than three seconds.

De Angelis's pass quite demoralised Dovizioso, who until then had been performing small miracles under braking and through the turns to make up for his obviously inferior power.

Now he gave up the unequal struggle, finishing ten seconds behind the leader, although comfortably clear of fourth. That had belonged to a lonely Luthi since lap nine.

There was a strong fight for fifth, won eventually by Bautista, who had a dreadful start from the second row and finished the first lap 13th. Debon had looked safe in the spot until he fell on lap 18, handing over to Kallio. At that point, he was two seconds clear of Bautista and Hiro Aoyama, but they closed quickly, and the battle was on.

Bautista used the draft to get ahead of Kallio as they started lap 22 and had the pace to keep the two KTMs behind to the flag, the trio covered by three-tenths. Barbera had been with the group, but ran wide and finished three seconds adrift.

Simon and Simoncelli had battled with Takahashi over ninth, Simoncelli narrowly prevailing over the line. Takahashi crashed out on the last lap, promoting Shuhei Aoyama to 11th.

A little way back, West and Espargaro also had tangled at the end of the back straight on the final lap, both remounting to finish out of the points. The rest of these were not hotly disputed, although there was a battle for 16th, which was won by the remounted Debon.

Lorenzo's fifth clear win stretched his lead over the increasingly disgruntled Dovizioso to 36, in spite of the former's problems at Mugello. The Italian's Honda was just not fast enough to beat the Aprilia. With both linked to a MotoGP move in 2008, there was increasing speculation that Dovizioso might jump ship from Honda, his loyalty to the marque having been so meagrely repaid.

125cc RACE – 22 laps

Talmacsi credited time spent at the track with Masterbike tests for his second pole of the year. 'I learned some secrets – seems they function,' he said. Team-mates Faubel and Gadea were alongside, and Bradley Smith was on the far end, his second front row.

The luckless Pasini had qualified eighth, but didn't make it past the first corner, spilling off into the gravel as his motor seized again, whereupon he gave the bike a thorough kicking.

The Aspar machines did all the leading from the start, with Gadea heading a pack of eight at half-distance. Faubel was second, Pesek now third, Talmacsi fourth, then Espargaro, rookie Randy Krummenacher, Koyama and Smith.

The infighting was constant, with Pesek pushing hard and leading on lap 13. On the 19th, he and Faubel tangled, and both slid off, Pesek remounting to save a couple of points. Smith was losing ground, little by little.

Koyama had been moving forward in the group and took the lead on the penultimate lap, with Krummenacher in second, continuing to amaze.

The last lap was a thriller. Gadea drafted past everyone to take the lead into the first corner, but at the end of the back straight, Koyama pushed back past him so hard that he lifted and ran wide, dropping straight to fourth.

Talmacsi and Krummenacher were the rostrum beneficiaries. Krummenacher's previous best had been 13th. Espargaro was still two seconds adrift, and Smith three more behind him. Corsi was at the head of the next gang.

Left: The Lorenzo's Land Three give a not-very-impromptu victory rock concert.

Below: The Spaniard stamps his authority on Dovizioso and early leader de Angelis.

Gold & Goose

Left: His first race win left Koyama beaming.

Below left: 'I've warned you often enough...' Pasini gives his bike what it deserves after yet another breakdown.

Below: Swiss rookie Randy Krummenacher took a surprise first podium, making two out for three for KTM.

Photographs: Gold & Goose

GRAN PREMI CINZANO DE CATALUNYA

10 JUNE 2007 • FIM WORLD CHAMPIONSHIP ROUND 7

CIRCUIT DE CATALUNYA

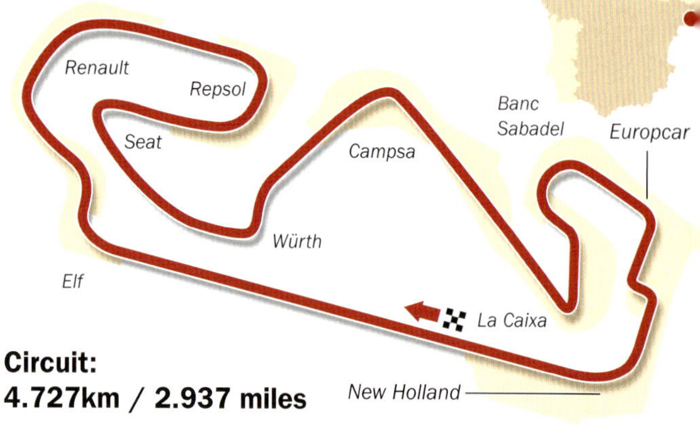

Circuit:
4.727km / 2.937 miles

MotoGP

RACE: 25 laps, 73.425 miles/118.175km • Weather: Dry • Air 31°C • Humidity 13% • Track 43°C

Pos.	Rider	Nat.	No.	Entrant	Machine	Tyres	Laps	Time & speed (mph/km/h)
1	Casey Stoner	AUS	27	Ducati Marlboro Team	Ducati	B	25	43m 16.907s 101.794mph/ 163.821km/h
2	Valentino Rossi	ITA	46	Fiat Yamaha Team	Yamaha	M	25	43m 16.976s
3	Dani Pedrosa	SPA	26	Repsol Honda Team	Honda	M	25	43m 17.297s
4	John Hopkins	USA	21	Rizla Suzuki MotoGP	Suzuki	B	25	43m 24.721s
5	Randy de Puniet	FRA	14	Kawasaki Racing Team	Kawasaki	B	25	43m 34.760s
6	Loris Capirossi	ITA	65	Ducati Marlboro Team	Ducati	B	25	43m 36.316s
7	Chris Vermeulen	AUS	71	Rizla Suzuki MotoGP	Suzuki	B	25	43m 36.402s
8	Alex Barros	BRA	4	Pramac d'Antin	Ducati	B	25	43m 41.769s
9	Marco Melandri	ITA	33	Honda Gresini	Honda	B	25	43m 41.870s
10	Colin Edwards	USA	5	Fiat Yamaha Team	Yamaha	M	25	43m 52.255s
11	Nicky Hayden	USA	1	Repsol Honda Team	Honda	M	25	43m 53.208s
12	Makoto Tamada	JPN	6	Dunlop Yamaha Tech 3	Yamaha	D	25	43m 55.627s
13	Alex Hofmann	GER	66	Pramac d'Antin	Ducati	B	25	43m 57.841s
14	Sylvain Guintoli	FRA	50	Dunlop Yamaha Tech 3	Yamaha	D	25	44m 01.306s
15	Shinya Nakano	JPN	56	Konica Minolta Honda	Honda	M	25	44m 11.010s
16	Kenny Roberts Jnr	USA	10	Team Roberts	KR212V	M	25	44m 16.562s
17	Carlos Checa	SPA	7	Honda LCR	Honda	M	25	44m 19.222s
18	Kurtis Roberts	USA	80	Team Roberts	KR212V	M	25	44m 20.229s
	Toni Elias	SPA	24	Honda Gresini	Honda	B	14	24m 23.184s

Fastest lap: John Hopkins, on lap 8, 1m 43.252s, 102.409mph/164.812km/h.

Lap record: Nicky Hayden, USA (Honda), 1m 43.048s, 102.612mph/165.138km/h (2006).

Event best maximum speed: Loris Capirossi, 199.5mph/321.1km/h (qualifying practice).

Grid order	1	2	3	4	5	6	7	8	9	10	11	12	13	14	15	16	17	18	19	20	21	22	23	24	25	•
46 ROSSI	26	27	27	27	27	27	27	27	27	27	27	27	27	27	27	27	27	46	27	46	27	46	46	27	27	1
14 de PUNIET	27	26	26	26	26	26	26	26	26	26	46	46	46	46	46	46	46	27	46	27	46	27	27	46	46	2
26 PEDROSA	21	21	46	46	46	46	46	46	46	46	26	26	26	26	26	26	26	26	26	26	26	26	26	26	26	3
27 STONER	46	46	21	21	21	21	21	21	21	21	21	21	21	21	21	21	21	21	21	21	21	21	21	21	21	4
21 HOPKINS	24	24	24	24	24	24	14	14	14	14	14	14	14	14	14	14	14	14	14	14	14	14	14	14	14	5
5 EDWARDS	14	14	14	14	14	14	24	24	24	24	24	24	24	24	65	65	65	65	65	65	65	65	65	65	65	6
1 HAYDEN	5	33	33	33	33	33	33	33	33	65	65	65	65	65	33	71	71	71	71	71	71	71	71	71	71	7
24 ELIAS	33	5	5	5	65	65	65	65	65	33	33	33	33	33	71	33	33	33	33	33	33	33	33	33	4	8
33 MELANDRI	1	1	65	65	5	1	1	1	1	1	1	1	71	71	1	1	1	4	4	4	4	4	4	4	33	9
66 HOFMANN	71	65	1	1	1	4	4	4	4	4	71	71	1	1	4	4	4	1	1	1	1	1	1	1	5	10
71 VERMEULEN	65	4	4	4	4	71	71	71	71	71	4	4	4	4	5	5	5	5	5	5	5	5	5	5	1	11
56 NAKANO	4	71	71	71	71	5	5	5	5	5	5	5	5	5	6	6	6	6	6	6	6	6	6	6	6	12
50 GUINTOLI	66	66	66	50	50	50	50	50	50	50	50	50	6	6	50	50	50	50	50	50	66	66	66	66	66	13
4 BARROS	56	56	50	66	66	66	66	66	66	66	66	6	50	50	66	66	66	66	66	66	50	50	50	50	50	14
7 CHECA	50	50	56	56	6	6	6	6	6	6	6	66	66	66	56	56	56	56	56	56	56	56	56	56	56	15
6 TAMADA	7	7	6	6	56	56	56	56	56	56	56	56	56	56	7	7	7	7	7	7	7	7	7	10	10	
65 CAPIROSSI	80	6	7	7	7	7	7	7	7	7	7	7	7	7	80	80	80	80	10	10	10	10	10	7	7	
10 ROBERTS Jnr	6	80	80	80	80	80	80	80	80	80	80	80	80	80	10	10	10	10	80	80	80	80	80	80	80	
80 ROBERTS	10	10	10	10	10	10	10	10	10	10	10	10	10	10												

FASTEST RACE LAPS

	Rider	Lap	Time
1	Hopkins	8	1m 43.252s
2	Stoner	14	1m 43.317s
3	Rossi	6	1m 43.324s
4	Pedrosa	3	1m 43.376s
5	de Puniet	6	1m 43.642s
6	Elias	4	1m 43.663s
7	Capirossi	5	1m 43.834s
8	Melandri	2	1m 43.836s
9	Hayden	6	1m 43.987s
10	Vermeulen	14	1m 43.996s
11	Barros	7	1m 44.111s
12	Tamada	5	1m 44.267s
13	Edwards	5	1m 44.466s
14	Guintoli	5	1m 44.478s
15	Hofmann	9	1m 44.600s
16	Nakano	5	1m 44.972s
17	Checa	5	1m 45.314s
18	Roberts Jnr	21	1m 45.354s
19	Roberts	20	1m 45.702s

QUALIFYING
9 June 2007
Weather: Dry
Air: 33°C Humidity: 11%
Track: 45°C

Pos.	Rider	Time
1	Rossi	1m 41.840s
2	de Puniet	1m 41.901s
3	Pedrosa	1m 42.002s
4	Stoner	1m 42.117s
5	Hopkins	1m 42.233s
6	Edwards	1m 42.283s
7	Hayden	1m 42.522s
8	Elias	1m 42.607s
9	Melandri	1m 42.623s
10	Hofmann	1m 42.860s
11	Vermeulen	1m 42.967s
12	Nakano	1m 43.334s
13	Guintoli	1m 43.557s
14	Barros	1m 43.722s
15	Checa	1m 43.729s
16	Tamada	1m 43.947s
17	Capirossi	1m 43.948s
18	Roberts Jnr	1m 44.263s
19	Roberts	1m 45.223s

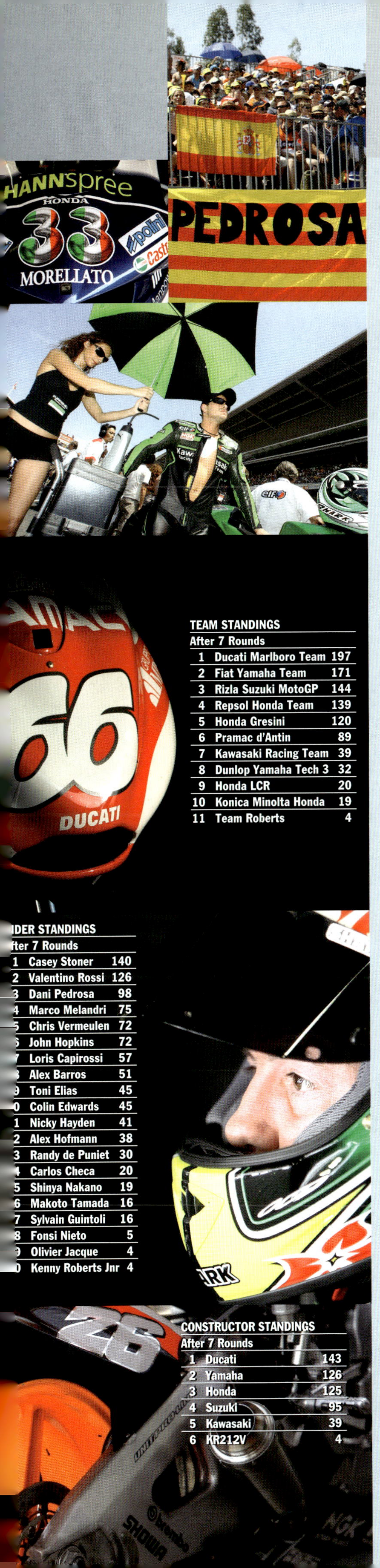

statistics

OFFICIAL TIMEKEEPER

250cc

23 laps, 67.551 miles/108.721km

Pos.	Rider (Nat.)	No.	Machine	Laps	Time & speed
1	Jorge Lorenzo (SPA)	1	Aprilia	23	40m 51.620s 99.200mph/ 159.647km/h
2	Alex de Angelis (RSM)	3	Aprilia	23	40m 54.814s
3	Andrea Dovizioso (ITA)	34	Honda	23	41m 02.216s
4	Thomas Luthi (SWI)	12	Aprilia	23	41m 08.720s
5	Alvaro Bautista (SPA)	19	Aprilia	23	41m 11.918s
6	Mika Kallio (FIN)	36	KTM	23	41m 12.186s
7	Hiroshi Aoyama (JPN)	4	KTM	23	41m 12.235s
8	Hector Barbera (SPA)	80	Aprilia	23	41m 15.204s
9	Marco Simoncelli (ITA)	58	Gilera	23	41m 28.323s
10	Julian Simon (SPA)	60	Honda	23	41m 28.387s
11	Shuhei Aoyama (JPN)	73	Honda	23	41m 31.212s
12	Roberto Locatelli (ITA)	15	Gilera	23	41m 39.648s
13	Jules Cluzel (FRA)	16	Aprilia	23	41m 58.705s
14	Karel Abraham (CZE)	17	Aprilia	23	42m 03.488s
15	Taro Sekiguchi (JPN)	44	Aprilia	23	42m 09.007s
16	Alex Debon (SPA)	6	Aprilia	23	42m 11.274s
17	Ratthapark Wilairot (THA)	8	Honda	23	42m 11.442s
18	Alex Baldolini (ITA)	25	Aprilia	23	42m 14.863s
19	Eugene Laverty (IRL)	50	Honda	23	42m 27.173s
20	Aleix Espargaro (SPA)	41	Aprilia	23	42m 34.149s
21	Anthony West (AUS)	14	Aprilia	23	42m 47.452s
22	Imre Toth (HUN)	10	Aprilia	22	40m 51.808s
23	Alvaro Molina (SPA)	31	Aprilia	22	40m 51.943s
	Yuki Takahashi (JPN)	55	Honda	22	DNF
	Dirk Heidolf (GER)	28	Aprilia	15	DNF
	Fabrizio Lai (ITA)	32	Aprilia	11	DNF
	Arturo Tizon (SPA)	9	Aprilia		DNS
	Santiago Barragan (SPA)	53	Honda		DNQ

Fastest lap: de Angelis, 1m 45.925s, 99.825mph/160.653km/h (record).

Previous lap record: Dani Pedrosa, SPA (Honda), 1m 47.302s, 98.544mph/158.591km/h (2004).

Event best maximum speed: Bautista, 172.5mph/277.6km/h (race).

Qualifying: 1 Lorenzo, 1m 45.098s; 2 Barbera, 1m 46.013s; 3 Dovizioso, 1m 46.201s; 4 Debon, 1m 46.333s; 5 Luthi, 1m 46.382s; 6 de Angelis, 1m 46.422s; 7 Bautista, 1m 46.436s; 8 Kallio, 1m 46.629s; 9 H. Aoyama, 1m 46.664s; 10 Simoncelli, 1m 46.666s; 11 Takahashi, 1m 46.667s; 12 Simon, 1m 46.836s; 13 S. Aoyama, 1m 47.037s; 14 Espargaro, 1m 47.100s; 15 Locatelli, 1m 47.820s; 16 West, 1m 47.894s; 17 Heidolf, 1m 47.903s; 18 Sekiguchi, 1m 47.932s; 19 Baldolini, 1m 48.180s; 20 Abraham, 1m 48.383s; 21 Lai, 1m 48.452s; 22 Wilairot, 1m 49.139s; 23 Laverty, 1m 49.310s; 24 Cluzel, 1m 49.347s; 25 Molina, 1m 49.416s; 26 Toth, 1m 49.729s; 27 Tizon, 1m 49.928s; 28 Barragan, 1m 54.203s.

Fastest race laps: 1 de Angelis, 1m 45.925s; 2 Lorenzo, 1m 45.949s; 3 Dovizioso, 1m 46.157s; 4 Luthi, 1m 46.408s; 5 Debon, 1m 46.546s; 6 H. Aoyama, 1m 46.663s; 7 Bautista, 1m 46.708s; 8 Kallio, 1m 46.717s; 9 Barbera, 1m 46.792s; 10 Simon, 1m 47.077s; 11 Simoncelli, 1m 47.100s; 12 Locatelli, 1m 47.375s; 13 S. Aoyama, 1m 47.407s; 14 Takahashi, 1m 47.746s; 15 Espargaro, 1m 47.939s; 16 West, 1m 48.003s; 17 Cluzel, 1m 48.476s; 18 Heidolf, 1m 48.717s; 19 Abraham, 1m 48.834s; 20 Wilairot, 1m 48.852s; 21 Sekiguchi, 1m 48.952s; 22 Baldolini, 1m 49.288s; 23 Lai, 1m 49.420s; 24 Laverty, 1m 49.581s; 25 Toth, 1m 50.163s; 26 Molina, 1m 50.355s.

World Championship: 1 Lorenzo, 153; 2 Dovizioso, 117; 3 de Angelis, 115; 4 Bautista, 100; 5 Barbera, 71; 6 Luthi, 56; 7 Simon, 52; 8 Kallio, 40; 9 Simoncelli, 38; 10 S. Aoyama, 37; 11 Lai, 28; 12 H. Aoyama, 26; 13 West, 25; 14 Takahashi, 22; 15 Espargaro, 19; 16 Wilairot, 16; 17 Locatelli, 14; 18 Debon, 11; 19 Heidolf, 10; 20 Baldolini, 10; 21 Abraham, 7; 22 Sekiguchi, 6; 23 Cluzel, 3; 24 Laverty, 3; 25 Tizon, 1.

125cc

22 laps, 64.614 miles/103.994km

Pos.	Rider (Nat.)	No.	Machine	Laps	Time & speed
1	Tomoyoshi Koyama (JPN)	71	KTM	22	41m 06.339s 94.321mph/ 151.795km/h
2	Gabor Talmacsi (HUN)	14	Aprilia	22	41m 06.388s
3	Randy Krummenacher (SWI)	34	KTM	22	41n 06.470s
4	Sergio Gadea (SPA)	33	Aprilia	22	41m 06.839s
5	Pol Espargaro (SPA)	44	Aprilia	22	41m 08.420s
6	Bradley Smith (GBR)	38	Honda	22	41m 11.131s
7	Simone Corsi (ITA)	24	Aprilia	22	41m 23.179s
8	Joan Olive (SPA)	6	Aprilia	22	41m 23.249s
9	Stefan Bradl (GER)	17	Aprilia	22	41m 23.258s
10	Michael Ranseder (AUT)	60	Derbi	22	41m 23.261s
11	Sandro Cortese (GER)	11	Aprilia	22	41m 23.451s
12	Esteve Rabat (SPA)	12	Honda	22	41m 23.594s
13	Lukas Pesek (CZE)	52	Derbi	22	41m 23.602s
14	Lorenzo Zanetti (ITA)	8	Aprilia	22	41m 30.046s
15	Dominique Aegerter (SWI)	77	Aprilia	22	41m 34.705s
16	Alexis Masbou (FRA)	7	Honda	22	41m 34.976s
17	Andrea Iannone (ITA)	29	Aprilia	22	41m 34.997s
18	Pere Tutusaus (SPA)	30	Aprilia	22	41m 35.365s
19	Mike di Meglio (FRA)	63	Honda	22	41m 35.958s
20	Pablo Nieto (SPA)	22	Aprilia	22	41m 38.139s
21	Federico Sandi (ITA)	15	Aprilia	22	41m 53.112s
22	Roberto Tamburini (ITA)	20	Aprilia	22	41m 53.700s
23	Nicolas Terol (SPA)	18	Derbi	22	42m 00.220s
24	Robert Muresan (ROU)	95	Derbi	22	42m 00.384s
25	Hugo van den Berg (NED)	56	Aprilia	22	42m 00.442s
26	Daniel Webb (GBR)	99	Honda	22	42m 26.509s
27	Ivan Masestro (SPA)	76	Aprilia	22	42m 43.273s
	Hector Faubel (SPA)	55	Aprilia	18	DNF
	Philipp Eitzinger (AUT)	85	Honda	12	DNF
	Simone Grotzkyj (ITA)	53	Aprilia	11	DNF
	Mattia Pasini (ITA)	75	Aprilia	2	DNF
	Raffaele de Rosa (ITA)	35	Aprilia	2	DNF
	Steve Bonsey (USA)	51	KTM	1	DNF
	Joey Litjens (NED)	37	Honda	0	DNF
	Dino Lombardi (ITA)	13	Honda		DNS

Fastest lap: Krummenacher, 1m 50.732s, 95.492mph/153.679km/h (record).

Previous lap record: Hector Faubel, SPA (Aprilia) 1m 50.773s, 95.456mph/153.622km/h (2006).

Event best maximum speed: Koyama, 146.0mph/235.0km/h (qualifying practice no. 2).

Qualifying: 1 Talmacsi, 1m 50.012s; 2 Faubel, 1m 50.336s; 3 Gadea, 1m 50.529s; 4 Smith, 1m 50.806s; 5 Pesek, 1m 50.933s; 6 de Rosa, 1m 50.945s; 7 Koyama, 1m 51.072s; 8 Pasini, 1m 51.170s; 9 Corsi, 1m 51.170s; 10 Iannone, 1m 51.295s; 11 Cortese, 1m 51.744s; 12 Rabat, 1m 51.799s; 13 Bradl, 1m 51.801s; 14 Olive, 1m 51.925s; 15 Krummenacher, 1m 51.930s; 16 di Meglio, 1m 51.985s; 17 Ranseder, 1m 51.995s; 18 Espargaro, 1m 52.050s; 19 Terol, 1m 52.069s; 20 Nieto, 1m 52.113s; 21 Zanetti, 1m 52.273s; 22 Masbou, 1m 52.383s; 23 Muresan, 1m 52.386s; 24 van den Berg, 1m 52.676s; 25 Tutusaus, 1m 52.677s; 26 Sandi, 1m 52.699s; 27 Aegerter, 1m 52.819s; 28 Grotzkyj, 1m 53.072s; 29 Tamburini, 1m 53.195s; 30 Eitzinger, 1m 53.619s; 31 Litjens, 1m 53.648s; 32 Bonsey, 1m 53.662s; 33 Lombardi, 1m 53.688s; 34 Maestro, 1m 53.859s; 35 Webb, 1m 54.939s.

Fastest race laps: 1 Krummenacher, 1m 50.732s; 2 Talmacsi, 1m 50.903s; 3 Pesek, 1m 50.903s; 4 Faubel, 1m 51.037s; 5 Espargaro, 1m 51.128s; 6 Koyama, 1m 51.131s; 7 Gadea, 1m 51.208s; 8 Smith, 1m 51.332s; 9 Ranseder, 1m 51.488s; 10 Zanetti, 1m 51.541s; 11 Olive, 1m 51.571s; 12 Pasini, 1m 51.572s; 13 Bradl, 1m 51.716s; 14 Cortese, 1m 51.799s; 15 Aegerter, 1m 51.919s; 16 Corsi, 1m 51.934s; 17 Nieto, 1m 51.941s; 18 Iannone, 1m 51.976s; 19 Rabat, 1m 51.978s; 20 Tutusaus, 1m 52.084s; 21 Terol, 1m 52.086s; 22 di Meglio, 1m 52.170s; 23 Masbou, 1m 52.175s; 24 Sandi, 1m 52.683s; 25 Grotzkyj, 1m 52.860s; 26 van den Berg, 1m 52.925s; 27 Tamburini, 1m 53.272s; 28 Muresan, 1m 43.277s; 29 Eitzinger, 1m 53.807s; 30 Webb, 1m 54.256s; 31 Maestro, 1m 54.842s; 32 de Rosa, 1m 57.981s; 33 Bonsey, 2m 01.419s.

World Championship: 1 Talmacsi, 115; 2 Faubel, 102; 3 Pesek, 94; 4 Corsi, 80; 5 Gadea, 79; 6 Koyama, 68; 7 Espargaro, 57; 8 Smith, 54; 9 Olive, 52; 10 Ranseder, 36; 11 de Rosa, 32; 12 Cortese, 32; 13 Rabat, 30; 14 Zanetti, 24; 15 Krummenacher, 23; 16 Nieto, 21; 17 Iannone, 17; 18 Pasini, 16; 19 Masbou, 13; 20 di Meglio, 11; 21 Bradl, 7; 22 Terol, 6; 23 Bianco, 5; 24 Bonsey, 3; 25 Aegerter, 2; 26 Grotzkyj, 1.

TEAM STANDINGS
After 7 Rounds

1	Ducati Marlboro Team	197
2	Fiat Yamaha Team	171
3	Rizla Suzuki MotoGP	144
4	Repsol Honda Team	139
5	Honda Gresini	120
6	Pramac d'Antin	89
7	Kawasaki Racing Team	39
8	Dunlop Yamaha Tech 3	32
9	Honda LCR	20
10	Konica Minolta Honda	19
11	Team Roberts	4

RIDER STANDINGS
After 7 Rounds

1	Casey Stoner	140
2	Valentino Rossi	126
3	Dani Pedrosa	98
4	Marco Melandri	75
5	Chris Vermeulen	72
6	John Hopkins	72
7	Loris Capirossi	57
8	Alex Barros	51
9	Toni Elias	45
10	Colin Edwards	45
11	Nicky Hayden	41
12	Alex Hofmann	38
13	Randy de Puniet	30
14	Carlos Checa	20
15	Shinya Nakano	19
16	Makoto Tamada	16
17	Sylvain Guintoli	16
18	Fonsi Nieto	5
19	Olivier Jacque	4
20	Kenny Roberts Jnr	4

CONSTRUCTOR STANDINGS
After 7 Rounds

1	Ducati	143
2	Yamaha	126
3	Honda	125
4	Suzuki	95
5	Kawasaki	39
6	KR212V	4

Main photograph: No easy way to make a living. Stoner heads Melandri and the Kawasakis of de Puniet and new boy West (13).

Right: Two out of three on the rostrum were from sunny Australia.

Centre right: Brolly good summer weather.

Far right: 250s in the gloom – Alex de Angelis leads the sufferers into Redgate.

Photographs: Gold & Goose

FIM WORLD CHAMPIONSHIP • ROUND 8

BRITISHGP

DONINGTON PARK

Welcome
NICKEL&DIME
NICKEL&DIME
NICKEL&DIME

NOLAN
27
73
alpinestars
DUCATI

Above: Nicky Hayden was an early victim of a treacherous Coppice Corner.

Top: Second-time pole starter Colin Edwards resists the temptation to pull a funny face on the grid.

Photographs: Gold & Goose

DONINGTON, opined Rossi on arrival, should be the perfect track for the 800s. The flowing corners would mean 'we can use all the good lines', while low overall gearing and a lack of long straights would mitigate against any relative lack of horsepower. As it turned out, pole time was quite a long way short of the 990s, but that was more down to circumstances. In a wet year, Britain laid on its summer worst for the GP, with drenching rain on Friday and Sunday, while Saturday's track was in no condition for fast times.

By the time the race rolled around, however, at least the track had rubbered up and dried slightly, although a number still went flying when they least expected it, including (again) Hayden, as well as newcomer/rainmaster Anthony West. On Friday, it had been even more treacherous, to the extent that Rossi, heading the safety commission for the regular meeting, demanded resurfacing. New boy West was too busy learning his new Kawasaki to bother, being fifth fastest in one session, and sixth overall for the day – quite a debut. He topped that by running fastest in wet morning warm-up, and with the leaders in the race, until his adventure at Coppice. He still finished 11th.

Rossi was one of several MotoGP riders who slid off in the first few minutes on Friday morning. He hadn't even been pushing, he said – the lack of grip was dangerous. This reflects years of problems of wet grip at Donington, clearly not solved by resurfacing three years ago. Various culprits have been blamed over the years, including the adjacent East Midlands airport and drifting unburnt fuel from aircraft on take-off. Race Director Paul Butler reminded the safety commission that, like any track, it improves during the course of a weekend. This mollified Rossi, who was able to joke about it the next day. 'We asked them to move the airport, but we don't have enough power,' he said. (He had fallen off again on Saturday morning, embarrassingly, on the way out of the pits. He explained he'd looked over his shoulder too long as Melandri came past at speed, and when he looked forward, he was already off the edge of the track. He slithered along at low speed in the mud. He said he felt so foolish that afterwards 'I tried to hide behind my bike.' He remounted and returned to the pits covered with mud, amid much mirth.)

The weekend began with the annual Day of Champions, again breaking records with a take of £217,000. Good support from the British fans, more than 84,000 of whom braved rainy race day. But they did themselves little credit by booing Stoner when he appeared on the auction stage, presumably because he had the temerity to be beating Rossi. The hostility was not confined to the Australian: Rossi's motorhome was among several daubed with angry graffiti after the race was over, by fans who had waited in vain for autographs.

They were denied the chance of a local hot-shot wild card when HRC put its foot down to prevent Johnny Rea from riding the second Roberts KR212V. Rea, who had recently taken his first BSB win, as well as victory in the Suzuka 300km, had been invited as much for publicity as anything: Team Roberts has a British sponsor, on-line car dealer Motorpoint.com, and Rea's presence would have guaranteed some TV time at last, as well as giving the youngster a taste of MotoGP. As Kenny Senior described it, 'It was a win-win situation for us. Honda Europe was very keen, and Honda Britain was very keen, but someone in Japan said no.' Presumably, they wanted to avoid risking a hot property for the forthcoming and all-important Suzuka eight-hour race. This left Kurtis as sole incumbent, since Kenny Junior had decided to withdraw from the team for the foreseeable future, with a proviso that he might return when the new chassis was ready. Why? 'The bike's too slow, and he's too old,' said his father, later explaining that his elder son was used to 1000cc bikes with ample horsepower, while Kurtis's background on 600cc racers suited him better for the relatively gutless new 800.

The Roberts privateer machine is particularly slow, but all the Hondas suffer from a lack of acceleration, among their other woes. Hayden had undergone some sort of a transformation, however, following his successful Catalunya tests of the new chassis. He qualified fourth, his best of the year, and was

fastest in the dry on Saturday morning. Among other things, he was backing off the traction control – not to encourage rear-wheel steering particularly, just for a better feel. 'We don't need near as much as the 990 – these things just don't have the power.' He had a new clutch too, better in the backshifts, but worse when you just closed the throttle, he said. It felt almost the same as the old clutch; the benefit was that it offered chances for improvement, whereas the old one was at the end of its development.

Team-mate Pedrosa may have been getting the parts sooner, but he had been winless for far too long for his liking, and was also smarting under his new nickname in the Spanish press. They called him The Voyeur, after his close spectator role at his home GP. Dominant winner at Donington in 2006, he had a disastrous race, suffering clutch trouble on the warm-up lap. He switched to his spare, set for the dry, and tailed off to eighth in the race. Back in the pit, he blew his top, threatening to walk away from Honda in 2008.

Luckless 125 ace Pasini, fresh from another seize and zero points the weekend before, claimed his fifth pole of the year, winning a fifth special-edition Tissot watch to add to his collection (two more from 2006). He'd have preferred race finishes, and quipped, 'If it all carries on going wrong for me, maybe next year I'll be selling watches for a living.'

Bridgestone not only flexed its muscles again in the wet, but also showed further development, with a new 16-inch rear that a few riders tried in the dry. Only Capirossi praised it, but it would be seen again in forthcoming races. In fact, pointed out Bridgestone racing boss Hiroshi Yamada, it was not the company's first tyre in that size, since it had made them for Kawasaki at Mugello in 2006.

It was another dire weekend for beleaguered Michelin, but its final act before leaving was accidental rather than deliberate revenge. During packing up for the rapid transfer to Assen, one of its trucks rolled forward, straight into one of the victorious Ducati team trucks, breaking the latter's windscreen. Ducati was obliged to find another towing unit in a hurry.

MOTOGP RACE – 30 laps

Colin Edwards took his second career pole by 'knocking his brain back to half speed'. Rossi was alongside and might have been ahead, had he not been baulked (he complained) on his fast lap by Roberts, running slowly on line. Pedrosa made for an all-Michelin front row; Hayden led row two from Stoner, the first Bridgestone man.

Warm-up was sodden, and while the rain was light as they lined up, the track was thoroughly wet. No question over tyre choice: full wets, although with numbers unrestricted, the range of compound choices was wide.

Edwards led into Redgate, Stoner slow away, after spinning up on a white line. By the end of the lap, Pedrosa was leading,

Main photograph: Loyal crowd risked bad weather, British Burgers and the Big Breakfast.

Below: The slip that cost West fourth place, after leading Rossi past Vermeulen.
Photographs: Gold & Goose

Above: Barros and team-mate Hofmann battled, until the Brazilian escaped.
Photograph: Gold & Goose

Top: Edwards led for 11 laps, but Stoner was not to be denied win number five.

Right: Rossi was lucky to survive this moment – and others.
Photographs: Clive Challinor Motorsport Photography

Rossi third, from Hopkins, Vermeulen and Hayden. Stoner was 1.5 seconds adrift, having got ahead of Melandri to lead the next group.

The Ducati closed up directly, with West following closely. Rossi was already losing places, troubled by a lack of feel. Both Hayden and Hopkins got by on the third lap, Stoner and West on the fourth.

Lap five saw a big shuffle: Pedrosa dropped from first to fifth – Edwards went past early in the lap, Stoner at the chicane, then both Suzukis at the Melbourne hairpin. This was the start of an inexorable slide backwards, sometimes losing two or three places a lap. His tyres were right, his bike settings very wrong.

Now Stoner was second, Hopkins with him, but Hayden had fallen trying to follow along, the first victim of the deceptively slippery brow leading on to Coppice corner. Vermeulen was having trouble with a fogged visor, but holding the pace.

Stoner stalked Edwards, the pair pulling out a lead of five seconds by lap ten. Now the Ducati rider started to apply some pressure, worried that the slowly drying track might destroy his tyres and wanting to build up a cushion. Edwards fought his rival and several front-wheel slides, and on lap 16 ran wide again into the Melbourne hairpin. Stoner was perfectly placed to take advantage and led from there to the end, pulling away at a second or more each lap to win by more than ten. Even though he had chosen the softest of Bridgestone's wet compounds, he said, the tyres had been faithful to the finish.

West was fourth behind the two Suzukis when he found the same slippery patch as Hayden, managing to stay on board for a rooster-tail, dirt-track ride across the gravel, only to fall finally at low speed. Now Rossi was fifth, busy putting some distance on a persistent de Puniet, and able to get past Vermeulen also on lap eight. In four more laps, he was past Hopkins and moving clear. Five seconds behind the leaders, and it was not yet half-distance. Definitely possible.

But no. The gap stretched instead, steadily at first, then faster. At the same time, Vermeulen's vision had improved; he had passed Hopkins and was speeding up. With four laps left, he caught and passed the fading Rossi quite easily. The Italian's tyre had been stripped bare on the drying track, he said later, the right side 'like a slick'.

Capirossi had qualified poorly again, but moved through steadily to take sixth off de Puniet on lap 20. He quickly demolished the three-second gap to fly past Hopkins three laps later.

Then he was down, having taken one too many risks. Hopkins regained fifth, with a strange tale. When a dry line did develop at the end, it didn't match his peculiar lines.

A few seconds behind, Pedrosa was under increasing pressure from Barros. They changed places more than once over the last two laps, Barros taking seventh by inches, Hofmann now right on Pedrosa's tail.

West had rejoined near the back and worked his way through to tenth. One of his victims, however, was Melandri, who gained confidence as the track dried and reversed the positions.

Elias was miles back, after narrowly surviving a high-speed run across the wet grass at Craner Curves. He set fastest lap at the end as he avoided being lapped.

Roberts was 13th, his best result, after running near the top ten in the first half of the race, then losing ground as the rain cleared. Nakano was close; Tamada and Guintoli another lap down, with Hayden four laps behind after rejoining, pitting, then cruising to the end with stones in his clutch among other damage. He'd hoped for a point or two just by finishing, but 17th was not good enough.

250cc RACE – 27 laps

De Angelis took his first pole of the year and was fastest also in the dry. Four-tenths down, Lorenzo headed Simon and Bautista, with Dovizioso sixth, alongside Kallio on row two. They lined up under heavy rain, for a race almost as gruelling for the spectators as the riders. Wet weather skills would be tested to the full, and frequently found wanting, with a huge number of crashes, several riders more than once – Barbera had the record, with three falls and remounts before he finally gave up.

De Angelis led away in a cloud of spray. Dovizioso and Lorenzo went with him, changing places on lap two, and all three stretching away. By lap ten, they were over 30 seconds clear, Bautista now fourth. A lap later, he was third – Lorenzo was down and out, another victim of Coppice's tricky entry. He ran back to try to rejoin, but his bike was too badly damaged.

De Angelis had a lead of two seconds at this point, and Dovizioso was content to let him set the pace as the laps clicked steadily away, the field thinning constantly. With seven laps to go, he started to push harder, nosing alongside now and then, until de Angelis fulfilled his reputation for vulnerability under pressure. As they started the penultimate lap, he tried that bit too hard through the notorious downhill Craner Curves. The front tucked under, and he was yet another to take the long slide across the wet grass.

At this point, they were over a minute clear of third place. He had time to jump back on and get going again without losing another place, finishing 22 seconds behind Dovizioso, whose second win of a hard year had showed real class. With Lorenzo no-scoring, it also revived his flagging title hopes.

Barbera had been the first of the fast men to fall, first time around the Melbourne Loop. Simoncelli had taken up the pursuit, only to experience the Craner roller-coaster on lap two, followed there one lap later by the dauntless Barbera again.

Now Simon led the chase, Bautista soon taking over; Hiro Aoyama was quickly past Simon too, Takahashi closing from behind, and Luthi still close. The gap to the leaders was growing fast, and Bautista had taken almost five seconds on his own account when he slipped of at McLeans.

Simon and Aoyama battled on, until the former fell at Coppice. Then the KTM rider had his hands full with Takahashi, battling all the way to claim the last rostrum spot by two-tenths.

Ten seconds behind, Kallio and Shuhei Aoyama had also been trading blows, until Kallio fell foul of Copse, although he remounted quickly enough to avoid being overtaken, He was the last rider on the same lap as the leaders; Simon was seventh, having also remounted.

Just finishing was a feat in itself, making an impressive achievement of Wilairot's career-best eighth. He had got away after good a battle with the impressive Dan Linfoot, who had taken over West's vacant Aprilia. Abraham was within sight in tenth; the rest were spread out, the last two being another lap behind. Luthi had also crashed, as well as Locatelli, Espargaro and Laverty.

125cc RACE – 25 laps

Pasini's pole was an imposing four-tenths ahead of Corsi and the rest, and it was time at last for his luck to turn.

Unusually, this was the last race of the day, and in luck with the weather. It had finally dried out, for a typically and furiously close Donington 125 race.

Pasini led the first lap, but dropped back to sixth in the brawl over the next two, as Corsi took over until lap 11. Pasini worked his way back through to pounce, however, and once leading, he gradually started to edge away. He had a second by lap 14 and then began to gain hand over fist, being almost five seconds clear before letting off to take a comfortable and long-awaited first win of the year.

'At last, my luck changes and I can show I am the fastest,' he said.

Koyama and Faubel disputed second, the KTM prevailing over the final laps by less than two seconds. Gadea had been close throughout, with Olive and di Meglio right there. Corsi had lost the group with a tumble at Melbourne on lap 14, but got back on quickly enough to finish that lap 12th and pull through to tenth. Smith led the next trio, taking seventh from de Rosa with a couple of laps to go, Nieto right behind.

Talmacsi had also been with the leaders, and was running sixth when he slowed suddenly and pitted – his turn to suffer the Aprilia disc-valve failure. He lost his points lead to Faubel as a result.

Espargaro fell twice, Masbou, Ranseder, van den Berg, Bianco and Rabat just once.

Below: Feather-footed; a questing Alex de Angelis and Andrea Dovizioso find the going very plashy.

Bottom: Pasini, flanked on the rostrum by Koyama and Faubel, at last turned his speed into victory.

Photographs: Gold & Goose

NICKEL & DIME BRITISH GRAND PRIX

24 JUNE 2007 • FIM WORLD CHAMPIONSHIP ROUND 8

DONINGTON PARK

Circuit 4.023km /2.500 miles

MotoGP

RACE: 30 laps, 75.000 miles/120.690km • Weather: Wet • Air 14°C • Humidity 90% • Track 18°C

Pos.	Rider	Nat.	No.	Entrant	Machine	Tyres	Laps	Time & speed (mph/km/h)
1	Casey Stoner	AUS	27	Ducati Marlboro Team	Ducati	B	30	51m 40.739s 87.068mph/ 140.122km/h
2	Colin Edwards	USA	5	Fiat Yamaha Team	Yamaha	M	30	51m 52.507s
3	Chris Vermeulen	AUS	71	Rizla Suzuki MotoGP	Suzuki	B	30	51m 56.417s
4	Valentino Rossi	ITA	46	Fiat Yamaha Team	Yamaha	M	30	52m 02.566s
5	John Hopkins	USA	21	Rizla Suzuki MotoGP	Suzuki	B	30	52m 16.257s
6	Randy de Puniet	FRA	14	Kawasaki Racing Team	Kawasaki	B	30	52m 17.213s
7	Alex Barros	BRA	4	Pramac d'Antin	Ducati	B	30	52m 18.833s
8	Dani Pedrosa	SPA	26	Repsol Honda Team	Honda	M	30	52m 19.731s
9	Alex Hofmann	GER	66	Pramac d'Antin	Ducati	B	30	52m 19.978s
10	Marco Melandri	ITA	33	Honda Gresini	Honda	B	30	52m 42.265s
11	Anthony West	AUS	13	Kawasaki Racing Team	Kawasaki	B	30	52m 47.225s
12	Toni Elias	SPA	24	Honda Gresini	Honda	B	30	53m 14.813s
13	Kurtis Roberts	USA	80	Team Roberts	KR212V	M	29	51m 47.281s
14	Shinya Nakano	JPN	56	Konica Minolta Honda	Honda	M	29	52m 50.579s
15	Makoto Tamada	JPN	6	Dunlop Yamaha Tech 3	Yamaha	D	28	52m 41.346s
16	Sylvain Guintoli	FRA	50	Dunlop Yamaha Tech 3	Yamaha	D	28	52m 54.413s
17	Nicky Hayden	USA	1	Repsol Honda Team	Honda	M	26	52m 58.768s
	Loris Capirossi	ITA	65	Ducati Marlboro Team	Ducati	B	24	41m 47.579s
	Carlos Checa	SPA	7	Honda LCR	Honda	M	4	7m 18.101s

Fastest lap: Toni Elias, on lap 28, 1m 41.428s, 88.724mph/142.788km/h.

Lap record: Dani Pedrosa, SPA (Honda), 1m 28.714s, 101.440mph/163.252km/h (2006).

Event best maximum speed: Casey Stoner, 169.8mph/273.2km/h (qualifying practice).

FASTEST RACE LAPS

	Rider	Lap	Time
1	Elias	28	1m 41.428s
2	Melandri	24	1m 41.473s
3	Capirossi	22	1m 41.794s
4	Stoner	21	1m 41.797s
5	Hofmann	27	1m 41.822s
6	Edwards	11	1m 41.843s
7	Rossi	9	1m 42.081s
8	Vermeulen	29	1m 42.102s
9	Barros	28	1m 42.213s
10	Pedrosa	23	1m 42.257s
11	de Puniet	30	1m 42.813s
12	Hopkins	9	1m 42.836s
13	West	7	1m 43.039s
14	Roberts	10	1m 44.531s
15	Hayden	4	1m 45.475s
16	Checa	4	1m 46.051s
17	Nakano	6	1m 46.069s
18	Tamada	7	1m 50.101s
19	Guintoli	11	1m 50.304s

Grid order	1	2	3	4	5	6	7	8	9	10	11	12	13	14	15	16	17	18	19	20	21	22	23	24	25	26	27	28	29	30	•
5 EDWARDS	26	26	26	26	5	5	5	5	5	5	5	5	5	5	5	27	27	27	27	27	27	27	27	27	27	27	27	27	27	27	1
46 ROSSI	5	5	5	5	27	27	27	27	27	27	27	27	27	27	27	5	5	5	5	5	5	5	5	5	5	5	5	5	5	5	2
26 PEDROSA	46	71	71	71	21	21	21	21	21	21	21	46	46	46	46	46	46	46	46	46	46	46	46	46	46	46	71	71	71	71	3
1 HAYDEN	21	46	1	21	71	71	71	46	46	46	46	21	21	21	21	71	71	71	71	71	71	71	71	71	71	71	46	46	46	46	4
27 STONER	71	1	21	27	26	13	13	71	71	71	71	71	71	71	71	21	21	21	21	21	21	21	65	65	21	21	21	21	21	21	5
21 HOPKINS	1	21	46	1	46	46	46	26	14	14	14	14	14	14	14	14	14	14	14	65	65	65	21	21	14	14	14	14	14	14	6
7 CHECA	27	27	27	13	13	26	26	14	26	26	26	26	26	65	65	65	65	65	65	14	14	14	14	14	26	26	26	26	26	4	7
14 de PUNIET	33	13	13	46	14	14	14	65	65	65	65	65	65	4	4	4	4	4	4	4	4	4	26	26	4	4	4	4	4	26	8
33 MELANDRI	13	14	14	14	65	65	65	4	4	4	4	4	4	26	26	26	26	26	26	26	26	26	4	4	66	66	66	66	66	66	9
24 ELIAS	14	33	65	65	66	4	4	66	66	66	66	66	66	66	66	66	66	66	66	66	66	66	66	66	13	33	33	33	33	33	10
56 NAKANO	7	65	33	7	4	66	66	33	33	80	80	80	80	80	80	80	13	13	13	13	13	13	13	13	33	13	13	13	13	13	11
71 VERMEULEN	65	7	7	66	33	33	33	56	80	33	33	33	33	13	13	13	80	80	80	33	33	33	33	33	80	24	24	24	24	24	12
65 CAPIROSSI	56	66	66	33	56	56	56	80	56	56	56	56	13	33	33	33	33	33	33	80	80	80	80	80	24	80	80	80	80		13
66 HOFMANN	66	4	4	4	80	80	80	24	24	13	13	13	56	56	56	56	56	56	24	24	24	24	24	24	56	56	56	56	56		14
4 BARROS	24	56	56	56	24	24	24	13	13	24	24	24	24	24	24	24	24	24	56	56	56	56	56	56	6	6	6	6			15
50 GUINTOLI	4	24	24	80	50	50	50	50	50	50	50	6	50	6	6	6	6	6	6	50	50	6	6	6	50	50	50	50			
13 WEST	80	80	80	24	6	6	6	6	6	6	6	50	6	50	50	50	50	50	50	6	6	50	50	50	1	1					
6 TAMADA	50	50	50	50	1	1	1	1	1	1	1	1	1	1	1	1	1	1	1	1	1	1	1	1							
80 ROBERTS	6	6	6	6																											

QUALIFYING
23 June 2007
Weather: Dry
Air: 18°C Humidity: 61%
Track: 29°C

Pos.	Rider	Time
1	Edwards	1m 28.531s
2	Rossi	1m 28.677s
3	Pedrosa	1m 28.863s
4	Hayden	1m 29.025s
5	Stoner	1m 29.061s
6	Hopkins	1m 29.073s
7	Checa	1m 29.281s
8	de Puniet	1m 29.415s
9	Melandri	1m 29.498s
10	Elias	1m 29.711s
11	Nakano	1m 29.718s
12	Vermeulen	1m 29.793s
13	Capirossi	1m 29.900s
14	Hofmann	1m 29.911s
15	Barros	1m 30.071s
16	Guintoli	1m 30.271s
17	West	1m 30.718s
18	Tamada	1m 30.800s
19	Roberts	1m 31.543s

statistics

RIDER STANDINGS
After 8 Rounds

1	Casey Stoner	165
2	Valentino Rossi	139
3	Dani Pedrosa	106
4	Chris Vermeulen	88
5	John Hopkins	83
6	Marco Melandri	81
7	Colin Edwards	65
8	Alex Barros	60
9	Loris Capirossi	57
10	Toni Elias	49
11	Alex Hofmann	45
12	Nicky Hayden	41
13	Randy de Puniet	40
14	Shinya Nakano	21
15	Carlos Checa	20
16	Makoto Tamada	17
17	Sylvain Guintoli	16
18	Anthony West	5
19	Fonsi Nieto	5
20	Olivier Jacque	4
21	Kenny Roberts Jnr	4
22	Kurtis Roberts	3

TEAM STANDINGS
After 8 Rounds

1	Ducati Marlboro Team	222
2	Fiat Yamaha Team	204
3	Rizla Suzuki MotoGP	171
4	Repsol Honda Team	147
5	Honda Gresini	130
6	Pramac d'Antin	105
7	Kawasaki Racing Team	54
8	Dunlop Yamaha Tech 3	33
9	Konica Minolta Honda	21
10	Honda LCR	20
11	Team Roberts	7

ONSTRUCTOR STANDINGS
fter 8 Rounds

1	Ducati	168
2	Yamaha	146
3	Honda	133
4	Suzuki	111
5	Kawasaki	49
6	KR212V	7

250cc

27 laps, 67.500 miles/108.621km

Pos.	Rider (Nat.)	No.	Machine	Laps	Time & speed
1	Andrea Dovizioso (ITA)	34	Honda	27	48m 40.173s 83.207mph/ 133.908km/h
2	Alex de Angelis (RSM)	3	Aprilia	27	49m 02.275s
3	Hiroshi Aoyama (JPN)	4	KTM	27	49m 43.310s
4	Yuki Takahashi (JPN)	55	Honda	27	49m 43.543s
5	Shuhei Aoyama (JPN)	73	Honda	27	50m 05.442s
6	Mika Kallio (FIN)	36	KTM	27	50m 47.506s
7	Julian Simon (SPA)	60	Honda	26	48m 46.333s
8	Ratthapark Wilairot (THA)	8	Honda	26	48m 53.923s
9	Dan Linfoot (GBR)	45	Aprilia	26	49m 03.623s
10	Karel Abraham (CZE)	17	Aprilia	26	49m 07.014s
11	Fabrizio Lai (ITA)	32	Aprilia	26	49m 40.756s
12	Dirk Heidolf (GER)	28	Aprilia	26	49m 44.105s
13	Taro Sekiguchi (JPN)	44	Aprilia	26	49m 55.840s
14	Alex Baldolini (ITA)	25	Aprilia	26	49m 57.649s
15	Imre Toth (HUN)	10	Aprilia	26	49m 58.272s
16	Efren Vazquez (SPA)	7	Aprilia	25	49m 08.436s
17	Toby Markham (GBR)	81	Yamaha	25	49m 12.039s
	Aleix Espargaro (SPA)	41	Aprilia	23	DNF
	Roberto Locatelli (ITA)	15	Gilera	14	DNF
	Jules Cluzel (FRA)	16	Aprilia	14	DNF
	Jorge Lorenzo (SPA)	1	Aprilia	10	DNF
	Thomas Luthi (SWI)	12	Aprilia	10	DNF
	Marco Simoncelli (ITA)	58	Gilera	9	DNF
	Alvaro Bautista (SPA)	19	Aprilia	8	DNF
	Eugene Laverty (IRL)	50	Honda	6	DNF
	Hector Barbera (SPA)	80	Aprilia	5	DNF
	Andrew Sawford (GBR)	82	Yamaha		DNQ
	Alex Kenchington (GBR)	83	Yamaha		DNQ

Fastest lap: de Angelis, 1m 45.461s, 85.332mph/137.328km/h.

Lap record: Andrea Dovizioso, ITA (Honda), 1m 33.029s, 96.735mph/155.680km/h (2006).

Event best maximum speed: Bautista, 149.3mph/240.3km/h (qualifying practice no. 2).

Qualifying: 1 de Angelis, 1m 32.391s; 2 Lorenzo, 1m 32.801s; 3 Simon, 1m 33.043s; 4 Bautista, 1m 33.096s; 5 Kallio, 1m 33.130s; 6 Dovizioso, 1m 33.170s; 7 Simoncelli, 1m 33.179s; 8 Barbera, 1m 33.209s; 9 Luthi, 1m 33.211s; 10 H. Aoyama, 1m 33.390s; 11 Takahashi, 1m 33.555s; 12 S. Aoyama, 1m 34.026s; 13 Locatelli, 1m 34.046s; 14 Lai, 1m 34.065s; 15 Laverty, 1m 34.489s; 16 Espargaro, 1m 34.634s; 17 Wilairot, 1m 34.857s; 18 Baldolini, 1m 35.033s; 19 Heidolf, 1m 35.237s; 20 Cluzel, 1m 35.398s; 21 Linfoot, 1m 35.448s; 22 Sekiguchi, 1m 35.705s; 23 Toth, 1m 35.812s; 24 Abraham, 1m 35.815s; 25 Vazquez, 1m 35.819s; 26 Markham, 1m 38.733s; 27 Sawford, 1m 39.602s; 28 Kenchington, 1m 40.695s.

Fastest race laps: 1 de Angelis, 1m 45.461s; 2 Dovizioso, 1m 45.839s; 3 Lorenzo, 1m 47.525s; 4 Takahashi, 1m 48.299s; 5 H. Aoyama, 1m 48.450s; 6 S. Aoyama, 1m 48.508s; 7 Kallio, 1m 48.629s; 8 Bautista, 1m 48.977s; 9 Luthi, 1m 49.395s; 10 Simon, 1m 49.406s; 11 Simoncelli, 1m 50.486s; 12 Wilairot, 1m 50.515s; 13 Locatelli, 1m 50.517s; 14 Linfoot, 1m 51.014s; 15 Espargaro, 1m 51.070s; 16 Abraham, 1m 51.079s; 17 Baldolini, 1m 51.779s; 18 Lai, 1m 52.008s; 19 Toth, 1m 52.049s; 20 Laverty, 1m 52.349s; 21 Sekiguchi, 1m 52.542s; 22 Heidolf, 1m 52.665s; 23 Cluzel, 1m 52.972s; 24 Vazquez, 1m 54.217s; 25 Markham, 1m 55.090s; 26 Barbera, 2m 11.134s.

World Championship: 1 Lorenzo, 153; 2 Dovizioso, 142; 3 de Angelis, 135; 4 Bautista, 100; 5 Barbera, 71; 6 Simon, 61; 7 Luthi, 56; 8 Kallio, 50; 9 S. Aoyama, 48; 10 H. Aoyama, 42; 11 Simoncelli, 38; 12 Takahashi, 35; 13 Lai, 33; 14 West, 25; 15 Wilairot, 24; 16 Espargaro, 19; 17 Locatelli, 14; 18 Heidolf, 14; 19 Abraham, 13; 20 Baldolini, 12; 21 Debon, 11; 22 Sekiguchi, 9; 23 Linfoot, 7; 24 Cluzel, 3; 25 Laverty, 3; 26 Tizon and Toth, 1.

125cc

25 laps, 62.500 miles/100.575km

Pos.	Rider (Nat.)	No.	Machine	Laps	Time & speed
1	Mattia Pasini (ITA)	75	Aprilia	25	41m 49.049s 89.667mph/ 144.305km/h
2	Tomoyoshi Koyama (JPN)	71	KTM	25	41m 52.302s
3	Hector Faubel (SPA)	55	Aprilia	25	41m 54.143s
4	Sergio Gadea (SPA)	33	Aprilia	25	41m 55.830s
5	Joan Olive (SPA)	6	Aprilia	25	41m 56.261s
6	Mike di Meglio (FRA)	63	Honda	25	41m 56.384s
7	Bradley Smith (GBR)	38	Honda	25	42m 02.554s
8	Raffaele de Rosa (ITA)	35	Aprilia	25	42m 02.934s
9	Pablo Nieto (SPA)	22	Aprilia	25	42m 03.416s
10	Simone Corsi (ITA)	24	Aprilia	25	42m 15.721s
11	Lorenzo Zanetti (ITA)	8	Aprilia	25	42m 16.109s
12	Sandro Cortese (GER)	11	Aprilia	25	42m 16.452s
13	Randy Krummenacher (SWI)	34	KTM	25	42m 27.261s
14	Enrique Jerez (SPA)	31	Honda	25	42m 30.954s
15	Andrea Iannone (ITA)	29	Aprilia	25	42m 37.831s
16	Robert Muresan (ROU)	95	Derbi	25	42m 54.049s
17	Simone Grotzkyj (ITA)	53	Aprilia	25	42m 54.769s
18	Lukas Pesek (CZE)	52	Derbi	25	42m 54.896s
19	Alexis Masbou (FRA)	7	Honda	25	43m 07.149s
20	Michael Ranseder (AUT)	60	Derbi	25	43m 07.487s
21	Joey Litjens (NED)	37	Honda	25	43m 12.271s
22	Luke Jones (GBR)	82	Honda	25	43m 13.050s
23	Steve Bonsey (USA)	51	KTM	25	43m 13.358s
24	Nicolas Terol (SPA)	18	Derbi	25	43m 16.440s
25	Daniel Webb (GBR)	99	Honda	25	43m 22.641s
26	Hugo van den Berg (NED)	56	Aprilia	25	43m 27.991s
27	Nikki Coates (GBR)	83	Honda	25	43m 29.452s
28	Robbie Stewart (GBR)	84	Honda	25	43m 29.602s
29	Roberto Tamburini (ITA)	20	Aprilia	24	42m 28.719s
30	Tom Hayward (GBR)	81	Honda	24	43m 00.549s
	Federico Sandi (ITA)	15	Aprilia	20	DNF
	Gabor Talmacsi (HUN)	14	Aprilia	19	DNF
	Kev Coghlan (GBR)	54	Honda	15	DNF
	Esteve Rabat (SPA)	12	Honda	13	DNF
	Stefano Bianco (ITA)	27	Aprilia	10	DNF
	Pol Espargaro (SPA)	44	Aprilia	10	DNF
	Dominique Aergerter (SWI)	77	Aprilia	4	DNF

Fastest lap: Pasini, 1m 38.188s, 91.652mph/147.500km/h.

Lap record: Alvaro Bautista, SPA (Aprilia), 1m 37.312s, 92.477mph/148.828km/h (2006).

Event best maximum speed: Tamburini, 133.4mph/214.7km/h (qualifying practice no. 2).

Qualifying: 1 Pasini, 1m 37.399s; 2 Corsi, 1m 37.846s; 3 Koyama, 1m 38.073s; 4 Talmacsi, 1m 38.153s; 5 Gadea, 1m 38.217s; 6 Faubel, 1m 38.238s; 7 Nieto, 1m 38.365s; 8 Masbou, 1m 38.386s; 9 Smith, 1m 38.394s; 10 Olive, 1m 38.427s; 11 Krummenacher, 1m 38.441s; 12 de Rosa, 1m 38.504s; 13 Espargaro, 1m 38.519s; 14 Iannone, 1m 38.813s; 15 di Meglio, 1m 38.990s; 16 Cortese, 1m 39.006s; 17 Zanetti, 1m 39.007s; 18 Ranseder, 1m 39.012s; 19 Tamburini, 1m 39.095s; 20 Bianco, 1m 39.229s; 21 Pesek, 1m 39.267s; 22 Terol, 1m 39.510s; 23 Sandi, 1m 39.640s; 24 Jerez, 1m 39.678s; 25 Aegerter, 1m 39.708s; 26 Muresan, 1m 40.065s; 27 van den Berg, 1m 40.126s; 28 Rabat, 1m 40.169s; 29 Litjens, 1m 40.184s; 30 Bonsey, 1m 40.566s; 31 Grotzkyj, 1m 40.771s; 32 Webb, 1m 41.131s; 33 Stewart, 1m 41.417s; 34 Jones, 1m 42.090s; 35 Coates, 1m 42.347s; 36 Coghlan, 1m 42.804s; 37 Hayward, 1m 43.800s.

Fastest race laps: 1 Pasini, 1m 38.188s; 2 Koyama, 1m 38.435s; 3 Olive, 1m 38.557s; 4 Faubel, 1m 38.600s; 5 Gadea, 1m 38.626s; 6 di Meglio, 1m 38.655s; 7 de Rosa, 1m 38.831s; 8 Smith, 1m 39.002s; 9 Krummenacher, 1m 39.220s; 10 Talmacsi, 1m 39.229s; 11 Cortese, 1m 39.287s; 12 Corsi, 1m 39.296s; 13 Zanetti, 1m 39.366s; 14 Nieto, 1m 39.394s; 15 Rabat, 1m 39.442s; 16 Masbou, 1m 39.605s; 17 Ranseder, 1m 39.923s; 18 Jerez, 1m 39.989s; 19 Iannone, 1m 40.277s; 20 Tamburini, 1m 40.298s; 21 Espargaro, 1m 40.375s; 22 Muresan, 1m 40.767s; 23 Bianco, 1m 40.869s; 24 Pesek, 1m 40.871s; 25 Grotzkyj, 1m 40.890s; 26 van den Berg, 1m 40.984s; 27 Bonsey, 1m 41.446s; 28 Litjens, 1m 41.453s; 29 Jones, 1m 41.498s; 30 Webb, 1m 41.516s; 31 Sandi, 1m 41.534s; 32 Stewart, 1m 42.091s; 33 Terol, 1m 42.104s; 34 Coates, 1m 42.145s; 35 Coghlan, 1m 42.765s; 36 Aegerter, 1m 44.540s; 37 Hayward, 1m 45.509s.

World Championship: 1 Faubel, 118; 2 Talmacsi, 115; 3 Pesek, 94; 4 Gadea, 92; 5 Koyama, 88; 6 Corsi, 86; 7 Olive, 63; 8 Smith, 63; 9 Espargaro, 57; 10 Pasini, 41; 11 de Rosa, 40; 12 Cortese, 36; 13 Ranseder, 36; 14 Rabat, 30; 15 Zanetti, 29; 16 Nieto, 28; 17 Krummenacher, 26; 18 di Meglio, 21; 19 Iannone, 18; 20 Masbou, 13; 21 Bradl, 7; 22 Terol, 6; 23 Bianco, 5; 24 Bonsey, 3; 25 Jerez, 2; 26 Aegerter, 2; 27 Grotzkyj, 1.

FIM WORLD CHAMPIONSHIP • ROUND 9

DUTCHTT ASSEN

Above: : Another brilliant performance, another fine win. Could Rossi turn his season around?

Right: The devil was in the detail of Yamaha's special Fiat livery.

Main photograph: Rossi stalked and eventually pounced; Stoner's race to second was faultless.

Photographs: Gold & Goose

agv
NOLAN
YAMAHA
27
DUCATI
SanDisk

Above: Hayden's revival carried him past team-mate Pedrosa and Hopkins to the first of three rostrum finishes.

Opposite, top right: Edwards on song, on his Yamaha of many colours.

Centre right: Rossi takes the lead from Stoner. Once ahead, he soon escaped.

Centre, far right: Team congratulations for Vermeulen's wet-weather pole.

Bottom right: Mid-field battle: Capirossi holds off Melandri, de Puniet, Hofmann and West.

Photographs: Gold & Goose

CLUB racers will be familiar with the system of drawing grid positions from a drawstring bag; cynics often suggest that racing would be more exciting if the fastest qualifiers were on the back row and the slowest up front. World Superbikes makes a one-lap individual shoot-out up front; Formula One has devised a complex triple-header system. MotoGP does it the old way, pole time being rewarded with the prime grid slot, on the inside for the first turn.

Since 2005, it's all been concentrated in the final session, and results are clouded by the qualifying tyres, the Michelins generally having an edge. The four-strokes compressed the grid, with ever-decreasing top-ten or top-15 time spans; the 800s have compressed it still more. At the same time, especially at tracks with few passing points, the starting position has become all the more important.

Rossi explained how improved tyre durability had diminished the value of another aspect of riding skill, and underlined the importance of a good start: 'Before, the race was more divided into different parts. At the end, the tyres slide a lot, so you have to control the bike more. Now the difference between the first lap and the last lap is a lot less.'

He was on row four, after Assen – her moods unaltered by recent radical surgery – added another imponderable. The final qualifying hour was wet, putting Vermeulen on pole and Melandri on row two, although both had been only average in the dry, while faster men, like Pedrosa, Rossi and Hayden, were ranged out behind wet-specialist neophyte Anthony West. Stoner, however, was second. The conditions had replicated the club-race lottery.

Rossi made a nonsense of his fears in a classic, inexorable surge from 11th on the grid to first past the flag. This time, it was his turn, after another vintage confrontation with second-placed Stoner. The Yamaha was no longer intimidated by the Ducati's surging power, while Rossi's corner speed and rhythm were smooth and unbeatable; Stoner did well to keep a cool head after his long-time lead and his dogged resistance were swept aside so comprehensively. At the half-way point of the season, however, he lost only five points of his significant championship lead.

There will come a time when riders will stop complaining about the emasculation of their beloved old Assen, and when MOTOCOURSE will cease reporting it, but that day is still some way off. The bad-mouthing was as widespread in 2007 as in 2006, following a lead set by a challenging Colin Edwards in the pre-event press conference: 'I don't know if the track builders are here, but they screwed it up. Every time they changed it. The old track was the best there ever was. Everything was cambered, everything had a little chicane in it. It'd be fine if they'd run it with crowns and cambers like the old track, but they just said: 'We'll make it flat!' But…here we are…'

Assen exacted revenge once more, singling out more than one rider for severe punishment. In 2006, it was Rossi and Elias; in 2007, it was Elias again, at the fast left Ramshoek (before the chicane), which had claimed Rossi – one of the few remaining parts of the old track. Elias suffered a spiral fracture to his left femur after catching his leg in the gravel trap; he would be out until after the summer break. Bradley Smith was the other to leave the track straight for hospital in Barcelona, where doctors added knee fractures to the list already comprising ankle and wrist. He'd been struck on the left side by Iannone during practice, the Italian running wide while Smith was travelling slowly on the outside line.

Fiat was launching its new Cinquecento minicar with worldwide celebrations of the 50th birthday of its iconic eponymous predecessor. The Yamaha team was integrated into the group launch, with bikes and riders in a special livery, for which words like 'bold' or 'challenging' do not go far enough. All pinks and greens, and line drawings and cartoons, the bikes looked great to some, hideous to others. It was for one race only, and an interesting demonstration of the commercial importance to Fiat of the Rossi connection. He did the company proud. The new Cinquecento and the MotoGP bike did have one other thing in common – neither is 500cc any more.

Now that things were turning around somewhat, at least for the factory Hondas, Nicky Hayden spoke for the first time of his reaction to HRC chief Satoru Horiike's revelation in China that his needs had not been considered at all with the new 800. 'It about broke my heart,' he told a press briefing. 'I hope he doesn't have anything else like that to say to me.' For Horiike was back in the paddock, to play down rumours of a post-Donington rift with Pedrosa, and to reiterate his earlier statements that the bike had been built with no particular rider in mind – neither Dani nor Nicky. Honda was working hard in all areas to improve its machine; had made 'many, many exhausts'; and was 'making plans to supply new parts to satellite teams step by step.' Nothing new there, except that the level of the factory machines at least continued to improve.

Schwantz, all-time lap record holder of the old traditional circuit, was at the track with the negative news that Suzuki would not field a second team in 2008 after all. His name had been linked increasingly with rumours of a Spanish-based outfit, to be run by 125 and 250 team magnate Jorge 'Aspar' Martinez.

There was another small step toward the envisaged MotoGP-only paddock of the future, with new, Dorna-issue, brushed-metal 'totem poles' outside each team hospitality unit, made to match the new paddock entry/exit gates. Only MotoGP teams had the poles.

MOTOGP RACE – 26 laps

Rossi eventually topped the three dry free sessions, but Vermeulen led the sodden qualifying hour. Second in both conditions was Stoner, flying from his very first out lap, a spill at the chicane in morning warm-up his only lapse of the weekend.

De Puniet was third in qualifying, pushing Melandri to head row two from Hopkins and Edwards; West (17th in the dry) impressed again by heading row three. Rossi had copied some of Edwards's rear settings, but his timing was wrong and he was 11th. Even more disgruntled, Hayden was 13th, although third in the dry and fastest in race-morning warm-up.

Stoner was clearly in front as they peeled into turn one, Rossi stuck mid-pack, but Hayden cut an orange streak around the

Above: A typically boisterous Assen crowd enjoys the action.

Below: All-time Assen lap record holder Kevin Schwantz.

Photographs: Gold & Goose

outside. He got into fifth, lost it to Edwards again, and took it back at the chicane at the end of a very aggressive first lap. 'My bike was as good as it's ever been; I decided to ride like a dog,' he explained.

Stoner was 1.2 seconds clear, but would not run away, Hopkins having taken second off Vermeulen; Melandri was fourth. Both would drop back almost at once, and by lap four, Hayden was up to third, with Pedrosa inches behind, following every move. The gap to Hopkins was 2.5 seconds, and he was more than keeping the leading Ducati in sight.

Rossi had finished lap one ninth, but on the fourth, he passed Capirossi, Melandri and Edwards one after the other. Next time around, he swept inside Vermeulen for fifth and started closing steadily on the Hondas. He was riding with fluid grace and visibly high corner speed. On lap seven, he scythed past Pedrosa into the chicane, and was poised and ready when Hayden's Honda took a little slide on the left-hander out on the old circuit. He dived straight past into the next double rights.

He was more than 2.5 seconds off Hopkins, but before half-distance, he was on the Suzuki and simply rode past on the inside coming out of the new Strubben hairpin. At the end of lap 12, Rossi was 1.528 seconds behind Stoner; he set fastest lap (short of the 990 record) next time around to cut the deficit to half a second.

The race was on. He pushed and probed, hoping to force an error. The young Australian was steadfast in defence, quite unruffled. Did he have something in reserve?

No. That was Rossi, after getting his breath back and easing off on his tyres. Several times, he had lunged threateningly alongside under braking for the chicane. With four laps to go, he did so decisively, pulling away immediately, by almost a second a lap for the next two. It was a magnificent performance, 'a greater race,' he said, than a similar ride from 11th to victory in Germany in 2006.

Hayden and Pedrosa had passed Hopkins as the Suzuki lost pace after half-distance. They were still just two seconds adrift of the leaders and inches apart, but by the end, sliding tyres forced Pedrosa to ease off, and eventually Hayden also. He was thrilled with his hard-won first podium of the year.

Edwards became stuck early on behind Melandri and then Vermeulen, finally getting ahead on lap nine, too late to get back with the Hondas. By then, De Puniet was closing fast on the Suzuki, having been left on the line from the front row. On lap 12, the Frenchman lined up a daring inside pass, but he was too far back, and when he got there, Vermeulen had already turned in. They collided; De Puniet went flying, Vermeulen weaved across the gravel to rejoin last.

This promoted Barros to seventh, after he had worked through from a bad start. Behind him, there was a brawl. Capirossi played a leading role, and Melandri had settled there; West was always prominent, Dunlop-shod Tamada having some rare fun, Checa and Hofmann catching up.

At half-distance, West was in front of Melandri, Hofmann and Checa looming. Tamada was off the back, Capirossi likewise, complaining of both clutch and front-tyre problems.

Hofmann escaped, while the Kawasaki novice held Melandri and Checa narrowly behind him through the chicane. Melandri was so angry at his continuing struggle with the new Honda that he smashed his screen as he crossed the line.

Nakano, having an even harder time adapting, had passed countryman Tamada with eight laps left; Guintoli was just three seconds behind his team-mate. Kurtis Roberts gained a distant final point, a major setting change proving adverse in terms of grip and confidence; Vermeulen was six seconds behind.

250cc RACE – 24 laps

After disaster at Donington, Lorenzo was in no mood to trifle, claiming his sixth pole in eight races by a full seven-tenths. His Aprilia's pace left Dovizioso's Honda trailing in second in practice, and would do worse in the race. Bautista and Hiro Aoyama were close front-row companions; Barbera led row two from Luthi, who had missed the second day after a thumping fall on the first.

Dovizioso led away, nimble through the first tight section. By the time they got to the end of the back straight, however, Lorenzo was ready to pounce. He would never be headed again, although the Italian rode the clearly slower Honda with exemplary courage and gusto to stay close for six laps or so. Even then, he was seldom closer than 1.5 seconds, and the effort would cost him dear later.

Barbera had been third away, but was about to be swamped. De Angelis was ahead of him on lap two, Bautista too; the apparently recuperated Luthi was snapping at his heels and also about to get by.

De Angelis was the fastest, and he stretched away steadily, at the same time closing up on Dovizioso. Once on his tail, he wasted no time, taking a daring dive at the flat-out Hoge Heide kink on the old track.

Dovizioso could do little but watch him disappear; de Angelis had his sights set on the leader, and after ten laps, he was within a second and getting ready to challenge. A lap later, Lorenzo got the message, and his usual late-race pace soon began to tell; he went on to win by nigh on four seconds.

The pursuit was a dour procession down to fifth. Bautista had also got ahead of the demoralised Dovizioso, but Aoyama had dropped back into a brawl. Simon had been prominent, but pitted after seven laps. At half-distance, Aoyama was heading team-mate Kallio, Simoncelli and Barbera. Then the last-named lost ground after one of his trademark narrow escapes – he nearly high-sided out of the chicane and had to fight to regain control for a good distance down the start-finish straight. Next Kallio suffered a big slide, saved it with his knee, but dropped out of the battle.

The remaining trio caught Luthi, who was swamped and retired directly. The fight went on to the end, but with no more changes of position, Aoyama, Simoncelli and Barbera being covered by less than three seconds.

Kallio was seven seconds away, and almost half a minute clear of the next group, where Locatelli took a popular ninth after an almost race-long battle with Takahashi and Lai.

Sekiguchi led the following gaggle from Shuhei Aoyama, Wilairot and Abraham (Cardion Aprilia), with Heidolf close, but out of the points.

West's replacement, Dan Linfoot, was the only person to crash, rather spectacularly.

Half-way through the year, another win for Lorenzo dashed any hopes Dovizioso might have had awakened at Donington. Now the Italian shared second overall with de Angelis, each of them 23 points behind Lorenzo.

Left: Chasing Lorenzo – de Angelis tucked in and going for it.

Below left: Retired rider Sebastian Porto re-accquaints himself with the 250cc grid.

Photographs: Gold & Goose

125cc RACE – 22 laps

There had always been the feeling that when everything went right for Pasini, the other riders would hardly see which way he had gone, and so it was at Assen. Starting from his fifth pole, he took the lead from Corsi half-way around lap one and motored away to win by more than six seconds. 'A perfect day. I was able to set my own pace,' he said.

Pesek was second on the grid, Corsi and Gadea completing row one.

Gadea had also passed Corsi on the first lap, with Talmacsi, Pesek and Faubel right behind; Koyama soon dropped off the back of the gang, only to rejoin again by race end.

Pasini kept pulling away as the battle for second went back and forth, with Gadea and Talmacsi doing most of the leading. The former led on to the last lap, team-mates Talmacsi and Faubel heading the gang in pursuit. It was decided in the final fumble through the chicane, Faubel getting the best of it from Talmacsi; Gadea led Koyama and Pesek.

Cortese was eighth, final victor in a long battle with Ranseder, while Bradl dropped out of it in the closing stages.

Danny Webb crashed heavily into the back of Bonsey at the end of the back straight, but the American survived to finish 27th place.

The title fight stayed close enough, although Faubel stretched his lead over Talmacsi to seven points. Gadea, Pesek and Koyama remained within striking distance, but Pasini remained 72 points adrift.

Above: An easy win for Pasini.

Above left: Barbera had another trademark narrow escape, to finish seventh.

Left: The 125 battle for second: Gadea heads Talmacsi, Corsi, Faubel and Pesek.

Photographs: Gold & Goose

A-STYLE TT ASSEN

30 JUNE 2007 • FIM WORLD CHAMPIONSHIP ROUND 9

TT ASSEN

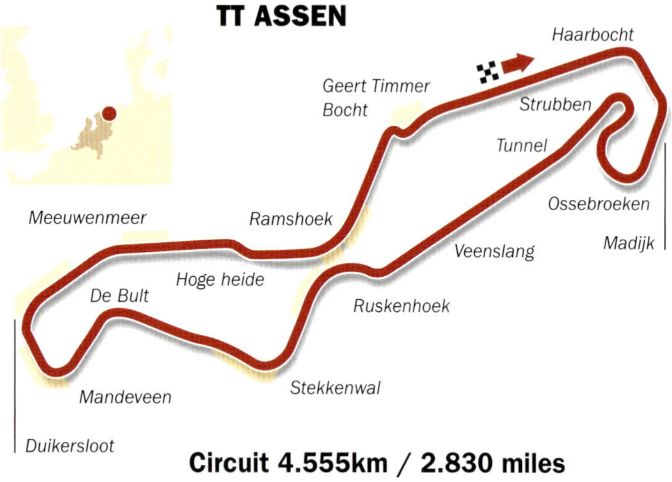

Circuit 4.555km / 2.830 miles

MotoGP

RACE: 26 laps, 73.580 miles/118.430km • Weather: Dry • Air 21°C • Humidity 38% • Track 32°C

Pos.	Rider	Nat.	No.	Entrant	Machine	Tyres	Laps	Time & speed (mph/km/h)
1	Valentino Rossi	ITA	46	Fiat Yamaha Team	Yamaha	M	26	42m 37.149s 103.599mph/ 166.727km/h
2	Casey Stoner	AUS	27	Ducati Marlboro Team	Ducati	B	26	42m 39.058s
3	Nicky Hayden	USA	1	Repsol Honda Team	Honda	M	26	42m 43.226s
4	Dani Pedrosa	SPA	26	Repsol Honda Team	Honda	M	26	42m 47.614s
5	John Hopkins	USA	21	Rizla Suzuki MotoGP	Suzuki	B	26	42m 50.287s
6	Colin Edwards	USA	5	Fiat Yamaha Team	Yamaha	M	26	42m 52.288s
7	Alex Barros	BRA	4	Pramac d'Antin	Ducati	B	26	43m 13.224s
8	Alex Hofmann	GER	66	Pramac d'Antin	Ducati	B	26	43m 18.917s
9	Anthony West	AUS	13	Kawasaki Racing Team	Kawasaki	B	26	43m 20.754s
10	Marco Melandri	ITA	33	Honda Gresini	Honda	B	26	43m 20.945s
11	Carlos Checa	SPA	7	Honda LCR	Honda	M	26	43m 20.975s
12	Shinya Nakano	JPN	56	Konica Minolta Honda	Honda	M	26	43m 25.045s
13	Makoto Tamada	JPN	6	Dunlop Yamaha Tech 3	Yamaha	D	26	43m 31.217s
14	Sylvain Guintoli	FRA	50	Dunlop Yamaha Tech 3	Yamaha	D	26	43m 34.867s
15	Kurtis Roberts	USA	80	Team Roberts	KR212V	M	26	44m 05.786s
16	Chris Vermeulen	AUS	71	Rizla Suzuki MotoGP	Suzuki	B	26	44m 11.957s
	Loris Capirossi	ITA	65	Ducati Marlboro Team	Ducati	B	17	28m 48.517s
	Randy de Puniet	FRA	14	Kawasaki Racing Team	Kawasaki	B	11	18m 14.507s

Fastest lap: Valentino Rossi, on lap 13, 1m 37.433s, 104.577mph/168.300km/h.

Lap record: Nicky Hayden, USA (Honda), 1m 37.106s, 104.929mph/168.867km/h (2006).

Event best maximum speed: Casey Stoner, 181.1mph/291.5km/h (race).

Grid order	1	2	3	4	5	6	7	8	9	10	11	12	13	14	15	16	17	18	19	20	21	22	23	24	25	26	•
71 VERMEULEN	27	27	27	27	27	27	27	27	27	27	27	27	27	27	27	27	27	27	27	27	27	27	46	46	46	46	1
27 STONER	21	21	21	21	21	21	21	21	21	21	21	46	46	46	46	46	46	46	46	46	46	46	27	27	27	27	2
14 de PUNIET	71	71	71	1	1	1	1	46	46	46	46	21	21	1	1	1	1	1	1	1	1	1	1	1	1	1	3
33 MELANDRI	33	1	1	26	26	26	46	1	1	1	1	1	1	26	26	26	26	26	26	26	26	26	26	26	26	26	4
21 HOPKINS	1	33	26	71	46	46	26	26	26	26	26	26	26	21	21	21	21	21	21	21	21	21	21	21	21	21	5
5 EDWARDS	5	26	33	46	71	71	71	71	5	5	5	5	5	5	5	5	5	5	5	5	5	5	5	5	5	5	6
13 WEST	26	5	5	5	5	5	5	5	71	71	71	4	4	4	4	4	4	4	4	4	4	4	4	4	4	4	7
66 HOFMANN	65	65	65	33	65	14	14	14	14	14	14	13	13	13	33	33	33	33	33	66	66	66	66	66	66	66	8
26 PEDROSA	46	46	46	65	14	65	33	33	33	4	4	33	66	33	13	13	13	13	66	33	33	13	13	13	13	13	9
65 CAPIROSSI	14	14	14	14	33	33	65	65	4	33	13	66	33	66	66	66	66	66	13	13	13	33	33	33	33	33	10
46 ROSSI	66	66	66	66	66	66	66	4	65	65	65	7	7	7	7	7	7	7	7	7	7	7	7	7	7	7	11
4 BARROS	13	13	13	13	13	4	4	66	13	13	33	6	6	6	6	6	6	6	56	56	56	56	56	56	56	56	12
1 HAYDEN	6	6	6	4	4	13	13	13	66	66	66	65	50	50	50	50	56	56	6	6	6	6	6	6	6	6	13
80 ROBERTS	56	4	4	6	6	6	6	6	6	6	6	50	56	56	56	56	50	50	50	50	50	50	50	50	50	50	14
56 NAKANO	4	50	50	50	50	50	50	50	50	50	7	56	65	65	65	65	65	80	80	80	80	80	80	80	80	80	15
7 CHECA	50	56	7	7	7	7	7	7	7	7	50	71	71	80	80	80	80	71	71	71	71	71	71	71	71	71	
50 GUINTOLI	7	7	56	56	56	56	56	56	56	56	56	80	80	71	71	71	71										
6 TAMADA	80	80	80	80	80	80	80	80	80	80	80																

FASTEST RACE LAPS

	Rider	Lap	Time
1	Rossi	13	1m 37.433s
2	Hayden	7	1m 37.797s
3	Pedrosa	11	1m 37.837s
4	Hopkins	3	1m 37.848s
5	Stoner	20	1m 37.906s
6	Edwards	11	1m 37.931s
7	de Puniet	7	1m 38.037s
8	Vermeulen	6	1m 38.582s
9	West	3	1m 38.835s
10	Barros	5	1m 38.845s
11	Hofmann	4	1m 38.878s
12	Capirossi	3	1m 38.922s
13	Tamada	6	1m 38.985s
14	Checa	10	1m 38.986s
15	Guintoli	7	1m 39.102s
16	Melandri	6	1m 39.114s
17	Nakano	6	1m 39.233s
18	Roberts	21	1m 40.213s

QUALIFYING

29 June 2007

Weather: Wet

Air: 14°C Humidity: 85%

Track: 16°C

Pos.	Rider	Time
1	Vermeulen	1m 48.555s
2	Stoner	1m 48.572s
3	de Puniet	1m 49.579s
4	Melandri	1m 49.679s
5	Hopkins	1m 49.684s
6	Edwards	1m 49.691s
7	West	1m 49.807s
8	Hofmann	1m 49.927s
9	Pedrosa	1m 50.132s
10	Capirossi	1m 50.169s
11	Rossi	1m 50.392s
12	Barros	1m 50.402s
13	Hayden	1m 50.581s
14	Roberts	1m 51.259s
15	Nakano	1m 51.827s
16	Checa	1m 53.271s
17	Guintoli	1m 54.253s
18	Tamada	1m 57.525s

statistics

TEAM STANDINGS

After 9 Rounds

1	Ducati Marlboro Team	242
2	Fiat Yamaha Team	239
3	Rizla Suzuki MotoGP	182
4	Repsol Honda Team	176
5	Honda Gresini	136
6	Pramac d'Antin	122
7	Kawasaki Racing Team	61
8	Dunlop Yamaha Tech 3	38
9	Honda LCR	25
10	Konica Minolta Honda	25
11	Team Roberts	8

IDER STANDINGS

fter 9 Rounds

1	Casey Stoner	185
2	Valentino Rossi	164
3	Dani Pedrosa	119
4	John Hopkins	94
5	Chris Vermeulen	88
6	Marco Melandri	87
7	Colin Edwards	75
8	Alex Barros	69
9	Loris Capirossi	57
0	Nicky Hayden	57
1	Alex Hofmann	53
2	Toni Elias	49
3	Randy de Puniet	40
4	Carlos Checa	25
5	Shinya Nakano	25
6	Makoto Tamada	20
7	Sylvain Guintoli	18
8	Anthony West	12
9	Fonsi Nieto	5
0	Olivier Jacque	4
1	Kurtis Roberts	4
2	Kenny Roberts Jnr	4

CONSTRUCTOR STANDINGS

After 9 Rounds

1	Ducati	188
2	Yamaha	171
3	Honda	149
4	Suzuki	122
5	Kawasaki	56
6	KR212V	8

250cc

24 laps, 67.920 miles/109.320km

Pos.	Rider (Nat.)	No.	Machine	Laps	Time & speed
1	Jorge Lorenzo (SPA)	1	Aprilia	24	40m 25.904s 100.804mph/ 162.229km/h
2	Alex de Angelis (RSM)	3	Aprilia	24	40m 29.761s
3	Alvaro Bautista (SPA)	19	Aprilia	24	40m 34.587s
4	Andrea Dovizioso (ITA)	34	Honda	24	40m 43.852s
5	Hiroshi Aoyama (JPN)	4	KTM	24	40m 56.704s
6	Marco Simoncelli (ITA)	58	Gilera	24	40m 57.039s
7	Hector Barbera (SPA)	80	Aprilia	24	40m 59.227s
8	Mika Kallio (FIN)	36	KTM	24	41m 06.711s
9	Roberto Locatelli (ITA)	15	Gilera	24	41m 37.733s
10	Yuki Takahashi (JPN)	55	Honda	24	41m 44.862s
11	Fabrizio Lai (ITA)	32	Aprilia	24	41m 45.265s
12	Taro Sekiguchi (JPN)	44	Aprilia	24	41m 52.714s
13	Shuhei Aoyama (JPN)	73	Honda	24	41m 52.754s
14	Ratthapark Wilairot (THA)	8	Honda	24	41m 54.621s
15	Karel Abraham (CZE)	17	Aprilia	24	41m 54.853s
16	Dirk Heidolf (GER)	28	Aprilia	24	41m 56.311s
17	Aleix Espargaro (SPA)	41	Aprilia	24	41m 59.716s
18	Efren Vazquez (SPA)	7	Aprilia	24	42m 03.610s
19	Alex Baldolini (ITA)	25	Aprilia	24	42m 10.829s
20	Jules Cluzel (FRA)	16	Aprilia	24	42m 13.277s
21	Eugene Laverty (IRL)	50	Honda	23	40m 34.583s
22	Imre Toth (HUN)	10	Aprilia	23	40m 52.632s
23	Ronald Beitler (NED)	69	Honda	23	42m 13.637s
24	Randy Gevers (NED)	68	Aprilia	21	41m 14.474s
	Thomas Luthi (SWI)	12	Aprilia	18	DNF
	Dan Linfoot (GBR)	45	Aprilia	11	DNF
	Hans Smees (NED)	72	Aprilia	10	DNF
	Julian Simon (SPA)	60	Honda	8	DNF
	Mike Velthuijzen (NED)	70	Honda		DNQ

Fastest lap: de Angelis, 1m 40.354s, 101.533mph/163.401km/h (record).

Previous lap record: Jorge Lorenzo, SPA (Aprilia), 1m 40.500s, 101.385mph/ 163.164km/h (2006).

Event best maximum speed: Bautista, 156.2mph/251.3km/h (qualifying practice no. 1).

Qualifying: 1 Lorenzo, 1m 39.958s; 2 Dovizioso, 1m 40.681s; 3 Bautista, 1m 41.128s; 4 H. Aoyama, 1m 41.226s; 5 Barbera, 1m 41.367s; 6 Luthi, 1m 41.408s; 7 de Angelis, 1m 41.443s; 8 Simoncelli, 1m 41.532s; 9 Simon, 1m 41.574s; 10 Kallio, 1m 41.892s; 11 Lai, 1m 41.986s; 12 Espargaro, 1m 42.924s; 13 Locatelli, 1m 42.938s; 14 S. Aoyama, 1m 42.987s; 15 Takahashi, 1m 42.996s; 16 Baldolini, 1m 43.079s; 17 Wilairot, 1m 43.115s; 18 Cluzel, 1m 43.649s; 19 Sekiguchi, 1m 43.781s; 20 Abraham, 1m 43.894s; 21 Laverty, 1m 44.148s; 22 Heidolf, 1m 44.314s; 23 Linfoot, 1m 44.569s; 24 Smees, 1m 44.652s; 25 Toth, 1m 44.787s; 26 Vazquez, 1m 44.959s; 27 Beitler, 1m 46.765s; 28 Gevers, 1m 46.887s; 29 Velthuijzen, 1m 48.800s.

Fastest race laps: 1 de Angelis, 1m 40.354s; 2 Lorenzo, 1m 40.432s; 3 Bautista, 1m 40.661s; 4 Dovizioso, 1m 40.934s; 5 Luthi, 1m 41.436s; 6 Kallio, 1m 41.526s; 7 H. Aoyama, 1m 41.554s; 8 Simoncelli, 1m 41.638s; 9 Barbera, 1m 41.659s; 10 Simon, 1m 41.853s; 11 Locatelli, 1m 42.845s; 12 S. Aoyama, 1m 43.085s; 13 Abraham, 1m 43.407s; 14 Takahashi, 1m 43.412s; 15 Heidolf, 1m 43.439s; 16 Wilairot, 1m 43.463s; 17 Cluzel, 1m 43.742s; 18 Lai, 1m 43.761s; 19 Sekiguchi, 1m 43.843s; 20 Baldolini, 1m 43.891s; 21 Espargaro, 1m 43.944s; 22 Vazquez, 1m 44.059s; 23 Laverty, 1m 44.152s; 24 Toth, 1m 44.826s; 25 Linfoot, 1m 44.967s; 26 Smees, 1m 45.292s; 27 Gevers, 1m 48.064s; 28 Beitler, 1m 48.836s.

World Championship: 1 Lorenzo, 178; 2 Dovizioso, 155; 3 de Angelis, 155; 4 Bautista, 116; 5 Barbera, 80; 6 Simon, 61; 7 Kallio, 58; 8 Luthi, 56; 9 H. Aoyama, 53; 10 S. Aoyama, 51; 11 Simoncelli, 48; 12 Takahashi, 41; 13 Lai, 38; 14 Wilairot, 26; 15 West, 25; 16 Locatelli, 21; 17 Espargaro, 19; 18 Heidolf, 14; 19 Abraham, 14; 20 Sekiguchi, 13; 21 Baldolini, 12; 22 Debon, 11; 23 Linfoot, 7; 24 Cluzel, 3; 25 Laverty, 3; 26 Tizon and Toth, 1.

125cc

22 laps, 62.260 miles/100.210km

Pos.	Rider (Nat.)	No.	Machine	Laps	Time & speed
1	Mattia Pasini (ITA)	75	Aprilia	22	38m 58.171s 95.871mph/ 154.289km/h
2	Hector Faubel (SPA)	55	Aprilia	22	39m 04.286s
3	Gabor Talmacsi (HUN)	14	Aprilia	22	39m 04.317s
4	Sergio Gadea (SPA)	33	Aprilia	22	39m 04.525s
5	Simone Corsi (ITA)	24	Aprilia	22	39m 04.625s
6	Tomoyoshi Koyama (JPN)	71	KTM	22	39m 04.804s
7	Lukas Pesek (CZE)	52	Derbi	22	39m 04.814s
8	Sandro Cortese (GER)	11	Aprilia	22	39m 15.867s
9	Michael Ranseder (AUT)	60	Derbi	22	39m 16.061s
10	Stefan Bradl (GER)	17	Aprilia	22	39m 19.951s
11	Pol Espargaro (SPA)	44	Aprilia	22	39m 21.038s
12	Randy Krummenacher (SWI)	34	KTM	22	39m 21.109s
13	Esteve Rabat (SPA)	12	Honda	22	39m 21.266s
14	Raffaele de Rosa (ITA)	35	Aprilia	22	39m 32.418s
15	Lorenzo Zanetti (ITA)	8	Aprilia	22	39m 35.162s
16	Alexis Masbou (FRA)	7	Honda	22	39m 35.316s
17	Nicolas Terol (SPA)	18	Derbi	22	39m 35.578s
18	Joan Olive (SPA)	6	Aprilia	22	39m 35.768s
19	Stefano Bianco (ITA)	27	Aprilia	22	39m 38.408s
20	Andrea Iannone (ITA)	29	Aprilia	22	39m 46.558s
21	Hugo van den Berg (NED)	56	Aprilia	22	39m 49.415s
22	Roberto Tamburini (ITA)	20	Aprilia	22	39m 49.545s
23	Enrique Jerez (SPA)	31	Honda	22	39m 50.094s
24	Federico Sandi (ITA)	15	Aprilia	22	39m 54.118s
25	Simone Grotzkyj (ITA)	53	Aprilia	22	39m 55.354s
26	Joey Litjens (NED)	37	Honda	22	39m 58.017s
27	Steve Bonsey (USA)	51	KTM	22	40m 16.929s
28	Dominique Aegerter (SWI)	77	Aprilia	22	40m 17.824s
29	Philipp Eitzinger (AUT)	85	Honda	22	40m 27.242s
30	Roy Pouw (NED)	90	Aprilia	21	39m 12.014s
31	Patrick vd Waarsenburg (NED)	72	Honda	21	39m 24.325s
32	Jasper Iwema (NED)	89	Honda	21	40m 12.447s
33	Ferry Stoffer (NED)	88	Honda	21	40m 12.722s
	Pablo Nieto (SPA)	22	Aprilia	19	DNF
	Robert Muresan (ROU)	95	Derbi	10	DNF
	Mike di Meglio (FRA)	63	Honda	10	DNF
	Daniel Webb (GBR)	99	Honda	5	DNF

Fastest lap: Faubel, 1m 45.551s, 96.534mph/155.356km/h.

Lap record: Sergio Gadea, SPA (Aprilia), 1m 45.098s, 96.949mph/ 156.025km/h (2006).

Event best maximum speed: Koyama, 132.4mph/213.0km/h (race).

Qualifying: 1 Pasini, 1m 45.603s; 2 Pesek, 1m 45.783s; 3 Corsi, 1m 46.198s; 4 Gadea, 1m 46.204s; 5 Cortese, 1m 46.216s; 6 Talmacsi, 1m 46.416s; 7 Faubel, 1m 46.853s; 8 de Rosa, 1m 46.946s; 9 Bradl, 1m 46.999s; 10 Ranseder, 1m 47.021s; 11 Olive, 1m 47.260s; 12 Terol, 1m 47.275s; 13 Koyama, 1m 47.344s; 14 Zanetti, 1m 47.400s; 15 Nieto, 1m 47.454s; 16 di Meglio, 1m 47.568s; 17 Espargaro, 1m 47.665s; 18 Bianco, 1m 47.841s; 19 Rabat, 1m 47.848s; 20 Masbou, 1m 47.972s; 21 Muresan, 1m 48.028s; 22 Litjens, 1m 48.248s; 23 Tamburini, 1m 48.303s; 24 Bonsey, 1m 48.617s; 25 Krummenacher, 1m 48.703s; 26 Jerez, 1m 48.719s; 27 Grotzkyj, 1m 49.061s; 28 Aegerter, 1m 49.113s; 29 Sandi, 1m 49.134s; 30 Webb, 1m 49.322s; 31 Pouw, 1m 50.025s; 32 van den Berg, 1m 50.244s; 33 Iwema, 1m 50.292s; 34 vd Waarsenburg, 1m 51.225s; 35 Stoffer, 1m 52.407s; 36 Eitzinger, 1m 52.862s; 37 Iannone, 2m 08.420s.

Fastest race laps: 1 Faubel, 1m 45.551s; 2 Pasini, 1m 45.558s; 3 Pesek, 1m 45.644s; 4 Talmacsi, 1m 45.675s; 5 Gadea, 1m 45.688s; 6 Corsi, 1m 45.715s; 7 Koyama, 1m 45.821s; 8 Cortese, 1m 46.110s; 9 Ranseder, 1m 46.178s; 10 Espargaro, 1m 46.212s; 11 de Rosa, 1m 46.240s; 12 Krummenacher, 1m 46.259s; 13 Bradl, 1m 46.260s; 14 Zanetti, 1m 46.406s; 15 Rabat, 1m 46.424s; 16 Bianco, 1m 46.468s; 17 Nieto, 1m 46.693s; 18 Masbou, 1m 46.758s; 19 Terol, 1m 46.815s; 20 Olive, 1m 46.840s; 21 Iannone, 1m 46.876s; 22 Tamburini, 1m 47.164s; 23 di Meglio, 1m 47.249s; 24 Jerez, 1m 47.401s; 25 Grotzkyj, 1m 47.402s; 26 van den Berg, 1m 47.445s; 27 Sandi, 1m 47.626s; 28 Muresan, 1m 47.694s; 29 Litjens, 1m 48.098s; 30 Aegerter, 1m 48.236s; 31 Bonsey, 1m 48.306s; 32 Webb, 1m 48.585s; 33 Eitzinger, 1m 48.754s; 34 Pouw, 1m 50.366s; 35 vd Waarsenburg, 1m 51.225s; 36 Stoffer, 1m 52.205s; 37 Iwema, 1m 52.351s.

World Championship: 1 Faubel, 138; 2 Talmacsi, 131; 3 Gadea, 105; 4 Pesek, 103; 5 Koyama, 98; 6 Corsi, 97; 7 Pasini, 66; 8 Olive, 63; 9 Smith, 63; 10 Espargaro, 62; 11 Cortese, 44; 12 Ranseder, 43; 13 de Rosa, 42; 14 Rabat, 33; 15 Krummenacher, 30; 16 Zanetti, 30; 17 Nieto, 28; 18 di Meglio, 21; 19 Iannone, 18; 20 Bradl, 13; 21 Masbou, 13; 22 Terol, 6; 23 Bianco, 5; 24 Bonsey, 3; 25 Jerez, 2; 26 Aegerter, 2; 27 Grotzkyj, 1.

FIM WORLD CHAMPIONSHIP • ROUND 10

GERMANGP

SACHSENRING

Pedrosa, Honda and Michelin won by the biggest margin of the MotoGP era. Even Stoner couldn't keep up.
Photograph: Gold & Goose

Above: Of all the Bridgestone runners, only Capirossi chose the right tyres. He was rewarded with second place.

Below: New HRC President Masumi Hamane looks anxiously over the pit wall for exploding Hondas. In the end, he was rewarded with a win.

Photographs: Gold & Goose

IF the unexpected is the most vital ingredient, then 2007's vintage was ratified at the Sachsenring's concentrated car-park Colditz. Two weeks before, Rossi had been close to divine; in Germany, he was all too human. All year, Honda had been struggling even for podiums. Today it was unbeatable. All year also, Bridgestone had put Michelin on the back foot, with frequent red faces. In Germany, it was quite the other way around. Until this race, Stoner's last laps had frequently been his fastest. This time, he faded to fifth. There was only one constant – his world championship points lead got bigger.

Last race of the almost non-stop European grind, and last before a long, long holiday for the smaller classes, the German GP was chiefly distinguished by punishing temperatures. Friday wasn't so bad, but Saturday became blistering, and Sunday peaked at 33 degrees ambient and a soaraway 41 degrees track temperature. Combined with the notorious series of endless left turns, leading on to the single right that precipitates riders headlong over the waterfall (the track's only memorable feature), this spelled doom for Stoner's hopes of even second, behind the uncatchable Pedrosa. He and fellow Bridgestone users Melandri and Hopkins couldn't sustain the pace at race end. Only that increasingly enigmatic rider Capirossi overcame the Bridgestone curse, on a tyre choice that was (nominally at least) softer, for a season-best second.

Honda's return to form included another rostrum for the reborn Hayden, but not before a gruesome Friday the Thirteenth proved almost as embarrassing for HRC as the win was welcome. Going for a fast time, Hayden suffered the worst kind of engine failure, right in front of the pits. It wasn't just smoky and oily, although it was all that. The factory RC212V shed intimate bits and pieces as Hayden looked for a place to park safely. Crowing TV reporters and (worse still) rival team members were able to garner souvenirs – bits of valve, con-rod, piston and casing. Things looked bad the next day too, when both factory Hondas produced prodigious quantities of smoke, although in each case it was something external fouling the exhausts.

And all in front of new HRC president Masumi Hamane, on hand to make his acquaintance with MotoGP, and to reassure beleaguered factory and satellite teams and riders. His speech was full of 'fighting spirit' and 'must work harder'. His return to Japan with a win in his pocket must have been very different from the outcome he had envisaged on Friday, as HRC's finest clattered itself wide open before the whole racing world.

But Hamane still had plenty to worry about, according to Hayden. Recent success had come not only with new parts and settings derived from post-Catalunya tests, but also at tracks where engine power is less significant. 'Here and Donington especially you only use five gears,' he said.

The new HRC boss's arrival coincided with the long-awaited delivery of new parts for satellite riders, especially Melandri, whose whole attitude was transformed by chassis and engine upgrades (including electronics and the longer exhaust pipes) that gave him a bike he could ride and place as he liked. Among other improvements were smoother throttle response and better control of engine braking on corner entry.

Hayden had also crashed in the morning over some new bumps after he had been put off line – the track had been partially resurfaced, and was also dirty and rather slick in the heat. Other riders had lucky escapes on the unpredictable and highly abrasive tar; Barros did not, trapping his right hand under the bar of his Ducati as it slid. Rapid treatment to a nasty open wound ensured that the veteran was back in the saddle in the afternoon. (Coincidentally, D'Antin team-mate Alex Hofmann had suffered an injury to his right hand when it was trapped in a car door, requiring surgery. Worse was to come for the German a week later.)

Fevered speculation about who goes where was hardly reduced by a very early announcement that John Hopkins would be leaving Suzuki for Kawasaki. It seems that the latter had been negotiating with Vermeulen as well, but stopped short of stealing both its commercial partner's riders. Increasingly strong links between Melandri and Ducati were revealed obliquely when Capirossi's manager suggested that his charge would be leaving the team in 2008 – all the more pressure on Melandri's team boss Fausto Gresini. He was already suffering from the possible loss of sponsor Hannspree, which was planning to increase its presence in World Superbike, and he had even found it quite hard to fill the vacancy left by Elias's injury. He'd offered

the Honda ride to Neil Hodgson, who rather unexpectedly had turned it down, preferring to concentrate on US Superbike possibilities, and had failed to reach the hibernating Kenny Roberts Junior. For this race, Michel Fabrizio was given his chance; for the next race, Miguel Duhamel would take over. Gresini got quite a shock when he found out just how old his '39-year-old' Laguna substitute looked. 'He may be old, but he's interesting,' he smiled.

Jim Redman was on hand for induction into the Hall of Fame. Now 75, Rhodesian Redman was four times 350 champion and twice 250, always on Hondas. He was also the first rider to take three GP wins in one day, at the Dutch TT in 1964. A lesson to today's pampered riders when they complain about the heat and exhaustion of one 45-minute gallop.

MOTOGP RACE – 30 laps

Rossi pronounced the fiddly Sachsenring better suited to 800s than 990s: 'You can use the bike more.' For once, however, qualifying did not yield faster times. That would have to wait for the race. Times were incredibly close – the top 16 covered by 0.835 second, and positions affected by a gust of wind or an inch too much enthusiasm.

Stoner was narrowly on pole, his second of the year, from a consistently fast Pedrosa and the re-enthused Melandri. Michelin qualifiers were having trouble making the full lap in the heat, with Rossi sixth after a slow final section, and likewise Hayden, down in 13th.

Stoner led the first few hundred yards, but Pedrosa passed him into the first corner, with a calm assurance that proved well justified. Melandri, Hopkins, Capirossi and de Puniet followed, with Rossi eighth and Hayden tenth. They would move forward together over the next three laps, until Hayden slowed, hearing a change in engine note and fearing he had split an exhaust. By

Left: **Italian Michel Fabrizio had one race for ex-125 champion Fausto Gresini (right), and made the top ten.**

Below left: **Melandri struggled in vain to keep Hayden behind.**

Bottom: **Hofmann, already hurt, was feeling the pressure at home.**

Photographs: Gold & Goose

Above: **A rejuvenated Hayden muscled his Honda to a second rostrum in a row.**

Top: **Crunch time. Rossi tried too hard to get past de Puniet. The smoke off the front tyre tells the story.**

Photographs: Gold & Goose

now, Rossi was seventh behind de Puniet, who was proving frustratingly hard to pass.

Checa was an early crasher, while Vermeulen pulled in for a ride-through after jumping the start. Rossi, seeing the three leaders breaking away, was getting desperate and worried also about overheating. He cut inside at the Omega curve at the bottom of the hill, had a little slide and was holding it tight for the second apex when he just leaned it over too far. He went down, de Puniet looking over his shoulder in astonishment. And that was it. With bent levers, his bike was unridable. He left the track on foot, his head cast down.

After ten giddying laps, Pedrosa's lead was more than a second, and he had already broken the 990 record. Another two and it was more than two seconds. His pace was steadfast, Stoner's fading, the Michelins better for once. Pedrosa finished 13.166 seconds ahead – the most crushing victory in the MotoGP four-stroke era.

Stoner held second, with Melandri losing out little by little behind him. Capirossi had taken fourth off Hopkins on lap two, sticking there for a while before his different tyre combination began to work better. He closed on Melandri, while at the same time Stoner was dropping back toward the Honda.

Capirossi took them both in one sweeping 21st lap: Melandri into the first corner (pushing the Honda way out wide), then Stoner at the bottom of the steep hill. He was off at once, the two troubled Bridgestone men falling into the hands of Hopkins, who had similar rear-tyre problems. 'It was like racing in the wet,' he said.

Barros had crashed on lap ten, promoting Hayden and Edwards behind him. The Honda man had got ahead before half-distance, the strange noise not having developed into anything worse. The pair began to close on de Puniet in sixth. Both got ahead of the Kawasaki and continued on toward the fading trio ahead. They caught them on lap 23, three seconds covering Melandri in third and Edwards in seventh. 'You could see they were in trouble…it was like bringing a gun to a knife fight,' said Hayden later.

He pushed through to third on lap 25, Edwards going with him. Capirossi was out of reach, but Hayden carried on gaining ground to the end. Edwards's efforts to catch him were thwarted by an unusual consequence of the abrasive surface: in spite of wearing double knee sliders, he had worn right through them on the left.

The hapless trio was losing ground fast, de Puniet also struggling some four or five seconds behind, and West stalking him after a near crash had urged caution. Then de Puniet was out, coasting to a stop with a faulty fuel pump.

Stoner won the battle of the lame for fifth, pushing past Melandri at the start of the penultimate lap. 'Half-way through, I was struggling – fifth is a positive, not a negative,' he said. Melandri and Hopkins were in line astern.

West was next, with Hofmann closing to within a couple of seconds at the end, bringing Fabrizio with him. Vermeulen, another 18 seconds down, had passed only Kurtis Roberts after his penalty. Tamada was two laps down after pitting for a new rear tyre and a cool drink; Checa was another one away, having remounted after his early crash and pitted for running repairs.

Nakano retired after 19 undistinguished laps.

250cc RACE – 29 laps

Kallio took his first pole by two-tenths from Dovizioso, then de Angelis, Lorenzo, Simon and the rest packed up close. The KTMs, near their Austrian home, had yet more new cylinders by Harald Bartol, last of the two-stroke believers, and clearly they worked well.

Dovizioso got the jump, Kallio chasing; de Angelis was third by the end of the lap, Hiro Aoyama fourth. In the pursuit pack, Bautista was tenth from row two, then ran off on lap three, re-joining next to last and never in contention.

Barbera was on the charge. When de Angelis found his way inside Dovizioso at the end of lap five, the Spaniard was fourth, ahead of Aoyama, with Simon following closely and Lorenzo losing ground at the head of the next group.

Barbera would play a leading role in the race, although not to his own benefit, with a series of entertaining but fruitless attacks into the first corner. He would outbrake everyone, including himself, then run wide, usually taking at least one of the group with him. In this way, they stayed close, shuffling back and forth as de Angelis built up a small lead.

Barbera's first victim was Kallio, on lap ten. Aoyama was now third, and on lap 13, he took the inside gap as Dovizioso ran wide out of the last corner and powered past. Into turn one, Barbera did it again, shuffling the orange bike straight back to fifth. Simon was sixth, but next time around out of the first corner, he was baulked by a back-marker and fell.

This stretched de Angelis's advantage to almost 1.5 seconds, but also put Dovizioso back into second; any hopes of a break-away were quashed as he closed up quickly, bringing the group with him. By this stage, Lorenzo was closing up, having got away from Simoncelli.

At the start of lap 18, Barbera did the same thing again, but the others were wiser now, and only he suffered. He lost fourth to Kallio and came within range of Lorenzo, who got ahead of his now-fading rival three laps later.

Meanwhile, Aoyama was back in front of Dovizioso and hounding the leader as the Italian struggled to stay close. The gap to third was more than a second when, on lap 27, Kallio took him at the first corner, then Lorenzo at the last.

Lorenzo made no more progress, but Kallio had more. He watched as team-mate Aoyama dived under de Angelis to the lead at the first corner, and was ready at the last one where the latter ran wide, aiming at a swooping faster exit. Instead, he let the second KTM through for the Finn's first podium in the class, and the marque's first one-two result. Kallio also set a new record on the last lap.

Lorenzo was close, Dovizioso less than a second behind him, but Barbera was another ten seconds down. The rest were spread out more or less evenly behind Simoncelli and 2006 winner Takahashi, with little change of position, although Locatelli took tenth off Espargaro with five laps left. Shuhei Aoyama's factory Honda was 12th.

Linfoot, Abraham, Laverty and wild card Walther swelled the crash list.

125cc RACE – 27 laps

Talmacsi took pole ahead of Pasini by a relatively huge four-tenths and ran away with the race. The Hungarian put it down to working at setting up his brother's 600 Supersport bike at the Hungaroring. 'Compared with a big bike, the 125 is easy,' he said.

Pasini's change of luck lasted only for the first few hundred yards, then he became tangled up in a clash with Espargaro and de Rosa. All three got going again, but to no avail.

For ten laps, Talmacsi concentrated on securing a lead of some five seconds, and after that on preserving it. He was still 3.5 seconds clear at the end.

The battle for second was seven-strong, from the start until a few laps before the finish. Faubel had control at first, then Pesek for a lap before Corsi took over for a long spell, from lap five until 24.

Gadea had a brief run in fourth just after half-distance, then fell back. All the time, Koyama was moving steadily forward through the group. On lap 18, he was fourth; on lap 20, third.

Just after the end of the next one, he drafted past Corsi, holding on to second to the end; Faubel took third off Corsi with one lap to go.

Corsi was still close, but the rest had dropped back in a private dispute, Krummenacher doing well again to resist the last-lap pressure of Pesek. Gadea had been ahead of both, but slid off on the penultimate corner. Smith was eighth.

Main photograph: Round and round the mulberry bush.

Below: Rampant Aoyama led KTM's first one-two.

Bottom: Joy for Harald Bartol, two-stroke believer.

Photographs: Gold & Goose

ALICE MOTORRAD GRAND PRIX DEUTSCHLAND

15 JULY 2007 • FIM WORLD CHAMPIONSHIP ROUND 10

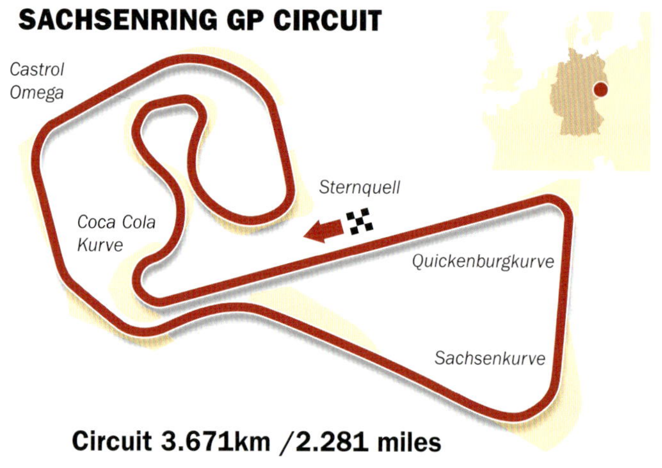

MotoGP

RACE: 30 laps, 68.430 miles/110.130km • Weather: Dry • Air 33°C • Humidity 28% • Track 41°C

Pos.	Rider	Nat.	No.	Entrant	Machine	Tyres	Laps	Time & speed (mph/km/h)
1	Dani Pedrosa	SPA	26	Repsol Honda Team	Honda	M	30	41m 53.196s 98.024mph/ 157.754km/h
2	Loris Capirossi	ITA	65	Ducati Marlboro Team	Ducati	B	30	42m 06.362s
3	Nicky Hayden	USA	1	Repsol Honda Team	Honda	M	30	42m 09.967s
4	Colin Edwards	USA	5	Fiat Yamaha Team	Yamaha	M	30	42m 11.495s
5	Casey Stoner	AUS	27	Ducati Marlboro Team	Ducati	B	30	42m 24.622s
6	Marco Melandri	ITA	33	Honda Gresini	Honda	B	30	42m 25.113s
7	John Hopkins	USA	21	Rizla Suzuki MotoGP	Suzuki	B	30	42m 26.591s
8	Anthony West	AUS	13	Kawasaki Racing Team	Kawasaki	B	30	42m 34.390s
9	Alex Hofmann	GER	66	Pramac d'Antin	Ducati	B	30	42m 36.410s
10	Michel Fabrizio	ITA	84	Honda Gresini	Honda	B	30	42m 37.655s
11	Chris Vermeulen	AUS	71	Rizla Suzuki MotoGP	Suzuki	B	30	42m 55.090s
12	Kurtis Roberts	USA	80	Team Roberts	KR212V	M	30	43m 03.917s
13	Makoto Tamada	JPN	6	Dunlop Yamaha Tech 3	Yamaha	D	28	42m 48.710s
14	Carlos Checa	SPA	7	Honda LCR	Honda	M	27	42m 34.089s
	Randy de Puniet	FRA	14	Kawasaki Racing Team	Kawasaki	B	29	41m 46.308s
	Shinya Nakano	JPN	56	Konica Minolta Honda	Honda	M	19	28m 40.361s
	Alex Barros	BRA	4	Pramac d'Antin	Ducati	B	9	12m 41.157s
	Valentino Rossi	ITA	46	Fiat Yamaha Team	Yamaha	M	5	7m 02.631s
	Sylvain Guintoli	FRA	50	Dunlop Yamaha Tech 3	Yamaha	D	3	4m 17.597s

Fastest lap: Dani Pedrosa, on lap 6, 1m 23.082s, 98.839mph/159.066km/h (record).

Previous lap record: Dani Pedrosa, 1m 23.355s, 98.515mph/158.54km/h (2006).

Event best maximum speed: Casey Stoner, 174.2mph/280.4km/h (qualifying practice).

Grid order	1	2	3	4	5	6	7	8	9	10	11	12	13	14	15	16	17	18	19	20	21	22	23	24	25	26	27	28	29	30	•
27 STONER	26	26	26	26	26	26	26	26	26	26	26	26	26	26	26	26	26	26	26	26	26	26	26	26	26	26	26	26	26	26	1
26 PEDROSA	27	27	27	27	27	27	27	27	27	27	27	27	27	27	27	27	27	27	27	27	65	65	65	65	65	65	65	65	65	65	2
33 MELANDRI	33	33	33	33	33	33	33	33	33	33	33	33	33	33	33	33	33	33	33	33	27	33	33	33	1	1	1	1	1	1	3
14 de PUNIET	21	65	65	65	65	65	65	65	65	65	65	65	65	65	65	65	65	65	65	65	33	27	27	1	5	5	5	5	5	5	4
21 HOPKINS	65	21	21	21	21	21	21	21	21	21	21	21	21	21	21	21	21	21	21	21	21	21	21	27	33	33	27	27	27	27	5
46 ROSSI	14	14	14	14	14	14	14	14	14	14	14	14	14	14	14	14	1	1	1	1	1	1	1	5	27	27	33	33	33	33	6
65 CAPIROSSI	4	4	46	46	46	4	4	4	4	5	5	5	1	1	1	1	14	14	5	5	5	5	5	21	21	21	21	21	21	21	7
4 BARROS	46	46	1	1	4	5	5	5	5	1	1	1	5	5	5	5	5	5	14	14	14	14	14	14	14	14	14	14	13	13	8
50 GUINTOLI	56	1	4	4	1	1	1	1	1	13	13	13	13	13	13	13	13	13	13	13	13	13	13	13	13	13	13	13	66	66	9
56 NAKANO	1	5	5	5	5	13	13	13	13	66	66	66	66	66	66	66	66	66	66	66	66	66	66	66	66	66	66	66	84	84	10
71 VERMEULEN	5	56	56	13	13	66	66	66	66	84	84	84	84	84	84	84	84	84	84	84	84	84	84	84	84	84	84	84	71	71	11
13 WEST	50	50	50	66	66	84	84	84	84	56	56	56	56	56	56	56	56	71	71	71	71	71	71	71	71	71	71	71	80	80	12
5 EDWARDS	13	7	13	71	84	56	56	56	56	80	80	80	80	80	71	71	71	80	80	80	80	80	80	80	80	80	80	80	14		13
1 HAYDEN	7	13	66	84	71	80	80	80	80	71	71	71	71	71	80	80	80	56	56	6	6	6	6	6	6	6	6	6			14
7 CHECA	66	66	71	56	56	6	6	71	71	6	6	6	6	6	6	6	6	6	6	7	7	7	7	7	7	7	7				15
66 HOFMANN	71	71	84	80	80	71	71	6	6	7	7	7	7	7	7	7	7	7	7												
84 FABRIZIO	84	84	6	6	6	7	7	7	7																						
6 TAMADA	6	6	80	7	7																										
80 ROBERTS	80	80	7																												

FASTEST RACE LAPS

	Rider	Lap	Time
1	Pedrosa	6	1m 23.082s
2	Stoner	6	1m 23.162s
3	Capirossi	4	1m 23.228s
4	Melandri	6	1m 23.246s
5	Hopkins	5	1m 23.456s
6	Rossi	3	1m 23.529s
7	Hayden	22	1m 23.617s
8	de Puniet	5	1m 23.799s
9	Vermeulen	17	1m 23.884s
10	Edwards	20	1m 23.886s
11	West	12	1m 23.938s
12	Barros	8	1m 24.003s
13	Hofmann	8	1m 24.087s
14	Checa	9	1m 24.148s
15	Fabrizio	5	1m 24.283s
16	Nakano	3	1m 24.421s
17	Guintoli	3	1m 24.683s
18	Roberts	6	1m 25.617s
19	Tamada	2	1m 25.844s

QUALIFYING

14 July 2007

Weather: Dry

Air: 28°C Humidity: 33%

Track: 38°C

Pos.	Rider	Time
1	Stoner	1m 22.384s
2	Pedrosa	1m 22.388s
3	Melandri	1m 22.397s
4	de Puniet	1m 22.539s
5	Hopkins	1m 22.561s
6	Rossi	1m 22.605s
7	Capirossi	1m 22.615s
8	Barros	1m 22.897s
9	Guintoli	1m 22.958s
10	Nakano	1m 22.969s
11	Vermeulen	1m 23.039s
12	West	1m 23.056s
13	Edwards	1m 23.090s
14	Hayden	1m 23.151s
15	Checa	1m 23.182s
16	Hofmann	1m 23.199s
17	Fabrizio	1m 23.491s
18	Tamada	1m 23.744s
19	Roberts	1m 24.209s

RIDER STANDINGS

After 10 Rounds		
1	Casey Stoner	196
2	Valentino Rossi	164
3	Dani Pedrosa	144
4	John Hopkins	103
5	Marco Melandri	97
6	Chris Vermeulen	93
7	Colin Edwards	88
8	Loris Capirossi	77
9	Nicky Hayden	73
10	Alex Barros	69
11	Alex Hofmann	60
12	Toni Elias	49
13	Randy de Puniet	40
14	Carlos Checa	27
15	Shinya Nakano	25
16	Makoto Tamada	23
17	Anthony West	20
18	Sylvain Guintoli	18
19	Kurtis Roberts	8
20	Michel Fabrizio	6
21	Fonsi Nieto	5
22	Olivier Jacque	4
23	Kenny Roberts Jnr	4

TEAM STANDINGS

After 10 Rounds		
1	Ducati Marlboro Team	273
2	Fiat Yamaha Team	252
3	Repsol Honda Team	217
4	Rizla Suzuki MotoGP	196
5	Honda Gresini	152
6	Pramac d'Antin	129
7	Kawasaki Racing Team	69
8	Dunlop Yamaha Tech 3	41
9	Honda LCR	27
10	Konica Minolta Honda	25
11	Team Roberts	12

CONSTRUCTOR STANDINGS

After 10 Rounds		
1	Ducati	208
2	Yamaha	184
3	Honda	174
4	Suzuki	131
5	Kawasaki	64
6	KR212V	12

statistics

250cc

29 laps, 66.149 miles/106.459km

Pos.	Rider (Nat.)	No.	Machine	Laps	Time & speed
1	Hiroshi Aoyama (JPN)	4	KTM	29	41m 16.191s 96.172mph/ 154.774km/h
2	Mika Kallio (FIN)	36	KTM	29	41m 16.310s
3	Alex de Angelis (RSM)	3	Aprilia	29	41m 16.465s
4	Jorge Lorenzo (SPA)	1	Aprilia	29	41m 16.770s
5	Andrea Dovizioso (ITA)	34	Honda	29	41m 17.487s
6	Hector Barbera (SPA)	80	Aprilia	29	41m 28.042s
7	Marco Simoncelli (ITA)	58	Gilera	29	41m 33.499s
8	Yuki Takahashi (JPN)	55	Honda	29	41m 38.500s
9	Thomas Luthi (SWI)	12	Aprilia	29	41m 45.049s
10	Roberto Locatelli (ITA)	15	Gilera	29	41m 52.174s
11	Aleix Espargaro (SPA)	41	Aprilia	29	41m 53.568s
12	Shuhei Aoyama (JPN)	73	Honda	29	41m 58.402s
13	Dirk Heidolf (GER)	28	Aprilia	29	42m 07.286s
14	Alex Baldolini (ITA)	25	Aprilia	29	42m 09.607s
15	Jules Cluzel (FRA)	16	Aprilia	29	42m 12.187s
16	Taro Sekiguchi (JPN)	44	Aprilia	29	42m 12.296s
17	Alvaro Bautista (SPA)	19	Aprilia	29	42m 23.626s
18	Fabrizio Lai (ITA)	32	Aprilia	29	42m 25.919s
19	Ratthapark Wilairot (THA)	8	Honda	29	42m 33.831s
	Karel Abraham (CZE)	17	Aprilia	19	DNF
	Thomas Walther (GER)	38	Honda	19	DNF
	Eugene Laverty (IRL)	50	Honda	18	DNF
	Julian Simon (SPA)	60	Honda	14	DNF
	Imre Toth (HUN)	10	Aprilia	13	DNF
	Dan Linfoot (GBR)	45	Aprilia	4	DNF
	Alvaro Molina (SPA)	31	Aprilia	4	DNF
	Joshua Sommer (GER)	18	Honda	3	DNF
	Efren Vazquez (SPA)	7	Aprilia	2	DNF

Fastest lap: Kallio, 1m 24.762s, 96.880mph/155.914km/h (record).

Previous lap record: Sebastian Porto, ARG (Aprilia), 1m 25.118s, 96.475mph/155.262km/h (2004).

Event best maximum speed: Kallio, 152.9mph/246.0km/h (free practice no. 2).

Qualifying: 1 Kallio, 1m 24.413s; 2 Dovizioso, 1m 24.643s; 3 de Angelis, 1m 24.647s; 4 Lorenzo, 1m 24.735s; 5 Simon, 1m 24.845s; 6 H. Aoyama, 1m 24.870s; 7 Barbera, 1m 24.910s; 8 Simoncelli, 1m 24.928s; 9 Bautista, 1m 25.082s; 10 Takahashi, 1m 25.099s; 11 Espargaro, 1m 25.213s; 12 Luthi, 1m 25.240s; 13 Heidolf, 1m 25.585s; 14 Locatelli, 1m 25.599s; 15 Baldolini, 1m 25.616s; 16 Lai, 1m 25.800s; 17 S. Aoyama, 1m 25.856s; 18 Sekiguchi, 1m 26.225s; 19 Vazquez, 1m 26.236s; 20 Abraham, 1m 26.685s; 21 Cluzel, 1m 26.890s; 22 Wilairot, 1m 26.960s; 23 Molina, 1m 27.066s; 24 Toth, 1m 27.644s; 25 Linfoot, 1m 27.886s; 26 Laverty, 1m 27.984s; 27 Sommer, 1m 28.840s; 28 Walther, 1m 28.962s.

Fastest race laps: 1 Kallio, 1m 24.762s; 2 H. Aoyama, 1m 24.814s; 3 Lorenzo, 1m 24.878s; 4 Simon, 1m 24.941s; 5 Barbera, 1m 24.948s; 6 de Angelis, 1m 25.017s; 7 Dovizioso, 1m 25.108s; 8 Simoncelli, 1m 25.162s; 9 Takahashi, 1m 25.516s; 10 Luthi, 1m 25.742s; 11 Espargaro, 1m 25.776s; 12 Locatelli, 1m 25.874s; 13 Bautista, 1m 25.942s; 14 S. Aoyama, 1m 25.944s; 15 Abraham, 1m 26.020s; 16 Heidolf, 1m 26.175s; 17 Baldolini, 1m 26.388s; 18 Lai, 1m 26.612s; 19 Cluzel, 1m 26.653s; 20 Sekiguchi, 1m 26.846s; 21 Vazquez, 1m 26.854s; 22 Wilairot, 1m 26.992s; 23 Laverty, 1m 27.944s; 24 Linfoot, 1m 27.979s; 25 Toth, 1m 28.179s; 26 Sommer, 1m 30.373s; 27 Walther, 1m 30.846s; 28 Molina, 1m 33.251s.

World Championship: 1 Lorenzo, 191; 2 de Angelis, 171; 3 Dovizioso, 166; 4 Bautista, 116; 5 Barbera, 90; 6 H. Aoyama, 78; 7 Kallio, 78; 8 Luthi, 63; 9 Simon, 61; 10 Simoncelli, 57; 11 S. Aoyama, 55; 12 Takahashi, 49; 13 Lai, 38; 14 Locatelli, 27; 15 Wilairot, 26; 16 West, 25; 17 Espargaro, 24; 18 Heidolf, 17; 19 Abraham, 14; 20 Baldolini, 14; 21 Sekiguchi, 13; 22 Debon, 11; 23 Linfoot, 7; 24 Cluzel, 4; 25 Laverty, 3; 26 Tizon and Toth, 1.

125cc

27 laps, 61.587 miles/99.117km

Pos.	Rider (Nat.)	No.	Machine	Laps	Time & speed
1	Gabor Talmacsi (HUN)	14	Aprilia	27	39m 30.802s 93.520mph/ 150.506km/h
2	Tomoyoshi Koyama (JPN)	71	KTM	27	39m 34.334s
3	Hector Faubel (SPA)	55	Aprilia	27	39m 34.412s
4	Simone Corsi (ITA)	24	Aprilia	27	39m 35.246s
5	Randy Krummenacher (SWI)	34	KTM	27	39m 42.653s
6	Lukas Pesek (CZE)	52	Derbi	27	39m 42.722s
7	Sandro Cortese (GER)	11	Aprilia	27	39m 48.073s
8	Bradley Smith (GBR)	38	Honda	27	39m 50.286s
9	Pablo Nieto (SPA)	22	Aprilia	27	39m 51.752s
10	Michael Ranseder (AUT)	60	Derbi	27	39m 53.430s
11	Joan Olive (SPA)	6	Aprilia	27	39m 56.846s
12	Esteve Rabat (SPA)	12	Honda	27	39m 57.898s
13	Stefan Bradl (GER)	17	Aprilia	27	40m 13.607s
14	Georg Froehlich (GER)	64	Honda	27	40m 14.305s
15	Mike di Meglio (FRA)	63	Honda	27	40m 15.204s
16	Stefano Bianco (ITA)	27	Aprilia	27	40m 17.188s
17	Robert Muresan (ROU)	95	Derbi	27	40m 24.010s
18	Steve Bonsey (USA)	51	KTM	27	40m 24.521s
19	Alexis Masbou (FRA)	7	Honda	27	40m 24.541s
20	Roberto Tamburini (ITA)	20	Aprilia	27	40m 24.689s
21	Dominique Aegerter (SWI)	77	Aprilia	27	40m 30.967s
22	Nicolas Terol (SPA)	18	Derbi	27	40m 31.427s
23	Federico Sandi (ITA)	15	Aprilia	27	40m 40.730s
24	Andrea Iannone (ITA)	29	Aprilia	27	40m 46.884s
25	Hugo van den Berg (NED)	56	Aprilia	27	40m 49.523s
26	Eric Huebsch (GER)	65	Aprilia	27	40m 49.638s
27	Daniel Webb (GBR)	99	Honda	27	40m 58.045s
28	Lorenzo Zanetti (ITA)	8	Aprilia	26	40m 16.495s
29	Sebastien Eckner (GER)	67	Honda	26	40m 33.475s
	Sergio Gadea (SPA)	33	Aprilia	26	DNF
	Joey Litjens (NED)	37	Honda	25	DNF
	Simone Grotzkyj (ITA)	53	Aprilia	15	DNF
	Mattia Pasini (ITA)	75	Aprilia	11	DNF
	Raffaele de Rosa (ITA)	35	Aprilia	8	DNF
	Patrick Unger (GER)	66	Aprilia	1	DNF
	Pol Espargaro (SPA)	44	Aprilia	1	DNF
	Dino Lombardi (ITA)	13	Honda		DNS

Fastest lap: Talmacsi, 1m 26.909s, 94.487mph/152.062km/h (record).

Previous lap record: Alvaro Bautista, SPA (Aprilia), 1m 27.519s, 93.828mph/151.002km/h (2006).

Event best maximum speed: Bradl, 128.4mph/206.6km/h (free practice no. 1).

Qualifying: 1 Talmacsi, 1m 26.839s; 2 Pasini, 1m 27.255s; 3 Faubel, 1m 27.266s; 4 Smith, 1m 27.576s; 5 Pesek, 1m 27.706s; 6 Cortese, 1m 27.728s; 7 Corsi, 1m 27.798s; 8 Krummenacher, 1m 27.829s; 9 Gadea, 1m 27.839s; 10 Rabat, 1m 28.094s; 11 Ranseder, 1m 28.108s; 12 Iannone, 1m 28.204s; 13 Espargaro, 1m 28.212s; 14 Olive, 1m 28.268s; 15 Koyama, 1m 28.277s; 16 Bradl, 1m 28.318s; 17 Nieto, 1m 28.343s; 18 Tamburini, 1m 28.689s; 19 di Meglio, 1m 28.711s; 20 Muresan, 1m 28.825s; 21 Froehlich, 1m 28.894s; 22 Bianco, 1m 28.905s; 23 de Rosa, 1m 29.038s; 24 Zanetti, 1m 29.076s; 25 Litjens, 1m 29.136s; 26 Masbou, 1m 29.431s; 27 Sandi, 1m 29.489s; 28 Terol, 1m 29.499s; 29 Grotzkyj, 1m 29.575s; 30 Bonsey, 1m 29.712s; 31 van den Berg, 1m 30.139s; 32 Unger, 1m 30.180s; 33 Aegerter, 1m 30.264s; 34 Webb, 1m 30.363s; 35 Lombardi, 1m 30.669s; 36 Huebsch, 1m 30.746s; 37 Eckner, 1m 32.176s.

Fastest race laps: 1 Talmacsi, 1m 26.909s; 2 Pesek, 1m 27.322s; 3 Corsi, 1m 27.334s; 4 Koyama, 1m 27.426s; 5 Krummenacher, 1m 27.432s; 6 Gadea, 1m 27.477s; 7 Cortese, 1m 27.534s; 8 Faubel, 1m 27.544s; 9 Nieto, 1m 27.860s; 10 Pasini, 1m 27.893s; 11 Iannone, 1m 27.925s; 12 Olive, 1m 28.094s; 13 Ranseder, 1m 28.150s; 14 Smith, 1m 28.169s; 15 Rabat, 1m 28.224s; 16 Zanetti, 1m 28.543s; 17 Bianco, 1m 28.595s; 18 Froehlich, 1m 28.748s; 19 Bonsey, 1m 28.749s; 20 Bradl, 1m 28.811s; 21 Tamburini, 1m 28.838s; 22 Aegerter, 1m 28.931s; 23 Litjens, 1m 28.970s; 24 Masbou, 1m 29.006s; 25 di Meglio, 1m 29.007s; 26 Muresan, 1m 29.044s; 27 Huebsch, 1m 29.257s; 28 Terol, 1m 29.345s; 29 Sandi, 1m 29.371s; 30 de Rosa, 1m 29.450s; 31 Grotzkyj, 1m 29.484s; 32 van den Berg, 1m 29.874s; 33 Webb, 1m 30.132s; 34 Eckner, 1m 31.728s; 35 Unger, 1m 37.645s.

World Championship: 1 Talmacsi, 156; 2 Faubel, 154; 3 Koyama, 118; 4 Pesek, 113; 5 Corsi, 110; 6 Gadea, 105; 7 Smith, 71; 8 Olive, 68; 9 Pasini, 66; 10 Espargaro, 62; 11 Cortese, 53; 12 Ranseder, 49; 13 de Rosa, 42; 14 Krummenacher, 41; 15 Rabat, 37; 16 Nieto, 35; 17 Zanetti, 30; 18 di Meglio, 22; 19 Iannone, 18; 20 Bradl, 16; 21 Masbou, 13; 22 Terol, 6; 23 Bianco, 5; 24 Bonsey, 3; 25 Froehlich and Jerez, 2; 27 Aegerter, 2; 28 Grotzkyj, 1.

FIM WORLD CHAMPIONSHIP • ROUND 11

UNITED STATES GP

LAGUNA SECA

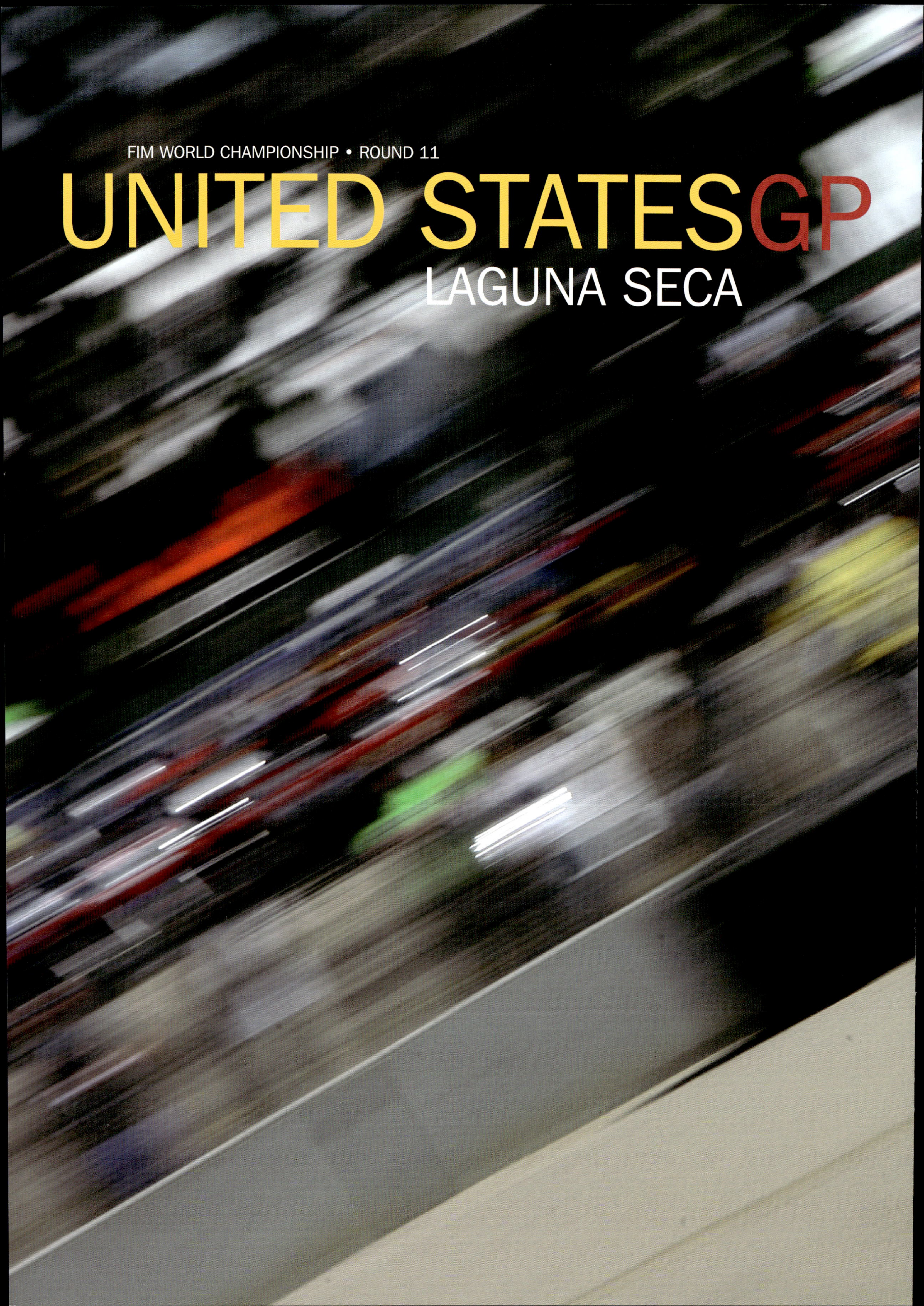

Uphill all the way, but Stoner made it look easy for his sixth win.
Photograph: Gold & Goose

FOR Dorna, America is the Holy Grail. Or, to choose a more fittingly Spanish image, the big windmill. Must race in America! Accordingly, as we have observed over the past two years, Dorna is willing to make huge compromises to ensure a race at Laguna Seca; by and large, the teams and riders follow suit. With some success: from 2008, as was announced in the week preceding 2007's third Red Bull US GP, there will be a second US race. And Indianapolis will be a real GP, hosting all three classes, rather than tagging MotoGP on to an AMA Superbike round, and at a circuit with facilities that are good enough for the vaultingly high standards of F1. There is a sense of a chill wind for the Californian circuit, which has tried so hard and spent so much trying to come up to scratch.

Controversy hovers over Laguna like the Pacific morning mists hang in the maritime valleys. The charming and challenging old track, and the overall organisation have only a finger-nail hold on the normal standards of MotoGP, and all the goodwill and compromise in the world can't stop them from losing their grip from time to time, in all sorts of ways.

The track surface is the starting point. After 2006's debacle, it had been resurfaced again, this time two months before the event. It was certainly much better in one respect, as Stoner said: 'We're not having chunks of it come off and hit us in the face. I think that's an improvement.' He found it bumpier than in 2006, however, which worked everyone's suspension to the stops, but also made an already intricate little track even more intriguing. Hayden: 'It's kind of weird. Some of the lines you used last year just to miss the bumps; this year, you're taking different lines to miss other bumps.' At least it continued to stay in one piece through the busy weekend of GP and AMA racing.

For 2007, the debacle was different, embarrassing and unsightly. It involved not just the trigger-happy and inexperienced Laguna track workers, but also their liaison with Race Director Paul Butler, who ultimately must share the blame for what happened to the especially unfortunate (again) Alex Hofmann.

Tight, swoopy and frequently blind, Laguna is a hard track to go fast on, and a hard track to learn. This year, there was just the one first-timer, sole class rookie Sylvain Guintoli. To cut a long story short, the Frenchman made a bad blunder early in first free practice, running into the Corkscrew way too fast. Hofmann, ahead of him on only his sixth lap, had just turned into the famous left-hand dive. The Yamaha speared into the left front of the Ducati, mashing the handlebar and trapping Hofmann's hand. Just a racing crash? Or an unpardonable amateurish error at this level? The questions would have to wait.

So too would Hofmann. His injuries were grievous: the thumb brake had inflicted a savage and gory diagonal gash across his hand, smashing a metacarpal so badly that it required a metal plate, 15 screws and 50 stitches in three hours of surgery. Close to passing out from pain, shock and heavy bleeding, the German remained at the trackside for the next 20 minutes as practice continued.

There is no full track ambulance access – one of the concessions made to race in America, and Butler insisted that he had been informed continually (misinformed, as it transpired) that Hofmann was being returned to the medical centre on a 'Mule' quad bike. Subsequently, Hofmann disputed this when he returned on Sunday for an emotional series of heartfelt com-

plaints against Race Direction. At one point while he waited, he said, he had taken a radio from a track worker to ask that practice be stopped. Eventually, the red flag was shown, and Hofmann was soon helicoptered off to hospital, where he was attended by Arthur Ting, a San Francisco surgeon well known to motorcycle racing, whose patient list included Lawson, Rainey and Doohan. Hofmann's last words were incontrovertible: 'It would not have happened if it had been Valentino Rossi.'

It was a serious break-down in communications, thankfully remedied when Melandri crashed heavily on Saturday morning – the red flag was shown immediately. This was a different kind of novice/expert clash: Kurtis Roberts had 'messed up coming out of Turn Two' and found himself stuck on the racing line, but travelling slowly. Just then, Melandri turned up going fast. He almost made it inside the Honda-powered hybrid, but just clipped Kurtis's boot, triggering a spectacular tumble into the gravel at Turn Three, his bike continuing into the barrier as the rider came to rest, suffering what at the time was thought to be only a dislocated ankle. Heroically, Melandri overcame the painful injury to race to his second rostrum of the season. After struggling to recuperate throughout the forthcoming summer break, however, his return at Brno would unearth an agonising neck injury, doubtless incurred at the same time.

Rossi was free with his criticism of Roberts, but then crashed himself, on the bump at Turn Six on the climb up toward the Corkscrew, where run-off had been clawed back from the hillside in 2006 in response to complaints from the riders. The crash happened at 180km/h, said Rossi, and the safety measures in every regard proved to be just enough. Rossi stopped sliding just before reaching the barriers, while his personal safety equipment also went right to the edge. Sliding along, he had worn his glove 'through the leather, through the carbon and through the fingernail, with just a small hole in the skin. So I used all the protection,' he smiled thankfully.

Hofmann's early elimination triggered a frantic game of hunt-the-rider, as Luis d'Antin sought a replacement during the lunch break. Kenny Roberts Junior had no difficulty in declining; Ben Bostrom accepted, but then was blocked because of his Yamaha contract; AMA Ducati racer Larry Pegram was on the list, but somehow unreachable in time. D'Antin then sought help from IRTA, which pointed out that Chaz Davies was at the track (to take part in the AMA Supersport race). The matter was arranged in a few minutes, and without even time to adjust footpegs or levers, the Welsh ex-250 hopeful was out with the big boys.

Also learners at MotoGP were two AMA regulars. Long-serving stalwart Miguel Duhamel was taking a run on Elias's vacant Gresini Honda, while hungry younger brother Roger Lee Hayden was wild-carding for Kawasaki, for whom he races in the USA. On a weekend when mixed fortunes kept on mixing, Roger Lee would end up not only with a top-ten finish, but also as best American, at a race won for the previous two years straight by brother Nicky. This time, Nicky was taken out on only the second corner by another ill-starred home hero, John Hopkins.

Emotions had run high in practice for Hopkins, who had been striving for a good grid slot on his second pair of qualifying tyres, only to run into Checa on the approach to the Corkscrew, cruising on the racing line. His lap was ruined, and as he passed the

Above: Laguna's signature corner is the Corkscrew, and nothing ever makes it any easier.

Above left: Duhamel, wide-eyed at the prospect of riding a MotoGP bike.

Left: Chaz Davies took over Hofmann's chair, leathers and motorbike at very short notice.

Far left: Hofmann looks aghast at his mutilated hand as he comes to rest.

All photographs: Gold & Goose

Above: Wish they all could be California girls.

Above centre: Rossi and Yamaha's previous world champion, Wayne Rainey.

Top: Vermeulen's second place made up for disappointment here last year.

Photographs: Gold & Goose

Spaniard, he made his feelings known by aiming a solid kick at him, though stopping short of actual contact. Caught on television, it roused the ire of beleaguered Race Director Butler, who slapped on an instant $2,000 fine. This provoked even more ire in Hopkins, who had been the victim of a previous Draconian decision in 2003 – he had been disqualified from the following race after triggering a first-corner pile-up at Motegi. 'I think Race Direction is a bunch of idiots. That's just my feeling. They know that,' he said, adding, 'Checa was on the racing line, just screwing around. I don't know why I get pin-pointed every time something bad goes on.'

The hoped-for Team Roberts resurgence stayed on hold. The awaited new chassis had been finished in time for team manager Chuck Aksland to bring it over as hand luggage, and it was fitted up forthwith. Kenny Junior had already pulled back from a vague suggestion that he might return at Laguna; Kurtis got on with setting up the new bike. 'It holds the line better coming out of the corner,' he said, rather wistfully. Without horsepower, however, it hardly mattered.

The very early silly season took another couple of steps forward, Vermeulen confirming on the rostrum that he would stay at Suzuki, Melandri beaming about a new two-year deal with Ducati. After the early Hopkins/Kawasaki announcement the week before in Germany, this further intensified speculation about the few remaining seats. And there was a nostalgic interlude, when local resident Wayne Rainey was inducted to the track's Hall of Fame, in a pre-weekend ceremony at Rainey Curve. In addition, the mayor of Monterey, Chuck Della Sala, issued a proclamation naming July 19 as Wayne Rainey Day.

A weekend with plenty going on, but in the end not enough of it on the race-track. By far the most important occurrence at Laguna was another more-or-less processional race. This time, Bridgestone emphatically regained the upper hand, controlling the rostrum, while Michelin was back to missing the target. For another race, tyres had controlled the outcome, effectively ruling out any dicing and the hoped-for strong ride from Pedrosa as well as Rossi, who made an impassioned plea after the race for a remedy from Michelin. TV viewers in Spain and Italy must have switched off in their thousands. It was a key moment in the formulation of the forthcoming control-tyre proposal.

MOTOGP RACE – 32 laps

There had now been a dozen races where someone other than pole qualifier had won. Stoner had twice been victim, but would have no truck with talk of a jinx, nor with doing anything but dominating every practice session. He ended up with a margin of two-tenths, large for this track, over Pedrosa and Vermeulen, with Hayden and Rossi peering over their shoulders. The jinx was in major jeopardy.

Race day was hot, but not as hot as in 2006, nor as in Germany the week before.

Pedrosa led away over the Turn One crest, Stoner chasing and Hayden swooping up around the outside into the next double-apex left. His late-entry trajectory carried him right into the path of early-entry Hopkins, who had already slipped off when his bike slammed into the double-winner's Honda, damaging the rear brake line. The defending Laguna champion was disconsolate – something similar had happened to him in China: 'It's just the way my season went – I mean, twice already this year. That's not normal.' Hopkins remounted, rode to the pits, then rejoined for a race-length test, to be rewarded with one point after further attrition ahead.

Stoner was in the lead by the time they reached the top of the hill, and would stay there until it was time to go home for the summer holidays. Not without some pressure. Pedrosa hung on to second and Vermeulen hung on to the Honda for a three-strong break-away. Rossi was fourth, but had been losing ground from the start, and was more than five seconds off the leader after just six laps. He had problems with rear grip, and they would not get better.

Pedrosa was suffering too, and Vermeulen was quick to pounce at the last corner on to the front straight, taking second on lap four. At this point, he was 1.3 seconds adrift of Stoner, and his pursuit would bring him tantalisingly closer, to within a second for the next five laps. 'At one point, I thought I was catching him, but I must have been kidding myself,' he said, for Stoner pulled out a few tenths on the 11th, keeping the pace while Vermeulen lost a shade here and there, and the pursuit was over.

'Everything was perfect this weekend. I just sort of kept my head down, made sure I reeled off a few more laps just to seal the victory,' Stoner explained, dauntingly for his rivals. He would stretch comfortably away so that he could ease off on the final lap and still win by almost ten seconds.

His sixth win not only broke the pole jinx, but also struck a decisive blow in the championship; he would go on holiday with a highly reassuring lead of 44 points. It was also the start of a triple hat-trick: he would get pole, best lap and victory at the next two races as well. At the beginning of the season, he said, he had hoped to be 'inside the top five in the championship. Which is looking pretty good now. I guess I had to set our goals a little bit higher.'

For Vermeulen also, the issue was sealed. He couldn't match Stoner, but he was already better than six seconds clear of Pedrosa, and was not to be threatened to the finish.

Pedrosa had his hands full, however. Melandri had finished lap one in sixth and had found sufficient rhythm to get ahead of the troubled Michelin runner Edwards; on lap ten, he also passed Rossi. He was only two seconds behind Pedrosa, and the gap gradually closed until by lap 15, he was on him and easily by him next time around. It was a remarkable ride. In the morning, unable to operate the gearshift without being pumped full of pain-killers, his only hope had been to make the finish. 'It's unbelievable to be here,' he said on the rostrum. 'It's been one of the best days in my life.'

There would be one more change to the top five. Pedrosa was finding it harder as chatter problems increased with the laps, and while Rossi was having similar tyre problems, it was to a lesser degree. He'd stayed close, and he reversed the positions on lap 20. He was still within sight of Melandri, but would drop back, while the dispirited Pedrosa would do the same behind him. Rossi smiled wryly as he sought solace in being at least 'the first Michelin. At the Sachsenring, all the Michelins finished up front, and the Bridgestones couldn't finish. Today, the difference between us and Bridgestone was big. I think that unfortunately it's too divided. A tyre should be an instrument, not the deciding factor, in a contest. People at home are fans of riders and bikes – Ducati or Rossi or Stoner – but they're not fans of Bridgestone or Michelin. Racing like this is pretty frustrating, but there's nothing we can do,' he said.

Edwards had led the pursuit early on; Capirossi had been ruled out of it on lap four after he had ceded seventh to de Puniet, when a gearbox glitch put him out. The second Yamaha rider was also battling with a serious lack of grip, however, and when de Puniet attacked with ten laps to go, he had no response. Nor on the next lap to Tamada and West, as his condition deteriorated.

West took seventh behind his team-mate, but Tamada stayed right up close for an impressive eighth, the best so far in his Dunlop year. Less than a second behind, Barros snitched ninth from Roger Lee Hayden on the last lap.

Edwards, the second American finisher, had dropped to 11th by the flag, with Nakano and Guintoli trailing in, then Checa a long way back, last rider on the same lap. Hopkins was two laps down after rejoining and took the last point; rookie Davies was another lap adrift after an experience in the deep end.

Hayden had been ahead of Hopkins when he finally gave up the unequal struggle on lap 23, his brake problems compounding tyre and other issues. Roberts had retired after just five laps with engine management problems. Duhamel also had pitted early, saying, 'My head wasn't in the race, and I didn't want to just ride around and mess it up for somebody.'

Below left: Roger Lee Hayden made an impressive top-ten debut.

Below centre left: Rossi, Melandri and Nakano get through safely as Hopkins crashes out. Hayden is heading for gravel.

Bottom left: Tamada heading for eighth, the former GP winner's best of the year.

Below: Tough guy Melandri crashed heavily on Saturday, made the rostrum on Sunday.

Photographs: Gold & Goose

RED BULL US GRAND PRIX

22 JULY 2007 • FIM WORLD CHAMPIONSHIP ROUND 11

LAGUNA SECA

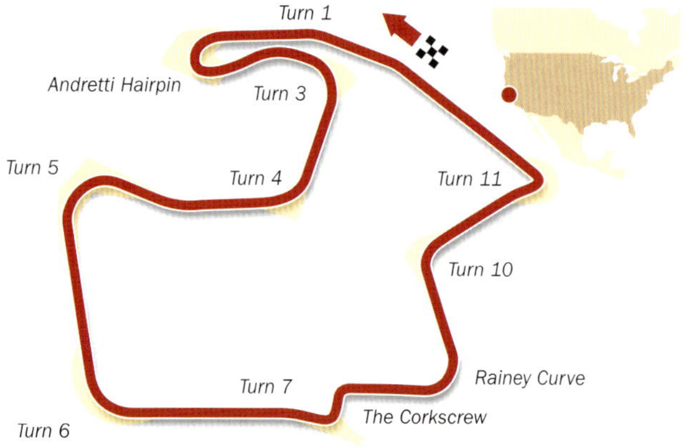

Circuit 3.602km /2.238 miles

MotoGP

RACE: 32 laps, 71.776 miles/115.520km • Weather: Dry • Air 30°C • Humidity 39% • Track 46°C

Pos.	Rider	Nat.	No.	Entrant	Machine	Tyres	Laps	Time & speed (mph/km/h)
1	Casey Stoner	AUS	27	Ducati Team	Ducati	B	32	44m 20.325s 97.135mph/ 156.323km/h
2	Chris Vermeulen	AUS	71	Rizla Suzuki MotoGP	Suzuki	B	32	44m 30.190s
3	Marco Melandri	ITA	33	Honda Gresini	Honda	B	32	44m 45.966s
4	Valentino Rossi	ITA	46	Fiat Yamaha Team	Yamaha	M	32	44m 50.989s
5	Dani Pedrosa	SPA	26	Repsol Honda Team	Honda	M	32	44m 55.947s
6	Randy de Puniet	FRA	14	Kawasaki Racing Team	Kawasaki	B	32	44m 58.631s
7	Anthony West	AUS	13	Kawasaki Racing Team	Kawasaki	B	32	45m 01.747s
8	Makoto Tamada	JPN	6	Dunlop Yamaha Tech 3	Yamaha	D	32	45m 02.680s
9	Alex Barros	BRA	4	Pramac d'Antin	Ducati	B	32	45m 03.845s
10	Roger Lee Hayden	USA	95	Kawasaki Racing Team	Kawasaki	B	32	45m 04.045s
11	Colin Edwards	USA	5	Fiat Yamaha Team	Yamaha	M	32	45m 07.701s
12	Shinya Nakano	JPN	56	Konica Minolta Honda	Honda	M	32	45m 13.173s
13	Sylvain Guintoli	FRA	50	Dunlop Yamaha Tech 3	Yamaha	D	32	45m 18.735s
14	Carlos Checa	SPA	7	Honda LCR	Honda	M	32	45m 35.691s
15	John Hopkins	USA	21	Rizla Suzuki MotoGP	Suzuki	B	30	45m 35.595s
16	Chaz Davies	GBR	57	Pramac d'Antin	Ducati	B	29	44m 34.640s
	Nicky Hayden	USA	1	Repsol Honda Team	Honda	M	22	31m 49.864s
	Miguel DuHamel	CAN	17	Honda Gresini	Honda	B	10	14m 29.711s
	Kurtis Roberts	USA	80	Team Roberts	KR212V	M	5	7m 16.822s
	Loris Capirossi	ITA	65	Ducati Team	Ducati	B	3	4m 21.970s

Fastest lap: Casey Stoner, on lap 19, 1m 22.542s, 97.833mph/157.447km/h (record).

Previous lap record: Dani Pedrosa, SPA (Honda), 1m 23.333s, 96.904mph/155.952km/h (2006).

Event best maximum speed: Alex Barros, 159.7mph/257.0km/h (race)

Grid order	1	2	3	4	5	6	7	8	9	10	11	12	13	14	15	16	17	18	19	20	21	22	23	24	25	26	27	28	29	30	31	32	•
27 STONER	27	27	27	27	27	27	27	27	27	27	27	27	27	27	27	27	27	27	27	27	27	27	27	27	27	27	27	27	27	27	27	27	1
26 PEDROSA	26	26	26	71	71	71	71	71	71	71	71	71	71	71	71	71	71	71	71	71	71	71	71	71	71	71	71	71	71	71	71	71	2
71 VERMEULEN	71	71	71	26	26	26	26	26	26	26	26	26	26	26	26	33	33	33	33	33	33	33	33	33	33	33	33	33	33	33	33	33	3
1 HAYDEN	46	46	46	46	46	46	46	46	46	33	33	33	33	33	33	26	26	26	26	46	46	46	46	46	46	46	46	46	46	46	46	46	4
46 ROSSI	5	5	5	5	33	33	33	33	33	46	46	46	46	46	46	46	46	46	46	26	26	26	26	26	26	26	26	26	26	26	26	26	5
65 CAPIROSSI	33	33	33	33	5	5	5	5	5	5	5	5	5	5	5	5	5	5	5	5	5	5	5	14	14	14	14	14	14	14	14	14	6
21 HOPKINS	65	65	14	14	14	14	14	14	14	14	14	14	14	14	14	14	14	14	14	14	14	14	14	5	6	6	6	6	13	13	13	13	7
5 EDWARDS	56	14	65	6	6	6	6	6	6	6	6	6	6	6	6	6	6	6	6	6	6	6	6	6	13	13	13	13	6	6	6	6	8
56 NAKANO	14	6	6	56	56	56	56	56	56	56	56	56	56	56	56	56	13	13	13	13	13	13	13	13	5	5	5	5	95	95	95	4	9
33 MELANDRI	6	56	56	7	7	7	7	95	13	13	13	13	13	13	13	13	56	56	56	56	95	95	95	95	95	95	95	95	4	4	4	95	10
6 TAMADA	7	7	7	95	95	95	95	13	95	95	95	95	95	95	95	95	95	95	95	95	56	4	4	4	4	4	4	4	5	5	5	5	11
13 WEST	95	95	95	13	13	13	13	4	4	4	4	4	4	4	4	4	4	4	4	4	4	56	56	56	56	56	56	56	56	56	56	56	12
14 de PUNIET	13	13	13	4	4	4	4	7	7	7	50	50	7	7	50	50	50	50	50	50	50	50	50	50	50	50	50	50	50	50	50	50	13
50 GUINTOLI	57	4	4	50	50	50	50	50	50	50	7	7	50	50	7	7	7	7	7	7	7	7	7	7	7	7	7	7	7	7	7	7	14
7 CHECA	4	57	57	57	57	1	1	1	1	57	57	57	57	1	1	1	1	1	1	1	1	1	21	21	21	21	21	21	21	21			15
95 HAYDEN	50	50	50	1	1	57	57	57	57	1	1	1	1	57	21	21	21	21	21	21	21	21	57	57	57	57	57	57	57				16
4 BARROS	80	1	1	80	80	17	17	17	17	17	21	21	21	21	57	57	57	57	57	57	57	57											
80 ROBERTS	1	80	80	17	17	21	21	21	21	21																							
17 DUHAMEL	17	17	17	21	21																												
57 DAVIES	21	21	21																														

FASTEST RACE LAPS

	Rider	Lap	Time
1	Stoner	19	1m 22.542s
2	Vermeulen	5	1m 22.636s
3	Hopkins	8	1m 22.848s
4	Melandri	28	1m 23.140s
5	Pedrosa	3	1m 23.339s
6	Rossi	27	1m 23.375s
7	West	11	1m 23.486s
8	de Puniet	19	1m 23.607s
9	R. Hayden	16	1m 23.615s
10	Barros	15	1m 23.628s
11	Tamada	20	1m 23.661s
12	Nakano	9	1m 23.695s
13	Edwards	4	1m 23.725s
14	Davies	27	1m 23.781s
15	Guintoli	7	1m 23.846s
16	Checa	5	1m 24.228s
17	Capirossi	2	1m 24.749s
18	N. Hayden	9	1m 24.710s
19	Roberts	5	1m 24.896s
20	DuHamel	5	1m 25.580s

QUALIFYING

21 July 2007

Weather: Dry

Air: 25°C Humidity: 49%

Track: 43°C

Pos.	Rider	Time
1	Stoner	1m 22.292s
2	Pedrosa	1m 22.501s
3	Vermeulen	1m 22.590s
4	N. Hayden	1m 22.624s
5	Rossi	1m 22.683s
6	Capirossi	1m 22.914s
7	Hopkins	1m 22.933s
8	Edwards	1m 22.943s
9	Nakano	1m 23.006s
10	Melandri	1m 23.018s
11	Tamada	1m 23.036s
12	West	1m 23.091s
13	de Puniet	1m 23.113s
14	Guintoli	1m 23.207s
15	Checa	1m 23.263s
16	R. Hayden	1m 23.425s
17	Barros	1m 23.557s
18	Roberts	1m 23.662s
19	DuHamel	1m 23.923s
20	Davies	1m 24.098s

statistics

RIDER STANDINGS
After 11 Rounds

1	Casey Stoner	221
2	Valentino Rossi	177
3	Dani Pedrosa	155
4	Chris Vermeulen	113
5	Marco Melandri	113
6	John Hopkins	104
7	Colin Edwards	93
8	Loris Capirossi	77
9	Alex Barros	76
10	Nicky Hayden	73
11	Alex Hofmann	60
12	Randy de Puniet	50
13	Toni Elias	49
14	Makoto Tamada	31
15	Carlos Checa	29
16	Anthony West	29
17	Shinya Nakano	29
18	Sylvain Guintoli	21
19	Kurtis Roberts	8
20	Roger Lee Hayden	6
21	Michel Fabrizio	6
22	Fonsi Nieto	5
23	Olivier Jacque	4
24	Kenny Roberts Jnr	4

TEAM STANDINGS
After 11 Rounds

1	Ducati Team	298
2	Fiat Yamaha Team	270
3	Repsol Honda Team	228
4	Rizla Suzuki MotoGP	217
5	Honda Gresini	168
6	Pramac d'Antin	136
7	Kawasaki Racing Team	88
8	Dunlop Yamaha Tech 3	52
9	Honda LCR	29
10	Konica Minolta Honda	29
11	Team Roberts	12

CONSTRUCTOR STANDINGS
After 11 Rounds

1	Ducati	233
2	Yamaha	197
3	Honda	190
4	Suzuki	151
5	Kawasaki	74
6	KR212V	12

An increasingly familiar sight – Stoner dashing away from the start. Hopkins would chase throughout, Pedrosa (26) succumb to team-mate Hayden behind him.
Photograph: Gold & Goose

FIM WORLD CHAMPIONSHIP • ROUND 12

CZECHGP
BRNO

RIZLA+
HOPPER
Arai
HELMET
MONSTER
ENERGY
HOPPER
RIZLA+
SUZUKI
MotoGP
Puig
Racing Screens
motogp

Above: **Ducati GP pioneer Loris Capirossi announced his departure to Suzuki.**

Top: **Toni Elias was back, and rode bravely to 11th.**

Left: **John Hopkins rode the race of his life. Only Stoner beat him.**

Photographs: Gold & Goose

MOTOGP got back to work at Brno, tanned and relaxed in most cases, still fighting for fitness in others. And failing unexpectedly, too, in the case of Marco Melandri, whose first outing on Friday morning triggered acute pain from a prolapsed disc in his neck, a legacy of his tumbling Laguna crash, which forced him to withdraw.

Everyone was hoping that the sweeping corners of the fine Brno circuit would reverse the trend of the previous two tight tracks and that we might see some close racing again. That hope would be confounded, as we shall see, although this time the tyre differences were not quite so clear cut as in Germany and America. The reason this time was something quite different – Stoner and a Ducati on such form that they just stretched everybody else into a hopeless pursuit. Shades of Mick Doohan and a time when (as he said himself) 'racing was as boring as sh*t.' Sadly, the 250 race was little different (this time chasing Lorenzo); it was left to the 125s again to show how exciting good motorcycle racing can be.

Never mind. With Rossi having another nightmare weekend – off form, off the pace and off the face of the earth when he was not on the bike, for reasons we shall return to – the shape of the championship became all but unalterable. This made it easier for the defeated to forget a rather bleak Sunday and think about Monday: the first chance for everybody to go testing since Barcelona, fully ten weeks before. And there was certainly plenty to test.

Michelin was back with a raft of new tyres – new construction especially, and compound too – after making good use of the break. They needed testing before use, however, which had to wait until Monday, much to the chagrin of Pedrosa and Rossi. Honda had new engine parts, as did most of the rest to some degree or another. Yamaha had the biggest news, kept under wraps until after the race: a pneumatic-valve-spring engine for Rossi to test. By now, he was so desperate, he would have been happy to test springs made from marshmallow.

Hayden couldn't wait until after the race, trying the new top-end engine parts on Friday and pronouncing himself disappointed. It may have been a bluff, for while he let it be known that he'd gone back to the old parts, his team said he'd raced the new engine and the new chassis. He certainly did something right, for he was top Michelin runner, adding to an interrupted trio of rostrums.

Rossi was in some kind of self-imposed purdah, giving none of his usual daily press briefings and avoiding formal conferences by neither qualifying on the front row nor finishing on the rostrum. The reason was yet another spectacular turn of fortune in an already Dickensian life. The way it's been running for Rossi recently, it was bad fortune, in the shape of the Italian tax department. Questioning the veracity of his status as a London resident, it had issued a demand for more than 100-million Euros, which included back taxes and penalties, with the threat of worse to come. Revelations to the press had been mounting over the past week, about his fleet of seven cars in Italy, his Pershing 50 boat moored near his home town of Tavullia and so on.

Rossi had declined to speak to the press, issuing a filmed statement that he was being exploited, a high-profile scapegoat in a political game played by Italy's new government. 'The professionals who handle my income declarations have assured me that they respected the rules,' he said. He wasn't about to succumb to the hungry pack of Italian pressmen at the circuit either – but this was a story that wasn't going to go away. Taking the worst finish of the year so far just added to the gloom.

Elias was back, his grin looking even bigger atop a visibly thinner frame, and walking on crutches. He was, he reckoned, only at about 60 per cent, still just 51 days after the spiral fracture of his femur, and had ridden a motorcycle for the first time only two days before. That had been at Misano, in a come-back test on a 600 Supersport, along with team-mate Melandri, having nursed his dislocated ankle through the summer break. Elias fell again in practice, but was unscathed and raced bravely to 11th.

That position was won from West, riding a Kawasaki that was back in lime green from the former darker metallic shade, after a corporate decree from Japan. Still finding his feet, West was short of set-up and still attempting to come to terms with qualifying tyres.

Hofmann's Ducati seat had been expected to go to Davies after his US GP debut, but instead the team went for their more regular substitute, Spaniard Ivan Silva.

More contract news: Marlboro graciously loaned its hospitality unit to Loris Capirossi so he could announce his move to Suzuki in 2008, a one-year contract. James Toseland had been confirmed for Tech 3 in the interim, and now it was released that his team-mate would be Colin Edwards. Still awaiting formal confirmation was the obvious – that Edwards was being moved aside to make way for Jorge Lorenzo. The prospect of the assertive 250 star sharing a pit with Rossi made for many a wry smile, but this time (not for the first time), Lorenzo's plans for extravagant celebration were undermined by events. Spain was about to record its 300th grand prix win, and Jorge's promo squad had all the paraphernalia ready. Jorge won the race alright, from pole position – his seventh of each so far – but an hour earlier, Hector Faubel had won the 125 race. Thus, Lorenzo was the 301st Spanish winner.

Race morning was interrupted by a sobering crash during 250 warm-up, when the perennially luckless Taro Sekiguchi suffered another major impact. Simoncelli had fallen on the right running out of the stadium section. The tumbling Gilera had gone on to the dirt, kicked up a cloud of dust, then slid back to come to rest on the track. A couple of riders passed safely, but Sekiguchi came through the dust cloud right on line and hit the fallen bike with explosive force. He rocketed over the handlebars and was stretchered away, still motionless, to be helicoptered to hospital. Later came the welcome news that, in spite of his injuries, which included a broken pelvis, he had regained consciousness and his life was not threatened. The debris and oil on the track took so long to clear that the 125 race was delayed.

MOTOGP RACE – 22 laps

For a third race in succession, Stoner took pole, having dominated every session except Friday afternoon's, when Dunlop-shod Guintoli fitted a qualifying tyre for a brief moment of glory. Michelin qualifiers hoisted Hayden and Pedrosa to the front row, from tenth and eighth respectively on race tyres. Hopkins had been set for a front-row spot, and perhaps even pole, after fastest section times – until he crashed. Even so, he led row two from de Puniet, with Rossi on the far end. He too might have improved, but his second qualifying tyre didn't hold up for a full lap.

Stoner was on the second race of a perfect set of three: pole position, fastest lap (not quite a new record) and victory. He began with a super start that meant he already had breathing space ahead of Pedrosa, Hopkins and Hayden by turn one. He'd stretched it to seven tenths by the end of the lap, while Hopkins was second, Pedrosa on the wrong side of the tyre equation again.

It was the start of a steadfast pursuit by the Suzuki rider, in his best ride and heading for a best-ever result. Only second, however. He held the gap at less than a second for the first five laps, and by the ninth, it was still less than 1.5 seconds. Stoner was equally steadfast, but had more weaponry. Over the next three laps, he gained another second, then kept on stretching. Hopkins, in turn, had more than five seconds on his pursuers and could afford to slacken off a little to be sure of a finish.

Hayden had dived underneath Pedrosa on the second lap, but again his pace was slightly slower than the leaders, and he also lost ground slowly, but steadily, in another processional race where the opposition was reduced to a vain pursuit of the flying Ducati.

On lap three, the second red Duke had displaced Pedrosa, but he couldn't make it stick, a sliding front tyre taking the blame; two laps later, Pedrosa was back to fourth, less than two seconds behind his team-mate. Try as he might, he couldn't prevent the gap from widening gradually, although he was less than three seconds behind at the end. His disquiet at the performance of the Michelins, like Rossi's, was growing.

Above: **Edwards tried too hard to make up for a bad start, and paid the price.**

Above right: **Even the crowd was colour-coded.**

Top: **A modern MotoGP race start: effective wheelie- and launch-control electronics mean only one bike, Randy de Puniet's Kawasaki, has a front wheel in the air.**

Photographs: Gold & Goose

Capirossi had been running wide and fell back into the grip of the next trio: Rossi, de Puniet and Vermeulen. Rossi appeared to be biding his time, and on lap eight, he ran underneath the Ducati at the chicane that starts the hill-climb. De Puniet also got ahead of Capirossi briefly, before dropping to the back of the group on lap ten.

As half-distance came and went, Vermeulen looked the strongest of the four, and by lap 14, the Suzuki had passed not only Capirossi, but also Rossi. This unusual event proved that Rossi was not waiting, but in trouble. Tyres, again, and one lap later, Capirossi got ahead at the first corner, in spite of running wide. Rossi lost touch at once, and it was all he could do to stay ahead of de Puniet.

It had been a disastrous weekend, and Rossi said that he had never really been on the pace, 'but it was worse than I expected.' They'd sacrificed some corner speed to a setting that improved traction. 'Then when the tyre made a big step down, I just had to wait for the end of the race. I am sad because I wasn't even able to fight today. At the end, I had to push to the limit to stay in front of de Puniet.'

The next big group had been led at half-distance by Guintoli, chased by Checa, Barros, Elias and West. The Yamaha slowed drastically five laps from the end, the tyres shot. By then, Barros had already got by and moved clear. Checa was next, by himself; heroic Elias and West were battling, the Spaniard in front over the last two laps. Guintoli was another five seconds away, then came the struggling Nakano, a long way down. Roberts was next, followed by Silva and Tamada.

Edwards was the only non-finisher. Pushing hard to make up for a bad start from the third row, he had lost the front on lap two and slid to earth. 'I've never lost the front so fast – it must not have been up to temperature,' he explained.

250cc RACE – 20 laps

Fast and spacious, Brno has always been kind to Aprilias, and Lorenzo was ready to emulate his hero, Biaggi, multiple Brno 250 winner. Lorenzo's seventh pole in 2007 was by a margin of more than half a second, with wild-card team-mate Alex Debon second and Dovizioso a close third. De Angelis completed the front row, shrugging off the effects of a heavy tumble on Friday.

The race up front was much as in the bigger class, or maybe even more processional. Lorenzo was in the lead by the first corner, Dovizioso behind him. Those positions would not change for the rest of the afternoon. De Angelis was next, then Kallio and Hiro Aoyama, the latter succumbing to Barbera on lap two as the Spaniard closed on the leaders. One lap later, Bautista ran past the KTM, charging hard from his row-three start.

For the next ten laps, the order stayed the same, except on the eighth, when Kallio changed places with de Angelis for third. At this point, Barbera was more than a second adrift, with Bautista closing remorselessly.

Dovizioso chased Lorenzo as hard as he could, remaining very close and threatening, within a tenth or two every time over the line. On lap 14, it was over. Lorenzo turned up the wick to set fastest lap, a new record. Dovizioso's efforts to follow suit were rewarded with a big slide that almost threw him out of the seat. The effort was beyond the capability of his slower motorcycle, and he was obliged to back off and settle for a safe second. His mood afterwards was blacker than ever.

A little way back, de Angelis and Kallio were battling it out, the Aprilia rider back in front until lap 18, when the KTM found a way past. Next time through the jam-packed stadium section, Kallio took a wide line through the second left-hander. De Angelis thought he saw a gap and tried to go through it, only for Kallio to come swinging back across his front wheel. De Angelis tried to tighten his line still further, but slipped off the edge of the tyre instead. He hit Kallio as he fell, the Finn lucky to stay on board.

Behind, Bautista had finally passed Barbera with six laps to go, but it wasn't over yet, and the compatriots battled hard enough to slow their pace, giving Hiro Aoyama a sniff at catching up. He never quite made it, but had a fine view as Barbera pushed ahead on the second-to-last lap, holding fourth at the finish by half a second.

Luthi was a lone seventh, still well clear of the next battling trio. They were headed over the line by a persistent Simon, finally edging ahead of team-mate Shuhei Aoyama, with Locatelli just over a second adrift.

De Angelis had got back on board quickly enough to save seventh, ahead of a group led by Lai.

Debon had got away badly to finish lap one in 12th, and had got back to eighth when he crashed hard and fast at the first corner at half-distance, rolling and tumbling all the way to the air-fence. Simoncelli and Takahashi also crashed out early on.

125cc RACE – 19 laps

Team-mates and title rivals Talmacsi and Faubel were first and second on the grid, the Hungarian rhapsodic at the (possibly hyperbolic) notion that 30,000 compatriots would attend the race. Local hero Pesek, who could count on rather more countrymen in the crowd, had recovered from a first-day crash to lead row two.

Talmacsi led away; Pasini took over for the next two laps, with Pesek working his way through to third by lap four, setting fastest lap (slower than Cecchinello's 2003 record).

On lap six, Gadea regained third and started to bring the chase group with him. At the half-way point, Pasini was back ahead of Talmacsi, with Gadea, Pesek and Faubel close behind. An inspired Ranseder had lost sixth to Koyama and would soon succumb also to Nieto, until the Spaniard slid off with eight laps left.

Now Gadea led for a lap before Pasini shoved past and looked as though he might escape. Not so. With three laps left, the front five were together again. Then Gadea fell from second at the first corner, adding a couple more tenths to Pasini's lead.

It didn't last. Pesek got up to second with two laps left, then Faubel dived past both of them to lead on to the final lap. Running three and even four abreast, the positions shuffled turn by turn. Talmacsi led at the first corner, but was third half-way around the lap. They all bustled into the last left-right combination, Faubel emerging in front from Pasini, Pesek holding Talmacsi narrowly at bay, all crossing the line in less than three-tenths. Faubel's win regained him the points lead.

Koyama was next and alone; Espargaro held off Corsi and Ranseder. Krummenacher was ninth, Cortese tenth, then came Rabat on the first Honda, leading a big group that included Smith in 13th.

Above: Locatelli and a Gilera crew member watch the timing screens.

Top: Lorenzo was too fast for Dovizioso in a processional 250 race.

Above left: Kallio survived a collision to secure another podium finish.

Left: Pasini demonstrates to a Czech model the hazards of the rostrum.

Below: Thrilling 125 race restored faith for the fans – Faubel narrowly heads Pasini to the line; Pesek (52) is about to pass half-hidden Talmacsi.

Photographs: Gold & Goose

CARDION AB GRAND PRIX CESKE REPUBLIKY

19 AUGUST 2007 • FIM WORLD CHAMPIONSHIP ROUND 12

AUTODROM BRNO

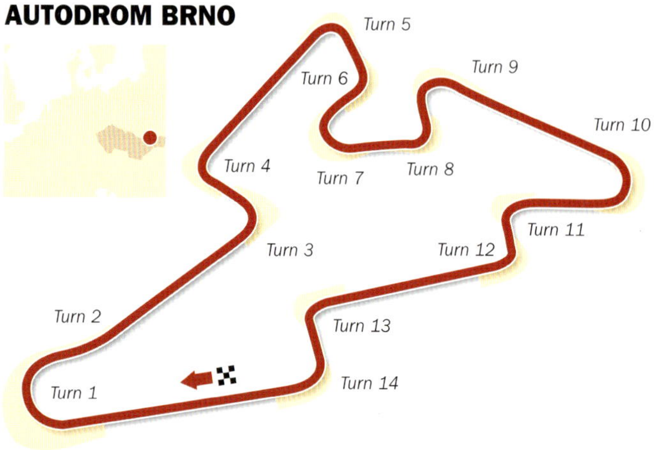

Circuit 5.403km / 3.357 miles

MotoGP

RACE: 22 laps, 73.854 miles/118.866km • Weather: Dry • Air 26°C • Humidity 40% • Track 35°C

Pos.	Rider	Nat.	No.	Entrant	Machine	Tyres	Laps	Time & speed (mph/km/h)
1	Casey Stoner	AUS	27	Ducati Marlboro Team	Ducati	B	22	43m 45.810s 101.262mph/ 162.965km/h
2	John Hopkins	USA	21	Rizla Suzuki MotoGP	Suzuki	B	22	43m 53.713s
3	Nicky Hayden	USA	1	Repsol Honda Team	Honda	M	22	43m 58.910s
4	Dani Pedrosa	SPA	26	Repsol Honda Team	Honda	M	22	44m 01.610s
5	Chris Vermeulen	AUS	71	Rizla Suzuki MotoGP	Suzuki	B	22	44m 03.113s
6	Loris Capirossi	ITA	65	Ducati Marlboro Team	Ducati	B	22	44m 05.173s
7	Valentino Rossi	ITA	46	Fiat Yamaha Team	Yamaha	M	22	44m 08.295s
8	Randy de Puniet	FRA	14	Kawasaki Racing Team	Kawasaki	B	22	44m 08.883s
9	Alex Barros	BRA	4	Pramac d'Antin	Ducati	B	22	44m 18.102s
10	Carlos Checa	SPA	7	Honda LCR	Honda	M	22	44m 20.963s
11	Toni Elias	SPA	24	Honda Gresini	Honda	B	22	44m 23.558s
12	Anthony West	AUS	13	Kawasaki Racing Team	Kawasaki	B	22	44m 24.060s
13	Sylvain Guintoli	FRA	50	Dunlop Yamaha Tech 3	Yamaha	D	22	44m 29.504s
14	Shinya Nakano	JPN	56	Konica Minolta Honda	Honda	M	22	44m 42.879s
15	Kurtis Roberts	USA	80	Team Roberts	KR212V	M	22	44m 55.413s
16	Ivan Silva	SPA	22	Pramac d'Antin	Ducati	B	22	45m 07.220s
17	Makoto Tamada	JPN	6	Dunlop Yamaha Tech 3	Yamaha	D	22	45m 11.614s
	Colin Edwards	USA	5	Fiat Yamaha Team	Yamaha	M	2	5m 25.074s
	Marco Melandri	ITA	33	Honda Gresini	Honda	B		DNQ

Fastest lap: Casey Stoner, on lap 13, 1m 58.301s, 102.164mph/164.41km/h.

Lap record: Loris Capirossi, ITA (Ducati), 1m 58.157s, 102.289mph/164.618km/h (2006).

Event best maximum speed: Dani Pedrosa, 182.7mph/294.1km/h (warm-up).

Grid order	1	2	3	4	5	6	7	8	9	10	11	12	13	14	15	16	17	18	19	20	21	22	•
27 STONER	27	27	27	27	27	27	27	27	27	27	27	27	27	27	27	27	27	27	27	27	27	27	1
1 HAYDEN	21	21	21	21	21	21	21	21	21	21	21	21	21	21	21	21	21	21	21	21	21	21	2
26 PEDROSA	26	1	1	1	1	1	1	1	1	1	1	1	1	1	1	1	1	1	1	1	1	1	3
21 HOPKINS	1	26	65	65	26	26	26	26	26	26	26	26	26	26	26	26	26	26	26	26	26	26	4
14 de PUNIET	65	65	26	26	65	65	65	46	46	46	46	46	46	71	71	71	71	71	71	71	71	71	5
46 ROSSI	46	46	46	46	46	46	46	14	65	65	65	71	71	46	46	65	65	65	65	65	65	65	6
65 CAPIROSSI	14	14	14	14	14	14	14	65	14	71	71	65	65	65	65	46	46	46	46	46	46	46	7
71 VERMEULEN	5	71	71	71	71	71	71	71	71	14	14	14	14	14	14	14	14	14	14	14	14	14	8
5 EDWARDS	71	24	7	7	7	7	7	7	7	50	50	50	50	4	4	4	4	4	4	4	4	4	9
50 GUINTOLI	24	7	24	50	50	50	50	50	50	7	7	4	4	50	50	50	7	7	7	7	7	7	10
56 NAKANO	7	50	50	24	24	24	24	24	24	4	4	7	7	24	7	7	50	13	13	13	24	24	11
7 CHECA	56	56	56	13	13	13	13	4	4	24	24	24	24	7	13	13	13	50	24	24	13	13	12
4 BARROS	50	13	13	56	4	4	4	13	13	13	13	13	13	13	24	24	24	24	50	50	50	50	13
24 ELIAS	4	4	4	4	56	56	56	56	56	56	56	56	56	56	56	56	56	56	56	56	56	56	14
6 TAMADA	13	6	6	6	6	80	80	80	80	80	80	80	80	80	80	80	80	80	80	80	80	80	15
13 WEST	6	80	80	80	80	22	22	22	22	6	6	6	6	6	6	6	6	6	6	22	22	22	
80 ROBERTS	22	22	22	22	22	6	6	6	6	22	22	22	22	22	22	22	22	22	22	6	6	6	
22 SILVA	80	5																					
33 MELANDRI																							

FASTEST RACE LAPS

	Rider	Lap	Time
1	Stoner	3	1m 58.301s
2	Hopkins	3	1m 58.306s
3	Hayden	2	1m 58.714s
4	Pedrosa	6	1m 58.964s
5	Capirossi	3	1m 59.016s
6	Rossi	4	1m 59.221s
7	de Puniet	3	1m 59.329s
8	Vermeulen	4	1m 59.399s
9	Guintoli	2	1m 59.771s
10	Checa	2	1m 59.894s
11	Barros	5	1m 59.930s
12	West	4	2m 00.017s
13	Elias	2	2m 00.128s
14	Nakano	4	2m 00.450s
15	Silva	5	2m 00.919s
16	Roberts	3	2m 00.952s
17	Tamada	3	2m 00.999s
18	Edwards	1	2m 06.884s

QUALIFYING

18 August 2007

Weather: Dry

Air: 25°C Humidity: 33%

Track: 32°C

Pos.	Rider	Time
1	Stoner	1m 56.884s
2	Hayden	1m 57.164s
3	Pedrosa	1m 57.179s
4	Hopkins	1m 57.567s
5	de Puniet	1m 57.599s
6	Rossi	1m 57.640s
7	Capirossi	1m 57.665s
8	Vermeulen	1m 57.699s
9	Edwards	1m 57.702s
10	Guintoli	1m 57.732s
11	Nakano	1m 57.969s
12	Checa	1m 58.143s
13	Barros	1m 58.204s
14	Elias	1m 58.264s
15	Tamada	1m 58.399s
16	West	1m 59.386s
17	Roberts	1m 59.446s
18	Silva	1m 59.721s

statistics

RIDER STANDINGS

After 12 Rounds		
1	Casey Stoner	246
2	Valentino Rossi	186
3	Dani Pedrosa	168
4	Chris Vermeulen	124
5	John Hopkins	124
6	Marco Melandri	113
7	Colin Edwards	93
8	Nicky Hayden	89
9	Loris Capirossi	87
10	Alex Barros	83
11	Alex Hofmann	60
12	Randy de Puniet	58
13	Toni Elias	54
14	Carlos Checa	35
15	Anthony West	33
16	Makoto Tamada	31
17	Shinya Nakano	31
18	Sylvain Guintoli	24
19	Kurtis Roberts	9
20=	Michel Fabrizio	6
20=	Roger Lee Hayden	6
22	Fonsi Nieto	5
23	Olivier Jacque	4
24	Kenny Roberts Jnr	4

EAM STANDINGS

ter 12 Rounds		
1	Ducati Marlboro Team	333
2	Fiat Yamaha Team	279
3	Repsol Honda Team	257
4	Rizla Suzuki MotoGP	248
5	Honda Gresini	173
6	Pramac d'Antin	143
7	Kawasaki Racing Team	100
8	Dunlop Yamaha Tech 3	55
9	Honda LCR	35
0	Konica Minolta Honda	31
1	Team Roberts	13

CONSTRUCTOR STANDINGS

After 12 Rounds		
1	Ducati	258
2	Yamaha	206
3	Honda	206
4	Suzuki	171
5	Kawasaki	82
6	KR212V	13

250cc

20 laps, 67.140 miles/108.060km

Pos.	Rider (Nat.)	No.	Machine	Laps	Time & speed
1	Jorge Lorenzo (SPA)	1	Aprilia	20	41m 04.954s 98.064mph/ 157.818km/h
2	Andrea Dovizioso (ITA)	34	Honda	20	41m 12.662s
3	Mika Kallio (FIN)	36	KTM	20	41m 16.061s
4	Hector Barbera (SPA)	80	Aprilia	20	41m 18.376s
5	Alvaro Bautista (SPA)	19	Aprilia	20	41m 18.898s
6	Hiroshi Aoyama (JPN)	4	KTM	20	41m 18.943s
7	Thomas Luthi (SWI)	12	Aprilia	20	41m 27.771s
8	Julian Simon (SPA)	60	Honda	20	41m 41.293s
9	Shuhei Aoyama (JPN)	73	Honda	20	41m 41.321s
10	Roberto Locatelli (ITA)	15	Gilera	20	41m 42.506s
11	Alex de Angelis (RSM)	3	Aprilia	20	42m 07.570s
12	Fabrizio Lai (ITA)	32	Aprilia	20	42m 18.483s
13	Aleix Espargaro (SPA)	41	Aprilia	20	42m 19.017s
14	Karel Abraham (CZE)	17	Aprilia	20	42m 19.529s
15	Efren Vazquez (SPA)	7	Aprilia	20	42m 19.597s
16	Ratthapark Wilairot (THA)	8	Honda	20	42m 20.119s
17	Dirk Heidolf (GER)	28	Aprilia	20	42m 20.428s
18	Jules Cluzel (FRA)	16	Aprilia	20	42m 45.018s
19	Imre Toth (HUN)	10	Aprilia	20	42m 58.752s
20	Dan Linfoot (GBR)	45	Aprilia	20	43m 02.057s
	Alex Baldolini (ITA)	25	Aprilia	18	DNF
	Eugene Laverty (IRL)	50	Honda	11	DNF
	Alex Debon (SPA)	6	Aprilia	10	DNF
	Yuki Takahashi (JPN)	55	Honda	3	DNF
	Marco Simoncelli (ITA)	58	Gilera	2	DNF
	Ho Wan Chow (CHN)	89	Aprilia		DNQ
	Jiri Mayer (CZE)	87	Honda		DNQ
	Zhu Wang (CHN)	88	Aprilia		DNQ

Fastest lap: Lorenzo, 2m 02.299s, 98.825mph/159.043km/h (record).

Previous lap record: Dani Pedrosa, SPA (Honda), 2m 02.554s, 98.619mph/ 158.712km/h (2005).

Event best maximum speed: Espargaro, 162.4mph/261.4km/h (qualifying practice no. 2).

Qualifying: 1 Lorenzo, 2m 01.368s; 2 Debon, 2m 02.026s; 3 Dovizioso, 2m 02.036s; 4 de Angelis, 2m 02.148s; 5 Barbera, 2m 02.568s; 6 Takahashi, 2m 02.690s; 7 Simon, 2m 02.907s; 8 S. Aoyama, 2m 02.945s; 9 Kallio, 2m 02.956s; 10 H. Aoyama, 2m 03.009s; 11 Bautista, 2m 03.026s; 12 Luthi, 2m 03.372s; 13 Espargaro, 2m 03.788s; 14 Simoncelli, 2m 03.890s; 15 Locatelli, 2m 04.057s; 16 Heidolf, 2m 04.535s; 17 Lai, 2m 04.797s; 18 Wilairot, 2m 04.853s; 19 Vazquez, 2m 05.157s; 20 Abraham, 2m 05.258s; 21 Cluzel, 2m 06.005s; 22 Baldolini, 2m 06.210s; 23 Toth, 2m 06.372s; 24 Laverty, 2m 06.543s; 25 Linfoot, 2m 07.120s; 26 Chow, 2m 09.932s; 27 Mayer, 2m 12.731s; 28 Wang, 2m 13.049s.

Fastest race laps: 1 Lorenzo, 2m 02.299s; 2 Dovizioso, 2m 02.539s; 3 Kallio, 2m 02.714s; 4 Bautista, 2m 02.797s; 5 Barbera, 2m 02.828s; 6 de Angelis, 2m 02.836s; 7 Simon, 2m 03.130s; 8 H. Aoyama, 2m 03.205s; 9 Debon, 2m 03.275s; 10 Luthi, 2m 03.418s; 11 Takahashi, 2m 03.704s; 12 S. Aoyama, 2m 04.108s; 13 Locatelli, 2m 04.282s; 14 Simoncelli, 2m 04.627s; 15 Abraham, 2m 05.166s; 16 Espargaro, 2m 05.214s; 17 Heidolf, 2m 05.342s; 18 Lai, 2m 05.486s; 19 Vazquez, 2m 05.558s; 20 Wilairot, 2m 06.004s; 21 Baldolini, 2m 06.414s; 22 Laverty, 2m 06.997s; 23 Cluzel, 2m 07.169s; 24 Toth, 2m 07.583s; 25 Linfoot, 2m 07.992s.

World Championship: 1 Lorenzo, 216; 2 Dovizioso, 186; 3 de Angelis, 176; 4 Bautista, 127; 5 Barbera, 103; 6 Kallio, 94; 7 H. Aoyama, 88; 8 Luthi, 72; 9 Simon, 69; 10 S. Aoyama, 62; 11 Simoncelli, 57; 12 Takahashi, 49; 13 Lai, 42; 14 Locatelli, 33; 15 Espargaro, 27; 16 Wilairot, 26; 17 West, 25; 18 Heidolf, 17; 19 Abraham, 16; 20 Baldolini, 14; 21 Sekiguchi, 13; 22 Debon, 11; 23 Linfoot, 7; 24 Cluzel, 4; 25 Laverty, 3; 26 Tizon, Toth and Vazquez, 1.

125cc

19 laps, 63.783 miles/102.657km

Pos.	Rider (Nat.)	No.	Machine	Laps	Time & speed
1	Hector Faubel (SPA)	55	Aprilia	19	40m 57.408s 93.447mph/ 150.388km/h
2	Mattia Pasini (ITA)	75	Aprilia	19	40m 57.478s
3	Lukas Pesek (CZE)	52	Derbi	19	40m 57.630s
4	Gabor Talmacsi (HUN)	14	Aprilia	19	40m 57.680s
5	Tomoyoshi Koyama (JPN)	71	KTM	19	41m 05.015s
6	Pol Espargaro (SPA)	44	Aprilia	19	41m 09.474s
7	Simone Corsi (ITA)	24	Aprilia	19	41m 09.802s
8	Michael Ranseder (AUT)	60	Derbi	19	41m 10.411s
9	Randy Krummenacher (SWI)	34	KTM	19	41m 17.172s
10	Sandro Cortese (GER)	11	Aprilia	19	41m 21.451s
11	Esteve Rabat (SPA)	12	Honda	19	41m 31.042s
12	Joan Olive (SPA)	6	Aprilia	19	41m 31.133s
13	Bradley Smith (GBR)	38	Honda	19	41m 31.271s
14	Alexis Masbou (FRA)	7	Honda	19	41m 31.671s
15	Stefano Bianco (ITA)	27	Aprilia	19	41m 36.442s
16	Steve Bonsey (USA)	51	KTM	19	41m 41.249s
17	Lorenzo Zanetti (ITA)	8	Aprilia	19	41m 41.529s
18	Raffaele de Rosa (ITA)	35	Aprilia	19	41m 41.821s
19	Federico Sandi (ITA)	15	Aprilia	19	41m 41.876s
20	Mike di Meglio (FRA)	63	Honda	19	41m 42.074s
21	Roberto Tamburini (ITA)	20	Aprilia	19	41m 49.436s
22	Nicolas Terol (SPA)	18	Derbi	19	41m 55.328s
23	Ricard Cardus (SPA)	86	Aprilia	19	41m 55.507s
24	Joey Litjens (NED)	37	Honda	19	41m 55.946s
25	Toni Wirsing (GER)	94	Honda	19	42m 08.015s
26	Dino Lombardi (ITA)	13	Honda	19	42m 10.190s
27	Hugo van den Berg (NED)	56	Aprilia	19	42m 14.003s
28	Daniel Webb (GBR)	99	Honda	19	42m 21.200s
29	Dominique Aegerter (SWI)	77	Aprilia	19	42m 21.287s
30	Simone Grotzkyj (ITA)	53	Aprilia	19	42m 27.387s
31	Karel Pesek (CZE)	92	Aprilia	18	41m 18.682s
	Sergio Gadea (SPA)	33	Aprilia	16	DNF
	Andrea Iannone (ITA)	29	Aprilia	15	DNF
	Pablo Nieto (SPA)	22	Aprilia	11	DNF
	Robert Muresan (ROU)	95	Derbi	8	DNF
	Michael Prasek (CZE)	93	Honda	7	DNF
	Karel Majek (CZE)	91	FGR	6	DNF

Fastest lap: L. Pesek, 2m 08.145s, 94.316mph/151.787km/h.

Lap record: Lucio Cecchinelllo, ITA (Aprilia), 2m 07.836s, 94.544mph/ 152.154km/h (2003).

Event best maximum speed: Espargaro, 137.1mph/220.7km/h (race).

Qualifying: 1 Talmacsi, 2m 06.861s; 2 Faubel, 2m 07.402s; 3 Pasini, 2m 07.429s; 4 Koyama, 2m 08.155s; 5 L. Pesek, 2m 08.200s; 6 Krummenacher, 2m 08.421s; 7 Gadea, 2m 08.578s; 8 Cortese, 2m 08.614s; 9 Nieto, 2m 08.694s; 10 Espargaro, 2m 08.712s; 11 Ranseder, 2m 08.952s; 12 Corsi, 2m 08.955s; 13 Smith, 2m 09.375s; 14 Tamburini, 2m 09.392s; 15 Masbou, 2m 09.463s; 16 Olive, 2m 09.652s; 17 Iannone, 2m 09.726s; 18 Rabat, 2m 09.729s; 19 di Meglio, 2m 09.734s; 20 Zanetti, 2m 09.845s; 21 Sandi, 2m 09.847s; 22 de Rosa, 2m 10.055s; 23 Muresan, 2m 10.328s; 24 Bianco, 2m 10.477s; 25 Terol, 2m 10.546s; 26 van den Berg, 2m 10.598s; 27 Bonsey, 2m 10.786s; 28 Litjens, 2m 10.820s; 29 Aegerter, 2m 11.121s; 30 Cardus, 2m 11.176s; 31 Wirsing, 2m 11.808s; 32 Webb, 2m 11.933s; 33 Grotzkyj, 2m 11.942s; 34 Lombardi, 2m 12.631s; 35 Prasek, 2m 13.786s; 36 Majek, 2m 15.108s; 37 K. Pesek, 2m 15.723s.

Fastest race laps: 1 L. Pesek, 2m 08.145s; 2 Pasini, 2m 08.221s; 3 Talmacsi, 2m 08.251s; 4 Gadea, 2m 08.268s; 5 Ranseder, 2m 08.283s; 6 Nieto, 2m 08.391s; 7 Faubel, 2m 08.406s; 8 Koyama, 2m 08.455s; 9 Espargaro, 2m 08.541s; 10 Corsi, 2m 08.655s; 11 Cortese, 2m 09.119s; 12 Muresan, 2m 09.210s; 13 Iannone, 2m 09.215s; 14 Krummenacher, 2m 09.216s; 15 Olive, 2m 09.504s; 16 Smith, 2m 09.692s; 17 Rabat, 2m 09.703s; 18 di Meglio, 2m 09.703s; 19 Sandi, 2m 09.768s; 20 Zanetti, 2m 09.772s; 21 Masbou, 2m 09.965s; 22 de Rosa, 2m 10.027s; 23 Bianco, 2m 10.307s; 24 Tamburini, 2m 10.440s; 25 Bonsey, 2m 10.548s; 26 Cardus, 2m 10.922s; 27 van den Berg, 2m 11.041s; 28 Litjens, 2m 11.396s; 29 Terol, 2m 11.573s; 30 Lombardi, 2m 11.729s; 31 Wirsing, 2m 11.937s; 32 Aegerter, 2m 12.223s; 33 Webb, 2m 12.585s; 34 Grotzkyj, 2m 12.587s; 35 K. Pesek, 2m 15.579s; 36 Prasek, 2m 15.899s; 37 Majek, 2m 15.957s.

World Championship: 1 Faubel, 179; 2 Talmacsi, 169; 3 Pesek, 129; 4 Koyama, 129; 5 Corsi, 119; 6 Gadea, 105; 7 Pasini, 86; 8 Smith, 74; 9 Olive, 72; 10 Espargaro, 72; 11 Cortese, 59; 12 Ranseder, 57; 13 Krummenacher, 48; 14 Rabat, 42; 15 de Rosa, 42; 16 Nieto, 35; 17 Zanetti, 30; 18 di Meglio, 22; 19 Iannone, 18; 20 Bradl, 16; 21 Masbou, 15; 22 Bianco, 6; 23 Terol, 6; 24 Bonsey, 3; 25 Froehlich and Jerez, 2; 27 Aegerter, 2; 28 Grotzkyj, 1.

Right and below right: **: Paddock by night – Yamaha and Pramac hospitality units.**

Below: **Flooded track – the water really was waist deep.**

Bottom right: **The sun came out again for race day.**

Photographs: Gold & Goose

Main photograph: **Lightning strike was one of many when a deluge stopped proceedings at lunctime on Friday.**

Photograph: Hidenobu Takeuchi

Left: **Stoner did it again. His wife, Adriana (black T-shirt), was always the first person he greeted after a race**

Photograph: Gold & Goose

FIM WORLD CHAMPIONSHIP • ROUND 13

SAN MARINOGP

MISANO

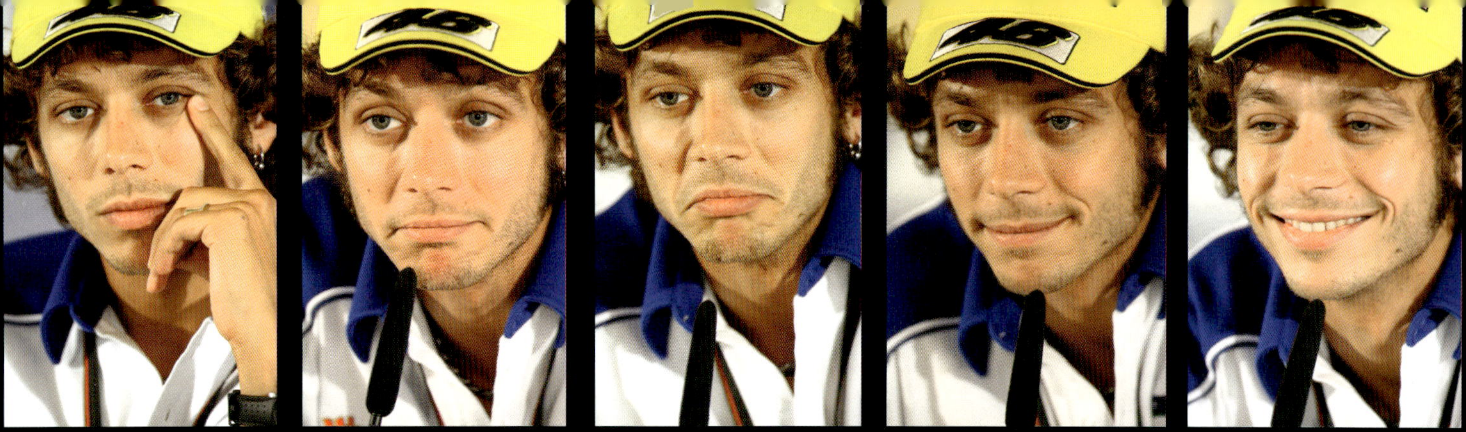

REPSOL
26
Kawasaki
14
48

REPSOL
26

Kawasaki
BRIDGESTONE
REPSOL

ROSSI must have been pleased with the return to Misano. The Santa Monica circuit is less than 10km from Tavullia, the town where he doesn't live any more (for tax purposes), but where he grew up, keeps at least one villa and where his fan base is centred. Something like 1,000 of those fans made the trip to the track on foot. But he could not have anticipated the circumstances of the second race in Italy – named rather grandiosely Gran Premio Cinzano di San Marino e della Riviera di Rimini (there was a special request to the press that the title be used in full, a gift to any journalist being paid by the word).

Firstly, there was his tax problem, with fresh revelations to come. He came out of purdah to attend the usual press debriefs and conferences, but tried to reduce the heat from his fervent home-country media by speaking only in English. Looking contrite, he said:, 'I have tried to make the best situation for me that is possible. If after this control, they understand I have done something wrong, I am ready to take responsibility.'

Secondly, he could have had no idea that the race, and by now the season, would be all about Casey Stoner, who took the third of a hat-trick of triples: pole, fastest lap and victory.

Finally, nobody (certainly nobody at Yamaha) could have expected that his new pneumatic-valve-spring engine would fail only four laps into the race – Rossi slowing suddenly and touring back to the pits. It was, Yamaha informed us immediately, nothing to do with the new pneumatics. Later, it emerged that it was a big-end bearing, a most unexpected failure. When it happened, a goodly proportion of those who had walked to the track turned right around and walked out again. After crashing in Germany and a downbeat Brno, this was the final nail in the coffin of any lingering title hopes.

By then, there were other reasons to lose interest in the race, since both factory Hondas had been put out by a precipitate first-lap crash triggered by an over-enthusiastic de Puniet, leaving Pedrosa and Hayden no chance to make the most of their new Michelins.

It would be nice, but inaccurate, to say that the return to Misano had all started so well. Quite the opposite. It went swimmingly, but in the literal sense. The circuit near the seaside had been dropped from the calendar after Wayne Rainey's career-ending crash there in 1993. The return came after the direction of travel had been reversed, nominally for safety reasons – although there was some doubt about the efficacy. The modern MotoGP carnival was greeted by extraordinary weather.

Only Barros and Capirossi had raced GP bikes at the old Misano, although Rossi also knew it well; only Anthony West had raced in the new clockwise direction, having won a 600 Supersport at the circuit earlier in the year. At the time, he'd expected to quit GP racing, so there was nothing underhand in circumventing the no-pre-testing rule. Race Direction turned a blind eye.

Whether the track was actually safer was a moot point. At the earlier SBK meeting, a Supersport bike had crashed at the end of the back straight, vaulting the railings and the safety fence, and ending up in a (mercifully empty) grandstand. Then Melandri suffered a similar crash, his own error, after touching the grass as he took a wide line through the same fast corners. He fell heavily, miraculously not exacerbating his neck injury; his spinning Honda was rotating so fast when it hit the tyre barriers that it climbed them and also slammed into the fence. It was contained, landing back on top of the tyres.

One reason was the adoption of paved run-off areas, something of a mixed blessing. Stoner explained that in some circumstances 'it gives you a second chance', but it also fails to slow you down if you have fallen off. 'It should be used corner by corner, not just everywhere,' he continued.

The reversed direction had introduced this hazard, with a set of three right-hand corners at the end of the back straight taken at reducing speed, under increasingly hard braking while leaned over. Extremely tricky. Previously, these had been increasing-speed left-handers, very popular with ex-dirt-trackers, for obvious reasons. Aside from this point of interest, the direction change had added little to what Stoner described as 'a go-kart track. It's not really a lot of fun. You can't really get flowing. It's more difficult to manage than enjoyable.'

Because of the new track, extra practice was planned: longer sessions for the smaller classes and a full extra hour on Friday for the big one. The MotoGP tyre allocation was also increased, with two extra rears and one more front. The weather had other ideas, and after rain on Friday morning, everything went haywire. The storm was of tropical, even biblical, proportions and was still going on long after the drainage had been overcome. Uniformed pit crews frantically cleared equipment on to the pit lane as the pit boxes became flooded; out on the track, it was even worse. Flooding was more than a metre deep on at least one corner. Clearly, no more practice on Friday, perhaps nor Saturday either.

Sterling efforts managed to get rid of the water by the next day, however, a hovering helicopter putting the finishing touches on Saturday morning. MotoGP free practice was extended to two hours.

The tyre complaints were getting louder, led by Rossi and Pedrosa from the other Michelin users. Privately, Rossi, deprived by the new rules of the 'Magic Bullet' Saturday-night-special tyre, was already lobbying for the adoption of a single tyre rule. Stoner's response, at a press conference, was a squelcher: 'Competition makes everybody push harder. If we go to a one-tyre rule...we may as well race the R6 cup.' A question was floated as to whether faster bikes should be penalised, or banned. Hayden smiled: 'I like the idea of banning the Ducati, now you mention it.'

Hayden was obliged also to dampen down a story emanating from the US: an employee of his father Earl's Second Chance Autos used-car lot had been implicated in a large-scale drug bust, laundering money and providing vehicles; rumours were growing that there was worse to come for the Hayden family. Happily, they turned out to be quite untrue.

More contract news: West was signed for Kawasaki for 2008, at the expense of de Puniet, who promptly signed for LCR Honda, Stoner's old team. 'It'll be the first winter without wondering what I will be doing next year,' said a beaming West, who had been the last of three to crash in the wet on Friday morning. Stoner had been the first, Vermeulen the second. 'I thought I'd better join my fellow-Australians,' joked West.

Hofmann was back, struggling somewhat with a still-awkward hand as well as a lack of race fitness. 'It's six weeks since I rode,' he said. Finally, the name Biaggi made a GP return – as a wild card in the 125 class. It was Max's nephew, Federico, who had adopted his uncle's surname for racing purposes. He qualified 32nd on his 'Friba' and finished in the same position.

MOTOGP RACE – 28 laps

Naturally, all were complaining of a lack of set-up time; the order of the names at the top of the list was shuffled only slightly: Stoner on a fourth successive pole, and Rossi back on the front row in second. Hayden was third, his second time on the front row all year, and in two races.

Race day was hot and dry, the stands being packed in anticipation of Rossi's chance to regain momentum and teach the young upstart a good lesson. The rider himself was less confident, saying after qualifying, 'To win will be difficult, but the rostrum is possible.'

Much of the heat was taken out of the race on the second corner. An over-enthusiastic de Puniet tagged fast-starter Vermeulen with his brake lever, flicked sideways and then into the air. His bike landed right on Pedrosa's, and the pair crashed out together. Hayden couldn't avoid the mêlée, but managed to stay on board in spite of almost hitting the barrier. He rejoined, but his race was also effectively over: the run across the gravel had put a cut in his rear tyre, and he was lucky to be able to run around disputing last with Kurtis Roberts, also put off by the incident, until the latter ran wide and let him go.

Rossi was still going, however, slotting into fourth as Stoner forged away after another superb start. As at Brno, the Australian wouldn't see another bike in front of him, but again he was hounded in the early stages by Hopkins's Suzuki, and then by the American's team-mate, Vermeulen, who had taken a flier off the third row.

Hopkins had been a close second at the end of lap one, and only a second behind when he had a scary front-wheel slide at

Opposite: **Rossi came out of purdah, and used his charm to the full in his first press appearance since the tax story broke.**

Photographs: Gold & Goose

Opposite centre and below: **De Puniet goes headlong in the first-corner crash. It also eliminated Pedrosa and spoiled HRC team-mate Hayden's race.**

Photographs: Martin Lauricella/Cello

Above: **Qualifying tyres, used one lap in anger – Rossi's Michelin (top) and Stoner's Bridgestone.**

Photographs: Gold & Goose

Inset above: Marco Melandri, here receiving remedial massage, was lucky not to have re-injured his neck in a heavy practice crash.

Above right: Lorenzo dressed as a centurion to celebrate win number eight.

Inset top right: The main 250 rivals get close up, Dovizioso ahead of Lorenzo.

Far right: Faubel blamed Talmacsi for punting him into Corsi's back wheel. Either way, the Hungarian survived to win. It was crucial for the championship.

Main photograph: Vermeulen apexes at speed and on the paint. His second place headed Suzuki's first MotoGP double rostrum.

Photographs: Gold & Goose

the end of the straight. This left him a bit detuned, and Vermeulen took advantage at the start of the next lap, the sixth, to dive underneath him.

Rossi was already out. He'd looked as though he was starting to move on the fourth lap, a second behind Vermeulen, and said later that his tyres had warmed up and he was feeling ready to push. The threat was never consummated. Next time around, 'I was braking hard, and I suddenly felt something let go. It felt like when a two-stroke seizes, although four-strokes always feel like that a bit. When I tried to start the engine again, it was blocked,' he said. He did get it going, to cruise back to the pits 'at 60km/h – with a noise like a salad bowl.'

Vermeulen chased hard, keeping the gap hovering at around a second. By lap 18, it was more than two seconds, and stretching. 'I thought for a while I might catch him. I don't know if I used my rear tyre too much getting into second, or if I was just kidding myself,' he said. Either way, shortly before half-distance, he settled for a safe second, his best-ever dry result.

Likewise, Hopkins was safe in third, giving Suzuki its first double rostrum in the four-stroke class, and demonstrating the growing strength of a factory that had rediscovered its commitment. It was already the only manufacturer to have more than one rider in the championship top five.

In the absence of both factory Hondas, the closest pursuit came from Melandri, on the charge after finishing the first lap ninth. He'd disposed of West and Edwards in the first couple of laps, then rapidly closed on Capirossi, passing him on lap five. By now, he was more than five seconds adrift of the leaders with no hope of catching up, let alone passing, at a track where opportunities are strictly limited. Capirossi stayed close, but never close enough to attack. Checa caught up around the middle of the race, but had dropped away again by the finish.

One of the few real scraps of the race was for seventh, with the same protagonists as at Brno, and the same result. Elias, finding this intensely physical track even harder than Brno because of the hard braking, prevailed once again over West, troubled with mid-corner chatter.

Edwards had lost out to both of them after mid-distance and was out of touch in ninth, blaming his tyres; Nakano trailed in behind. Hofmann had passed the latter on the penultimate lap, but his injuries had meant that his braking was weak, and the Japanese rider passed him back before the end. Guintoli was 12th, followed by Hayden, who had passed a fading Tamada, then Roberts.

Another strong ride came to nothing – Barros had qualified 17th, finished lap one 13th and had been pushing through ever since. He was up to eighth on lap 15, ahead of West and about to pounce on Edwards when his Ducati stopped with an electrical failure. Yet more excitement taken out of a very dull race.

250cc RACE – 26 laps

Lorenzo's eighth pole of the year (in the single Saturday qualifying session) was by a narrow margin of a couple of tenths, from Dovizioso, who was hoping that a slow and twisty circuit, for once, might leave his Honda at less than the usual disadvantage. But there was to be no joy for the home boy in this class either. Barbera and Hiro Aoyama completed the front row; second KTM rider Kallio led the second.

The race should have been better, but it too was processional, thanks to a mechanical failure. Dovizioso had led Lorenzo and Kallio away, with a gang of eight close for almost the first ten laps. Barbera was strong, up to third almost immediately, then briefly ahead of Lorenzo as well on lap three. At the same time, Bautista was closing fast, fourth ahead of Kallio on lap four, passing Barbera also five laps later. A step too far: on the very next tight corner, he lost the rear and slid out.

This gave the two up front a couple of seconds on Barbera, and they were soon stretching the gap further. With ten laps to go, they started to trade blows. They changed places twice on lap 17, and three times on the next, Lorenzo leading over the line for the first time. And from then on.

Next time around, Dovizioso suddenly sat up and pulled off, narrowly preventing a crash as the engine seized and locked the rear wheel. He coasted to a stop, slumped in visible despair. Lorenzo was now more than 2.5 seconds clear of the pursuit, his eighth win of 2007 and a 54-point lead in the bag. 'I'm sorry Andrea didn't finish, because he is a strong rider, and I would have had a lot of fun if I'd beat him, but this is racing... I crashed at Donington and Mugello, so now I have to be happy,' said Lorenzo.

The pursuit at the point of Dovizioso's departure was led by Kallio, from Hiro Aoyama, Barbera dropping back, his hands full with a persistent de Angelis; Luthi was closing on the pair.

With four laps left, the KTMs had an internecine battle. Aoyama had got ahead of Kallio for two laps, the Finn looking for a chance to swap back again when he got off line, had a major slide and a big high-sider. He remounted, but the crash had fractured his rear rim, and he pulled in with a puncture. Aoyama then took the lap record, chasing the distant Lorenzo.

The battle for third raged to the finish, Barbera eventually prevailing for the last rostrum place, from Luthi and de Angelis.

The field was well spaced: almost 30 seconds away, Shuhei Aoyama finally displaced Locatelli. Bautista had remounted and tagged on to Aoyama for an eventual eighth, with Takahashi following for ninth. They had dropped off Simon by four seconds at the end.

125cc RACE – 23 laps

As with the 250s, the loss of Friday afternoon meant just one qualifying session, with Pesek taking his first pole of the year by three-thousandths, from Faubel. Pasini and Talmacsi filled the front row.

Pasini stormed off the line with a pack of five in pursuit – Faubel, from Corsi, Talmacsi, Pesek and Koyama, the last-named soon dropping back.

They quickly closed down on Pasini, Faubel being the first to go ahead, then Corsi for two laps, then Faubel again. On lap eight, Pasini regained the lead and began a remarkable demonstration. Eight-tenths ahead after one lap, he took another half-second next time around with fastest lap of the race – unusually, faster than his pole time. He just kept on stretching away, putting all the bad luck from earlier in the year as far behind him as were his pursuers.

The remaining quartet were still at each other's throat, while Koyama was closing up again. With five laps left, he had rejoined the group, but next time around Pesek slid off on a slow corner, pushing the KTM rider right off the track and out of contention for second.

Corsi had made most of the running, and still led, with Faubel and Talmacsi right with him. Then came the defining moment, at the fast corners. Faubel's view was that Talmacsi had run into him, punting him off line and into Corsi's back wheel. Talmacsi (not surprisingly) blamed Faubel for swerving across in front of him. The result was that the Hungarian survived, while the other two crashed. Talmacsi was second, Koyama third.

Gadea was a lonely fourth; fifth to 13th was covered by just over two seconds after a huge race-long battle. Espargaro finally prevailed over Krummenacher, Bradl and Smith, after hanging back and attacking at the end.

GP CINZANO DI SAN MARINO E RIVIERA DI RIMINI

2 SEPTEMBER 2007 • FIM WORLD CHAMPIONSHIP ROUND 13

MISANO WORLD CIRCUIT

Circuit 4.180km /2.597 miles

MotoGP

RACE: 28 laps, 72.716 miles/117.040km • Weather: Dry • Air 26°C • Humidity 48% • Track 42°C

Pos.	Rider	Nat.	No.	Entrant	Machine	Tyres	Laps	Time & speed (mph/km/h)
1	Casey Stoner	AUS	27	Ducati Marlboro Team	Ducati	B	28	44m 34.720s 97.883mph/ 157.528km/h
2	Chris Vermeulen	AUS	71	Rizla Suzuki MotoGP	Suzuki	B	28	44m 39.571s
3	John Hopkins	USA	21	Rizla Suzuki MotoGP	Suzuki	B	28	44m 50.722s
4	Marco Melandri	ITA	33	Honda Gresini	Honda	B	28	44m 57.457s
5	Loris Capirossi	ITA	65	Ducati Marlboro Team	Ducati	B	28	44m 59.507s
6	Carlos Checa	SPA	7	Honda LCR	Honda	M	28	45m 09.706s
7	Toni Elias	SPA	24	Honda Gresini	Honda	B	28	45m 15.616s
8	Anthony West	AUS	13	Kawasaki Racing Team	Kawasaki	B	28	45m 16.494s
9	Colin Edwards	USA	5	Fiat Yamaha Team	Yamaha	M	28	45m 21.866s
10	Shinya Nakano	JPN	56	Konica Minolta Honda	Honda	M	28	45m 23.528s
11	Alex Hofmann	GER	66	Pramac d'Antin	Ducati	B	28	45m 24.019s
12	Sylvain Guintoli	FRA	50	Dunlop Yamaha Tech 3	Yamaha	D	28	45m 43.896s
13	Nicky Hayden	USA	1	Repsol Honda Team	Honda	M	28	45m 55.144s
14	Makoto Tamada	JPN	6	Dunlop Yamaha Tech 3	Yamaha	D	28	46m 08.943s
15	Kurtis Roberts	USA	80	Team Roberts	KR212V	M	27	45m 14.795s
	Alex Barros	BRA	4	Pramac d'Antin	Ducati	B	15	24m 17.361s
	Valentino Rossi	ITA	46	Fiat Yamaha Team	Yamaha	M	5	8m 58.083s
	Randy de Puniet	FRA	14	Kawasaki Racing Team	Kawasaki	B	0	
	Dani Pedrosa	SPA	26	Repsol Honda Team	Honda	M	0	

Fastest lap: Casey Stoner, on lap 12, 1m 34.649s, 98.790mph/158.987km/h (record).

Previous lap record: New circuit.

Event best maximum speed: Casey Stoner, 155.5mph/250.2km/h (race).

Grid order		1	2	3	4	5	6	7	8	9	10	11	12	13	14	15	16	17	18	19	20	21	22	23	24	25	26	27	28	•
27	STONER	27	27	27	27	27	27	27	27	27	27	27	27	27	27	27	27	27	27	27	27	27	27	27	27	27	27	27	27	1
46	ROSSI	21	21	21	21	21	71	71	71	71	71	71	71	71	71	71	71	71	71	71	71	71	71	71	71	71	71	71	71	2
1	HAYDEN	71	71	71	71	71	21	21	21	21	21	21	21	21	21	21	21	21	21	21	21	21	21	21	21	21	21	21	21	3
14	de PUNIET	46	46	46	46	33	33	33	33	33	33	33	33	33	33	33	33	33	33	33	33	33	33	33	33	33	33	33	33	4
21	HOPKINS	65	65	65	65	65	65	65	65	65	65	65	65	65	65	65	65	65	65	65	65	65	65	65	65	65	65	65	65	5
26	PEDROSA	5	5	33	33	7	7	7	7	7	7	7	7	7	7	7	7	7	7	7	7	7	7	7	7	7	7	7	7	6
7	CHECA	7	13	5	7	13	13	13	13	5	5	5	5	5	5	4	13	13	13	13	13	13	13	13	13	13	24	24	24	7
71	VERMEULEN	13	33	13	13	5	5	5	5	13	13	4	4	4	4	5	24	24	24	24	24	24	24	24	24	24	13	13	13	8
5	EDWARDS	33	7	7	5	24	24	4	4	4	4	13	13	13	13	13	5	5	5	5	5	5	5	5	5	5	5	5	5	9
13	WEST	24	24	24	24	4	4	24	24	24	24	24	24	24	24	24	56	56	56	56	56	56	56	56	56	56	56	56	56	10
50	GUINTOLI	56	56	56	4	56	56	56	56	56	56	56	56	56	56	56	66	66	66	66	66	66	66	66	66	66	66	66	66	11
33	MELANDRI	50	50	4	56	50	50	50	50	50	50	50	50	50	66	66	50	50	50	50	50	50	50	50	50	50	50	50	50	12
65	CAPIROSSI	4	4	50	50	6	6	6	6	6	6	6	66	66	50	50	6	6	6	6	6	1	1	1	1	1	1	1	1	13
56	NAKANO	6	6	6	6	66	66	66	66	66	66	66	6	6	6	6	1	1	1	1	1	6	6	6	6	6	6	6	6	14
24	ELIAS	66	66	66	66	1	1	1	1	1	1	1	1	1	1	1	80	80	80	80	80	80	80	80	80	80	80	80		15
6	TAMADA	80	1	1	1	80	80	80	80	80	80	80	80	80	80	80														
4	BARROS	1	80	80	80	46																								
80	ROBERTS																													
66	HOFMANN																													

FASTEST RACE LAPS

	Rider	Lap	Time
1	Stoner	12	1m 34.649s
2	Vermeulen	6	1m 34.709s
3	Hopkins	8	1m 34.945s
4	Rossi	3	1m 35.225s
5	Melandri	4	1m 35.572s
6	Capirossi	16	1m 35.652s
7	Edwards	10	1m 35.717s
8	Checa	9	1m 35.846s
9	Barros	6	1m 36.053s
10	Elias	28	1m 36.222s
11	West	14	1m 36.246s
12	Nakano	11	1m 36.334s
13	Hofmann	23	1m 36.461s
14	Guintoli	8	1m 36.560s
15	Tamada	6	1m 36.645s
16	Hayden	19	1m 36.706s
17	Roberts	6	1m 37.020s

QUALIFYING

1 September 2007

Weather: Dry

Air: 23°C Humidity: 46%

Track: 42°C

Pos.	Rider	Time
1	Stoner	1m 33.918s
2	Rossi	1m 34.094s
3	Hayden	1m 34.469s
4	de Puniet	1m 34.506s
5	Hopkins	1m 34.536s
6	Pedrosa	1m 34.580s
7	Checa	1m 34.628s
8	Vermeulen	1m 34.717s
9	Edwards	1m 34.768s
10	West	1m 34.939s
11	Guintoli	1m 35.202s
12	Melandri	1m 35.236s
13	Capirossi	1m 35.283s
14	Nakano	1m 35.389s
15	Elias	1m 35.632s
16	Tamada	1m 35.865s
17	Barros	1m 35.897s
18	Roberts	1m 36.605s
19	Hofmann	1m 36.659s

statistics

RIDER STANDINGS

After 13 Rounds

1	Casey Stoner	271
2	Valentino Rossi	186
3	Dani Pedrosa	168
4	Chris Vermeulen	144
5	John Hopkins	140
6	Marco Melandri	126
7	Colin Edwards	100
8	Loris Capirossi	98
9	Nicky Hayden	92
10	Alex Barros	83
11	Alex Hofmann	65
12	Toni Elias	63
13	Randy de Puniet	58
14	Carlos Checa	45
15	Anthony West	41
16	Shinya Nakano	37
17	Makoto Tamada	33
18	Sylvain Guintoli	28
19	Kurtis Roberts	10
20=	Michel Fabrizio	6
20=	Roger Lee Hayden	6
22	Fonsi Nieto	5
23	Olivier Jacque	4
24	Kenny Roberts Jnr	4

TEAM STANDINGS

After 13 Rounds

1	Ducati Marlboro Team	369
2	Fiat Yamaha Team	286
3	Rizla Suzuki MotoGP	284
4	Repsol Honda Team	260
5	Honda Gresini	195
6	Pramac d'Antin	148
7	Kawasaki Racing Team	108
8	Dunlop Yamaha Tech 3	61
9	Honda LCR	45
10	Konica Minolta Honda	37
11	Team Roberts	14

CONSTRUCTOR STANDINGS

After 13 Rounds

1	Ducati	283
2	Honda	219
3	Yamaha	213
4	Suzuki	191
5	Kawasaki	90
6	KR212V	14

250cc

26 laps, 67.522 miles/108.680km

Pos.	Rider (Nat.)	No.	Machine	Laps	Time & speed
1	Jorge Lorenzo (SPA)	1	Aprilia	26	42m 54.427s 94.432mph/ 151.974km/h
2	Hiroshi Aoyama (JPN)	4	KTM	26	42m 58.005s
3	Hector Barbera (SPA)	80	Aprilia	26	43m 01.468s
4	Thomas Luthi (SWI)	12	Aprilia	26	43m 01.640s
5	Alex de Angelis (RSM)	3	Aprilia	26	43m 02.091s
6	Shuhei Aoyama (JPN)	73	Honda	26	43m 30.661s
7	Roberto Locatelli (ITA)	15	Gilera	26	43m 31.345s
8	Alvaro Bautista (SPA)	19	Aprilia	26	43m 31.363s
9	Yuki Takahashi (JPN)	55	Honda	26	43m 31.569s
10	Julian Simon (SPA)	60	Honda	26	43m 34.720s
11	Jules Cluzel (FRA)	16	Aprilia	26	43m 46.147s
12	Aleix Espargaro (SPA)	41	Aprilia	26	43m 51.047s
13	Ratthapark Wilairot (THA)	8	Honda	26	43m 54.487s
14	Karel Abraham (CZE)	17	Aprilia	26	43m 55.927s
15	Eugene Laverty (IRL)	50	Honda	26	44m 04.377s
16	Efren Vazquez (SPA)	7	Aprilia	26	44m 04.486s
17	Imre Toth (HUN)	10	Aprilia	25	44m 12.292s
18	Omar Menghi (ITA)	64	Aprilia	25	44m 18.042s
	Mika Kallio (FIN)	36	KTM	23	DNF
	Alex Baldolini (ITA)	25	Aprilia	19	DNF
	Andrea Dovizioso (ITA)	34	Honda	19	DNF
	Dan Linfoot (GBR)	45	Aprilia	17	DNF
	Dirk Heidolf (GER)	28	Aprilia	13	DNF
	Fabrizio Lai (ITA)	32	Aprilia	4	DNF
	Marco Simoncelli (ITA)	58	Gilera	3	DNF

Fastest lap: H. Aoyama, 1m 38.074s, 95.340mph/153.435km/h (record).

Previous lap record: New circuit.

Event best maximum speed: Lorenzo, 153.4mph/246.8km/h (race).

Qualifying: 1 Lorenzo, 1m 38.395s; 2 Dovizioso, 1m 38.558s; 3 Barbera, 1m 38.733s; 4 H. Aoyama, 1m 38.826s; 5 Kallio, 1m 39.007s; 6 Bautista, 1m 39.023s; 7 Luthi, 1m 39.031s; 8 Simon, 1m 39.087s; 9 Simoncelli, 1m 39.180s; 10 de Angelis, 1m 39.182s; 11 S. Aoyama, 1m 39.506s; 12 Takahashi, 1m 39.694s; 13 Espargaro, 1m 40.056s; 14 Locatelli, 1m 40.206s; 15 Lai, 1m 40.329s; 16 Wilairot, 1m 40.408s; 17 Cluzel, 1m 40.768s; 18 Laverty, 1m 40.912s; 19 Heidolf, 1m 41.290s; 20 Abraham, 1m 41.545s; 21 Vazquez, 1m 41.717s; 22 Baldolini, 1m 41.749s; 23 Linfoot, 1m 42.426s; 24 Toth, 1m 42.944s; 25 Menghi, 1m 44.745s.

Fastest race laps: 1 H. Aoyama, 1m 38.074s; 2 Lorenzo, 1m 38.311s; 3 Kallio, 1m 38.419s; 4 de Angelis, 1m 38.431s; 5 Luthi, 1m 38.454s; 6 Dovizioso, 1m 38.461s; 7 Barbera, 1m 38.577s; 8 Bautista, 1m 38.640s; 9 Takahashi, 1m 39.348s; 10 S. Aoyama, 1m 39.454s; 11 Simon, 1m 39.502s; 12 Locatelli, 1m 39.574s; 13 Cluzel, 1m 39.832s; 14 Espargaro, 1m 40.075s; 15 Wilairot, 1m 40.168s; 16 Abraham, 1m 40.259s; 17 Vazquez, 1m 40.493s; 18 Heidolf, 1m 40.649s; 19 Baldolini, 1m 40.719s; 20 Laverty, 1m 40.860s; 21 Lai, 1m 41.297s; 22 Linfoot, 1m 41.585s; 23 Toth, 1m 43.904s; 24 Menghi, 1m 44.332s; 25 Simoncelli, 1m 44.798s.

World Championship: 1 Lorenzo, 241; 2 de Angelis, 187; 3 Dovizioso, 186; 4 Bautista, 135; 5 Barbera, 119; 6 H. Aoyama, 108; 7 Kallio, 94; 8 Luthi, 85; 9 Simon, 75; 10 S. Aoyama, 72; 11 Simoncelli, 57; 12 Takahashi, 56; 13 Locatelli, 42; 14 Lai, 42; 15 Espargaro, 31; 16 Wilairot, 29; 17 West, 25; 18 Abraham, 18; 19 Heidolf, 17; 20 Baldolini, 14; 21 Sekiguchi, 13; 22 Debon, 11; 23 Cluzel, 9; 24 Linfoot, 7; 25 Laverty, 4; 26 Tizon, Toth and Vazquez, 1.

125cc

23 laps, 59.731 miles/96.140km

Pos.	Rider (Nat.)	No.	Machine	Laps	Time & speed
1	Mattia Pasini (ITA)	75	Aprilia	23	39m 47.944s 90.060mph/ 144.938km/h
2	Gabor Talmacsi (HUN)	14	Aprilia	23	39m 52.718s
3	Tomoyoshi Koyama (JPN)	71	KTM	23	39m 56.520s
4	Sergio Gadea (SPA)	33	Aprilia	23	40m 03.763s
5	Pol Espargaro (SPA)	44	Aprilia	23	40m 11.916s
6	Randy Krummenacher (SWI)	34	KTM	23	40m 13.103s
7	Stefan Bradl (GER)	17	Aprilia	23	40m 13.335s
8	Bradley Smith (GBR)	38	Honda	23	40m 13.457s
9	Raffaele de Rosa (ITA)	35	Aprilia	23	40m 13.938s
10	Michael Ranseder (AUT)	60	Derbi	23	40m 14.183s
11	Esteve Rabat (SPA)	12	Honda	23	40m 14.637s
12	Joan Olive (SPA)	6	Aprilia	23	40m 14.916s
13	Mike di Meglio (FRA)	63	Honda	23	40m 15.437s
14	Andrea Iannone (ITA)	29	Aprilia	23	40m 20.838s
15	Sandro Cortese (GER)	11	Aprilia	23	40m 27.249s
16	Lorenzo Zanetti (ITA)	8	Aprilia	23	40m 27.979s
17	Hector Faubel (SPA)	55	Aprilia	23	40m 28.069s
18	Nicolas Terol (SPA)	18	Derbi	23	40m 28.101s
19	Roberto Tamburini (ITA)	20	Aprilia	23	40m 36.235s
20	Lukas Pesek (CZE)	52	Derbi	23	40m 37.565s
21	Alexis Masbou (FRA)	7	Honda	23	40m 38.440s
22	Simone Sancioni (ITA)	42	Aprilia	23	40m 45.463s
23	Dominique Aegerter (SWI)	77	Aprilia	23	40m 45.610s
24	Ferruccio Lamborghini (ITA)	79	Aprilia	23	40m 47.624s
25	Roberto Lacalendola (ITA)	87	Aprilia	23	40m 53.053s
26	Steve Bonsey (USA)	51	KTM	23	40m 53.220s
27	Joey Litjens (NED)	37	Honda	23	40m 56.701s
28	Simone Grotzkyj (ITA)	53	Aprilia	23	40m 58.339s
29	Robert Muresan (ROU)	95	Derbi	23	41m 06.516s
30	Daniel Webb (GBR)	99	Honda	23	41m 08.907s
31	Hugo van den Berg (NED)	56	Aprilia	23	41m 09.620s
32	Federico Biaggi (ITA)	80	Friba	23	41m 42.172s
	Simone Corsi (ITA)	24	Aprilia	21	DNF
	Stefano Bianco (ITA)	27	Aprilia	16	DNF
	Dino Lombardi (ITA)	13	Honda	11	DNF
	Pablo Nieto (SPA)	22	Aprilia	9	DNF
	Federico Sandi (ITA)	15	Aprilia	0	DNF

Fastest lap: Pasini, 1m 42.811s, 90.947mph/146.365km/h (record).

Previous lap record: New circuit.

Event best maximum speed: Corsi, 137.8mph/221.7km/h (warm-up).

Qualifying: 1 Pesek, 1m 43.370s; 2 Faubel, 1m 43.373s; 3 Pasini, 1m 43.381s; 4 Talmacsi, 1m 43.541s; 5 Corsi, 1m 43.611s; 6 Koyama, 1m 43.695s; 7 Rabat, 1m 44.095s; 8 Cortese, 1m 44.242s; 9 Smith, 1m 44.385s; 10 Gadea, 1m 44.529s; 11 di Meglio, 1m 44.546s; 12 Ranseder, 1m 44.635s; 13 de Rosa, 1m 44.762s; 14 Espargaro, 1m 44.895s; 15 Olive, 1m 44.917s; 16 Krummenacher, 1m 44.928s; 17 Bradl, 1m 44.966s; 18 Terol, 1m 45.054s; 19 Bianco, 1m 45.071s; 20 Zanetti, 1m 45.074s; 21 Tamburini, 1m 45.191s; 22 Iannone, 1m 45.396s; 23 Sancioni, 1m 45.627s; 24 Grotzkyj, 1m 45.719s; 25 Aegerter, 1m 45.782s; 26 Sandi, 1m 45.821s; 27 Masbou, 1m 45.856s; 28 Nieto, 1m 45.861s; 29 Bonsey, 1m 45.911s; 30 Lacalendola, 1m 46.107s; 31 Litjens, 1m 46.183s; 32 Biaggi, 1m 46.513s; 33 Webb, 1m 46.614s; 34 Lombardi, 1m 46.777s; 35 van den Berg, 1m 46.833s; 36 Muresan, 1m 46.890s; 37 Lamborghini, 1m 47.147s.

Fastest race laps: 1 Pasini, 1m 42.811s; 2 Talmacsi, 1m 43.097s; 3 Pesek, 1m 43.103s; 4 Corsi, 1m 43.156s; 5 Faubel, 1m 43.165s; 6 Koyama, 1m 43.231s; 7 Gadea, 1m 43.285s; 8 Rabat, 1m 43.410s; 9 Espargaro, 1m 43.743s; 10 Olive, 1m 43.816s; 11 Bradl, 1m 43.831s; 12 Iannone, 1m 43.848s; 13 Krummenacher, 1m 43.857s; 14 Smith, 1m 43.888s; 15 di Meglio, 1m 43.920s; 16 Ranseder, 1m 44.085s; 17 de Rosa, 1m 44.213s; 18 Cortese, 1m 44.214s; 19 Masbou, 1m 44.224s; 20 Zanetti, 1m 44.429s; 21 Bianco, 1m 44.450s; 22 Terol, 1m 44.487s; 23 Bonsey, 1m 44.783s; 24 Sancioni, 1m 44.901s; 25 Biaggi, 1m 44.976s; 26 Tamburini, 1m 45.062s; 27 Aegerter, 1m 45.178s; 28 Lamborghini, 1m 45.223s; 29 Muresan, 1m 45.449s; 30 Lacalendola, 1m 45.451s; 31 Litjens, 1m 45.509s; 32 Nieto, 1m 45.542s; 33 Grotzkyj, 1m 45.559s; 34 Webb, 1m 46.048s; 35 van den Berg, 1m 46.077s; 36 Lombardi, 1m 46.750s.

World Championship: 1 Talmacsi, 189; 2 Faubel, 179; 3 Koyama, 145; 4 Pesek, 129; 5 Corsi, 119; 6 Gadea, 118; 7 Pasini, 111; 8 Espargaro, 83; 9 Smith, 82; 10 Olive, 76; 11 Ranseder, 63; 12 Cortese, 60; 13 Krummenacher, 58; 14 de Rosa, 49; 15 Rabat, 47; 16 Nieto, 35; 17 Zanetti, 30; 18 di Meglio, 25; 19 Bradl, 25; 20 Iannone, 20; 21 Masbou, 15; 22 Bianco, 6; 23 Terol, 6; 24 Bonsey, 3; 25 Froehlich and Jerez, 2; 27 Aegerter, 2; 28 Grotzkyj, 1.

Forza! Rossi's first win for five races would be his last of the season.
Photograph: Gold & Goose

FIM WORLD CHAMPIONSHIP • ROUND 14

PORTUGUESEGP
ESTORIL

Above: With Stoner in trouble, the stage was left to Pedrosa and Rossi. They made the most of it.

Opposite top: Too late, things began to look up for Dani. He would finish the year on a high.

Opposite bottom: Carlos Checa's seventh place reflected generally improving fortunes for Honda.

Photographs: Gold & Goose

IF it was a turning of the tide, the last race of the European season meant that it had come rather late. Or was it just a ripple? For almost 42,000 at the Estoril track, many of them Rossi fans, it hardly mattered. For a second year in succession, it was a thriller from the quirky slow-and-fast mixed track (epic fast corner on to a long downhill straight, dizzying first-gear two-and-fro corners up the other side). In 2006, Elias had beaten Rossi by two-thousandths – a moment that the Italian now laughingly recalled: 'Cost me the f*cking championship.' On this occasion, it was Rossi narrowly in front – for the first time, amazingly, in five races.

Rossi dedicated victory to his rallying hero and later friendly acquaintance, Colin McRae, whose tragic death in a helicopter accident had saddened the paddock the previous day. 'Colin was the Kevin Schwantz of rallying,' said Rossi. He could pay no higher compliment.

The composition of the rostrum, indeed of the first four, suggested that Michelin's work over the summer and the tyres tested for the first time after Brno were, if not the complete answer to Bridgestone, at least a big step in the right direction. Three out of the top four were on the French tyres, including the top two, for it was Pedrosa second, and Stoner only third. Funnily enough, they'd actually raced on older-generation rear tyres, being short of the right compound in the new tyres, but hopes were raised anyway.

The same hopes of late relief applied to the beleaguered Japanese manufacturers. It seemed that at the second asking, Yamaha's new pneumatic-valve-spring motor, still just a one-off and only for Rossi, was a real improvement, and that Honda's work also had born fruit for Pedrosa and Hayden.

For those hoping for a change in the course of the season, it was a false dawn, and with a plausible scientific explanation. Stoner described how, after the first five laps, he had been battling a slipper clutch fault that had him almost freewheeling into some corners. Funnily enough, this is not unlike the system Ducati tested early in 2005, until it precipitated journeys into the gravel for both Capirossi and Checa. It forced a rethink of his riding style and braking points, but by the end of the race, he had adjusted: 'I started to feel more comfortable at the same time as the Bridgestones started to come better.'

That last comment mirrored an explanation given earlier by Rossi, expounding (as so often) on the topic of tyres, the tyre rules and the Michelin/Bridgestone divide. 'It's the quality of the tyre that's a problem, not the quantity. Our main problem is that Bridgestone have maximum performance on the first lap, but Michelin must wait two or three laps. The second problem is the life of the tyre. We have maximum performance for ten or 12 laps only, so Bridgestone are alone for the last laps. It's about the beginning and the end of the race. The middle of the race, we are okay.'

He had more of interest to say on that other tyre battle – for qualifying. Michelin, with front and rear special softies, had an edge, but Bridgestone had been creeping up, exploiting slightly harder two-lap tyres that gave the rider a chance to get his eye in for the massively increased grip levels. Rossi: 'It is difficult to arrive at the limit of qualifying tyres on just one lap, because it is so much more than with race tyres.' He'd tried the harder-softy route in the hope of getting two laps, but the tactic failed. 'It was a bad card to play,' he said. 'The tyre didn't work for the full second lap.'

Tyres, tyres! It was now known that both Yamaha and Honda had approached Bridgestone about the possibility of supply for 2008, and been knocked back. Team manager Davide Brivio confirmed that Yamaha would stay with Michelin for 2008 – a prediction that would soon be overtaken by events. Asked by pressmen if he was happy to hear about this, Rossi paused, looked mischievous and said, 'For you, I am happy.' This was also untrue.

Off-track, there was an experiment, a sort of faltering step up the social ladder, with a trial run of an 'exclusive' MotoGP-only paddock. Once inside, it was all fine and dandy, but the elitist enclave was secured behind makeshift barriers draped with green mesh and looked much like a building site from the outside, especially since the inward-facing hospitality units revealed their ugly backsides, all air-conditioning vents, kitchen annexes and massive rubbish bins.

Another new signing for 2008 saved 2007's only rookie, Sylvain Guintoli, whose place at Tech 3 had gone to James Tose-

land. The Frenchman signed for Pramac d'Antin Ducati. Bad news for Chaz Davies. The Welsh ex-250 rider, who had subbed for the injured Hofmann in America, had tested a Desmosedici at Mugello in the week before the Portuguese race, arranged by his old friend Stoner, and taken a tumble. He had some hopes of a slot in the team, but was back in the States to fulfil his 600 Supersport duties when the door was closed in his face.

There was even worse news for Hofmann. Still in pain and having had bike trouble on the warm-up lap, he started on his spare. Plumb last, he lost heart and pitted. Team boss, d'Antin, was outraged. 'Lack of motivation is not an excuse for us,' he said. Hofmann was summarily dropped for the rest of the year.

There was a flash of the younger Jorge Lorenzo when the 250 leader was badly baulked on his fast lap of the last session, foiling any chances of him regaining pole from Dovizioso. The feisty Spaniard gestured angrily at the unidentified rider, and when he stopped after the session, he insisted, 'I am going to speak to Race Direction about this.' When he got there, he was on the carpet instead, fined US $5,000 for making 'a gesture prejudicial to the interest of the sport'.

MOTOGP RACE – 28 laps

'I know it's just qualifying, but I'm happy,' said Hayden, after a blistering lap that shaded an earlier battle for pole between Stoner and Rossi. Another remarkable performance came from Tamada, who claimed a best yet for his Dunlop effort to head row two from Pedrosa.

Stoner was away first as usual, another brilliant start, chased hard by the Repsol Hondas, Pedrosa ahead. Melandri was fourth, ahead of Rossi, although he had scythed past by the time they crossed the line on the first run down the long downhill straight.

Rossi's next move was a pushy one, past Hayden at the cor-

Above: Former Estoril winner Tamada ran strongly in seventh, only to fall back and then off before the finish.
Photograph: Gold & Goose

ners before the tight uphill chicane on the third lap. By then, Stoner and Pedrosa were almost 1.5 seconds clear, but after three laps of settling in, Rossi began to close it down. Hayden had dropped out of touch.

The start of lap seven saw the first signs of life for a long-awaited battle for the lead, Pedrosa drafting past Stoner to outbrake him into the first corner. One lap later, Rossi did the same to the troubled Australian. Stoner stayed close, and on lap ten, Rossi pulled the same outbraking move on Pedrosa to lead for the first time.

A little way back, Hayden had an entertaining exchange of blows with Melandri, finally prevailing on lap eight and setting off once again. The leaders, Stoner at the rear, were just over two seconds away, well within sight. The champion set a new record as he gradually closed on the Ducati, and was on his tail by lap 17, when the lead had just changed hands again, in favour of Pedrosa.

That was at the usual place, into the first corner, and Pedrosa sprinted away, taking Rossi with him. By lap 20, the duo were two seconds clear of Stoner, but it wasn't over yet. The oil flags came out after de Puniet's Kawasaki suffered a smoky blow-up, and Stoner regained lost speed. He shook off Hayden and began closing on the leaders. Within seven-tenths over the last couple of laps, he was never close enough to challenge.

Up front was a classic battle. Rossi outbraked Pedrosa into turn one at the start of lap 26, but ran wide and lost the place immediately. Then he found a different place, braking for the left-hander at the end of the back straight (the very corner where Pedrosa had taken down team-mate Hayden a year before). This time, it was for keeps. Rossi had it under control, if narrowly, although Pedrosa chased hard to the end, Stoner in his shadow.

Melandri had lost Hayden, blaming chatter on a rear tyre that was too hard, but he never did shake off Hopkins. Nor could the Suzuki rider challenge him: 'He was just gapping me coming out of the corners, and I couldn't get close enough to pass.' In fact, Hopkins did get in front briefly, only to lose the position at the next corner.

Tamada managed to hold back the pursuit in the early laps, a huge jostling pack, with the leaders disappearing in the distance. Elias, 2006's winner, was weaving and bobbing behind the yellow bike until somebody tagged him from behind; he ran off track, rejoining in 13th.

Checa was next up, behind the inspired Japanese, with West following him briefly. The Spaniard got ahead on lap six, the pair gaining a little ground as Capirossi and Barros took up the pursuit. By now, West was dropping back fast from the gang; Edwards even faster behind him, in reverse gear after his second-row start.

By lap 18, Tamada's heroic and close pursuit was over, his tyres all used up, and he had lost three seconds when he slipped off with five laps remaining. It was still strong proof of continuing progress for Dunlop, a background player in the current tyre dramatics.

Capirossi started to lose pace from the 11th lap. Barros took over, followed by the resurgent Elias next time around, and then de Puniet too. By the 19th, Elias was ahead of the Brazilian in what was now a close pack of nine; Vermeulen had tagged on behind de Puniet and Capirossi, then Guintoli, Nakano, Edwards and West.

De Puniet had gone next time around, in a cloud of smoke, splitting the group a little. Barros and Elias were trading places when the Brazilian's Ducati also blew up on lap 22. Capirossi managed to fend off Edwards, who had taken tenth off Nakano on the last lap. West was 12th, back ahead of the fading Vermeulen at the end.

Guintoli took the last point, a lap adrift after pitting for a tyre change; Roberts retired early with a slipping clutch. Hofmann retired in pain and all out of motivation, a decision that ended his career with the team. He only needed to have finished to have earned a point.

250cc RACE – 26 laps

Dovizioso claimed only his second pole of the season, the slow corners somewhat compensating for his lack of top speed. Also that Lorenzo was baulked on his fast lap, leading to second place, and the angry gestures that cost him so dear. Barbera and Kallio completed the first row; Bautista was on the second after crashing on Friday.

The race seemed to be settled early, Dovizioso and Lorenzo forging away ahead as Kallio and Simon bickered over third, the

KTM prevailing. But his pace was slow, caused by a problem that would prove terminal. A sticking float bowl flooded the carburettors so badly that eventually the airbox was inundated. He retired on lap five, leaving a now-distant pursuit to Barbera, Hiro Aoyama and Simon.

There was a growing storm behind. Bautista had finished lap one way down in 12th, but was charging through, bringing with him the other Aoyama, de Angelis and Luthi. By the eighth lap, Bautista had cut through to the front of the group and was going away from them.

Dovizioso was about a second clear of Lorenzo, Bautista 2.7 seconds adrift. He made short work of that, the leaders getting frantic pit signals of his approach, and Lorenzo closing up accordingly. But there was no stopping Bautista. On lap 16, he passed Lorenzo into the first corner, and Dovizioso at the chicane to take a lead he would extend all the way to the end. He set one fastest lap after another, his 24th being a new record by almost a full second. 'I think it was my greatest victory ever,' he beamed.

Lorenzo faded from pursuit, while Dovizioso chased as best he could, the rostrum finishers well spaced at the end. It was the first time in seven races that Dovizioso had actually crossed the line ahead of Lorenzo, and he cut back the Spaniard's lead by four points. The gap was still 51, and if he was to get back on terms, the Italian's only hope was that Lorenzo would fail to finish at least two of the remaining four races.

The pack behind had dwindled, Shuhei Aoyama pitting with eight laps left, his brother four laps later. The three remaining were laying on a fine display of to-and-fro through the tight sections. At the end, Luthi pipped Barbera, who had passed de Angelis by inches on the run to the line.

Simoncelli was a long way down, ahead of Simon for seventh. Lai led the next gang from Abraham, Heidolf, Espargaro and Cluzel; Laverty had a steady ride to 14th from 17th on the grid, equalling his best so far. Toth was a lap down, but still got a point; only 17 finished, including Chinese wild-card Ho Wan Chow, two laps adrift.

Locatelli and Takahashi had crashed out on the second and third laps; Vazquez and Wilairot each with three laps to go, the former in the midst of the gang going for eighth.

125cc RACE – 23 laps

It was pole number seven for Pasini, from Pesek and the Aprilias of Corsi and Talmacsi, whose team-mate/rival, Faubel, was right behind him, eighth on the grid.

Pasini led Corsi at the end of lap one, but Faubel moved straight into second and kept close. Olive led the pursuit, but Talmacsi was moving rapidly through after finishing the first lap eighth. By lap six, he was fourth and working on a gap of less than two seconds.

Pasini had started to move away when he overdid it on the brakes for the uphill chicane on lap 11. The bike was undamaged, and he was straight back on board, rejoining in 13th.

The pace now eased, Corsi heading Faubel and Talmacsi; Olive and Espargaro were catching up to make a group of five on lap 14, Talmacsi ahead for the first time.

For the next eight laps, they were all over one another, Espargaro ahead from laps 16 to 20. Now the title rivals took over, both of them outbraking him into the first corner, Faubel taking his first taste of the lead.

He would hold it from there to the end, interrupted briefly on the final lap by a doughty attack from Talmacsi at the chicane. It left Faubel perfectly placed to get a better run out of the final corner and draft past over the line, to win by better than a tenth. He cut the Hungarian's lead by five points to just five.

An ecstatic Espargaro was almost as close in third, taking his first rostrum. Corsi and Olive were hardly further away, the first five covered by little more than a second.

Bradl gained two places on the last lap for a best-ever sixth, heading Koyama, the vengeful Pasini and de Rosa. Krummenacher led the next gang from Rabat, Smith a little way back after battling a loose brake lever from the start. Pesek, 13th, had been put on the gravel from the group disputing sixth.

Above and left: Pol Espargaro relished his first 125 rostrum; earlier he had led several laps – here from Simone Corsi and Gabor Talmacsi.

Top: Brilliant 250 winner Bautista, through from behind, has just taken the lead ahead of Dovizioso and Lorenzo.

Photographs: Gold & Goose

bwin.com GRANDE PREMIO DE PORTUGAL

16 SEPTEMBER 2007 • FIM WORLD CHAMPIONSHIP ROUND 14

CIRCUITO DO ESTORIL

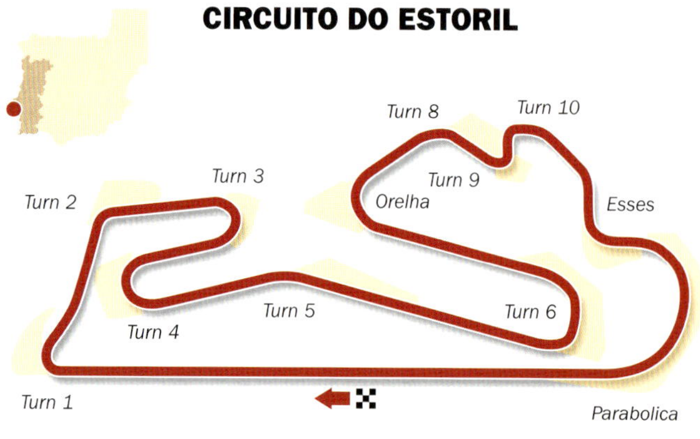

Circuit 4.182km /2.598 miles

MotoGP

RACE: 28 laps, 72.772 miles/117.096km • Weather: Dry • Air 28°C • Humidity 42% • Track 34°C

Pos.	Rider	Nat.	No.	Entrant	Machine	Tyres	Laps	Time & speed (mph/km/h)
1	Valentino Rossi	ITA	46	Fiat Yamaha Team	Yamaha	M	28	45m 49.911s 95.252mph/ 153.294km/h
2	Dani Pedrosa	SPA	26	Repsol Honda Team	Honda	M	28	45m 50.086s
3	Casey Stoner	AUS	27	Ducati Marlboro Team	Ducati	B	28	45m 51.388s
4	Nicky Hayden	USA	1	Repsol Honda Team	Honda	M	28	46m 02.862s
5	Marco Melandri	ITA	33	Honda Gresini	Honda	B	28	46m 07.254s
6	John Hopkins	USA	21	Rizla Suzuki MotoGP	Suzuki	B	28	46m 08.768s
7	Carlos Checa	SPA	7	Honda LCR	Honda	M	28	46m 21.435s
8	Toni Elias	SPA	24	Honda Gresini	Honda	B	28	46m 30.446s
9	Loris Capirossi	ITA	65	Ducati Marlboro Team	Ducati	B	28	46m 33.018s
10	Colin Edwards	USA	5	Fiat Yamaha Team	Yamaha	M	28	46m 34.585s
11	Shinya Nakano	JPN	56	Konica Minolta Honda	Honda	M	28	46m 35.314s
12	Anthony West	AUS	13	Kawasaki Racing Team	Kawasaki	B	28	46m 44.473s
13	Chris Vermeulen	AUS	71	Rizla Suzuki MotoGP	Suzuki	B	28	46m 49.913s
14	Sylvain Guintoli	FRA	50	Dunlop Yamaha Tech 3	Yamaha	D	27	46m 57.523s
	Makoto Tamada	JPN	6	Dunlop Yamaha Tech 3	Yamaha	D	23	38m 04.958s
	Alex Barros	BRA	4	Pramac d'Antin	Ducati	B	22	36m 37.792s
	Randy de Puniet	FRA	14	Kawasaki Racing Team	Kawasaki	B	19	31m 36.089s
	Alex Hofmann	GER	66	Pramac d'Antin	Ducati	B	11	18m 41.437s
	Kurtis Roberts	USA	80	Team Roberts	KR212V	M	2	3m 47.574s

Fastest lap: Nicky Hayden, on lap 13, 1m 37.493s, 95.954mph/154.423km/h (record).

Previous lap record: Kenny Roberts Jnr, USA (KR211V), 1m 37.914s, 95.541mph/153.759km/h (2006).

Event best maximum speed: Casey Stoner, 198.3mph/319.1km/h (warm-up).

FASTEST RACE LAPS

	Rider	Lap	Time
1	Hayden	13	1m 37.493s
2	Rossi	9	1m 37.508s
3	Stoner	3	1m 37.600s
4	Pedrosa	5	1m 37.671s
5	Hopkins	2	1m 37.831s
6	Melandri	2	1m 38.006s
7	Checa	4	1m 38.286s
8	Tamada	10	1m 38.523s
9	Edwards	28	1m 38.650s
10	de Puniet	16	1m 38.718s
11	Capirossi	5	1m 38.833s
12	Elias	21	1m 38.870s
13	Barros	4	1m 38.979s
14	Guintoli	11	1m 38.997s
15	Vermeulen	5	1m 39.013s
16	Nakano	19	1m 39.016s
17	West	13	1m 39.179s
18	Hofmann	3	1m 39.468s
19	Roberts	1	1m 49.703s

QUALIFYING

15 September 2007

Weather: Dry

Air: 27°C Humidity: 41%

Track: 36°C

Pos.	Rider	Time
1	Hayden	1m 36.301s
2	Stoner	1m 36.341s
3	Rossi	1m 36.576s
4	Tamada	1m 36.736s
5	Pedrosa	1m 36.829s
6	Edwards	1m 36.904s
7	Melandri	1m 37.157s
8	Guintoli	1m 37.189s
9	Elias	1m 37.246s
10	Hopkins	1m 37.280s
11	Checa	1m 37.296s
12	Vermeulen	1m 37.365s
13	Nakano	1m 37.530s
14	Barros	1m 37.550s
15	Capirossi	1m 37.733s
16	West	1m 37.885s
17	Hofmann	1m 37.959s
18	de Puniet	1m 38.271s
19	Roberts	1m 39.017s

Grid order	1	2	3	4	5	6	7	8	9	10	11	12	13	14	15	16	17	18	19	20	21	22	23	24	25	26	27	28	•
1 HAYDEN	27	27	27	27	27	27	26	26	26	46	46	46	46	46	46	46	26	26	26	26	26	26	26	26	26	26	46	46	1
27 STONER	26	26	26	26	26	26	27	27	46	26	26	26	26	26	26	26	46	46	46	46	46	46	46	46	46	46	26	26	2
46 ROSSI	1	1	46	46	46	46	46	46	27	27	27	27	27	27	27	27	27	27	27	27	27	27	27	27	27	27	27	27	3
6 TAMADA	46	46	1	33	1	1	1	1	1	1	1	1	1	1	1	1	1	1	1	1	1	1	1	1	1	1	1	1	4
26 PEDROSA	33	33	33	1	33	33	33	33	33	33	33	33	33	33	33	33	33	33	33	33	33	33	33	33	33	33	33	33	5
5 EDWARDS	21	21	21	21	21	21	21	21	21	21	21	21	21	21	21	21	21	21	21	21	21	21	21	21	21	21	21	21	6
33 MELANDRI	24	6	6	6	6	7	7	7	7	7	7	7	7	7	7	7	7	7	7	7	7	7	7	7	7	7	7	7	7
50 GUINTOLI	6	24	24	7	7	6	6	6	6	6	6	6	6	6	6	6	6	6	6	6	6	6	6	24	24	24	24	24	8
24 ELIAS	5	13	7	13	65	65	65	65	65	65	4	4	4	4	4	24	4	4	24	24	24	24	24	65	65	65	65	65	9
21 HOPKINS	13	5	13	65	13	4	4	4	4	4	65	24	24	24	24	4	24	24	4	4	4	65	65	56	56	56	56	5	10
7 CHECA	7	7	5	4	4	13	24	24	24	24	24	65	14	14	14	14	14	14	14	65	65	4	56	5	5	5	5	56	11
71 VERMEULEN	65	65	65	5	5	24	13	71	71	14	14	14	65	65	65	65	65	65	65	71	71	71	5	71	13	13	13	13	12
56 NAKANO	4	4	4	24	24	5	71	13	14	71	71	71	71	71	71	71	71	71	71	50	56	56	71	13	71	71	71	71	13
4 BARROS	56	56	56	14	71	71	5	14	13	13	50	50	50	50	50	50	50	50	50	56	5	5	13	50	50	50	50		14
65 CAPIROSSI	71	71	14	56	14	14	14	50	50	50	13	13	13	13	13	13	56	56	56	5	13	13	50						15
13 WEST	14	14	71	71	56	50	50	56	56	56	56	56	56	56	56	56	13	13	5	13	50	50							
66 HOFMANN	50	50	50	50	50	56	56	5	5	5	5	5	5	5	5	5	5	5	13										
14 de PUNIET	80	66	66	66	66	66	66	66	66	66	66																		
80 ROBERTS	66	80																											

statistics

EAM STANDINGS

fter 14 Rounds		
1	Ducati Marlboro Team	392
2	Fiat Yamaha Team	317
3	Rizla Suzuki MotoGP	297
4	Repsol Honda Team	293
5	Honda Gresini	214
6	Pramac d'Antin	148
7	Kawasaki Racing Team	112
8	Dunlop Yamaha Tech 3	63
9	Honda LCR	54
0	Konica Minolta Honda	42
1	Team Roberts	14

RIDER STANDINGS

After 14 Rounds		
1	Casey Stoner	287
2	Valentino Rossi	211
3	Dani Pedrosa	188
4	John Hopkins	150
5	Chris Vermeulen	147
6	Marco Melandri	137
7	Colin Edwards	106
8	Loris Capirossi	105
9	Nicky Hayden	105
10	Alex Barros	83
11	Toni Elias	71
12	Alex Hofmann	65
13	Randy de Puniet	58
14	Carlos Checa	54
15	Anthony West	45
16	Shinya Nakano	42
17	Makoto Tamada	33
18	Sylvain Guintoli	30
19	Kurtis Roberts	10
20=	Michel Fabrizio	6
20=	Roger Lee Hayden	6
22	Fonsi Nieto	5
23	Olivier Jacque	4
24	Kenny Roberts Jnr	4

CONSTRUCTOR STANDINGS

After 14 Rounds		
1	Ducati	299
2	Honda	239
3	Yamaha	238
4	Suzuki	201
5	Kawasaki	94
6	KR212V	14

250cc

26 laps, 67.574 miles/108.732km

Pos.	Rider (Nat.)	No.	Machine	Laps	Time & speed
1	Alvaro Bautista (SPA)	19	Aprilia	26	43m 56.458s 92.255mph/ 148.470km/h
2	Andrea Dovizioso (ITA)	34	Honda	26	44m 00.825s
3	Jorge Lorenzo (SPA)	1	Aprilia	26	44m 02.606s
4	Thomas Luthi (SWI)	12	Aprilia	26	44m 09.143s
5	Hector Barbera (SPA)	80	Aprilia	26	44m 09.869s
6	Alex de Angelis (RSM)	3	Aprilia	26	44m 09.898s
7	Marco Simoncelli (ITA)	58	Gilera	26	44m 26.780s
8	Julian Simon (SPA)	60	Honda	26	44m 27.092s
9	Fabrizio Lai (ITA)	32	Aprilia	26	45m 08.711s
10	Karel Abraham (CZE)	17	Aprilia	26	45m 08.777s
11	Dirk Heidolf (GER)	28	Aprilia	26	45m 10.518s
12	Aleix Espargaro (SPA)	41	Aprilia	26	45m 10.617s
13	Jules Cluzel (FRA)	16	Aprilia	26	45m 11.033s
14	Eugene Laverty (IRL)	50	Honda	26	45m 27.436s
15	Imre Toth (HUN)	10	Aprilia	25	44m 04.722s
16	Alvaro Molina (SPA)	31	Aprilia	25	44m 29.638s
17	Ho Wan Chow (CHN)	89	Aprilia	24	44m 07.470s
	Efren Vazquez (SPA)	7	Aprilia	23	DNF
	Ratthapark Wilairot (THA)	8	Honda	23	DNF
	Hiroshi Aoyama (JPN)	4	KTM	22	DNF
	Shuhei Aoyama (JPN)	73	Honda	18	DNF
	Dan Linfoot (GBR)	45	Aprilia	18	DNF
	Alex Baldolini (ITA)	25	Aprilia	7	DNF
	Mika Kallio (FIN)	36	KTM	4	DNF
	Yuki Takahashi (JPN)	55	Honda	2	DNF
	Roberto Locatelli (ITA)	15	Gilera	1	DNF
	Luke Lawrence (GBR)	84	Aprilia		DNQ
	Santiago Barragan (SPA)	53	Honda		DNQ
	Zhu Wang (CHN)	88	Aprilia		DNQ

Fastest lap: Bautista, 1m 40.521s, 93.063mph/149.771km/h (record).

Previous lap record: Hiroshi Aoyama, JPN (KTM), 1m 41.676s, 92.006mph/ 148.070km/h (2006).

Event best maximum speed: Bautista, 170.9mph/275.0km/h (race).

Qualifying: 1 Dovizioso, 1m 40.355s; 2 Lorenzo, 1m 40.480s; 3 Barbera, 1m 40.699s; 4 Kallio, 1m 40.851s; 5 H. Aoyama, 1m 40.856s; 6 Bautista, 1m 40.884s; 7 Simon, 1m 41.093s; 8 de Angelis, 1m 41.100s; 9 Takahashi, 1m 41.157s; 10 Luthi, 1m 41.176s; 11 Simoncelli, 1m 41.370s; 12 S. Aoyama, 1m 41.531s; 13 Locatelli, 1m 41.552s; 14 Espargaro, 1m 42.200s; 15 Lai, 1m 42.334s; 16 Heidolf, 1m 43.074s; 17 Laverty, 1m 43.132s; 18 Wilairot, 1m 43.150s; 19 Vazquez, 1m 43.336s; 20 Toth, 1m 43.664s; 21 Abraham, 1m 43.703s; 22 Cluzel, 1m 43.981s; 23 Baldolini, 1m 44.069s; 24 Linfoot, 1m 44.539s; 25 Molina, 1m 44.570s; 26 Chow, 1m 47.044s; 27 Lawrence, 1m 48.335s; 28 Barragan, 1m 49.307s; 29 Wang, 1m 49.413s.

Fastest race laps: 1 Bautista, 1m 40.521s; 2 Dovizioso, 1m 40.926s; 3 de Angelis, 1m 41.008s; 4 Lorenzo, 1m 41.102s; 5 Luthi, 1m 41.119s; 6 H. Aoyama, 1m 41.134s; 7 Kallio, 1m 41.199s; 8 Barbera, 1m 41.211s; 9 S. Aoyama, 1m 41.236s; 10 Simon, 1m 41.411s; 11 Simoncelli, 1m 41.483s; 12 Abraham, 1m 43.310s; 13 Lai, 1m 43.369s; 14 Wilairot, 1m 43.420s; 15 Espargaro, 1m 43.424s; 16 Heidolf, 1m 43.453s; 17 Cluzel, 1m 43.537s; 18 Vazquez, 1m 43.571s; 19 Takahashi, 1m 43.779s; 20 Laverty, 1m 43.947s; 21 Baldolini, 1m 44.221s; 22 Toth, 1m 44.381s; 23 Linfoot, 1m 45.238s; 24 Molina, 1m 45.390s; 25 Chow, 1m 47.180s; 26 Locatelli, 1m 51.021s.

World Championship: 1 Lorenzo, 257; 2 Dovizioso, 206; 3 de Angelis, 197; 4 Bautista, 160; 5 Barbera, 130; 6 H. Aoyama, 108; 7 Luthi, 98; 8 Kallio, 94; 9 Simon, 83; 10 S. Aoyama, 72; 11 Simoncelli, 66; 12 Takahashi, 56; 13 Lai, 49; 14 Locatelli, 42; 15 Espargaro, 35; 16 Wilairot, 29; 17 West, 25; 18 Abraham, 24; 19 Heidolf, 22; 20 Baldolini, 14; 21 Sekiguchi, 13; 22 Cluzel, 12; 23 Debon, 11; 24 Linfoot, 7; 25 Laverty, 6; 26 Toth, 2; 27 Tizon and Vazquez, 1.

125cc

23 laps, 59.777 miles/96.186km

Pos.	Rider (Nat.)	No.	Machine	Laps	Time & speed
1	Hector Faubel (SPA)	55	Aprilia	23	40m 46.337s 87.953mph/ 141.546km/h
2	Gabor Talmacsi (HUN)	14	Aprilia	23	40m 46.469s
3	Pol Espargaro (SPA)	44	Aprilia	23	40m 46.572s
4	Simone Corsi (ITA)	24	Aprilia	23	40m 47.338s
5	Joan Olive (SPA)	6	Aprilia	23	40m 47.525s
6	Stefan Bradl (GER)	17	Aprilia	23	40m 53.916s
7	Tomoyoshi Koyama (JPN)	71	KTM	23	40m 54.634s
8	Mattia Pasini (ITA)	75	Aprilia	23	40m 55.294s
9	Raffaele de Rosa (ITA)	35	Aprilia	23	40m 55.321s
10	Randy Krummenacher (SWI)	34	KTM	23	41m 00.389s
11	Esteve Rabat (SPA)	12	Honda	23	41m 00.460s
12	Bradley Smith (GBR)	38	Honda	23	41m 04.482s
13	Lukas Pesek (CZE)	52	Derbi	23	41m 07.455s
14	Alexis Masbou (FRA)	7	Honda	23	41m 17.858s
15	Stefano Bianco (ITA)	27	Aprilia	23	41m 17.949s
16	Mike di Meglio (FRA)	63	Honda	23	41m 17.985s
17	Lorenzo Zanetti (ITA)	8	Aprilia	23	41m 18.282s
18	Andrea Iannone (ITA)	29	Aprilia	23	41m 18.323s
19	Federico Sandi (ITA)	15	Aprilia	23	41m 30.654s
20	Danny Webb (GBR)	99	Honda	23	41m 47.903s
21	Simone Grotzkyj (ITA)	53	Aprilia	23	41m 50.246s
22	Roberto Tamburini (ITA)	20	Aprilia	23	41m 50.339s
23	Robert Muresan (ROU)	95	Derbi	23	41m 52.553s
24	Louis Rossi (FRA)	62	Honda	23	41m 55.687s
	Dino Lombardi (ITA)	13	Honda	18	DNF
	Pere Tutusaus (SPA)	30	Aprilia	15	DNF
	Sergio Gadea (SPA)	33	Aprilia	12	DNF
	Sandro Cortese (GER)	11	Aprilia	9	DNF
	Michel Ranseder (AUT)	60	Derbi	9	DNF
	Steve Bonsey (USA)	51	KTM	8	DNF
	Nicolas Terol (SPA)	18	Derbi	7	DNF
	Pablo Nieto (SPA)	22	Aprilia	5	DNF
	Dominique Aegerter (SWI)	77	Aprilia	4	DNF
	Joey Litjens (NED)	37	Honda		DNS
	Ricard Cardus (SPA)	86	Aprilia		DNQ
	Ivo Relvas (POR)	61	Aprilia		DNQ

Fastest lap: Talmacsi, 1m 45.027s, 89.070mph/143.345km/h (record).

Previous lap record: Alvaro Bautista, SPA (Aprilia), 1m 45.746s, 88.465mph/ 142.371km/h (2006).

Event best maximum speed: Krummenacher, 146.6mph/235.9km/h (race).

Qualifying: 1 Pasini, 1m 44.675s; 2 Pesek, 1m 44.933s; 3 Corsi, 1m 45.158s; 4 Talmacsi, 1m 45.176s; 5 Cortese, 1m 45.288s; 6 Gadea, 1m 45.339s; 7 Espargaro, 1m 45.365s; 8 Faubel, 1m 45.378s; 9 Bradl, 1m 45.479s; 10 Olive, 1m 45.621s; 11 Koyama, 1m 45.695s; 12 Krummenacher, 1m 45.970s; 13 Terol, 1m 45.971s; 14 di Meglio, 1m 46.010s; 15 Smith, 1m 46.048s; 16 Iannone, 1m 46.062s; 17 Rabat, 1m 46.164s; 18 de Rosa, 1m 46.192s; 19 Ranseder, 1m 46.374s; 20 Masbou, 1m 46.374s; 21 Nieto, 1m 46.756s; 22 Zanetti, 1m 46.798s; 23 Bianco, 1m 46.869s; 24 Aegerter, 1m 46.982s; 25 Tamburini, 1m 47.183s; 26 Litjens, 1m 47.215s; 27 Muresan, 1m 47.351s; 28 Sandi, 1m 47.375s; 29 Webb, 1m 47.520s; 30 Lombardi, 1m 47.874s; 31 Tutusaus, 1m 48.003s; 32 Bonsey, 1m 48.236s; 33 Grotzkyj, 1m 48.697s; 34 Rossi, 1m 49.679s; 35 Cardus, 1m 50.854s; 36 Relvas, 1m 52.088s.

Fastest race laps: 1 Talmacsi, 1m 45.027s; 2 Corsi, 1m 45.287s; 3 Faubel, 1m 45.287s; 4 Pasini, 1m 45.317s; 5 Olive, 1m 45.347s; 6 Espargaro, 1m 45.360s; 7 Cortese, 1m 45.464s; 8 Bradl, 1m 45.507s; 9 Rabat, 1m 45.540s; 10 Gadea, 1m 45.623s; 11 Pesek, 1m 45.708s; 12 de Rosa, 1m 45.734s; 13 Koyama, 1m 45.790s; 14 Ranseder, 1m 45.791s; 15 Terol, 1m 45.943s; 16 Krummenacher, 1m 46.083s; 17 Smith, 1m 46.386s; 18 Iannone, 1m 46.388s; 19 Zanetti, 1m 46.456s; 20 Sandi, 1m 46.493s; 21 Bianco, 1m 46.513s; 22 di Meglio, 1m 46.554s; 23 Masbou, 1m 46.715s; 24 Nieto, 1m 47.655s; 25 Tutusaus, 1m 47.719s; 26 Lombardi, 1m 47.749s; 27 Tamburini, 1m 47.762s; 28 Webb, 1m 47.852s; 29 Muresan, 1m 48.041s; 30 Grotzkyj, 1m 48.093s; 31 Aegerter, 1m 48.239s; 32 Rossi, 1m 48.265s; 33 Bonsey, 1m 48.339s.

World Championship: 1 Talmacsi, 209; 2 Faubel, 204; 3 Koyama, 154; 4 Pesek, 132; 5 Corsi, 132; 6 Pasini, 119; 7 Gadea, 118; 8 Espargaro, 99; 9 Olive, 87; 10 Smith, 86; 11 Krummenacher, 64; 12 Ranseder, 63; 13 Cortese, 60; 14 de Rosa, 56; 15 Rabat, 52; 16 Bradl, 35; 17 Nieto, 35; 18 Zanetti, 30; 19 di Meglio, 25; 20 Iannone, 20; 21 Masbou, 17; 22 Bianco, 7; 23 Terol, 6; 24 Bonsey, 3; 25 Froehlich and Jerez, 2; 27 Aegerter, 2; 28 Grotzkyj, 1.

BRIDGESTONE
Alice

FIM WORLD CHAMPIONSHIP • ROUND 15

JAPANESEGP

TWIN-RING MOTEGI

Above: **Dreams come true – part one: Capirossi redeemed his season and made it three in a row at Motegi.**

Main photograph: **Dreams come true – part two: Stoner's faultless and dominant season was rewarded with a resounding first world championship. A red-letter day for Ducati.**

Photographs: Gold & Goose

Above: De Puniet's second place gave him his biggest smile in two years.

Top: Loris Capirossi's judgement was perfect, his riding controlled. They made him unbeatable.

Photographs: Gold & Goose

SEVERAL important things happened at Motegi. Paramount among them was that Casey Stoner won the championship. He did so with three races to spare, a resounding victory backed up by a 100-per-cent finishing record, and a rags-to-riches story that, as Stoner said, 'proves that if you never give up, anything can happen.'

It wasn't quite as expected, in a supremely difficult wet-to-dry race when the blazing heat of the preceding two days gave way to persistent rain. Success hinged on the timing of one's bike swap, and failure was readily available in several different forms (West, for instance, threw away his first-ever MotoGP lead after having jumped the start; Rossi lost all his chances when he pitted because he mistakenly thought he had a puncture). Stoner, showing some signs of stress for almost the first time all year, rode a dogged and safe race to sixth. All he needed to do was to beat Valentino, and the Yamaha rider accomplished that for him. The first Australian champion was Wayne Gardner in 1987; then Mick Doohan reigned supreme from 1994 to 1998. Stoner shows many of the character traits of his feisty forebears, including an unquenchable determination.

It was a red-letter day for Ducati. Capirossi's canny race win meant three in a row at Motegi for the Italian rider and factory – a sweet taste in the heartland of the dominant Japanese, at Honda's own track. And for Bridgestone, claiming four in a row at home. The first was by Tamada on a Honda in 2004, in a year with just one other win, by the same rider in Rio. This was the tenth of the season so far, showing just how far the company had come in three years.

Another important event was that Dani Pedrosa finally signed on the dotted line for Honda, for two years. He had been holding back while complaining bitterly about his duff machine and tyres. Like Stoner's title, the deal had been inevitable for some time. In the background, heads had rolled at HRC after the new 800's dismal debut season. Personable and popular vice-president Satoru Horiike had been moved to R&D, and general manager Sutomu Ishii had also gone elsewhere.

At the time, all of this was overshadowed by the tyre news, after Dorna's Carmelo Ezpeleta had swung down from on high with an extraordinary and totally unexpected decree on Saturday afternoon. In short, Dorna was proposing a one-tyre rule for the 2008 season.

It wasn't a *fait accompli*, said Ezpeleta, merely a proposal. But many insiders pointed to the desperate knee-jerk politics behind it and the almost impossibly tight time schedule (all to be decided in Malaysia four weeks hence), and assumed that it was already inevitable. A chorus of aggrieved hostility was loud, centring on the sullying of the ivory tower of the World Championship for short-term advantage. It was not unanimous. The tyre companies wanted competition, as did most observers. There was an important tradition to be preserved: racing as a contest between engineers, and as a valued development tool. But satellite team owners, for example, welcomed it as a first-ever chance to have equal tyres.

Riders necessarily take a short-term view, unclouded by sentiment, and they were generally more accepting. Especially those who had been disadvantaged in 2007 by having to use Michelins. Of these, Hayden thought of the fans: 'In Germany and Laguna, I think we should have given their money back. Though it's also cool to see Michelin fighting back.' Pedrosa was unequivocally in favour. 'I think now it is not equal for riders and teams,' he said. Rossi was philosophical: 'For me, one tyre is not worse.' Bridgestone riders mainly thought like Hopkins: 'I don't care, as long as it's Bridgestones.' But Stoner repeated his condemnation: 'It's like running the R6 Cup. GPs are about prototypes, and it's the competition between the manufacturers that brings out the best in these bikes.'

Positions could and would change, however, and in one case already had. Back in April in Istanbul, Ezpeleta himself had come out strongly against control tyres as a way of seeking closer racing. Events since then had forced a rethink, most notably because Honda and Yamaha, who between them supply half the grid, had expressed concern. This proposal was his radical way of taking control, of taking the championship out of the tyre stalemate.

As it transpired, it was no foregone conclusion. Ezpeleta's proposal was only a first step in a plan that would continue to unfold over the coming weeks.

Race-track business went on more or less as usual. Hofmann was out of the d'Antin team, and Davies invited back. Sadly, an elbow injury sustained when testing with the factory at Mugello, was playing up and he had to decline; veteran factory tester Shinichi Itoh took his place. Rare MotoGP wild-cards were Kawasaki's veteran Akira Yanagawa and Suzuki tester Kousuke Akiyoshi.

Another pneumatic-valve-spring engine blow-up in practice for Rossi proved the last outing of the year for the new motor. 'The performance is a little better, but the reliability is not so good,' he said, adding that he had already been considering switching back to the old motor, which was better able to cope with the high stress of a track with a great deal of hard first-gear acceleration.

Stoner's stress? That came on Friday afternoon, after Checa got in his way. He treated the Spaniard to a series of angry gestures, including a raised finger. Lorenzo had been fined for something similar the race before, but Stoner got away with a 'cool it' wigging from Race Direction. Hopkins was fined US $2,000 at Laguna for aiming what he said was a mock kick at the same rider. Now he recalled his Motegi history – he had been suspended in 2003 after triggering a first-corner pile-up, when Capirossi got away scot-free for doing the same thing a year later. The American wasn't impressed. 'They have no consistency in their calls,' he said.

Obligingly, the target of all this abuse (plus more at Motegi, after baulking Vermeulen and de Puniet in practice) announced the end of his GP career. Checa had signed to ride a Ten Kate Honda in World Superbikes instead. He'd chosen that over a testing berth with Ducati. 'I am still a racer,' he said.

MOTOGP RACE – 24 laps

Blazing heat in qualifying made the same showcase for Michelin's softies as Pedrosa had made for its latest race tyres in free practice. He was on pole by four-tenths from Rossi; Hayden completed the front row, his fourth in succession, saying, 'I'm

Below: **Tyres meant everything at Motegi. From left to right: Bridgestone's Hiroshi Yamada, Dunlop's Jeremy Ferguson and Michelin's Jean-Philippe Weber are all smiles over their new proposal; Hopkins receives a special soft qualifying Bridgestone; Dunlop was improving markedly, but too late.**

Bottom: **Hard braking – de Puniet's rear tyre skims the surface, while Elias's distinctive sideways style is more brutal.**

Photographs: Gold & Goose

really bummed there's only four races left to go in the season.'

Stoner was ninth, on row three – his worst of the year and the first time not up front since Donington. 'Couldn't get comfortable,' he explained. He'd also missed a gear at the final chicane on his already flawed fast lap. Race conditions were so different it hardly mattered.

The track was wet, but already with a drying line as Pedrosa led away, displaced on lap two by West, on the right-hander into the second tunnel. Sadly, the new kid had quite obviously jumped the start from his second-row slot. He pitted from the lead on the third lap for a race-ruinous ride-through penalty.

Stoner got to the front on lap four, with Melandri and de Puniet also ahead of Pedrosa; the Italian took over on the fifth, by which time, the two had a gap approaching four seconds on the pursuit. That was now led by Rossi, who had gained places rapidly, helped by fast-starting Hayden and Suzuki wild-card Akiyoshi dropping back, the former quite quickly, already having tyre problems. He would be the first significant rider to pit for a change, after seven laps.

The conditions were desperate – drying over the first part of the track, but still quite wet on the second, with more rain threatening. De Puniet had slipped back from the leading group on lap five, then took an ever bigger excursion on the seventh, lucky to regain the track.

Checa was first into the pits, after his sixth lap, then Guintoli and Hayden on the seventh. It would do the last-named little good, as his Michelin cut slick proved treacherous in the extreme, and he wouldn't regain pace until right at the end. Then de Puniet, Elias, Itoh and Tamada called in. Capirossi waited until the end of lap nine. As it turned out, he timed it perfectly.

Up front, the decision was not so easy. Those fighting for points and prizes couldn't afford to take the risk that the track would keep on drying. Meanwhile, some riders' intermediate tyres were working better than others.

After ten laps, Stoner was dropping back from Melandri, while Rossi was closing fast on the Ducati. He caught him on the 11th at the bottom of the hill and was easily past. Two laps later, he was in a spirited ding-dong with Melandri, but just as he prevailed on lap 14, the Honda rider dived into the pits, as did Stoner.

At this stage, Capirossi had moved up from ninth to fifth. Next time around, he passed Melandri, Edwards and Rossi in one lap to take a lead he would never lose. He might have passed Pedrosa as well, but the Spaniard removed the need, crashing out on his ruined wet tyres.

Rossi's Michelins were also shot, and he admitted that he should have changed them earlier. Instead, he waited a lap longer. The gap to leader Capirossi had been five seconds. Next time around, second to fourth dived into the pits, and the Ducati was almost 15 seconds clear of… the revived de Puniet!

Rossi's out-lap saw him so wide at the bottom of the hill that he pitted again, thinking he had a flat. Not so, and he rejoined, way out of contention.

De Puniet had Elias and Guintoli just behind him, but he escaped over the final laps, leaving the two of them to battle to the end. Guintoli did get ahead with two laps left, but the Spaniard snatched it straight back. Fourth was still a best-for-years for Dunlop.

Melandri was next, also leaving his bike change too late, then taking time to get used to his dry set-up. He caught Stoner, bringing Akiyoshi with him, until the luckless Japanese pitted to retire. Melandri prevailed with five laps to go and was a couple of seconds ahead at the end. It had been a tense race for the new champion, but when he saw that Rossi was gone after 17 laps, he 'started to relax a little bit more and concentrate on finishing.'

West was next, well adrift; Barros was close, after battling with Hayden to the end. Hopkins was within sight and not far ahead of team-mate Vermeulen. Next came Tamada, with Rossi trying and failing to pass the Japanese in the closing laps, bamboozled again by a bad Michelin. Edwards, two seconds back, had a similar story, but just managed to keep Itoh behind him in 15th. Nakano was well back and out of the points; wild-card Yanagawa and Checa were a lap down. Kurtis Roberts retired early on, when neither wet nor cut slick tyres would work worth a damn.

Opposite left: Light at the end of the tunnel: underpass illumination is reflected in his screen as Elias rides to third – a rostrum return after his season was ruined by injury.

Left and below: A first-class win for 250 rookie Kallio; below, the Finn leads KTM team-mate Aoyama and Dovisioso on the Honda. Aoyama would not make the finish.

Photographs: Gold & Goose

250cc RACE – 23 laps

There was some relief for Honda at its own track: a pair heading the front row, home hero Shuhei Aoyama on pole with Dovizioso alongside. Next came the Aprilias of Lorenzo and Barbera, with Kallio heading row two from his team-mate, and then two more Hondas – Simon and Takahashi.

Warm-up gave a chance for practice in the wet, which was just as well. It was Dovizioso away first, with nigh on 1.5 seconds on Hiro Aoyama, Kallio, Takahashi and Simon. Aoyama would soon peg him back, Takahashi then also getting past Kallio to do the same.

By lap seven, the lead group had been swelled to five and shuffled by the arrival of Barbera from eighth on lap one. Takahashi took the lead next time around, and they crossed the line with Barbera second, then Dovizioso, Kallio and Hiro Aoyama, covered by less than 1.2 seconds.

Takahashi was bent on escape and had better than two seconds when Kallio managed to displace Barbera for second. His pace was faster, and by lap 15, he and Dovizioso were pressing Takahashi; Aoyama was a couple of seconds off in fourth, Barbera soon to drop away behind him.

There were several changes of position, Kallio leading for the first time on lap 17, and Takahashi third. Now Aoyama had also closed. At the same time, it started to drizzle again. In the changing conditions, the two Japanese contenders would not survive up front.

Dovizioso led once more on lap 18, but Kallio took control next time around as Takahashi finally succumbed to the pressure, running off, but regaining the circuit and momentum, having lost only one place.

Next to go was Aoyama, touching a white line under braking and sliding out on the second-to-last lap. By now, Kallio had a margin of almost a second, but the final run through traffic was decisive as he kept his head down, taking his first 250 victory by almost five seconds.

Barbera was 15 seconds back for his fourth rostrum of the year; Takahashi was another three seconds away, with de Angelis all but overtaking him on the last lap. The Aprilia rider had made his way through the group chasing the leaders, but had lost too much time waiting for his tyre to warm up, 13th on lap three before finding his rhythm.

His adversaries on the way through had been Simon, Simoncelli, Shuhei Aoyama and Luthi, and they finished in that order, a little spread at the finish, but with the remounted Hiro Aoyama slotting into eighth, ahead of his brother.

Lorenzo was 11th, still close to Luthi and stripping another shred from Dovizioso's forlorn title hopes as he closed the gap to 36 points.

Former 125 star and now wild-card Youichi Ui was 14th on one of two Yamahas in the field, after slipping off and remounting in the early stages – a sentimental journey in more than one way; Bautista recovered for one point in 15th after running off track and out of the top ten before half-distance.

Linfoot was among six to crash out, as was Takumi Takahashi on the Burning Blood Racing Honda.

125cc RACE – 21 laps

Practice had been dry and Pasini was on pole again (number eight); warm-up and the race were sodden, for a confusing crash-fest of wildly changing fortunes. The first of 20 crashes came on the warm-up lap; Pesek crashed and remounted twice, and still finished in the points, Faubel only once, and was still on the rostrum.

Pasini set off at speed, Talmacsi in pursuit, closing down over the first half of the race to less than a second. Faubel and Gadea stayed within touch for the first six laps, but the former slipped off, rejoining in 16th. This opened the way for di Meglio, fastest in warm-up, to attack first Faubel, and then Talmacsi on lap 14, although the Hungarian was straight back in front. That put him out of touch with Pasini, however, who drew away to win at his ease, master of slippery track.

Di Meglio also slipped off briefly, hitting the ground running to remount, which put Faubel back on the rostrum, but the former retained fourth. Olive was next, having been in the thick of a battle before half-distance. De Rosa crashed after setting fastest lap; Pesek got up to fifth before the first of two spills, handing the place to Smith, who slid off on lap ten. Olive survived it all and held off Corsi for fifth, then came a lone Nieto. Gadea had been storming through, gaining five places in one lap alone, and was eighth.

Ranseder and Iannone completed the top ten; Cortese, Bonsey, Rabat and Pol Espargaro were among the many crashers.

Opposite bottom: Guintoli gives Pedrosa a good spanking – bad conditions, good riding and improved tyres gave the Dunlop class rookie a best-ever fourth.

Below: Master of the wet track, Pasini pulled away from the 125 crash-fest. Aspar team-mates Talmacsi, Faubel and Gadea head the early pursuit.

Photographs: Gold & Goose

A-STYLE GRAND PRIX OF JAPAN

23 SEPTEMBER 2007 • FIM WORLD CHAMPIONSHIP ROUND 15

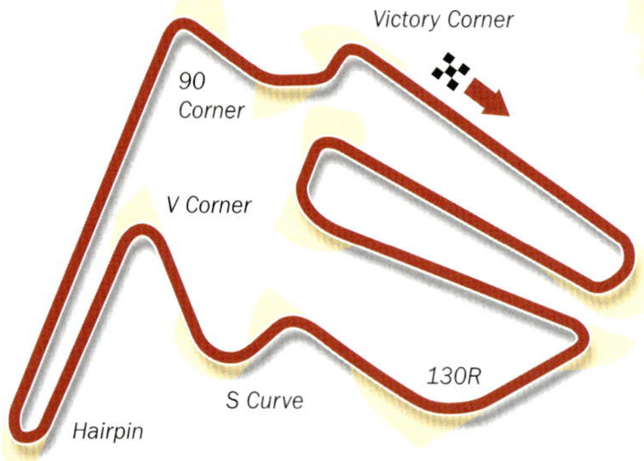

TWIN RING MOTEGI

Circuit 4.801km /2.983 miles

MotoGP

RACE: 24 laps, 71.592 miles/115.224km • Weather: Dry • Air 21°C • Humidity 90% • Track 24°C

Pos.	Rider	Nat.	No.	Entrant	Machine	Tyres	Laps	Time & speed (mph/km/h)
1	Loris Capirossi	ITA	65	Ducati Marlboro Team	Ducati	B	24	47m 05.484s 91.222mph/ 146.808km/h
2	Randy de Puniet	FRA	14	Kawasaki Racing Team	Kawasaki	B	24	47m 16.337s
3	Toni Elias	SPA	24	Honda Gresini	Honda	B	24	47m 17.010s
4	Sylvain Guintoli	FRA	50	Dunlop Yamaha Tech 3	Yamaha	D	24	47m 17.676s
5	Marco Melandri	ITA	33	Honda Gresini	Honda	B	24	47m 34.053s
6	Casey Stoner	AUS	27	Ducati Marlboro Team	Ducati	B	24	47m 36.663s
7	Anthony West	AUS	13	Kawasaki Racing Team	Kawasaki	B	24	47m 55.485s
8	Alex Barros	BRA	4	Pramac d'Antin	Ducati	B	24	47m 57.827s
9	Nicky Hayden	USA	1	Repsol Honda Team	Honda	M	24	47m 59.113s
10	John Hopkins	AUS	21	Rizla Suzuki MotoGP	Suzuki	B	24	48m 05.199s
11	Chris Vermeulen	AUS	71	Rizla Suzuki MotoGP	Suzuki	B	24	48m 08.288s
12	Makoto Tamada	JPN	6	Dunlop Yamaha Tech 3	Yamaha	D	24	48m 14.797s
13	Valentino Rossi	ITA	46	Fiat Yamaha Team	Yamaha	M	24	48m 15.183s
14	Colin Edwards	USA	5	Fiat Yamaha Team	Yamaha	M	24	48m 17.219s
15	Shinichi Ito	JPN	72	Pramac d'Antin	Ducati	B	24	48m 17.774s
16	Shinya Nakano	JPN	56	Konica Minolta Honda	Honda	M	24	48m 38.463s
17	Akira Yanagawa	JPN	87	Kawasaki Racing Team	Kawasaki	B	23	47m 34.190s
18	Carlos Checa	SPA	7	Honda LCR	Honda	M	23	48m 03.727s
	Kousuke Akiyoshi	JPN	64	Rizla Suzuki MotoGP	Suzuki	B	20	40m 07.818s
	Dani Pedrosa	SPA	26	Repsol Honda Team	Honda	M	14	28m 09.647s
	Kurtis Roberts	USA	80	Team Roberts	KR212V	M	1	2m 47.984s

Fastest lap: Toni Elias, on lap 23, 1m 50.718s, 96.999mph/156.104km/h.

Lap record: Valentino Rossi, ITA (Yamaha), 1m 47.288s, 100.099mph/161.095km/h (2006).

Event best maximum speed: Dani Pedrosa, 179.8mph/289.4km/h (free practice no. 3).

Grid order	1	2	3	4	5	6	7	8	9	10	11	12	13	14	15	16	17	18	19	20	21	22	23	24	•
26 PEDROSA	26	13	13	27	33	33	33	33	33	33	33	33	33	46	65	65	65	65	65	65	65	65	65	65	1
46 ROSSI	13	27	27	33	27	27	27	27	27	27	27	46	46	26	46	14	14	14	14	14	14	14	14	14	2
1 HAYDEN	27	26	33	14	46	46	46	46	46	46	46	27	27	5	5	24	24	24	24	24	24	24	24	24	3
14 de PUNIET	64	64	26	26	26	26	26	26	26	26	26	26	26	33	33	50	50	50	50	50	50	50	50	50	4
24 ELIAS	1	33	64	46	64	64	64	64	64	5	5	5	5	65	14	27	27	27	27	33	33	33	33	33	5
13 WEST	24	46	14	64	5	5	5	5	5	64	64	65	65	27	24	33	33	33	33	27	27	27	27	27	6
5 EDWARDS	46	14	46	5	65	65	65	65	13	13	13	14	14	14	50	64	64	64	64	64	13	13	13	13	7
65 CAPIROSSI	5	1	5	65	14	14	14	13	65	56	65	24	24	24	27	5	1	1	1	1	1	1	4	4	8
27 STONER	33	5	1	24	24	24	13	4	21	65	56	64	50	50	64	1	13	13	13	13	4	4	1	1	9
33 MELANDRI	14	24	24	1	1	13	24	21	56	14	14	50	64	64	1	13	4	4	4	4	71	71	21	21	10
21 HOPKINS	21	56	65	56	56	1	4	71	14	24	24	13	1	1	13	46	5	71	71	71	21	21	71	71	11
56 NAKANO	56	4	56	4	4	4	56	56	24	50	50	1	13	13	4	4	71	21	21	21	6	6	6	6	12
64 AKIYOSHI	4	65	4	21	21	56	21	14	71	21	1	71	71	71	71	71	21	5	5	6	5	46	46	46	13
7 CHECA	65	21	21	13	13	21	71	24	4	71	71	4	4	4	21	21	6	6	6	5	46	5	5	5	14
4 BARROS	6	72	72	72	72	50	72	1	50	1	4	56	21	21	6	6	46	46	46	46	72	72	72	72	15
6 TAMADA	72	7	7	7	50	72	6	50	1	4	21	21	6	6	72	72	72	72	72	72	56	56	56	56	
71 VERMEULEN	7	6	50	50	71	71	1	72	72	72	72	6	56	72	56	56	56	56	56	56	87	87	87		
50 GUINTOLI	50	50	6	6	6	6	50	6	6	6	6	72	72	56	7	7	87	87	87	87	7	7	7		
87 YANAGAWA	87	71	71	71	7	7	7	7	7	7	7	7	7	7	87	87	7	7	7	7					
72 ITO	71	87	87	87	87	87	87	87	87	87	87	87	87	87											
80 ROBERTS	80																								

FASTEST RACE LAPS

	Rider	Lap	Time
1	Elias	23	1m 50.718s
2	Guintoli	24	1m 50.758s
3	de Puniet	22	1m 50.806s
4	Melandri	23	1m 51.002s
5	Capirossi	20	1m 51.146s
6	Rossi	24	1m 51.153s
7	Stoner	22	1m 51.235s
8	Hopkins	23	1m 51.254s
9	Barros	22	1m 51.316s
10	West	22	1m 51.499s
11	Edwards	24	1m 51.574s
12	Ito	24	1m 51.977s
13	Akiyoshi	20	1m 52.195s
14	Vermeulen	22	1m 52.270s
15	Yanagawa	21	1m 52.477s
16	Hayden	24	1m 52.840s
17	Tamada	23	1m 52.857s
18	Nakano	23	1m 54.182s
19	Checa	17	1m 56.124s
20	Pedrosa	13	1m 58.519s

QUALIFYING

22 September 2007

Weather: Dry*

*Declared a wet race, permitting bike changes, because the track was wet at the start

Air: 32°C Humidity: 45%

Track: 45°C

Pos.	Rider	Time
1	Pedrosa	1m 45.864s
2	Rossi	1m 46.255s
3	Hayden	1m 46.575s
4	de Puniet	1m 46.643s
5	Elias	1m 46.804s
6	West	1m 46.912s
7	Edwards	1m 46.997s
8	Capirossi	1m 47.047s
9	Stoner	1m 47.121s
10	Melandri	1m 47.136s
11	Hopkins	1m 47.163s
12	Nakano	1m 47.295s
13	Akiyoshi	1m 47.316s
14	Checa	1m 47.334s
15	Barros	1m 47.367s
16	Tamada	1m 47.714s
17	Vermeulen	1m 47.914s
18	Guintoli	1m 48.085s
19	Yanagawa	1m 48.569s
20	Ito	1m 49.548s
21	Roberts	1m 50.035s

statistics

OFFICIAL TIMEKEEPER

RIDER STANDINGS

After 15 Rounds

1	Casey Stoner	297
2	Valentino Rossi	214
3	Dani Pedrosa	188
4	John Hopkins	156
5	Chris Vermeulen	152
6	Marco Melandri	148
7	Loris Capirossi	130
8	Nicky Hayden	112
9	Colin Edwards	108
10	Alex Barros	91
11	Toni Elias	87
12	Randy de Puniet	78
13	Alex Hofmann	65
14	Carlos Checa	54
15	Anthony West	54
16	Sylvain Guintoli	43
17	Shinya Nakano	42
18	Makoto Tamada	37
19	Kurtis Roberts	10
20=	Michel Fabrizio	6
20=	Roger Lee Hayden	6
22	Fonsi Nieto	5
23	Olivier Jacque	4
24	Kenny Roberts Jnr	4
25	Shinichi Ito	1

TEAM STANDINGS

After 15 Rounds

1	Ducati Marlboro Team	427
2	Fiat Yamaha Team	322
3	Rizla Suzuki MotoGP	308
4	Repsol Honda Team	300
5	Honda Gresini	241
6	Pramac d'Antin	157
7	Kawasaki Racing Team	141
8	Dunlop Yamaha Tech 3	80
9	Honda LCR	54
10	Konica Minolta Honda	42
11	Team Roberts	14

CONSTRUCTOR STANDINGS

After 15 Rounds

1	Ducati	324
2	Honda	255
3	Yamaha	251
4	Suzuki	207
5	Kawasaki	114
6	KR212V	14

250cc

23 laps, 68.609 miles/110.423km

Pos.	Rider (Nat.)	No.	Machine	Laps	Time & speed
1	Mika Kallio (FIN)	36	KTM	23	48m 28.585s 84.924mph/ 136.672km/h
2	Andrea Dovizioso	34	Honda	23	48m 33.478s
3	Hector Barbera (SPA)	80	Aprilia	23	48m 50.112s
4	Yuki Takahashi (JPN)	55	Honda	23	48m 52.073s
5	Alex de Angelis (RSM)	3	Aprilia	23	48m 53.963s
6	Julian Simon (SPA)	60	Honda	23	49m 10.849s
7	Marco Simoncelli (ITA)	58	Gilera	23	49m 17.367s
8	Hiroshi Aoyama (JPN)	4	KTM	23	49m 26.367s
9	Shuhei Aoyama (JPN)	73	Honda	23	49m 37.634s
10	Thomas Luthi (SWI)	12	Aprilia	23	49m 39.422s
11	Jorge Lorenzo (SPA)	1	Aprilia	23	49m 41.620s
12	Seijin Oikawa (JPN)	76	Yamaha	23	49m 54.956s
13	Jules Cluzel (FRA)	16	Aprilia	23	50m 04.821s
14	Youichi Ui (JPN)	75	Yamaha	23	50m 15.683s
15	Alvaro Bautista (SPA)	19	Aprilia	23	50m 18.666s
16	Roberto Locatelli (ITA)	15	Gilera	23	50m 27.326s
17	Aleix Espargaro (SPA)	41	Aprilia	23	50m 35.367s
18	Imre Toth (HUN)	10	Aprilia	23	50m 39.000s
19	Eugene Laverty (IRL)	50	Honda	22	48m 36.503s
20	Yuki Hamamoto (JPN)	77	Yamaha	22	48m 37.028s
	Dan Linfoot (GBR)	45	Aprilia	19	DNF
	Fabrizio Lai (ITA)	32	Aprilia	17	DNF
	Takumi Takahashi (JPN)	20	Honda	3	DNF
	Ratthapark Wilairot (THA)	8	Honda	2	DNF
	Dirk Heidolf (GER)	28	Aprilia	1	DNF
	Karel Abraham (CZE)	17	Aprilia	0	DNF
	Alex Baldolini (ITA)	25	Aprilia	0	DNF
	Efren Vazquez (SPA)	7	Aprilia	0	DNF

Fastest lap: Dovizioso, 2m 04.160s, 86.497mph/139.204km/h.

Lap record: Shinya Nakano, JPN (Yamaha), 1m 52.253s, 95.673mph/ 153.970km/h (2000).

Event best maximum speed: Barbera, 155.9mph/250.9km/h (free practice no. 2).

Qualifying: 1 S. Aoyama, 1m 51.327s; 2 Dovizioso, 1m 51.466s; 3 Lorenzo, 1m 51.765s; 4 Barbera, 1m 51.828s; 5 Kallio, 1m 52.053s; 6 H. Aoyama, 1m 52.169s; 7 Simon, 1m 52.261s; 8 Y. Takahashi, 1m 52.328s; 9 de Angelis, 1m 52.329s; 10 Luthi, 1m 52.441s; 11 Bautista, 1m 52.711s; 12 Simoncelli, 1m 52.825s; 13 Locatelli, 1m 52.830s; 14 Wilairot, 1m 54.124s; 15 Lai, 1m 54.418s; 16 T. Takahashi, 1m 54.487s; 17 Ui, 1m 54.779s; 18 Baldolini, 1m 54.914s; 19 Abraham, 1m 55.032s; 20 Heidolf, 1m 55.182s; 21 Laverty, 1m 55.352s; 22 Espargaro, 1m 55.451s; 23 Toth, 1m 55.485s; 24 Vazquez, 1m 55.690s; 25 Cluzel, 1m 56.042s; 26 Hamamoto, 1m 56.692s; 27 Linfoot, 1m 56.705s; 28 Oikawa, 1m 56.973s.

Fastest race laps: 1 Dovizioso, 2m 04.160s; 2 Kallio, 2m 04.203s; 3 Y. Takahashi, 2m 04.587s; 4 H. Aoyama, 2m 04.620s; 5 de Angelis, 2m 05.422s; 6 Barbera, 2m 05.459s; 7 Ui, 2m 06.243s; 8 Luthi, 2m 06.514s; 9 S. Aoyama, 2m 06.618s; 10 Simon, 2m 06.854s; 11 Simoncelli, 2m 07.061s; 12 Bautista, 2m 07.375s; 13 Lorenzo, 2m 07.862s; 14 T. Takahashi, 2m 08.013s; 15 Oikawa, 2m 08.066s; 16 Cluzel, 2m 08.194s; 17 Locatelli, 2m 08.525s; 18 Toth, 2m 09.040s; 19 Hamamoto, 2m 09.317s; 20 Wilairot, 2m 09.769s; 21 Lai, 2m 10.131s; 22 Espargaro, 2m 10.529s; 23 Linfoot, 2m 10.753s; 24 Laverty, 2m 11.363s; 25 Heidolf, 2m 25.888s.

World Championship: 1 Lorenzo, 262; 2 Dovizioso, 226; 3 de Angelis, 208; 4 Bautista, 161; 5 Barbera, 146; 6 Kallio, 119; 7 H. Aoyama, 116; 8 Luthi, 104; 9 Simon, 93; 10 S. Aoyama, 79; 11 Simoncelli, 75; 12 Y. Takahashi, 69; 13 Lai, 49; 14 Locatelli, 42; 15 Espargaro, 35; 16 Wilairot, 29; 17 West, 25; 18 Abraham, 24; 19 Heidolf, 22; 20 Cluzel, 15; 21 Baldolini, 14; 22 Sekiguchi, 13; 23 Debon, 11; 24 Linfoot, 7; 25 Laverty, 6; 26 Oikawa, 4; 27 Ui, 2; 28 Toth, 2; 29 Tizon and Vazquez, 1.

125cc

21 laps, 62.643 miles/100.821km

Pos.	Rider (Nat.)	No.	Machine	Laps	Time & speed
1	Mattia Pasini (ITA)	75	Aprilia	21	46m 29.900s 80.838mph/ 130.096km/h
2	Gabor Talmacsi (HUN)	14	Aprilia	21	46m 32.885s
3	Hector Faubel (SPA)	55	Aprilia	21	46m 52.305s
4	Mike di Meglio (FRA)	63	Honda	21	47m 03.651s
5	Joan Olive (SPA)	6	Aprilia	21	47m 07.251s
6	Simone Corsi (ITA)	24	Aprilia	21	47m 08.962s
7	Pablo Nieto (SPA)	22	Aprilia	21	47m 14.388s
8	Sergio Gadea (SPA)	33	Aprilia	21	47m 18.801s
9	Michael Ranseder (AUT)	60	Derbi	21	47m 20.572s
10	Andrea Iannone (ITA)	29	Aprilia	21	47m 26.574s
11	Dominique Aegerter (SWI)	77	Aprilia	21	47m 33.488s
12	Lukas Pesek (CZE)	52	Derbi	21	47m 40.234s
13	Danny Webb (GBR)	99	Honda	21	47m 44.479s
14	Tomoyoshi Koyama (JPN)	71	KTM	21	47m 49.449s
15	Stefan Bradl (GER)	17	Aprilia	21	47m 53.155s
16	Roberto Tamburini (ITA)	20	Aprilia	21	47m 58.189s
17	Nicolas Terol (SPA)	18	Derbi	21	47m 59.961s
18	Kazuma Watanabe (JPN)	74	Honda	21	48m 00.454s
19	Randy Krummenacher (SWI)	34	KTM	21	48m 05.306s
20	Nayuta Mizuno (JPN)	69	Yamaha	21	48m 12.693s
21	Alexis Masbou (FRA)	7	Honda	21	48m 35.869s
22	Shouya Tomizawa (JPN)	58	Honda	17	48m 05.067s
	Simone Grotzkyj (ITA)	53	Aprilia	20	DNF
	Pol Espargaro (SPA)	44	Aprilia	17	DNF
	Iori Namihira (JPN)	59	Honda	14	DNF
	Lorenzo Zanetti (ITA)	8	Aprilia	12	DNF
	Bradley Smith (GBR)	38	Honda	9	DNF
	Esteve Rabat (SPA)	12	Honda	9	DNF
	Stefano Bianco (ITA)	27	Aprilia	8	DNF
	Robert Muresan (ROU)	95	Derbi	8	DNF
	Steve Bonsey (USA)	51	KTM	7	DNF
	Sandro Cortese (GER)	11	Aprilia	7	DNF
	Federico Sandi (ITA)	15	Aprilia	6	DNF
	Raffaele de Rosa (ITA)	35	Aprilia	5	DNF
	Yuuchi Yanagisawa (JPN)	57	Honda	5	DNF
	Dino Lombardi (ITA)	13	Honda	3	DNF

Fastest lap: de Rosa, 2m 10.998s, 81.982mph/131.937km/h.

Lap record: Mika Kallio, FIN (KTM), 1m 57.666s, 91.271mph/146.886km/h (2006).

Event best maximum speed: Koyama, 135.9mph/218.7km/h (qualifying practice no. 2).

Qualifying: 1 Pasini, 1m 57.301s; 2 Koyama, 1m 57.892s; 3 Talmacsi, 1m 58.175s; 4 Faubel, 1m 58.571s; 5 Smith, 1m 58.752s; 6 Corsi, 1m 58.764s; 7 Olive, 1m 58.958s; 8 Pesek, 1m 58.981s; 9 de Rosa, 1m 59.073s; 10 Cortese, 1m 59.206s; 11 Gadea, 1m 59.259s; 12 di Meglio, 1m 59.316s; 13 Bradl, 1m 59.346s; 14 Terol, 1m 59.377s; 15 Rabat, 1m 59.496s; 16 Espargaro, 1m 59.603s; 17 Krummenacher, 1m 59.615s; 18 Zanetti, 1m 59.639s; 19 Iannone, 1m 59.704s; 20 Nieto, 1m 59.752s; 21 Ranseder, 2m 00.087s; 22 Masbou, 2m 00.364s; 23 Bianco, 2m 00.420s; 24 Tamburini, 2m 00.570s; 25 Bonsey, 2m 00.836s; 26 Aegerter, 2m 00.935s; 27 Grotzkyj, 2m 01.457s; 28 Muresan, 2m 01.587s; 29 Webb, 2m 01.786s; 30 Tomizawa, 2m 01.947s; 31 Namihira, 2m 01.966s; 32 Watanabe, 2m 01.978s; 33 Lombardi, 2m 02.056s; 34 Sandi, 2m 02.096s; 35 Yanagisawa, 2m 02.127s; 36 Mizuno, 2m 03.964s.

Fastest race laps: 1 de Rosa, 2m 10.998s; 2 Pasini, 2m 11.069s; 3 di Meglio, 2m 11.546s; 4 Talmacsi, 2m 11.588s; 5 Pesek, 2m 12.084s; 6 Faubel, 2m 12.265s; 7 Gadea, 2m 12.297s; 8 Espargaro, 2m 12.549s; 9 Corsi, 2m 12.816s; 10 Olive, 2m 12.949s; 11 Grotzkyj, 2m 13.001s; 12 Ranseder, 2m 13.006s; 13 Nieto, 2m 13.092s; 14 Iannone, 2m 13.097s; 15 Aegerter, 2m 13.127s; 16 Smith, 2m 13.128s; 17 Bradl, 2m 13.562s; 18 Terol, 2m 13.607s; 19 Krummenacher, 2m 13.645s; 20 Tomizawa, 2m 13.812s; 21 Tamburini, 2m 14.008s; 22 Rabat, 2m 14.163s; 23 Bianco, 2m 14.164s; 24 Muresan, 2m 14.173s; 25 Bonsey, 2m 14.537s; 26 Zanetti, 2m 14.580s; 27 Webb, 2m 14.597s; 28 Watanabe, 2m 14.625s; 29 Lombardi, 2m 15.130s; 30 Koyama, 2m 15.288s; 31 Masbou, 2m 15.868s; 32 Mizuno, 2m 15.964s; 33 Yanagisawa, 2m 16.889s; 34 Sandi, 2m 17.183s; 35 Namihira, 2m 17.322s; 36 Cortese, 2m 18.310s.

World Championship: 1 Talmacsi, 229; 2 Faubel, 220; 3 Koyama, 156; 4 Pasini, 144; 5 Corsi, 142; 6 Pesek, 136; 7 Gadea, 126; 8 Espargaro, 99; 9 Olive, 98; 10 Smith, 86; 11 Ranseder, 70; 12 Krummenacher, 64; 13 Cortese, 60; 14 de Rosa, 56; 15 Rabat, 52; 16 Nieto, 44; 17 di Meglio, 38; 18 Bradl, 36; 19 Zanetti, 30; 20 Iannone, 26; 21 Masbou, 17; 22 Aegerter and Bianco, 7; 24 Terol, 6; 25 Bonsey and Webb, 3; 27 Froehlich and Jerez, 2; 29 Grotzkyj, 1.

FIM WORLD CHAMPIONSHIP • ROUND 16

AUSTRALIANGP

PHILLIP ISLAND

Champion, and spoils. Stoner gave the adoring crowd exactly what it wanted – another clear and masterful victory.
Photograph: Gold & Goose

Above: **Rossi's mixed-up Aboriginal "Guido" caused some offence.**

Above centre: **Chris Vermeulen with Freddie Sheene, on the Suzuki painted as a tribute to his ever-popular father Barry.**

Top: **When Capirossi blew by, Rossi thought he might be in for some fun. Instead, he was left behind.**

Above centre right: **A minute of silence was in memory of Norick Abe, killed in a scooter crash the preceding week. In the front row, from left: Claude Danis (FIM and Race Direction), Lin Jarvis (Yamaha), Carmelo Ezpeleta (Dorna), Masahiko Nakajima (Yamaha), Hervé Poncharal (IRTA and Tech 3) and Makoto Tamada.**

Photographs: Gold & Goose

IF there was any sense of ennui among the regulars now that the championship was settled, it certainly wasn't shared by the Australian fans. They might have preferred it for Stoner to have secured the title at home, but that wasn't to be. The national rugby team had come home defeated from the World Cup, but the latest Australian champion was nothing but triumphant. Before the race, and after it.

The fans, 50,425 of them, flocked to the track in a major revival of interest, although not equal in numbers to the 90,000-odd claimed for the first Australian race, when Gardner won in 1989; and Stoner was the rider of choice for the fans just as Rossi is in Italy. Was it modesty, or a growing feeling that all the adulation was 'a bit much, really', that caused Stoner conscientiously to mention that there were three Australians in MotoGP, not just one? Both Vermeulen and West had done their share in raising the profile of bike racing in Australian once again.

He also clearly thought that was enough Australiana for now, and was not amused when Rossi poached some indigenous icons for his bike decoration: his cartoon had been blacked up and decorated with Aboriginal dot art.

The island at the foot of the island continent laid on quite a welcome: icy winds and horizontal rain showers marred both days of practice, especially the first. Race day was mild and dry, however, and Monday (inevitably) bathed in glorious sunshine.

The conditions gave Stoner a chance to demonstrate at home what observers have noted everywhere else, in 2006 as well – that the new champion never rides at anything but the limit. Over the treacherous wet Lukey Heights, he was reliably the only rider going hard enough to have the traction control working. Every lap. He also crashed twice, once at low speed on some spillage at the hairpin, the second time a more serious high-sider when his rear wheel slipped off the dry line at Siberia.

The big one had gone, but there were a couple of major-league titles remaining: those for constructor and team. Ducati's miraculous year continued when Capirossi stormed through to take second place. Their second-ever one-two secured both of them, with two races to spare. The smaller classes were still open however, the 125 more so than the 250, and a fascinating battle between team-mates became even closer.

Rossi's cartoon faux pas came on a specially-liveried factory Yamaha, for a second time painted at the behest of sponsor Fiat. He and Edwards rode machines in the colours of the Italian flag, bearing a bold Scorpion logo, made famous in the 1950s and 1960s by car tuner and constructor Carlo Abarth. Fiat now owns the brand and badged the fairings; Yamaha might have done better to get the famous Italian to work some of his magic inside the motor. Pedrosa's Honda was in among the Ducatis for top speed – Stoner's weekend best 324.6km/h, Pedrosa second on 321.4, then three more Ducatis, while Rossi was seventh, behind de Puniet's Kawasaki on 317.2.

Another livery played off the image of Barry Sheene in Australia – the annual memorial ride was again popular – and his association with Suzuki, not to mention with Chris Vermeulen, whose early international career he had fostered. Chris's bike retained the Rizla light blue, but gained some white stripes that were reminiscent of the very first square-four RG500 Suzukis, ridden in 1974 by Sheene, Paul Smart and Jack Findlay.

The last of the Australian trio, West, had a tricky weekend, which began when he made the press laugh with his earthy response to the turn-around in his career, from unpaid privateer to factory Kawasaki rider. 'Even half-way through the year, I didn't know if I'd be working at Maccers [MacDonald's] now, or still on a bike,' he said. On Friday evening, his father was involved in a fracas in the hospitality suites, and on Sunday, the rider's efforts were scotched by wheelspin and slides. Nothing that wouldn't further endear this down-to-earth rider to his loyal home fans, though.

The tyre story had turned another revolution, in that the major protagonists were now quietly confident that the issue would be resolved without the single-tyre option going ahead. That was only half the story. Behind closed doors, a complex deal was being forced through: a special one-rider (Rossi) on Bridgestones deal. The rumour seemed barely plausible when it surfaced on Sunday night. Watch this space.

Honda and Ducati each had new bodywork: a larger nose cowl for the former, preferred by Hayden, and a smaller for the latter, which was Stoner's choice. Cross-winds are always an issue at Phillip Island, but nobody resorted to drilling holes as in the past.

Rossi had one consolation: by edging ahead of Stoner on the grid, he took over on the BMW M-Award cumulative times, for all qualifying plus the IRTA tests. His total of 28m 49.18s was half a tenth inside Stoner's 28m 49.87s. Pedrosa was next, a full 2.72 seconds slower.

Red face of the weekend belonged to Pedrosa, courtesy of a glitch in his clutch. He stopped at the end of warm-up, as permitted, to practice a start. Hopkins stopped behind to await his turn. Pedrosa revved up, engaged the clutch, and the RS212V went straight skyward. Pedrosa fell off the back; the Honda fell on to its side, holing its radiator. Hopkins could hardly believe his eyes, putting a hand on his hips as he looked around to see if he had been the only spectator. He wasn't; it had been filmed from every angle, including on-bike, and he was joined by millions more when the shots circulated on Internet video sites.

MOTOGP RACE – 27 laps

Stoner was fastest in free practice and third on the grid, but for a second race in a row, it was Pedrosa on pole, Rossi alongside him; Hayden led row two, missing the cut by a tenth.

The hoped-for good weather prevailed at the start, and everyone anticipated another of the close races for which Phillip Island is so famous. It was not to be, however, as once again Stoner stretched everybody's legs. In Hayden's case, to breaking point.

Stoner started with another trade-mark flier off the grid, firmly in control as they peeled into the daunting first corner. He tore off with Hayden in hot pursuit, closing slightly on the second half of the lap to show this would not necessarily be another runaway. Rossi was behind Pedrosa and pushed past at the hairpin on lap two. Then he was too hard on the throttle through

Above: Abarth's Scorpion led the way on the Fiat Yamahas. Would have been more useful inside the M1 motor.

Below: Barros claimed a strong fifth as his career drew towards an end.

Photographs: Gold & Goose

the signature triple left-handers on to the straight, running on to the grass at close to top speed and dropping back again. It cost vital tenths, and it was not until lap four that he got back in front again, by which time he was more than 1.6-seconds off the leading pair.

Capirossi had finished lap one in fifth, ahead of Barros and a fighting Melandri, the last ahead of both by lap three. He took Pedrosa also next time around. Next, Rossi was his target, but he stayed out of reach, and by lap seven, Melandri was running into familiar chatter problems. He resisted Pedrosa fiercely, but in vain, and at one-third-distance, he was dropping back at an ever-increasing rate.

Hayden was having a fine ride, sticking within half a second of Stoner without apparent difficulty. 'It was the closest I'd been to the lead all year.' It all went wrong on lap ten. The Honda V4 dropped a valve, this time without wholesale destruction. Hayden continued gamely on three cylinders. 'In Germany, it slowed and I still finished. Even on three cylinders, I did a 1:31.9. Then it went tight and stopped.' The time came on lap 12, but the bike didn't finish the 13th.

Rossi had scythed past into turn one after his first slow lap, but Stoner was almost three seconds clear and would keep pulling away. 'I made one of my best starts, so I had the first corner to myself, and I could concentrate on getting the tyres warmed up and ready to go. Nicky was really pushing in the beginning, but I managed to get away,' he smiled. 'This is the most special of my wins. Standing on the podium with all the crowd was fantastic. I've worked a long time to win this race.'

Out of touch with the Ducati, Rossi instead found himself engaged with Pedrosa once more, the Honda getting ahead for laps 18 and 19. Both complained afterwards of worsening wheelspin at the end, but Rossi had the compensation of claiming fastest lap, slower than the 990 time, and preserving a perfect Phillip Island rostrum record.

On lap 18, Capirossi took fourth off the slowing Melandri and directly closed on the pair up ahead. He was on them at the start of lap 19, blowing by them on the run down the straight to take a second place he would hold to the end. Rossi did manage to leave Pedrosa, but the Ducati was already well out of reach. 'Honestly, I'm not too disappointed today, because I know I did everything I could, and it is always a great pleasure on the podium here. When Loris came, I thought we could have a good race, like the old days…but I had to slow down again,' he said.

Barros had been circulating steadily a little way behind, gaining fifth on lap 21 as Melandri dropped back. Hopkins followed at a respectful distance, having escaped from West in the early stages. Nakano had been heading the next gang, but gave way to de Puniet and Checa, both of whom were ahead of West by lap eight. The Frenchman kept going, closing on Hopkins over the next three laps and finding a way past, then holding the position to the end.

Checa and West were trading blows, while Vermeulen and Edwards were catching up before half-distance. The four went back and fourth until, with fewer than ten laps to go, Vermeulen finally prevailed, Edwards still with him. Both passed the still-slowing Melandri on the last lap.

Nakano dropped away, alone in 13th; Guintoli was another six seconds down; Elias was a long way back for the last point. Close behind, Tamada prevailed narrowly again over Roberts, who had got ahead earlier.

Chaz Davies joined Hayden on the retirement list, in only his second ride as replacement for Alex Hofmann on the Pramac D'Antin Ducati.

250cc RACE – 25 laps

Lorenzo took his 23rd career pole in his 46th start – a 50-per-cent hit rate. The margin was huge and ominous, almost nine-tenths, over the Aprilias of Barbera, Bautista and de Angelis. Dovizioso was seventh, on row two.

The title leader led away from Dovizioso and almost at once began a display of mastery, pulling out almost a second every lap to win by almost 20 seconds. There was nobody to touch him. It was his ninth of the season, equalling the best totals set by his boyhood heroes, Rossi and Biaggi. With two races left, he could still equal the season record, set by Kato in 2001.

It was a solitary affair, but the battle for second made up for it. Dovizioso was displaced on the first run down the straight, his Honda clearly short of top speed compared with Bautista's

Aprilia. Soon he was also under pressure from Simoncelli, until the Gilera rider suffered a big slide on lap five and dropped to the back of the group in seventh, with Shuhei Aoyama, de Angelis and Luthi now hounding Dovizioso.

Aoyama was fired up, and on lap seven had got through to second. Then he had a near high-sider at Honda Hairpin, only regaining control when on the grass; he rejoined in tenth.

By now, Dovizioso and Bautista were disputing second; Luthi was poised behind, while Simon and Hiro Aoyama had caught up, passing de Angelis, who would soon lose touch.

At the mid-point, Bautista had been in control, and Dovizioso would soon be displaced by Luthi, then Simon. Some hard riding ensued, the Italian back up to third and threatening Bautista on lap 19. Then he missed a gear out of Siberia and dropped back to fifth.

Luthi held second for the 21st and 22nd laps, then it was Bautista again over the line. They started the last with Dovizioso up front. He changed places with Bautista twice on that lap, but in the end could do nothing about Bautista's faster run out on to the straight and was hard pressed to hang on to third, ahead of Hiro Aoyama, Luthi and Simon. It was just enough to keep his title chances, if not his hopes, alive, with Lorenzo now 45 points ahead.

De Angelis had come under attack from Simoncelli and Shuhei Aoyama, moving up again; he lost out to both of them as they crossed the line almost abreast.

Takahashi eventually outpaced Locatelli for tenth; then they trailed in – Cluzel, Abraham, Espargaro and Heidolf completing the points. Laverty was just out of them, by three seconds.

Barbera's race had soon been over, his engine taking him only as far as the hairpin on the first lap before dying; Kallio crashed out a lap later, one of only two riders to fall. The other was rookie Vazquez, on lap four.

125cc RACE – 21 laps

The weather had the worst effect on practice and qualifying for the smallest class, while Pasini took his ninth pole of the year, only narrowly from de Rosa. Pesek and Koyama completed the front row; title rivals Faubel and Talmacsi were on the second and third rows respectively.

The familiar light blue bike of Pasini led the pack into the first corner, but they were all over one another, and it was Koyama's orange KTM ahead over the line for the first time. Positions were changing constantly, with a pack of ten riders all still covered by 2.1 seconds after 12 laps. There had been several different leaders over the line, Pasini, Faubel, Pesek and Talmacsi all taking at least one turn. Ranseder had been with the group, but had crashed out and rejoined near the back.

The group broke up only a little over the remaining laps. Pesek and Faubel were making the running up front, while Olive, Talmacsi and Rabat stayed close, Koyama and the others dropping back a little. Then they all closed up again for an epic final lap.

Faubel led over the line; Pesek took over into the first corner and managed somehow to prevent anyone else from getting past. 'It was like a beautiful game that I played,' he said after the race. A canny Olive managed to snitch second from Faubel, while Corsi also finished strongly to take fourth, ahead of Rabat, Pasini, Koyama and a thoroughly bamboozled Talmacsi, with only Gadea behind him. The first nine were covered by less than 1.5 seconds.

Tenth-placed Cortese had lost touch only in the closing laps. Some way back, rookie Bonsey managed to foil Smith for 15th and the last points, his second score of the year.

Eighth place against Faubel's third meant that Talmacsi retained the title lead by a single excruciating point. An inter-team-mate cliff-hanger, for sure.

Above: Talmacsi leads Pesek and Rabat over the skyline in a fraught 125 race.

Above left: Nine, count 'em, nine wins for Lorenzo, 250 champion elect.

Centre far left: Nakano's difficult year wasn't improving as it approached an end.

Top: Over Lukey Heights and down to MG hairpin, Shuhei Aoyama (73) seizes a short-lived second from Bautista, Dovizioso, Luthi and de Angelis.

Far left: Another skirmish between Pedrosa and Rossi was determined by tyre wear.

Photographs: Gold & Goose

GMC AUSTRALIAN GRAND PRIX

14 OCTOBER 2007 • FIM WORLD CHAMPIONSHIP ROUND 16

PHILLIP ISLAND

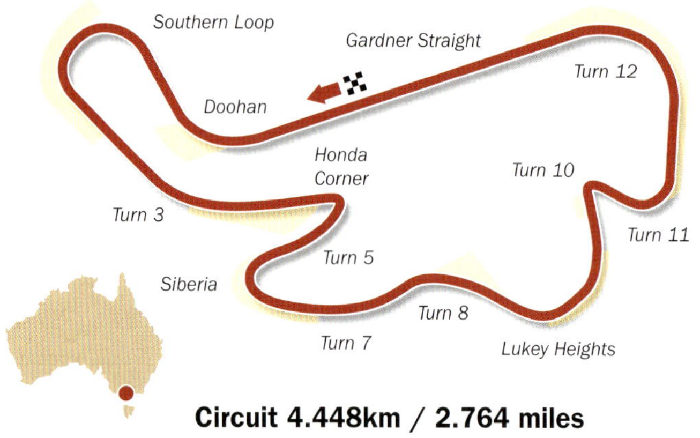

Circuit 4.448km / 2.764 miles

MotoGP

RACE: 27 laps, 74.628 miles/120.096km • Weather: Dry • Air 20°C • Humidity 47% • Track 31°C

Pos.	Rider	Nat.	No.	Entrant	Machine	Tyres	Laps	Time & speed (mph/km/h)
1	Casey Stoner	AUS	27	Ducati Marlboro Team	Ducati	B	27	41m 12.244s 108.665mph/ 174.879km/h
2	Loris Capirossi	ITA	65	Ducati Marlboro Team	Ducati	B	27	41m 19.007s
3	Valentino Rossi	ITA	46	Fiat Yamaha Team	Yamaha	M	27	41m 22.282s
4	Dani Pedrosa	SPA	26	Repsol Honda Team	Honda	M	27	41m 23.907s
5	Alex Barros	BRA	4	Pramac d'Antin	Ducati	B	27	41m 31.719s
6	Randy de Puniet	FRA	14	Kawasaki Racing Team	Kawasaki	B	27	41m 39.557s
7	John Hopkins	USA	21	Rizla Suzuki MotoGP	Suzuki	B	27	41m 41.487s
8	Chris Vermeulen	AUS	71	Rizla Suzuki MotoGP	Suzuki	B	27	41m 47.077s
9	Colin Edwards	USA	5	Fiat Yamaha Team	Yamaha	M	27	41m 47.317s
10	Marco Melandri	ITA	33	Honda Gresini	Honda	B	27	41m 49.215s
11	Carlos Checa	SPA	7	Honda LCR	Honda	M	27	41m 49.965s
12	Anthony West	AUS	13	Kawasaki Racing Team	Kawasaki	B	27	41m 50.670s
13	Shinya Nakano	JPN	56	Konica Minolta Honda	Honda	M	27	41m 59.674s
14	Sylvain Guintoli	FRA	50	Dunlop Yamaha Tech 3	Yamaha	D	27	42m 06.568s
15	Toni Elias	SPA	24	Honda Gresini	Honda	B	27	42m 22.715s
16	Makoto Tamada	JPN	6	Dunlop Yamaha Tech 3	Yamaha	D	27	42m 25.148s
17	Kurtis Roberts	USA	80	Team Roberts	KR212V	M	27	42m 25.264s
	Nicky Hayden	USA	1	Repsol Honda Team	Honda	M	12	18m 22.054s
	Chaz Davies	GBR	57	Pramac d'Antin	Ducati	B	12	18m 45.841s

Fastest lap: Valentino Rossi, on lap 7, 1m 30.801s, 109.579mph/176.350km/h.

Lap record: Marco Melandri, ITA (Honda), 1m 30.332s, 110.148mph/177.266km/h (2005).

Event best maximum speed: Casey Stoner, 201.7mph/324.6km/h (warm-up).

Grid order		1	2	3	4	5	6	7	8	9	10	11	12	13	14	15	16	17	18	19	20	21	22	23	24	25	26	27	•
26	PEDROSA	27	27	27	27	27	27	27	27	27	27	27	27	27	27	27	27	27	27	27	27	27	27	27	27	27	27	27	1
46	ROSSI	1	1	1	1	1	1	1	1	1	1	46	46	46	46	46	46	46	26	26	65	65	65	65	65	65	65	65	2
27	STONER	26	26	26	46	46	46	46	46	46	46	1	1	26	26	26	26	26	46	46	46	46	46	46	46	46	46	46	3
1	HAYDEN	46	46	46	33	33	33	26	26	26	26	26	26	33	33	33	33	33	65	65	26	26	26	26	26	26	26	26	4
65	CAPIROSSI	65	65	33	26	26	26	33	33	33	33	33	33	65	65	65	65	65	33	33	33	4	4	4	4	4	4	4	5
14	de PUNIET	4	33	65	65	65	65	65	65	65	65	65	65	4	4	4	4	4	4	4	4	33	33	33	14	14	14	14	6
4	BARROS	33	4	4	4	4	4	4	4	4	4	4	4	14	14	14	14	14	14	14	14	14	14	14	21	21	21	21	7
56	NAKANO	21	21	21	21	21	21	21	21	21	21	21	21	21	21	21	21	21	21	21	21	21	21	21	33	33	33	71	8
50	GUINTOLI	56	56	13	13	13	13	13	14	14	14	14	14	13	13	13	13	13	7	7	13	13	71	71	71	71	71	5	9
13	WEST	14	13	56	56	56	56	56	7	7	7	7	7	7	7	7	7	7	13	13	71	71	13	13	5	5	5	33	10
5	EDWARDS	13	14	14	14	14	14	14	13	13	13	13	13	71	71	71	71	71	71	71	7	5	5	5	13	13	7	7	11
33	MELANDRI	5	71	71	71	7	7	7	56	56	56	71	71	5	5	5	5	5	5	5	5	7	7	7	7	7	13	13	12
7	CHECA	71	5	7	7	71	71	71	71	71	71	56	5	56	56	56	56	56	56	56	56	56	56	56	56	56	56	56	13
21	HOPKINS	24	7	57	57	5	5	5	5	5	5	5	56	50	50	50	50	50	50	50	50	50	50	50	50	50	50	50	14
6	TAMADA	7	24	5	5	57	57	57	57	57	50	50	50	24	24	24	24	24	24	24	24	24	24	24	24	24	24	24	15
71	VERMEULEN	57	57	24	24	50	50	50	50	50	57	57	57	6	6	6	6	6	6	6	6	6	6	80	80	80	80	6	
57	DAVIES	50	50	50	50	24	24	24	24	24	24	24	24	80	80	80	80	80	80	80	80	80	80	6	6	6	6	80	
24	ELIAS	6	6	6	6	6	6	6	6	6	6	6	6																
80	ROBERTS	80	80	80	80	80	80	80	80	80	80	80	80																

FASTEST RACE LAPS

	Rider	Lap	Time
1	Rossi	7	1m 30.801s
2	Melandri	4	1m 30.806s
3	Hayden	6	1m 30.816s
4	Stoner	10	1m 30.871s
5	Pedrosa	8	1m 30.956s
6	Capirossi	18	1m 31.073s
7	Barros	5	1m 31.364s
8	de Puniet	3	1m 31.572s
9	Hopkins	15	1m 31.719s
10	Checa	7	1m 31.751s
11	West	3	1m 31.871s
12	Vermeulen	7	1m 31.920s
13	Edwards	14	1m 31.987s
14	Nakano	4	1m 32.043s
15	Davies	4	1m 32.302s
16	Guintoli	2	1m 32.479s
17	Elias	2	1m 32.492s
18	Tamada	3	1m 33.373s
19	Roberts	15	1m 33.594s

QUALIFYING

13 October 2007

Weather: Dry

Air: 16°C Humidity: 46%

Track: 24°C

Pos.	Rider	Time
1	Pedrosa	1m 29.201s
2	Rossi	1m 29.419s
3	Stoner	1m 29.816s
4	Hayden	1m 29.932s
5	Capirossi	1m 30.090s
6	de Puniet	1m 30.110s
7	Barros	1m 30.325s
8	Nakano	1m 30.612s
9	Guintoli	1m 30.621s
10	West	1m 30.649s
11	Edwards	1m 30.676s
12	Melandri	1m 31.078s
13	Checa	1m 31.203s
14	Hopkins	1m 31.386s
15	Tamada	1m 31.595s
16	Vermeulen	1m 31.810s
17	Davies	1m 32.043s
18	Elias	1m 32.442s
19	Roberts	1m 32.948s

statistics

RIDER STANDINGS

After 16 Rounds

1	Casey Stoner	322
2	Valentino Rossi	230
3	Dani Pedrosa	201
4	John Hopkins	165
5	Chris Vermeulen	160
6	Marco Melandri	154
7	Loris Capirossi	150
8	Colin Edwards	115
9	Nicky Hayden	112
10	Alex Barros	102
11	Toni Elias	88
12	Randy de Puniet	88
13	Alex Hofmann	65
14	Carlos Checa	59
15	Anthony West	58
16	Sylvain Guintoli	45
17	Shinya Nakano	45
18	Makoto Tamada	37
19	Kurtis Roberts	10
20=	Michel Fabrizio	6
20=	Roger Lee Hayden	6
22	Fonsi Nieto	5
23	Olivier Jacque	4
24	Kenny Roberts Jnr	4
25	Shinichi Ito	1

TEAM STANDINGS

After 16 Rounds

1	Ducati Marlboro Team	472
2	Fiat Yamaha Team	345
3	Rizla Suzuki MotoGP	325
4	Repsol Honda Team	313
5	Honda Gresini	248
6	Pramac d'Antin	168
7	Kawasaki Racing Team	155
8	Dunlop Yamaha Tech 3	82
9	Honda LCR	59
10	Konica Minolta Honda	45
11	Team Roberts	14

CONSTRUCTOR STANDINGS

After 16 Rounds

1	Ducati	349
2	Honda	268
3	Yamaha	267
4	Suzuki	216
5	Kawasaki	124
6	KR212V	14

250cc

25 laps, 69.100 miles/111.200km

Pos.	Rider (Nat.)	No.	Machine	Laps	Time & speed
1	Jorge Lorenzo (SPA)	1	Aprilia	25	39m 25.727s 105.146mph/ 169.216km/h
2	Alvaro Bautista (SPA)	19	Aprilia	25	39m 45.361s
3	Andrea Dovizioso (ITA)	34	Honda	25	39m 45.451s
4	Hiroshi Aoyama (JPN)	4	KTM	25	39m 45.524s
5	Thomas Luthi (SWI)	12	Aprilia	25	39m 45.793s
6	Julian Simon (SPA)	60	Honda	25	39m 46.772s
7	Marco Simoncelli (ITA)	58	Gilera	25	39m 58.687s
8	Shuhei Aoyama (JPN)	73	Honda	25	39m 58.770s
9	Alex de Angelis (RSM)	3	Aprilia	25	39m 58.778s
10	Yuki Takahashi (JPN)	55	Honda	25	40m 10.541s
11	Roberto Locatelli (ITA)	15	Gilera	25	40m 14.460s
12	Jules Cluzel (FRA)	16	Aprilia	25	40m 19.737s
13	Karel Abraham (CZE)	17	Aprilia	25	40m 28.945s
14	Aleix Espargaro (SPA)	41	Aprilia	25	40m 35.095s
15	Dirk Heidolf (GER)	28	Aprilia	25	40m 43.534s
16	Eugene Laverty (IRL)	50	Honda	25	40m 46.966s
17	Fabrizio Lai (ITA)	32	Aprilia	25	40m 56.972s
18	Taro Sekiguchi (JPN)	11	Aprilia	25	40m 59.302s
19	Ratthapark Wilairot (THA)	8	Honda	25	40m 59.643s
20	Federico Sandi (ITA)	21	Aprilia	24	39m 32.275s
	Alex Baldolini (ITA)	25	Aprilia	18	DNF
	Imre Toth (HUN)	10	Aprilia	5	DNF
	Efren Vazquez (SPA)	7	Aprilia	3	DNF
	Mika Kallio (FIN)	36	KTM	1	DNF
	Ho Wan Chow (CHN)	89	Aprilia	1	DNF
	Hector Barbera (SPA)	80	Aprilia	0	DNF

Fastest lap: Lorenzo, 1m 33.761s, 106.120mph/170.783km/h.

Lap record: Sebastian Porto, ARG (Aprilia), 1m 33.381s, 106.551mph/ 171.478km/h (2004).

Event best maximum speed: Bautista, 171.7mph/276.4km/h (warm-up).

Qualifying: 1 Lorenzo, 1m 32.884s; 2 Barbera, 1m 33.770s; 3 Bautista, 1m 33.820s; 4 de Angelis, 1m 33.824s; 5 Simoncelli, 1m 33.854s; 6 H. Aoyama, 1m 33.932s; 7 Dovizioso, 1m 34.153s; 8 Luthi, 1m 34.185s; 9 Simon, 1m 34.299s; 10 S. Aoyama, 1m 34.412s; 11 Kallio, 1m 34.527s; 12 Takahashi, 1m 34.990s; 13 Locatelli, 1m 35.372s; 14 Espargaro, 1m 35.788s; 15 Cluzel, 1m 35.860s; 16 Lai, 1m 35.903s; 17 Heidolf, 1m 36.238s; 18 Toth, 1m 36.463s; 19 Baldolini, 1m 36.512s; 20 Vazquez, 1m 36.842s; 21 Abraham, 1m 37.076s; 22 Sekiguchi, 1m 37.106s; 23 Wilairot, 1m 37.376s; 24 Laverty, 1m 37.476s; 25 Sandi, 1m 37.623s; 26 Chow, 1m 38.981s.

Fastest race laps: 1 Lorenzo, 1m 33.761s; 2 Simon, 1m 34.376s; 3 H. Aoyama, 1m 34.384s; 4 S. Aoyama, 1m 34.462s; 5 Bautista, 1m 34.466s; 6 Luthi, 1m 34.526s; 7 Simoncelli, 1m 34.553s; 8 Dovizioso, 1m 34.676s; 9 de Angelis, 1m 34.683s; 10 Locatelli, 1m 35.184s; 11 Takahashi, 1m 35.252s; 12 Cluzel, 1m 35.863s; 13 Abraham, 1m 36.031s; 14 Espargaro, 1m 36.135s; 15 Heidolf, 1m 36.471s; 16 Baldolini, 1m 36.646s; 17 Laverty, 1m 36.786s; 18 Wilairot, 1m 36.870s; 19 Vazquez, 1m 37.130s; 20 Lai, 1m 37.187s; 21 Sekiguchi, 1m 37.283s; 22 Sandi, 1m 37.431s; 23 Toth, 1m 38.582s; 24 Kallio, 1m 43.541s; 25 Chow, 1m 58.388s.

World Championship: 1 Lorenzo, 287; 2 Dovizioso, 242; 3 de Angelis, 215; 4 Bautista, 181; 5 Barbera, 146; 6 H. Aoyama, 129; 7 Kallio, 119; 8 Luthi, 115; 9 Simon, 103; 10 S. Aoyama, 87; 11 Simoncelli, 84; 12 Takahashi, 75; 13 Lai, 49; 14 Locatelli, 47; 15 Espargaro, 37; 16 Wilairot, 29; 17 Abraham, 27; 18 West, 25; 19 Heidolf, 23; 20 Cluzel, 19; 21 Baldolini, 14; 22 Sekiguchi, 13; 23 Dehon, 11; 24 Linfoot, 7; 25 Laverty, 6; 26 Oikawa, 4; 27 Ui, 2; 28 Toth, 2; 29 Tizon and Vazquez, 1.

125cc

23 laps, 63.572 miles/102.304km

Pos.	Rider (Nat.)	No.	Machine	Laps	Time & speed
1	Lukas Pesek (CZE)	52	Derbi	23	38m 03.020s 100.238mph/ 161.318km/h
2	Joan Olive (SPA)	6	Aprilia	23	38m 03.110s
3	Hector Faubel (SPA)	55	Aprilia	23	38m 03.210s
4	Simone Corsi (ITA)	24	Aprilia	23	38m 03.425s
5	Esteve Rabat (SPA)	12	Honda	23	38m 03.935s
6	Tomoyoshi Koyama (JPN)	71	KTM	23	38m 04.335s
7	Mattia Pasini (ITA)	75	Aprilia	23	38m 04.336s
8	Gabor Talmacsi (HUN)	14	Aprilia	23	38m 04.391s
9	Sergio Gadea (SPA)	33	Aprilia	23	38m 04.477s
10	Sandro Cortese (GER)	11	Aprilia	23	38m 17.672s
11	Pol Espargaro (SPA)	44	Aprilia	23	38m 24.765s
12	Randy Krummenacher (SWI)	34	KTM	23	38m 25.707s
13	Nicolas Terol (SPA)	18	Derbi	23	38m 29.511s
14	Mike di Meglio (FRA)	63	Honda	23	38m 29.583s
15	Steve Bonsey (USA)	51	KTM	23	38m 40.843s
16	Bradley Smith (GBR)	38	Honda	23	38m 41.001s
17	Joey Litjens (NED)	37	Honda	23	38m 43.426s
18	Lorenzo Zanetti (ITA)	9	Aprilia	23	38m 43.473s
19	Dominique Aegerter (SWI)	77	Aprilia	23	38m 47.291s
20	Andrea Iannone (ITA)	29	Aprilia	23	38m 47.851s
21	Simone Grotzkyj (ITA)	53	Aprilia	23	38m 54.502s
22	Michael Ranseder (AUT)	60	Derbi	23	39m 04.173s
23	Roberto Tamburini (ITA)	20	Aprilia	23	39m 06.634s
24	Dino Lombardi (ITA)	13	Honda	23	39m 21.544s
25	Ferruccio Lamborghini (ITA)	79	Aprilia	23	39m 40.578s
26	Glenn Scott (AUS)	68	Aprilia	22	39m 27.083s
	Stefan Bradl (GER)	17	Aprilia	19	DNF
	Pablo Nieto (SPA)	22	Aprilia	17	DNF
	Alexis Masbou (FRA)	7	Honda	15	DNF
	Danny Webb (GBR)	99	Honda	13	DNF
	Raffaele de Rosa (ITA)	35	Aprilia	5	DNF
	Blake Leigh-Smith (AUS)	70	Honda		DNQ
	Rhys Moller (AUS)	96	Honda		DNQ
	Jackson Leigh-Smith (AUS)	73	Honda		DNQ
	Robert Muresan (ROU)	95	Derbi		DNQ

Fastest lap: Talmacsi, 1m 38.061s, 101.466mph/163.294km/h.

Lap record: Alvaro Bautista, SPA (Aprilia), 1m 36.927s, 102.653mph/ 165.204km/h (2006).

Event best maximum speed: Pasini, 150.3mph/241.9km/h (race).

Qualifying: 1 Pasini, 1m 38.078s; 2 de Rosa, 1m 38.104s; 3 Pesek, 1m 38.106s; 4 Koyama, 1m 38.382s; 5 Corsi, 1m 38.528s; 6 Faubel, 1m 38.587s; 7 Gadea, 1m 38.974s; 8 Olive, 1m 38.977s; 9 Talmacsi, 1m 39.134s; 10 Cortese, 1m 39.189s; 11 Rabat, 1m 39.354s; 12 di Meglio, 1m 39.477s; 13 Smith, 1m 39.697s; 14 Zanetti, 1m 39.708s; 15 Ranseder, 1m 39.750s; 16 Nieto, 1m 39.775s; 17 Espargaro, 1m 39.797s; 18 Bonsey, 1m 39.945s; 19 Terol, 1m 39.983s; 20 Krummenacher, 1m 40.305s; 21 Masbou, 1m 40.377s; 22 Iannone, 1m 40.424s; 23 Litjens, 1m 40.544s; 24 Grotzkyj, 1m 40.659s; 25 Webb, 1m 41.197s; 26 Bradl, 1m 41.240s; 27 Lombardi, 1m 41.476s; 28 Aegerter, 1m 41.949s; 29 Tamburini, 1m 42.330s; 30 Lamborghini, 1m 42.612s; 31 Scott, 1m 43.415s; 32 B. Leigh-Smith, 1m 44.971s; 33 Moller, 1m 45.536s; 34 J. Leigh-Smith, 1m 48.459s; 35 Muresan, 2m 13.903s.

Fastest race laps: 1 Talmacsi, 1m 38.061s; 2 Faubel, 1m 38.157s; 3 Cortese, 1m 38.167s; 4 Koyama, 1m 38.223s; 5 Olive, 1m 38.237s; 6 Pesek, 1m 38.279s; 7 Pasini, 1m 38.284s; 8 Rabat, 1m 38.380s; 9 Gadea, 1m 38.387s; 10 Corsi, 1m 38.409s; 11 Ranseder, 1m 38.483s; 12 Terol, 1m 38.892s; 13 Espargaro, 1m 39.022s; 14 di Meglio, 1m 39.070s; 15 Krummenacher, 1m 39.271s; 16 de Rosa, 1m 39.532s; 17 Litjens, 1m 39.559s; 18 Webb, 1m 39.722s; 19 Bonsey, 1m 39.724s; 20 Smith, 1m 39.757s; 21 Zanetti, 1m 39.882s; 22 Nieto, 1m 39.897s; 23 Masbou, 1m 39.962s; 24 Iannone, 1m 40.175s; 25 Aegerter, 1m 40.221s; 26 Bradl, 1m 40.304s; 27 Grotzkyj, 1m 40.535s; 28 Tamburini, 1m 40.589s; 29 Lombardi, 1m 41.339s; 30 Lamborghini, 1m 42.085s; 31 Scott, 1m 44.428s.

World Championship: 1 Talmacsi, 237; 2 Faubel, 236; 3 Koyama, 166; 4 Pesek, 161; 5 Corsi, 155; 6 Pasini, 153; 7 Gadea, 133; 8 Olive, 118; 9 Espargaro, 104; 10 Smith, 86; 11 Ranseder, 70; 12 Krummenacher, 68; 13 Cortese, 66; 14 Rabat, 63; 15 de Rosa, 56; 16 Nieto, 44; 17 di Meglio, 40; 18 Bradl, 36; 19 Zanetti, 30; 20 Iannone, 26; 21 Masbou, 17; 22 Terol, 9; 23 Aegerter and Bianco, 7; 25 Bonsey, 4; 26 Webb, 3; 27 Froehlich and Jerez, 2; 29 Grotzkyj, 1.

FIM WORLD CHAMPIONSHIP • ROUND 17

MALAYSIAN GP

SEPANG

Knock-out: Lorenzo secured his second straight 250 title with third, and awarded himself a prize-fighter's belt to celebrate.
Photograph: Gold & Goose

Above: Doe-eyed grid girls.

Top: Almost always first away, Stoner heads de Puniet, Melandri and West – but second-row starter West had jumped the start again.

Above right: Sweet nothings – or strong blackmail? Dorna's Ezpeleta in discussion with Bridgestone senior executive Hiroshi Yasukawa.

Above far right: US double champion Ben Spies was waiting his chance to test the Suzuki. The weather made it a wasted trip.

Right: Pedrosa got to the rostrum again. His mood was improving slightly.

Photographs: Gold & Goose

STEAMY Sepang is a regular call for the grand prix troops, as a prime close-season testing circuit. They found something more reminiscent of the USA this time: a resurfacing gone wrong, covered with patches. The first flawed attempt had been done directly after the car GP in April, but at several key points – notably the hairpins at the ends of the connected straights – the surface hadn't taken and had to be done again, barely a week before the race. That much was known beforehand. What was unexpected was how, Laguna-like, instead of smoothing out the wide and interesting track, which takes much punishment from both F1 and from the heat, they had managed to introduce new bumps.

The first day brought forth a chorus of complaint from riders, the poor grip not helped by several rain showers. The new surface dried quickly, but they even complained about that: the extensive patching was in such a dark material that you could hardly see if it was wet or dry. It was bumpy, dirty and slippery, they all said. Predictably, the grip improved with use, although some old hands remembered a time when no GP could take place at a track that had not previously been raced on and rubbered-up a bit. And when testing on Monday was spoiled by heavy rain, the verdict of Chris Vermeulen was that it would have been unraceable if it had been wet on Sunday.

The grip was one thing, the bumps quite another. Dani Pedrosa, on pole for a third race in a row, described gloomily the relearning process involved: 'The track is changing all the time and is bumpier than before. We did a lot of testing here, and now we have to learn it again, because the bumps are in different places.'

Same for everybody, of course, but the factory Honda riders had another cross to bear. After Hayden's dropped valve of the previous weekend, the service life of the engines had been cut yet again, by a massive 50 per cent, according to the American. 'I'm happy, because I get to keep using the engine. They just cut the miles in half, they didn't cut back on rpm or change anything.' Asked if speculation that the current life between rebuilds was now down to just 300km – much less distance than a rider covers in a weekend – he loyally demurred, 'I'm not sure exactly, okay? I won't tell you how much I make, either.'

One effect was to throw a planned day or two of post-race testing into doubt, to avoid running short of motors for Valencia. Hayden is an inveterate tester, applying himself to the task with

more dedication than any other rider, but the problem was solved by Monday's rain. At least he did go out. Another foiled by the weather was new double US champion Ben Spies, who had overcome his dislike of air travel to visit the race and endure the frustration of watching other people riding so that he could get a first full test on the MotoGP Suzuki. He'd been promised 'as many laps and as many tyres as I can', a consolation for not getting the wild-card rides he'd been hoping for. In the end, he got no laps at all.

The expected climax to the tyre story arrived with many elements of farce, and confirmation that the crazy rumours of Australia were well founded.

The first expected step had been an IRTA meeting to determine the teams' vote on the matter, but when Dorna informed them that the one-tyre proposal had not been finalised in detail, the meeting was cancelled. 'There was nothing to vote on,' said President Hervé Poncharal. The MSMA meeting directly afterwards did go ahead, but tyres were off the agenda. Instead, they discussed the 250 class, agreeing to continue with two-strokes until 2010 (a slight reprieve), by when they would have decided on a replacement – 500cc four-stroke twins seemed to be the current flavour of choice, ousting the previous notion of production-based 600cc motors.

The real tyre business was going on in secret – until Bridgestone's Hiroshi Yamada revealed how the company had been skewered by Dorna. Ezpeleta had told him, he said, that if Bridgestone was not willing to supply Rossi with tyres, he would revive the one-tyre proposal, with Michelin as the supplier.

Rossi tried, without much success, to distance himself from the machinations. He dealt only with Yamaha chief Masao Furusawa, he said ('Although we are agreed.'), and Furusawa with Bridgestone. 'I don't know how the name of Carmelo (Ezpeleta) came into this,' he continued. Either way, the weekend ended with the assumption that he alone in the Yamaha squad would be on Bridgestones for 2008; a few days later, Dorna announced that the one-tyre proposal had been withdrawn.

Suzuki's factory tester, Nobu Aoki, was riding the 2008 prototype as a wild-card. Understandably, the veteran was lacking somewhat on pace, but the bike showed a nifty turn of speed. Weekend speed-trap figures put Aoki sixth at 301.5km/h, with Stoner fastest at 307.0. By comparison, the '07 Suzukis were languishing near the bottom, 14th and 15th fastest, at around 298km/h. Aoki was using the '07 engine, and credited hard work on aerodynamics in Suzuki's new wind-tunnel.

The 2008 season will be Suzuki's third with pneumatic valve springs. From another part of the paddock came a strong hint that Honda also intended to switch to pneumatics, putting the biggest manufacturer in the unusual position of following rivals with new technology, rather than leading the way. The hint came in a briefing by new HRC MD Kosuke Yasutake. The 2008 bike, he said, would have the same configuration and vee angle as the current RC212V, but would have a new engine and a new chassis, aimed at better cornering and acceleration. Would it retain steel valve springs, asked MOTOCOURSE? 'We will follow the modern trend of technology,' he replied.

A good crowd of almost 37,500, encouraged by entry prices as low as ten ringgit (just over £1.50), enjoyed crucial and exciting races in the smaller classes. Lorenzo didn't need to win, and third was enough for him to take his second 250 title in a row, and to trigger another of his post-Rossi theatrical displays. He donned the golden gloves and gown of a victorious boxer, and brandished a prize-fighter's belt over his head. 'This is the culmination of years of hard work, since I was three,' he said. It was Dunlop's 15th 250 title in succession.

Lorenzo, who has a reputation among the teams of being difficult to work with, names Max Biaggi as a role model, and Max's name resurfaced in the rumour mill, Fausto Gresini revealing that he was a strong candidate for his satellite Honda team in 2008. HRC's man poured cold water on the idea of giving Max another chance however, and this may have been

Above: **Chasing Casey – Melandri heads West, with Vermeulen, Elias, Capirossi and Rossi prominent in pursuit.**

Below: **Hopkins had some special stickers to liven up his changing-room door.**

Photographs: Gold & Goose

decisive, for the rumour didn't survive the weekend.

Talmacsi won the 125 race, taking nine points back from third-placed team-mate Faubel, but the disappointment in victory from team owner Jorge 'Aspar' Martinez and staff was extraordinary to see. Clearly, they would have preferred fellow Spaniard Faubel to have won the championship, for sponsorship as well as chauvinistic reasons.

MOTOGP RACE – 21 laps

Stoner and fellow Bridgestone users de Puniet and Hopkins got the best of free practice, but the champion complained that the track's many bumps had upset his traction-control system on his qualifying lap. He was still second, but Pedrosa took a third pole in succession. A fired-up Melandri was third; de Puniet, West (his best ever) and Hayden completed row two.

West's hopes didn't even survive the green light. He'd lined up on the wrong grid slot – for the four-strong 250 rather than the three-strong MotoGP second row. This put him ahead of his correct position, and meant that he had jumped the start again, without even turning a wheel. Another stop-and-go penalty spoiled his chances.

Stoner got his usual flier to lead Pedrosa, de Puniet, Melandri and West into the first tight corners. At the end of lap one, Pedrosa moved through inside at the hairpin, but Stoner simply passed him again on the way out. He never saw another back wheel, unless he was lapping someone, but he had to work to the end to stay ahead of a closer-than-usual pursuit. The reason was his own condition: stricken by the heat, he was feeling dizzy and might not have lasted much longer.

The pack behind West was led by Hopkins from Vermeulen, Elias, Capirossi, Rossi and Hayden, and was already more than a second adrift. Rossi was moving through rapidly as Hopkins ran off to lose six places on lap two. Next time around, he was ahead of new group leader Elias as well, and closing on West, who was fading slightly. His mood was clear as he barged past the Australian on lap five, at the end of which West went into the pits for his penalty. Rossi was three seconds adrift of de Puniet and would never get a great deal closer.

Ahead, Melandri had an odd problem that had slowed his progress. He'd tried to adjust the valve for his drinking tube on the warm-up lap, but instead pulled it off completely. 'Every time I braked, water was coming inside my visor. I tried to disconnect the tube, but for the first two laps, the water was still coming out.' Now the liberated tube was flapping in his wake as he regained speed and passing momentum, breathing down Pedrosa's neck for three laps before passing him at the first hairpin. He was less than three seconds behind Stoner, who was setting a string of fastest laps. But Melandri closed slightly to keep the pressure on, and was only just over a second adrift with three laps to go, forcing the Australian to push again.

Hayden had been following Rossi at a little distance, a little slower through the traffic, passing Vermeulen for seventh on lap five. Next time around, he was on Elias, always a hard man to pass because of his stunning late braking: 'probably the hardest guy to pass apart from Stoner'. For the next five laps, he tried everything without success, and then finally he outbraked him for the final hairpin. He was travelling much too fast when he got there, however, and ran straight on into the gravel, rejoining in tenth, behind the Suzukis and Edwards.

On the 18th lap, Hayden finally got by Edwards, but lost a second to the Suzukis in the process. He pegged them back and was nibbling at Hopkins at the flag. Vermeulen had escaped, as one of several riders whose fastest laps came at the end, completely confounding predictions that the tyres wouldn't last the distance and showing how the track had improved lap by lap. Rossi's best lap was the second to last; Stoner's new lap record came on the 15th lap.

Edwards faded, another struggling with the extreme heat, after fighting off illness earlier in the week.

Behind him, Capirossi had fallen back into a battle with Barros. He succumbed, but got ahead again on lap 17, to stay there by less than a second over the line. Aoki was ten seconds behind, finally getting ahead of Checa with five laps to go after a race-long duel. Then came West, coming through from last on lap six to pass Nakano for the last point two laps from the end.

Davies was seven seconds adrift, holding off Tamada to the end. Guintoli had been ahead, but faded rapidly at the end to 19th; Roberts was miles behind after running off early on. With nothing to lose, he had tried switching off the traction control and actually had lapped slightly faster without it. 'This is the first year I've ridden with it, and I've never liked it,' he said. There were no retirements or crashes.

250cc RACE – 20 laps

KTM dominated the front row for the 250 race, Aoyama three-hundredths faster than Kallio. Lorenzo was a tenth adrift, Dovizioso alongside and Bautista heading row two. The scene was set for a fine battle, with a big leading group fighting to the very end.

Dovizioso led away and had pulled almost 2.5 seconds after three laps, the pursuit piling up behind Kallio. Lorenzo got ahead on lap four, Hiro Aoyama and Bautista also passing Kallio later in the lap; Luthi followed suit on the next one, charging straight up to third. Bautista was even more impressive just behind him, but his progress was cut short at the end of lap seven when his engine died; he ran off the track at the final hairpin to retire.

Now Lorenzo and Luthi started to close on Dovizioso, leaving the rest by two seconds as they did so, Barbera now leading the group. But it was not all over yet.

At half-distance, Lorenzo was looming over Dovizioso, and he took him at the first tight right-left corners. The pair drew away from Luthi slightly, but on lap 14, Lorenzo was out of the saddle and almost off the track. He didn't lose the lead, but it gave everyone else the chance to catch up again by three-quarter-distance. Aoyama was now third, then Kallio, Luthi and Barbera, with Simon dropping back out of touch.

Dovizioso got ahead again for a couple more laps, his speed through the technical sections making up for any deficit on the two straights; on lap 18, Lorenzo got back ahead, and Kallio moved up to second, the next three right with them. The outcome was far from clear.

As they approached the hairpin at the end of the penultimate lap, Lorenzo had dropped cautiously to the back of the group, Aoyama leading for the first time from Dovizioso. Behind the Italian, Kallio took a tight line into the hairpin, only to find Dovizioso turning right across in front of him. He braked, lost it and, while fighting the slide, tagged the Italian's back wheel to ruinous effect. Dovizioso fell as his assailant ran into the gravel, remaining upright.

Thus, Aoyama could hold on by better than two seconds for his second win of the year. Barbera took advantage of the confusion for second, with Lorenzo close behind, Kallio almost alongside him. Luthi had dropped back by the end.

Simon had closed again on Luthi by the finish; Locatelli had caught and passed team-mate Simoncelli for seventh, Takahashi right behind. Dovizioso had remounted in tenth, but lost the place to Espargaro on the final lap.

De Angelis was lying seventh at half-distance when he slipped off, his fourth crash of the weekend; Vazquez was the only other faller.

Lorenzo's title came after nine wins and just one no-pointer: 'We will have to celebrate this like the end of the world.' Dovizioso's second was unassailable, while Bautista led a distant battle for third overall.

125cc RACE – 19 laps

Faubel took pole for the 125 race, his second of the year, a tenth clear of Talmacsi. Cortese and front-row first-timer Espargaro completed an all-Aprilia row.

Espargaro may have been a bit overcome. He charged off the line to lead into the first corner, but ran wide directly. Pasini took over, but by the end of the lap, Talmacsi and Faubel were ahead of him, gaining a little gap over the next two laps – until Faubel ran wide at the last hairpin. He lost almost a second, and Talmacsi made the most of it. He started to pull away at more than half a second a lap; after ten, he was more than six seconds clear and still stretching. He was able to slacken off by the end and still win by almost seven seconds.

The group disputing second got bigger and bigger as the laps counted down. On the 14th, there were eight in the group – Olive, Pasini, Faubel, Corsi, Koyama, Gadea, Cortese and Espargaro. Pesek was closing and would soon tag on.

Espargaro was the first to go, crashing with four laps remaining, while Cortese broke down and retired on the last lap. All the rest made it, rather surprisingly.

By the finish, Koyama had escaped from the mêlée, but Faubel was in the thick of it. It took all his efforts to get ahead of Olive at the finish. Gadea was right behind; Pesek, Corsi and Pasini were a second away, but still all over each other.

Smith headed the next group for ninth, from Masbou, Terol and Nieto. Ranseder and de Rosa joined the crash list.

Above: Supplications notwithstanding, Faubel lost nine valuable points to 125 race winner Talmacsi.

Top: Hiro Aoyama's clear win was the KTM rider's second.

Photographs: Gold & Goose

POLINI MALAYSIAN MOTORCYCLE GRAND PRIX

21 OCTOBER 2007 • FIM WORLD CHAMPIONSHIP ROUND 17

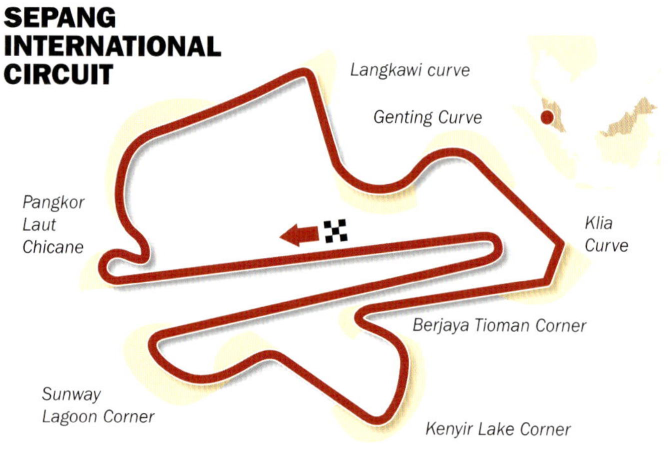

Circuit 5.548km /3.447 miles

MotoGP

RACE: 21 laps, 72.387 miles/116.508km • Weather: Dry • Air 32°C • Humidity 51% • Track 38°C

Pos.	Rider	Nat.	No.	Entrant	Machine	Tyres	Laps	Time & speed (mph/km/h)
1	Casey Stoner	AUS	27	Ducati Marlboro Team	Ducati	B	21	43m 04.405s 100.844mph/ 162.292km/h
2	Marco Melandri	ITA	33	Honda Gresini	Honda	B	21	43m 06.106s
3	Dani Pedrosa	SPA	26	Repsol Honda Team	Honda	M	21	43m 06.731s
4	Randy de Puniet	FRA	14	Kawasaki Racing Team	Kawasaki	B	21	43m 08.170s
5	Valentino Rossi	ITA	46	Fiat Yamaha Team	Yamaha	M	21	43m 09.178s
6	Toni Elias	SPA	24	Honda Gresini	Honda	B	21	43m 22.072s
7	Chris Vermeulen	AUS	71	Rizla Suzuki MotoGP	Suzuki	B	21	43m 25.355s
8	John Hopkins	USA	21	Rizla Suzuki MotoGP	Suzuki	B	21	43m 26.603s
9	Nicky Hayden	USA	1	Repsol Honda Team	Honda	M	21	43m 26.855s
10	Colin Edwards	USA	5	Fiat Yamaha Team	Yamaha	M	21	43m 34.151s
11	Loris Capirossi	ITA	65	Ducati Marlboro Team	Ducati	B	21	43m 39.328s
12	Alex Barros	BRA	4	Pramac d'Antin	Ducati	B	21	43m 40.072s
13	Nobuatsu Aoki	JPN	9	Rizla Suzuki MotoGP	Suzuki	B	21	43m 48.518s
14	Carlos Checa	SPA	7	Honda LCR	Honda	M	21	43m 48.891s
15	Anthony West	AUS	13	Kawasaki Racing Team	Kawasaki	B	21	43m 54.063s
16	Shinya Nakano	JPN	56	Konica Minolta Honda	Honda	M	21	43m 56.131s
17	Chaz Davies	GBR	57	Pramac d'Antin	Ducati	B	21	44m 03.310s
18	Makoto Tamada	JPN	6	Dunlop Yamaha Tech 3	Yamaha	D	21	44m 04.001s
19	Sylvain Guintoli	FRA	50	Dunlop Yamaha Tech 3	Yamaha	D	21	44m 27.524s
20	Kurtis Roberts	USA	80	Team Roberts	KR212V	M	21	44m 55.365s

Fastest lap: Casey Stoner, on lap 15, 2m 02.108s, 101.635mph/163.566km/h (record).

Previous lap record: Loris Capirossi, ITA (Ducati), 2m 02.127s, 101.620mph/163.541km/h (2006).

Event best maximum speed: Casey Stoner, 190.8mph/307.0km/h (free practice no. 3).

Grid order	1	2	3	4	5	6	7	8	9	10	11	12	13	14	15	16	17	18	19	20	21	•
26 PEDROSA	27	27	27	27	27	27	27	27	27	27	27	27	27	27	27	27	27	27	27	27	27	1
27 STONER	26	26	26	26	26	26	26	26	33	33	33	33	33	33	33	33	33	33	33	33	33	2
33 MELANDRI	14	14	14	14	33	33	33	33	26	26	26	26	26	26	26	26	26	26	26	26	26	3
14 de PUNIET	33	33	33	33	14	14	14	14	14	14	14	14	14	14	14	14	14	14	14	14	14	4
13 WEST	13	13	13	13	46	46	46	46	46	46	46	46	46	46	46	46	46	46	46	46	46	5
1 HAYDEN	21	24	46	46	24	24	24	24	24	24	24	24	24	24	24	24	24	24	24	24	24	6
71 VERMEULEN	71	46	24	24	1	1	1	1	1	1	1	71	21	71	71	71	71	71	71	71	71	7
24 ELIAS	24	71	71	1	71	71	71	71	71	71	71	21	71	21	21	21	21	21	21	21	21	8
46 ROSSI	65	1	1	71	21	21	21	21	21	21	21	5	5	5	5	5	5	1	1	1	1	9
21 HOPKINS	46	65	21	21	65	5	5	5	5	5	5	1	1	1	1	1	1	5	5	5	5	10
65 CAPIROSSI	1	21	65	65	5	65	65	4	4	4	4	4	4	4	4	4	65	65	65	65	65	11
4 BARROS	4	5	5	5	4	4	4	65	65	65	65	65	65	65	65	65	4	4	4	4	4	12
5 EDWARDS	5	4	4	4	13	9	7	7	7	7	7	7	7	7	7	9	9	9	9	9	9	13
56 NAKANO	7	7	7	9	9	7	56	56	9	9	9	9	9	9	9	7	7	7	7	7	7	14
50 GUINTOLI	9	9	9	7	7	56	9	9	56	56	56	56	56	56	56	56	56	56	56	13	13	15
7 CHECA	56	56	56	56	56	57	57	57	57	57	57	57	57	57	57	13	13	13	13	56	56	
57 DAVIES	57	57	57	57	57	6	6	50	50	50	50	50	50	6	13	57	57	57	57	57	57	
6 TAMADA	6	6	6	6	6	50	50	6	6	6	6	6	6	50	6	6	6	6	6	6	6	
9 AOKI	80	50	50	50	50	80	13	13	13	13	13	13	13	13	50	50	50	50	50	50	50	
80 ROBERTS	50	80	80	80	80	13	80	80	80	80	80	80	80	80	80	80	80	80	80	80	80	

FASTEST RACE LAPS

	Rider	Lap	Time
1	Stoner	15	2m 02.108s
2	Rossi	20	2m 02.303s
3	Melandri	14	2m 02.330s
4	Hayden	17	2m 02.349s
5	Pedrosa	17	2m 02.487s
6	de Puniet	16	2m 02.503s
7	Elias	9	2m 02.738s
8	Edwards	9	2m 03.013s
9	Vermeulen	21	2m 03.023s
10	West	14	2m 03.046s
11	Hopkins	17	2m 03.112s
12	Capirossi	19	2m 03.398s
13	Barros	20	2m 03.421s
14	Aoki	12	2m 03.975s
15	Checa	13	2m 04.154s
16	Nakano	19	2m 04.580s
17	Tamada	7	2m 04.728s
18	Guintoli	7	2m 04.828s
19	Davies	15	2m 04.866s
20	Roberts	14	2m 05.251s

QUALIFYING

20 October 2007

Weather: Dry

Air: 33°C Humidity: 50%

Track: 38°C

Pos.	Rider	Time
1	Pedrosa	2m 01.877s
2	Stoner	2m 01.918s
3	Melandri	2m 01.944s
4	de Puniet	2m 02.107s
5	West	2m 02.202s
6	Hayden	2m 02.225s
7	Vermeulen	2m 02.301s
8	Elias	2m 02.432s
9	Rossi	2m 02.466s
10	Hopkins	2m 02.697s
11	Capirossi	2m 02.708s
12	Barros	2m 03.022s
13	Edwards	2m 03.040s
14	Nakano	2m 03.233s
15	Guintoli	2m 03.408s
16	Checa	2m 03.525s
17	Davies	2m 04.197s
18	Tamada	2m 04.314s
19	Aoki	2m 04.604s
20	Roberts	2m 05.404s

statistics

250cc

20 laps, 68.940 miles/110.960km

Pos.	Rider (Nat.)	No.	Machine	Laps	Time & speed
1	Hiroshi Aoyama (JPN)	4	KTM	20	43m 09.316s 95.859mph/ 154.270km/h
2	Hector Barbera (SPA)	80	Aprilia	20	43m 11.567s
3	Jorge Lorenzo (SPA)	1	Aprilia	20	43m 12.273s
4	Mika Kallio (FIN)	36	KTM	20	43m 12.281s
5	Thomas Luthi (SWI)	12	Aprilia	20	43m 16.621s
6	Julian Simon (SPA)	60	Honda	20	43m 18.063s
7	Roberto Locatelli (ITA)	15	Gilera	20	43m 25.421s
8	Marco Simoncelli (ITA)	58	Gilera	20	43m 35.417s
9	Yuki Takahashi (JPN)	55	Honda	20	43m 37.348s
10	Aleix Espargaro (SPA)	41	Aprilia	20	43m 44.070s
11	Andrea Dovizioso (ITA)	34	Honda	20	43m 45.204s
12	Karel Abraham (CZE)	17	Aprilia	20	43m 51.830s
13	Shuhei Aoyama (JPN)	73	Honda	20	43m 57.336s
14	Alex Baldolini (ITA)	25	Aprilia	20	43m 57.374s
15	Dirk Heidolf (GER)	28	Aprilia	20	43m 58.506s
16	Ratthapark Wilairot (THA)	8	Honda	20	43m 58.589s
17	Eugene Laverty (IRL)	50	Honda	20	44m 02.784s
18	Taro Sekiguchi (JPN)	11	Aprilia	20	44m 11.981s
19	Jules Cluzel (FRA)	16	Aprilia	20	44m 24.941s
20	Fabrizio Lai (ITA)	32	Aprilia	20	44m 26.340s
21	Imre Toth (HUN)	10	Aprilia	20	44m 41.962s
	Doni Tata Pradita (INA)	35	Yamaha	16	DNF
	Alex de Angelis (RSM)	3	Aprilia	10	DNF
	Efren Vazquez (SPA)	7	Aprilia	9	DNF
	Alvaro Bautista (SPA)	19	Aprilia	6	DNF

Fastest lap: H. Aoyama, 2m 08.266s, 96.755mph/155.713km/h.

Lap record: Dani Pedrosa, SPA (Honda), 2m 08.015s, 96.946mph/ 156.019km/h (2004).

Event best maximum speed: Luthi, 162.7mph/261.9km/h (warm-up).

Qualifying: 1 H. Aoyama, 2m 07.429s; 2 Kallio, 2m 07.461s; 3 Lorenzo, 2m 07.621s; 4 Dovizioso, 2m 07.675s; 5 Bautista, 2m 07.785s; 6 Luthi, 2m 07.939s; 7 Barbera, 2m 08.148s; 8 Simon, 2m 08.496s; 9 de Angelis, 2m 08.745s; 10 Locatelli, 2m 08.953s; 11 Simoncelli, 2m 09.557s; 12 Takahashi, 2m 09.570s; 13 Abraham, 2m 10.501s; 14 Espargaro, 2m 10.549s; 15 Wilairot, 2m 10.587s; 16 S. Aoyama, 2m 10.664s; 17 Baldolini, 2m 10.685s; 18 Cluzel, 2m 10.698s; 19 Heidolf, 2m 10.854s; 20 Laverty, 2m 10.926s; 21 Lai, 2m 11.110s; 22 Vazquez, 2m 11.176s; 23 Sandi, 2m 11.333s; 24 Toth, 2m 11.596s; 25 Sekiguchi, 2m 12.051s; 26 Pradita, 2m 14.439s.

Fastest race laps: 1 H. Aoyama, 2m 08.266s; 2 Luthi, 2m 08.272s; 3 Lorenzo, 2m 08.456s; 4 Simon, 2m 08.479s; 5 de Angelis, 2m 08.613s; 6 Barbera, 2m 08.617s; 7 Dovizioso, 2m 08.644s; 8 Kallio, 2m 08.660s; 9 Bautista, 2m 08.676s; 10 Locatelli, 2m 08.703s; 11 Simoncelli, 2m 09.023s; 12 Takahashi, 2m 09.272s; 13 S. Aoyama, 2m 09.876s; 14 Wilairot, 2m 09.978s; 15 Espargaro, 2m 10.099s; 16 Abraham, 2m 10.408s; 17 Heidolf, 2m 10.583s; 18 Baldolini, 2m 10.805s; 19 Laverty, 2m 11.062s; 20 Sekiguchi, 2m 11.133s; 21 Cluzel, 2m 11.246s; 22 Lai, 2m 11.367s; 23 Toth, 2m 12.292s; 24 Sandi, 2m 12.317s; 25 Vazquez, 2m 13.357s; 26 Pradita, 2m 14.578s.

World Championship: 1 Lorenzo, 303; 2 Dovizioso, 247; 3 de Angelis, 215; 4 Bautista, 181; 5 Barbera, 166; 6 H. Aoyama, 154; 7 Kallio, 132; 8 Luthi, 126; 9 Simon, 113; 10 Simoncelli, 92; 11 S. Aoyama, 90; 12 Takahashi, 82; 13 Locatelli, 56; 14 Lai, 49; 15 Espargaro, 43; 16 Abraham, 31; 17 Wilairot, 29; 18 West, 25; 19 Heidolf, 24; 20 Cluzel, 19; 21 Baldolini, 16; 22 Sekiguchi, 13; 23 Debon, 11; 24 Linfoot, 7; 25 Laverty, 6; 26 Oikawa, 4; 27 Ui, 2; 28 Toth, 2; 29 Tizon and Vazquez, 1.

125cc

19 laps, 65.493 miles/105.412km

Pos.	Rider (Nat.)	No.	Machine	Laps	Time & speed
1	Gabor Talmacsi (HUN)	14	Aprilia	19	42m 50.831s 91.721mph/ 147.611km/h
2	Tomoyoshi Koyama (JPN)	71	KTM	19	42m 57.584s
3	Hector Faubel (SPA)	55	Aprilia	19	42m 58.624s
4	Joan Olive (SPA)	6	Aprilia	19	42m 59.011s
5	Sergio Gadea (SPA)	33	Aprilia	19	42m 59.778s
6	Lukas Pesek (CZE)	52	Derbi	19	43m 00.766s
7	Simone Corsi (ITA)	24	Aprilia	19	43m 00.963s
8	Mattia Pasini (ITA)	75	Aprilia	19	43m 01.166s
9	Bradley Smith (GBR)	38	Honda	19	43m 14.257s
10	Alexis Masbou (FRA)	7	Honda	19	43m 15.639s
11	Nicolas Terol (SPA)	18	Derbi	19	43m 15.740s
12	Pablo Nieto (SPA)	22	Aprilia	19	43m 17.025s
13	Stefan Bradl (GER)	17	Aprilia	19	43m 20.321s
14	Mike di Meglio (FRA)	63	Honda	19	43m 20.606s
15	Esteve Rabat (SPA)	12	Honda	19	43m 21.842s
16	Stefano Bianco (ITA)	27	Aprilia	19	43m 26.286s
17	Randy Krummenacher (SWI)	34	KTM	19	43m 26.660s
18	Andrea Iannone (ITA)	29	Aprilia	19	43m 45.497s
19	Lorenzo Zanetti (ITA)	8	Aprilia	19	43m 47.787s
20	Simone Grotzkyj (ITA)	53	Aprilia	19	43m 48.187s
21	Roberto Tamburini (ITA)	20	Aprilia	19	43m 56.257s
22	Danny Webb (GBR)	99	Honda	19	43m 59.372s
23	Robert Muresan (ROU)	95	Derbi	19	43m 59.380s
24	Joey Litjens (NED)	37	Honda	19	44m 10.308s
25	Cyril Carrillo (FRA)	36	Honda	19	44m 13.213s
26	Steve Bonsey (USA)	51	KTM	19	44m 21.205s
27	Ferruccio Lamborghini (ITA)	79	Aprilia	19	44m 24.567s
28	Raffaele de Rosa (ITA)	35	Aprilia	19	44m 31.844s
	Dino Lombardi (ITA)	13	Honda	19	45m 07.312s*
	Sandro Cortese (GER)	11	Aprilia	18	DNF
	Pol Espargaro (SPA)	44	Aprilia	15	DNF
	Dominique Aegerter (SWI)	77	Aprilia	5	DNF
	Michael Ranseder (AUT)	60	Derbi	0	DNF

* Finished through the pits.

Fastest lap: Talmacsi, 2m 13.987s, 92.625mph/149.065km/h.

Lap record: Alvaro Bautista, SPA (Aprilia), 2m 13.118s, 93.229mph/ 150.038km/h (2006).

Event best maximum speed: Bradl, 137.3mph/221.0km/h (free practice no. 2).

Qualifying: 1 Faubel, 2m 13.327s; 2 Talmacsi, 2m 13.443s; 3 Cortese, 2m 14.141s; 4 Espargaro, 2m 14.166s; 5 Corsi, 2m 14.347s; 6 Koyama, 2m 14.440s; 7 Pesek, 2m 14.630s; 8 Olive, 2m 14.723s; 9 Nieto, 2m 14.738s; 10 Pasini, 2m 14.798s; 11 Gadea, 2m 14.967s; 12 Masbou, 2m 15.061s; 13 Terol, 2m 15.385s; 14 de Rosa, 2m 15.476s; 15 Smith, 2m 15.635s; 16 Ranseder, 2m 15.676s; 17 Rabat, 2m 15.835s; 18 di Meglio, 2m 15.895s; 19 Bradl, 2m 16.150s; 20 Tamburini, 2m 16.483s; 21 Iannone, 2m 16.546s; 22 Aegerter, 2m 16.778s; 23 Krummenacher, 2m 16.822s; 24 Bianco, 2m 16.835s; 25 Webb, 2m 16.866s; 26 Zanetti, 2m 17.267s; 27 Litjens, 2m 17.616s; 28 Bonsey, 2m 17.772s; 29 Carrillo, 2m 18.030s; 30 Grotzkyj, 2m 18.420s; 31 Muresan, 2m 19.004s; 32 Lombardi, 2m 19.189s; 33 Lamborghini, 2m 19.972s.

Fastest race laps: 1 Talmacsi, 2m 13.987s; 2 Olive, 2m 13.993s; 3 Pesek, 2m 14.188s; 4 Cortese, 2m 14.227s; 5 Koyama, 2m 14.305s; 6 Faubel, 2m 14.334s; 7 Corsi, 2m 14.336s; 8 Pasini, 2m 14.359s; 9 Gadea, 2m 14.664s; 10 Nieto, 2m 14.857s; 11 Espargaro, 2m 14.923s; 12 de Rosa, 2m 14.988s; 13 Terol, 2m 15.053s; 14 Masbou, 2m 15.144s; 15 Smith, 2m 15.165s; 16 Bianco, 2m 15.228s; 17 Bradl, 2m 15.310s; 18 Rabat, 2m 15.423s; 19 di Meglio, 2m 15.800s; 20 Krummenacher, 2m 15.971s; 21 Aegerter, 2m 16.096s; 22 Iannone, 2m 16.207s; 23 Zanetti, 2m 16.229s; 24 Grotzkyj, 2m 16.644s; 25 Tamburini, 2m 17.360s; 26 Webb, 2m 17.689s; 27 Muresan, 2m 17.716s; 28 Litjens, 2m 17.728s; 29 Carrillo, 2m 17.847s; 30 Lombardi, 2m 18.318s; 31 Bonsey, 2m 18.337s; 32 Lamborghini, 2m 18.605s.

World Championship: 1 Talmacsi, 262; 2 Faubel, 252; 3 Koyama, 186; 4 Pesek, 171; 5 Corsi, 164; 6 Pasini, 161; 7 Gadea, 144; 8 Olive, 131; 9 Espargaro, 104; 10 Smith, 93; 11 Ranseder, 70; 12 Krummenacher, 68; 13 Cortese, 66; 14 Rabat, 64; 15 de Rosa, 56; 16 Nieto, 48; 17 di Meglio, 42; 18 Bradl, 39; 19 Zanetti, 30; 20 Iannone, 26; 21 Masbou, 23; 22 Terol, 14; 23 Aegerter and Bianco, 7; 25 Bonsey, 4; 26 Webb, 3; 27 Froehlich and Jerez, 2; 29 Grotzkyj, 1.

RIDER STANDINGS

After 17 Rounds

1	Casey Stoner	347
2	Valentino Rossi	241
3	Dani Pedrosa	217
4	Marco Melandri	174
5	John Hopkins	173
6	Chris Vermeulen	169
7	Loris Capirossi	155
8	Colin Edwards	121
9	Nicky Hayden	119
10	Alex Barros	106
11	Randy de Puniet	101
12	Toni Elias	98
13	Alex Hofmann	65
14	Carlos Checa	61
15	Anthony West	59
16	Sylvain Guintoli	45
17	Shinya Nakano	45
18	Makoto Tamada	37
19	Kurtis Roberts	10
20=	Michel Fabrizio	6
20=	Roger Lee Hayden	6
22	Fonsi Nieto	5
23	Olivier Jacque	4
24	Kenny Roberts Jnr	4
25	Nobuatsu Aoki	3
26	Shinichi Ito	1

TEAM STANDINGS

After 17 Rounds

1	Ducati Marlboro Team	502
2	Fiat Yamaha Team	362
3	Rizla Suzuki MotoGP	342
4	Repsol Honda Team	336
5	Honda Gresini	278
6	Pramac d'Antin	172
7	Kawasaki Racing Team	169
8	Dunlop Yamaha Tech 3	82
9	Honda LCR	61
10	Konica Minolta Honda	45
11	Team Roberts	14

CONSTRUCTOR STANDINGS

After 17 Rounds

1	Ducati	374
2	Honda	288
3	Yamaha	278
4	Suzuki	225
5	Kawasaki	137
6	KR212V	14

FIM WORLD CHAMPIONSHIP • ROUND 18

VALENCIAGP

VALENCIA

Belatedly, Honda matched Ducati on speed, and Michelin matched Bridgestone on tyres. Pedrosa did the rest – reducing Stoner to a background blur.
Photograph: Gold & Goose

THE last undecided championship came to a fine climax at the final round. The (almost) all-Spanish team of former multi-champion Jorge Martinez was riven with split loyalties, while two of its three riders faced a tactical battle that was tense for every inch of the way. In the end, Spanish team owner, sponsors and national loyalists were all winners and losers when the wrong one of the three riders prevailed. Ex-boxer and frequent fall-guy Gabor Talmacsi resisted every attempt by Hector Faubel, and thus became a popular first-ever Hungarian world champion in motorcycle racing history.

However, the significance was overshadowed by other events. With the major titles sewn up, attention was largely focused on 2008. Tests would start on the Tuesday after the race – new riders on new bikes and new tyres. It was not until after the race, though, that Rossi was able to admit, 'Yes, I think we will be on Bridgestone next year.'

There was significance also in the longer term, and a feeling that the tide may be turning in several respects. It was not just a victory for Michelin, only the sixth of the year, but also the manner in which Pedrosa achieved it – blowing past Stoner's Ducati on sheer speed before they had reached the end of the front straight to brake for the first corner. What a change from the start of the season.

And in another sphere, there was Rossi's story, at the track where he had lost the title in 2006 with a headstrong race crash. He fell again, this time during qualifying, and quite heavily on the way out of the first corner, after a manful battle to save the viciously flicking bike. This not only left him at the back of the grid, but also with three fractures in his throttle hand.

Being Rossi, he raced anyway, with a shorter brake lever that allowed him to use his first two fingers only, the other two being taped together and painful. As the last ten laps came along, he was 14th and already in the points, and still with three Yamahas in front of him that could be called in if necessary. And circulating comfortably: his best lap (his tenth) put him tenth overall and less than a second off Pedrosa's new record. Then, in a final kick in the teeth, his M1 Yamaha, already one of the slower bikes on the track, did what it had done to him at his home GP at Misano. It quit. It locked up going into Turn One, which put him off the track, and although it started again, allowing him to return to the pits, it was only to retire.

With Pedrosa winning, this cost Rossi second place in the championship, by one point. It made 2007 his worst overall result and his worst year in racing since he had arrived as a 125 rookie in 1996, to finish ninth. No wonder he ended the evening by announcing, 'I have a great big battle with this bike that is not over yet.' He didn't need to repeat his earlier veiled threat to quit or, worse still, switch machines, 'if Yamaha don't demonstrate to me next year that it's possible to be competitive, to help me decide my future.'

The 100th race of the MotoGP era was marked with the presentation of a new world champion's trophy – a sort of Meccano vase to which the name of each new champion can be bolted, year by year. It also marked a century of four-stroke starts for three riders who have not missed a race since 2002: Rossi, Checa and Nakano. It was a landmark weekend for oldest inhabitant Alex Barros, whose 276th start would be his last. The 37-year-old Brazilian confirmed his retirement, but even now was hedging his bets, just in case a good offer came out of the blue from World Superbikes or AMA. Carlos Checa was also saying an emotional goodbye, in a weekend marred by a stomach problem so severe that it entailed several trips to hospital. Carlos rejected a testing offer from Ducati, saying, 'I am still a racer' – he had taken the coveted ex-Toseland SBK seat at Ten Kate Honda. Several other riders – Capirossi, Hopkins, de Puniet, Melandri and Elias among them – were also about to say goodbye to their teams.

And one whole team was still wavering on the brink of saying goodbye: Team Roberts was hanging on to its oft-deferred hopes of securing a big-money deal for 2008, allowing it to lease bikes for two riders. If this did not come off, it would be their last race. Kenny Roberts was not there for the occasion, having hurt his foot in a quad-bike accident (while saving his dog) at his Montana home in the USA.

The race also marked a gloomy milestone for what was once a cornerstone nation in motorbike racing. When Hofmann substitute Chaz Davies withdrew after a second crash in two days, he ended the last chance of a British rider scoring even a single point for the season. Thus, 2007 was the first year since Englishman Les Graham won the opening World Championship in 1949 that there was not a single Briton on the points table.

Rossi's belated tyre 'revelation' came after the whole furore

had been brought to an end, the GP Commission announcing revised tyre rules: extra tyres (total up by nine), and extra testing for tyre manufacturers and at new or fully resurfaced circuits.

Stoner took one final prize. Rossi's crash before putting on qualifying tyres had allowed the Australian to draw decisively clear in the season-long contest for best qualifier – Rossi had taken the lead in Australia. By the end, the total qualifying time for all races, plus the IRTA tests, won Stoner the BMW M-Award – a 70,000-euro, 425-horsepower, BMW M-Series coupe, which he passed straight on to his 18-year-old wife of less than a year, Adriana.

The last GP brought forth a bike-racing first: airbags for riders. The Dainese 'D-Air Race System' is worn rather like a life-jacket, being triggered by gyroscopes and accelerometers to deploy – hopefully – before the wearer hits the ground. A couple of riders were testing them in the smaller classes and managed to set them off, the loss of dignity more than compensated for by intact collarbones.

MOTOGP RACE – 30 laps

After four races, the pattern of qualifying was becoming familiar: Stoner dominating free practice (interrupted by Guintoli's Yamaha on Dunlop qualifiers); Pedrosa coming in with a late-session pole. Hayden sacrificed a race tyre for an extra (third) qualifier, to help him get closer to the far-distant limits of the tyres, rather hard to learn in just two laps. The tactic took him from 12th in free practice to the front row.

De Puniet led row two from the pair of best-yet Dunlop runners – too little too late to save the tyre supplier.

Stoner's pace off the line was such that he was nine-tenths

Above: **Reflections of pain as Rossi takes his injured right hand into the Clinica Mobile, Dr Costa in close attendance.**

Left: **This could be the last time… Kurtis Roberts on the back-marker KR212V.**

Below left: **Last time also for GP stalwarts Carlos Checa (on bike) and Alex Barros. Lucio Cecchinello (left) looks on as they share a last moment on the grid.**

Far left: **Hayden got away well, but lost the pace. He will succumb to Hopkins, Melandri and Capirossi, looming behind.**

Photographs: Gold & Goose

Above: **After five years, Hopkins left Suzuki with a fourth rostrum to celebrate with his loyal crew.**

Below: **Capirossi – bound for Suzuki in two days time – had no more than an average last race for Ducati.**

Photographs: Gold & Goose

clear by the second timing point, but Pedrosa had closed up by the end of the lap and stayed there for the next four, the last of which brought him a new record. It was then that the most surprising move of the race took his Honda out of Stoner's slipstream before the end of the main straight and sent it sailing past, well into the braking zone. This was a new twist.

Hayden was already dropping away as now it was Stoner's turn to stay close. Another surprise – obviously, he wasn't finding it easy. It was a clear display of 800cc racing: each rider so close to the edge that the occasional front-wheel slide was inevitable; both riding so well that they recovered immediately. But Pedrosa had something more. On lap nine, the gap grew to a second, swung around 1.5 seconds for the next ten laps, and then started to stretch again.

Stoner pushed again, to close to within 1.7 seconds on lap 24, but that was that. 'It was very close, then with a handful of laps to go, the left of my rear tyre seemed to give way on me. I had a couple of rear-end loses, so I just decided to give up at that point,' he said. Pedrosa had ample time to slow for a wheelie over the line.

Hopkins, full of good intentions after five years with Suzuki, leapt off the third row and tucked in behind Hayden, but it took him until lap four before a decisive move at turn two put him ahead. By then, the leaders were well over two seconds away, and would keep on stretching. But Hopkins was not to be troubled from behind, and his fourth rostrum appearance of the season was well won.

On lap seven, Melandri finally passed the troubled Hayden, the only Michelin runner to choose the 16-inch rear. Hayden kept on him, and at two-thirds-distance was ahead again, beginning a to-and-fro battle that would occupy the next four laps. As they slowed one another, Capirossi was coming from behind, after besting Barros and then de Puniet. With eight laps to go, Melandri finally got away.

Hayden kept Capirossi behind him for as long as possible, but on lap 26, deteriorating grip caused him to succumb. By now, Vermeulen had picked his way steadily through from 12th on lap one, and he too got ahead of the slowing Honda to start nibbling at Capirossi's heels, the pair of them closing up again on Melandri, all crossing the line in little more than a second.

Hayden was still losing speed, and the next trio were catching him fast. Barros, at the head of it, passed him with two laps to go, but the outgoing World Champion managed to fend off de Puniet and Elias. Guintoli had been between Barros and Elias until lap 19 in a strong ride, and was just eight seconds adrift at the end.

Checa and Edwards disputed 12th for most of the race, the Spaniard finally taking a decisive advantage; Nakano was three seconds behind Edwards after a typically downbeat race, then came Tamada and West, who had been struggling all weekend. He claimed some benefit – in the steady laps of the race, he had achieved a new understanding of his problems: 'All weekend, I thought it was rear grip, but actually I've been lacking confidence in pushing the front.'

Roberts retired after ten laps with worsening engine problems that saw him going slower and slower.

The other retirement was Rossi. He had been, he said later, 'in quite good shape – not at the maximum, but I was able to ride.' He'd passed West and then Nakano, and was sitting pretty in 14th when it all went wrong. He cruised into the pits and slumped into his chair. There was nothing more he could do after his worst-ever season. With no obvious fault, puzzled Yamaha engineers sent the motor to Japan for investigation.

250cc RACE – 27 laps

Champion Lorenzo seemed set for pole until the last moments, and from that point had trouble maintaining his enthusiasm for his last 250 race. His mind was set on his forthcoming MotoGP career, due to begin in earnest in tests two days hence.

Kallio was his qualifying nemesis, for a second pole of the year on a mixed front row of four different makes; Takahashi's Honda and Simoncelli's Gilera rounded it out. Dovizioso was in the middle of row two.

Lorenzo took off at the head of a pack of eight, all over one another for the first nine laps. Barbera was second, then Dovizioso took over, Kallio also getting ahead of the Spaniard. Bautista was in the group, with fast wild-card Debon and Simon. De Angelis was there too, making steady progress from seventh on lap one to second by lap eight.

On the tenth, he took the lead. Once displaced, Lorenzo started to drop back immediately, blaming a bad tyre choice.

Dovizioso took up the chase as de Angelis moved steadily clear, the gap more than a second on lap 11, and more than two on lap 16. By now, Bautista had been in second for two laps, and over the next four, he whittled away at the gap, Kallio tight up behind him, Dovizioso also dropping away as the pursuit became spaced out.

Bautista seemed certain to catch his team-mate, but his faster pace was achieved only with greater risk, and on the 21st lap, he finally succumbed to physics, sliding off on the fast left leading to the final corner.

Kallio's orange KTM was now equally close, his comfort increasing with a lighter fuel load – he'd set a new record on lap 20, and said later, 'I dropped back at the beginning, but I knew it would get better. It's more important to be fast at the end of the race.' He closed up at once and pounced with two laps left, holding the Aprilia behind him to the line. The taciturn Finn's second win of the year equalled two for the other brightest of the ex-125 class rookies, Bautista.

A little way back, Dovizioso had come under attack from Debon, who took third with four laps left. The Italian stayed with him, planning an attack on the last corner of the last lap. Debon was ready for it, however, and pushed the Honda wide on the exit, then used his speed to take his first rostrum in a nine-year career by a tenth.

The next group had Barbera heading Simon and Lorenzo, Takahashi and Luthi closing up to within a couple of seconds over the last laps. Aoyama was never close enough, a lonely tenth. Next came Simoncelli after an adventurous race. He had been with the leaders until running off on lap nine, when he dropped to 14th, but he had made progress from then on. He'd passed and outdistanced Espargaro and earlier Locatelli, who were a couple of seconds apart.

Laverty qualified 26th and had a steady ride to 20th, the last rider on the same lap as the leaders; Lai, Cluzel and Abraham joined the crash list.

125cc RACE – 24 laps

The mathematics of the 125 championship battle were simple: Talmacsi led by ten points. If Faubel was to win, he had to finish at least third. Lower than that, and the Spaniard would take the crown. The battle commenced in qualifying. Faubel held the upper hand right until the end, but Talmacsi's pole was by an intimidating 0.373 second. Team-mate Gadea was next, with strict orders not to interfere, and above all not to finish between the pair.

Talmacsi took off from the start, 1.2 seconds clear after four laps. But Faubel was in second, having finished lap one fifth and taken three laps to close up.

They were more than four seconds clear of a pack led by Pesek from Nieto and a charging Pasini, with Smith back to seventh after a flying start that saw him finish lap one in third. Gadea had been 11th at the end of lap one and was moving forward, bringing Espargaro along.

Faubel needed them all to catch up. Over and over, he drafted past Talmacsi on the straight, then blocked him over the next tight turns. Often, they came close to colliding; Talmacsi led over the line every time.

Slowly, a chase pack of five, led by Pasini, closed up. Too slowly for Faubel; at two-thirds-distance, they were still almost three seconds adrift, with Gadea a close seventh, behind Nieto and Pesek. Gadea took third on lap 19, and two laps later, led a gang only a second adrift and closing.

At the start of the last lap, Talmacsi led his team-mates, Gadea tucked right in, with Pasini and Pesek still a second behind. Could Faubel slow Talmacsi enough for one of them to pass him? He tried, and Gadea came within inches of running into Talmacsi's back wheel. But the chasers just weren't close enough. The team-mates crossed the line within three-tenths, Faubel ahead and Talmacsi second. Pasini was half a second down, Pesek likewise. Rabat came through to defeat Nieto and Smith; Espargaro had joined the lead group, but ran off to finish in tenth.

And Talmacsi was champion, by five points.

Left: Kallio concluded KTM's strong finish to the season with his own second win.

Below: Fast wild-card Debon got a top-three finish, after nine years of trying.

Photographs: Gold & Goose

Left: Team Aspar riders made a rostrum full-house: new champion Talmacsi at the far end, race winner Faubel in the centre, and third-placed Gadea nearest the camera.

Below: Strength in depth: racing at the back of the 125 class was often more intense than up front: former race winner di Meglio leads Litjens, Lombardi and wild-cards Saez and Tutusaus. They were disputing 23rd place.

Photographs: Gold & Goose

GP bwin.com DE LA COMUNITAT VALENCIANA

4 NOVEMBER 2007 • FIM WORLD CHAMPIONSHIP ROUND 18

CIRCUITO DE LA COMUNITAT VALENCIANA

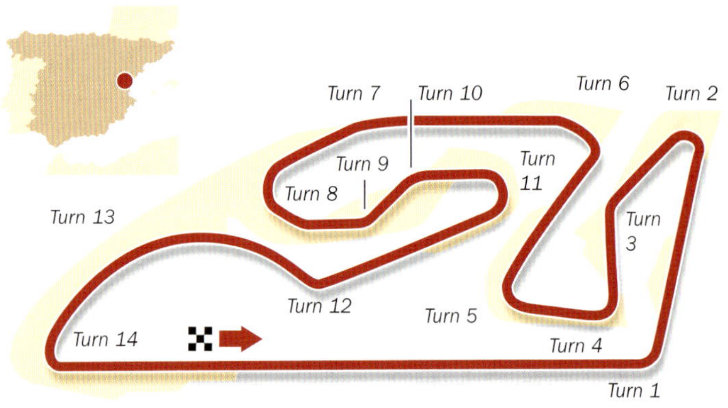

Circuit 4.005km /2.489 miles

MotoGP

RACE: 30 laps, 74.670 miles/120.150km • Weather: Dry • Air 19°C • Humidity 43% • Track 25°C

Pos.	Rider	Nat.	No.	Entrant	Machine	Tyres	Laps	Time & speed (mph/km/h)
1	Dani Pedrosa	SPA	26	Repsol Honda Team	Honda	M	30	46m 43.533s 95.867mph/ 154.283km/h
2	Casey Stoner	AUS	27	Ducati Marlboro Team	Ducati	B	30	46m 48.980s
3	John Hopkins	USA	21	Rizla Suzuki MotoGP	Suzuki	B	30	47m 03.937s
4	Marco Melandri	ITA	33	Honda Gresini	Honda	B	30	47m 08.360s
5	Loris Capirossi	ITA	65	Ducati Marlboro Team	Ducati	B	30	47m 09.337s
6	Chris Vermeulen	AUS	71	Rizla Suzuki MotoGP	Suzuki	B	30	47m 09.395s
7	Alex Barros	BRA	4	Pramac d'Antin	Ducati	B	30	47m 13.003s
8	Nicky Hayden	USA	1	Repsol Honda Team	Honda	M	30	47m 13.866s
9	Randy de Puniet	FRA	14	Kawasaki Racing Team	Kawasaki	B	30	47m 14.428s
10	Toni Elias	SPA	24	Honda Gresini	Honda	B	30	47m 14.563s
11	Sylvain Guintoli	FRA	50	Dunlop Yamaha Tech 3	Yamaha	D	30	47m 22.296s
12	Carlos Checa	SPA	7	Honda LCR	Honda	M	30	47m 26.039s
13	Colin Edwards	USA	5	Fiat Yamaha Team	Yamaha	M	30	47m 30.105s
14	Shinya Nakano	JPN	56	Konica Minolta Honda	Honda	M	30	47m 33.753s
15	Makoto Tamada	JPN	6	Dunlop Yamaha Tech 3	Yamaha	D	30	47m 40.412s
16	Anthony West	AUS	13	Kawasaki Racing Team	Kawasaki	B	30	47m 58.902s
	Valentino Rossi	ITA	46	Fiat Yamaha Team	Yamaha	M	19	30m 32.477s
	Kurtis Roberts	USA	80	Team Roberts	KR212V	M	10	16m 15.099s

Fastest lap: Dani Pedrosa, on lap 5, 1m 32.748s, 96.594mph/155.453km/h (record).

Previous record: Loris Capirossi, ITA (Ducati), 1m 32.924s, 96.411mph/155.159km/h (2006).

Event best maximum speed: Dani Pedrosa, 188.9mph/304.0km/h (free practice no. 3).

Grid order	1	2	3	4	5	6	7	8	9	10	11	12	13	14	15	16	17	18	19	20	21	22	23	24	25	26	27	28	29	30	•
26 PEDROSA	27	27	27	27	27	26	26	26	26	26	26	26	26	26	26	26	26	26	26	26	26	26	26	26	26	26	26	26	26	26	1
27 STONER	26	26	26	26	26	27	27	27	27	27	27	27	27	27	27	27	27	27	27	27	27	27	27	27	27	27	27	27	27	27	2
1 HAYDEN	1	1	1	21	21	21	21	21	21	21	21	21	21	21	21	21	21	21	21	21	21	21	21	21	21	21	21	21	21	21	3
14 de PUNIET	21	21	21	1	1	1	33	33	33	33	33	33	33	33	33	33	33	33	33	1	1	33	33	33	33	33	33	33	33	33	4
50 GUINTOLI	33	33	33	33	33	33	1	1	1	1	1	1	1	1	1	1	1	1	1	33	33	1	1	1	1	65	65	65	65	65	5
6 TAMADA	65	65	65	65	65	65	65	65	65	65	65	65	65	65	65	65	65	65	65	65	65	65	65	65	65	1	71	71	71	71	6
21 HOPKINS	4	4	4	4	4	4	4	14	14	14	14	14	14	14	14	14	14	14	14	14	71	71	71	71	71	71	1	1	4	4	7
65 CAPIROSSI	6	14	14	14	14	14	14	4	4	4	4	71	71	71	71	71	71	71	71	71	14	14	14	14	4	4	4	4	1	1	8
7 CHECA	14	6	50	50	50	50	50	50	50	50	71	4	4	4	4	4	4	4	4	4	4	4	4	4	14	14	14	14	14	14	9
33 MELANDRI	50	50	6	6	6	71	71	71	71	71	50	50	50	50	50	50	50	50	24	24	24	24	24	24	24	24	24	24	24	24	10
71 VERMEULEN	24	24	71	71	71	6	24	24	24	24	24	24	24	24	24	24	24	24	50	50	50	50	50	50	50	50	50	50	50	50	11
4 BARROS	71	71	24	24	24	24	6	6	6	6	6	6	6	5	5	7	5	5	5	5	5	5	7	7	7	7	7	7	7	7	12
56 NAKANO	56	56	56	56	56	56	56	56	56	56	56	56	5	7	7	5	7	7	7	7	7	7	5	5	5	5	5	5	5	5	13
24 ELIAS	7	13	13	5	5	5	5	5	5	5	5	5	7	6	6	46	46	56	56	56	56	56	56	56	56	56	56	56	56	56	14
5 EDWARDS	13	7	5	7	7	7	7	7	7	7	7	7	56	46	46	6	6	6	6	6	6	6	6	6	6	6	6	6	6	6	15
13 WEST	5	5	7	13	13	46	46	46	46	46	46	46	46	56	56	56	56	46	13	13	13	13	13	13	13	13	13	13	13	13	
46 ROSSI	46	46	46	46	46	13	13	13	13	13	13	13	13	13	13	13	13	13	46												
80 ROBERTS	80	80	80	80	80	80	80	80	80	80																					
57 DAVIES																															

FASTEST RACE LAPS

	Rider	Lap	Time
1	Pedrosa	5	1m 32.748s
2	Stoner	2	1m 32.775s
3	Hopkins	5	1m 33.064s
4	de Puniet	5	1m 33.199s
5	Melandri	2	1m 33.244s
6	Barros	3	1m 33.347s
7	Hayden	2	1m 33.435s
8	Capirossi	2	1m 33.463s
9	Vermeulen	8	1m 33.598s
10	Rossi	10	1m 33.696s
11	Guintoli	3	1m 33.759s
12	Elias	9	1m 33.811s
13	Checa	6	1m 33.913s
14	Edwards	8	1m 33.985s
15	Nakano	3	1m 34.137s
16	Tamada	2	1m 34.159s
17	Roberts	3	1m 34.768s
18	West	3	1m 34.802s

QUALIFYING

3 November 2007

Weather: Dry

Air: 21°C Humidity: 34%

Track: 26°C

Pos.	Rider	Time
1	Pedrosa	1m 31.517s
2	Stoner	1m 31.603s
3	Hayden	1m 31.903s
4	de Puniet	1m 31.963s
5	Guintoli	1m 32.074s
6	Tamada	1m 32.151s
7	Hopkins	1m 32.165s
8	Capirossi	1m 32.261s
9	Checa	1m 32.273s
10	Melandri	1m 32.367s
11	Vermeulen	1m 32.617s
12	Barros	1m 32.714s
13	Nakano	1m 32.730s
14	Elias	1m 32.790s
15	Edwards	1m 33.021s
16	West	1m 33.231s
17	Rossi	1m 33.290s
18	Roberts	1m 33.431s

statistics

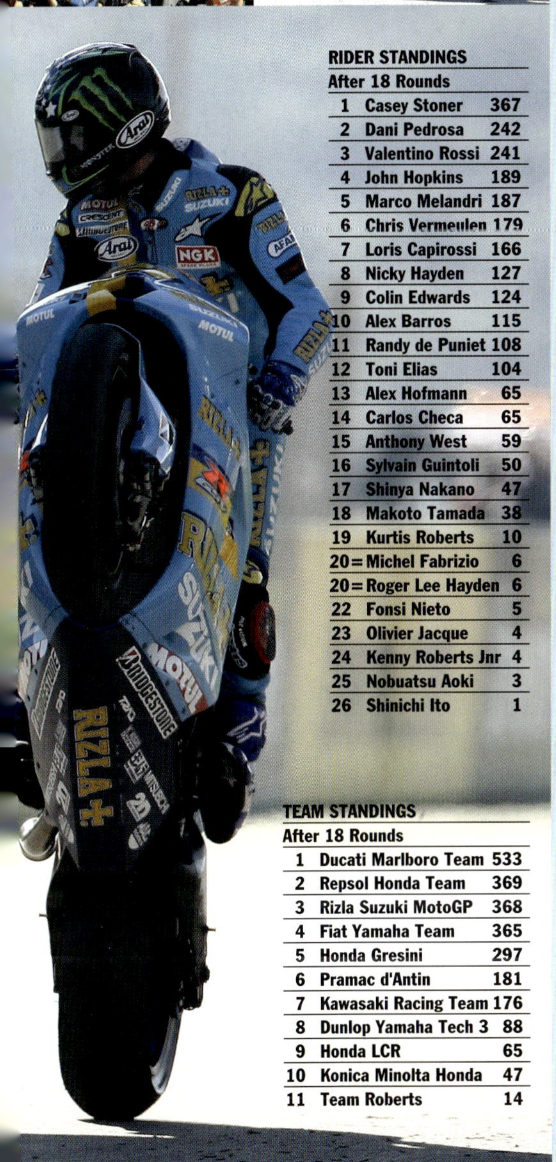

RIDER STANDINGS

After 18 Rounds

1	Casey Stoner	367
2	Dani Pedrosa	242
3	Valentino Rossi	241
4	John Hopkins	189
5	Marco Melandri	187
6	Chris Vermeulen	179
7	Loris Capirossi	166
8	Nicky Hayden	127
9	Colin Edwards	124
10	Alex Barros	115
11	Randy de Puniet	108
12	Toni Elias	104
13	Alex Hofmann	65
14	Carlos Checa	65
15	Anthony West	59
16	Sylvain Guintoli	50
17	Shinya Nakano	47
18	Makoto Tamada	38
19	Kurtis Roberts	10
20=	Michel Fabrizio	6
20=	Roger Lee Hayden	6
22	Fonsi Nieto	5
23	Olivier Jacque	4
24	Kenny Roberts Jnr	4
25	Nobuatsu Aoki	3
26	Shinichi Ito	1

TEAM STANDINGS

After 18 Rounds

1	Ducati Marlboro Team	533
2	Repsol Honda Team	369
3	Rizla Suzuki MotoGP	368
4	Fiat Yamaha Team	365
5	Honda Gresini	297
6	Pramac d'Antin	181
7	Kawasaki Racing Team	176
8	Dunlop Yamaha Tech 3	88
9	Honda LCR	65
10	Konica Minolta Honda	47
11	Team Roberts	14

ONSTRUCTOR STANDINGS

er 18 Rounds

Ducati	394
Honda	313
Yamaha	283
Suzuki	241
Kawasaki	144
KR212V	14

250cc

27 laps, 67.203 miles/108.135km

Pos.	Rider (Nat.)	No.	Machine	Laps	Time & speed
1	Mika Kallio (FIN)	36	KTM	27	43m 28.349s 92.737mph/ 149.246km/h
2	Alex de Angelis (RSM)	3	Aprilia	27	43m 28.720s
3	Alex Debon (SPA)	6	Aprilia	27	43m 35.146s
4	Andrea Dovizioso (ITA)	34	Honda	27	43m 35.229s
5	Hector Barbera (SPA)	80	Aprilia	27	43m 41.116s
6	Julian Simon (SPA)	60	Honda	27	43m 41.379s
7	Jorge Lorenzo (SPA)	1	Aprilia	27	43m 43.100s
8	Yuki Takahashi (JPN)	55	Honda	27	43m 44.786s
9	Thomas Luthi (SWI)	12	Aprilia	27	43m 44.900s
10	Hiroshi Aoyama (JPN)	4	KTM	27	43m 48.572s
11	Marco Simoncelli (ITA)	58	Gilera	27	43m 51.975s
12	Aleix Espargaro (SPA)	41	Aprilia	27	44m 00.154s
13	Roberto Locatelli (ITA)	15	Gilera	27	44m 02.659s
14	Alex Baldolini (ITA)	25	Aprilia	27	44m 27.174s
15	Ratthapark Wilairot (THA)	8	Honda	27	44m 27.194s
16	Dirk Heidolf (GER)	28	Aprilia	27	44m 28.037s
17	Shuhei Aoyama (JPN)	73	Honda	27	44m 29.859s
18	Efren Vazquez (SPA)	7	Aprilia	27	44m 47.969s
19	Taro Sekiguchi (JPN)	11	Aprilia	27	44m 48.947s
20	Federico Sandi (ITA)	21	Aprilia	27	44m 52.761s
21	Eugene Laverty (IRL)	50	Honda	27	44m 55.878s
22	Alvaro Molina (SPA)	31	Aprilia	26	43m 49.821s
23	Imre Toth (HUN)	10	Aprilia	26	43m 56.395s
24	Santiago Barragan (SPA)	53	Honda	26	44m 11.861s
	Alvaro Bautista (SPA)	19	Aprilia	20	DNF
	Karel Abraham (CZE)	17	Aprilia	20	DNF
	Joshua Sommer (GER)	18	Honda	19	DNF
	Jules Cluzel (FRA)	16	Aprilia	15	DNF
	Fabrizio Lai (ITA)	32	Aprilia	0	DNF

Fastest lap: Kallio, 1m 35.659s, 93.654mph/150.722km/h (record).

Previous lap record: Dani Pedrosa, SPA (Honda), 1m 35.792s, 93.524mph/ 150.513km/h (2005).

Event best maximum speed: Barbera, 162.6mph/261.6km/h (race).

Qualifying: 1 Kallio, 1m 35.166s; 2 Lorenzo, 1m 35.333s; 3 Takahashi, 1m 35.623s; 4 Simoncelli, 1m 35.712s; 5 Barbera, 1m 35.727s; 6 Bautista, 1m 35.766s; 7 Simon, 1m 35.958s; 8 Debon, 1m 35.962s; 9 de Angelis, 1m 35.985s; 10 Dovizioso, 1m 35.985s; 11 H. Aoyama, 1m 36.077s; 12 S. Aoyama, 1m 36.103s; 13 Espargaro, 1m 36.318s; 14 Luthi, 1m 36.344s; 15 Locatelli, 1m 36.688s; 16 Lai, 1m 37.580s; 17 Cluzel, 1m 37.680s; 18 Heidolf, 1m 37.770s; 19 Wilairot, 1m 37.792s; 20 Baldolini, 1m 37.922s; 21 Abraham, 1m 38.090s; 22 Sekiguchi, 1m 38.557s; 23 Vazquez, 1m 38.589s; 24 Molina, 1m 38.683s; 25 Sandi, 1m 38.904s; 26 Laverty, 1m 38.919s; 27 Toth, 1m 39.080s; 28 Barragan, 1m 40.427s; 29 Sommer, 1m 41.692s.

Fastest race laps: 1 Kallio, 1m 35.659s; 2 Bautista, 1m 35.810s; 3 de Angelis, 1m 35.978s; 4 Debon, 1m 36.097s; 5 Dovizioso, 1m 36.114s; 6 Barbera, 1m 36.199s; 7 Luthi, 1m 36.218s; 8 Simon, 1m 36.218s; 9 Lorenzo, 1m 36.375s; 10 Simoncelli, 1m 36.380s; 11 Takahashi, 1m 36.473s; 12 H. Aoyama, 1m 36.503s; 13 Espargaro, 1m 36.743s; 14 Locatelli, 1m 36.828s; 15 S. Aoyama, 1m 37.202s; 16 Wilairot, 1m 37.415s; 17 Heidolf, 1m 37.574s; 18 Abraham, 1m 37.857s; 19 Baldolini, 1m 37.956s; 20 Sekiguchi, 1m 38.457s; 21 Vazquez, 1m 38.532s; 22 Sandi, 1m 38.711s; 23 Laverty, 1m 38.897s; 24 Cluzel, 1m 38.967s; 25 Toth, 1m 39.856s; 26 Molina, 1m 39.925s; 27 Barragan, 1m 40.740s; 28 Sommer, 1m 40.967s.

Final World Championship Standings: See table on page 221.

125cc

24 laps, 59.736 miles/96.120km

Pos.	Rider (Nat.)	No.	Machine	Laps	Time & speed
1	Hector Faubel (SPA)	55	Aprilia	24	40m 14.228s 89.061mph/ 143.330km/h
2	Gabor Talmacsi (HUN)	14	Aprilia	24	40m 14.413s
3	Sergio Gadea (SPA)	33	Aprilia	24	40m 14.514s
4	Mattia Pasini (ITA)	75	Aprilia	24	40m 15.054s
5	Lukas Pesek (CZE)	52	Derbi	24	40m 15.106s
6	Esteve Rabat (SPA)	12	Honda	24	40m 20.078s
7	Pablo Nieto (SPA)	22	Aprilia	24	40m 23.266s
8	Bradley Smith (GBR)	38	Honda	24	40m 27.262s
9	Tomoyoshi Koyama (JPN)	71	KTM	24	40m 34.962s
10	Pol Espargaro (SPA)	44	Aprilia	24	40m 35.230s
11	Nicolas Terol (SPA)	18	Derbi	24	40m 35.574s
12	Simone Corsi (ITA)	24	Aprilia	24	40m 46.306s
13	Michael Ranseder (AUT)	60	Derbi	24	40m 53.770s
14	Alexis Masbou (FRA)	7	Honda	24	40m 53.776s
15	Randy Krummenacher (SWI)	34	KTM	24	40m 53.934s
16	Steve Bonsey (USA)	51	KTM	24	40m 54.108s
17	Stefano Bianco (ITA)	27	Aprilia	24	40m 55.105s
18	Dominique Aegerter (SWI)	77	Aprilia	24	40m 55.226s
19	Roberto Tamburini (ITA)	20	Aprilia	24	40m 58.397s
20	Andrea Iannone (ITA)	29	Aprilia	24	40m 58.401s
21	Danny Webb (GBR)	99	Honda	24	41m 09.140s
22	Robert Muresan (ROU)	95	Derbi	24	41m 23.463s
23	Mike di Meglio (FRA)	63	Honda	24	41m 26.436s
24	Joey Litjens (NED)	37	Honda	24	41m 26.543s
25	Dino Lombardi (ITA)	13	Honda	24	41m 26.998s
26	Daniel Saez (SPA)	78	Aprilia	24	41m 27.014s
27	Pere Tutusaus (SPA)	30	Aprilia	24	41m 27.096s
28	Ferruccio Lamborghini (ITA)	79	Aprilia	24	41m 30.423s
29	Alen Gyorfi (HUN)	40	Aprilia	24	41m 53.078s
30	Joan Olive (SPA)	6	Aprilia	23	40m 23.616s
	Lorenzo Zanetti (ITA)	8	Aprilia	11	DNF
	Simone Grotzkyj (ITA)	53	Aprilia	11	DNF
	Sandro Cortese (GER)	11	Aprilia	9	DNF
	Takaaki Nakagami (JPN)	98	Honda	9	DNF
	Raffaele de Rosa (ITA)	35	Aprilia	7	DNF
	Stefan Bradl (GER)	17	Aprilia	1	DNF
	Ivan Maestro (SPA)	76	Aprilia	0	DNF

Fastest lap: Faubel, 1m 39.380s, 90.148mph/145.079km/h (record).

Previous lap record: Hector Faubel, SPA (Aprilia), 1m 39.574s, 89.972mph/ 144.796km/h (2006).

Event best maximum speed: Gadea, 138.1mph/222.3km/h (race).

Qualifying: 1 Talmacsi, 1m 39.029s; 2 Faubel, 1m 39.402s; 3 Gadea, 1m 39.745s; 4 Pesek, 1m 39.792s; 5 Nieto, 1m 39.877s; 6 Corsi, 1m 40.000s; 7 Terol, 1m 40.048s; 8 Pasini, 1m 40.059s; 9 Espargaro, 1m 40.279s; 10 Cortese, 1m 40.287s; 11 Rabat, 1m 40.488s; 12 Smith, 1m 40.528s; 13 Olive, 1m 40.551s; 14 Bradl, 1m 40.660s; 15 Koyama, 1m 40.743s; 16 Ranseder, 1m 40.927s; 17 Krummenacher, 1m 40.951s; 18 Masbou, 1m 40.999s; 19 Bianco, 1m 41.161s; 20 Nakagami, 1m 41.200s; 21 di Meglio, 1m 41.222s; 22 de Rosa, 1m 41.291s; 23 Aegerter, 1m 41.321s; 24 Zanetti, 1m 41.327s; 25 Iannone, 1m 41.344s; 26 Tamburini, 1m 41.349s; 27 Bonsey, 1m 41.600s; 28 Webb, 1m 41.843s; 29 Muresan, 1m 42.171s; 30 Maestro, 1m 42.257s; 31 Saez, 1m 42.378s; 32 Litjens, 1m 42.420s; 33 Tutusaus, 1m 42.567s; 34 Lombardi, 1m 43.075s; 35 Grotzkyj, 1m 43.276s; 36 Lamborghini, 1m 43.335s; 37 Gyorfi, 1m 43.807s.

Fastest race laps: 1 Faubel, 1m 39.380s; 2 Talmacsi, 1m 39.632s; 3 Gadea, 1m 39.711s; 4 Pesek, 1m 39.724s; 5 Pasini, 1m 39.733s; 6 Rabat, 1m 39.738s; 7 Nieto, 1m 39.964s; 8 Cortese, 1m 40.136s; 9 Smith, 1m 40.166s; 10 Terol, 1m 40.439s; 11 Espargaro, 1m 40.506s; 12 Koyama, 1m 40.726s; 13 Olive, 1m 40.792s; 14 Corsi, 1m 40.894s; 15 Bonsey, 1m 41.010s; 16 de Rosa, 1m 41.220s; 17 Aegerter, 1m 41.230s; 18 Tamburini, 1m 41.250s; 19 Masbou, 1m 41.283s; 20 Ranseder, 1m 41.288s; 21 Iannone, 1m 41.346s; 22 Krummenacher, 1m 41.425s; 23 Bianco, 1m 41.485s; 24 Zanetti, 1m 41.529s; 25 Webb, 1m 41.541s; 26 Nakagami, 1m 41.658s; 27 Litjens, 1m 41.945s; 28 Muresan, 1m 42.012s; 29 Lamborghini, 1m 42.352s; 30 Saez, 1m 42.484s; 31 Tutusaus, 1m 42.488s; 32 Lombardi, 1m 42.568s; 33 di Meglio, 1m 42.626s; 34 Grotzkyj, 1m 43.521s; 35 Gyorfi, 1m 43.592s; 36 Bradl, 1m 54.470s.

Final World Championship Standings: See table on page 221.

WORLD CHAMPIONSHIP POINTS 2007

MOTOGP

Position	Rider	Nationality	Machine	Qatar	Spain	Turkey	China	France	Italy	Catalunya	Great Britain	Netherlands	Germany	United States	Czech Republic	San Marino	Portugal	Japan	Australia	Malaysia	Valencia	Points total
1	Casey Stoner	AUS	Ducati	25	11	25	25	16	13	25	25	20	11	25	25	25	16	10	25	25	20	367
2	Dani Pedrosa	SPA	Honda	16	20	–	13	13	20	16	8	13	25	11	13	–	20	–	13	16	25	242
3	Valentino Rossi	ITA	Yamaha	20	25	6	20	10	25	20	13	25	–	13	9	–	25	3	16	11	–	241
4	John Hopkins	USA	Suzuki	13	–	10	16	9	11	13	11	11	9	1	20	16	10	6	9	8	16	189
5	Marco Melandri	ITA	Honda	11	8	11	11	20	7	7	6	6	10	16	–	13	11	11	6	20	13	187
6	Chris Vermeulen	AUS	Suzuki	9	7	5	9	25	8	9	16	–	5	20	11	20	3	5	8	9	10	179
7	Loris Capirossi	ITA	Ducati	–	4	16	10	8	9	10	–	–	20	–	10	11	7	25	20	5	11	166
8	Nicky Hayden	USA	Honda	8	9	9	4	–	6	5	–	16	16	–	16	3	13	7	–	7	8	127
9	Colin Edwards	USA	Yamaha	10	16	–	5	4	4	6	20	10	13	5	–	7	6	2	7	6	3	124
10	Alex Barros	BRA	Ducati	7	5	13	2	–	16	8	9	9	–	7	7	–	–	8	11	4	9	115
11	Randy de Puniet	FRA	Kawasaki	–	3	8	8	–	–	11	10	–	–	10	8	–	–	20	10	13	7	108
12	Toni Elias	SPA	Honda	2	13	20	–	–	10	–	4	–	–	–	5	9	8	16	1	10	6	104
13	Alex Hofmann	GER	Ducati	5	–	7	7	11	5	3	7	8	7	–	–	5	–	–	–	–	–	65
14	Carlos Checa	SPA	Honda	–	10	4	6	–	–	–	–	5	2	2	6	10	9	–	5	2	4	65
15	Anthony West	AUS	Kawasaki	–	–	–	–	–	–	–	5	7	8	9	4	8	4	9	4	1	–	59
16	Sylvain Guintoli	FRA	Yamaha	1	1	1	3	6	2	2	–	2	–	3	3	4	2	13	2	–	5	50
17	Shinya Nakano	JPN	Honda	6	6	3	–	–	3	1	2	4	–	4	2	6	5	–	3	–	2	47
18	Makoto Tamada	JPN	Yamaha	–	2	2	–	7	1	4	1	3	3	8	–	2	–	4	–	–	1	38
19	Kurtis Roberts	USA	KR212V	–	–	–	–	–	–	–	3	1	4	–	1	1	–	–	–	–	–	10
20=	Michel Fabrizio	ITA	Honda	–	–	–	–	–	–	–	–	–	6	–	–	–	–	–	–	–	–	6
20=	Roger Lee Hayden	USA	Kawasaki	–	–	–	–	–	–	–	–	–	–	6	–	–	–	–	–	–	–	6
22	Fonsi Nieto	SPA	Kawasaki	–	–	–	–	5	–	–	–	–	–	–	–	–	–	–	–	–	–	5
23	Olivier Jacque	FRA	Kawasaki	4	–	–	–	–	–	–	–	–	–	–	–	–	–	–	–	–	–	4
24	Kenny Roberts Jnr	USA	KR212V	3	–	–	1	–	–	–	–	–	–	–	–	–	–	–	–	–	–	4
25	Nobuatsu Aoki	JPN	Suzuki	–	–	–	–	–	–	–	–	–	–	–	–	–	–	–	–	3	–	3
26	Shinichi Ito	JPN	Ducati	–	–	–	–	–	–	–	–	–	–	–	–	–	–	1	–	–	–	1

Above: The three world champions of 2007, from left to right: Gabor Talmacsi, Casey Stoner, Jorge Lorenzo.
Photograph: Gold & Goose

250cc

Position	Rider	Nationality	Machine	Qatar	Spain	Turkey	China	France	Italy	Catalunya	Great Britain	Netherlands	Germany	Czech Republic	San Marino	Portugal	Japan	Australia	Malaysia	Valencia	Points total
1	Jorge Lorenzo	SPA	Aprilia	25	25	20	25	25	8	25	–	25	13	25	25	16	5	25	16	9	312
2	Andrea Dovizioso	ITA	Honda	11	16	25	16	20	13	16	25	13	11	20	–	20	20	16	5	13	260
3	Alex de Angelis	RSM	Aprilia	20	13	13	13	16	20	20	20	20	16	5	11	10	11	7	–	20	235
4	Alvaro Bautista	SPA	Aprilia	–	20	16	20	8	25	11	–	16	–	11	8	25	1	20	–	–	181
5	Hector Barbera	SPA	Aprilia	16	–	8	10	13	16	8	–	9	10	13	16	11	16	–	20	11	177
6	Hiroshi Aoyama	JPN	KTM	–	10	–	7	–	–	9	16	11	25	10	20	–	8	13	25	6	160
7	Mika Kallio	FIN	KTM	–	–	10	11	9	–	10	10	8	20	16	–	–	25	–	13	25	157
8	Thomas Luthi	SWI	Aprilia	13	–	11	8	–	11	13	–	–	7	9	13	13	6	11	11	7	133
9	Julian Simon	SPA	Honda	8	–	9	9	11	9	6	9	–	–	8	6	8	10	10	10	10	123
10	Marco Simoncelli	ITA	Gilera	7	–	7	–	10	7	7	–	10	9	–	–	9	9	9	8	5	97
11	Yuki Takahashi	JPN	Honda	9	8	–	–	–	5	–	13	6	8	–	7	–	13	6	7	8	90
12	Shuhei Aoyama	JPN	Honda	6	9	–	–	7	10	5	11	3	4	7	10	–	7	8	3	–	90
13	Roberto Locatelli	ITA	Gilera	10	–	–	–	–	–	4	–	7	6	6	9	–	–	5	9	3	59
14	Fabrizio Lai	ITA	Aprilia	4	5	6	6	4	3	–	5	5	–	4	–	7	–	–	–	–	49
15	Aleix Espargaro	SPA	Aprilia	5	–	5	5	–	4	–	–	–	5	3	4	4	–	2	6	4	47
16	Karel Abraham	CZE	Aprilia	–	1	4	–	–	–	2	6	1	–	2	2	6	–	3	4	–	31
17	Ratthapark Wilairot	THA	Honda	2	4	1	4	5	–	–	8	2	–	–	3	–	–	–	–	1	30
18	Alex Debon	SPA	Aprilia	–	11	–	–	–	–	–	–	–	–	–	–	–	–	–	–	16	27
19	Anthony West	AUS	Aprilia	3	7	–	3	6	6	–	–	–	–	–	–	–	–	–	–	–	25
20	Dirk Heidolf	GER	Aprilia	1	6	3	–	–	–	–	4	–	3	–	–	5	–	1	1	–	24
21	Jules Cluzel	FRA	Aprilia	–	–	–	–	–	–	3	–	–	1	–	5	3	3	4	–	–	19
22	Alex Baldolini	ITA	Aprilia	–	3	2	–	3	2	–	2	–	2	–	–	–	–	–	2	2	18
23	Taro Sekiguchi	JPN	Aprilia	–	–	–	2	2	1	1	3	4	–	–	–	–	–	–	–	–	13
24	Dan Linfoot	GBR	Aprilia	–	–	–	–	–	–	–	7	–	–	–	–	–	–	–	–	–	7
25	Eugene Laverty	IRL	Honda	–	2	–	–	1	–	–	–	–	–	–	1	2	–	–	–	–	6
26	Seijin Oikawa	JPN	Yamaha	–	–	–	–	–	–	–	–	–	–	–	–	–	4	–	–	–	4
27	Youichi Ui	JPN	Yamaha	–	–	–	–	–	–	–	–	–	–	–	–	–	2	–	–	–	2
28	Imre Toth	HUN	Aprilia	–	–	–	–	–	–	–	1	–	–	–	–	1	–	–	–	–	2
29=	Arturo Tizon	SPA	Aprilia	–	–	–	1	–	–	–	–	–	–	–	–	–	–	–	–	–	1
29=	Efren Vazquez	SPA	Aprilia	–	–	–	–	–	–	–	–	–	–	1	–	–	–	–	–	–	1

125cc

Position	Rider	Nationality	Machine	Qatar	Spain	Turkey	China	France	Italy	Catalunya	Great Britain	Netherlands	Germany	Czech Republic	San Marino	Portugal	Japan	Australia	Malaysia	Valencia	Points total
1	Gabor Talmacsi	HUN	Aprilia	20	25	11	13	13	13	20	–	16	25	13	20	20	20	8	25	20	282
2	Hector Faubel	SPA	Aprilia	25	16	6	20	10	25	–	16	20	16	25	–	25	16	16	16	25	277
3	Tomoyoshi Koyama	JPN	KTM	10	–	16	–	6	11	25	20	10	20	11	16	9	2	10	20	7	193
4	Lukas Pesek	CZE	Derbi	16	20	10	25	20	–	3	–	9	10	16	–	3	4	25	10	11	182
5	Mattia Pasini	ITA	Aprilia	–	–	–	6	–	10	–	25	25	–	20	25	8	25	9	8	13	174
6	Simone Corsi	ITA	Aprilia	11	–	25	11	8	16	9	6	11	13	9	–	13	10	13	9	4	168
7	Sergio Gadea	SPA	Aprilia	–	11	–	10	25	20	13	13	13	–	–	13	–	8	7	11	16	160
8	Joan Olive	SPA	Aprilia	5	8	20	–	11	–	8	11	–	5	4	4	11	11	20	13	–	131
9	Pol Espargaro	SPA	Aprilia	9	13	5	7	5	7	11	–	5	–	10	11	16	–	5	–	6	110
10	Bradley Smith	GBR	Honda	4	–	8	8	16	8	10	9	–	8	3	8	4	–	–	7	8	101
11	Esteve Rabat	SPA	Honda	8	–	2	16	–	–	4	–	3	4	5	5	5	–	11	1	10	74
12	Michael Ranseder	AUT	Derbi	3	7	4	9	2	5	6	–	7	6	8	6	–	7	–	–	3	73
13	Randy Krummenacher	SWI	KTM	–	–	1	–	3	3	16	3	4	11	7	10	6	–	4	–	1	69
14	Sandro Cortese	GER	Aprilia	–	9	–	–	9	9	5	4	8	9	6	1	–	–	6	–	–	66
15	Pablo Nieto	SPA	Aprilia	7	10	3	–	1	–	–	7	–	7	–	–	–	9	–	4	9	57
16	Raffaele de Rosa	ITA	Aprilia	13	–	13	4	–	2	–	8	2	–	–	7	7	–	–	–	–	56
17	Mike di Meglio	FRA	Honda	2	–	–	2	7	–	–	10	–	1	–	3	–	13	2	2	–	42
18	Stefan Bradl	GER	Aprilia	–	–	–	–	–	–	7	–	6	3	–	9	10	1	–	3	–	39
19	Lorenzo Zanetti	ITA	Aprilia	–	6	9	1	–	6	2	5	1	–	–	–	–	–	–	–	–	30
20	Andrea Iannone	ITA	Aprilia	1	4	7	5	–	–	–	1	–	–	–	2	–	6	–	–	–	26
21	Alexis Masbou	FRA	Honda	6	–	–	3	4	–	–	–	–	–	2	–	2	–	–	6	2	25
22	Nicolas Terol	SPA	Derbi	–	2	–	–	–	4	–	–	–	–	–	–	–	–	3	5	5	19
23=	Dominique Aegerter	SWI	Aprilia	–	–	–	–	–	1	1	–	–	–	–	–	–	5	–	–	–	7
23=	Stefano Bianco	ITA	Aprilia	–	5	–	–	–	–	–	–	–	–	1	–	1	–	–	–	–	7
25	Steve Bonsey	USA	KTM	–	3	–	–	–	–	–	–	–	–	–	–	–	–	1	–	–	4
26	Danny Webb	GBR	Honda	–	–	–	–	–	–	–	–	–	–	–	–	–	3	–	–	–	3
27=	Georg Froehlich	GER	Honda	–	–	–	–	–	–	–	–	–	2	–	–	–	–	–	–	–	2
27=	Enrique Jerez	SPA	Honda	–	–	–	–	–	–	–	2	–	–	–	–	–	–	–	–	–	2
29	Simone Grotzkyj	ITA	Aprilia	–	1	–	–	–	–	–	–	–	–	–	–	–	–	–	–	–	1

WORLD SUPERBIKE CHAMPIONSHIP REVIEW

THAT'S ENTERTAINMENT

By GORDON RITCHIE

LOTS of people in World Superbike had good reason to be cheerful in 2007. Especially the race winners, and such was the level of entertaining competition at the top that even double champion Troy Corser could not quite win a race on his factory bike. The only privateer victory of the year was really a semi-factory effort, with extra-special X-man Xaus's old factory 999F06 also playing its part in his home victory.

The real top men of 2007, James Toseland, Noriyuki Haga, Max Biaggi and Troy Bayliss, were all in avaricious winning form from the off, and they finished within 43 points of each other; the top three were within 18 points, the top two within two cliffhanging digits.

Four manufacturers won races, five took podiums, six scored points (a single came along for the private MV Agusta, if you can't think of the final one).

The top four competitors finished not just densely packed in the Riders' Championship, but the most successful manufacturers were only 48 points apart in their own contest in the order of Yamaha, Honda, Ducati and Suzuki – thus, Yamaha won this particular battle for the very first time. And this being World Superbike, with two races per race day (except for a washed-out Silverstone race two), the season was a MotoGP-busting 25 races long, which usually exaggerates machinery supremacies or deficiencies, not negates them.

The great paradoxes, unlike previous years, were that although comparatively few riders won races in the 2007 season, they won them mostly at record pace, and that each of the big four manufacturers really could have won the title – albeit with only one of their respective top two riders capable of ultimate honours.

The few chances we had to compare the Pirelli control tyres with the full factory Honda/Michelin or Ducati/Dunlop combos came in the three UK rounds, and the comparison was inescapably more favourable to the supposedly development-unfriendly control rubber. Another step for Pirelli, and the world took notice to the point of looking toward jumping on the single-tyre bandwagon, in both MotoGP and BSB series.

Only 20–25 bikes on the grid was well short of FGSport's 2006 boast of maybe 30 for 2007, but closer inspection showed that quality, in terms of riders and machines, was generally very much on the up – again. This was in spite of some remarkably Machiavellian escapades from – mainly – those whacky mid-field Italians: hijackings and harsh sackings, pay-for-play riders and sponsors not paying at all. It could have been a soap opera, except for the fact that it felt so unclean at times.

What we can look forward to is a deep, wide and tall entry in 2008; that is almost guaranteed, especially by the new 1200cc twin-cylinder rules, with attendant handicapping caveats already laid down in the rulebook.

Cheaper to run, more production-based Ducatis would have been welcome a couple of years ago, but they should be a straightforward conduit to affordable privateer performance and full grids once again.

Importantly for SBK's global push, there will be a return to America in 2008, making a respectable total of 14 events, barring unforeseen disasters.

The new mid-season partnership with Infront, Swiss-based TV marketing gurus, had little effect in 2007, but much more is expected in the future.

And in the mid-term? There will be what is missing currently from the world's premier manufacturer-based championship – more manufacturer teams. Certainly, BMW is coming in 2009, because what it says, it invariably does. Other manufacturers, more certain than ever that there will never be a chance of running properly in the unrealistically expensive MotoGP world, at least now know where to go when they need to combine specific product marketing with status building global competition.

Despite every motorsport this side of NASCAR and F1 struggling hard for sponsorship cash in the modern era, SBK is still the world's affordable alternative, has attracted big-spending Taiwanese TV company Hannspree as a title sponsor for three years (after the unforeseen loss of Corona Extra) and can only become more sponsor-friendly as TV exposure expands.

All in all, 2007 was a very good 20th year for SBK racing.

James Toseland and friends: The new Superbike World Champion is joined in celebration by the Ten Kate team and friendly associates at Magny-Cours.
Photograph: Gold & Goose

JAMES TOSELAND

TWO-FOUR TIME

Above: **Onward and upward – Toseland moves to MotoGP after his second title.**

Main picture: **Harder than he looks: James Toseland's narrow victory came through hard work and clear focus.**

Photographs: Gold & Goose

OVERALL statistics and two world championships in seven years (one on a factory Ducati twin, the other on a largely private Honda four) tell us everything we need to know about James Toseland, the SBK racer. He's never been the fastest learner in the world, not since he left the UK in a blaze of 'Next-Hailwood!' glory at the end of 1997 anyway. But a surer learner, a more dedicated and self-sacrificial student of racing there has seldom been.

No pain, no gain seems to be his personal dictum, and no amount of virtuoso AOR piano playing or guileless public outbursts of affection for his mum or his manager can deflect from the fact that they don't come in a harder grade of stainless steel than Toseland.

Just like 2004, he wrapped up this one at Magny-Cours. Unlike 2004, he had a points advantage in 2007. He didn't get enough credit for his first championship win, for reasons beyond his control, and a bad year in 2005 saw him looking for a job. Ten Kate took him up, with some reservations, but James turned into the team's ideal type of rider – one who was eager to learn, to make some packages work when others wanted to junk them, but most of all one who was willing and able to win races, to overcome setbacks, to share Ten Kate's desire for nothing less than win-win, and win again.

In 2006, on a bike that was nothing like as sophisticated in electronics as virtually everyone else's, Toseland was the closest man to interstellar Bayliss. No disgrace, especially after Bayliss went over and whupped ass in MotoGP at the Valencia finale.

In 2007, Toseland was the one handing out Dutch-accented cloggings to his rivals most weekends. Furthermore, he kept his momentum through the potential disasters of a machine failure at Donington, an eighth place after crashing and rejoining in the wet at Silverstone, curious rear tyre spin issues at Lausitz and a self-inflicted points abrasion after falling at Biaggi's home circuit. And in coming back from another potential disaster in race one at Magny-Cours, Toseland proved that he was utterly incapable of being fazed when suddenly everything was to play for.

Strange then that some observers will still look back on the 2007 season convinced that maybe Haga was robbed, or that Biaggi would definitely have won it had he known all the tracks, or that Bayliss would have won it with another 20bhp.

The fact is that Toseland won the title, not any of the other hotshots, albeit by the narrowest margin ever, but also in one of the hardest years ever. Late season may have been a trial, but the earlier stats clarify the situation somewhat, showing Toseland in a better, truer light.

He scored more race wins than any of his rivals, with probably less direct factory support than any of them, using unfashionable suspension, braking and electronics components for the most part. He had been required to jump between PI/home-brewed (in testing), HRC (until Brno), and then again PI/home-brewed traction control and engine management packages. In a year when the sophistication and familiarity of a rider's traction control seemed even more important than in 2006, this was no mean feat for Sheffield man Toseland and his well-backed Dutch dealer team. It is a key aspect of Toseland's season that should not go unrecognised.

It was not a settled end of season for Toseland of course, not the vast winning margin we may have expected at one stage, but definitely a season in which he was the most consistent and toughest, even if sometimes his overall Sunday race package and simple good fortune were found wanting.

Toseland now says he can move to MotoGP with his head held high, and few of those who get to look at SBK racing close up doubt that he will take his unquenchable desire to learn and work hard into GP racing. At 27, he may or may not be too late going, but he is certainly the best Britain has got right now.

He will more than do justice to whatever machine is put under him, and if he is looking for a marker to follow, how about the rider who didn't quite win World Superbike on a Ten Kate Honda, and yet has won a MotoGP race, Chris Vermeulen? Or ex-AMA man Nicky Hayden, whom few saw as a potential champion in 2003. Or, dare we say it, Casey Stoner, thoroughly deserving surprise 2007 champion, after a crashtastic first MotoGP season in 2006.

No matter what the outcome of the next couple of James Toseland's seasons, he'll be a huge asset, wherever and whatever he rides.

Ten Kate

james toseland

noriyuki haga

troy bayliss

2007 TEAMS AND RIDERS

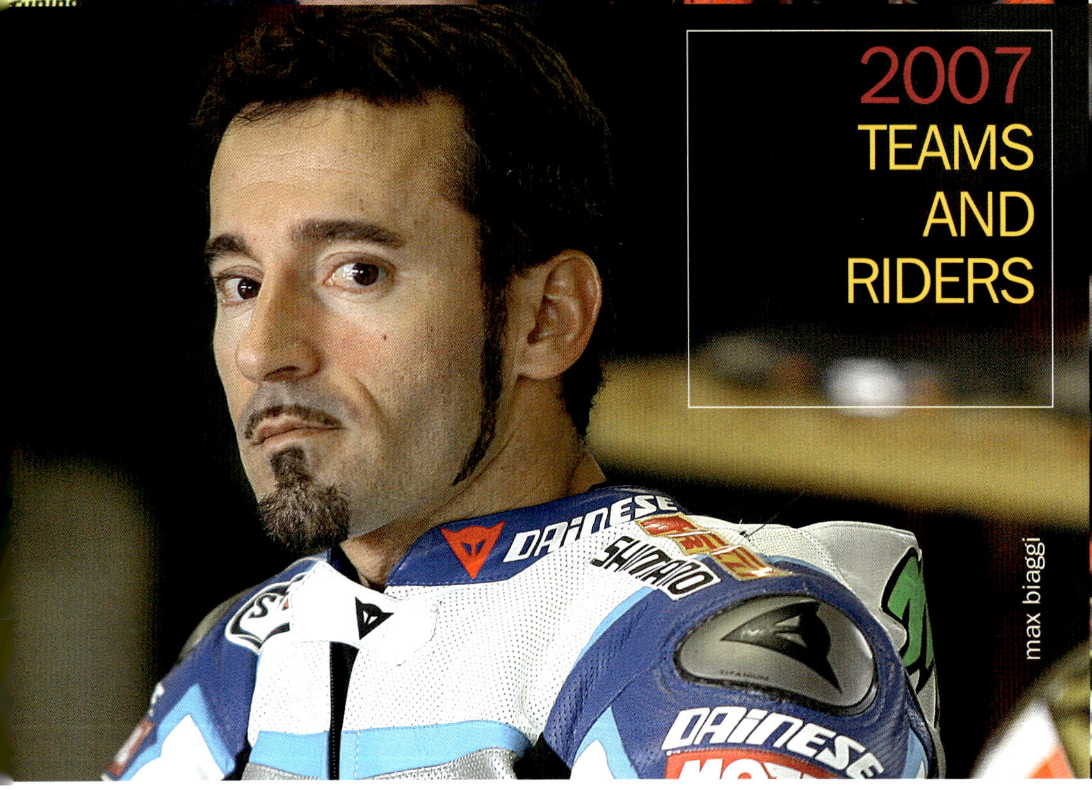
max biaggi

troy corser

Ducati Xerox

Troy Bayliss (37) was back for another bite, even if he did go on record many times to say that 2007 was almost a wasted year – he was just hanging about, waiting for the 1200cc twin era to begin in 2008. He was fast as ever, the 999F07 still potent 80 per cent of the time, and once again his exuberance was both his making and his occasional downfall. He's growing old disgracefully and rides to wins on pieces of tarmac other riders only see when crashing – and he's loved for it. Lorenzo Lanzi (25) had another 'nothing-special' season, a single podium and two front-row starts – much less than he and his team had hoped for.

Team Caracchi Ducati SC

Jakub Smrz (23) showed flashes on the creakingly old 999F05, actually of uncertain vintage, component by component. 'Kuba' made a respected name for himself in SBK guise and was another welcome refugee from the GPs. Fourteenth overall made him best of the riders on a third-ranking machine set-up – so we couldn't ask for more.

Team Sterilgarda Ducati

Ruben Xaus (29) was the effervescent, ever-present single prong in the semi-factory-bike/fully private-budget team. His old team-mate and current team owner, Marco Borciani (31), was a wild-card at Monza, Misano and Vallelunga on the normal Italian championship machine, with Giovanni Bussei (34) a wild-card at Donington and Valencia, looking for sponsorship that didn't turn up, despite two Superpole starts and points in every race.

Team Pedercini Ducati

Dean Ellison (26) battled in a no-hoper 999RS set-up, the enthusiasm to race from the father-and-son Pedercini team unabated by their much-reduced 2007 effort. Difficult to imagine what lining up on the grid merely trying not to be last does to rider's spirit, but Ellison wins gilded prizes for tenacity and bulldog spirit.

Hannspree Ten Kate Honda

James Toseland (26) we know all about, and in going from second in 2006 to champion in 2007, occasionally it seemed that he was in a one-man team. Roby Rolfo (26) pushed Toseland hard in the nicest-guy-in-the-paddock stakes, and at Monza looked like the tiger we saw in 250GPs. Finishing on the same points as Lanzi was largely the start and finish of how his riding was rated in the paddock, but he still has time to make a flight from the wrong side of the elite wire to the winning bull's-eye bed.

DFX Corse Honda

Michel Fabrizio (22) was there or thereabouts, scoring a single podium in the year when the factory teams became impregnable, and did enough to get a factory Ducati ride in 2008. His nationality and youth helped, but he needs his rough edges and cocky undertone trimmed to progress further; Tardozzi will be the man to do it, we assume. The DFX team, hit by the late and unexpected pull-out of two top sponsors, was understaffed, shambolic and ever changing. That caused Steve Martin (38) to depart, by mutual agreement, after Australia. He went on to wild-card for the factory Yamaha WSS team, a combined Team YZF and Virgin Yamaha team at Brands Hatch, and ended 2007 with Celani Suzuki in SBK. Luca Morelli (19) bought a ride for the Martin-less part of the season, from Donington onward, and scored points on occasion.

Alto Evolution Honda

Karl Muggeridge (32) didn't quite know what he had got himself into at the start of the season, but his previous employ at Ten Kate could not have looked more attractive after a disrupted season unsurpassed in SBK history. There were accusations of international hijacking of trucks and even kidnapping, the exit of original signing Joshua Brookes (23) after the Silverstone race (injured after crashing on his team-mate's oil spills), a revolving

ruben xaus

max neukirchner

fonsi nieto

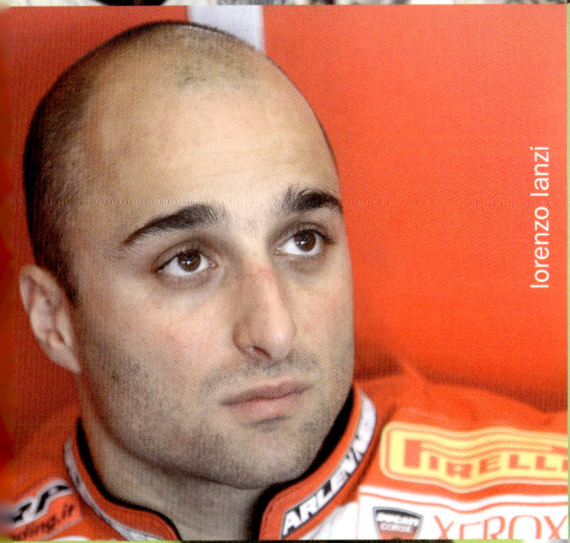
lorenzo lanzi

regis laconi

yukio kagayama

michel fabrizio

shinichi nakatomi

door of team personnel maybe also unequalled in SBK history, and eventually two security guards following the one-time 'liberated' trucks on their travels across Europe, then guarding the team's pit boxes in rottweiler fashion. A more conventional line-up for the last third of the season included a new chief engineer in Marco Nicotari, and he rated the abilities of eventual Brookes replacement Yoann Tiberio (20).

Kawasaki PSG-1 Corse

Regis Laconi (31) and Fonsi Nieto (28) were in the least official of the factory squads once more, so much so that they were ignored in the discussions on the 1200cc twin rules, much to the chagrin of team owner Pierguido Pagani. The bikes were no better in relative terms than in 2006, and only a single podium came along, from Nieto running on the edge of adhesion and reason at the very last round. Too many technical issues and an elusive set-up held them all back. To add to their difficulties, they added wild-card riders to dilute the effort all the more: Mauro Sanchini (36) dressed in green at Monza, Misano and Vallelunga, and Vittorio Iannuzzo (25) at Silverstone and Brno.

Alstare Suzuki Corona Extra

A real dream team, with four-time 250GP champion and series 500/MotoGP race winner Max Biaggi (35) out of enforced retirement and into the winner's circle first time out. The continuation of Yukio Kagayama (32) was a more painful journey, one that took him to many medical centres. His propensity for crashing left him on two podiums only, and his race wins from 2006 seemed a long way away, despite winning the Suzuka Eight-Hour at mid-season.

Suzuki Germany

Max Neukirchner (23) rode a year-old Suzuki to the best privateer/privateer slot of ninth (but only if we count Xaus in overall seventh as semi-factory). A great all-round effort, on not a huge amount of money.

Celani Team Suzuki Italia

Last year's big Superstock winner, Alessandro Polita (22), ended his year early by making more of an impact on the track than the points. Thus, super-sub Steve Martin was drafted in for a period. Stefano Cruciani (28) also had two rides for the team, at Brands and Brno

Yamaha Motor Italia

Noriyuki Haga (31) had a new bike to deal with and, predictably, didn't deal with the novelty any better than he ever does, at least at first. Enter, stage left, Troy Corser (35), development ace and fierce racer – if still sometimes enigmatic in the middle of races. That Yamaha won the manufacturers' crown for the first time in its 20-year SBK history said everything about the general efficacy of the official factory team.

Yamaha YZF Team

Shinichi Nakatomi (28) was the single French-based representative for most of the year. Even when Steve Martin made his one-off ride at Brands, Nakatomi stayed on the bike he had been riding all year. Riding hurt at times, and he was not up front too often. The team saw 2007 as its last year of racing and developing parts for Yamaha all at once. In 2008, it will be racing at races, testing at tests.

Yamaha Junior Pro SBK Racing

Czech rider Jiri Drazdak (27) was not an all-season entry and was replaced at Assen by Marek Svoboda (36). However, he returned to finish the last few races, albeit as a wild-card.

LBR MV Agusta

An entirely private team, running home-brewed MV Agusta F4s, then what was stated to be the new 312R. Austrian privateer Christian Zaiser (33) rode the bikes until they became frustrated with a lack of factory support.

THE BIKES OF 2007

DUCATI 999F07

OTHER than refinement and re-engineering of a few details, the 2007 factory Ducati was largely identical to the 2006 version, the 999F06. It was something of an 'F06-and-a-half,' quipped Ducati team boss Davide Tardozzi.

If we take Ducati's word literally, the venerable desmo would have made 194bhp at 12,500rpm from its well-established 104 x 58.8mm engine, with the usual improvements to the Termignoni exhaust designs coming along as time passed – and lots of work on mapping for the Magneti Marelli Marvel 4 ECU/EFI, which vaporised fuel through one IWF1 injector per cylinder. Combined with other electronic refinements, theoretically these made it easier to ride.

Despite all this, a combination of advances in tyre technology and the inexorable march of the four-cylinder machines left Ducati behind at some tracks.

Attempting to re-invent its well-worn wheel, Ducati even displayed some uncharacteristic inconsistency of race set-up performance from track to track. A particularly sticky patch was evident at Brno and Brands, despite Bayliss's ability to post stunning single lap times in tests, Superpole and qualifying.

Where Ducati usually scores over its rivals is in the support a factory team commands from its ancillary suppliers, but with the bike largely unchanged, even that factor was less significant. For example, the Öhlins 42mm, gas-pressurised, TTX20 upside-down forks and TTX36 damper were only lightly breathed upon.

There was even a 2006-spec factory machine on the grid, supposedly a full 999F06, for Ruben Xaus and the Sterilgarda team. Despite the appearance of a full-time track electronics expert as part of the deal, the Xerox boys always seemed to have a lead in mapping and sophistication.

The Caracchi squad had a supposed 999F05 for Jakub Smrz, but in reality it was a mix of many parts, from several vintages, kept going relatively quickly by Ducati legend Franco Farne's ever-changing troop of men in black. Given the limitations, Smrz was often impressive in his debut season.

The Pedercini team continued in single-rider guise, but its machines were very much of private 999RS level, no fancy electronics or real factory parts. Oh, how they all prayed for 1200cc twins.

HONDA CBR1000RR

IN its second World Superbike season, the current model CBR1000RR came in three different colours and flavours. The officially supported white, blue and green meanie from Hannspree Ten Kate was very much a home distilled and perennially potent Dutch spirit, while the privateer Italian versions from DFX and Alto Evolution were heavily inconsistent, only occasionally heady, and frustratingly variable in quantity and quality.

The official entry made up for any deficiencies in the other Honda packages. Gerrit Ten Kate and his team of dyno warriors found around 225bhp at the rear tyre when required, and improved throttle linearity in most instances.

Central to any winning package in 2007 was the electronics ensemble, and that was largely the story of the Ten Kate season. HRC 'anti-spin' EFI and ignition technology arrived in time for Qatar, and this system was used until Misano, where patently it could not deal with the twisty circuit and hot track temperatures.

Instant help was at hand from a PI Research ECU system that had been under development by both PI and Ten Kate for months. At Brno, they produced their more sophisticated and immediately effective electronics suite, and the bike was right back on the race-long pace again.

The way Ten Kate operates means that it would rather develop and build its own equipment than merely buy parts over the counter. This has led to a highly individualistic chassis package, which continued with WP 48mm forks and new rear shocks. At Brno, the rear shocks even included electronic damping control in compression and rebound, although they could be swapped from conventional to electronic versions, thanks to the full-time presence of a dedicated WP technician.

The rear shock operated on an exquisitely fabricated KR rear swing-arm. This was more expensive than other options, but back-to-back tests gave it the edge, especially over full race distance. The KR arm's removable linkage and bracket system meant that even if the machine's mounting points changed, the main body of the rear swing-arm could remain in use. Ten Kate was the only truly top team to use Nissin brake rotors and calipers.

The Alto Evolution Honda team had the most bizarre season imaginable off-track, and it told on the machinery. The former Klaffi Hondas proved unreliable early on, and with a shortage of full-race engines, at a few events, they ran with relatively standard motors.

Then the machines were impounded for some time in the team truck, on the orders of a Belgian court, and they had to be completely revamped before Brno. Suspension issues and differences of opinion over set-up in the often changing team sometimes stopped the quicker engines from being put to best use. It was a troubled season, to say the least.

DFX almost had it worse. Original rider Steve Martin's entirely reasonable demands for a comprehensive traction control system and a crew of professional mechanics to look after his machinery caused a rift that became a split.

The machines improved slowly as the season went on, to the point that Fabrizio was on the podium at Brno, and nearly there at Brands. Overall set-up and tyre life may have been problems for the team, but the DFX machine was capable of a World Superbike top-speed breakthrough, Fabrizio going over 200mph at Monza for the first time in history.

SUZUKI GSX-R1000K7

A new bike, but not an all-new bike. Much of 2006's engine was carried forward, but the 2007 chassis went from a combination of extrusions and forgings to a mix of cast and welded sections. Again, it was supported by full factory Showa suspension: 42mm USD forks up front and a more compact 2007 rear shock. Braking was by 320/290mm Brembos.

With a claimed 210PS at 13,000rpm, the engine was no more powerful than the 2006 version at the start, and it lagged behind the fastest Yamahas and Hondas all year. But there were several differences in the details of the K6 and K7. The main one was the twin-exhaust design, even if one silencer on the race-bike was a dummy, there to match the silhouette of the new, twin-pipe road machine.

The main engine equipment change during the year was the adoption of the increasingly ubiquitous Magneti Marelli EFI and attendant electronic rider aids, replacing the Suzuki/Mitsubishi system that politics had decreed should continue to be used until mid-season. An evolution not a revolution, and full fly-by-wire remained a long-distant illusion.

KAWASAKI ZX-10R

THE second year for the ZX-10R was tougher than the first. The machine was unable to make best use of the advances in tyres, especially over race distance, when compared to the best of the rest.

The 76 x 55mm, 998cc engine was fast, but once more the power was mostly found up high, even though season-long work with Pectel PI SQ6M ECU and a data-acquisition system helped the team to moderate power. There were two major steps in the engine spec through the year, and the machine may have made even more than the claimed 200bhp at 13,500rpm posted early in the season, especially with a new Akira designed airbox, which fed 43mm throttle bodies.

On the cycle parts front, Australian ex-all-round racer Peter Goddard was the Öhlins engineer who looked after the 42mm FGR46 forks and TTX rear shocks. Brembo brakes hauled the big and slightly brutish ZX-10R down from high speed.

The machine was said to be on the 165kg weight limit, but it appeared that nothing could overcome the bike's dated overall design, and it was the least manoeuvrable, making it consistently the hardest on tyres.

YAMAHA YZF-R1

YAMAHA waved goodbye to the five-valve-head R1 in some style, with a beautiful, new M1-inspired machine, which, on the face of it, drew the straightest line from MotoGP to World Superbike.

The old five-valve head had been a marketing inspired arrangement for many years; seemingly, the 2007 four-valve head was an instant improvement, if not as much as Haga had expected.

Yamaha was justifiably proud of its road-bike advances in fly-by-wire throttles, variable intake trumpets, EXUP valves and suchlike, but the simple fact is that on the race-bike, all this clever stuff, designed to make 170bhp smoother and more usable on the road, was immediately junked. The Yamaha Motor Italia team did experiment with the variable intakes (a two-stage affair, short or long) toward the final third of the year.

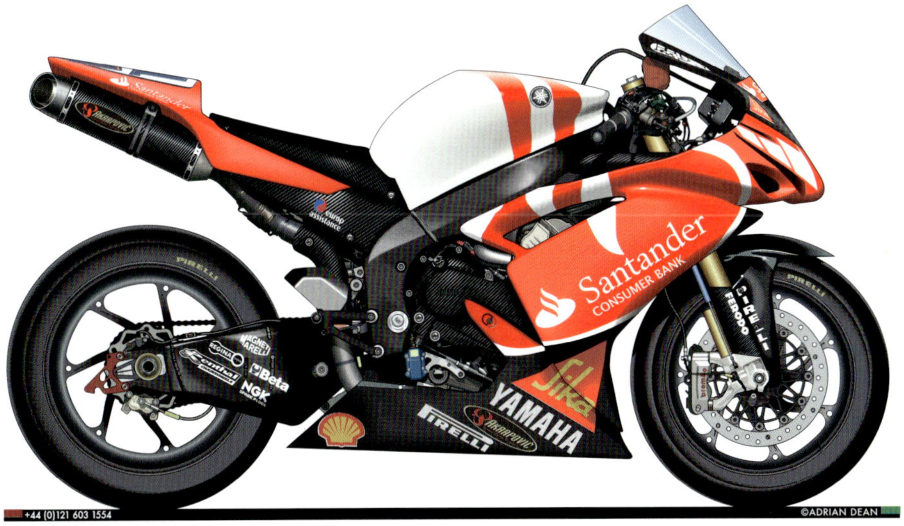

A Magneti Marelli Marvel 4 ECU controlled the engine again, and the machine did use its twin rear exhausts in anger all year, with Akrapovic units in the seat hump. The team, which does most of its own development in-house, rather than being a true factory team like Ducati, spent much time with the Akrapovic crew.

The engine was still thought to produce less than the 225bhp of the Ten Kate Honda, and the machine was not quite on the 165kg limit, probably needing a full winter to get there, not the short close season available to get the largely new bike ready.

Factory Öhlins suspension was used, and exhaustive work in testing delivered the all-important in-house swing-arm design. Tyre life was an occasional issue if the riders had to mix it up early in the races, something that appeared to cause other top teams less trouble.

WORLD SUPERBIKE CHAMPIONSHIP • ROUND 1

LOSAIL

QATAR

Above: First-lap scratchings of the first race of the year: Toseland leads Corser, Haga and Biaggi.

Right: Troy Corser claimed the opening Superpole of the season.

Centre right: Biaggi's debut victory wrote his name large in his new class.

Below right: Two top tens for Max Neukirchner.

Photographs: Gold & Goose

Above: Desert blooms.

Top: Toseland opened his account with a win in race two.

Below: Desert climes provided a fine warm start to the year.

Bottom: A pair of Kawasakis awaiting their marching orders.

Photographs: Gold & Goose

PRE-SEASON testing uncertainties ended with a high-pitched sonic boom in Qatar, announcing a new world disorder – even if the latest WSB signature tune featured a generous spread of old chords.

First up was the very latest R1 tuning fork from Yamaha, a red rhapsody in four-valve time that took Haga to the best lap on day one, then carried his team-mate, Corser, to his 39th Superpole career win. New force number two was – very firmly – Biaggi, a promising rookie who arrived talking quietly, but then proceeded to birch everyone with his new big stick, a 2007 Alstare GSX-R. A batch of improved Pirelli control tyres helped the top men incinerate the previous best lap times in practice and race, over three days of largely warm and dry conditions in the desert.

In reality, when they started racing, there were only two top men and machines: Biaggi and Toseland, running for Suzuki and Honda respectively.

In the first race, Toseland, who had vastly improved both his own performance and that of his machine in winter testing, made great use of his recently arrived electronics package from HRC. Early on, he looked to have run away with the first 18-lap battle, but he fell prey to Biaggi's impressively patient advance. Laden with self-confident guile and inexorable pace, Biaggi was showing why he was a four-time 250 champion and, on occasion, one of the few riders ever to have truly challenged the likes of Doohan and Rossi in GPs. Due credit should be given to this, one of the best victories he has ever scored, akin to his debut 500-class win.

It was almost easy to forget that this was the first of his WSB career. He even survived the usual first couple of laps of elbow flailing and paintwork deflowering in each race with good grace and a cool head.

The target on Biaggi's back, a tempting roundel, which had been verbally stabbed by some of his new rivals from the second he showed up, suddenly was propelled out of range by his first golden shot in Superbike. The earlier cynical cracks and veiled threats were left echoing gracelessly across the desert towards oblivion. Max was for real again, even in an all-new class.

Close behind came a determined, but firmly vanquished, Toseland, while in third, the appearance of a Xerox Ducati was no surprise. The more unusual development was that it belonged to Lanzi, not Bayliss, but at 13s from the win, the return of the rider after a dreadful 2006 hardly rippled the oasis, given the seismic events up front.

Kagayama, a factor at Losail in 2006, held on to Lanzi's contrails for fourth, while reigning champ Bayliss, the man who had seemed the best bet to draw Biaggi's sting after winter testing, ended a distant fifth.

While others muttered grimly and stared at the data sheets for clues after race one, a lone rider swept in on his white steed to defend the honour of the WSB establishment in the second outing. It was the last one to be put to Biaggi's short sword a few hours earlier – Toseland. The 2004 champion was in an even more resolute mood than had been evident in the opener, leading every lap across the line and preventing a debut double from the rapidly closing Biaggi.

Corser gave the new R1 its first podium, with Haga fourth and Fonsi Nieto scoring a notable fifth, on a Kawasaki that didn't seem to be on the same level as the others as a basic package.

As the ever-present Qatari dust settled, Toseland and Biaggi exited stage centre with a share of the championship lead, and the honour of their teams and manufacturers not merely intact, but dazzlingly burnished.

Round 1
LOSAIL, Qatar
24 February 2007, 3.343-mile/5.380km circuit

Race 1 18 laps, 60.174 miles/96.840km
Dry, Air 25°C Humidity 56% Track 43°C

Pl.	Name Nat. (Machine)	No.	Time & gap	Laps
1	Max Biaggi, ITA (Suzuki)	3	36m 10.115s 99.822mph/160.648km/h	18
2	James Toseland, GBR (Honda)	52	1.483s	18
3	Lorenzo Lanzi, ITA (Ducati)	57	13.906s	18
4	Yukio Kagayama, JPN (Suzuki)	71	14.819s	18
5	Troy Bayliss, AUS (Ducati)	21	17.305s	18
6	Max Neukirchner, GER (Suzuki)	76	24.931s	18
7	Roberto Rolfo, ITA (Honda)	44	25.165s	18
8	Noriyuki Haga, JPN (Yamaha)	41	27.320s	18
9	Troy Corser, AUS (Yamaha)	11	31.237s	18
10	Ruben Xaus, SPA (Ducati)	111	31.669s	18
11	Steve Martin, AUS (Honda)	99	42.355s	18
12	Shinichi Nakatomi, JPN (Yamaha)	38	46.845s	18
13	Alessandro Polita, ITA (Suzuki)	53	59.207s	18
14	Jakub Smrz, CZE (Ducati)	96	1m 00.296s	18
15	Dean Ellison, GBR (Ducati)	42	1m 21.043s	18
16	Christian Zaiser, AUT (MV Agusta)	73	1m 44.306s	18
17	Mashel Al Naimi, QAT (Kawasaki)	95	1 lap	17

DNF: Regis Laconi, FRA (Kawasaki) 55, 11 laps; Fonsi Nieto, SPA (Kawasaki) 10, 11 laps; Joshua Brookes, AUS (Honda) 25, 11 laps; Jiri Drazdak, CZE (Yamaha) 36, 7 laps; Karl Muggeridge, AUS (Honda) 31, 0 laps; Michel Fabrizio, ITA (Honda) 84, 0 laps.

Fastest lap: Biaggi, 1m 59.275s, 100.899mph/162.381km/h (record).

Superpole: Corser, 1m 58.402s, 101.643mph/163.578km/h.

Race 2 18 laps, 60.174 miles/96.840km
Dry, Air 26°C Humidity 44% Track 47°C

Pl.	Name Nat. (Machine)	No.	Time & gap	Laps
1	James Toseland, GBR (Honda)	52	36m 09.433s 99.853mph/160.698km/h	18
2	Max Biaggi, ITA (Suzuki)	3	0.738s	18
3	Troy Corser, AUS (Yamaha)	11	7.386s	18
4	Norikyuki Haga, JPN (Yamaha)	41	14.984s	18
5	Fonsi Nieto, SPA (Kawasaki)	10	15.033s	18
6	Yukio Kagayama, JPN (Suzuki)	71	15.911s	18
7	Lorenzo Lanzi, ITA (Ducati)	57	16.664s	18
8	Troy Bayliss, AUS (Ducati)	21	23.249s	18
9	Ruben Xaus, SPA (Ducati)	111	24.282s	18
10	Max Neukirchner, GER (Suzuki)	76	33.480s	18
11	Regis Laconi, FRA (Kawasaki)	55	34.004s	18
12	Michel Fabrizio, ITA (Honda)	84	37.297s	18
13	Joshua Brookes, AUS (Honda)	25	42.064s	18
14	Karl Muggeridge, AUS (Honda)	31	42.359s	18
15	Alessandro Polita, ITA (Suzuki)	53	46.206s	18
16	Jakub Smrz, CZE (Ducati)	96	46.467s	18
17	Shinichi Nakatomi, JPN (Yamaha)	38	51.300s	18
18	Steve Martin, AUS (Honda)	99	1m 03.411s	18
19	Dean Ellison, GBR (Ducati)	42	1m 42.715s	18
20	Mashel Al Naimi, QAT (Kawasaki)	95	1 lap	17

DNF: Jiri Drazdak, CZE (Yamaha) 36, 6 laps; Roberto Rolfo, ITA (Honda) 44, 0 laps; Christian Zaiser, AUT (MV Agusta) 73, 0 laps.

Fastest lap: Biaggi, 1m 59.194s, 100.967mph/162.491km/h (record).

Lap record: Norikyuki Haga, JPN (Yamaha), 2m 00.061s, 100.238mph/161.318km/h (2006).

Championship points: 1 Biaggi and Toseland, 45; 3 Lanzi, 25; 4 Corser, 23; 5 Kagayama, 23; 6 Haga, 21; 7 Bayliss, 19; 8 Neukirchner, 16; 9 Xaus, 13; 10 Nieto, 11; 11 Rolfo, 9; 12 Laconi and Martin, 5; 14 Fabrizio and Nakatomi, 4.

WORLD SUPERBIKE CHAMPIONSHIP • ROUND 2

PHILLIP ISLAND

AUSTRALIA

Above and right: Touchingly close – James Toseland and Troy Bayliss were so fierce that the Australian collected tyre rubber on his leathers.

Centre right: The lap record was poor consolation for Corser at home.

Centre right, below: Flame-out, but no points for Laconi's Kawasaki.

Top far right: Xaus (111) and Lanzi had a private-v-factory duel in both legs.

Centre far right: Go-kart diversion for (back row, from left) Martin, Brookes, Muggeridge, Parkes, Curtain and Toseland; (front row) Kagayama, Nieto, Bayliss, Corser and Biaggi.

Bottom far right: Haga celebrates his first rostrum of the season.

Photographs: Gold & Goose

ONE weekend and only two-thirds of a world away from Qatar, the Australian round of the championship saw the first Australian winner of the year, when Bayliss took the lead on lap 18 of race one, quickly pushing away from early force of the field Toseland, who in turn was making his 2007 tactics plain for all to see. No espionage needed, clearly he was going to go balls to the tyre wall in every race; few could match his race-long pace anyway.

On this particular weekend, only Bayliss would prove equal to Toseland come race day, and occasionally it was a touchingly close affair. Tyre marks on Bayliss's leathers showed the intensity of the fight between the English usurper and the hometown Aussie battler, but in race one, when Bayliss finally passed a fast starting, but ultimately creatively defensive, Toseland, the contest was simply all over bar the ecstatic local shouting. Toseland hardly gave up; Bayliss, for one, did not expect him to, but the winning margin of two seconds could have been more.

Bayliss, like Biaggi before him in Qatar, was to find Toseland in even more competitive mood in race two, and the Englishman's flinty grit earned him the second race win, after another marvellous late-race holding job.

Outrageous misfortune was waiting to ambush the other Aussie candidate for new Victorian Regent, Corser's rear tyre traction dropping off so badly at the end of the opener that he was losing three seconds per lap at one stage. Things improved in race two, but an eventual pair of fifths felt like no more than 40 per cent of his realistic pre-race expectations. He took home a new lap record, 1m 31.826s, but when you wanted two big trophies, it was no consolation.

Even more galling for Corser was the strong overall performance of his new team-mate, Haga. Fourth in race one, he rode like a battling top to take third in a brilliant triple-header for the last podium slot in the second 22-lap slug-out, behind Toseland and Bayliss. Corser did not even have the pleasure of winning Superpole number 40. The pre-race award went to Bayliss, who took a far from lucky win number 13.

Biaggi lacked the brilliance of Qatar, and Haga won the three-way duel in race two. But Max was hungry enough to get his teeth into the lowest podium step in race one, albeit crossing the line ten seconds from Bayliss.

The 'men-from-boys' nature of this beautiful circuit obviously played a firm, but fair, hand in proceedings, aiding the flight of the top handful, who dropped Lanzi from the podium fights. The second factory equipped Italian was a distant sixth and a lacklustre seventh.

The flowing track has always been good for Ducatis, even if they are seriously outgunned for power, if not always speed, down the straight. This allowed Ruben Xaus to get his nose into the top six, on a bike with top-notch electronics, but with a team that had little experience in using them. Ex-GP rider Xaus made up for the temporary shortfall by beating his race-one nemesis, Lanzi, in race two.

A bizarre timekeeping error at the end spoiled an otherwise impressive day for World Superbike again. Max Neukirchner was credited with the wrong finishing place, and no one in charge of proceedings noticed that the photo-finish picture clearly featured Neukirchner and Lanzi, rather than the quoted Neukirchner and Fabrizio. It transpired (although clearly it didn't transpond) that Fabrizio was just behind, out of shot.

The inglorious muddle was finally sorted, with Lanzi seventh (dead-heated to the thousandth), Neukirchner eighth and Fabrizio ninth. The gap from Lanzi to Neukirchner, only measurable by the photo-finish pic? Three-ten-thousandths of a second. Or 0.0003s, if you like your figures in figures.

Round 2

PHILLIP ISLAND, Australia

4 March 2007, 2.762-mile/4.445km circuit

Race 1 22 laps, 60.764 miles/97.790km
Dry, Air 23°C Humidity 50% Track 37°C

Pl.	Name Nat. (Machine)	No.	Time & gap	Laps
1	Troy Bayliss, AUS (Ducati)	21	34m 11.276s 106.641mph/171.622km/h	22
2	James Toseland, GBR (Honda)	52	2.096s	22
3	Max Biaggi, ITA (Suzuki)	3	10.143s	22
4	Noriyuki Haga, JPN (Yamaha)	41	18.923s	22
5	Troy Corser, AUS (Yamaha)	11	19.742s	22
6	Lorenzo Lanzi, ITA (Ducati)	57	24.765s	22
7	Ruben Xaus, SPA (Ducati)	111	27.404s	22
8	Max Neukirchner, GER (Suzuki)	76	34.614s	22
9	Fonsi Nieto, SPA (Kawasaki)	10	35.339s	22
10	Steve Martin, AUS (Honda)	99	36.238s	22
11	Roberto Rolfo, ITA (Honda)	44	38.067s	22
12	Joshua Brookes, AUS (Honda)	25	47.078s	22
13	Shinichi Nakatomi, JPN (Yamaha)	38	58.571s	22
14	Jakub Smrz, CZE (Ducati)	96	1m 08.000s	22
15	Alessandro Polita, ITA (Suzuki)	53	1m 22.584s	22
16	Christian Zaiser, AUT (MV Agusta)	73	1m 28.374s	22
17	Dean Ellison, GBR (Ducati)	42	1m 30.184s	22
18	Jiri Drazdak, CZE (Yamaha)	36	1 lap	17

DNF: Regis Laconi, FRA (Kawasaki) 55, 16 laps; Michel Fabrizio, ITA (Honda) 84, 5 laps.

Fastest lap: Corser, 1m 31.826s, 108.283mph/174.264km/h (record).

Race 2 22 laps, 60.764 miles/97.790 km
Dry, Air 21°C Humidity 55% Track 40°C

Pl.	Name Nat. (Machine)	No.	Time & gap	Laps
1	James Toseland, GBR (Honda)	52	34m 16.990s 106.345 mph/171.145 km/h	22
2	Troy Bayliss, AUS (Ducati)	21	0.274s	22
3	Noriyuki Haga, JPN (Yamaha)	41	6.916s	22
4	Max Biaggi, ITA (Suzuki)	3	7.013s	22
5	Troy Corser, AUS (Yamaha)	11	7.052s	22
6	Ruben Xaus, SPA (Ducati)	111	23.176s	22
7	Lorenzo Lanzi, ITA (Ducati)	57	26.471s	22
8	Michel Fabrizio, ITA (Honda)	84	26.486s	22
9	Max Neukirchner, GER (Suzuki)	76	26.486s	22
10	Roberto Rolfo, ITA (Honda)	44	37.936s	22
11	Jakub Smrz, CZE (Ducati)	96	41.308s	22
12	Joshua Brookes, AUS (Honda)	25	48.672s	22
13	Shinichi Nakatomi, JPN (Yamaha)	38	48.717s	22
14	Fonsi Nieto, SPA (Kawasaki)	10	1m 13.095s	22
15	Alessandro Polita, ITA (Suzuki)	53	1m 13.882s	22
16	Christian Zaiser, AUT (MV Agusta)	73	1m 17.925s	22

DNF: Dean Ellison, GBR (Ducati) 42, 16 laps; Drazdak, CZE (Yamaha) 36, 6 laps; Steve Martin, AUS (Honda) 99, 1 lap.

Fastest lap: Haga, 1m 32.621s, 107.354mph/172.769km/h.

Superpole: Bayliss, 1m 32.145s, 107.908mph/173.661km/h.

Lap record: Troy Bayliss, AUS (Ducati), 1m 32.402s, 107.608mph/173.178km/h (2006).

Championship points: 1 Toseland, 90; 2 Biaggi, 74; 3 Bayliss, 64; 4 Haga, 50; 5 Corser, 45; 6 Lanzi, 44; 7 Xaus, 32; 8 Neukirchner, 31; 9 Kagayama, 23; 10 Nieto, 20; 11 Rolfo, 20; 12 Fabrizio, 12; 13 Martin, 11; 14 Brookes, 11; 15 Nakatomi, 10.

WORLD SUPERBIKE CHAMPIONSHIP • ROUND 3

DONINGTON PARK

GREAT BRITAIN

Above: Ducati team chief Davide Tardozzi shows sheer dismay as Bayliss crashes out of the lead in race one.

Top: Haga leads the pack into Redgate. Note Toseland (half-hidden), Biaggi (3) and Laconi (55), with Corser (11) between them, and Nieto (10) in pursuit.

Right: First-race winner Toseland soaks up the applause of an appreciative home crowd.

Above centre right: Dean Ellison on his privateer Ducati.

Centre right: Two podiums for Corser, and another lap record. But still no win.

Bottom far right: Toseland sits up and slows as his Honda runs out of sparks.

Photographs: Gold & Goose

Left: Bayliss is helped away from his ruinous and costly Coppice crash.

Below: Race two trio: Xaus (111) will keep Laconi behind him, but Biaggi's yellow Suzuki is coming through.

Below centre: Red-carpet treatment – the Team Italia Yamaha's pristine pit.

Photographs: Gold & Goose

DESPITE an otherwise welcome return to Donington, scene of World Superbike's first ever worldwide production-based playtime in 1988, it's difficult to credit quite how miserable the venue was in late March. It was starkly cold and frequently wet, and perhaps because of those combined factors, riders went down hard and often during practice. Across all the classes, too many hurt themselves on a surface that was still shaking off the grip of winter.

For the uninitiated (it was 2001 when WSB last visited Donington), a favourite place to fall was the fearsome drop down Craner, as riders flicked right and left. The most significant place on race day – April 1st, but nobody was fooling – was Coppice where, during race one, Bayliss fell, trapping his right hand under the handlebar. This ground both knuckles off his little finger, as well as bashing his family jewels injuriously on the fuel tank. He lost not only his finger and the lead, but also any chance of taking part in race two. Alessandro Polita also fell and injured himself in the opener, dislocating his collarbone severely.

The chief benefactor of the Australian's misfortune, even though he was full of public sympathy for his fallen rival, was Toseland, who was the only rider near Bayliss at the time. Thus he took the first Donington race win while the 2001 and 2006 champion was being removed to Derby Royal Infirmary. It was similar to the soothing hometown tonic Bayliss had poured into the grin-soaked Phillip Island crowds during Round Two, but on this occasion the Union Jack occupied all of the flag that was hoisted highest towards the jets passing overhead from nearby East Midlands Airport.

On either side of Toseland's Union Jack was Corser's Southern Cross and the *tricolore* of Max Biaggi's native Italy. Corser was 1.3s behind, Biaggi another second or so back, with Haga fourth and Lanzi fifth.

Haga did not rank Donington highest on his list of all-time favourite circuits, but he probably should have, as he followed what could be considered an unlucky fourth in race one (having chosen a tyre that took a while to warm up) with a win in the second 23-lap freezathon. The race was held in positively balmy ambient conditions of 13°C, rather than the first race's barmy nine degrees.

The manner of Haga's win, Biaggi being second by only 0.111s, was pleasing, as the pair battled it out right to the frequently portentous last corner, Goddards. When Biaggi ran wide, Haga had it, with the ever close Corser just a second from what was proving to be an elusive first 2007 victory.

But what of the local hero? Toseland had already taken his first and last finish of the day when his bike – leading at the time – ran out of sparks on lap four. Originally, his quick shifter was blamed, but whatever the real cause, he left Donington with a minor dent in his championship lead, if still no double win in his SBK career.

The second race proved the worth of Xaus, who was as high as any rational person would expect him to be at this early stage, fourth.

Donington was a welcome sight for all, especially now that some of its Second World War supply depot 'charm' has been replaced by modernist industrial units, which at least fit the current millennium. The track's pit-lane make-over doesn't quite make it Monza or Assen, but with British fans in surprisingly dense numbers in spite of the weather, and a superb layout for bikes of any kind, it was good for everyone to be back racing WSB at the GP track again. For all except Bayliss and Polita, we can surmise.

Round 3
DONINGTON PARK, Great Britain
1 April 2007, 2.500-mile/4.023km circuit

Race 1 23 laps, 57.500 miles/92.529km
Dry, Air 9°C Humidity 68% Track 15°C

Pl.	Name Nat. (Machine)	No.	Time & gap	Laps
1	James Toseland, GBR (Honda)	52	35m 28.222s 97.256mph/156.518km/h	23
2	Troy Corser, AUS (Yamaha)	11	1.368s	23
3	Max Biaggi, ITA (Suzuki)	3	2.448s	23
4	Noriyuki Haga, JPN (Yamaha)	41	9.249s	23
5	Lorenzo Lanzi, ITA (Ducati)	57	18.028s	23
6	Fonsi Nieto, SPA (Kawasaki)	10	18.956s	23
7	Regis Laconi, FRA (Kawasaki)	55	29.998s	23
8	Max Neukirchner, GER (Suzuki)	76	30.296s	23
9	Roberto Rolfo, ITA (Honda)	44	30.525s	23
10	Jakub Smrz, CZE (Ducati)	96	36.661s	23
11	Karl Muggeridge, AUS (Honda)	31	39.389s	23
12	Joshua Brookes, AUS (Honda)	25	48.045s	23
13	Michel Fabrizio, ITA (Honda)	84	51.290s	23
14	Giovanni Bussei, ITA (Ducati)	159	51.402s	23
15	Dean Ellison, GBR (Ducati)	42	1m 00.156s	23
16	Luca Morelli, ITA (Ducati)	22	1 lap	22
17	Shinichi Nakatomi, JPN (Yamaha)	38	1 lap	22
18	Aaron Zanotti, GBR (Yamaha)	64	1 lap	22
19	Steve Martin, AUS (Honda)	99	5 laps	18

DNF: Ruben Xaus, SPA (Ducati) 111, 21 laps; Christian Zaiser, AUT (MV Agusta) 73, 11 laps; Alessandro Polita, ITA (Suzuki) 53, 10 laps; Troy Bayliss, AUS (Ducati) 21, 5 laps.

Fastest lap: Bayliss, 1m 31.575s, 98.271mph/158.152km/h (record).

Race 2 23 laps, 57.500 miles/92.529km
Dry, Air 13°C Humidity 55% Track 21°C

Pl.	Name Nat. (Machine)	No.	Time & gap	Laps
1	Noriyuki Haga, JPN (Yamaha)	41	35m 26.734s 97.324mph/156.627km/h	23
2	Max Biaggi, ITA (Suzuki)	3	0.111s	23
3	Troy Corser, AUS (Yamaha)	11	1.100s	23
4	Ruben Xaus, SPA (Ducati)	111	5.927s	23
5	Lorenzo Lanzi, ITA (Ducati)	57	9.834s	23
6	Regis Laconi, FRA (Kawasaki)	55	12.203s	23
7	Roberto Rolfo, ITA (Honda)	44	22.287s	23
8	Jakub Smrz, CZE (Ducati)	96	30.060s	23
9	Karl Muggeridge, AUS (Honda)	31	37.734s	23
10	Max Neukirchner, GER (Suzuki)	76	39.893s	23
11	Giovanni Bussei, ITA (Ducati)	159	41.524s	23
12	Michel Fabrizio, ITA (Honda)	84	45.617s	23
13	Steve Martin, AUS (Honda)	99	52.547s	23
14	Shinichi Nakatomi, JPN (Yamaha)	38	1m 01.669s	23
15	Joshua Brookes, AUS (Honda)	25	1m 20.586s	23
16	Aaron Zanotti, GBR (Yamaha)	64	1m 26.912s	23
17	Luca Morelli, ITA (Ducati)	22	1m 27.181s	23

DNF: Fonsi Nieto, SPA (Kawasaki) 10, 11 laps; Dean Ellison, GBR (Ducati) 42, 7 laps; James Toseland, GBR (Honda) 52, 3 laps; Christian Zaiser, AUT (MV Agusta) 73, 0 laps.

DNS: Troy Bayliss, AUS (Ducati) 21; Alessandro Polita, ITA (Suzuki) 53.

Fastest lap: Haga, 1m 31.634s, 98.208mph/158.051km/h.

Superpole: Bayliss, 1m 30.370s, 99.582mph/160.261km/h.

Lap record: Troy Corser, AUS (Ducati), 1m 33.470s, 96.281mph/154.950km/h (1996).

Championship points: 1 Toseland, 115; 2 Biaggi, 110; 3 Haga, 88; 4 Corser, 81; 5 Lanzi, 66; 6 Bayliss, 64; 7 Neukirchner, 46; 8 Xaus, 45; 9 Rolfo, 36; 10 Nieto, 30; 11 Laconi, 24; 12 Kagayama, 23; 13 Smrz, 23; 14 Fabrizio, 18; 15 Brookes, 16.

WORLD SUPERBIKE CHAMPIONSHIP • ROUND 4

VALENCIA

SPAIN

Above: Surprise winner Xaus shows Haga he is not to be intimidated.

Right: Toseland claimed a single win for a fourth meeting in a row.

Centre right: Haga leads a sliding Toseland, with Biaggi barely visible behind him.

Below right: Fabrizio made an impression on his privateer Honda.

Opposite page, from top: Bayliss was part of one finger lighter, and back on the rostrum; Brookes fights for control of his wayward Honda; Xaus gave a small Spanish crowd something to celebrate.

Photographs: Gold & Goose

Valencia had become comfortable as the first WSB round in Europe after the long-hauls. Now displaced, it went into an occasional weather induced sulk. The first race of the day was run in largely dry conditions, albeit punctuated by occasional damp patches; even so, the 2003 lap record was still scared, although not quite to death.

The weather further reduced the crowd in what remains the hardest market for World Superbike, but every Spaniard who stayed in bed, instead of choosing from a vast array of available viewing options trackside, would have reason to regret his lazy lie-in.

Xaus chose his home round to prove that his 2006-spec factory Ducati was able to win (eventually, in convincing fashion), and also to show quite categorically that his team now knew how to get the best out of both bike and rider, not to mention their new full-time electronics engineer from Ducati.

Race one had four potential winners at one stage, until Xaus broke the challenge of eventual second-placed Haga. It was processional towards the end, but nonetheless it was a regal procession for Sterilgarda's very own prince of multi-lingual popularity. Xaus ran fourth in race two, underlining his return to the top flight.

The reigning King of Superbike also went well. Remarkably for a rider who had arrived in Spain with one less digit than at Donington, and who had been lucky not to lose a testicle, Bayliss was a convincing third in race one.

Riding with a stump for a right pinkie and a protective cricket box over his still delicate groin, Bayliss was sixth in race two because of a less-than-ideal shift in set-up, but considering all his recent misadventures, leaving Spain with 26 points was more than many had imagined possible. He even won Superpole (for the third weekend in a row), bringing the fleeting possibility of a repeat of his MotoGP race win here, the ghost of which lingered for all who had witnessed the seemingly impossible at first hand in October 2006.

After Toseland's machinery machinations at Donington, a tyre that had spun on the rim held him back in fifth in race one at Valencia. He made up for it with a superb win in race two, after a close battle right to the end of the 23 laps.

It was a thriller at the beginning, and even though the contest for the win saw four riders drop off the final pace, Toseland only just fought off the charge of Biaggi and Haga. The leading four-cylinder contenders crossed the line within 0.375s. At one time, Valencia had been the ultimate twins' circuit, but in 2007, the fours showed that good electronics and a sharp set-up more than allowed them to challenge, despite the track surface not being perfect.

Some of the fours' horsemen were still in bother, however. Once more, Corser was blighted, being fourth in the opener after leading with conviction for a time; then he slipped to ninth in race two, complaining about his rear tyre.

Xaus's success was difficult for the other big-name Superbike Spaniard to take. In fact, Valencia was somewhat disastrous all round for Nieto, who scored not a single point. His bike was 'unridable' because of poor set-up in race one, while a bad choice of tyre caused him to tumble during race two. The Kawasaki guys always knew that they would have a struggle at Valencia, after Nieto was 14th and Laconi 15th in Superpole. That made Laconi's second-race eighth seem a decent result.

To summarise: Rain in Spain. Local gain in Spain.

Round 4
VALENCIA, Spain
15 April 2007, 2.489-mile/4.005km circuit

Race 1 23 laps, 57.247 miles/92.115km
Dry, Air 17°C Humidity 70% Track 17°C

Pl.	Name Nat. (Machine)	No.	Time & gap	Laps
1	Ruben Xaus, SPA (Ducati)	111	37m 14.606s 92.211mph/148.399km/h	23
2	Noriyuki Haga, JPN (Yamaha)	41	1.997s	23
3	Troy Bayliss, AUS (Ducati)	21	6.330s	23
4	Troy Corser, AUS (Yamaha)	11	8.780s	23
5	James Toseland, GBR (Honda)	52	17.040s	23
6	Lorenzo Lanzi, ITA (Ducati)	57	24.272s	23
7	Michel Fabrizio, ITA (Honda)	84	25.822s	23
8	Max Biaggi, ITA (Suzuki)	3	26.087s	23
9	Joshua Brookes, AUS (Honda)	25	28.778s	23
10	Roberto Rolfo, ITA (Honda)	44	32.754s	23
11	Regis Laconi, FRA (Kawasaki)	55	37.084s	23
12	Max Neukirchner, GER (Suzuki)	76	37.141s	23
13	Giovanni Bussei, ITA (Ducati)	159	37.563s	23
14	Jakub Smrz, CZE (Ducati)	96	38.544s	23
15	Yukio Kagayama, JPN (Suzuki)	71	53.049s	23

DNF: Shinichi Nakatomi, JPN (Yamaha) 38, 17 laps; Karl Muggeridge, AUS (Honda) 31, 12 laps; Carmelo Morales, SPA (Yamaha) 131, 12 laps; Luca Morelli, ITA (Ducati) 22, 11 laps; Fonsi Nieto, SPA (Kawasaki) 10, 10 laps; Steve Martin, AUS (Honda) 99, 8 laps; Christian Zaiser, AUT (MV Agusta) 73, 3 laps; Dean Ellison, GBR (Ducati) 42, 3 laps.

Fastest lap: Bayliss, 1m 36.092s, 93.233mph/150.044km/h.

Race 2 23 laps, 57.247 miles/92.115km
Dry, Air 19°C Humidity 50% Track 23°C

Pl.	Name Nat. (Machine)	No.	Time & gap	Laps
1	James Toseland, GBR (Honda)	52	37m 02.596s 92.709mph/149.201km/h	23
2	Max Biaggi, ITA (Suzuki)	3	0.287s	23
3	Noriyuki Haga, JPN (Yamaha)	41	0.375s	23
4	Ruben Xaus, SPA (Ducati)	111	6.637s	23
5	Lorenzo Lanzi, ITA (Ducati)	57	7.991s	23
6	Troy Bayliss, AUS (Ducati)	21	10.210s	23
7	Joshua Brookes, AUS (Honda)	25	10.861s	23
8	Regis Laconi, FRA (Kawasaki)	55	14.366s	23
9	Troy Corser, AUS (Yamaha)	11	15.511s	23
10	Max Neukirchner, GER (Suzuki)	76	19.716s	23
11	Michel Fabrizio, ITA (Honda)	84	25.287s	23
12	Roberto Rolfo, ITA (Honda)	44	26.437s	23
13	Yukio Kagayama, JPN (Suzuki)	71	34.992s	23
14	Carmelo Morales, SPA (Yamaha)	131	39.987s	23
15	Giovanni Bussei, ITA (Ducati)	159	42.445s	23
16	Shinichi Nakatomi, JPN (Yamaha)	38	43.467s	23
17	Jakub Smrz, CZE (Ducati)	96	1m 08.350s	23

DNF: Luca Morelli, ITA (Ducati) 22, 16 laps; Fonsi Nieto, SPA (Kawasaki) 10, 16 laps; Steve Martin, AUS (Honda) 99, 13 laps; Dean Ellison, GBR (Ducati) 42, 12 laps; Christian Zaiser, AUT (MV Agusta) 73, 7 laps; Karl Muggeridge, AUS (Honda) 31, 0 laps.

Fastest lap: Haga, 1m 35.746s, 93.570mph/150.586km/h.

Superpole: Bayliss, 1m 51.982s, 80.003mph/128.753km/h.

Lap record: Neil Hodgson, GBR (Ducati), 1m 35.007s, 94.297mph/151.757km/h (2003).

Championship points: 1 Toseland, 151; 2 Biaggi, 138; 3 Haga, 124; 4 Corser, 101; 5 Bayliss, 90; 6 Lanzi, 87; 7 Xaus, 83; 8 Neukirchner, 56; 9 Rolfo, 46; 10 Laconi, 37; 11 Fabrizio, 32; 12 Brookes, 32; 13 Nieto, 30; 14 Kagayama, 27; 15 Smrz, 25.

WORLD SUPERBIKE CHAMPIONSHIP • ROUND 5

ASSEN

NETHERLANDS

Left: Eventual winner by inches, Bayliss heads Toseland in race two.

Below: The championship leader kept his record – a win in every round.

Photographs: Gold & Goose

Above: Rolfo heads Neukirchner and Fabrizio in a strong battle for fifth.

Left: Biaggi made up for a disappointing first race with champagne in the second.

Far left: Corser led Bayliss in race one, but would crash out near the end.

Photographs: Gold & Goose

ASSEN may only have some of its sabre-toothed fast swings and kinks left from the golden ages of its many previous incarnations, but the last few corners are still distinctly, uniquely, Assenesque. The last chicane has been a particular catalyst in many a memorable SBK race, and so it would prove once more.

No prizes for knowing which crew was under most pressure during the run-up to the Assen race weekend – Hannspree Ten Kate Honda. Bizarre in some ways, what with Toseland still leading, not to mention having won a race at every previous round, but the air of expectation had become heavy, despite the fine weather in practice. Air temperature of 27°C on Friday? In May? In the northern Netherlands? We must have missed the turn for Assen and arrived in Misano by accident.

Toseland did not disappoint pre-race, scoring the Superpole win after strong showings in all sessions. It was all the more impressive because his team-mate, Rolfo, was still languishing, barely in the fight for the top ten.

A relatively cool race one ended up in a straight fight between Toseland and Haga, with some tough passes and extravagant overtaking. Toseland toughed it out to win by 0.6s, once more besting a rider he had been battling for championship placings for seasons. Xaus was eventually three seconds down, in a lonely third. Clearly, Valencia was no flash in the pan for Ruben, who had started from row two.

Bayliss, still recovering, but still fast, was fourth, two seconds up on Lanzi and Biaggi, having started from the front row in third, alongside his team-mate.

Max was finding the week-in/week-out grind of Superbike racing not as straightforward as might have been expected after his victory in Qatar, but like Bayliss, he would be glad of the SBK format, which offers a second race each day to recover composure and points. Corser was similarly grateful for a second bite, as he went out after falling on lap 21. But he climbed on to his spare R1 to record fourth in race two.

The fire in Toseland's belly was stoked by the knowledge that he had never scored a double race win in SBK racing. After he led on the exit of the final fateful chicane, overhauling long-term leader Bayliss firmly to do so, he was a cast-iron certainty for two wins in one day.

Although Toseland denied it afterwards, it looked like he pulled a celebratory wheelie a tad too early on the exit, allowing Bayliss, ever a monster of competitiveness, to sneak inside and steal the win by only nine-thousandths of a second. Hardly a disaster in the grand scheme for Toseland, but certainly careless – even if his wheelie had been inadvertent.

Biaggi put his personal redemption of championship points back on track a little, finishing third and lonely, with Corser five seconds behind him.

It was particularly pleasing for Rolfo to be fifth, at the head of a quarrelling pack of four hard-case riders, Fabrizio, Neukirchner and Nieto crossing the line within 1.1s of a rejuvenated Roby.

Haga was particularly upset, understandably, his Assen jinx having struck again in race two, especially when it wasn't his fault this time. He had worked his way through from 15th on the grid in each race, all after crashing at high speed in Superpole.

Nearly all of the top championship contenders got a taste of champagne at some stage, slurring the predictions of the final-placing soothsayers, with one notable exception. Once more, Toseland had stretched his lead, despite his last-corner loss of concentration. Behind, things were going from close to squeaking, as Bayliss appeared on the top-four radar again, at the expense of Corser and Lanzi.

Round 5
ASSEN, Holland
29 April 2007, 2.830-mile/4.555km circuit

Race 1 22 laps, 62.260 miles/100.210km
Dry, Air 17°C Humidity 33% Track 25°C

Pl.	Name Nat. (Machine)	No.	Time & gap	Laps
1	James Toseland, GBR (Honda)	52	37m 02.097s 100.879mph/162.349km/h	22
2	Noriyuki Haga, JPN (Yamaha)	41	0.663s	22
3	Ruben Xaus, SPA (Ducati)	111	3.698s	22
4	Troy Bayliss, AUS (Ducati)	21	7.134s	22
5	Lorenzo Lanzi, ITA (Ducati)	57	9.312s	22
6	Max Biaggi, ITA (Suzuki)	3	9.534s	22
7	Yukio Kagayama, JPN (Suzuki)	71	18.286s	22
8	Fonsi Nieto, SPA (Kawasaki)	10	18.403s	22
9	Roberto Rolfo, ITA (Honda)	44	19.873s	22
10	Max Neukirchner, GER (Suzuki)	76	22.914s	22
11	Jakub Smrz, CZE (Ducati)	96	29.602s	22
12	Michel Fabrizio, ITA (Honda)	84	40.961s	22
13	Shinichi Nakatomi, JPN (Yamaha)	38	41.008s	22
14	Dean Ellison, GBR (Ducati)	42	1m 12.714s	22
15	Marek Svoboda, CZE (Yamaha)	85	2 laps	20
16	Regis Laconi, FRA (Kawasaki)	55	2 laps	20

DNF: Troy Corser, AUS (Yamaha) 11, 20 laps; Karl Muggeridge, AUS (Honda) 31, 10 laps; Joshua Brookes, AUS (Honda) 25, 8 laps; Luca Morelli, ITA (Ducati) 22, 0 laps; Christian Zaiser, AUT (MV Agusta) 73, 0 laps.

Fastest lap: Bayliss, 1m 39.906s, 101.988mph/164.134km/h (record).

Race 2 22 laps, 62.260 miles/100.210km
Dry, Air 21°C Humidity 26% Track 34°C

Pl.	Name Nat. (Machine)	No.	Time & gap	Laps
1	Troy Bayliss, AUS (Ducati)	21	36m 54.133s 101.242mph/162.933km/h	22
2	James Toseland, GBR (Honda)	52	0.009s	22
3	Max Biaggi, ITA (Suzuki)	3	7.439s	22
4	Troy Corser, AUS (Yamaha)	11	12.379s	22
5	Roberto Rolfo, ITA (Honda)	44	23.052s	22
6	Michel Fabrizio, ITA (Honda)	84	23.158s	22
7	Max Neukirchner, GER (Suzuki)	76	23.311s	22
8	Fonsi Nieto, SPA (Kawasaki)	10	24.147s	22
9	Jakub Smrz, CZE (Ducati)	96	29.660s	22
10	Regis Laconi, FRA (Kawasaki)	55	32.301s	22
11	Yukio Kagayama, JPN (Suzuki)	71	32.389s	22
12	Shinichi Nakatomi, JPN (Yamaha)	38	39.091s	22
13	Joshua Brookes, AUS (Honda)	25	39.128s	22
14	Luca Morelli, ITA (Ducati)	22	1 lap	21
15	Marek Svoboda, CZE (Yamaha)	85	1 lap	21
16	Dean Ellison, GBR (Ducati)	42	3 laps	19

DNF: Lorenzo Lanzi, ITA (Ducati) 57, 18 laps; Karl Muggeridge, AUS (Honda) 31, 16 laps; Noriyuki Haga, JPN (Yamaha) 41, 10 laps; Ruben Xaus, SPA (Ducati) 111, 3 laps.

DNS: Christian Zaiser, AUT (MV Agusta) 73.

Fastest lap: Haga, 1m 39.770s, 102.127mph/164.358km/h (record).

Superpole: Toseland, 1m 38.603s, 103.336mph/166.303km/h.

Lap record: Troy Bayliss, AUS (Ducati), 1m 40.767s, 101.117mph/162.732km/h (2006).

Championship points: 1 Toseland, 196; 2 Biaggi, 164; 3 Haga, 144; 4 Bayliss, 128; 5 Corser, 114; 6 Xaus, 99; 7 Lanzi, 98; 8 Neukirchner, 71; 9 Rolfo, 64; 10 Nieto, 46; 11 Fabrizio, 46; 12 Laconi, 43; 13 Kagayama, 41; 14 Smrz, 37; 15 Brookes, 35.

WORLD SUPERBIKE CHAMPIONSHIP • ROUND 6

MONZA

ITALY

Above: Bayliss had managed to shake off Biaggi by the finish of race one.

Left: Before the event, title rivals Bayliss and Toseland posed back to back. By the end of the weekend, the man on the left would have been Haga.

Opposite page: Masked marvel Haga used all his superpowers to claim the year's first double.

Below: Rolfo and Corser get serious in a fight over the same piece of tarmac.

Bottom: Umbrella girls were on hand for any emergency.

Photographs: Gold & Goose

SOMETHING remarkable happened at Monza, and it all revolved around the new threat to Toseland's half-season supremacy, Haga. At his team's home race, Haga completed the double that Toseland had not quite made secure at Assen, the first rider to double up in the season. It was an utterly convincing performance from the Japanese rider, who had taken only his fourth ever Superpole on Saturday afternoon, with a new track best of 1m 44.941s.

Something even more remarkable had happened earlier that day, at the end of the official qualifying sessions. Eleven-times World Superbike race winner Laconi had manhandled his fast, but flighty, Kawasaki around Monza quicker than anyone in official pre-Superpole qualifying. It was a short fairy tale, however, as he was seventh in Superpole, and he would only finish eighth in race two, after taking a DNF in race one.

At the healthier end of the final-results sheets, Haga's winning margins of eight seconds in race one, and two seconds in race two were emphatic enough. Only Bayliss would join him on the podium more than once.

The Aussie capitalised on a problem for Toseland in race one, the English rider having gone for the softest, 200mm-section Monza special rears, against advice from Pirelli. His aggressive choice worked well until the tyre started to lose rubber from the crown, allowing Toseland to slide inexorably back to fourth.

In the first race, Hannspree Ten Kate Honda was in bother all round, Toseland being almost out of gas over the line, and Rolfo's best ride since joining SBK in 2006 ending because of a fuel problem on the last lap. He had been lying second at the time, after a superb race filled with aggression and élan. With Bayliss second, there was still going to be a local rider on the podium, Max Biaggi, dressed in muscle-painted red leathers, designed to cut through the air with great efficiency. He was fast enough to stick with Bayliss, after the Aussie's run-through from eighth on lap one. Bayliss finished in Toseland's slipstream in race two, the latter suddenly discovering that Haga was his closest challenger in the overall points table.

Sixth on lap one, Haga had also beaten Biaggi's race-one lap record, hitting the front on lap seven after setting a stunning 1m 46.064s.

Monza presented the riders with the highest top speeds of the season, easily so since Hockenheim has become a distant memory. Haga averaged 198km/h in Superpole, but in terms of sheer top speed, the 200mph barrier had been busted open for the first time in SBK history.

Michel Fabrizio was the unlikely high-velocity stacker, on an even more unlikely privateer Honda DFX Corse machine. Nonetheless, they hit 322.7km/h (200.5mph) in race trim. Xaus and Bayliss were also over 320km/h at some stages, showing the importance of the 999 Ducati's skinny, low-drag design.

In the off-podium dust-ups, race one saw Corser fifth, just ahead of the otherwise largely invisible 2007 version of Kagayama. Four riders flogged around the last lap in a position to take a podium in race two, and such was the vehemence of the last-lap push that Biaggi's clutch lever was pinged off by Bayliss after contact on the way out of Ascari, when Biaggi had run wide and swept back across the track to recover position. Max only found out that he was clutchless on the approach to the Parabolica; it put him off enough to lose his ideal line and finish fifth, yet still less than a second away from Toseland. The Englishman was also experiencing a slight problem with a warped brake disc and a slipper-clutch issue. Bayliss was third, with Rolfo agonisingly close to the last podium step, only losing out by 0.3s.

Round 6
MONZA, Italy
13 May 2007, 3.600-mile/5.793km circuit

Race 1 18 laps, 64.800 miles/104.274km
Dry, Air 26°C Humidity 57% Track 36°C

Pl.	Name Nat. (Machine)	No.	Time & gap	Laps
1	Noriyuki Haga, JPN (Yamaha)	41	32m 04.428s	18
			121.207mph/195.064km/h	
2	Troy Bayliss, AUS (Ducati)	21	8.403s	18
3	Max Biaggi, ITA (Suzuki)	3	9.703s	18
4	James Toseland, GBR (Honda)	52	13.587s	18
5	Troy Corser, AUS (Yamaha)	11	14.898s	18
6	Yukio Kagayama, JPN (Suzuki)	71	14.954s	18
7	Lorenzo Lanzi, ITA (Ducati)	57	19.517s	18
8	Michel Fabrizio, ITA (Honda)	84	24.120s	18
9	Karl Muggeridge, AUS (Honda)	31	24.682s	18
10	Max Neukirchner, GER (Suzuki)	76	29.197s	18
11	Joshua Brookes, AUS (Honda)	25	32.654s	18
12	Ruben Xaus, SPA (Ducati)	111	34.054s	18
13	Marco Borciani, ITA (Ducati)	20	37.386s	18
14	Alessandro Polita, ITA (Suzuki)	53	37.704s	18
15	Jakub Smrz, CZE (Ducati)	96	41.377s	18
16	Steve Martin, AUS (Honda)	99	42.730s	18
17	Mauro Sanchini, ITA (Kawasaki)	92	59.096s	18

DNF: Roberto Rolfo, ITA (Honda) 44, 17 laps; Regis Laconi, FRA (Kawasaki) 55, 15 laps; Luca Morelli, ITA (Ducati) 22, 12 laps; Robertino Pietri, ITA (Yamaha) 40, 12 laps; Marek Svoboda, CZE (Yamaha) 85, 11 laps; Dean Ellison, GBR (Ducati) 42, 8 laps; Fonsi Nieto, SPA (Kawasaki) 10, 7 laps.

Fastest lap: Biaggi, 1m 46.172s, 122.053mph/196.425km/h (record).

Race 2 18 laps, 64.800 miles/104.274km
Dry, Air 28°C Humidity 40% Track 44°C

Pl.	Name Nat. (Machine)	No.	Time & gap	Laps
1	Noriyuki Haga, JPN (Yamaha)	41	32m 05.318s	18
			121.151mph/194.974km/h	
2	James Toseland, GBR (Honda)	52	2.691s	18
3	Troy Bayliss, AUS (Ducati)	21	2.841s	18
4	Roberto Rolfo, ITA (Honda)	44	3.188s	18
5	Max Biaggi, ITA (Suzuki)	3	3.551s	18
6	Troy Corser, AUS (Yamaha)	11	13.034s	18
7	Yukio Kagayama, JPN (Suzuki)	71	17.246s	18
8	Regis Laconi, FRA (Kawasaki)	55	18.410s	18
9	Karl Muggeridge, AUS (Honda)	31	29.017s	18
10	Jakub Smrz, CZE (Ducati)	96	29.686s	18
11	Michel Fabrizio, ITA (Honda)	84	30.371s	18
12	Max Neukirchner, GER (Suzuki)	76	31.982s	18
13	Ruben Xaus, SPA (Ducati)	111	32.165s	18
14	Robertino Pietri, ITA (Yamaha)	40	1m 32.292s	18
15	Dean Ellison, GBR (Ducati)	42	1m 41.840s	18

DNF: Marco Borciani, ITA (Ducati) 20, 15 laps; Steve Martin, AUS (Honda) 99, 11 laps; Joshua Brookes, AUS (Honda) 25, 9 laps; Mauro Sanchini, ITA (Kawasaki) 92, 7 laps; Alessandro Polita, ITA (Suzuki) 53, 5 laps; Marek Svoboda, CZE (Yamaha) 85, 1 lap; Fonsi Nieto, SPA (Kawasaki) 10, 1 lap; Lorenzo Lanzi, ITA (Ducati) 57, 0 laps.

DNS: Luca Morelli, ITA (Ducati) 22.

Fastest lap: Haga, 1m 46.064s, 122.177mph/196.625km/h (record).

Superpole: Haga, 1m 44.941s, 123.484mph/198.729km/h.

Lap record: Troy Bayliss, AUS (Ducati), 1m 46.815s, 121.318mph/195.242km/h (2006).

Championship points: 1 Toseland, 229; 2 Haga, 194; 3 Biaggi, 191; 4 Bayliss, 164; 5 Corser, 135; 6 Lanzi, 107; 7 Xaus, 106; 8 Neukirchner, 81; 9 Rolfo, 77; 10 Kagayama, 60; 11 Fabrizio, 59; 12 Laconi, 51; 13 Nieto, 46; 14 Smrz, 44; 15 Brookes, 40.

WORLD SUPERBIKE CHAMPIONSHIP • ROUND 7

SILVERSTONE

GREAT BRITAIN

Above: Above: Sam and son – the rest of the Corser family.

Top: It was raining stair-rods for the only start of the day. Biaggi, Lanzi, Toseland, Haga and Bayliss fan out for Copse Corner.

Right: Crash-recovery man Toseland took an inadvertently air-cooled Honda from 18th to eighth.

Photographs: Gold & Goose

Below: Having narrowly survived a high-side moment, Max was never a factor.

Below centre: Lanzi sees off a splashy challenge from Xaus.

Bottom: Heated debate – SBK men Paolo Flammini and Paolo Ciabatti (ex-Ducati), and Yamaha's Davide Tardozzi, before the cancellation of race two.

Bottom right: Where are they? Winner Bayliss looks for any signs of pursuit.

Photographs: Gold & Goose

IT wouldn't have been England without rain at some stage. Just as Donington had shivered in the cold in March, Silverstone eventually disappeared under a deluge of malevolence from the rain gods.

It all had started so well: Thursday's event launch helped along by an aerobatic display, riders such as Bayliss and Corser merrily strapped into tandem stunt planes before looping loops at a nearby airfield. But for the first qualifying session, the weather had turned up, and it started wet. All the same, it finished dry enough for Haga to score a new track best lap in the class.

On day two, it was almost pleasantly dry, with track temperatures that were good enough for a new absolute track best from Bayliss in Superpole. His 1m 24.558s was a whopping 1.7s faster than 2006.

Race day's incessant rain slaughtered any illusion of an English summer, and all the good work from dry qualifying was scrapped. Everyone had to start again from scratch in the 20-minute morning warm-up session.

Fabrizio was fastest, but little good it did him, as he was the first rider to crash out of the race. With standing water at some corner apexes and no end to the rain in sight, many felt that there wouldn't be a race at all, but the first full 28-lapper started bang on time.

Bayliss is a man who likes rain, and with a series of Silverstone wet dramas under his belt already, he took an early lead, from Corser and Haga, Toseland in fourth. Until lap three that is, when Toseland fell down – and seemingly out, after his engine's coolant was clearly caught on camera being pumped out. His problems continued, as his clip-on had been bent and come loose, causing him problems for the rest of the race. His restart ended in eighth (it was a miracle that his engine lasted with no water), after working his way back through from 18th. He was still lapped by everyone down to seventh.

A strange day indeed; it would be a short one too.

For the most part, the top men still in the race kept it wheels down, Corser and Bayliss swapping the lead until the latter picked up and ran to a clear margin of victory of just over two seconds. Not from Corser, but from Haga, who was two seconds clear of his Aussie team-mate.

Ten Kate's day was almost saved by Rolfo, who scored an equal career best in fourth, albeit a monstrous 50 seconds from Bayliss.

Laconi, another recognised rain dancer, could not match Walker's wet-weather Kawasaki win from Assen in 2006, and went fifth, while Biaggi was an unhappy sixth, having suffered a near highside so bad that when he landed back on his Suzuki, he broke his foot peg with the inside of his rapidly descending lower leg. Pained, he carried on nonetheless, on a day when that was pretty much all anyone could do.

Lanzi was seventh, with Toseland behind. Xaus was another crasher and restarter, while Neukirchner held off the warring Italian factions of Vittorio Iannuzzo (the weekend's third PSG-1 rider, for some never quite explained reason) and Luca Morelli (paying for the DFX Honda ride that Steve Martin lost due to lack of sponsorship).

With the rains hardly abating through the day, a track surface with all the drainage properties of a brand-new bucket, and a redoubling of the rainfall shortly before race two, the start of the second drenching was delayed. The track was inspected and re-inspected, the race cut to 20 laps, the start delayed yet again...until, finally, sense and the advance of time prevailed – race two was aborted. It was an unpopular move for some, but it was based on safety first. Never a priority to be criticised too seriously.

Round 7

SILVERSTONE, Great Britain

27 May 2007, 2.213-mile/3.561km circuit

Race 1 28 laps, 61.964 miles/99.708km

Wet, Air 10°C Humidity 95% Track 12°C

Pl.	Name Nat. (Machine)	No.	Time & gap	Laps
1	Troy Bayliss, AUS (Ducati)	21	46m 02.875s 80.728mph/129.919km/h	28
2	Noriyuki Haga, JPN (Yamaha)	41	2.035s	28
3	Troy Corser, AUS (Yamaha)	11	4.568s	28
4	Roberto Rolfo, ITA (Honda)	44	50.039s	28
5	Regis Laconi, FRA (Kawasaki)	55	1m 09.634s	28
6	Max Biaggi, ITA (Suzuki)	3	1m 20.982s	28
7	Lorenzo Lanzi, ITA (Ducati)	57	1m 33.061s	28
8	James Toseland, GBR (Honda)	52	1 lap	27
9	Ruben Xaus, SPA (Ducati)	111	1 lap	27
10	Max Neukirchner, GER (Suzuki)	76	1 lap	27
11	Vittorio Iannuzzo, ITA (Kawasaki)	13	1 lap	27
12	Luca Morelli, ITA (Honda)	22	1 lap	27
13	Shinichi Nakatomi, JPN (Yamaha)	38	2 laps	26

DNF: Fonsi Nieto, SPA (Kawasaki) 10, 21 laps; Yukio Kagayama, JPN (Suzuki) 71, 20 laps; Jakub Smrz, CZE (Ducati) 96, 17 laps; Joshua Brookes, AUS (Honda) 25, 13 laps; Alessandro Polita, ITA (Suzuki) 53, 12 laps; Dean Ellison, GBR (Ducati) 42, 6 laps; Karl Muggeridge, AUS (Honda) 31, 1 lap; Michel Fabrizio, ITA (Honda) 84, 0 laps.

Fastest lap: Haga, 1m 37.005s, 82.117mph/132.154km/h.

Race 2

Cancelled due to extreme weather conditions.

Superpole: Bayliss, 1m 24.558s, 94.204mph/151.607km/h.

Lap record: Troy Bayliss, AUS (Ducati), 1m 26.299s, 92.304mph/148.549km/h (2006).

Championship points: 1 Toseland, 237; 2 Haga, 214; 3 Biaggi, 201; 4 Bayliss, 189; 5 Corser, 151; 6 Lanzi, 116; 7 Xaus, 113; 8 Rolfo, 90; 9 Neukirchner, 87; 10 Laconi, 62; 11 Kagayama, 60; 12 Fabrizio, 59; 13 Nieto, 46; 14 Smrz, 44; 15 Brookes, 40.

WORLD SUPERBIKE CHAMPIONSHIP • ROUND 8

MISANO

ITALY

Above: **Mid-field battle: Lanzi heads Laconi's Kawasaki, Neukirchner (76), Nakatomi (38), Zanotti (64), Nieto (10) and Polita (53). Kawasakis were blue for one race, in honour of San Marino sponsorship of the team.**

Right: **Ex-racer old-pals act: Superbike legend Carl Fogarty and Yamaha's Davide Tardozzi.**

Below right: **Max Biaggi had all the comforts of home.**

Centre right: **Kagayama was on the rostrum for the first time all year.**

Centre far right: **High-speed wreckage: Haga and Biaggi make dust after the latter's indiscretion.**

Bottom centre right: **Almost incognito, Rossi watched his old rival's downfall.**

Bottom far right: **Resurgent Bayliss's double for Ducati made it three races in a row for the defending champion.**

Photographs: Gold & Goose

OUT of the washing-up pan into the fire; from the ducking stools of Silverstone to Misano's tarmac cauldron. The action followed suit in a sizzling pair of ace races. Bayliss was top scorer in each.

The championship chase, closer with every passing lap in the previous weeks, continued to be so after the first leg, until a smash and mistimed brake lever grab from Biaggi, who took out Haga too. After the crash, a furious debate ensued between the partisan Italians and the rest, but no matter how vociferous the defence of Max, the TV coverage showed that Biaggi had run in way too deep and fast as he tried to pass the unsurpassable, high-speed obstacle that was Haga as both riders pursued leader Bayliss.

Understandably, Haga was incandescent and would have kicked a lot more than just gravel in Biaggi's direction had he not been restrained. The feud would continue for a while, on track and off.

The cameras caught something else as Biaggi and Haga impacted, the remarkable sight of one Valentino Rossi standing trackside in 'disguise'. The red crash helmet hid most of his unruly mop of hair, the cinema-screen-scale sunglasses most of his face, but the blue and white Yamaha T-shirt and the inimitable gangly frame were unmistakable.

At the Tavullia lad's old home track of Misano, it was nothing short of Shakespearean that Rossi – for so long Biaggi's younger, more popular nemesis in GPs – was not only on site, but also at the very corner Biaggi chose to stumble over his own impatience and take out the man who had been closest to leader Toseland.

The drama on lap 21, on the revised and reversed Misano world circuit, allowed Corser to score second place, while the lonely Kagayama was third for a first podium of the year.

Biaggi and Haga's gravel disturbance also did a massive favour for Toseland, who was in bother with his Honda, spinning, then going sideways in a fashion that those with better, more comprehensive traction control technology must have found puzzling. He was 11 seconds behind winner Bayliss, while his team-mate, Rolfo, was a further seven seconds down, with Lanzi in sixth.

The expected challenge by Ruben Xaus, who had won a race at the similarly tight and tricky Valencia circuit, came to little: eighth behind Laconi in race one, seventh in the second.

In race two, the hammer on the red Ducati sickle led from start to finish, Bayliss beating Haga and then Biaggi on track this time, while Kagayama got the best of a scrap with a fading Corser. Toseland, in the deep stuff and quietly raging against his machine, was sixth. He ended his day a mere 21 points up on Bayliss, who had won the previous three contests. Again, the tin-pot Bologna single-track tractor was the world's best two-cylinder 'MotoGP' bike, even at the end of its long sub-1000cc guise, and once more Bayliss looked like the best rider in the pack.

Haga disappeared from Biaggi, who had started well, fell away for a time and eventually got back on to terms. He was not to take the new lap record; Bayliss went away with that, as well as his two wins, on a 1m 36.022s.

Corser, the superb Superpole man, as he has been so often, artfully splattered ink all over the record books again, his 1m 34.948s edging out Bayliss, Haga and Toseland.

Only 15 riders finished race one, giving LBR MV Agusta rider Christian Zaiser and the MV Agusta F4 312 R their first points – almost within a backfire crack of its birthplace, the Cagiva Research Centre, in nearby San Marino.

Round 8

MISANO, Italy

17 June 2007, 2.597-mile/4.180km circuit

Race 1 24 laps, 62.328 miles/100.320km

Dry, Air 31°C Humidity 38% Track 48°C

Pl.	Name Nat. (Machine)	No.	Time & gap	Laps
1	Troy Bayliss, AUS (Ducati)	21	38m 52.856s 96.195mph/154.811km/h	24
2	Troy Corser, AUS (Yamaha)	11	2.374s	24
3	Yukio Kagayama, JPN (Suzuki)	71	8.965s	24
4	James Toseland, GBR (Honda)	52	11.110s	24
5	Roberto Rolfo, ITA (Honda)	44	18.709s	24
6	Lorenzo Lanzi, ITA (Ducati)	57	20.467s	24
7	Regis Laconi, FRA (Kawasaki)	55	22.072s	24
8	Ruben Xaus, SPA (Ducati)	111	25.424s	24
9	Max Neukirchner, SPA (Suzuki)	76	30.891s	24
10	Jakub Smrz, CZE (Ducati)	96	37.724s	24
11	Marco Borciani, ITA (Ducati)	20	44.898s	24
12	Mauro Sanchini, ITA (Kawasaki)	92	1m 01.538s	24
13	Luca Morelli, ITA (Honda)	22	1m 37.781s	24
14	Dean Ellison, GBR (Ducati)	42	1 lap	23
15	Christian Zaiser, AUT (MV Agusta)	73	1 lap	23

DNF: Noriyuki Haga, JPN (Yamaha) 41, 21 laps; Max Biaggi, ITA (Suzuki) 3, 21 laps; Fonsi Nieto, SPA (Kawasaki) 10, 14 laps; Luca Conforti, ITA (Honda) 34, 10 laps; Shinichi Nakatomi, JPN (Yamaha) 38, 6 laps; Alessandro Polita, ITA (Suzuki) 53, 5 laps; Michel Fabrizio, ITA (Honda) 84, 4 laps.

Fastest lap: Haga, 1m 36.356s, 97.040mph/156.171km/h (record).

Superpole: Corser, 1m 34.948s, 98.479mph/158.487km/h.

Race 2 24 laps, 62.328 miles/100.320km

Dry, Air 27°C Humidity 46% Track 46°C

Pl.	Name Nat. (Machine)	No.	Time & gap	Laps
1	Troy Bayliss, AUS (Ducati)	21	38m 43.506s 96.582mph/155.434km/h	24
2	Noriyuki Haga, JPN (Yamaha)	41	2.537s	24
3	Max Biaggi, ITA (Suzuki)	3	6.386s	24
4	Yukio Kagayama, JPN (Suzuki)	71	8.905s	24
5	Troy Corser, AUS (Yamaha)	11	9.130s	24
6	James Toseland, GBR (Honda)	52	13.967s	24
7	Ruben Xaus, SPA (Ducati)	111	16.708s	24
8	Roberto Rolfo, ITA (Honda)	44	16.781s	24
9	Lorenzo Lanzi, ITA (Ducati)	57	17.312s	24
10	Max Neukirchner, GER (Suzuki)	76	33.065s	24
11	Regis Laconi, FRA (Kawasaki)	55	33.605s	24
12	Fonsi Nieto, SPA (Kawasaki)	10	41.251s	24
13	Jakub Smrz, CZE (Ducati)	96	42.723s	24
14	Shinichi Nakatomi, JPN (Yamaha)	38	56.644s	24
15	Mauro Sanchini, ITA (Kawasaki)	92	1m 00.739s	24
16	Luca Conforti, ITA (Honda)	34	1m 16.641s	24
17	Alessandro Polita, ITA (Suzuki)	53	1m 17.714s	24
18	Luca Morelli, ITA (Honda)	22	1m 34.886s	24
19	Dean Ellison, GBR (Ducati)	42	1 lap	23

DNF: Marco Borciani, ITA (Ducati) 20, 15 laps; Christian Zaiser, AUS (MV Agusta) 73, 11 laps; Michel Fabrizio, ITA (Honda) 84, 2 laps.

Fastest lap: Bayliss, 1m 36.022s, 97.378mph/156.714km/h (record).

Lap record: New track.

Championship points: 1 Toseland, 260; 2 Bayliss, 239; 3 Haga, 234; 4 Biaggi, 217; 5 Corser, 182; 6 Lanzi, 133; 7 Xaus, 130; 8 Rolfo, 109; 9 Neukirchner, 100; 10 Kagayama, 89; 11 Laconi, 76; 12 Fabrizio, 59; 13 Smrz, 53; 14 Nieto, 50; 15 Brookes, 40.

WORLD SUPERBIKE CHAMPIONSHIP • ROUND 9

BRNO

CZECH REPUBLIC

Above: Early laps, and Lanzi is between Toseland and Biaggi, the real protagonists.

Right: Kagayama, rostrum-bound again.

Below right: One non-finish and 13th place for Smrz in his home race.

Centre right: Fabrizio made the Brno podium once more.

Opposite page, from top: Laconi was still struggling with the Kawasaki; Biaggi tucked in tight at a favourite track; compatriots Haga and Kagayama dispute third in race one.

Photographs: Gold & Goose

FOR Brno 2007, read Qatar 2007, as the battle between Toseland and Biaggi to share the wins had almost identical outcomes, except this time around, it was Toseland first, then Biaggi. That Biaggi and Suzuki had tested at Brno, and that Max had an enviable GP record at the Czech circuit, were enough to make the rest a little restive before the weekend had even started; Biaggi duly set the fastest time in the first practice session of the weekend.

It was Superpole that gave us the biggest story pre-race, however, Haga sweeping away even Biaggi's impressive time with a 1m 59.603s, the first Superbike to break two minutes. On race day, though, Haga and his Yamaha Motor Italia team were to suffer.

Toseland tried his usual front-running on a bike with a new version of the PI electronics package that the English company and Ten Kate had been working on since they'd put it into back-room development in favour of the Honda anti-spin version. It paid instant dividends, although Brno is not a particularly tough place for traction control to get its sensor triggering teeth into.

Toseland had to succumb after a few laps, and Haga, who was to finish fourth on two occasions, even had a chance to lead at one stage, after Biaggi had been first to pass Toseland. It was only for one lap, and he slid back to fourth, 2.4 seconds from Toseland and his resurgent Honda package.

Biaggi lost the duel with Toseland in race one, but only by 0.2 second; in race two, he would have his revenge by a larger margin of 1.5 seconds.

An early leader in race two was Lorenzo Lanzi, but it was another young Italian – the man who had beaten Lanzi to the European Superstock crown in 2003 – who would get his name on some silverware after the second 20-lap race. Michel Fabrizio finally had turned around an excruciatingly difficult season in the cash- and personnel-strapped DFX Honda team with a charging sixth in race one. Just like 2006, however, he was to get on the podium at Brno, finishing third, ahead of Haga and all the other Honda riders bar Toseland.

Third place in race one had gone to Brno's double winner from the 2006 season, Kagayama.

If Haga was in bother during the latter stages of each race, fast starter Corser was in trouble all day – only seventh in race one, and a frustrated retiree in race two, from a comfy second place, after a cover bolt had come undone and oil sprayed on his rear tyre."

For a change, it was not a good day for the Aussies, Bayliss only scoring sixth in race one, after crashing into fellow Australian Karl Muggeridge's sliding, spinning machine. Muggeridge and Regis Laconi – who stayed upright – blamed each other for the contact, but as it was not caught on TV, the rest of the world will never get the chance to judge for themselves.

Bayliss's brilliant Misano seemed a long way off after Brno, a track the Ducati team knew might be a struggle. Part of the reason was the famous hill running up to the final chicane, where the 220bhp four-cylinder cheetah's made the 190+bhp twin-cylinder gazelle's look more than vulnerable.

What was supposed to be a good track for the Kawasaki runners (three this weekend, with Silverstone third man Vittorio Iannuzzo back as well) proved to be just another green hell. Reliability issues, set-up imperfections and prematurely wrecked tyres littered the post-race conversations again. Best ZX-10 finisher Nieto – eighth in race two – even had oil all over his boots.

Round 9
BRNO, Czech Republic
22 July 2007, 3.357-mile/5.403km circuit

Race 1 20 laps, 67.140 miles/108.060km
Dry, Air 25°C Humidity 52% Track 37°C

Pl.	Name Nat. (Machine)	No.	Time & gap	Laps
1	James Toseland, GBR (Honda)	52	41m 02.730s	20
			98.152mph/157.961km/h	
2	Max Biaggi, ITA (Suzuki)	3	0.237s	20
3	Yukio Kagayama, JPN (Suzuki)	71	1.185s	20
4	Noriyuki Haga, JPN (Yamaha)	41	2.403s	20
5	Roberto Rolfo, ITA (Honda)	44	3.472s	20
6	Michel Fabrizio, ITA (Honda)	84	3.758s	20
7	Troy Corser, AUS (Yamaha)	11	18.235s	20
8	Lorenzo Lanzi, ITA (Ducati)	57	19.653s	20
9	Max Neukirchner, GER (Suzuki)	76	22.230s	20
10	Shinichi Nakatomi, JPN (Yamaha)	38	31.662s	20
11	Regis Laconi, FRA (Kawasaki)	55	32.796s	20
12	Ruben Xaus, SPA (Ducati)	111	47.360s	20
13	Vittorio Iannuzzo, ITA (Kawasaki)	13	1m 01.983s	20
14	Jiri Drazdak, CZE (Yamaha)	36	1m 02.052s	20
15	Stefano Cruciani, ITA (Suzuki)	112	1m 48.872s	20

DNF: Milos Cihak, CZE (Suzuki) 15, 19 laps; Jakub Smrz, CZE (Ducati) 96, 12 laps; Troy Bayliss, AUS (Ducati) 21, 11 laps; Karl Muggeridge, AUS (Honda) 31, 11 laps; Fonsi Nieto, SPA (Kawasaki) 10, 4 laps; Christian Zaiser, AUT (MV Agusta) 73, 3 laps; Dean Ellison, GBR (Ducati) 42, 2 laps; Luca Morelli, ITA (Honda) 22, 2 laps.

Fastest lap: Haga, 2m 01.543s, 99.439mph/160.032km/h (record).

Race 2 19 laps, 63.783 miles/102.657km
Dry, Air 27°C Humidity 33% Track 43°C

Pl.	Name Nat. (Machine)	No.	Time & gap	Laps
1	Max Biaggi, ITA (Suzuki)	3	38m 53.022s	19
			98.429mph/158.406km/h	
2	James Toseland, GBR (Honda)	52	1.510s	19
3	Michel Fabrizio, ITA (Honda)	84	5.419s	19
4	Noriyuki Haga, JPN (Yamaha)	41	6.765s	19
5	Roberto Rolfo, ITA (Honda)	44	7.910s	19
6	Troy Bayliss, AUS (Ducati)	21	9.241s	19
7	Lorenzo Lanzi, ITA (Ducati)	57	19.424s	19
8	Fonsi Nieto, SPA (Kawasaki)	10	24.191s	19
9	Shinichi Nakatomi, JPN (Yamaha)	38	26.680s	19
10	Ruben Xaus, SPA (Ducati)	111	28.095s	19
11	Karl Muggeridge, AUS (Honda)	31	33.256s	19
12	Max Neukirchner, GER (Suzuki)	76	33.352s	19
13	Jakub Smrz, CZE (Ducati)	96	33.495s	19
14	Regis Laconi, FRA (Kawasaki)	55	40.453s	19
15	Vittorio Iannuzzo, ITA (Kawasaki)	13	57.284s	19
16	Luca Morelli, ITA (Honda)	22	1m 17.657s	19
17	Milos Cihak, CZE (Suzuki)	15	1m 35.801s	19
18	Stefano Cruciani, ITA (Suzuki)	112	1m 37.346s	19

DNF: Christian Zaiser, AUT (MV Agusta) 73, 14 laps; Yukio Kagayama, JPN (Suzuki) 71, 10 laps; Jiri Drazdak, CZE (Yamaha) 36, 7 laps; Troy Corser, AUS (Yamaha) 11, 6 laps; Dean Ellison, GBR (Ducati) 42, 1 lap.

Fastest lap: Corser, 2m 00.674s, 100.156mph/161.185km/h (record).

Superpole: Haga, 1m 59.603, 101.052mph/162.628km/h.

Lap record: Noriyuki Haga, JPN (Yamaha), 2m 02.594s, 98.587mph/158.660km/h (2006).

Championship points: 1 Toseland, 305; 2 Biaggi, 262; 3 Haga, 260; 4 Bayliss, 249; 5 Corser, 191; 6 Lanzi, 150; 7 Xaus, 140; 8 Rolfo, 131; 9 Neukirchner, 111; 10 Kagayama, 105; 11 Fabrizio, 85; 12 Laconi, 83; 13 Nieto, 58; 14 Smrz, 56; 15 Brookes, 40.

WORLD SUPERBIKE CHAMPIONSHIP • ROUND 10

BRANDS HATCH

GREAT BRITAIN

Left: Toseland abandons his leathers to the Brands Hatch multitude after a career-first double race win.

Bottom left: Out of the shadows: Haga leads Toseland.

Bottom centre: Biaggi's first visit to Brands yielded a jubilant podium finish.

Bottom: Fabrizio repeated his best-of-the-rest performance – twice.

Below: Ronald Ten Kate looks thoughtful. The weekend could hardly have gone better for the chief Honda team.

Photographs: Gold & Goose

AMAZING to think that before Brands Hatch, the 2004 world champion had never quite scored a double win, but that was the monkey on Toseland's back at the biggest race and most intense venue. Or perhaps we should say, one of many potentially disruptive and distracting monkeys.

It had been a busy season already, especially at home – a disastrous Silverstone, a half-way brilliant Donington until his bike let him down in race two. Only a week before Brands, there had been a crash in front of the Japanese top brass at the Suzuka eight-hour, predating an announcement that he was leaving Honda and WSB to ride in MotoGP for Yamaha. Press attention became a heavy anvil, expectation from the home crowd a potential hammer. With Toseland desperate to win his first SBK race at Brands, you might not have been surprised if he had allowed the pressure to become too much for him.

But Brands was an impressive gloves-off rebuke to those who thought he had lost focus and even his legendary self-belief, especially after his very public error at Suzuka. It came in the form of two wins, a great leap forward in his championship lead and many ambitions fulfilled in the space of the afternoon. British racing's very own white knight.

Another rider hoping to bounce back at Brands was not so fortunate, as the frequently unforgiving track simply butchered the 2006 champion, Bayliss, who fell in one race after being passed with seeming ease by Toseland and Haga, losing concentration inversely to the pull he made on his front brake lever as he entered Druids. Bayliss had clearly jumped the start, but it was not declared, and he blamed the crash in part on a loss of concentration due to the expectation of being flagged in any time. A seventh in race two was no great help to his recovery.

You could argue that Max Biaggi was brilliant in race one, or that he lost a golden opportunity in race two. Or both points with equal veracity. His podium on his first visit to Brands was amazing to behold, yet an eighth in race two was less impressive, following a ride-through penalty for a jump start. His rip through the field from 16th when he rejoined was fun to watch, but doubtless no fun for Max.

Serial Brands race winner Haga was only seventh after falling and restarting at Surtees in the opener, but netted a second place in race two; his team-mate, Corser, speared two podium fish. Although the latter did not really get on terms with Toseland, he did not allow him to get too far away or too relaxed either.

Xaus, a threat in qualifying and seventh off the grid, made fourth in race one and sixth in race two, putting Lanzi in the shade, as the diminutive Italian finished a dowdy ninth and 12th. The factory team from Ducati was in serious trouble for the second weekend in succession, especially when you factor in Xaus, the semi-privateer in a private team, who was much more effective on a much less well-cosseted race package.

Kagayama, former BSB rider, scored a fifth in race two after a flight and crash landing at the fast right of Clearways, but even the Suzuka eight-hour winner and his factory Suzuki were outperformed by Michel Fabrizio on the private DFX Honda. He rattled in a fifth, then followed with a superb fourth, on a bike that is usually fast in a straight line, but not always the best around the corners, or the most reliable.

Rolfo was a respectable sixth in race one, a technically handicapped 11th in race two, suffering brake problems for what he said was the third time in 2007.

Round 10
BRANDS HATCH, Great Britain
5 August 2007, 2.301-mile/3.703km circuit

Race 1 25 laps, 57.525 miles/92.575km
Dry, Air 27°C Humidity 48% Track 38°C

Pl.	Name Nat. (Machine)	No.	Time & gap	Laps
1	James Toseland, GBR (Honda)	52	36m 35.120s	25
			94.313mph/151.782km/h	
2	Troy Corser, AUS (Yamaha)	11	1.554s	25
3	Max Biaggi, ITA (Suzuki)	3	2.917s	25
4	Ruben Xaus, SPA (Ducati)	111	10.202s	25
5	Michel Fabrizio, ITA (Honda)	84	14.133s	25
6	Roberto Rolfo, ITA (Honda)	44	14.323s	25
7	Noriyuki Haga, JPN (Yamaha)	41	19.380s	25
8	Regis Laconi, FRA (Kawasaki)	55	22.676s	25
9	Lorenzo Lanzi, ITA (Ducati)	57	24.259s	25
10	Max Neukirchner, GER (Suzuki)	76	24.423s	25
11	Steve Martin, AUS (Yamaha)	99	33.365s	25
12	Fonsi Nieto, SPA (Kawasaki)	10	33.373s	25
13	Shinichi Nakatomi, JPN (Yamaha)	38	33.548s	25
14	Jakub Smrz, CZE (Ducati)	96	48.283s	25
15	Marty Nutt, GBR (Yamaha)	77	1m 04.655s	25
16	Stefano Cruciani, ITA (Suzuki)	112	1m 08.886s	25
17	Luca Morelli, ITA (Honda)	22	1m 08.953s	25
18	Dean Ellison, GBR (Ducati)	42	1m 09.057s	25

DNF: Karl Muggeridge, AUS (Honda) 31, 23 laps; Yukio Kagayama, JPN (Suzuki) 71, 21 laps; Troy Bayliss, AUS (Ducati) 21, 4 laps.

Fastest lap: Haga, 1m 26.590s, 95.636mph/153.912km/h.

Superpole: Bayliss, 1m 25.607s, 96.734mph/155.679km/h.

Race 2 25 laps, 57.525 miles/92.575km
Dry, Air 28°C Humidity 40% Track 44°C

Pl.	Name Nat. (Machine)	No.	Time & gap	Laps
1	James Toseland, GBR (Honda)	52	36m 34.177s	25
			94.353mph/151.847km/h	
2	Noriyuki Haga, JPN (Yamaha)	41	1.686s	25
3	Troy Corser, AUS (Yamaha)	11	1.760s	25
4	Michel Fabrizio, ITA (Honda)	84	8.456s	25
5	Yukio Kagayama, JPN (Suzuki)	71	8.988s	25
6	Ruben Xaus, SPA (Ducati)	111	9.470s	25
7	Troy Bayliss, AUS (Ducati)	21	18.313s	25
8	Max Biaggi, ITA (Suzuki)	3	19.116s	25
9	Regis Laconi, FRA (Kawasaki)	55	20.501s	25
10	Max Neukirchner, GER (Suzuki)	76	20.586s	25
11	Roberto Rolfo, ITA (Honda)	44	21.808s	25
12	Lorenzo Lanzi, ITA (Ducati)	57	24.883s	25
13	Fonsi Nieto, SPA (Kawasaki)	10	31.988s	25
14	Karl Muggeridge, AUS (Honda)	31	33.253s	25
15	Shinichi Nakatomi, JPN (Yamaha)	38	36.868s	25
16	Steve Martin, AUS (Yamaha)	99	37.972s	25
17	Dean Ellison, GBR (Ducati)	42	1m 07.216s	25
18	Luca Morelli, ITA (Honda)	22	1m 08.297s	25

DNF: Jakub Smrz, CZE (Ducati) 96, 5 laps; Stefano Cruciani, ITA (Suzuki) 112, 0 laps.

DNS: Marty Nutt, GBR (Yamaha) 77.

Fastest lap: Toseland, 1m 26.689s, 95.527mph/153.736km/h.

Lap record: James Toseland, GBR (Honda), 1m 26.351s, 95.927mph/154.379km/h (2006).

Championship points: 1 Toseland, 355; 2 Haga, 289; 3 Biaggi, 286; 4 Bayliss, 258; 5 Corser, 227; 6 Xaus, 163; 7 Lanzi, 161; 8 Rolfo, 146; 9 Neukirchner, 123; 10 Kagayama, 116; 11 Fabrizio, 109; 12 Laconi, 98; 13 Nieto, 65; 14 Smrz, 58; 15 Nakatomi, 41.

WORLD SUPERBIKE CHAMPIONSHIP • ROUND 11

LAUSITZ

GERMANY

Above: Corser slips underneath the struggling Toseland, Fabrizio close behind.

Left: Good timing gave Fonsi Nieto his first Superpole.

Opposite page: An austere venue – empty grandstands frown down as Biaggi leads Haga, Toseland, Xaus, Bayliss, Nieto and the rest.

Below: Bayliss and Haga battle it out.

Bottom left: Pirellis galore – was it Toseland's turn for a bad one?

Bottom right: Ice-cool model sets the tone.

Photographs: Gold & Goose

BATHING in a 66-point advantage after Brands, no one in Toseland's squad could predict their fate on race day – only a ninth and a fourth. The former was blamed by JT on an inexplicably duff rear tyre, the latter was maybe all he could have hoped for. Thus, the three chasing riders, once struggling in Toseland's con-trail, suddenly jumped into his shadow.

Practice was the reason why not everyone was ready for race day: frequent rain meant that Sunday's occasional sunshine saw many riders on a final set-up that was not really tried and tested. Hence, this may have been Toseland's real problem in race one, but so furious was he, and so keen to show that the tyre and not his bike was to blame, that he went out in race two on his spare bike, which had the same spec of rear and overall settings as his number-one machine from the opener. All he proved, however, was that maybe fourth was all he would have got in race one as well.

The Lausitz Eurospeedway proved weird and often wet in practice, the rain eventually falling on a largely dry track at the start of the 'wet' Superpole, only just following Fonsi Nieto's blitz out of the inflatable exit at the end of the pit lane. His deliberate early-bird cleverness would be rewarded, as he set the fastest lap of the session straight off, just before the endless grey skies opened once more.

The rest made do in pre-race training, but at the end of each race, the names at the top were familiar. Haga was an immense 11 seconds up on first-time Lausitzer Biaggi; Corser finished 0.6 second behind the Suzuki, with Bayliss a whopping 22 seconds from the win, having pushed too hard early on. He had been two seconds in the lead after a single lap, but this pace merely fried his tyres, and he slipped back as the race ground on to its 24-lap conclusion.

Biaggi was lucky to go at all, his machine having stalled on the warm-up lap. He restarted as the rest headed off, but made it back in time to join the grid on the second row.

In the second race, the the usual five names were at the top, Bayliss (peerlessly into the 1.35s in qualifying) leading for most of the outing. Haga took the point for six laps at two-thirds distance, but lost out by 1.3 seconds. Biaggi was 13 seconds from Bayliss, Toseland 1.6 second from a podium finish. In the era of control tyres, big gaps between riders are always an indication of either a very disparate choice of the tyre options on offer, or machine set-up being way off for those riders who would normally be somewhere in the hunt. The lack of dry practice time definitely played a puckish part on this stage, in both regards. Thus, some argued that a less-than-ideal set-up, not a bad tyre, had caused Toseland to be 44 seconds from Haga, almost two seconds per lap slower overall. Others simply pointed out that every now and again, everyone gets a less-than-perfect tyre, and this was Toseland's turn.

Whatever the reason, the main points all went to Toseland's rivals, and despite a gritty recovery in race two, full of concentration and focus, the championship leader left Germany mentally battered and grimly silent. And 'only' 41 points ahead. The rest left almost daring to dream.

Biaggi, who had never seen the place before, proved once more that he was as adept an instant Superbike racer in his first season as he had been a GP rider for over ten – not something most of the previous big-name GP refugees could say, not of year one at least. With two free weekends to ponder his return home to Rome, at Vallelunga, Biaggi joined Haga in the 'maybe, just maybe' club.

Round 11

LAUSITZ, Germany

9 September 2007, 2.650-mile/4.265km circuit

Race 1 24 laps, 63.600 miles /102.360km
Dry, Air 17°C Humidity 55% Track 24°C

Pl.	Name Nat. (Machine)	No.	Time & gap	Laps
1	Noriyuki Haga, JPN (Yamaha)	41	40m 02.923s 95.289mph/153.353km/h	24
2	Max Biaggi, ITA (Suzuki)	3	11.007s	24
3	Troy Corser, AUS (Yamaha)	11	11.628s	24
4	Troy Bayliss, AUS (Ducati)	21	22.156s	24
5	Roberto Rolfo, ITA (Honda)	44	26.082s	24
6	Regis Laconi, FRA (Kawasaki)	55	26.381s	24
7	Fonsi Nieto, SPA (Kawasaki)	10	36.870s	24
8	Lorenzo Lanzi, ITA (Ducati)	57	43.465s	24
9	James Toseland, GBR (Honda)	52	44.258s	24
10	Karl Muggeridge, AUS (Honda)	31	45.233s	24
11	Shinichi Nakatomi, JPN (Yamaha)	38	52.553s	24
12	Ruben Xaus, SPA (Ducati)	111	1m 01.959s	24
13	Jakub Smrz, CZE (Ducati)	96	1m 17.989s	24
14	Steve Martin, AUS (Suzuki)	99	1m 19.224s	24
15	Yoann Tiberio, FRA (Honda)	32	1m 36.627s	24
16	Jiri Drazdak, CZE (Yamaha)	36	1m 36.879s	24

DNF: Dean Ellison, GBR (Ducati) 42, 14 laps; Luca Morelli, ITA (Honda) 22, 10 laps; Michel Fabrizio, ITA (Honda) 84, 9 laps; Max Neukirchner, GER (Suzuki) 76, 6 laps; Martin Bauer, AUT (Honda) 45, 6 laps.

Fastest lap: Haga, 1m 39.033s, 96.337mph/155.039km/h.

Race 2 24 laps, 63.600 miles/102.360km
Dry, Air 20°C Humidity 50% Track 29°C

Pl.	Name Nat. (Machine)	No.	Time & gap	Laps
1	Troy Bayliss, AUS (Ducati)	21	39m 49.291s 95.833mph/154.228km/h	24
2	Noriyuki Haga, JPN (Yamaha)	41	1.353s	24
3	Max Biaggi, ITA (Suzuki)	3	13.001s	24
4	James Toseland, GBR (Honda)	52	14.641s	24
5	Troy Corser, AUS (Yamaha)	11	15.210s	24
6	Ruben Xaus, SPA (Ducati)	111	25.830s	24
7	Roberto Rolfo, ITA (Honda)	44	29.752s	24
8	Fonsi Nieto, SPA (Kawasaki)	10	29.947s	24
9	Max Neukirchner, GER (Suzuki)	76	30.552s	24
10	Karl Muggeridge, AUS (Honda)	31	33.815s	24
11	Regis Laconi, FRA (Kawasaki)	55	39.323s	24
12	Lorenzo Lanzi, ITA (Ducati)	57	42.592s	24
13	Michel Fabrizio, ITA (Honda)	84	50.755s	24
14	Steve Martin, AUS (Suzuki)	99	53.598s	24
15	Shinichi Nakatomi, JPN (Yamaha)	38	56.284s	24
16	Jakub Smrz, CZE (Ducati)	96	57.818s	24
17	Martin Bauer, AUT (Honda)	45	1m 18.407s	24
18	Yoann Tiberio, FRA (Honda)	32	1m 32.030s	24
19	Jiri Drazdak, CZE (Yamaha)	36	1m 36.702s	24

DNF: Luca Morelli, ITA (Honda) 22, 7 laps; Dean Ellison, GBR (Ducati) 42, 2 laps.

Fastest lap: Haga, 1m 38.622s, 96.738mph/155.685km/h (record).

Superpole: Nieto, 1m 50.681s, 86.198mph/138.723km/h.

Previous record: Troy Bayliss, AUS (Ducati), 1m 38.635s, 96.726mph/155.665km/h (2006).

Championship points: 1 Toseland, 375; 2 Haga, 334; 3 Biaggi, 322; 4 Bayliss, 296; 5 Corser, 254; 6 Xaus, 177; 7 Lanzi, 173; 8 Rolfo, 166; 9 Neukirchner, 130; 10 Kagayama, 116; 11 Laconi, 113; 12 Fabrizio, 112; 13 Nieto, 82; 14 Smrz, 61; 15 Muggeridge and Nakatomi, 47.

WORLD SUPERBIKE CHAMPIONSHIP • ROUND 12

VALLELUNGA

ITALY

Right: Rolfo got nowhere in the first race, was a happier fifth at the second attempt.

Centre right: Bayliss was back on top form, winning race two.

Below: Too-tight corners and too much stress put Toseland horizontal.

Photographs: Gold & Goose

Left: Bayliss, Haga, Biaggi – the big guns thunder away.

Below: Third and fourth were enough to keep Haga's title chances alive.

Below centre: Fellow Australians Karl Muggeridge and Steve Martin battle over 13th in race two.

Bottom: Laconi fends off Fabrizio in race one – but not for long.

Photographs: Gold & Goose

IT was inevitable that some day Rome-based FGSport would get its dreamed-of home race, and with Biaggi joining the crew for 2007, the controllers of SBK decreed that 2007 would be the year. The venue had a lot going for it: a great layout in places and some great spectator vantage points, including a vast white and grey grandstand that allowed everyone clinging to their rolled-up race programmes to feel like an elevated member of the old Republic's Senate for the day.

Vallelunga also had a lot against it, notably safety in some FIM sanctioned blind-spot areas, a paddock that was more like an unlit council car-park than a global working arena, an access and parking 'plan' that made Brands Hatch look generous by comparison, and a mountain of other teething problems. None of this was helped by occasional Eternal City haughtiness and a general lack of urgency. The racing was exciting, however, often close and ultimately, for the second time in succession, pivotal. And yet again, the weather spoiled practice completely – for the soaked crowd and jittery riders alike.

It did not affect the dry Superpole too badly, and despite the effects of torrential rain on Thursday, and jabbing punches of real rain thereafter, race day was dry, although race two proved slippery after oil was spilled in the Supersport race, on the two fastest parts of the track.

The first lap of the first race was either shambolic or showtime, depending on how much leather-on-leather contact you like of an average Sunday lunchtime. Rolfo went out after someone hit his rear so hard it punctured his rim, deflating the tyre; an overexcited Corser crashed out near the front, and the closely following Neukirchner was forced to join him on the terminally horizontal axis.

Hosting a mix of liberally applied block passes, elbow wrestling and front-wheel chopping into the slower corners, Vallelunga, with its schizophrenic layout of superfast and comically slow corners, was having instantly memorable effects.

Bayliss, fastest man in qualifying and Superpole winner yet again, was out front, but right with him was Biaggi, egged-on in the pit lane by his period-dressed legionary guard and attendant female muses. On lap four, he took the lead; on lap 24, he received the freedom of Rome, having beaten Bayliss by five seconds, Toseland by seven and Haga by ten. The next would-be Roman Emperor, Michel Fabrizio, was fifth, albeit 22 seconds down.

The haves and the have-nots were all in the mix again. Some, however, were showing either an appetite for self-destruction or too great a desire to win when the odds were against them. James Toseland had been adept in overall qualifying – for 66 per cent of the lap anyway. The remaining part, designed by a short-sighted kart driver who had evidently received less asphalt from the tarmac supplier than he had ordered, was not exactly Honda-friendly. Having lost all his speed there in qualifying, Toseland finally lost the front in the second race, at the apex of the chicane that leaves the impossibly tight mid-section. Nerves and expectation were finally taking hold in the normally unshakeable Toseland/Ten Kate world. The fall cost him dear, and despite battling his way back with a broken gear-lever and a clutch lever in a difficult position, Toseland finished the second race 11th, scoring five points, which would prove invaluable later.

Up front in race two, Bayliss got the better of Biaggi as the latter made a mistake going into the slowest left in the place (where Toseland had fallen), losing time and space even a charged-up, hometown Max could not regain. Thus, Bayliss scored a win, while Biaggi was second and Haga third. Corser was fourth and Rolfo fifth, having dusted off Xaus (a race-one faller, restarter and eventual retiree).

Round 12
VALLELUNGA, Italy
30 September 2007, 2.554-mile/4.110km circuit

Race 1 24 laps, 61.296 miles/98.640km
Dry, Air 21°C Humidity 47% Track 31°C

Pl.	Name Nat. (Machine)	No.	Time & gap	Laps
1	Max Biaggi, ITA (Suzuki)	3	39m 24.967s 93.300mph/150.152km/h	24
2	Troy Bayliss, AUS (Ducati)	21	5.638s	24
3	James Toseland, GBR (Honda)	52	7.452s	24
4	Noriyuki Haga, JPN (Yamaha)	41	10.079s	24
5	Michel Fabrizio, ITA (Honda)	84	22.257s	24
6	Lorenzo Lanzi, ITA (Ducati)	57	25.662s	24
7	Regis Laconi, FRA (Kawasaki)	55	34.811s	24
8	Fonsi Nieto, SPA (Kawasaki)	10	38.075s	24
9	Shinichi Nakatomi, JPN (Yamaha)	38	39.070s	24
10	Vittorio Iannuzzo, ITA (Kawasaki)	13	47.702s	24
11	Jakub Smrz, CZE (Ducati)	96	47.806s	24
12	Marco Borciani, ITA (Ducati)	20	53.488s	24
13	Karl Muggeridge, AUS (Honda)	31	54.509s	24
14	Steve Martin, AUS (Suzuki)	99	1m 01.967s	24
15	Yoann Tiberio, FRA (Honda)	32	1m 08.291s	24
16	Luca Morelli, ITA (Honda)	22	1m 08.517s	24
17	Dean Ellison, GBR (Ducati)	42	1 lap	23

DNF: Ruben Xaus, SPA (Ducati) 111, 9 laps; Norino Brignola, ITA (Ducati) 117, 3 laps; Max Neukirchner, GER (Suzuki) 76, 0 laps; Troy Corser, AUS (Yamaha) 11, 0 laps; Roberto Rolfo, ITA (Honda) 44, 0 laps.

Fastest lap: Haga, 1m 37.419s, 94.374mph/151.880km/h (record).

Superpole: Bayliss, 1m 35.890s, 95.879mph/154.302km/h.

Race 2 24 laps, 61.296 miles/98.640km
Dry, Air 26°C Humidity 32% Track 40°C

Pl.	Name Nat. (Machine)	No.	Time & gap	Laps
1	Troy Bayliss, AUS (Ducati)	21	39m 30.861s 93.068mph/149.778km/h	24
2	Max Biaggi, ITA (Suzuki)	3	1.431s	24
3	Noriyuki Haga, JPN (Yamaha)	41	4.466s	24
4	Troy Corser, AUS (Yamaha)	11	13.766s	24
5	Roberto Rolfo, ITA (Honda)	44	20.848s	24
6	Ruben Xaus, SPA (Ducati)	111	21.930s	24
7	Lorenzo Lanzi, ITA (Ducati)	57	29.847s	24
8	Fonsi Nieto, SPA (Kawasaki)	10	29.986s	24
9	Shinichi Nakatomi, JPN (Yamaha)	38	40.126s	24
10	Max Neukirchner, GER (Suzuki)	76	40.733s	24
11	James Toseland, GBR (Honda)	52	42.544s	24
12	Vittorio Iannuzzo, ITA (Kawasaki)	13	54.504s	24
13	Karl Muggeridge, AUS (Honda)	31	55.024s	24
14	Steve Martin, AUS (Suzuki)	99	55.304s	24
15	Yoann Tiberio, FRA (Honda)	32	59.781s	24
16	Norino Brignola, ITA (Ducati)	117	1m 00.609s	24
17	Luca Morelli, ITA (Honda)	22	1m 06.922s	24
18	Marco Borciani, ITA (Ducati)	20	1m 18.228s	24
19	Dean Ellison, GBR (Ducati)	42	1 lap	23

DNF: Regis Laconi, FRA (Kawasaki) 55, 12 laps; Michel Fabrizio, ITA (Honda) 84, 8 laps; Jakub Smrz, CZE (Ducati) 96, 1 lap.

Fastest lap: Biaggi, 1m 37.727s, 94.076mph/151.401km/h.

Previous record: New circuit.

Championship points: 1 Toseland, 396; 2 Biaggi, 367; 3 Haga, 363; 4 Bayliss, 341; 5 Corser, 267; 6 Lanzi, 192; 7 Xaus, 187; 8 Rolfo, 177; 9 Neukirchner, 136; 10 Fabrizio, 123; 11 Laconi, 122; 12 Kagayama, 116; 13 Nieto, 98; 14 Smrz, 66; 15 Nakatomi, 61.

WORLD SUPERBIKE CHAMPIONSHIP • ROUND 13

MAGNY-COURS

FRANCE

Above: Lanzi goes flying after colliding with Toseland, battling to stay on board on the left. Corona Suzuki substitute Neukirchner gets past safely on the inside.

Above right: No hard feelings. A hobbling Lanzi visited Toseland on the grid before race two.

Right: Nieto, here leading team-mate Laconi, put the unfancied Kawasaki on the podium.

Photographs: Gold & Goose

Left: Double winner Haga, here heading Corser and Biaggi, missed the title by just two points.

Below: FGSport chief Paolo Flammini could look back on a mammoth season.

Bottom: The burden lifted, new double World Champion James Toseland lifts his burden.

Photographs: Gold & Goose

ON race morning, fog swathed us in a cloak of impending doom. Cancellation of the event was not impossible, because racing proved to be just that, until past midday. The low cloud finally lifted its voluminous underskirts long enough to start the first-leg can-can. Race one set off into the residue of the gloom some 20 minutes late. It lasted only half a corner for Lorenzo Lanzi, as he and Toseland touched, Lanzi falling hard at high-speed, and continuing to bounce and slap for a great distance. It looked bad, and it was bad – enough to see him miss race two. Thankfully unbroken, he recovered enough to hobble to the start line and wish Toseland good luck (or something) for race two.

Oh yeah, race two still mattered.

Somehow, incredibly, race 25 of the season had become the championship decider. You see, another match point for Toseland had been withheld by a deranged Lady Luck and the relentless push of one Noriyuki Haga in race one.

While Toseland and Biaggi were getting back into contention from the back of the grid after the mêlée at turn one, Haga passed team-mate Corser on lap two and led every subsequent lap. Ultimately, Bayliss took second place, only 2.7 seconds from the determined Haga, and just a second up on Corser.

Toseland rammed his way back to seventh, in Biaggi's slipstream, but at the front, the heavy braking, fast direction changing track brought some other names to the fore, all of them with an eye on 2008.

Max Neukirchner battled his way to fourth, having been up to second for a short time, in his first ride for the major Suzuki team – he had replaced the injured Kagayama. He had to give best to Corser, but was four seconds up on fifth-placed Nieto, who was finding his Kawasaki remarkably adept for a change. Biaggi almost got to him, a slowing Toseland did not seem able to. After race one, it was just Toseland and Haga, 17 points between them, going for the biggest Superbike prize.

Having seen his once vast points lead evaporate, largely, but not exclusively, through no fault of his own, Magny-Cours Superpole winner Toseland had arrived in France looking to win and adorn his championship with two more gilt handles. After race one, there was an urgent need simply to make sure he really did get the world title, never mind planning any adornments to the trophy, which was in some danger of slipping from his grasp.

After the second race, Toseland said that he was surprised to find himself in a position where he could not quite stay with the leading pack. Nonetheless, after all the recent problems and afflictions, in the end he appeared simply to have ridden as safely as possible to the finish. He even had a near traffic jam of potential *bête noires* on his back tyre for much of the race, but at the last gasp, he finished just ahead of team-mate Rolfo, in sixth, and two points clear of double winner Haga after a mammoth season.

At the front of race two, Haga was in a class of his own once more, needing to win and doing so brilliantly. Biaggi was a determined second, but rider of the day – on a day when there were quite a few candidates – was third-placed Nieto, on the unfancied and frequently afflicted Kawasaki. Corser was unhappy to see him ahead at the end, having been run off track by Biaggi in race one, then pushed wide by Nieto, only for the two to come together on the racing line with a hard crunch, which Corser believed was entirely deliberate on Nieto's part.

Thus, it ended: a heady double sake in the last two races, and a deserved – if narrowly so in the final analysis – glass of victory champagne for Toseland and Ten Kate Honda.

Round 13
MAGNY-COURS, France
7 October 2007, 2.741-mile/4.411km circuit

Race 1 23 laps, 63.043 miles/101.453km
Dry, Air 15°C Humidity 94% Track 19°C

Pl.	Name Nat. (Machine)	No.	Time & gap	Laps
1	Noriyuki Haga, JPN (Yamaha)	41	38m 33.762s 98.084mph/157.851km/h	23
2	Troy Bayliss, AUS (Ducati)	21	2.770s	23
3	Troy Corser, AUS (Yamaha)	11	3.735s	23
4	Max Neukirchner, GER (Suzuki)	76	8.570s	23
5	Fonsi Nieto, SPA (Kawasaki)	10	12.925s	23
6	Max Biaggi, ITA (Suzuki)	3	13.283s	23
7	James Toseland, GBR (Honda)	52	16.395s	23
8	Ruben Xaus, SPA (Ducati)	111	22.581s	23
9	Regis Laconi, FRA (Kawasaki)	55	22.828s	23
10	Roberto Rolfo, ITA (Honda)	44	32.729s	23
11	Shinichi Nakatomi, JPN (Yamaha)	38	38.305s	23
12	Karl Muggeridge, AUS (Honda)	31	53.685s	23
13	Yoann Tiberio, FRA (Honda)	32	53.799s	23
14	Michel Fabrizio, ITA (Honda)	84	53.915s	23
15	Guillaume Dietrich, FRA (Suzuki)	83	56.474s	23
16	Steve Martin, AUS (Suzuki)	99	1m 11.402s	23

DNF: Luca Morelli, ITA (Honda) 22, 19 laps; Jakub Smrz, CZE (Ducati) 96, 4 laps; Dean Ellison, GBR (Ducati) 42, 4 laps; Lorenzo Lanzi, ITA (Ducati) 57, 0 laps.

Fastest lap: Neukirchner, 1m 39.844s, 98.825mph/159.044km/h (record).

Race 2 23 laps, 63.043 miles/101.453km
Dry, Air 24°C Humidity 57% Track 31°C

Pl.	Name Nat. (Machine)	No.	Time & gap	Laps
1	Noriyuki Haga, JPN (Yamaha)	41	38m 35.353s 98.017mph/157.743km/h	23
2	Max Biaggi, ITA (Suzuki)	3	3.518s	23
3	Fonsi Nieto, SPA (Kawasaki)	10	9.142s	23
4	Troy Corser, AUS (Yamaha)	11	9.257s	23
5	Troy Bayliss, AUS (Ducati)	21	12.825s	23
6	James Toseland, GBR (Honda)	52	19.316s	23
7	Roberto Rolfo, ITA (Honda)	44	20.994s	23
8	Regis Laconi, FRA (Kawasaki)	55	22.452s	23
9	Michel Fabrizio, ITA (Honda)	84	22.505s	23
10	Ruben Xaus, SPA (Ducati)	111	28.352s	23
11	Karl Muggeridge, AUS (Honda)	31	44.333s	23
12	Yoann Tiberio, FRA (Honda)	32	48.077s	23
13	Guillaume Dietrich, FRA (Suzuki)	83	1m 23.307s	23
14	Luca Morelli, ITA (Honda)	22	1m 23.826s	23
15	Dean Ellison, GBR (Ducati)	42	1m 37.631s	23

DNF: Max Neukirchner, GER (Suzuki) 76, 6 laps; Shinichi Nakatomi, JPN (Yamaha) 38, 5 laps; Steve Martin, AUS (Suzuki) 99, 1 lap; Jakub Smrz, CZE (Ducati) 96, 0 laps.

Fastest lap: Biaggi, 1m 40.040s, 98.632mph/158.733km/h.

Superpole: Toseland, 1m 38.501s, 100.173mph/161.213km/h.

Previous record: Troy Bayliss, AUS (Ducati), 1m 40.370s, 98.308mph/158.211km/h (2006).

Final World Championship points: See page 257.

SUOMY
ids
HANNspree
HONDA
Puig
HANNspree
52
HANNspree
HONDA
PIRELLI

WORLD SUPERBIKE CHAMPIONSHIP

Photograph: Gold & Goose

RESULTS 2007

Position	Rider	Nationality	Machine	Qatar/1	Qatar/2	Phillip Island/1	Phillip Island/2	Donington/1	Donington/2	Valencia/1	Valencia/2	Assen/1	Assen/2	Monza/1	Monza/2	Silverstone/1	Silverstone/2	Misano/1	Misano/2	Brno/1	Brno/2	Brands Hatch/1	Brands Hatch/2	Lausitz/1	Lausitz/2	Vallelunga/1	Vallelunga/2	Magny-Cours/1	Magny-Cours/2	Points total
1	James Toseland	GBR	Honda	20	25	20	25	25	–	11	25	25	20	13	20	8	–	13	10	25	20	25	25	7	13	16	5	9	10	415
2	Noriyuki Haga	JPN	Yamaha	8	13	13	16	13	25	20	16	20	–	25	25	20	–	–	20	13	13	9	20	25	20	13	16	25	25	413
3	Max Biaggi	ITA	Suzuki	25	20	16	13	16	20	8	20	10	16	16	11	10	–	–	16	20	25	16	8	20	16	25	20	10	20	397
4	Troy Bayliss	AUS	Ducati	11	8	25	20	–	–	16	10	13	25	20	16	25	–	25	25	–	10	–	9	13	25	20	25	20	11	372
5	Troy Corser	AUS	Yamaha	7	16	11	11	20	16	13	7	–	13	11	10	16	–	20	11	9	–	20	16	16	11	–	13	16	13	296
6	Reuben Xaus	SPA	Ducati	6	7	9	10	–	13	25	13	16	–	4	3	7	–	8	9	4	6	13	10	4	10	–	10	8	6	201
7=	Lorenzo Lanzi	ITA	Ducati	16	9	10	9	11	11	10	11	11	–	9	–	9	–	10	7	8	9	7	4	8	4	10	9	–	–	192
7=	Roberto Rolfo	ITA	Honda	9	–	5	6	7	9	6	4	7	11	–	13	13	–	11	8	11	11	10	5	11	9	–	11	6	9	192
9	Max Neukirchner	GER	Suzuki	10	6	8	8	8	6	4	6	6	9	6	4	6	–	7	6	7	4	6	6	–	7	–	6	13	–	149
10	Regis Laconi	FRA	Kawasaki	5	–	–	9	10	5	8	–	6	–	8	11	–	9	5	5	2	8	7	10	5	9	–	7	8	–	137
11	Michel Fabrizio	ITA	Honda	–	4	–	7	3	4	9	5	4	10	8	5	–	–	–	–	10	16	11	13	–	3	11	–	2	7	132
12	Fonsi Nieto	SPA	Kawasaki	11	7	2	10	–	–	–	8	8	–	–	–	–	–	4	–	8	4	3	9	8	8	8	11	16	–	125
13	Yukio Kagayama	JPN	Suzuki	13	10	–	–	–	–	1	3	9	5	10	9	–	–	16	13	16	–	–	11	–	–	–	–	–	–	116
14=	Jakub Smrz	CZE	Ducati	2	–	2	5	6	8	2	–	5	7	1	6	–	–	6	3	–	3	2	–	3	–	5	–	–	–	66
14=	Shinichi Nakatomi	JPN	Yamaha	4	–	3	3	–	2	–	–	3	4	–	–	3	–	–	2	6	7	3	1	5	1	7	7	5	–	66
16	Karl Muggeridge	AUS	Honda	–	2	–	–	5	7	–	–	–	–	7	7	–	–	–	–	–	5	–	2	6	6	3	3	4	5	62
17	Joshua Brookes	AUS	Honda	–	3	4	4	4	1	7	9	–	3	5	–	–	–	–	–	–	–	–	–	–	–	–	–	–	–	40
18	Steve Martin	AUS	Honda/Yamaha/ Suzuki	5	–	6	–	–	3	–	–	–	–	–	–	–	–	–	–	–	–	5	–	2	2	2	2	–	–	27
19	Vittorio Iannuzzo	ITA	Kawasaki	–	–	–	–	–	–	–	–	–	–	–	–	5	–	–	–	3	1	–	–	–	–	6	4	–	–	19
20	Marco Borciani	ITA	Ducati	–	–	–	–	–	–	–	–	–	–	3	–	–	–	5	–	–	–	–	–	–	–	4	–	–	–	12
21=	Giovanni Bussei	ITA	Ducati	–	–	–	–	2	5	3	1	–	–	–	–	–	–	–	–	–	–	–	–	–	–	–	–	–	–	11
21=	Luca Morelli	ITA	Ducati/Honda	–	–	–	–	–	–	–	–	–	2	–	–	4	–	3	–	–	–	–	–	–	–	–	–	–	2	11
23	Yoann Tiberio	FRA	Honda	–	–	–	–	–	–	–	–	–	–	–	–	–	–	–	–	–	–	–	–	1	–	1	1	3	4	10
24=	Alessandro Polita	ITA	Suzuki	3	1	1	1	–	–	–	–	–	–	2	–	–	–	–	–	–	–	–	–	–	–	–	–	–	–	8
24=	Dean Ellison	GBR	Ducati	1	–	–	–	1	–	–	–	2	–	–	1	–	–	2	–	–	–	–	–	–	–	–	–	–	1	8
26	Mauro Sanchini	ITA	Kawasaki	–	–	–	–	–	–	–	–	–	–	–	–	–	–	4	1	–	–	–	–	–	–	–	–	–	–	5
27	Guillaume Dietrich	FRA	Suzuki	–	–	–	–	–	–	–	–	–	–	–	–	–	–	–	–	–	–	–	–	–	–	–	–	1	3	4
28=	Jiri Drazdak	CZE	Yamaha	–	–	–	–	–	–	–	–	–	–	–	–	–	–	–	–	2	–	–	–	–	–	–	–	–	–	2
28=	Robertino Pietri	ITA	Yamaha	–	–	–	–	–	–	–	–	–	–	–	2	–	–	–	–	–	–	–	–	–	–	–	–	–	–	2
28=	Carmelo Morales	SPA	Yamaha	–	–	–	–	–	–	–	2	–	–	–	–	–	–	–	–	–	–	–	–	–	–	–	–	–	–	2
28=	Marek Svoboda	CZE	Yamaha	–	–	–	–	–	–	–	–	1	1	–	–	–	–	–	–	–	–	–	–	–	–	–	–	–	–	2
32=	Marty Nutt	GBR	Yamaha	–	–	–	–	–	–	–	–	–	–	–	–	–	–	–	–	–	–	1	–	–	–	–	–	–	–	1
32=	Stefano Cruciani	ITA	Suzuki	–	–	–	–	–	–	–	–	–	–	–	–	–	–	–	–	1	–	–	–	–	–	–	–	–	–	1
32=	Christian Zaiser	AUT	MV Agusta	–	–	–	–	–	–	–	–	–	–	–	–	–	–	1	–	–	–	–	–	–	–	–	–	–	–	1

WORLD SUPERSPORT CHAMPIONSHIP REVIEW

TURKISH DELIGHT

By GORDON RITCHIE

Above: Kenan Sofuoglu, runaway World Supersport Champion.

Top: 'Superglue' leads runner-up Broc Parkes's Yamaha in Germany.

Above right: Former champion Sebastien Charpentier was unable to sustain a championship challenge after inury.

Photographs: Gold & Goose

FOR a championship littered with potential champions and championship winning teams, the theoretically most closely contested series in the world has been far from that in recent years. Even in 2006, champion Sebastien Charpentier only had to rely on his team-mate, Kenan Sofuoglu, helping him in the last two rounds because of potentially disastrous injury from mid-season testing, since he had scored a high points advantage already. In 2007, with Charpentier as his team-mate again, and another new Honda CBR600RR for Gerrit Ten Kate to get his grinding-wheel teeth into, Sofuoglu started out as only one of many potential champions.

There was history man Charpentier himself, the only double champion and still in competitive Ten Kate captivity. Broc Parkes and Kevin Curtain, in the World Supersport Racing Team, now owned by Yamaha NV, were never to be discounted.

Darkest of dark green horses were former champion Fabien Foret and Pere Riba, in the newly official Kawasaki ZX-6R Ninja team, on a new model and faster than they should have been in early testing. There was also a supported Suzuki effort from Hoegee Suzuki, running Barry Veneman and Vesa Kallio. Add in Gianluca Nannelli on the venerable, but occasionally virile, Caracchi SC 749R Ducati twin and you had a few possible race winners right there. Unlike Superbike, however, when you cast the net wider, you didn't catch smaller fry, you got even more riders capable of spawning not just wins, but maybe a strong title challenge as well.

Honda had Althea (ex-Megabike) as a supported team, and again it fielded Supersport royalty in Katsuaki Fujiwara. He was on the new '07 bike also (not all were to start, nor some to finish) and he had been helping development of the bike all along.

Stiggy Motorsports had been hard at it in winter development and fielded Robbin Harms from Denmark; he was nothing if not a potential top-three finisher. In the greater tuning-fork fraternity, Yamaha's Massimo Roccoli (Lorenzini by Leoni) and Gianluca Vizziello (RG Racing) were also podium princes in waiting.

With the surprise packages who always appear in any WSS season, like maybe Craig Jones (Revè Ekerold Honda), we had the ingredients for knock-down, drag-out mayhem – and too many good riders and bikes for any one to dominate.

Once more, we were all wrong.

Sofuoglu had a bike under him that he loved from the outset, but team-mate Charpentier would grow to loath in races, after – paradoxically – playing sweet music on it in qualifying.

From the outset, Sofuoglu – 'Superglue' as friendly elements in his Ten Kate team had nicknamed him – stuck to the points like that very substance. He had to give best to Curtain, Charpentier and Fujiwara in qualifying in Qatar, but made a meze of them come race day. Indeed, in addition to scoring five poles, he was never once off the front row in qualifying in 13 attempts.

Behind him in Qatar came Curtain, Fujiwara and Foret, the new Kawasaki proving potent in its youth, surely to become stronger as the season wore on.

Fabien Foret, Monsieur Mercurial himself, scored a race win from a distant fifth a week later in Oz, after the first half of the race had given him no chance. Suffering chatter in qualifying, he opted for a normal road-spec Pirelli SC rear for the race, the same one you and I can buy from a shop for real-world conditions, rather than the DOT Approved (but more overtly racy) tyre more often used for competition. Even his own team were stunned. Understandably, Pirelli was overjoyed. Sofuoglu was second, Parkes third and Charpentier fourth.

Same old faces winning races? Well, not at Donington, back on the calendar, but at an unseasonably early stage of the proceedings. April Fool's Day is the traditional time to play jokes on your mates in the UK, but few except Sofuoglu left England with a smile.

On a track surface that registered 7°C during the first untimed WSS session, three of the regular top contenders put themselves out of the running after crashing hard. Curtain only managed two laps before breaking his collarbone, Charpentier six before breaking his pelvis and collarbone, and Parkes a fulsome ten before he went out with a cracked his clavicle.

In the Sunday race, Sofuoglu won, Harms was second, Fujiwara third and Jones fourth, a big boost to the Englishman's low-budget/high-ability team.

After trips to the surgeons to have their collarbones filled with what appeared to be industrial curtain hooks and old pillion footrests, the Yamaha pairing of Parkes and Curtain showed grit and commitment to race at all.

In Spain, fifth place awaited Parkes, behind Sofuoglu, Andrew Pitt (Charpentier's stand-in, 2001 champion and not quite Ilmor MotoGP rider), the ever unpredictable Nannelli and still flying Foret, but pain and a truncated career was the reward for Curtain after a hideous crash on lap three. Pere Riba lost the front, slid into Curtain and subsequently they both collected Fujiwara on the outside line. Curtain's footpeg first pierced his inner/upper thigh, then twisted obscenely one way and another, leaving him with an internal and external wound that could be likened most closely to the aftermath of a shark attack.

A series of subs replaced him from then on. Steve Martin was the first to be drawn across the soon-to-be worn-out entrance matting of the Yamaha World Supersport Racing Team pit garage; tenth at Assen.

Having been perfect at Valencia (pole and race winner), Sofuoglu continued the trend at Ten Kate's home track, winning once more from Pitt and Foret (and not forgetting local man Veneman in fourth), as the two beaten ex-champions unwittingly bolstered the man who was already champion elect. He was 53 points ahead at this stage, not even half-way through another astounding year.

Another perfect performance by Kenan the Unstoppable at Monza allowed him to draw even further ahead of the field, including a second-placed Foret, and latest Yamaha sub Anthony West, who qualified 14th and finished a slipstreaming third.

Even better awaited wild wild-card West at Silverstone, a subaquatic sliver of slipperiness, where his bike's webbed feet allowed him to capitalise on a first-corner mistake from faller Sofuoglu. He went from 16th on the dry grid to victory on a wet surface, 33 seconds and countless Olympic swimming-pool lengths from Harms, 48 seconds from Fujiwara, and a water world from Foret in fourth.

West made it dry-race win number one at a rerouted Misano, from Parkes and Sofuoglu in an aggregate race, as Foret failed to finish, having collided with Jones early on.

Podium redemptions for both Jones (second) and Foret (third) at Brno were damned overall, however, by the fact that Sofuoglu won again, by 11 seconds, stretching out one hand toward the trophy in England two weeks later.

He duly won the title, if not the Brands race, Parkes scoring the first of two wins on the trot, from Sofuoglu and Massimo Roccoli, the Italian finally joining the ranks of the trophy takers. BSB regular Tommy Hill was now on the second works Yamaha and took fifth at home.

At Lausitz, nobody's favourite anything, Parkes won, Sofuoglu was second and Czech Intermoto wild-card/long-term replacement Matthieu Lagrive scored a blinding third. He set a trend, because at the new track of Vallelunga, Spanish privateer Joan Lascorz (Glaner Motocard.com Honda) was good value for his third place. Craig Jones was utterly robbed of his first win after the race was stopped, due to an oil spill, with Sofuoglu ahead, for the only time all race.

With the scent of a new historical high point in his nostrils, Sofuoglu rode with all the fury he could muster to win the final race at Magny-Cours, his race-long contest with Parkes ending with a new WSS record of eight wins. Parkes, second in France, was also promoted to second in the title run. Foret's mechanical DNF at home put him third overall, while the still-injured Fujiwara was fourth. Another assured podium of third from Jones put him fifth overall, an outstanding final reward for rider and team, who started with 2006 bikes and ended up with six top tens, three podiums and a moral victory at Vallelunga.

However, the numbers game belonged to Sofuoglu. He may have had two more opportunities than previous record holder Karl Muggeridge to score race wins in his particular championship season, but all the same, a 143-point margin of victory may be eternally unbeatable, if only because that much liberally applied bad luck cannot strike most of the other would-be champions quite that often ever again. But this is World Supersport, so never say never.

The first Turkish World Champion, Kenan Sofuoglu, was brilliantly worthy and courtesy of the class that so often amazes, even for some utterly unforeseen reasons.

In the Superstock 1000 FIM Cup class, the all-new Ducati 1098 won first time out, after a stunning last-day, last-lap sort-out, with Niccolo Canepa (Ducati Xerox Junior Team) finishing third at Magny-Cours and thus beating four other potential champs to the top spot.

The Superstock 600 European Championship went to Maxime Berger (Trasimeno Yamaha) with one race to spare.

Above: Broc Parkes (Yamaha YZF R6) took two late-season wins for second overall.

Centre below left: Former champion Fujiwara (Honda CBR600RR) was fourth in the table.

Below left: Dane Robbin Harms was a rostrum finisher on his CBR600RR.

Photographs: Gold & Goose

Below: Flag-waving Turkish fans support Sofuoglu at Brands Hatch.

Photograph: Martin Lauricello/Cello

WORLD ENDURANCE CHAMPIONSHIP

THE ULTIMATE ENDURANCE MACHINE

By MARTIN GELDER

Above: **Unbeatable again – Mathieu Lagrive asserts his authority on the SERT Suzuki GSX-R1000 at Oschersleben.**

Top centre: **Australian Glen Richards wheels the Phase One Endurance Yamaha into the Le Mans dusk.**

Bottom centre: **First race for the BMW Motorrad Motorsport R1200S at Le Mans brought an impressive 16th place.**

Top right: **Bol d'Or winner Gimbert leaves the Le Mans pit on the GMT94 Yamaha.**

Below: **The final showdown. Philippe on the Suzuki (left) and Giabbani on the Kawasaki line up for first practice at the Bol d'Or.**

Photographs: Martin Gelder

FOLLOWING the return of the classic Le Mans and Bol d'Or 24-hour races in 2006, 2007 was to be another year of change, the organisation of the championship passing back to the sport's governing body, the FIM, and the individual circuits. Some hailed this as a return to the good old days of the previous decade, while others were concerned that the change of management would reduce the profile of the series.

The addition of a new race at the Doha circuit in Qatar lifted everyone's spirits, but it was the return of a single team to the championship that caused the most discussion before the season started.

Team Kawasaki France had been a force to be reckoned with in the days of Fogarty, Rymer and Hislop, but it had not run in the full championship for more than five years. Its announcement of a full season of competition for 2007, and the head-hunting of Yamaha Austria's star rider, Frenchman Gwen Giabbani, to run alongside Brit Steve Plater and Spaniard Julian Mazuecos, convinced the endurance paddock that finally there would be a serious challenge to SERT Suzuki's recent dominance of the championship. Surely, fast riders, a well-supported machine and a team with endurance experience to spare would be able to carry the fight to the untouchable Suzuki…

Le Mans 24-Hour – France – 21/22 April

SERT Suzuki entered two machines for Le Mans. Regulars Philippe, Lagrive and Da Costa were on the No.1 GSX-R1000, while the No.2 machine was ridden by Costes, Dietrich and SBK's Neukirchner.

The two Suzukis were split in the opening hours of the race by Yamaha GMT94's Gimbert, Checa (David) and Four, with the Kawasaki France riders and Yamaha Austria's Jerman, Scarnato and Cudlin jostling for position behind them. A minor oil-line problem cost the No.1 Suzuki the lead during the night, dropping it behind the No.2 bike and Kawasaki France's entry. These three teams were still close at the end of the race, Suzuki No.2 finally taking the chequered flag ahead of No.1 in second place, Kawasaki France in third, GMT94 fourth and Yamaha Austria fifth.

A series of oil leaks left Yamaha Phase One fighting back to ninth overall. A big surprise was that the Open class BMW R1200S prototype finished 16th overall.

Albacete 6-Hour – Spain – 5 May

Taking advantage of home-track knowledge, Mazuecos took the lead for Kawasaki France in the first hour of the race, quickly opening a gap on the SERT Suzuki, with the Spanish-run Qatar Racing Team Kawasaki (Cardoso, Silva and Al Naimi) close behind. Yamaha Austria's Scarnato and Yamaha Phase One's Van Keymeulen tangled while fighting for third early in the race, allowing FCC TSR Honda – competing in its first European endurance race – to move up into the top five. Local team Folch Yamaha is always a strong performer at Albacete, and it finished third, behind Kawasaki France and SERT Suzuki. Qatar Kawasaki was fourth and Swiss Kawasaki team Bolliger fifth.

FCC TSR finished in a strong sixth, showing that Suzuka 8-Hour experience is just as valid outside Japan. Yamaha Austria was ninth, and Yamaha Phase One a disappointing 18th.

Suzuka 8-Hour – Japan – 29 July

The change of series organiser led to a record number of European teams making the long trip to Suzuka, but the Japanese race proved as tough as ever for the visitors.

The race win went to the Yoshimura Suzuki team of Kagayama and Akiyoshi, breaking a ten-year run of victories for

Honda and giving Suzuki its first win at Suzuka since 1983. Checa (Carlos) and Okada, on the HRC Honda, were second, with the No.788 FCC TSR Honda of Yeshima and Itoh third overall and first in the points; the dominant Japanese Superbike-class machines do not score in the World Championship .

SERT Suzuki was seventh overall and second in the points, ahead of the FCC TSR Honda that had raced at Albacete, which was eighth. Yamaha Phase One (Nowland, Richards and Nebel) was fourth, Bolliger Kawasaki (Morillon, Muff and Saiger) fifth, and Diablo Kawasaki (Hutchins, Cudlin Junior and Mason) sixth.

Despite a good opening to the season, Team Kawasaki France didn't compete at Suzuka, apparently because of disagreements between Kawasaki Japan and the local organiser. It was a strange decision that would cost the team dearly later in the year.

Oschersleben 24-Hour – Germany – 11/12 August

With Scarnato still suffering from injuries received at Albacete, Yamaha Austria drafted in Steve Martin for the German round, while date clashes with the British championship led to Stefan Nebel and Pedro Valcaneras joining Phase One. The race started on a drying track, and Yamaha Austria lost time changing to slicks, then crashed shortly afterwards. This left SERT Suzuki to establish an early lead over Kawasaki France, before Phase One moved up to second. Giabbani crashed the Kawasaki four hours into the race, leaving Yamaha Austria and Phase One to fight through the night for second place, behind SERT Suzuki.

With fewer than four hours to run, disaster struck Phase One when an oil-pump failure followed earlier clutch problems. Kawasaki France inherited second after third-placed Yamaha Austria's engine began to overheat. Kawasaki Bolliger was fourth, while a brilliant performance from the BMW Motorrad Motorsport R1200S ensured fifth; the second BMW R1200S finished ninth. British team Kawasaki Diablo took seventh, the best result of the season at what used to be its bogey track.

But it was no surprise to see SERT Suzuki's Philippe, Lagrive and Da Costa on the top step of the podium once again.

Bol d'Or 24-Hour – France – 15/16 September

The second SERT Suzuki was back for the Bol d'Or, presumably with team orders for the riders to stay between their team-mates on the No.1 SERT bike and the rest of the field. They did this from the start of the race, despite the best efforts of Yamaha Austria, Team Kawasaki France and wild-card Yamaha GMT94. A series of setbacks hit the Kawasaki, which lost ten laps after pushing in early in the race; it retired in the early hours of the morning with a blown engine.

SERT Suzuki's luck also failed at the Bol, a crash leaving the No.1 bike to fight its way back through the field. By dawn, it was up to third, and the gremlins switched their attention to SERT No.2, which crashed while in the lead, letting GMT94 through to first. GMT94 held its advantage to the finish, with SERT No.1 second and taking the championship. SERT No.2 was third, and Yamaha Phase One fourth, after a race-long fight with Bolliger Kawasaki.

Bolliger had looked set for fifth until rider Horst Saiger crashed on the pit-lane exit after the final stop of the race. The marshals would not help him move the bike, so the team was forced to retire 20 minutes before the end of the race. A bitter disappointment for the normally stoic Swiss outfit.

Qatar 8-Hour – Qatar – 10 November

Although SERT Suzuki had already taken the 2007 QMMF Endurance World Championship, the final race of the year – and the first visit to the dusty Losail circuit for the endurance series – proved to be one of the closest of the season.

Philippe, on the SERT Suzuki, took the lead at the start, but he was quickly reeled in and passed by former Kawasaki France rider Steve Plater, now on the Phase One Yamaha. Plater led for the rest of the first hour, until he was skittled off by Philippe as both riders prepared to make their first fuel and tyre stop. This let Yamaha Austria through into first place, with local squad Qatar Racing Team Kawasaki taking second.

SERT Suzuki began an epic climb-back from almost dead last, finally passing Yamaha Austria – surely preparing to celebrate its first world endurance victory – just 40 minutes before the end of the race, when the Austrians made their final stop. The Qatari Kawasaki was third; the French Suzuki fire-brigade team (Sapeurs Pompiers) fourth; and the Italian/American squad, Amadeus X One Yamaha, fifth. The BMW Boxer team finished a remarkable year with seventh overall, ahead of Suzuki Sweden, Yamaha Phase One and Slovakian team Maco Moto.

The Dust Settles

The Kawasaki challenge that we had all been expecting at the start of the year failed to materialise, seemingly because the team could not – or would not – commit to the full season. A good result at Suzuka might have been enough to pressurise SERT Suzuki into more of the kind of mistakes we saw at the Bol d'Or, and the fight could have come down to an eight-hour sprint at the final round.

Instead, Dominique Meliand's SERT Suzuki proved once again to be the ultimate endurance machine. The championship was not easy for the team – particularly the 24-hour races – but it remains the team to beat in 2008.

The 2008 championship will dispense with the 'Superbike' class. Instead, SuperProduction (full endurance chassis with limited engine tuning) will fight for the Endurance World Championship, and SuperStock (similar specifications to European SuperStock) machines will compete for an Endurance World Cup. Will this rule change mean that Yamaha Austria, Yamaha Phase One, Endurance Moto38 and Bolliger Kawasaki will be able to mount a credible challenge to SERT Suzuki? Team Kawasaki France might have something to say about that...

TOP TEN TEAMS

1: Suzuki Endurance Racing Team – SERT (FRA) – Suzuki GSX-R1000 – Vincent Philippe (FRA), Matthieu Lagrive (FRA), Julien Da Costa (FRA)
The only team to score points in every round of the championship.

2: Team Kawasaki France (FRA) – Kawasaki ZX10R – Gwen Giabbani (FRA), Steve Plater (GBR), Julian Mazuecos (SPA)
Pre-season contender, but only finished three races.

3: Yamaha Austria Racing Team(AUT) – Yamaha YZF-R1 – Igor Jerman (SLO), Sebastien Scarnato (FRA), Damian Cudlin (AUS), Steve Martin (AUS)
Scored at every race except the Bol d'Or; missed second overall by just one point.

4: Suzuki Endurance Racing Team No.2 – SERT (FRA) – Suzuki GSX-R1000 – William Costes (FRA), Guillame Dietrich (FRA), Max Neukirchner (GER)
Only entered two races, but took home a win and a third place.

5: Endurance Moto38 Yamaha (FRA) – Yamaha YZF-R1 – Erwin Nigon (FRA), Julien Millet (FRA), João Contente Fernandes (POR)
The stalwart French team was as consistent as ever, scoring everywhere except Le Mans

6: Yamaha Phase One Endurance (GBR) – Yamaha YZF-R1 – Warwick Nowland (AUS), Glen Richards (AUS), Didier Van Keymeulen (BEL), Stefan Nebel (GER), Pedro Valcaneras (SPA), Steve Plater (GBR)
Consistency would have given Phase One third in the championship, possibly second. It only missed fourth by three points.

7: Yamaha GMT94 (FRA) – Yamaha YZF-R1 – Sebastien Gimbert (FRA), David Checa (SPA), Olivier Four (FRA)
The former world endurance champion team still had what it takes, gaining a first-ever Bol d'Or win.

8: Bolliger Team Switzerland (SUI) – Kawasaki ZX10R – David Morillon (FRA), Patric Muff (SUI), Horst Saiger (AUT), Eric Mizera (GER)
Bad luck at the two French 24-hour races let down the usually unflappable Swiss squad.

9: Team 18 Sapeurs Pompiers (FRA) – Suzuki GSX-R1000 – Stephane Molinier (FRA), Guillaume Pialoux (FRA), David Briere (FRA)
Not a permanent team, but with extensive endurance experience, which shows in the results.

10: FCC TSR (JPN) – Honda CBR1000RR – Satoru Iwata (JPN), Yoshiyuki Sugai (JPN), Takeshi Tsujimura (JPN), Heinz Platacis (SUI)
Rumours have the Japanese team back in the full championship in 2008, with a new European partner team and a determination to make its mark on the world scene.

SIDECAR WORLD CHAMPIONSHIP

TRIPLE ECHO

By JOHN McKENZIE

AFTER two fairly comfortable world title wins in 2005 and 2006 with races in hand, Tim Reeves started the 2007 season confidently. In 2006, most serious competition had come from Finnish part-time ice-racing pair Pekka Paivarinta and Timo Karttiala (LCR Suzuki), and although Reeves entered the campaign as favourite, eyes were also on the growing speed and experience of the Finns. Stretched resources caused by under-funding contributed to their lack of ultimate success, but not before they had pushed Reeves to new limits.

Long-standing track records set by Steve Webster were broken, and it wasn't until the eighth of the 11 races that Reeves topped the table. In true world champion style, however, he matched consistency with determination and skill to win through, recording six wins and ten rostrums.

Prospects for the future were revealed when Ben and Tom Birchall notched up a pair of second places, and Seb Delannoy recorded a single victory to keep the French flag flying. Series returnee Markus Schlosser, a veteran of the old two-stroke days, ended up third, his passenger being sidecar's own 'Peter Pan', Adolf Hanni.

Round One, 13 May – Schleiz, Germany

Kent-based Tim Reeves returned to the fray with his Team Eastern Airways livery shrouding a new 2007 LCR chassis and Suzuki GSXR1000K7 motor – a combination that was some 25kg lighter than his 2006 machine. He also had a new passenger in Stuart Graham, brother Tim having quit due to work and family commitments. Graham's tenure on the carbon-fibre platform proved short, however, as he withdrew after injuring his hip in a collision with a verge marker during qualifying. A phone call and a hurried flight just delivered Patrick Far rance to Reeve's aid, 30 minutes before the final qualifying session; he stayed put for the whole season.

The duo qualified sixth for a third-row start in the Gold race on Sunday, having scythed through the Match-race quarter- and semi-finals to smash Steve Webster's long-standing track record in a time of 1m 29.867s.

In the Match-race final, Reeves took the win from the Finnish title contenders, Paivarinta and Karttiala, once again setting fastest race lap.

In Sunday's dramatic 22-lap Gold race, Reeves fought his way through from the third row to head the field at the end on the opening lap. He extended the lead lap on lap, despite Paivarinta striving to make up ground, and had pulled out a five-second gap before suffering fuel-pump problems on lap seven, which caused him to drop back and limp home in seventh.

Gold race winners were the returning – and deserving – Swiss pair of Markus Schlosser and the ever-young Adolf Hanni, who just pipped Delannoy and Cluze; the Birchall brothers completed the rostrum.

Round Two, 10 June – Brands Hatch, UK

The sidecars were added to the German Touring Car Championship (DTM) event as an unusual, but well-received, sideshow, and the flying Finns, Paivarinta and Karttiala, steered their machine to a flag-to-flag victory in the 36-lap race. Although chased hard by local hero and pole man Reeves, desperate for a win on his home track, Paivarinta was first into Paddock bend and never lost his iron grip on the race. In three laps, the Finn had pulled out a 4.6-second advantage over the world champion, and although the latter battled through the field to reduce the advantage, the inevitable backmarkers gave Paivarinta a breathing space.

With ten laps to go, Reeves finally began to make inroads on the race leader, closing to within 1.5 seconds as they began the last lap. But it was all too late; Paivarinta and Karttiala crossed the finish line to take both the race win and the championship lead, by four points from Reeves and Farrance. Meanwhile, the second Eastern Airways outfit of Sean and Mark Hegarty scored a superb third place in their first actual race finish in a full-distance world championship event.

Round Three, 30 June – Assen, Netherlands

It was back with the MotoGP series for the trip to Assen, scene of so many fantastic sidecar battles. The return was eventful, with a thrilling two-part race.

Points leader Paivarinta had grabbed pole with an impressive 1m 27.984s. Under bright sunshine, there was a close start, but the race had to be curtailed after 11 laps when the red flags came out following a three-outfit crash down the field. That gave a provisional result for Reeves from Schlosser and Paivarinta in third.

Fortunately, there were no serious injuries, and the race was restarted. This time, however, it was Paivarinta who got away to a flyer, chased hard by Reeves, but a change in the weather proved to be the deciding factor – Paivarinta got to grips with the slippery surface, while Reeves was forced to back off.

The Finnish pair were Finland's ice racing champions, and Paivarinta's experience gives an unbelievable confidence in the rain. He made light work of the slippery conditions and, as the rain became heavier, appeared to cruise to his second successive victory. Reeves, on the other hand, was fighting with huge slides and barely keeping the machine on the tarmac. Paivarinta's heroic efforts increased his title lead to nine points over the reigning champion.

Round Four, July 15 – Sachsenring, Germany

The searing heat at the Sachsenring, the half-way point in the season, would require a huge effort from Reeves to put his title ambitions back on track. A hard-fought win and a second did just that, clipping the points gap back to just five.

Saturday's 11-lap Sprint race was an exciting interlude, Reeves' 2006 lap record of 1m 29.546s being broken unofficially by Seb Delannoy on lap three.

Reeves headed the field on the opening lap, but dropped back to second as Paivarinta charged through from third. By lap four, he had retaken the lead, going on to take the win and 25 points, a fraction ahead of hard charging Markus Schlosser. Series leader Paivarinta followed home in third place.

Sunday saw the temperature soar to 33 degrees with a track temperature of 41 degrees, leaving the sidecar teams extremely concerned about the effects over a 22-lap race. The Gold race was run directly after the MotoGP round, and although many spectators had drifted away after Valentino Rossi crashed out, they returned en masse to watch the sidecar race – and they were not disappointed, cheering loudly for the three-wheelers.

As the race got under way, Reeves settled into second, behind Delannoy, but took the lead when the French duo destroyed their engine. The Eastern Airways pair pulled away from Paivarinta, who had moved up into second, but by half-distance, Reeves was beginning to falter, initially with a rear-tyre problem, but increasingly because of the heat.

On lap 13, Paivarinta grabbed the initiative, taking the race win by 17 seconds. As the race had progressed, Reeves had slowed visibly, and although he held second to the chequered flag, it was obvious that he had a serious problem. Seconds after pulling into the pit lane after the slow-down lap, he climbed from the outfit and promptly fainted from heat exhaustion. Farrance was also overcome, and both were quickly removed to the medical centre for rehydration treatment.

'I can't remember riding the last couple of laps,' recounted Reeves. 'I was feeling shivery and dizzy, and must have been on auto-pilot! I remember someone talking to me when I was laid in pit lane, but although I opened my mouth to speak, nothing came out.'

Round Five, 22 July – Salzburgring, Austria

In Austria, another two-race weekend and two wins for Reeves, who capitalised on Paivarinta's engine problems, saw the pendulum swing back in the world champion's favour.

Reeves had a perfect weekend, qualifying on pole and unofficially breaking the lap record by a massive 1.7 seconds. Setting the fastest time of the weekend at 1m 23s.

In Saturday's ten-lap Sprint race, Paivarinta was forced to follow on all but one tour before Reeves took the win with a two-second advantage.

It was a different story in the Gold race on Sunday, however, Reeves shooting away to lead the field around the first corner, leaving the luckless Paivarinta to pull out at turn three with an expensive blown engine, which would effectively seal his championship challenge.

Left: Reeves and Farrance had to work hard to make it three titles in a row.
Photograph: John McKenzie

Right: Sidecars stayed true to idiosyncrasy, the creed kept alive by a hard core of survivors, and some good close action.

Below: Paivarinta has the line, but Delannoy is cutting grass on the inside trying to steal the lead. Sprint races had plenty of rough and tumble.

Below right: Kentish sidecar stalwart Tim Reeves changed passengers and scored a hat-trick.
Photographs: Mark Walters

It wasn't all plain sailing for the world champion, though, as the rapidly improving Ben and Tom Birchall stepped up a gear mid-race to move into second place, shadowing his every move. The more experienced Reeves controlled the race from the front, however, and took his second win of the weekend, crossing the line just under a second ahead of the brothers.

The two wins and Paivarinta's non-finish handed the championship impetus to Reeves, and with a 25-point advantage, he topped the table for the first time in the season.

Round 6, 19 August – Rijeka, Croatia

Reeves clinched his third successive FIM Superside World Sidecar title after taking the win and a third place in the penultimate round in Croatia.

The win in Saturday's Match race followed a blistering performance from the world champion, who broke Markus Boesiger's 1998 lap record with a time of 1m 30.802s, winning by just 0.26 second from Paivarinta over the three laps.

Sunday morning saw the track temperature sizzle up to 50 degrees as the 20-lap Gold race loomed. Tyre choice would prove crucial; the broiling heat's effects on the rubber necessitated the hardest compounds available.

After the start, Reeves remained in third place for the first two laps, before forging ahead of Paivarinta to slot into second, behind Delannoy. By lap seven, he had grabbed the lead, but was unable to forge any discernable advantage over Delannoy and Paivarinta as the backmarkers hove into view.

Vicious slides indicated that the tyres were beginning to succumb to the melting track. By lap 16, Delannoy had begun to fade, leaving Paivarinta and Reeves locked in a battle that, with the title at stake, could only end in the gravel or recriminations.

Paivarinta finally snatched the lead, but on the last lap, the paint swapping became serious, losing Reeves his wheel-arch, and Paivarinta his nose-cone. Both outfits continued to the final corner, where Paivarinta caught the back of Reeves's outfit and then ran off the track.

Reeves took the win, followed by Delannoy and the Birchalls. Subsequently, Paivarinta tabled a protest, resulting in a 20-second penalty for Reeves, which dropped him down to third place. That made Delannoy the first French sidecar race winner since Alain Michel at Mugello in 1991.

'There were two incidents on that last lap,' said Reeves. 'I had been following Paivarinta closely, and was right on his back wheel as we approached the fast left-hander and then the right turn. He went towards the left and left a gap wide enough to drive a lorry through. But then he turned back in on me and took my wheel-arch off, and also his nose-cone. Although both outfits were damaged, we were able to continue towards the final corner. But he ran into the back of me, causing his fairing to tuck under the front wheel, leaving me to complete the race for the win. But when we got back to the paddock, Paivarinta lodged a protest, and the jury upheld it. We intend to appeal...'

He did, but the decision stood. Even so, with a lead of 46 points and only one round to go, Reeves had regained his title.

Round Seven, 9 September – Le Mans, France

Newly crowned World Champions Tim Reeves and Patrick Farrance rounded off the 2007 FIM World Sidecar Championship in style by taking the win in the final round. As the race unfolded, the usual three front runners were involved in a battle for the lead, Reeves and Farrance coming out on top to lead from Ben and Tom Birchall, with Paivarinta and Karttiala holding on to third place.

The three outfits pulled away from the rest of the field once again, and when they happened upon backmarkers Adam Treasure and Kees Endeveled in the final stages, it was Reeves who found a way through to make it to the flag with less than a second to spare over Birchall. It was his sixth win of the series, and 21st overall.

Paivarinta and Karttiala were third, three seconds adrift of the leading two outfits. They completed their world championship campaign as runners-up, some 55 points adrift of Reeves's total of 235.

ISLE OF MAN TT RACES

STILL THE MAN

By MAC McDIARMID

'Keep on past the grocer…' McGuinness speeds past the unique trackside furniture of Kirk Michael village.

Photograph: Gavan Caldwell Photography

Above: Muscling his Honda through the Mountain swerves, Guy Martin gave his all in trying to keep McGuinness in sight during the Superbike race.
Photograph: Dave Collister/www.photocycles.com

It may be that the most momentous aspect of the centenary TT was not the crowds, nor the festival, nor the dazzling array of past stars, nor even the fitting landmark of John McGuinness's 130mph lap, but what occurred at the bend named after the TT's favourite son, Joey Dunlop, at the 26th Milestone, on the last lap of the last race of the century. Mark Ramsbotham, a newcomer from Norfolk, was killed when he lost control of his machine, which cartwheeled off the track, killing two spectators, 33-year-old Dean Jacob from Kidderminster and a 52-year-old Australian, John Kenzig, visiting the races for the first time. Far from being commonplace, as some might suppose, these are believed to be the first spectator fatalities in the long history of the event. Two marshals were also injured, Hilary Musson and Janice Phillips. A former TT racer herself, Musson suffered grave injuries. An enquiry into the incident was pending.

JOHN McGuinness certainly is a class act, but sometimes he verges on the monotonous. In 2007, he dominated practice again on the Honda Superbike, pronouncing himself more or less ready to race before practice week was half over. Indeed, over the past four years, two with Yamaha and two with Honda, he's shown himself so adept at finding the right set-up by the middle of practice week that it's hard to escape the conclusion that he knows something the rest don't.

Or perhaps it's merely that the fluency of his riding style, his Hislop-like capacity for 'letting it run', lends itself to a lack of histrionics around the Mountain Course. Lougher, you suspect, is just as smooth, but perhaps lacks the physical size and strength to muscle the Superbike when it does get leery. The rest, with the possible exception of Hutchinson, are still learning the art of riding Superbikes as if they were 250s on steroids, which, with the notable exception of big Dave Jefferies, has usually been the key to TT success.

It helped, of course, that – give or take new yokes and revised electronics – he was riding precisely the same old friend on which he'd taken two wins in 2006. In a week of mixed weather, on Tuesday he lapped on the HM Plant Fireblade at 128.5mph, way ahead of the field. After Wednesday's washout, he upped that to 129mph on Thursday evening. Of the rest, Guy Martin impressed on the Hydrex Honda, just 7.5 seconds in arrears, followed by Ians Lougher and Hutchinson, and Martin Finnegan, all also Honda mounted. All four bettered their previous personal bests. Of the non-Honda riders, Michael Rutter, returning to the island for the first time in seven years, struggled with a succession of engine problems, while Yamaha's abbreviated efforts lay in the hands of cheerful rookie Steve Plater. In other words, both the Superbike and Senior races were pretty much in the Honda bag.

Although Bruce Anstey was oddly absent from the Superbike leaderboard, the Kiwi amply compensated in the Superstock and Supersport classes. Riding again for TAS Suzuki – rebranded and repainted in black 'Relentless' livery – he topped both classes during Thursday's fast session, at 125.3mph and 122.6mph respectively. On Friday evening, however, Hutchinson took the Superstock Fireblade around at 125.6mph, remarkable for a model that had been so palpably off the pace the year before. Finnegan, riding an MV Agusta not a million miles from the machine that won the 2006 WSB Superstock series, wasn't far behind at 124.3mph. Both were speeds that failed to hint at what would happen come race week. The same could be said for the Supersport class, where McGuinness ranked second to Anstey, both some way off the Morecambe man's lap record of a shade under 124mph.

In the sidecar class, many wondered how the legacy of last year's horrific Rhencullen crash would weigh on Dave Molyneux, this year riding with Rick Long, Rob Fisher's former passenger. It was a question never answered, for a succession of mechanical and electrical problems ravaged the Manxman's week. Hours before Saturday's opening practice session, he blew up his race engine at Jurby, emerging two days later with a roadbike engine borrowed from Tommy Leonard's shop. On Tuesday, they bolted in a new race motor, only to break down by Bray Hill. Not until Thursday did the 11-times winner put in a half-decent lap, 111.9mph. Although he improved this to 112.8mph on Friday, it was some way off his own 116mph record.

So instead, we watched impressed as the Manxman, who's usually played second fiddle to Moly, dominated the field. Nick Crowe, riding with Molyneux's former passenger, Dan Sayle, lapped at over 114mph on both Tuesday and Thursday evenings – the only crew to dip under the 20-minute mark by some distance. With Klaus Klaffenbock enduring a week as wretched as Moly's, John Holden was best of the rest.

Practice week concluded bizarrely with a three-bike pile-up at the notorious Black Dub, where Michael Weynand slid off, and Victor Gilmore and Jim Hodson came to grief on the wreckage. None was badly hurt, but the Peel fire engine had to attend to the resulting blaze, more or less curtailing the session.

SUPERBIKE TT

The opening race began amid speculation and controversy, but concluded by proving what we already knew – that McGuinness is still The Man. Scheduled to run on Saturday, the race was postponed, allegedly because of poor visibility on the Mountain, although much paddock muttering suggested that Dunlop had been unable to supply legal intermediate tyres to suit the mixed conditions prevailing at the time. Race organisers were prompt to scotch such suggestions, although this did little to quell wagging tongues.

So the first race of the Centennial began on Monday, causing the postponement of the Superstock event to Tuesday.

In other respects, it was business as usual. Despite tricky conditions with damp patches under trees and on the Mountain, McGuinness rattled into an immediate lead with an opening lap at 127.8mph, and he wasn't headed for the next 226 miles. Of the pretenders, Guy Martin clung most convincingly to his shirt-tail, just two seconds adrift at Glen Helen and 4.5 seconds after one lap, with Hutchinson a comfortable third.

First man away, Michael Rutter, riding in his first TT for seven years, compounded a practice week that had been blighted by engine problems with an early retirement, while Bruce Anstey's ambitions expired even earlier at Crosby. Local man Paul Hunt crashed out at Kerrowmoar on lap two, luckily without serious injury.

McGuiness's second lap, a record at 128.279mph and a slow first refuelling stop for Martin further extended the HM Plant rider's lead. From then on, the Morecambe man rode coolly to his signals, to win by 26 seconds from Martin. Third, a further 40 seconds down, was Hutchinson, with Finnegan, Lougher and Ryan Farquhar completing the leaderboard. The final silver replica went to newcomer Steve Plater in 11th place, a remarkable performance.

McGuiness conceded that the 48-hour delay had heaped extra pressure on him, and that conditions had been testing. 'I tried everything at the start,' he said of his customary demoralising opening lap, 'and had a real good go. There were damp patches that needed respect in places, and I had a huge slide at the 13th.' For his part, Martin admitted that he'd had his sights on a maiden TT win, but didn't quite have the pace of the HM Plant Honda, especially with two tardy pit stops.

SIDECARS

For a while in Race 'A', it looked as though Molyneux's practice misfortunes would continue, for within 12 miles of the start, he was overtaken on the road by Nicky Crowe, riding with a fervour previously unseen. Yet just a few miles later, Crowe was reported as touring at Quarry Bends, pulling in half a mile later at Sulby Crossroads, conveniently next to the pub run by passenger Dan Sayle's mum. Meanwhile, Klaus Klaffenbock's miserable week continued when he retired at Ballacraine, just seven miles into the opening lap.

Crowe's departure far from handed the result to Molyneux, however, for at Ramsey on lap one, John Holden led by six seconds from Steve Norbury, with Moly a similar margin behind in an unfamiliar third place.

On lap two, Molyneux upped the pace, taking seven seconds out of the leader, to lie second. Then, in one of the grittiest displays of his illustrious career, he flogged his underpowered Honda to the fastest lap of the race, 112.738mph, to win by 15 seconds from Holden and Winkle. Steve Norbury placed third, a further 24 seconds down, with Neary, Schofield and Connole completing the top six.

After perhaps the most bloody-minded and belligerent of all his wins, an oddly humble Molyneux paid generous tribute to the Manxman whose nemesis he has so often been. 'It was weird...Nick had it in the bag on talent and speed. To be honest, I'd have been happy with sixth. I rode my heart out and have never been so committed.'

Holden, who had seemed so close to a maiden win, was given a '+12' signal late on the second lap and just couldn't comprehend how his lead had disappeared. 'I can't believe I lost ten seconds on one lap,' he mused. The victory was Moly's 12th and Long's seventh, the latter equalling the performance of Wolfgang Kaulich three decades before.

The second sidecar race reaped more historic achievement for Molyneux, and even more heartache for Crowe in yet another dramatic duel. This time, Moly's good fortune included a track incursion by a dog at Glen Lough, causing the start to be postponed by 15 minutes and allowing the Manxman to change a malfunctioning instrument pod on the start line.

For this race, Molyneux was using Hutchinson's spare Supersports engine, but even this failed to prevent Crowe from blasting into an early lead. At Glen Helen first time around, it was Crowe, Klaffenbock and Holden, with Moly in an uncharacteristic fourth. After one lap, Crowe led by 14.7 seconds, by now from a fired-up Molyneux, with Holden and Klaffi close behind.

If this was the cue for another lap record, it came from an unexpected source, for Crowe and Sayle scorched around the second lap at a staggering 116.687mph – six seconds under Moly's 2005 mark – to extend their lead to 24 seconds. Just three miles later, though, it was all over for the local pairing, as they clattered to a halt at Ballahutchin. A moment or so later, Klaffi, looking good for his first TT rostrum finish, went out at the same spot. Molyneux and Long hung on to win by 26 seconds, again from Holden and Winkle who, for all the mechanical mayhem around them, used the same GSX-R600 engine for the whole of practice and both races. Remarkably, the entire leaderboard was identical to Race 'A', for Norbury, Neary, Schofield and Connole completed the top six.

So, ironically, the man who'd had the most troubled TT, Molyneux, benefited from the two biggest slices of luck to finish with 13 career wins, behind only Dunlop and Hailwood. 'To be honest, I wasn't even sure if we'd finish,' he said after the race. 'I saw Dan and Nicky go out and couldn't believe their bad luck.' Rick Long, now the most successful passenger of all time, with eight wins, echoed the sentiment. 'My heart went out to Nick and Dan when we saw them pulled up.'

Above: Haircut 100

Photograph: Gavan Caldwell Photography

Below: Double good fortune took Manxman Dave Molyneux (with passenger Dave Long) to his 13th sidecar win.

Photograph: Dave Purves

Bottom: Unlucky lap-record pair Nick Crowe and Dan Sayle were leading the field by 24 seconds when they broke down on the last lap.

Photograph: Dave Collister/www.photocycles.com

SUPERSTOCK TT

Perfect weather prevailed again for the Superstock TT, third running of the class that replaced the previous production categories as the world's toughest road test.

Having won the same race in the two previous years, Bruce Anstey was emphatically the man in charge in the Superstock race, which he led from start to finish. By Glen Helen, ten miles into the first lap, the Kiwi already led by five seconds. He overtook McGuinness on the road just a few miles later at Ballaugh, and completed the lap at 128.297mph, faster than McGuinness's new Superbike record – from a standing start on a barely modified road bike. A marginally faster second lap, 128.349mph, sealed the result.

'The bike went well, but could have handled better,' said the deadpan Anstey of his Relentless TAS Suzuki GSX-R1000. He need hardly have added that he 'really went for it for the first two laps'. McGuinness, who placed second, fully 40 seconds behind the winner, paid tribute to Anstey's 'sensational' lap speeds, adding that he 'pushed hard to Glen Helen on lap one, and wasn't expecting to be five seconds down when I got my next signal. The bike was good enough today, but the rider wasn't.'

McGuinness's HM Plant Honda team-mate, Hutchinson, held third place throughout, having 'ridden the wheels off' the Fireblade, but he had a few dicey moments on damp patches under the trees. Both results confounded the poor showing of the Honda, essentially an identical model, in the 2006 Superstock TT.

Fourth, 20 seconds behind the Yorkshireman, was Martin Finnegan on the MV Agusta, with 20-year-old Manxman Conor Cummins the first Yamaha man home in fifth, after overhauling sixth-placed Mark Parrett – still aching from a crash at Cruikshanks in the Superbike race – only on the final lap. Initially, Cummins was credited as being the fastest-ever local lapper, although veteran Maughold rider Gary Carswell lapped marginally faster, at 124.621mph, on the way to ninth place on his final lap.

SUPERSPORT (JUNIOR)

As happens so often, the Supersport race was the least predictable, and the most riveting, of the entire week. It featured lap records galore, speeds – on modified street machines on treaded tyres – faster than the outright record of a mere eight years before and, as with the sidecar events, rotten luck for the most deserving rider.

That man was Bruce Anstey, who, from a standing start, took his Relentless Suzuki around at a record 124.055mph, bettering that one lap later at 125.041mph, to leave the rest of the field's ambitions in shreds. Then, at the half-distance pit-stops, McGuinness, Hutchinson and Martin made clean getaways, but the Kiwi's bike refused to fire up. When finally it did, he'd lost 23 seconds and any realistic chance of victory. That effectively put McGuinness in the lead, but by Glen Helen, Hutchinson was in front, by a slender 0.3 second, extended to five seconds by the end of the lap. Meanwhile, Anstey was riding angry, only two seconds behind Martin.

We may look back on that final lap as the one in which road racing's two tyros finally cut their teeth. Despite McGuinness lapping at over 125mph, Hutchinson clung on to win from his illustrious team-mate by 2.84 seconds. And Martin dug deep to hold off the Anstey charge with a new lap record, 125.161mph, while Anstey himself lapped only 0.12 second slower. Indeed, Anstey, whose blistering pace inspired this captivating race, broke the lap record three times – on laps one, two and four – only to finish off the rostrum. Local rider Nigel Beattie placed fifth, 85 seconds behind Anstey, and six seconds ahead of local rival Cummins. Hutchinson's winning time was fully 35 seconds faster than McGuinness's 2006 race record.

A breathless and 'over the moon' Hutchinson described it as a race of 'ridiculous speed. When I got the "P3" signal, I wondered what on earth was going on, but got cracking and was helped by a good pit stop.' Martin confessed himself equally super-lunar, while even McGuinness agreed that it was 'wicked'.

SENIOR TT

If the Junior TT allowed the young upstarts a taste of champagne, the week's concluding event, the Senior, put them firmly back on the beer. It was, as so often of late, the John McGuinness Show. And he was as good as his word, having predicted that a 130mph lap was possible, provided conditions were right.

And they were. A two-second McGuinness advantage by Glen Helen on lap one was stretched to almost ten seconds after one lap, completed at a tantalising 129.883mph. On the second, flying lap, he clocked 17 minutes, 21.99 seconds, rapturously converted to 130.354mph by commentator Charlie Lambert. This landmark came almost 20 years after the 120mph barrier was broken by Steve Hislop.

With Anstey retiring early with handling problems and only Martin able to come anywhere near McGuinness's pace, it was all over bar the shouting. The HM Plant Honda rider claimed his 13th TT win – equalling Molyneux – by 32 seconds, at an average speed of 127.255mph. Martin placed second from Hutchinson, Lougher, Archibald and Cummins, with Plater an impressive seventh.

It was an emotional win for McGuinness, who savours TT history rather more than most of his opponents. 'I remember sitting on the hedge at Rhencullen when Hizzie did the first 120mph lap in '89… and never thought for a moment that I'd be the guy to break 130. If ever there was a time to crack it, lap two was it, with a rolling start and near-perfect conditions. I'm so proud to have achieved these landmarks…it's a day I'll cherish forever.' As he spoke, little did he know of the awful and perhaps momentous events unfolding over the Mountain at the 26th Milestone.

Although both Honda and Yamaha began TT week with 130 TT wins apiece (although Yamaha hybrids arguably added two to its tally), Honda's five wins in the week put it convincingly top of the all-time manufacturers' rankings. In a distant third place was Norton, with 43, just two ahead of Suzuki.

Above: **Fastest yet – John McGuinness won the Centenary Senior TT with a landmark record speed. Admiring young team-mate Ian Hutchinson, third, shares the moment.**
Photograph: Gavan Caldwell Photography

Top left: **Superstock winner for a third straight year, Bruce Anstey launches his Suzuki GSX-R.**
Photograph: Dave Purves

Centre left: **Archibald was out of luck in the Superstock race.**

Bottom left: **Hutchinson came of age with his narrow Supersport win.**
Photograph: Dave Collister/www.photocycles.com

KICKER
HJC
SUZUKI
GSX
ヨシムラ
ZERO GRAVITY
SUZUKI
SUZUKI

US RACING REVIEW

DOWN TO THE WIRE

By PAUL CARRUTHERS Cycle News

Ben Spies made it two in a row, with his one-point win over Suzuki team-mate Mat Mladin.
Photograph: Andrew Wheeler

SUZUKI
66
DUNLOP
DUNLOP
SUZUKI
DUNLOP
KBC

THERE'S nothing like a little intra-team rivalry to put life into a championship fight. Throw in the fact that the two antagonists have a general dislike of each other – and will do practically anything to make sure the other doesn't win – and you have all the ingredients for a heated battle. Welcome to the 2007 AMA Superbike Series, a championship that wavered back and forth all season long between Yoshimura Suzuki team-mates Mat Mladin and Ben Spies; a championship in which the rest of the field were just bit players; and a championship that was decided at the very last round, and by just a single point.

And when that last round at Laguna Seca came to a close, the two came together on the cool-down lap, the defeated Mladin gracious in defeat and taking the time to congratulate Spies on his second successive AMA crown. And why wouldn't he? Mladin knows that it's because of Spies that he has had to raise his game; the Australian likes a good battle, both on and off the track, and he knows that without Spies there wouldn't have been one. And what good is winning another title if you didn't have anyone to beat?

As much as they dislike each other, antagonise each other and each other's crews, and cause the Suzuki brass to fall on their knees every night and pray that the entire operation doesn't implode right in front of them, these two are good for each other. They push each other to levels that the rest of the field can't come close to matching, and this turns out to be a rather fruitful exercise for Suzuki, given the fact that it didn't lose a single race the entire season. Scrap on, boys!

Both Spies and Mladin came away with what they wanted – or at least what they said they wanted. From day one at Daytona, Mladin was steadfast in his claim that he no longer cared about winning championships. He was here to win races – and lots of them. Spies also wanted to win races, but he had his eye on the prize of being champion again, and was willing to do whatever it took to get it.

Mladin ended up winning 12 races, which was a new single-season record. He crashed twice trying to win more – at Daytona and Miller Motorsports Park – although he remounted and still scored points in both rounds. Good to his word, Mladin pushed and pushed, and he's never ridden better.

Spies won seven times over the year and never finished worse than second, putting together a more consistent season that resulted in the title. He also earned more pole positions, and this championship pays a point for each pole. Ditto for most laps led. Spies also had some crashes, and both men were fortunate in that the AMA is usually quick to throw a red flag, yet slow to restart a race, which meant there were a few occasions when both were able to restart after crashing – not something that would be possible in most other series. That said, the championship remained in doubt until the bitter end.

Yoshimura Suzuki entered 2007's series as the all-conquering team with its all-conquering motorcycle – the GSX-R1000. And that wasn't about to change. There was one change, however, and that was the inclusion in the team of Tommy Hayden, the eldest of the three Hayden brothers. Tommy was there to replace long-time Yosh man Aaron Yates, who in turn would head up Michael Jordan's Suzuki team.

While Spies and Mladin continued to roll on, Hayden struggled for most of the year after hurting himself at the first test for the team in Malaysia. He would end the season fifth in the championship, but it was far less than what he and the team had expected. He did serve as a good buffer between Mladin and Spies, and their respective crews, Hayden's crew usually being slotted between the pair in the pit garages. Hayden was 'Switzerland' in the Yoshimura team, generally staying out of the fight, but providing a neutral zone for those who wanted to visit without threat of warfare.

The American Honda team was back for more with the same two riders: Miguel Duhamel and Jake Zemke. They would battle all season long with a motorcycle that neither of them particularly liked, Zemke ending up third in the championship, and Duhamel eighth. Duhamel was actually the stronger, until he was badly injured late in the season during a test session at Road Atlanta. That forced him out of the final races and dropped him in the series point standings. The bottom line: Duhamel did enough to keep his ride for 2008, but Zemke did not; the Californian is set to be replaced in the factory squad by Briton Neil Hodgson.

Kawasaki was back in full force with Roger Lee Hayden and newcomer Jamie Hacking. Both fared well at times, although Hacking struggled mightily with the ZX-10R for most of the season. But when he got the bike to where he liked it, he excelled with several third-place finishes, and he was able to climb to sixth by season's end.

Meanwhile, Roger Lee ended up tenth, although he did miss a few rounds to concentrate on winning the Supersport title for a first time, joining his brothers Tommy and Nicky as AMA title winners. He also earned a wild-card ride at the US Grand Prix, impressing many with tenth.

Yamaha returned to the Superbike wars with its R1, with Eric Bostrom and Jason DiSalvo at the controls. Bostrom's season was typical – up and down – although it was mostly down, and he ended it as the seventh-ranked rider. Both he and DiSalvo struggled to get the R1 to where they wanted it, DiSalvo being totally off the pace in most races and ultimately finishing ninth in the series.

Yates thrived in his new surroundings at Team Jordan, getting on the podium in Superbike races and finishing the season fourth, only three points behind Zemke in third.

The other big team in the pits was the Corona Honda effort,

Main photograph: Mladin won more races, but failed to regain the title that he has won five times before.

Bottom left: Serial champ Mladin could smile in defeat. 'We're bad for each other's health," he told Spies.

Bottom: The Yoshimura Suzuki pair dominated the AMA Superbike series.

Below: Second-time winner Ben Spies has ambitions for MotoGP.

Photographs: Andrew Wheeler

Above: **Aaron Yates gave Michael Jordan's Suzuki team its first rostrum on his way to fourth overall.**
Photograph: Tom Hnatiw/Flick of the Wrist Photography

Right: **Veteran Miguel Duhamel on the Honda. His season was spoiled by a late testing injury.**
Photograph: Andrew Wheeler

with British rider James Ellison going it alone – well, except for a one-off ride at Laguna Seca, where he was seriously upstaged by Neil Hodgson. Ellison finished the year in 11th place on the points table.

Eraldo Ferracci brought MV into AMA Superbike racing in 2007, with Italian Luca Scassa and Georgian Matt Lynn. The pair had some good runs in the top ten, but both suffered numerous crashes that had Ferracci scratching his head. Still, the pair ended up tied for 14th in the championship.

As always, it was off to Daytona for the start of the season and – again – the Superbike race played second fiddle to the Daytona 200, which now uses the modified 600s of the Formula Xtreme class as the basis for what was once America's premier event. In 2006, Spies was outsmarted by Mladin, beaten to the line in a race the Texan had thought he was going to win. A year later, he got that win. And more.

Spies won his first-ever Daytona Superbike race by three seconds over Duhamel, the French Canadian well ahead of Zemke. Fourth place ultimately went to Kawasaki's Akira Yanagawa, the Japanese visitor riding a steady race to take advantage of the woes of so many others. Team M4 EMGO Suzuki's Geoff May rounded out the top five.

If Spies was smiling after winning, that smile probably started on the fifth lap, when he watched Mladin crash out of the lead. The Aussie would remount and climb to as high as eighth before giving up two spots on the final lap with a badly chunked front tyre.

So Spies left Florida with a healthy points lead of 17 over Mladin. As is often said, you can't necessarily win the championship at Daytona, but you can lose it there, and Mladin was starting his season in a deep hole. Ditto for several others.

On the opening lap, a miscue in the International Horseshoe put Hacking on the ground, and he took Yates with him. Hayden was also affected, as he had to take to the dirt to avoid the carnage. Yates would remount to finish 11th, and Hayden would rejoin to end up eighth. Hacking, though, was out of his first Superbike race with the Kawasaki team after just half a lap. His team-mate, Hayden, also ran afoul of things, high-siding out of the battle for third on lap five – the same lap that Mladin fell. The next of the top men to face problems was Bostrom. Running at the front for the first two laps and then in the top three throughout, Bostrom had a front tyre go bad on the 12th lap and he had to pit to have it changed. He would end up 21st when all was said and done.

No one is ever very sad to see Daytona disappear in their rear-view mirrors, especially since the next round takes place at a real race-track – Barber Motorsports Park. Barber saw Mladin bounce back in a big way, holding off Spies for 28 pressure packed laps to win the first race of the double-header. Duhamel was third, his season off to a good start. Although he was the best of the rest, no one could keep pace with the two factory Suzukis, which was a theme that held steadfast for the season.

Mladin got the jump on pole-sitter Spies and the pair took off, quickly gapping the field. Their lead grew by seconds, but there was little between them. Spies kept it close throughout, but a pass never came and Mladin recorded his record building 52nd Superbike victory by 0.116 second. The next day featured more of the same, Mladin putting himself back in the championship hunt by winning again. The podium was the same as the day before, with Spies second and Duhamel third.

'That was a nice win for us,' Mladin said after his 53rd Superbike win. 'It was nice to get the double. We put in some hard work during the off-season. My guys put in some hard work.'

After three of 18 races, Spies continued to lead with 103 points, but his lead on Mladin was down to just eight.

California Speedway in Fontana, California, has a sterile feel.

Situated within a giant NASCAR oval, the road course is rather dull, and the action seems distant to the spectators. But Spies and Mladin did their very best to make things interesting as the series made its only stop in Southern California – at least for the first ten laps. Those laps were magical to watch – unless you were Suzuki brass – as the two were acting like anything but team-mates as they pushed and shoved each other with reckless abandon. But it all changed on the 11th lap as Spies found his way around Mladin and simply took off, turning a 0.008-second deficit into a one-second lead as he clicked off a 1m 24.335s to Mladin's 1m 25.413s. From there, he would stretch until the finish, leading over the stripe by 6.7 seconds.

Yamaha's Bostrom put his R1 on the podium in third, with Tommy Hayden besting Duhamel.

If Mladin appeared dead in the water after being soundly beaten by Spies the day before, that wasn't the case a day later when he stormed back to beat his young team-mate by 0.035 second. Mladin took off at the start and actually led by over three seconds on the 13th of 28 laps, but that lead evaporated in lapped traffic, and once Spies got the bit between his teeth, the race was on. For the last eight laps, the pair ran together, separated by less than half a second for the duration. But try as he might, Spies couldn't get past Mladin, and the result was the pair splitting race wins over the course of the weekend.

Bostrom finished third again, with Hayden fourth – for the second successive race.

Mladin continued his roll as the series headed to Infineon Raceway, the gritty Australian winning both races to leave Northern California's wine country tied on points with Spies. It was as if those two other races hadn't even been held.

The first win, the 55th of Mladin's AMA Superbike career, was rather easy. Instead of the expected duel with Spies, it was a runaway, the veteran winning by 19.1 seconds in what was the dullest Superbike race of the season to date. Spies was second, but any chance he had of staying with Mladin ended early. On just the second lap, the Texan ran off on the exit of Turn One and got into the dirt. He lost almost three seconds, and from there, the six-times AMA Superbike Champion simply pulled away, gapping Spies by half a second a lap, sometimes more, to win his seventh AMA Superbike race at Infineon.

Third went to Duhamel, the French Canadian battling with Yamaha's DiSalvo before ultimately pulling clear. At the finish, he was almost five seconds clear of DiSalvo, the New Yorker holding on for fourth, his best ever AMA Superbike finish.

Mladin dominated again on the Sunday, beating Spies by 9.4 seconds after controlling the race from the outset. Spies kept him honest early on, but could never make serious inroads. Zemke held off the advances of Roger Lee Hayden for third, until the latter's Kawasaki expired on the 23rd of 28 laps. That moved Duhamel to fourth, although he just beat Tommy Hayden's Suzuki by 0.08 second to the flag.

Spies's season hit a snag at Road America, but he came out of it much better than anyone thought possible. In an extra practice session put on because of an expected wet race, Spies tossed his GSX-R1000 down the road and injured his right foot. He was fortunate to be healthy enough to finish second to Mladin in Saturday's first race, with Tommy Hayden getting his first podium for the team and making it a complete factory Suzuki sweep of the top three.

'I didn't' break anything, but it threw me down pretty good,' Spies said. 'My whole crew, they've got to rebuild a whole new bike, and I've made them do that two weekends in a row.'

Win 57 extended Mladin's championship lead to six points after eight of 19 rounds.

Bottom left: **Jamie Hacking switched to Kawasaki, and five rostrum visits put him sixth overall.**

Below centre left: **Jason DiSalvo got a best of fourth on the Yamaha.**

Below: **Roger Lee Hayden won the Supersport crown for Kawasaki.**

Photographs: Andrew Wheeler

Bottom: **Eric Bostrom (Yamaha) had an up-and-down year, finished seventh.**

Photograph: Tom Hnatiw/Flick of the Wrist Photography

Above: Neil Hodgson leads fellow Honda rider Duhamel and Yates's Suzuki in his one-off Superbike ride at Laguna.
Photograph: Andrew Wheeler

Top left: Ex-250 GP rider Chaz Davies found refuge riding a Yamaha in the Supersport class, with a best of fourth place.
Photograph: Tom Htniw/Flick of the Wrist Photography

Right: Another British GP refugee, James Ellison, made his US Superbike debut, and was 11th overall.
Photograph: Andrew Wheeler

Below right: Spies took the Superstock title as well.
Photograph: Tom Htniw/Flick of the Wrist Photography

Sunday dawned wet and rainy, and Spies surprised everyone with his effort, the Texan taking his first wet-weather win with a brilliant ride in an attrition filled race on the soaked Road America road course. Not only did Spies win, but also he regained the championship lead he'd lost the day before. He realised it after he took the chequered flag and found that his friend Hacking had finished second on the Kawasaki, pushing Mladin to third. That meant a two-point lead – and a weekend well and truly saved when things had looked so bleak just a day earlier.

When you have two riders on identical motorcycles and tyres, turning almost identical lap times, the race can be won or lost at the start. Case in point: the first race at the Miller Motorsports Park in Utah. Spies got a holeshot, while Mladin botched it. And from there, it was all Spies as he rode away from his team-mate to win the first of two AMA Superbike races at the new facility by 7.273 seconds.

Zemke's third was his third podium. The Californian had his hands full, however, with Roger Lee Hayden, who backed off the pace only in the final laps to finish fourth.

Spies did the Miller double a day later, on an afternoon that very nearly ended Mladin's season. While Spies ran away and hid, things behind him – and especially with Mladin – were topsy-turvy. Mladin was fortunate to have made the finish at all, having crashed out of the lead on the sixth lap in the very fast second corner, bringing out the red flags. Although initially he appeared injured, Mladin got out of the ambulance and ran back to the paddock, where his crew frantically went about fixing his badly beaten motorcycle in time to make the restart. Then he bravely rode on, battling with Duhamel and Roger Lee Hayden for third place. He ended up fourth. Impressive indeed.

Suddenly, the championship lead had grown again, with Spies out in front by 18 points.

Miss Momentum stayed in the Spies corner at Laguna Seca, where the AMA boys took the support role as the Red Bull US Grand Prix came Stateside. For the second year in a row, Spies was the man, and his performances there, in front of the most important people in road racing, definitely can't have hurt his chances of moving one day to the big stage of MotoGP. The Texan owned Mladin at Laguna, beating him by 4.9 seconds and grabbing a boatload of championship points, having earned a point for pole, a point for laps led and the points for winning the race. Spies left the Monterey Peninsula leading the championship by 24 points, 420–396, after 12 of 19 rounds. But there was still a long way to go, and Mladin would quickly show that this wasn't a fight from which he planned to walk away.

The battle for third at Laguna was the most entertaining of the day, Yates, Duhamel and Neil Hodgson fighting for the duration. When all was said and done, however, it was Yates, who gave Michael Jordan his first-ever AMA Superbike podium. Duhamel was fourth, with Honda mounted Hodgson fifth in his one-off return to the AMA series.

Mladin took full advantage of a red flag to end Spies's winning streak at four on a hot, overcast afternoon at the Mid-Ohio Sports Car Course. Mladin had blown the first start, going from second on the grid to seventh, but was granted a reprieve when David Weber suffered a vicious high-side on the 13th lap, stopping the race near the mid-point, with Spies holding a comfortable 6.539-second lead. On the second try, Mladin got away better – he was fourth and he quickly dispatched the riders between himself and Spies. When Spies bobbled going on to the front straight at the end of the fifth lap, Mladin pounced, taking the lead with an inside pass into Turn One.

Duhamel ended up third, with Yates fourth and Roger Lee Hayden fifth; third to seventh places were covered by less than a second.

The following day's race was delayed by rain and ended up being the longest day in recent memory of AMA road racing. But it was also a day when Mladin continued his surge back toward the front in the points standings. He did so with another victory, giving himself a perfect two-race sweep of the weekend to inch back into title contention.

After a long day of delays caused by wet weather in central Ohio, Mladin managed to beat Spies by 1.868 seconds in the shortened 18-lap final, the Australian taking over the lead on the sixth of 18 laps. From there, he was never headed, although Spies kept him honest for the duration.

Hacking was third, the Kawasaki rider's best race of the season. Although he was over 16 seconds behind the two Suzukis at the finish, he was able to hold off Yates. In taking the two victories, Mladin did what he had to do to pull back points on Spies. He now trailed by 17.

The gap would be diminished even further by Mladin's win at Virginia International Raceway. Just like that, it was down to 11 points, and then six points when he won again the next day. Things were getting tight, especially around the neck of Spies.

'It is amazing,' Mladin said of his landmark 60th victory. 'It was only maybe three years ago that I was at 30-something wins, and we've had a number of wins over the past three or four years and really boosted that number up. As I said yesterday, or whenever it was, in no way shape or form do I think 60's going to be the last. I'm certainly working as hard as I can to extend my career and be a force in AMA Superbike for as long as possible.'

With Spies finishing second on both days, third on Saturday went to Hacking after a race-long battle with Yates. On Sunday, Yates turned the tables and finished third over Hacking. Fast by Ferracci MV Agusta riders, meanwhile, had their best days of the season, Luca Scassa taking seventh and Matt Lynn eighth.

If Spies owns Laguna Seca, than Mladin owns Road Atlanta. With his two wins there, Mladin made certain that the championship would come down to a winner-take-all affair in the season finale.

Mladin closed to within two points of the lead with a victory over a battered Spies on a sunny and warm Saturday afternoon at the Braselton, Georgia, circuit, then left with a three-point lead on the Texan after winning again on Sunday.

Mladin was in control on the sixth of 25 scheduled laps on Saturday, when Spies crashed in the downhill Turn Four, bringing out a red flag. Neither Spies nor the bike was badly damaged, and he was able to make the restart. He was on the back row, however, which meant Mladin got a head start, and he took full advantage of the situation.

'I said to Ben, "We're not good for each other's health,"' Mladin said. As for the remainder of the season: 'We've got a couple more races to go. Hopefully we can keep it together.'

Spies's race was nothing short of heroic. From the back of the grid, he quickly made his way through the pack. Eighth at the end of the first lap of the restart, Spies had made his way into second by the sixth lap. By then, Mladin had over five seconds in hand, and Spies had no hope of cutting into it.

On Sunday, it was more of the same, Mladin sweeping the shortened second leg and setting up the Californian finale. 'That's the way we wanted to be heading to Laguna Seca,' Mladin said. The victory was his sixth in a row and twelfth of the season, breaking his own record of 11 wins from 2005. It was also his 63rd career victory.

Hacking was a distant third, 20.34 seconds behind Spies.

The pressure heading to Laguna was at an all-time high, and most of it seemed to fall on young Spies's shoulders. But he did what many felt he couldn't do – he withstood the pressure of Mladin not only to win the race, but also to take the championship, his second in a row in the AMA Superbike class.

Spies and Mladin had battled for a good portion of the race, Mladin doing most of the leading. But it all changed on the 16th of 28 laps, when Spies took over in the Corkscrew and then pulled away, leading by over five seconds before his last-lap celebration allowed Mladin to get to 2.5 seconds at the finish line.

When all was said and done, Spies had won the title by just a single point, 652–651. 'Once I got into the lead, that was the longest 12 laps of my life,' he said.

Yates narrowly defeated Zemke for third. The order was reversed in the final points standings, however, as Zemke beat Yates, 468–465.

Both factory Kawasakis crashed out of the race, Roger Lee Hayden going down in Turn Three on the opening lap, just moments after winning the AMA Supersport crown. Hacking went out in Turn Five on lap five.

In the other support classes, Spies did the double by capturing the Superstock title; Josh Hayes was impressive in winning Formula Xtreme while also battling for the Supersport title to the very end; and Roger Lee Hayden won that Supersport title in the final race at Laguna.

Below: **Formula Extreme champion Josh Hayes holds off his Honda team-mate Aaron Gobert.**

Photograph: Tom Hnatiw/Flick of the Wrist Photography

BRITISH SUPERBIKES REVIEW

HIGHS AND LOWS

By LOUISE CAIN

Above: Defending champion Kiyonari did it again for Honda.
Photograph: Gavan Caldwell Photography

Inset right: Kiyo and team celebrate the hard-fought win.
Photograph: Clive Challinor

BENNETTS British Superbike Championship delivered all the emotions that only racing can provide. In a season that saw the high of Honda and Ryuichi Kiyonari retaining the title, nothing could have prepared the paddock for the low of losing two young riders. It was all there in 13 weekends, which varied from fast furious fun to gut-wrenching sorrow.

For 2007, there was a shift in power, with a new young breed of rider starting to emerge. The rider who mixed things up the most with the usual suspects was Jonathan Rea. In his second year in the premier class, the Ulsterman became a force to be reckoned with, challenging his HM Plant Honda team-mate, Kiyonari, all season to the final round at Brands Hatch.

Apart from Rea, there was an influx of talent from the Supersport class – Cal Crutchlow, Leon Camier and Tom Sykes all made the step up. Crutchlow slotted into the Rizla Suzuki team with World Superbike star Chris Walker. Camier joined the Bike Animal Honda team, while Sykes went to Stobart Vent Axia Honda with Shane Byrne.

Battle commenced at Brands Hatch on the full GP circuit, with a surprising front row. Rea secured pole with the fastest-ever two-wheeled lap, a blistering 1m 25.235s. Camier took third, with second and fourth positions going to Airwaves Ducati's Gregorio Lavilla and Leon Haslam.

At the end of race day, Lavilla had notched up two wins and walked away with the fledgling championship lead. Rea and Camier shared the podium spoils with a second and third each, leaving the Brands Hatch crowd enthralled at the audacity of these youngsters forcing their way on to the podium.

Camier prepared for his Superbike debut by banging in consistent laps all weekend. 'I was expecting top ten, top eight. I've been working really hard with the team and Dunlop during testing to understand the bike and find a set-up,' he said.

He had quite a battle with Lavilla, as he explained, 'When I was in front, I was making a couple of mistakes and I was just trying to find some more grip, because I could hear Lavilla behind me. I was trying wide lines, then standing the bike up and cutting in, but he obviously thought I went wide and stuck it underneath me! I then turned to hit a really late apex and we clouted. No one fell off or was hurt, so no worries.'

With the unsettled feeling of new blood on the podium, the Superbikes moved on to high-speed Thruxton. Tommy Hill, on the Virgin Media Optoma Loans Yamaha, put one across the bows of the top three by taking pole position. Sadly, he only managed eighth and tenth in the races. Normal service was almost resumed with another double from Lavilla, with Kiyo joining him on the podium. The latter took a third and a second, but the other two podium places went to Camier, who was second in race one, and Byrne, third in race two.

'I wanted to get into the lead and try and pull away, but those factory Hondas are quick. I had to just try and hang in there. I wasn't quite fast enough to put a move on Lavilla, but we're back and on the podium, which is great,' said Byrne.

When Walker came back to the UK, there was a lot of talk of the 2001 season, when he was pipped to the title by Neil Hodgson. The glory days were back, and Walker's first podium came at Silverstone during round three, when he finished third behind Kiyonari and Rea. A repeat podium performance looked on the cards for race two, but he had to settle for fourth while Lavilla picked up second and Rea took third.

This was the first round in which Kiyonari showed his hand, claiming his first double win of the year. It was also where Haslam's lacklustre start to the year went from bad to worse due to a high-speed off during free practice. 'I knew the Ducati was capable of much more, so in the second session, I pushed a bit too hard and came off,' recalled Haslam. He suffered heavy bruising in the fall, but bounced back in qualifying to finish second.

'I am happy enough,' declared Haslam after the second race. 'I had a few problems in race one, and having lost the lead, I dropped back and finished up sixth, but it gave me confidence for the second race. I got a good start in race two and was feeling good chasing Kiyo, but getting bumped by Shakey caused me to fall back again. After that, I was just starting to catch Johnny Rea and Chris Walker when the red flag came out, leaving me in fifth.' The red flag was caused by Steve Plater crashing and leaving fluid on the track, causing two other riders to crash out.

Lavilla still held the title lead ahead of Camier, but Kiyonari was beginning to close in as the teams headed north to Oulton Park. The Virgin Media Optoma Loans Yamaha team had signed James Haydon for 2007 as they had worked well together in the past. However, the change to Pirelli tyres from his usual Dunlop rubber was producing poor finishes. Uninspiring results, coupled with an untimely mountain-biking accident, saw him leave the team. The vacancy was filled by former South African Superbike Champion Hudson Kennaugh.

Championship leader Lavilla took pole position and was joined on the front row by young Sykes on the Stobart Honda. The race turned into an Airwaves Ducati house battle, the duelling pair almost coming to blows. Haslam was leading until the hairpin, where Lavilla put a very late move on him, running underneath the Brit and forcing him to lift his machine. 'It was a harsh move, but he had lost his braking point and left his tyre mark on my fairing. Greg apologised to me straightaway – it was one of those things,' shrugged Haslam, who came home less than a quarter of a second from victory.

With Lavilla and Haslam in first and second, that left the final step of the podium open for Kiyo. In race two, Kiyonari fought back and secured the top spot, with Haslam second and Byrne third. Although race two ended with the regulars at the front, it started out with Sykes taking the hole-shot and Hill jumping on his tail – their dash for the front was impressive, but normal service was soon resumed. On the points front, Kiyonari was in second place and homing in on Lavilla. The championship was hotting up as everyone headed to Snetterton, where things would really change.

As the Stobart Honda improved, so did the results. Byrne took a superb pole position at Snetterton and looked set for his first win of the year. Camier, on the other hand, suffered a nightmare in qualifying, a technical problem keeping him off the track and leaving him to start from the back row of the grid. Bad luck was widespread, and for Lavilla, it hit during morning warm-up. The weather conditions had been mixed all weekend, and when he went out in warm-up, he discovered that he had slightly more grip, which caused his forks to bottom out at Sears corner, pushing the front and causing him to crash.

Lavilla only managed a sixth in race one and a very unfortunate DNF in race two. His team manager, Wright, said, 'It was an electrical problem that caused fuel starvation. Obviously, we are all devastated for Greg for the second race.' While Lavilla was having a bad day at the office, Kiyo wasn't. Double race wins were all he needed to take the championship lead, and that is what he delivered.

Byrne also had a disappointing day, with a DNF in race one due to a stone damaging a sensor on his bike, which made the machine think the traction control was on, preventing it from revving. He delivered the goods in race two, however, with a third-place finish. Ride of the day had to go to Camier. He managed to turn his back-row start into two sixth-place finishes. The Bridewell brothers also made an appearance in the top ten; Tommy was tenth in race one, while his older brother, Ollie, took tenth in race two.

It was now time to cross the water to the slowest circuit on the calendar, Mondello Park in the Republic of Ireland. Local rider Rea did the honourable thing and grabbed pole position from his team-mate, Kiyo. Haslam was in third place, while Karl Harris on the Hydrex Honda graced the front row in fourth.

Johnny Rae flies high at Cadwell. After his first win, more would follow.
Photograph: Clive Challinor

Above: **Leon Haslam had a mixed year on the Ducati, but a double at Donington preserved his challenge to the end.**
Photograph: Clive Challinor

Rea was hoping for the win first time out, but it wasn't to be. Haslam took the top step from Byrne and Lavilla in third place. However, the hard riding Ulsterman got what he wanted in race two – his maiden win.

'It feels mega!' Rea said excitedly. 'It's a long time coming, but now it's here, I'm really glad. They say after your first win, it's a bit easier to win again, but we'll just keep our heads down. One win isn't enough really. To do it here at home is a little bit special.'

Although Rea was on a high, the paddock was about to hit a low. Guy Sanders high-sided his Gearlink Kawasaki Supersport bike and was picking himself up off the track when he was hit head on by the oncoming riders. Sadly, he succumbed to his injuries, leaving a huge gap in the paddock and a feeling of shock that resonated throughout motorcycle racing.

As the year progressed, the same could not be said of the Rizla Suzuki team, so it decided to bring in Neil Hodgson to test the Suzuki at Cadwell Park. The rumours started immediately: 'Hodgson to ride for Rizla Suzuki, Walker out!' As it turned out, that wasn't the case, as the team's PR explained: 'All rumours I'm afraid. It started off at World Superbikes at Silverstone. The team owner and the team manager, Simon Buckmaster, met up with Yukio Kagayama. They were quite interested in putting Yuki on the bike just to give us another opinion on it, as he knows the bike very well. It was just to get another opinion and assistance on developing the bike.'

The team went with Hodgson as the next best thing.

Next up was Knockhill in Scotland. No one could have foreseen the wet weather, of almost Biblical proportions, that hit the event. The singular qualifying session was hit by rain, leaving Rea on pole, as no one was able to better his time. Once again, the front row of the grid was littered with newcomers – HM Plant occupied one and two, with Sykes in third and Camier in fourth.

Ahead of race one, the heavens opened, delaying the start. Once under way, Rea dominated, getting the hole-shot and simply pulling away from the chasing pack. He finished 6.848 seconds clear of Kiyo to take his second win on the trot. Haslam was in third place, while his team-mate and early championship leader, Lavilla, languished in seventh place. Just behind him was Ollie Bridewell and the NB Suzuki, who were turning into top-ten regulars.

Race two was similar, Rea disappearing into the distance to pick up his first double and his third win on the bounce. Haslam and Kiyonari joined him on the podium in second and third places respectively. Kiyo almost missed out on third due to a late charge from Sykes. The pair had a drag race to the line, with Kiyo pipping Sykes by 0.055 second. A visibly disappointed Sykes slumped over his tank, his gallant charge for a podium having been thwarted once again.

'I think a podium will be there or thereabouts some time. I just need to keep plugging away and gaining experience, and every time I get more experience, a few more tenths drop off my times,' said Sykes.

Lavilla's championship was going from bad to worse, a crash in race two robbing him of points. He tumbled out of contention just two laps in when he clipped the damp white line. Since Rea pulled in maximum points and Lavilla lost out, Rea took over second place in the championship.

More wet weather hurled itself at the BSB paddock at Oulton Park for round eight. Sykes started on the front row of the grid and did lead for a short time until the chasing pack engulfed him. Lavilla suffered a horrifying start-line crash, falling mid-pack and being run over by an oncoming rider. He crawled off the track, leaving his Airwaves Ducati sprawled across it. This incident brought out the safety car, which bunched up the field.

Rea was doing his best to romp away with the race lead, but a big moment lost him two places. He was still in the running, however, until he high-sided at Druids, allowing his team-mate to stretch the points lead over him. The wet weather played into the hands of the Michelin running Japanese star, and he pulled a magnificent lead of 20.075 seconds over second-place man Shane Byrne.

It had been a tough weekend for Byrne, with numerous crashes ahead of race day. 'It was a difficult race. I've had so little time on the bike, as I keep falling off it! I really wanted a podium,' he said.'

Walker picked up his second podium finish of the year in third. 'We are getting there with the bike; we are still a little bit off in the dry. The boys came up with a good wet set-up, which we tried in warm-up, and it worked,' he beamed.

The second outing for the Superbike boys was equally exciting, but this time, the HM Plant Honda riders experienced a role reversal, Rea taking the win and Kiyo crashing. Like his team-mate in race one, Rea pulled a huge lead, crossing the line 12.1903 seconds clear of Karl Harris in second. He even had time to mimic a pair of binoculars and look behind him as he took the chequered flag. Byrne was in third place. This was the first all-British podium for quite some time, and surprising considering it is the British Superbike Championship! The antics of the Honda team had left the title chase even closer, with Kiyo just 11 points ahead of Rea.

Also joining the top ten in both races was Ollie Bridewell, who was becoming a familiar face there. Following his off in race one, Lavilla delivered a gritty performance in race two, finishing in tenth and salvaging some points.

Mallory Park hosted round nine of the championship, which was morphing into an HM Plant internal brawl, with Kiyo and Rea going head to head. The British weather had a massive impact on proceedings, and heavy rain hit first free practice, the session being reduced to just 20 minutes. During that time, Ollie Bridewell took to the track on his NB Racing Suzuki. He tried to save a high-side, but it didn't work and he was thrown head-on into the barriers at the Esses.

It was a crash that he wasn't able to walk away from. He was treated at the trackside by the medical staff before being transferred to the medical centre. There, he lost the fight for life, leaving the paddock a much sadder place.

The night before, Ollie had been getting up to mischief with his brother, Tommy, throwing water bombs around the paddock and having a good time. Qualifying for race day was abandoned and the grid set from championship points.

Ollie would have been on the fourth row of the grid, a spot that was left open. Circuit commentator Fred Clarke summed up the feeling in the paddock when he said, 'Ollie Bridewell was a welcome breath of fresh air in this all-too-frequently serious world. Very, very rarely to be seen without that engaging smile upon his face. Simply to have been in his company was to gain, a treasured memento. It is a cliché I know, but you will be missed. God bless you Ollie.'

The race weekend continued in a subdued fashion, and the outcome pulled the championship even closer. The race-one winner was Byrne, nailing his first victory of the season. Rea nabbed second place from Haslam, while Kiyonari committed a cardinal sin by crashing out, which handed the title lead to Rea.

Race two saw further drama as Rea made a last minute lunge in an attempt to pass Haslam, which resulted in him burying his black Honda in the barriers, along with his title lead. The second win went to Kiyo, who romped home with it. Haslam took second place, and Byrne stepped on the podium once again.

Croft, in the north-east, was to yield some interesting results for the young riders who were starting to mature. Crutchlow made the biggest impact of the weekend, securing his first Superbike pole position at a circuit he had always claimed to be his bogey track. It was the team's first pole position since Brands Hatch in October 2005 with Haydon. 'Before the session, I had a discussion with Pete Jennings, my chief technician, about what tyres I should use during qualification. I wasn't sure about his idea, but I have to say it worked a treat – my first ever front row is a pole position, and you can't ask for any more than that,' said Crutchlow.

Although that much sought-after podium finish didn't happen for Crutchlow, he was fourth in race one, his highest finish of the year. Another young gun finally stepped on to the rostrum, not once, but twice. Sykes on the Stobart Honda rode two hard races and finished third in both.

'It's great to repay the team with a double podium, and I'm over the moon,' grinned Sykes. 'I got a good start in both races, and in the first race, I realised I had a little bit left and thought about going for second, but it was a bit of a do-or-die manoeuvre, and I didn't want to risk anything.'

Kiyo was thrilled with his double result, saying, 'I am so happy because we have proved we can win in both the wet and dry. In the first race, I got a good start and followed Jonathan until I found a suitable passing point. Once I passed him, I pushed as hard as possible and maintained the gap between us. I am pleased that we have a point's lead going to Cadwell Park, as this is not one of my strongest circuits.'

Rea was also happy to take two second places, but not so pleased about the championship: 'I'm a bit disappointed with the championship scenario, as we were unable to close down the points gap on Kiyo. I gave it 110 per cent, but he was on fire today and definitely had the edge over us.'

With just three rounds remaining, Kiyo was 26 points clear of Rea, and 60 points ahead of Haslam.

The next stop was the challenging Cadwell Park, Honda's home ground. James Haydon made his return, joining the Hawk Colchester Kawasaki team. Kennaugh, who had replaced Haydon at the Virgin team, left after Knockhill, deciding to return to the Raceways Yamaha Superstock team. Haydon managed two

Below far left: Rookie of the year Tom Sykes came of age on the flaming Fireblade, narrowly missing a first win.

Below left: Injury prematurely ended Leon Camier's impressive run.

Below: Former champion Shane Byrne regained momentum through the year.

Photographs: Clive Challinor

Bottom: Former champion Gregorio Lavilla had a torrid season.

Photograph: Martin Lauricello/Cello

Above: **Chris Walker, back from SBK, and Suzuki team-mate Cal Crutchlow form a blue barrier for Michael Rutter.**
Photograph: Clive Challinor

strong results, completing both races in the top ten, and being the first Kawasaki home each time. Returning to his favoured Dunlop tyres seemed to be the key to his success.

Haslam grabbed pole and proceeded to beat Honda at its home track. Meanwhile, Lavilla jumped the start and was given a 20-second penalty. However, he still managed to complete the race in seventh. The battle raged between Rea, Sykes, Haslam and Camier. The lap record tumbled six times during the race, finally being set at 1m 26.911s by Camier.

The race took a dramatic turn for the worse when Camier put a move on Rea at the chicane and it went wrong. The former wasn't committed enough with his move, and as Rea changed direction through the chicane, he clipped Camier's bike, taking them both down. Rea looked furious, but picked up his stricken black Honda. He did return to the action, but it all ended when he tumbled off at Park corner. Haslam took the win from Kiyo, and Sykes slotted into third place once again. With Rea out, Kiyo now had clear 46-point lead over his team-mate, who was just nine points ahead of Haslam.

Rea pulled it back in race two, taking the win from Kiyo, with Lavilla in third place. Camier suffered a huge off over the Mountain and landed badly, dislocating his knee, breaking his femur and cracking his pelvis. Haslam and Sykes took it in turns to run wide, losing several places. In his efforts to regain position, Haslam over-cooked it and crashed at Park corner on the last lap. Rea's win left the points situation thus: Kiyo 388, Rea 347 and Haslam 313.

The penultimate round of the Bennetts British Superbike Championship took place at Donington Park. No one ever could have predicted the outcome. The surprises began in qualifying, when Sykes picked up pole position. He had gained five front-row starts, but this was his first pole. He was hoping it would translate into a win, but his luck was out on that front.

Kiyo could have wrapped up the title at Donington – all he needed to do was pick up a double win. Sounds simple, but as the racing got under way, it was anything but. Haslam took the win from an eventful race one, with Sykes and Byrne in second and third respectively. There was not a single HM Plant Honda on the podium.

Rea looked uncomfortable on his black bike, and he had admitted to having tyre and suspension issues. Haslam nabbed the lead from Rea at the Esses, Rea braked very late into the Melbourne loop and was preparing to slide under Haslam when it all went wrong. His rear tyre started to slide, but then caught, almost high-siding him, and his foot slipped off the peg. As he regained control, he ran straight across the front of Haslam, nearly taking him off. Both rejoined the race, and Haslam wasted no time in regaining the lead, while Rea had to settle for fifth.

Honda was not out of the woods yet, as Kiyo was getting a lot of attention from Crutchlow, who was lining him up for a move at Goddards. Crutchlow dived under Kiyo, but missed a gear, which was just enough to speed him up and cause him to crash, taking Kiyo with him.

Thanks to his fall in race one, Kiyo was absolutely on it in race two. He got out of shape at Goddards while challenging Walker for second place. Once in the lead, he had another moment at Redgate, where he got on the gas early and almost high-sided. He ran wide on to the grass, giving the lead to Haslam and putting himself back to fourth place, behind Walker.

The action was still thick and fast, with Haslam and Sykes squaring up to one another on the last lap. Sykes tried to take Haslam at Goddards, and it was a real drag to the line with Haslam winning by just 0.056 second. This superb double win, and HM Plant's run of bad luck, put Haslam back into contention for the title. After the exciting weekend, the points stood at Kiyo 404, Rea 367 and Haslam 363.

The fight would go to the wire at the Brands Hatch Indy circuit. 'I'm over the moon. To do it at Donington in front of my home crowd… I'm thrilled,' Haslam said. 'It has kept the championship alive for at least one more round, and I have taken a big chunk of points back on Kiyo,' he concluded.

Tommy Bridewell made his return to the track at Donington Park following the loss of his brother, Ollie. Even a 130mph crash at the infamous Craner Curves couldn't stop him. He finished both races in the top 20 saying, 'It's been a difficult weekend at times for everyone, but we needed to get back to doing what we do, and that's to go racing.'

As the fight was heading into the final round, it was Kiyo's title to lose, and everyone else's to gain. Lavilla stormed to pole with the fastest two-wheeled lap of the Brands Hatch Indy circuit, turning a time of 45.19 seconds. He was joined by Sykes, then Rea, with Byrne taking up the last place. This left the other two key players on the second row.

Kiyo needed to finish in the top five to clinch the title, and he did just that, coming home in third. Lavilla took the win from Rea, who had tried to break away at the start, but the Spaniard reeled him in. Sykes, who had hoped for his first win of the year, had a spectacular off on the run on to the Cooper Straight, which left his bike in a ball of flames.

'I am so happy to have won the championship again for HM Plant Honda,' said a relieved Kiyo. 'I feel quite emotional, as we have worked so closely for the last four seasons, and I like this team and championship, so I am very sad to be leaving. Thank you so much to Honda for all of their support, the sponsors, the British fans and everyone who has helped me achieve this. Thank you everyone for a fantastic four years. The British Championship is a very competitive series, and it hasn't been easy, but so much work has gone into this and I am very pleased to have won again.'

With the pressure now off for the title, the battle was on between Rea and Haslam for second place. Once again, the race win went to Lavilla, giving him at least a fairy-tale ending to his tempestuous season. The race was red-flagged after James Buckingham's bike blew on the run through Paddock Hill, spewing oil everywhere.

After the restart, Byrne was running in third place, with Crutchlow in fourth, while Lavilla was picking his way forward to take the lead. Byrne ran out of luck at Paddock Hill on lap 13, when he lost the rear and slid off at high speed into the gravel. This gifted Crutchlow third place and his first podium of the year. Kiyo had to settle for fourth place; after the race, he admitted that he had relaxed a little bit too much.

Leon Haslam didn't have the race weekend he had hoped for and finished in fifth place. With Rea on the podium twice, he secured second place in the championship, giving HM Plant Honda the top two spots.

The 2008 season is shaping up to be a transition year for BSB, with a one-make tyre rule, plus new tuning regulations to curb both performance and costs – all the bikes will be restricted to the same level as current Supersport regulations, while chassis rules remain unchanged. On the rider front, Kiyo is off to World Superbike with Ten Kate, while Rea is joining him in the same team, but in the Supersport class.

GSE has announced that it will not be racing next year unless the BSB organisers allow the new 1098 Ducati to run non-standard pistons. It was thought that the team would switch to World Superbikes, but it cannot find sponsors who want European exposure.

The fall-out from this announcement will have a big impact on the paddock and who goes where. Haslam is tipped to move to HM Plant Honda; Lavilla may well return to Rizla Suzuki, as Walker is out. As for Crutchlow, Sykes and Camier, where they will land is yet unclear.

SUPPORT CLASSES

Michael Laverty and his team-mate, Ian Lowry, dominated the Maxxis Supersport class all season. The Relentless Suzuki team finished on the podium at every round with the exception of the second visit to Oulton Park. There, the spoils were shared by road racing specialist Ian Hutchinson on the Bike Animal Honda and TT legend John McGuinness on the Padgetts Honda.

The only man to challenge the Ulstermen was Dennis Hobbs, team-mate to John McGuinness. Hobbs had been coming on strong all year and pushing both riders hard; unfortunately, he crashed at Cadwell Park and broke his collar bone. He did ride through the pain in an attempt to keep his title fight alive, but it wasn't to be.

Laverty took the title one round early at Donington Park, while Lowry wrapped up second in the championship at Brands Hatch at the end of the year. Hobbs finished in third.

Former British Superbike rider Glen Richards joined forces with Embassy Racing to pick up the Metzeler National Superstock Championship. He had to keep Liverpudlian Steve Brogan on the Teng Tools Honda at bay, as he was his closest rival at the final round.

Hudson Kennaugh on the Raceways Yamaha finished third overall, despite missing several rounds while racing for the Virgin Superbike team. He was still in with a mathematical chance of the title at the last round, but he had set-up issues that put him 16th on the grid and unable to challenge.

The British 125GP Championship was also decided early, Luke Jones on the SP125/KGD Racing machine becoming the new champion at Donington Park. Young Scot Robbie Stewart came home in second place for the KRP team, and Kev Coghlan finished in third place on the UK1 bike. He could well have been second, but suffered a technical problem during the final round at Brands Hatch, which put him out of the race.

Below left: Glen Richards (Yamaha) took victory in the Superstock series.
Photograph: Clive Challinor

Above: Above: Relentless Suzuki teammates Michael Laverty and Ian Lowry dominated the Supersport class.
Photograph: Gavan Caldwell Photography

Left: Luke Jones tied up the 125 championship early.
Photograph: Clive Challinor

MAJOR RESULTS

OTHER CHAMPIONSHIP RACING SERIES WORLDWIDE

Compiled by KAY EDGE

AMA Championship Road Race Series (Superbike)

DAYTONA INTERNATIONAL SPEEDWAY, Daytona Beach, Florida, 10 March, 44.250 miles/71.212km
1 Mat Mladin (Suzuki); **2** Ben Spies (Suzuki); **3** Miguel Duhamel (Honda); **4** Aaron Yates (Suzuki); **5** Tommy Hayden (Suzuki); **6** Jake Zemke (Honda); **7** Jamie Hacking (Kawasaki); **8** Eric Bostrom (Yamaha); **9** Jason DiSalvo (Yamaha); **10** James Ellison (Honda); **11** Roger Lee Hayden (Kawasaki); **12** Matt Lynn (MV); **13** Jake Holden (Suzuki).

BARBER MOTORSPORTS PARK, Leeds, Alabama, 21-22 April, 64.400 miles/103.040km
Race 1
1 Mat Mladin (Suzuki); **2** Ben Spies (Suzuki); **3** Miguel Duhamel (Honda); **4** Aaron Yates (Suzuki); **5** Tommy Hayden (Suzuki); **6** Jake Zemke (Honda); **7** Jamie Hacking (Kawasaki); **8** Eric Bostrom (Yamaha); **9** Jason DiSalvo (Yamaha); **10** James Ellison (Honda); **11** Roger Lee Hayden (Kawasaki); **12** Matt Lynn (MV); **13** Jake Holden (Suzuki).

Race 2
1 Mat Mladin (Suzuki); **2** Ben Spies (Suzuki); **3** Miguel Duhamel (Honda); **4** Tommy Hayden (Suzuki); **5** Aaron Yates (Suzuki); **6** Eric Bostrom (Yamaha); **7** Jason DiSalvo (Yamaha); **8** Jamie Hacking (Kawasaki); **9** Roger Lee Hayden (Kawasaki); **10** Jake Zemke (Honda).

CALIFORNIA SPEEDWAY, Fontana, California, 28-28 April, 66.080 miles/106.345km
Race 1
1 Ben Spies (Suzuki); **2** Mat Mladin (Suzuki); **3** Eric Bostrom (Yamaha); **4** Tommy Hayden (Suzuki); **5** Miguel Duhamel (Honda); **6** Jake Zemke (Honda); **7** Aaron Yates (Suzuki); **8** Roger Lee Hayden (Kawasaki); **9** Jason DiSalvo (Yamaha); **10** Matt Lynn (MV Agusta).

Race 2
1 Mat Mladin (Suzuki); **2** Ben Spies (Suzuki); **3** Eric Bostrom (Yamaha); **4** Tommy Hayden (Suzuki); **5** Jake Zemke (Honda); **6** Miguel Duhamel (Honda); **7** Roger Lee Hayden (Kawasaki); **8** Jamie Hacking (Kawasaki); **9** Aaron Yates (Suzuki); **10** Jason DiSalvo (Yamaha).

INFINEON RACEWAY, Sonoma, California, 19-20 May, 60.320 miles/97.060km
Race 1
1 Mat Mladin (Suzuki); **2** Ben Spies (Suzuki); **3** Miguel Duhamel (Honda); **4** Jason DiSalvo (Yamaha); **5** Jake Zemke (Honda); **6** Roger Lee Hayden (Kawasaki); **7** Tommy Hayden (Suzuki); **8** Jamie Hacking (Kawasaki); **9** James Ellison (Honda); **10** Matt Lynn (MV Agusta).

Race 2
1 Mat Mladin (Suzuki); **2** Ben Spies (Suzuki); **3** Jake Zemke (Honda); **4** Miguel Duhamel (Honda); **5** Tommy Hayden (Suzuki); **6** Jason DiSalvo (Yamaha); **7** Eric Bostrom (Yamaha); **8** James Ellison (Honda); **9** Jake Holden (Suzuki); **10** Jamie Hacking (Kawasaki).

ROAD AMERICA, Elkhart Lake, Wisconsin, 2-3 June, 64.000 miles/102.998km
Race 1
1 Mat Mladin (Suzuki); **2** Ben Spies (Suzuki); **3** Tommy Hayden (Suzuki); **4** Miguel Duhamel (Honda); **5** Jake Zemke (Honda); **6** Eric Bostrom (Yamaha); **7** Roger Lee Hayden (Kawasaki); **8** Jason DiSalvo (Yamaha); **9** Jamie Hacking (Kawasaki); **10** Jake Holden (Suzuki).

Race 2
1 Ben Spies (Suzuki); **2** Jamie Hacking (Kawasaki); **3** Mat Mladin (Suzuki); **4** Aaron Yates (Suzuki); **5** James Ellison (Honda); **6** Jake Zemke (Honda); **7** Jake Holden (Suzuki); **8** John Haner (Suzuki); **9** Eric Bostrom (Yamaha); **10** Dominic Jones (Honda).

MILLER MOTORSPORTS PARK, Tooele, Utah, 23-24 June, 64.200 miles/103.54km
Race 1
1 Ben Spies (Suzuki); **2** Mat Mladin (Suzuki); **3** Jake Zemke (Honda); **4** Roger Lee Hayden (Kawasaki); **5** Miguel Duhamel (Honda); **6** Jamie Hacking (Kawasaki); **7** Tommy Hayden (Suzuki); **8** Aaron Yates (Suzuki); **9** Jason DiSalvo (Yamaha); **10** James Ellison (Honda).

Race 2
1 Ben Spies (Suzuki); **2** Jake Zemke (Honda); **3** Miguel Duhamel (Honda); **4** Mat Mladin (Suzuki); **5** Roger Lee Hayden (Kawasaki); **6** Tommy Hayden (Suzuki); **7** Jason DiSalvo (Yamaha); **8** Aaron Yates (Suzuki); **9** Jamie Hacking (Kawasaki); **10** Luca Scassa (MV Agusta).

MAZDA RACEWAY LAGUNA SECA, Monterey, California, 22 July, 61.600 miles/98.560km.
1 Ben Spies (Suzuki); **2** Mat Mladin (Suzuki); **3** Aaron Yates (Suzuki); **4** Miguel Duhamel (Honda); **5** Neil Hodgson (Honda); **6** Jamie Hacking (Kawasaki); **7** Jason DiSalvo (Yamaha); **8** Jake Holden (Suzuki); **9** Eric Bostrom (Yamaha); **10** James Ellison (Honda).

MID-OHIO SPORTS CAR COURSE, Lexington, Ohio, 4-5 August, 62.400 miles/99.840km.
Race 1
1 Mat Mladin (Suzuki); **2** Ben Spies (Suzuki); **3** Miguel Duhamel (Honda); **4** Aaron Yates (Suzuki); **5** Roger Lee Hayden (Kawasaki); **6** Eric Bostrom (Yamaha); **7** Jason DiSalvo (Yamaha); **8** Jake Zemke (Honda); **9** Tommy Hayden (Suzuki); **10** James Ellison (Honda).

Race 2
1 Mat Mladin (Suzuki); **2** Ben Spies (Suzuki); **3** Jamie Hacking (Kawasaki); **4** Aaron Yates (Suzuki); **5** Jake Zemke (Honda); **6** Miguel Duhamel (Honda); **7** Eric Bostrom (Yamaha); **8** Roger Lee Hayden (Kawasaki); **9** Tommy Hayden (Suzuki); **10** Matt Lynn (MV Agusta).

VIRGINIA INTERNATIONAL RACEWAY, Alton, Virginia, 18-19 August, 62.300 miles/99.680km.
Race 1
1 Mat Mladin (Suzuki); **2** Ben Spies (Suzuki); **3** Jamie Hacking (Kawasaki); **4** Aaron Yates (Suzuki); **5** Roger Lee Hayden (Kawasaki); **6** Eric Bostrom (Yamaha); **7** Jason DiSalvo (Yamaha); **8** Jake Zemke (Honda); **9** Tommy Hayden (Suzuki); **10** James Ellison (Honda).

Race 2
1 Mat Mladin (Suzuki); **2** Ben Spies (Suzuki); **3** Aaron Yates (Suzuki); **4** Jamie Hacking (Kawasaki); **5** Tommy Hayden (Suzuki); **6** Jake Zemke (Honda); **7** Luca Scassa (MV Agusta); **8** Matt Lynn (MV Agusta); **9** Jake Holden (Suzuki); **10** Roger Lee Hayden (Kawasaki).

ROAD ATLANTA, Braselton, Georgia, 1-2 September, 63.500 miles/101.389km
Race 1
1 Mat Mladin (Suzuki); **2** Ben Spies (Suzuki); **3** Jamie Hacking (Kawasaki); **4** Aaron Yates (Suzuki); **5** Jake Zemke (Honda); **6** Roger Lee Hayden (Kawasaki); **7** Matt Lynn (MV Agusta); **8** Jake Holden (Suzuki); **9** Luca Scassa (MV Agusta); **10** Ben Thompson (Suzuki).

Race 2
1 Mat Mladin (Suzuki); **2** Ben Spies (Suzuki); **3** Jamie Hacking (Kawasaki); **4** Aaron Yates (Suzuki); **5** Roger Lee Hayden (Kawasaki); **6** Jake Zemke (Honda); **7** Tommy Hayden (Suzuki); **8** James Ellison (Honda); **9** Jake Holden (Suzuki); **10** Eric Bostrom (Yamaha).

MAZDA RACEWAY LAGUNA SECA, Monterey, California, 16 September, 61.600 miles/98.560km.
1 Ben Spies (Suzuki); **2** Mat Mladin (Suzuki); **3** Aaron Yates (Suzuki); **4** Jake Zemke (Honda); **5** Eric Bostrom (Yamaha); **6** Tommy Hayden (Suzuki); **7** Jason DiSalvo (Yamaha); **8** James Ellison (Honda); **9** Jake Holden (Suzuki); **10** Matt Lynn (MV Agusta).

Final Championship Points

1	Ben Spies	652
2	Mat Mladin	651
3	Jake Zemke	468
4	Aaron Yates	465
5	Tommy Hayden	454
6	Jamie Hacking	403

7 Eric Bostrom, 363; **8** Miguel Duhamel, 360; **9** Jason DiSalvo, 359; **10** Roger Lee Hayden, 344.

Endurance World Championship

24 HEURES DU MANS, Le Mans Bugatti Circuit, France, 21-22 April 2007.
Endurance World Championship, round 1. 818 laps of the 2.597-mile/4.180km circuit, 2124.346 miles/3419.240km
1 Suzuki Endurance Racing Team 2, FRA: William Costes/Guillaume Dietrich/Max Neukirchner (Suzuki GSX-R1000), 24h 01m 40.609s, 88.423mph/142.303km/h.
2 Suzuki Endurance Racing Team 1, FRA: Vincent Philippe/Julien Da Costa/Matthieu Lagrive (Suzuki GSX-R1000), 818 laps; **3** Kawasaki Motor France, FRA: Steve Plater/Julian Mazuecos/Gwen Giabbani (Kawasaki ZX10R), 817; **4** Yamaha GMT 94, FRA: Sébastien Gimbert/David Checa/Olivier Four (Yamaha YZF-R1), 811; **5** Yamaha Austria Racing Team, AUT: Igor Jerman/Sébastien Scarnato/Damian Cudlin (Yamaha YZF-R1), 810; **6** Junior Team Suzuki LMS, FRA: Freddy Foray/Emeric Jonchiere/Anthony Delhalle (Suzuki GSX-R1000), 795; **7** Acropolis Moto Expert, FRA: Jakub Smrz/Christophe Cogan/Stefan Nebel (Yamaha YZF-R1), 791; **8** Team LTG 57, FRA: Anthony Moreno/Mickael Lalevee/Anthony Dos Santos (Yamaha YZF R-1), 788; **9** Yamaha Phase One Endurance, GBR: Warwick Nowland/Glen Richards/Didier van Keymeulen (Yamaha YZF-R1), 788; **10** Team 18 Sapeurs Pompiers, FRA: Stéphane Molinier/Guillaume Pialoux/David Brière (Suzuki GSX-R1000), 787; **11** Jadoul Motorsport, BEL: Didier Jadoul/Gregory Fastre/Denny Lannoo (Kawasaki ZX10R), 782; **12** Select Machines, FRA: Jocelyn Henry/Emmanuel Parisse/Jerome Gueno (Honda CBR1000RR), 780; **13** Team Zone Rouge, BEL: Oliver Depoorter/Serge Fischer/Patrick Marey (Yamaha YZF-R1), 779; **14** 3D Endurance Moto Center, FRA: Christian Haquin/Emmanuel Labussiere/Baptiste Guittet (Kawasaki ZX10R), 778; **15** Village Motos Honka, FRA: Sami Penna/David Le Bail/Jerome Danton (Suzuki GSX-R1000), 778.
Fastest lap: Kawasaki Motor France, 1m 39.860s, on lap 613.
Championship points: **1** Suzuki Endurance Racing Team 2, 35; **2** Suzuki Endurance Racing Team 1, 28; **3** Kawasaki Motor France, 22; **4** Yamaha GMT 94, 18; **5** Yamaha Austria Racing Team, 15; **6** Junior Team Suzuki LMS, 14.

6 HORAS DE ALBACETE, Albacete, Spain, 5 May 2007.
Endurance World Championship, round 2. 227 laps of the 2.199-mile/3.539km circuit, 499.173 miles/803.353km
1 Kawasaki Motor France, FRA: Steve Plater/Gwen Giabbani/Julian Mazuecos (Kawasaki ZX10R), 6h 01m 27.173s, 82.860mph/133.350km/h.
2 Suzuki Endurance Racing Team 1, FRA: Vincent Philippe/Matthieu Lagrive/Julien Da Costa (Suzuki GSX-R1000), 226 laps; **3** Yamaha Folch Endurance, SPA: David Tomas/Victor Casas/David Fouloi (Yamaha YZF-R1), 224; **4** Qatar Endurance Racing Team, QAT: José Luis Cardoso/Ivan Silva (Kawasaki ZX10R), 222; **5** Bolliger Team Switzerland Kawasaki, SWI: David Morillon/Patric Muff/Horst Saiger (Kawasaki ZX10R), 222; **6** FCC TSR, JPN: Takeshi Tsujimura/Yoshiyuki Sugai (Honda CBR1000RR), 221; **7** Endurance Moto 38, FRA: Erwan Nigon/Julien Millet/Joao Contente Fernandes (Yamaha YZF-R1), 220; **8** Team 18 Sapeurs Pompiers, FRA: Stéphane Molinier/Guillaume Pialoux/David Brière (Suzuki GSX-R1000), 219; **9** Yamaha Austria Racing Team, AUT: Igor Jerman/Sébastien Scarnato/Damian Cudlin (Yamaha YZF-R1), 218; **10** Suzuki Sweden, SWE: Tobias Andersson/Andi Notman/Nicklas Carlberg (Suzuki GSX-R1000), 216; **11** Amadeus X-One, ITA: Paolo Tessari/Will Gruy/Riccaro Ricci (Yamaha YZF-R1), 216; **12** Raffin Motos, FRA: Damien Chene/Stéphane Kokes/Pascal Grosjean (Kawasaki ZX10R), 216; **13** Genous Team, FRA: Alexandre Lagrive/Yvan Genestier/Bruce Rulfo (Suzuki GSX-R1000), 216; **14** Team LTG 57, FRA: Mickael Lalevee/Anthony Dos Santos/Louis Alexandre Tachon (Yamaha YZF-R1), 216; **15** Diablo 666 Bolliger Kawasaki, GBR: James Hutchins/Olivier Ulmann/Alexander Cudlin (Kawasaki ZX10R), 215.
Fastest lap: Kawasaki Motor France, 1m 32.541s, 85.546mph/137.673km/h, on lap 166.
Championship points: **1** Suzuki Endurance Racing Team 1, 48; **2** Kawasaki Motor France, 47; **3** Suzuki Endurance Racing Team 2, 35; **4** Yamaha Austria Racing Team, 22; **5** Yamaha GMT 94, 18; **6** Team 18 Sapeurs Pompiers and Yamaha Folch Endurance, 16.

SUZUKA EIGHT HOURS, Suzuka International Circuit, Japan, 29 July 2007.
Endurance World Championship, round 3. 216 laps of the 3.617-mile/5.821km circuit, 781.272 miles/1257.336km
1 Yoshimura Suzuki with Jomo 34, JPN: Yukio Kagayama/Kousuke Akiyoshi (Suzuki GSX-R1000), 8h 01m 35.077s, 97.338mph/156.650km/h.
2 Team HRC 33, JPN: Tadayuki Okada/Carlos Checa (Honda CBR1000RR), 216 laps; **3** (1st SBK class) FCC TSR, JPN: Yusuke Teshima/Shinichi Ito (Honda CBR1000RR), 215; **4** Yoshimura Suzuki with Jomo 12, JPN: Atsushi Watanabe/D. Sakai (Suzuki GSX-R1000), 215; **5** Moriwaki Motul Racing, JPN: Tatsuya Yamaguchi/Leon Camier (Honda CBR1000RR), 212; **6** Masked Rider Den-O Honda Dream RT, JPN: Kazuki Tokudome/Gaku Kamada (Honda CBR1000RR), 211; **7** (2nd SBK class) Suzuki Endurance Racing Team 1, FRA: Vincent Philippe/Matthieu Lagrive/Julien Da Costa (Suzuki GSX-R1000), 210; **8** (3rd SBK class) FCC TSR Eurosport Benelux, NED: Satoru Iwata/Yoshiyuki Sugai/Heinz Platacis (Honda CBR1000RR), 210; **9** Yamaha Racing 81, JPN: J. Stauffer/Norick Abe (Yamaha YZF-R1), 210; **10** Team Sakurai Honda 71, JPN: Yuichi Takeda/Kazuma Tsuda (Honda CBR1000RR), 209; ... **15** (4th SBK class) Yamaha Phase One Endurance, GBR: Warwick Nowland/Glen Richards/Stefan Nebel (Yamaha YZF-R1); ... 18 (5th SBK class) Bolliger Team Switzerland Kawasaki, SWI: David Morillon/Patric Muff/Horst Saiger (Kawasaki ZX10R), 205; ... 21 (6th SBK class) Diablo 666 Bolliger Kawasaki, GBR: James Hutchins/Alexander Cudlin/Gary Mason (Kawasaki ZX10R), 203; ... 24 (7th SBK class) RMT 21 Racing, GER: Jakub Smrz/Franck Heidger/Henry Meyer (Honda CBR1000RR), 202; 29 (8th SBK class) Endurance Moto 38, FRA: Erwan Nigon/Julien Millet/Joao Contente Fernandes (Yamaha YZF-R1), 201; 34 (9th SBK class) Suzuki Sweden, SWE: Tobias Andersson/Paul Young (Suzuki GSX-R1000), 200; 35 (10th SBK class) Maco Moto Racing, SLO: Tomas Miksovsky/Damian Rowley/Leroy Verboven (Yamaha YZF-R1), 198; 36 (11th SBK class) Yamaha Austria Racing Team, AUT: Igor Jerman/Damian Cudlin/Steve Martin (Yamaha YZF-R1), 198.
Fastest lap: FCC TSR, 2m 09.227s, 100.762mph/162.160km/h, on lap 3.
Championship points: **1** Suzuki Endurance Racing Team 1, 72; **2** Kawasaki Motor France, 47; **3** FCC TSR, 40; **4** Suzuki Endurance Racing Team 2, 35; **5** Yamaha Austria Racing Team, 28; **6** Yamaha Phase One Endurance, 26.

24 STUNDEN VON OSCHERSLEBEN, Oschersleben Circuit, Germany, 11-12 August 2007.
Endurance World Championship, round 4. 905 laps of the 2.279-mile/3.667km circuit, 2062.495 miles/3318.635km
1 Suzuki Endurance Racing Team 1, FRA: Vincent Philippe/Matthieu Lagrive/Julien Da Costa (Suzuki GSX-R1000), 24h 01m 14.798s, 86.520mph/139.240km/h.
2 Kawasaki Motor France, FRA: Steve Plater/Gwen Giabbani/Julian Mazuecos (Kawasaki ZX10R), 893 laps; **3** Yamaha Austria Racing Team, AUT: Igor Jerman/Sébastien Scarnato/Damian Cudlin (Yamaha YZF-R1), 885; **4** Bolliger Team Switzerland Kawasaki, SWI: David Morillon/Patric Muff/Horst Saiger (Kawasaki ZX10R), 878; **5** Raffin Motos, FRA: Damien Chene/Stéphane Kokes/Pascal Grosjean (Kawasaki ZX10R), 871; **6** Diablo 666 Bolliger Kawasaki, GBR: James Hutchins/Alexander Cudlin/Olivier Ulmann (Kawasaki ZX10R), 870; **7** Jadoul Motorsport, BEL: Didier Jadoul/Gregory Fastre/Denny La Undo (Kawasaki ZX10R), 868; **8** Endurance Moto 38, FRA: Erwan Nigon/Julien Millet/Joao Contente Fernandes (Yamaha YZF-R1), 866; **9** RMT 21 Racing, GER: Matti Seidel/Henry Meyer/Marco Apel (Honda CBR1000RR), 860; **10** Racing Team Hepelmann, GER: Hans-Josef Hepelmann/Reinhard Krachter/Oliver Wrede (Yamaha YZF-R1), 854; **11** AM Moto Racing, FRA: Sullivan Hernandez/Pierre Guersillon/Pierre Donischal (Suzuki GSX-R1000), 853; **12** Endurance Moto 45, FRA: Nicolas Jaulneau/Marcel Levrel/Cedric

Louvel (Suzuki GSX-R1000), 852; **13** Maco Moto Racing, SLO: Tomas Miksovsky/Damian Rowley/Leroy Verboven (Yamaha YZF-R1), 840; **14** RT Racing Team & Moto Virus, FRA: Frédéric Jond/Eric Monot/Jean-Luc Devoyon (Suzuki GSX-R1000), 831; **15** Team Fraikin/Pro Bike 25, FRA: Pierre Bergot/Regis Bonjean/Frédéric Demilly (Honda CBR1000RR), 825.
Fastest lap: Kawasaki Motor France, 1m 29.678s.
Championship points: **1** Suzuki Endurance Racing Team 1, 107; **2** Kawasaki Motor France, 75; **3** Yamaha Austria Racing Team, 50; **4** Bolliger Team Switzerland Kawasaki, 42; **5** FCC TSR, 40; **6** Suzuki Endurance Racing Team 2, 35.

BOL D'OR 24 HOURS, Circuit de Nevers, Magny Cours, France, 15-16 September 2007.
Endurance World Championship, round 5. 801 laps of the 2.741-mile/4.411km circuit, 2195.541 miles/3533.211km
1 Yamaha GMT 94, FRA: David Checa/Sébastien Gimbert/Olivier Four (Yamaha YZF-R1), 24h 00m 21.085s.
2 Suzuki Endurance Racing Team 1, FRA: Vincent Philippe/Matthieu Lagrive/Julien Da Costa (Suzuki GSX-R1000), 794 laps; **3** Suzuki Endurance Racing Team 2, FRA: William Costes/Guillaume Dietrich/Max Neukirchner (Suzuki GSX-R1000), 791; **4** Yamaha Phase One Endurance, GBR: Warwick Nowland/Glen Richards/Federico Vallcaneras (Yamaha YZF-R1), 789; **5** Acropolis Moto Expert, FRA: Laurry Fremy/Gregory Fastre/Gregory Leblanc (Yamaha YZF-R1), 782; **6** National Motos, FRA: Frédéric Protat/Daniel Ribalta/Denis Bouan (Honda CBR1000RR), 779; **7** Endurance Moto 38, FRA: Julien Millet/Cyril Brivet/Fabric Auger (Yamaha YZF-R1), 772; **8** Junior Team Suzuki LMS, FRA: Freddy Foray/Emeric Jonchiere/Anthony Delhalle (Suzuki GSX-R1000), 771; **9** Team 18 Sapeurs Pompiers, FRA: Stéphane Molinier/Guillaume Pialoux/David Brière (Suzuki GSX-R1000), 769; **10** AM Moto Racing, FRA: Sullivan Hernandez/Pierre Guersillon/Olivier Ulmann (Suzuki GSX-R1000), 768; **11** Endurance Moto 45, FRA: Nicolas Jaulneau/Cedric Louvel/Nicolas Grilli (Suzuki GSX-R1000), 764; **12** 3D Endurance Moto Center, FRA: Christian Haquin/Emmanuel Labussiere/Baptiste Guittet (Kawasaki ZX10R), 764; **13** Jadoul Motorsport, BEL: Didier Jadoul/Pierrot Lerat Vanstaen/Denny Lannoo (Kawasaki ZX10R), 763; **14** Infini Team Yohann Moto, FRA: Christophe Michel/Marc Fissette/Vincent Bocquet (Suzuki GSX-R1000), 760; **15** RT Racing Team & Moto Virus, FRA: Jean-Luc Devoyon/Frédéric Jond/Eric Monot (Suzuki GSX-R1000), 754.
Fastest lap: Yamaha GMT 94, 1m 42.714s, 96.064mph/154.600km/h.
Championship points: **1** Suzuki Endurance Racing Team 1, 135; **2** Kawasaki Motor France, 75; **3** Suzuki Endurance Racing Team 2, 57; **4** Yamaha GMT 94, 53; **5** Yamaha Austria Racing Team, 50; **6** Yamaha Phase One Endurance, 44.

8 HOURS OF DOHA, Losail Circuit, Qatar, 10 November 2007.
Endurance World Championship, round 6. 222 laps of the 3.343-mile/5.380km circuit, 742.146 miles/1194.360km
1 Suzuki Endurance Racing Team, 1, FRA: Vincent Philippe/Matthieu Lagrive (Suzuki GSX-R1000), 8h 00m 30.281s, 93.015mph/149.693km/h.
2 Yamaha Austria Racing Team, AUT: Steve Martin/Igor Jerman/Damian Cudlin (Yamaha YZF-R1), 222 laps; **3** Qatar Endurance Racing Team, QAT: Ivan Silva/Victor Carrasco/Mishel Al Naimi (Kawasaki ZX10R), 219; **4** Team 18 Sapeurs Pompiers, FRA: Stéphane Molinier/Guillaume Pialoux/David Brière (Suzuki GSX-R1000), 217; **5** Amadeus X-One, ITA: Paolo Tessari/Will Gruy/Riccardo Ricci (Yamaha YZF-R1), 217; **6** Endurance Moto 38, FRA: Julien Millet/Cyril Brivet/Joao Contente Fernandes (Yamaha YZF-R1), 217; **7** Suzuki Sweden, SWE: Tobias Andersson/Paul Young/Andi Notman (Suzuki GSX-R1000), 216; **8** Yamaha Phase One Endurance, GBR: Warwick Nowland/Glen Richards/Steve Plater (Yamaha YZF-R1), 215; **9** Maco Motor Racing, SLO: Patrick Piot/Tomas Miksovsky/Leroy Verboven (Yamaha YZF-R1), 215; **10** Team LTG 57, FRA: Anthony Dos Santos/Amaury Baratin/Cyril Huvier (Yamaha YZF-R1), 214; **11** RT Racing Team & Moto Virus, FRA: Jean-Luc Devoyon/Frédéric Jond (Suzuki GSX-R1000), 214; **12** Raffin Motos, FRA: Serge Fisher/Stéphane Kokes/Pascal Grosjean (Kawasaki ZX10R), 214; **13** Endurance Moto 45, FRA: Nicolas Jaulneau/Cedric Louvel/Emeric Jonchiere (Suzuki GSX-R1000), 212; **14** Eurosport Benelux Nedestaete, NED: Martin Hoogenraad/Mike Velthuijzen/Mario van Vossel (Yamaha YZF-R1), 207; **15** Bolliger Team Switzerland Kawasaki, SWI: David Morillon/Patric Muff/Eric Mizera (Kawasaki ZX10R), 204.
Fastest lap: Suzuki Endurance Racing Team 1, 2m 03.263s, 97.998mph/157.712km/h, on lap 77.

Final World Championship points

1	Suzuki Endurance Racing Team 1, FRA	165
2	Kawasaki Motor France, FRA	75
3	Yamaha Austria Racing Team, AUT	74
4	Suzuki Endurance Racing Team, 2, FRA	57
5	Endurance Moto 38, FRA	55
6	Yamaha Phase One Endurance, GBR	54

7 Yamaha GMT 94, FRA, 53; **8** Bolliger Team Switzerland Kawasaki, SWI, 43; **9** Team 18 Sapeurs Pompiers, FRA, 42; **10** FCC TSR, JPN, 40; **11** Qatar Endurance Racing Team, QAT, 32; **12** Acropolis Moto Expert, FRA, 28; **13** Diablo 666 Bolliger Kawasaki, GBR, 27; **14** Junior Team Suzuki LMS, FRA, 25; **15** Suzuki Sweden, SWE, 25.

Isle of Man Tourist Trophy Races

ISLE OF MAN TOURIST TROPHY COURSE, 2-8 June 2007. 37.73-mile/60.72km course.
Bennetts Superbike TT (6 laps, 226.38 miles/ 364.32km)
1 John McGuinness (1000 Honda Fireblade), 1h 48m 11.17s, 125.550mph/202.053km/h.
2 Guy Martin (1000 Honda), 1h 48m 37.11s; **3** Ian Hutchinson (1000 Honda CBR), 1h 49m 17.33s; **4** Martin Finnegan (1000 Honda CBR), 1h 49m 35.71s; **5** Ian Lougher (1000 Honda CBR), 1h 50m 34.23s; **6** Ryan Farquhar (1000 Honda Fireblade), 1h 50m 54.77s; **7** Adrian Archibald (1000 Suzuki GSXR), 1h 51m 27.25s; **8** Conor Cummins (1000 Yamaha YZF R1), 1h 52m 19.00s; **9** Ian Armstrong (1000 Yamaha R1), 1h 53m 07.65s; **10** Steve Plater (1000 Yamaha R1), 1h 53m 30.84s.
Fastest lap: McGuinness, 17m 38.85s, 128.279mph/206.445km/h, on lap 2 (record).

Pokerstars Supersport TT (4 laps, 150.92 miles/ 242.88km)
1 Ian Hutchinson (600 Honda CBR), 1h 13m 29.11s, 123.225mph/198.311km/h.
2 John McGuinness (600 Honda CBR), 1h 13m 31.95s; **3** Guy Martin (600 Honda), 1h 13m 35.92s; **4** Bruce Anstey (600 Suzuki GSXR), 1h 13m 38.27s; **5** Nigel Beattie (600 Yamaha R6), 1h 15m 03.59s; **6** Conor Cummins (600 Yamaha YZF R6), 1h 15m 10.08s; **7** Ryan Farquhar (600 Kawasaki ZX6), 1h 15m 14.46s; **8** Steve Plater (600 Yamaha R6), 1h 15m 14.93s; **9** Chris Palmer (600 Honda CBR), 1h 15m 15.20s; **10** Ian Lougher (600 Honda CBR), 1h 15m 34.94s; **11** Dan Stewart (600 Yamaha R6), 1h 15m 41.99s; **12** Keith Amor (600 Honda RR), 1h 15m 45.03s; **13** Martin Finnegan (600 Honda CBR), 1h 16m 05.56s; **14** Ian Pattinson (600 Honda CBR), 1h 16m 08.61s; **15** Jimmy Moore (600 Honda CBR), 1h 16m 22.98s; **16** Ian Armstrong (600 Honda CBR), 1h 16m 23.94s; **17** Roy Richardson (600 Yamaha R6), 1h 16m 34.44s; **18** Les Shand (600 Yamaha R6), 1h 16m 51.20s; **19** James McBride (600 Yamaha R6), 1h 16m 51.94s.
Fastest lap: Martin, 18m 05.23s, 125.161mph/ 201.427km/h, on lap 4 (record).

Pokerstars Superstock TT (4 laps, 150.92 miles/ 242.88km)
1 Bruce Anstey (1000 Suzuki GSXR), 1h 11m 56.29s, 125.875mph/202.576km/h.
2 John McGuinness (1000 Honda Fireblade), 1h 12m 36.59s; **3** Ian Hutchinson (1000 Honda CBR), 1h 12m 58.91s; **4** Martin Finnegan (1000 MV Agusta), 1h 13m 18.61s; **5** Conor Cummins (1000 Yamaha YZF R1), 1h 14m 00.26s; **6** Mark Parrett (1000 Yamaha R1), 1h 14m 03.65s; **7** James McBride (1000 Yamaha R1), 1h 14m 21.17s; **8** Ian Pattinson (1000 Suzuki GSXR), 1h 14m 24.54s; **9** Gary Carswell (1000 Suzuki GSXR), 1h 14m 51.91s; **10** Dan Stewart (1000 Yamaha R1), 1h 14m 53.32s; **11** Ian Armstrong (1000 Suzuki GSX K7), 1h 15m 03.51s; **12** Gary Johnson (1000 Yamaha R1), 1h 15m 16.11s; **13** Nigel Beattie (1000 Yamaha R1), 1h 15m 21.68s; **14** Ian Lougher (1000 Honda CBR), 1h 15m 28.81s; **15** Steve Plater (1000 Yamaha R1), 1h 15m 30.20s.
Fastest lap: Anstey, 17m 37.85s, 128.400mph/ 206.640km/h, on lap 2 (record).

Pokerstars Senior TT (6 laps, 226.38 miles/ 364.32km)
1 John McGuinness (1000 Honda Fireblade), 1h 46m 44.23s, 127.255mph/204.797km/h.
2 Guy Martin (1000 Honda), 1h 47m 16.96s; **3** Ian Hutchinson (1000 Honda CBR), 1h 48m 04.60s; **4** Ian Lougher (1000 Honda CBR), 1h 49m 08.12s; **5** Adrian Archibald (1000 Suzuki GSXR), 1h 49m 21.61s; **6** Conor Cummins (1000 Yamaha YZF R1), 1h 49m 47.86s; **7** Steve Plater (1000 Yamaha R1), 1h 50m 21.67s; **8** Michael Rutter (1000 Kawasaki ZX10 R), 1h 50m 42.22s; **9** Ian Armstrong (1000 Yamaha R1), 1h 51m 56.08s; **10** James McBride (1000 Yamaha R1), 1h 51m 59.14s.
Fastest lap: McGuinness, 17m 21.99s, 130.354mph/209.784km/h, on lap 2 (record).

Bavaria Sidecar TT: Race A (3 laps, 113.19 miles/ 182.16km)
1 Dave Molyneux/Rick Long (600 Honda CBR), 1h 00m 49.06s, 111.668mph/179.712km/h.
2 John Holden/Andrew Winkle (600 Suzuki K6), 1h 00m 55.56s; **3** Steve Norbury/Scott Parnell (600 Yamaha YZF R6), 1h 01m 19.73s; **4** Simon Neary/Stuart Bond (600 Yamaha R6), 1h 01m 43.11s; **5** Allan Schofield/Peter Founds (600 Suzuki K6), 1h 01m 44.97s; **6** Nigel Connole/Jamie Winn (600 Honda RR), 1h 02m 20.23s; **7** Conrad Harrison/Kerry Williams (600 Honda CBR RR), 1h 02m 32.54s; **8** Tony Elmer/Darren Marshall (600 Yamaha R6), 1h 02m 49.49s; **9** Glyn Jones/Chris Lake (600 Honda RR), 1h 03m 18.12s; **10** Andy Laidlow/Patrick Farrance (600 Suzuki GSXR), 1h 03m 20.19s; **11** Gary Bryan/Ivan Murray (600 Yamaha R6), 1h 03m 30.66s; **12** Roy Hanks/Dave Wells (600 Suzuki K6), 1h 03m 48.57s.
Fastest lap: Molyneux/Long, 20m 04.83s, 112.736mph/181.431km/h, on lap 3.

Bavaria Sidecar TT: Race B (3 laps, 113.19 miles/ 182.16km)
1 Dave Molyneux/Rick Long (600 Honda CBR), 59m 39.11s, 113.851mph/183.225km/h.
2 John Holden/Andrew Winkle (600 Suzuki K6), 1h 00m 05.26s; **3** Steve Norbury/Scott Parnell (600 Yamaha YZF R6), 1h 01m 07.80s; **4** Simon Neary/Stuart Bond (600 Yamaha R6), 1h 01m 21.70s; **5** Allan Schofield/Peter Founds (600 Suzuki K6), 1h 01m 44.80s; **6** Nigel Connole/Jamie Winn (600 Honda RR), 1h 01m 49.55s; **7** Conrad Harrison/Kerry Williams (600 Honda CBR RR), 1h 02m 01.81s; **8** Glyn Jones/Chris Lake (600 Honda RR), 1h 02m 35.84s; **9** Tony Elmer/Darren Marshall (600 Yamaha R6), 1h 02m 37.52s.
Fastest lap: Nick Crowe/Dan Sayle (600 Honda RR), 19m 24.24s, 116.667mph/187.757km/h, on lap 2 (record).

British Championships

BRANDS HATCH GRAND PRIX CIRCUIT, 9 April 2007. 2.301-mile/3.703km circuit.
Bennetts British Superbike Championship, rounds 1 and 2
Race 1 (20 laps, 46.020 miles/74.060km)
1 Gregorio Lavilla (Ducati), 28m 56.903s, 95.38mph/153.50km/h.
2 Leon Camier (Honda); **3** Jonathan Rea (Honda); **4** Shane Byrne (Honda); **5** Chris Walker (Suzuki); **6** Leon Haslam (Ducati); **7** Tom Sykes (Honda); **8** Ryuichi Kiyonari (Honda); **9** Tommy Hill (Yamaha); **10** Michael Rutter (Kawasaki); **11** Simon Andrews (Yamaha); **12** Tommy Bridewell (Suzuki); **13** Cal Crutchlow (Suzuki); **14** Karl Harris (Honda); **15** Peter Hickman (Kawasaki).
Fastest lap: Lavilla, 1m 25.724s, 96.63mph/ 155.51km/h (record).

Race 2 (21 laps, 48.321 miles/77.763km)
1 Gregorio Lavilla (Ducati), 31m 09.132s, 93.07mph/149.78km/h.
2 Jonathan Rea (Honda); **3** Leon Camier (Honda); **4** Leon Haslam (Ducati); **5** Tom Sykes (Honda); **6** Karl Harris (Honda); **7** Michael Rutter (Kawasaki); **8** Chris Walker (Suzuki); **9** Simon Andrews (Yamaha); **10** Dean Thomas (Suzuki); **11** Ryuichi Kiyonari (Honda); **12** Peter Hickman (Kawasaki); **13** Shane Byrne (Honda); **14** Steve Plater (Yamaha); **15** Ollie Bridewell (Suzuki).
Fastest lap: Rea, 1m 25.755s, 96.59mph/ 155.45 km/h.
Championship points: **1** Lavilla, 50; **2** Camier and Rea, 36; **4** Haslam, 23; **5** Sykes, 20; **6** Walker, 19.

Maxxis British Supersport Championship, round 1 (8 laps, 18.408 miles/29.624km)
1 Michael Laverty (Suzuki), 13m 01.199s, 84.83mph/136.52km/h.
2 Jamie Robinson (Honda); **3** Ian Lowry (Suzuki); **4** Aaron Walker (Honda); **5** Stuart Easton (Kawasaki); **6** John McGuinness (Honda); **7** Richard Cooper (Yamaha); **8** Steven Neate (Honda); **9** Ian Hutchinson (Honda); **10** James Westmoreland (Honda); **11** Daniel Cooper (Honda); **12** Sam Owens (Honda); **13** Craig Fitzpatrick (Yamaha); **14** Jack Kennedy (Honda); **15** Ben Wylie (Yamaha).
Fastest lap: Billy McConnell (Yamaha), 1m 29.865s, 92.18mph/148.35km/h.
Championship points: **1** Laverty, 25; **2** Robinson, 20; **3** Lowry, 16; **4** Walker, 13; **5** Easton, 11; **6** McGuinness, 10.

British 125GP Championship, round 1 (15 laps, 34.515 miles/55.545km)
1 Ashley Beech (Honda), 23m 56.432s, 86.50mph/139.21 km/h.
2 Kev Coghlan (Honda); **3** Anthony Rogers (Honda); **4** Robbie Stewart (Honda); **5** Luke Mossey (Honda); **6** Luke Jones (Honda); **7** Matthew Hoyle (Honda); **8** Deane Brown (Honda); **9** Nikki Coates (Honda); **10** Tom Hayward (Honda); **11** Michael Wilcox (Honda); **12** James Ford (Honda); **13** Lee Costello (Honda); **14** Jenny Tinmouth (Honda); **15** Rhys Moller (Honda).
Fastest lap: Coghlan, 1m 34.610s, 87.55mph/ 140.90km/h.
Championship points: **1** Beech, 25; **2** Coghlan, 20; **3** Rogers, 16; **4** Stewart, 13; **5** Mossey, 11; **6** Jones, 10.

THRUXTON CIRCUIT, 15 April 2007. 2.356-mile/ 3.792km circuit.
Bennetts British Superbike Championship, rounds 3 and 4 (2 x 22 laps, 51.832 miles/ 83.424km)
Race 1
1 Gregorio Lavilla (Ducati), 27m 52.872s, 106.45mph/171.31km/h.
2 Leon Camier (Honda); **3** Ryuichi Kiyonari (Honda); **4** Shane Byrne (Honda); **5** Tom Sykes (Honda); **6** Leon Haslam (Ducati); **7** Cal Crutchlow (Suzuki); **8** Tommy Hill (Yamaha); **9** Chris Walker (Suzuki); **10** Karl Harris (Honda); **11** Michael Rutter (Kawasaki); **12** Peter Hickman (Kawasaki); **13** Steve Plater (Yamaha); **14** Scott Smart (Kawasaki); **15** Tommy Bridewell (Suzuki).
Fastest lap: Lavilla, 1m 15.114s, 112.90mph/ 181.69km/h.

Race 2
1 Gregorio Lavilla (Ducati), 29m 01.593s, 107.12mph/172.39km/h.
2 Ryuichi Kiyonari (Honda); **3** Shane Byrne (Honda); **4** Jonathan Rea (Honda); **5** Leon Camier (Honda); **6** Leon Haslam (Ducati); **7** Tom Sykes (Honda); **8** Michael Rutter (Kawasaki); **9** Karl Harris (Honda); **10** Tommy Hill (Yamaha); **11** Scott Smart (Kawasaki); **12** Peter Hickman (Kawasaki); **13** Steve Plater (Yamaha); **14** Cameron Donald (Honda); **15** Guy Martin (Honda).
Fastest lap: Byrne, 1m 15.382s, 112.50mph/ 181.05km/h.
Championship points: **1** Lavilla, 100; **2** Camier, 67; **3** Kiyonari and Rea, 49; **5** Byrne, 45; **6** Haslam, 43.

Maxxis British Supersport Championship, round 2 (20 laps, 47.120 miles/75.840km)
1 Michael Laverty (Suzuki), 26m 12.443s, 107.86mph/173.58km/h.
2 Jamie Robinson (Honda); **3** Billy McConnell (Yamaha); **4** James Westmoreland (Honda); **5** Stuart Easton (Kawasaki); **6** Ian Hutchinson

(Honda); **7** Martin Jessopp (Ducati); **8** Daniel Cooper (Honda); **9** Jack Kennedy (Honda); **10** Alex Lowes (Honda); **11** Guy Sanders (Kawasaki); **12** Aaron Walker (Honda); **13** Ben Wylie (Yamaha); **14** Paul Young (Triumph); **15** Craig Fitzpatrick (Yamaha).
Fastest lap: Laverty, 1m 17.835s, 108.95mph/175.34 km/h.
Championship points: **1** Laverty, 50; **2** Robinson, 40; **3** Easton, 22; **4** Westmoreland, 19; **5** Hutchinson and Walker, 17.

British 125GP Championship, round 2 (16 laps, 37.696 miles/60.672km)
1 Luke Mossey (Honda), 22m 06.118s, 102.32mph/164.67km/h.
2 Luke Jones (Honda); **3** Kev Coghlan (Honda); **4** Nikki Coates (Honda); **5** Ashley Beech (Honda); **6** Michael Wilcox (Honda); **7** James Ford (Honda); **8** Jenny Tinmouth (Honda); **9** Lee Costello (Honda); **10** Michael Hill (Honda); **11** Alec Wright (Honda); **12** Ian Stanford (Honda); **13** Sam Neate (Honda); **14** Luke Hinton (Honda); **15** Tim Hastings (Honda).
Fastest lap: Coates, 1m 21.037s, 104.70mph/168.50km/h.
Championship points: **1** Beech, Coghlan and Mossey, 36; **4** Jones, 30; **5** Coates, 20; **6** Rogers, 16.

SILVERSTONE INTERNATIONAL CIRCUIT, 29 April 2007. 2.213-mile/3.561km circuit.
Bennetts British Superbike Championship, rounds 5 and 6
Race 1 (20 laps, 44.260 miles/71.220km)
1 Ryuichi Kiyonari (Honda), 28m 49.500s, 92.12mph/148.25km/h.
2 Jonathan Rea (Honda); **3** Chris Walker (Suzuki); **4** Leon Camier (Honda); **5** Gregorio Lavilla (Ducati); **6** Leon Haslam (Ducati); **7** Tom Sykes (Honda); **8** Tommy Hill (Yamaha); **9** Karl Harris (Honda); **10** Michael Rutter (Kawasaki); **11** Cal Crutchlow (Suzuki); **12** Tommy Bridewell (Suzuki); **13** Ollie Bridewell (Suzuki); **14** Dean Thomas (Suzuki); **15** James Haydon (Yamaha).
Fastest lap: Lavilla, 1m 25.645s, 93.01mph/149.68km/h.

Race 2 (13 laps, 28.769 miles/46.293km)
1 Ryuichi Kiyonari (Honda), 18m 37.312s, 92.68mph/149.15km/h.
2 Gregorio Lavilla (Ducati); **3** Jonathan Rea (Honda); **4** Chris Walker (Suzuki); **5** Leon Haslam (Ducati); **6** Tom Sykes (Honda); **7** Cal Crutchlow (Suzuki); **8** Tommy Hill (Yamaha); **9** Michael Rutter (Kawasaki); **10** Tommy Bridewell (Suzuki); **11** Ollie Bridewell (Suzuki); **12** Karl Harris (Honda); **13** Dean Thomas (Suzuki); **14** Scott Smart (Kawasaki); **15** Guy Martin (Honda).
Fastest lap: Lavilla, 1m 25.377s, 93.30mph/150.15km/h (record).
Championship points: **1** Lavilla, 131; **2** Kiyonari, 99; **3** Rea, 85; **4** Camier, 80; **5** Haslam, 64; **6** Sykes, 59.

Maxxis British Supersport Championship, round 3 (18 laps, 39.834 miles/64.098km)
1 Dennis Hobbs (Honda), 27m 36.571s, 86.55mph/139.29km/h.
2 Ian Lowry (Suzuki); **3** Michael Laverty (Suzuki); **4** Ian Hutchinson (Honda); **5** Tom Grant (Yamaha); **6** John McGuinness (Honda); **7** Billy McConnell (Yamaha); **8** Martin Jessopp (Ducati); **9** Stuart Easton (Kawasaki); **10** Richard Cooper (Yamaha); **11** Sam Owens (Honda); **12** Jack Kennedy (Honda); **13** James Westmoreland (Honda); **14** Guy Sanders (Kawasaki); **15** James Hillier (Kawasaki).
Fastest lap: McConnell, 1m 29.117s, 89.39mph/143.86km/h.
Championship points: **1** Laverty, 66; **2** Robinson, 40; **3** Lowry, 36; **4** Hutchinson, 30; **5** Easton, 29; **6** Hobbs and McConnell, 25.

British 125GP Championship, round 3 (15 laps, 33.195 miles/53.415km)
1 Luke Jones (Honda), 23m 51.054s, 83.50mph/134.38km/h.
2 Kev Coghlan (Honda); **3** Ashley Beech (Honda); **4** Nikki Coates (Honda); **5** Tom Hayward (Honda); **6** Michael Wilcox (Honda); **7** Scott Rogers (Honda); **8** James Ford (Honda); **9** Alec Wright (Honda); **10** Jonathan Lodge (Honda); **11** Luke Hinton (Honda); **12** Michael Smith (Honda); **13** Michael Hill (Honda); **14** Sam Neate (Honda); **15** Ian Stanford (Honda).
Fastest lap: Luke Mossey (Aprilia), 1m 34.024s, 84.72mph/136.34km/h.
Championship points: **1** Coghlan, 56; **2** Jones, 55; **3** Beech, 52; **4** Mossey, 36; **5** Coates, 33; **6** Wilcox, 25.

OULTON PARK INTERNATIONAL, 7 May 2007. 2.692-mile/4.332km circuit.
Bennetts British Superbike Championship, rounds 7 and 8 (2 x 17 laps, 45.764 miles/73.644km)
Race 1
1 Gregorio Lavilla (Ducati), 27m 29.245s, 99.89mph/160.76km/h.
2 Leon Haslam (Ducati); **3** Ryuichi Kiyonari (Honda); **4** Jonathan Rea (Honda); **5** Tom Sykes (Honda); **6** Shane Byrne (Honda); **7** Cal Crutchlow (Suzuki); **8** Leon Camier (Honda); **9** Karl Harris (Honda); **10** Tommy Hill (Yamaha); **11** Scott Smart (Kawasaki); **12** Simon Andrews (Yamaha); **13** Ollie Bridewell (Suzuki); **14** Tommy Bridewell (Suzuki); **15** Michael Rutter (Kawasaki).
Fastest lap: Byrne, 1m 36.206s, 100.73mph/162.10km/h.

Race 2
1 Ryuichi Kiyonari (Honda), 27m 33.097s, 99.65mph/160.37km/h.
2 Leon Haslam (Ducati); **3** Shane Byrne (Honda); **4** Gregorio Lavilla (Ducati); **5** Jonathan Rea (Honda); **6** Tom Sykes (Honda); **7** Tommy Hill (Yamaha); **8** Leon Camier (Honda); **9** Chris Walker (Suzuki); **10** Dean Thomas (Suzuki); **11** Ollie Bridewell (Suzuki); **12** Tommy Bridewell (Suzuki); **13** Michael Rutter (Kawasaki); **14** Simon Andrews (Yamaha); **15** Chris Martin (Honda).
Fastest lap: Rea, 1m 35.479s, 101.49mph/163.33km/h.
Championship points: **1** Lavilla, 169; **2** Kiyonari, 140; **3** Rea, 109; **4** Haslam, 104; **5** Camier, 96; **6** Sykes, 80.

Maxxis British Supersport Championship, round 4 (16 laps, 43.072 miles/69.312km)
1 Dennis Hobbs (Honda), 26m 52.676s, 96.14mph/154.72km/h.
2 Ian Lowry (Suzuki); **3** Michael Laverty (Suzuki); **4** Guy Sanders (Kawasaki); **5** John McGuinness (Honda); **6** Tom Grant (Yamaha); **7** Sam Owens (Honda); **8** Paul Young (Triumph); **9** Jamie Robinson (Honda); **10** Stuart Easton (Kawasaki); **11** Guy Martin (Honda); **12** James Hillier (Kawasaki); **13** Steven Neate (Honda); **14** Richard Cooper (Yamaha); **15** Ben Wylie (Yamaha).
Fastest lap: Billy McConnell (Yamaha), 1m 39.939s, 96.96mph/156.04km/h.
Championship points: **1** Laverty, 82; **2** Lowry, 56; **3** Hobbs, 50; **4** Robinson, 47; **5** Easton, 35; **6** McGuinness, 31.

British 125GP Championship, round 4 (14 laps, 37.688 miles/60.648km)
1 Luke Jones (Honda), 25m 10.592s, 89.81mph/144.54km/h.
2 Kev Coghlan (Honda); **3** Luke Mossey (Aprilia); **4** Ashley Beech (Honda); **5** Robbie Stewart (Honda); **6** Nikki Coates (Honda); **7** Michael Wilcox (Honda); **8** Tom Hayward (Honda); **9** Lee Costello (Honda); **10** Stewart Finlay (Honda); **11** Jenny Tinmouth (Honda); **12** Michael Smith (Honda); **13** Luke Hinton (Honda); **14** Matthew Hoyle (Honda); **15** Sam Neate (Honda).
Fastest lap: Mossey, 1m 46.731s, 90.79mph/146.11km/h.
Championship points: **1** Jones, 80; **2** Coghlan, 76; **3** Beech, 65; **4** Mossey, 52; **5** Coates, 43; **6** Wilcox, 34.

SNETTERTON CIRCUIT, 20 May 2007. 1.952-mile/3.141km circuit.
Bennetts British Superbike Championship, rounds 9 and 10
Race 1 (22 laps, 42.944 miles/69.102km)
1 Ryuichi Kiyonari (Honda), 24m 00.140s, 107.33mph/172.73km/h.
2 Jonathan Rea (Honda); **3** Leon Haslam (Ducati); **4** Tom Sykes (Honda); **5** Leon Camier (Honda); **6** Gregorio Lavilla (Ducati); **7** Tommy Hill (Yamaha); **8** Cal Crutchlow (Suzuki); **9** Chris Walker (Suzuki); **10** Tommy Bridewell (Suzuki); **11** Michael Rutter (Kawasaki); **12** Simon Andrews (Yamaha); **13** Karl Harris (Honda); **14** Scott Smart (Kawasaki); **15** Steve Plater (Yamaha).
Fastest lap: Lavilla, 1m 04.730s, 108.54mph/174.68km/h.

Race 2 (24 laps, 46.848 miles/75.384km)
1 Ryuichi Kiyonari (Honda), 26m 56.071s, 104.34mph/167.92km/h.
2 Jonathan Rea (Honda); **3** Shane Byrne (Honda); **4** Tom Sykes (Honda); **5** Leon Haslam (Ducati); **6** Leon Camier (Honda); **7** Tommy Hill (Yamaha); **8** Scott Smart (Kawasaki); **9** Chris Walker (Suzuki); **10** Ollie Bridewell (Suzuki); **11** Aaron Zanotti (Yamaha); **12** Hudson Kennaugh (Yamaha); **13** Dean Thomas (Suzuki); **14** Chris Martin (Honda); **15** Karl Harris (Honda).
Fastest lap: Kiyonari, 1m 04.777s, 108.46mph/174.55km/h.
Championship points: **1** Kiyonari, 190; **2** Lavilla, 179; **3** Rea, 149; **4** Haslam, 131; **5** Camier, 117; **6** Sykes, 106.

Maxxis British Supersport Championship, round 5 (20 laps, 39.040 miles/62.820km)
1 Ian Lowry (Suzuki), 22m 58.589s, 101.93mph/164.04km/h.
2 Michael Laverty (Suzuki); **3** Dennis Hobbs (Honda); **4** Billy McConnell (Yamaha); **5** Jamie Robinson (Honda); **6** Paul Young (Triumph); **7** Guy Sanders (Kawasaki); **8** James Westmoreland (Honda); **9** John McGuinness (Honda); **10** Tom Grant (Yamaha); **11** Daniel Cooper (Honda); **12** Ian Hutchinson (Honda); **13** Sam Owens (Honda); **14** Steven Neate (Honda); **15** Christian Elkin (Honda).
Fastest lap: Lowry, 1m 08.069s, 103.22mph/166.11km/h.
Championship points: **1** Laverty, 102; **2** Lowry, 81; **3** Hobbs, 66; **4** Robinson, 58; **5** McConnell and McGuinness, 38.

British 125GP Championship, round 5 (16 laps, 31.232 miles/50.256km)
1 Robbie Stewart (Honda), 20m 02.838s, 93.46mph/150.41km/h.
2 Michael Wilcox (Honda); **3** Luke Jones (Honda); **4** Kev Coghlan (Honda); **5** Tom Hayward (Honda); **6** Matthew Hoyle (Honda); **7** Rob Guiver (Honda); **8** Lee Costello (Honda); **9** Jamie Mossey (Honda); **10** Jordan Malton (Honda); **11** Sam Neate (Honda); **12** James Maguire (Honda); **13** Jess Trayler (Honda); **14** Rhys Moller (Honda); **15** Ross Constable (Honda).
Fastest lap: Ashley Beech (Honda), 1m 13.946s, 95.01mph/152.91km/h.
Championship points: **1** Jones, 96; **2** Coghlan, 89; **3** Beech, 65; **4** Wilcox, 54; **5** Mossey, 52; **6** Stewart, 49.

MONDELLO PARK, 17 June 2007. 2.176-mile/3.502-km circuit.
Bennetts British Superbike Championship, rounds 11 and 12 (2 x 18 laps, 39.168 miles/63.036km)
Race 1
1 Leon Haslam (Ducati), 30m 02.146s, 78.26mph/125.95km/h.
2 Shane Byrne (Honda); **3** Gregorio Lavilla (Ducati); **4** Jonathan Rea (Ducati); **5** Ryuichi Kiyonari (Honda); **6** Karl Harris (Honda); **7** Leon Camier (Honda); **8** Cal Crutchlow (Suzuki); **9** Chris Walker (Suzuki); **10** Tommy Hill (Yamaha); **11** Chris Martin (Honda); **12** Scott Smart (Kawasaki); **13** Hudson Kennaugh (Yamaha); **14** Dean Thomas (Suzuki); **15** Stuart Easton (Kawasaki).
Fastest lap: Byrne, 1m 39.215s, 78.97mph/127.10km/h (record).

Race 2
1 Jonathan Rea (Honda), 30m 14.164s, 77.74mph/125.11km/h.
2 Shane Byrne (Honda); **3** Gregorio Lavilla (Ducati); **4** Leon Haslam (Ducati); **5** Ryuichi Kiyonari (Honda); **6** Leon Camier (Honda); **7** Tom Sykes (Honda); **8** Karl Harris (Honda); **9** Tommy Hill (Yamaha); **10** Scott Smart (Kawasaki); **11** Ollie Bridewell (Suzuki); **12** Steve Plater (Yamaha); **13** Dean Thomas (Suzuki); **14** Peter Hickman (Kawasaki); **15** Tristan Palmer (Honda).
Fastest lap: Rea, 1m 38.604s, 79.46mph/127.88km/h (record).
Championship points: **1** Kiyonari, 212; **2** Lavilla, 211; **3** Rea, 187; **4** Haslam, 169; **5** Camier, 136; **6** Byrne, 127.

Maxxis British Supersport Championship, round 6 (9 laps, 19.584 miles/31.518km)
1 Dennis Hobbs (Honda), 15m 22.686s, 76.43mph/123.00km/h.
2 Jamie Robinson (Honda); **3** Ian Lowry (Suzuki); **4** John McGuinness (Honda); **5** Stuart Easton (Kawasaki); **6** Tom Grant (Yamaha); **7** Craig Fitzpatrick (Yamaha); **8** James Westmoreland (Honda); **9** Martin Jessopp (Ducati); **10** Sam Owens (Honda); **11** Ian Hutchinson (Honda); **12** Joe Dickinson (Honda); **13** Paul Young (Triumph); **14** Aaron Walker (Honda); **15** Daniel Cooper (Honda).
Fastest lap: Hobbs, 1m 41.039s, 77.55mph/124.80km/h (record).
Championship points: **1** Laverty, 102; **2** Lowry, 97; **3** Hobbs, 91; **4** Robinson, 78; **5** McGuinness, 51; **6** Easton, 46.

British 125GP Championship, round 6 (16 laps, 34.816 miles/56.032km)
1 Nikki Coates (Honda), 29m 46.954s, 70.15mph/112.90km/h.
2 Robbie Stewart (Honda); **3** Luke Jones (Honda); **4** Michael Wilcox (Honda); **5** Anthony Rogers (Honda); **6** Tom Hayward (Honda); **7** Kev Coghlan (Honda); **8** James Maguire (Honda); **9** Lee Costello (Honda); **10** Alec Wright (Honda); **11** Stewart Finlay (Honda); **12** Jenny Tinmouth (Honda); **13** James Ford (Honda); **14** Tim Hastings (Honda); **15** Sam Shorrock (Honda).
Fastest lap: Stewart, 1m 47.810s, 72.68mph/116.96km/h.
Championship points: **1** Jones, 112; **2** Coghlan, 98; **3** Stewart, 69; **4** Coates, 68; **5** Wilcox, 67; **6** Beech, 65.

KNOCKHILL CIRCUIT, 1 July 2007. 1.271-mile/2.045km circuit.
Bennetts British Superbike Championship, rounds 13 and 14
Race 1 (24 laps, 30.504 miles/49.080km)
1 Jonathan Rea (Honda), 21m 28.015s, 85.28mph/137.24km/h.
2 Ryuichi Kiyonari (Honda); **3** Leon Haslam (Ducati); **4** Shane Byrne (Honda); **5** Chris Walker (Suzuki); **6** Tom Sykes (Honda); **7** Gregorio Lavilla (Ducati); **8** Ollie Bridewell (Suzuki); **9** Sean Emmett (Suzuki); **10** Karl Harris (Honda); **11** Cal Crutchlow (Suzuki); **12** Hudson Kennaugh (Yamaha); **13** Tommy Hill (Yamaha); **14** Stuart Easton (Kawasaki); **15** Paul Barron (Yamaha).
Fastest lap: Rea, 52.578s, 87.04mph/140.08km/h.

Race 2 (26 laps, 33.046 miles/53.170km)
1 Jonathan Rea (Honda), 22m 56.710s, 86.43mph/139.09km/h.
2 Leon Haslam (Ducati); **3** Ryuichi Kiyonari (Honda); **4** Tom Sykes (Honda); **5** Shane Byrne (Honda); **6** Chris Walker (Suzuki); **7** Leon Camier (Honda); **8** Karl Harris (Honda); **9** Sean Emmett (Suzuki); **10** Ollie Bridewell (Suzuki); **11** Stuart Easton (Kawasaki); **12** Steve Plater (Yamaha); **13** Hudson Kennaugh (Yamaha); **14** Tristan Palmer (Honda); **15** Marty Nutt (Yamaha).
Fastest lap: Rea, 51.971s, 88.06mph/141.72km/h.
Championship points: **1** Kiyonari, 248; **2** Rea, 237; **3** Lavilla, 220; **4** Haslam, 205; **5** Byrne, 151; **6** Camier, 145.

Maxxis British Supersport Championship, round 7 (20 laps, 25.420 miles/40.900km)
1 Michael Laverty (Suzuki), 18m 53.493s, 80.75mph/129.95km/h.
2 Paul Young (Triumph); **3** Tom Grant (Yamaha); **4** Billy McConnell (Yamaha); **5** Ian Lowry (Suzuki); **6** Martin Jessopp (Ducati); **7** Dennis Hobbs (Honda); **8** Ian Hutchinson (Honda); **9** Keith Amor (Honda); **10** Sam Owens (Honda); **11** Craig Fitzpatrick (Yamaha); **12** James Hillier (Kawasaki); **13** Christian Elkin (Honda); **14** Jamie Robinson (Honda); **15** Joe Dickinson (Honda).
Fastest lap: Robinson, 52.819s, 86.65mph/139.45km/h.
Championship points: **1** Laverty, 127; **2** Lowry, 108; **3** Hobbs, 100; **4** Robinson, 80; **5** Grant, 53; **6** McConnell and McGuinness, 51.

British 125GB Championship, round 7 (16 laps, 20.336 miles/32.720km)
1 Kev Coghlan (Honda), 15m 05.053s, 80.91mph/130.21km/h.
2 Luke Jones (Honda); **3** Rob Guiver (Honda); **4** Michael Wilcox (Honda); **5** Robbie Stewart (Honda); **6** Anthony Rogers (Honda); **7** Lee Costello (Honda); **8** Tom Hayward (Honda); **9** James Lodge (Honda); **10** Alec Wright (Honda); **11** Tim Hastings (Honda); **12** Ashley Beech (Honda); **13** Jenny Tinmouth (Honda); **14** Nikki Coates (Honda); **15** James Ford (Honda).
Fastest lap: Coghlan, 55.061s, 83.12mph/133.77km/h.
Championship points: **1** Jones, 132; **2** Coghlan, 123; **3** Stewart amd Wilcox, 80; **5** Coates, 70; **6** Beech, 69.

OULTON PARK INTERNATIONAL, 15 July 2007. 2.692-mile/4.332km circuit.
Bennetts British Superbike Championship, rounds 15 and 16
Race 1 (17 laps, 45.764 miles/73.644km)
1 Ryuichi Kiyonari (Honda), 31m 03.104s, 88.42mph/142.30km/h.

2 Shane Byrne (Honda); 3 Chris Walker (Suzuki); 4 Leon Haslam (Ducati); 5 Cal Crutchlow (Suzuki); 6 Leon Camier (Honda); 7 Scott Smart (Kawasaki); 8 Tommy Hill (Yamaha); 9 Ollie Bridewell (Suzuki); 10 Guy Martin (Honda); 11 Tristan Palmer (Honda); 12 Malcolm Ashley (Kawasaki); 13 Peter Hickman (Kawasaki); 14 Tom Tunstall (Honda); 15 James Buckingham (Honda).
Fastest lap: Kiyonari, 1m 43.960s, 93.22mph/150.02km/h.

Race 2 (14 laps, 37.688 miles/60.648km)
1 Jonathan Rea (Honda), 24m 33.750s, 92.06mph/148.16km/h.
2 Karl Harris (Honda); 3 Shane Byrne (Honda); 4 Leon Haslam (Ducati); 5 Leon Camier (Honda); 6 Tom Sykes (Honda); 7 Michael Rutter (Kawasaki); 8 Chris Walker (Suzuki); 9 Ollie Bridewell (Suzuki); 10 Gregorio Lavilla (Ducati); 11 Scott Smart (Kawasaki); 12 Tristan Palmer (Honda); 13 Peter Hickman (Kawasaki); 14 Tom Tunstall (Honda); 15 Marty Nutt (Yamaha).
Fastest lap: Kiyonari, 1m 43.501s, 93.63mph/150.68km/h.
Championship points: 1 Kiyonari, 273; 2 Rea, 262; 3 Haslam, 231; 4 Lavilla, 226; 5 Byrne, 187; 6 Camier, 166.

Maxxis British Supersport Championship, round 8 (14 laps, 37.688 miles/60.648km)
1 Ian Hutchinson (Honda), 26m 03.600s, 86.77mph/139.64km/h.
2 John McGuinness (Honda); 3 Jamie Robinson (Honda); 4 Michael Laverty (Suzuki); 5 Billy McConnell (Yamaha); 6 Aaron Walker (Honda); 7 James Westmoreland (Honda); 8 Daniel Cooper (Honda); 9 Dennis Hobbs (Honda); 10 Joe Dickinson (Honda); 11 Ian Lowry (Suzuki); 12 Craig Fitzpatrick (Yamaha); 13 Alan O'Connor (Honda); 14 Gary Johnson (Kawasaki); 15 Grahame Frear (Honda).
Fastest lap: Robinson, 1m 50.143s, 87.98mph/141.60km/h.
Championship points: 1 Laverty, 140; 2 Lowry, 113; 3 Hobbs, 107; 4 Robinson, 96; 5 Hutchinson, 72; 6 McGuinness, 71.

British 125GP Championship, round 8 (8 laps, 21.536 miles/34.656km)
1 Rob Guiver (Honda), 16m 26.340s, 78.60mph/126.49km/h.
2 Luke Jones (Honda); 3 Kev Coghlan (Honda); 4 Stewart Finlay (Honda); 5 Ashley Beech (Honda); 6 Nikki Coates (Honda); 7 Sam Shorrock (Honda); 8 Lee Costello (Honda); 9 Jenny Tinmouth (Honda); 10 Sam Neate (Honda); 11 Tom Hayward (Honda); 12 Connor Behan (Honda); 13 James Ford (Honda); 14 Ross Constable (Honda); 15 Jon Vincent (Honda).
Fastest lap: Guiver, 2m 00.566s, 80.38mph/129.36km/h.
Championship points: 1 Jones, 152; 2 Coghlan, 139; 3 Beech, Coates, Stewart and Wilcox, 80.

MALLORY PARK CIRCUIT, 22 July 2007. 1.410-mile/2.270km circuit.
Bennetts British Superbike Championship, rounds 17 and 18
Race 1 (30 laps, 42.300 miles/68.100km)
1 Shane Byrne (Honda), 28m 21.458s, 89.50mph/144.04km/h.
2 Jonathan Rea (Honda); 3 Leon Haslam (Ducati); 4 Chris Walker (Suzuki); 5 Gregorio Lavilla (Ducati); 6 Tom Sykes (Honda); 7 Tommy Hill (Yamaha); 8 Leon Camier (Honda); 9 Cal Crutchlow (Suzuki); 10 Scott Smart (Kawasaki); 11 Simon Andrews (Yamaha); 12 Dean Thomas (Suzuki); 13 Tristan Palmer (Honda); 14 Peter Hickman (Kawasaki); 15 Chris Martin (Honda).
Fastest lap: Ryuichi Kiyonari (Honda), 55.845s, 90.98mph/146.42km/h (record).

Race 2 (22 laps, 31.020 miles/49.940km)
1 Ryuichi Kiyonari (Honda), 21m 24.315s, 86.95mph/139.93km/h.
2 Leon Haslam (Ducati); 3 Shane Byrne (Honda); 4 Tom Sykes (Honda); 5 Cal Crutchlow (Suzuki); 6 Chris Walker (Suzuki); 7 Gregorio Lavilla (Ducati); 8 Michael Rutter (Kawasaki); 9 Tommy Hill (Yamaha); 10 Scott Smart (Kawasaki); 11 Leon Camier (Honda); 12 Simon Andrews (Yamaha); 13 Karl Harris (Honda); 14 Dean Thomas (Suzuki); 15 Chris Martin (Honda).
Fastest lap: Kiyonari, 55.890s, 90.82mph/146.16km/h.
Championship points: 1 Kiyonari, 298; 2 Rea, 282; 3 Haslam, 267; 4 Lavilla, 246; 5 Byrne, 228; 6 Camier, 179.

Maxxis British Supersport Championship, round 9 (28 laps, 39.480 miles/63.560km)
1 Michael Laverty (Suzuki), 27m 20.538s, 86.63mph/139.42km/h.
2 Ian Lowry (Suzuki); 3 Dennis Hobbs (Honda); 4 Billy McConnell (Yamaha); 5 Ian Hutchinson (Honda); 6 John McGuinness (Honda); 7 Stuart Easton (Kawasaki); 8 Joe Dickinson (Honda); 9 Jamie Robinson (Honda); 10 Tom Grant (Yamaha); 11 Martin Jessopp (Ducati); 12 James Westmoreland (Honda); 13 Daniel Cooper (Honda); 14 Aaron Walker (Honda); 15 Paul Young (Triumph).
Fastest lap: Laverty, 57.518s, 88.25mph/142.02km/h.
Championship points: 1 Laverty, 165; 2 Lowry, 133; 3 Hobbs, 123; 4 Robinson, 103; 5 Hutchinson, 83; 6 McGuinness, 81.

British 125GP Championship, round 9 (20 laps, 28.200 miles/45.400km)
1 Ashley Beech (Honda), 20m 23.312s, 82.98mph/133.54km/h.
2 Luke Jones (Honda); 3 Nikki Coates (Honda); 4 Michael Wilcox (Honda); 5 Lee Costello (Honda); 6 Tom Hayward (Honda); 7 Kev Coghlan (Honda); 8 Rob Guiver (Honda); 9 Deane Brown (Honda); 10 Matthew Hoyle (Honda); 11 Alec Wright (Honda); 12 Robbie Stewart (Honda); 13 Stewart Finlay (Honda); 14 James Maguire (Honda); 15 Sam Neate (Honda).
Fastest lap: Stewart, 59.886s, 84.76mph/136.41km/h (record).
Championship points: 1 Jones, 172; 2 Coghlan, 148; 3 Beech, 105; 4 Coates, 96; 5 Wilcox, 93; 6 Stewart, 84.

CROFT CIRCUIT, 12 August 2007. 2.125-mile/3.420km circuit.
Bennetts British Superbike Championship, rounds 19 and 20 (2 x 20 laps, 42.500 miles/68.400km)
Race 1
1 Ryuichi Kiyonari (Honda), 26m 51.398s, 94.94mph/152.79km/h.
2 Jonathan Rea (Honda); 3 Tom Sykes (Honda); 4 Cal Crutchlow (Suzuki); 5 Leon Haslam (Ducati); 6 Gregorio Lavilla (Ducati); 7 Leon Camier (Honda); 8 Chris Walker (Suzuki); 9 Shane Byrne (Honda); 10 Tommy Hill (Yamaha); 11 Karl Harris (Honda); 12 Simon Andrews (Yamaha); 13 Michael Rutter (Kawasaki); 14 Scott Smart (Kawasaki); 15 Chris Martin (Honda).
Fastest lap: Haslam, 1m 19.898s, 95.74mph/154.09km/h (record).

Race 2
1 Ryuichi Kiyonari (Honda), 26m 51.188s, 94.96mph/152.82km/h.
2 Jonathan Rea (Honda); 3 Tom Sykes (Honda); 4 Gregorio Lavilla (Ducati); 5 Leon Camier (Honda); 6 Leon Haslam (Ducati); 7 Shane Byrne (Honda); 8 Michael Rutter (Kawasaki); 9 Simon Andrews (Yamaha); 10 Chris Walker (Suzuki); 11 Scott Smart (Kawasaki); 12 Dean Thomas (Suzuki); 13 Cal Crutchlow (Suzuki); 14 Aaron Zanotti (Yamaha); 15 James Buckingham (Honda).
Fastest lap: Kiyonari, 1m 19.695s, 95.99mph/154.48km/h (record).
Championship points: 1 Kiyonari, 348; 2 Rea, 322; 3 Haslam, 288; 4 Lavilla, 269; 5 Byrne, 244; 6 Sykes, 203.

Maxxis British Supersport Championship, round 10 (18 laps, 38.250 miles/61.560km)
1 Billy McConnell (Yamaha), 25m 45.686s, 89.08mph/143.36km/h.
2 Dennis Hobbs (Honda); 3 Ian Lowry (Suzuki); 4 Ian Hutchinson (Honda); 5 Stuart Easton (Kawasaki); 6 John McGuinness (Honda); 7 Tom Grant (Yamaha); 8 James Westmoreland (Honda); 9 Paul Young (Triumph); 10 Aaron Walker (Honda); 11 Alex Lowes (Honda); 12 Jack Kennedy (Honda); 13 James Hillier (Kawasaki); 14 Pauli Pekkanen (Triumph); 15 Martin Jessopp (Ducati).
Fastest lap: McConnell, 1m 22.689s, 92.51mph/148.88km/h (record).
Championship points: 1 Laverty, 165; 2 Lowry, 149; 3 Hobbs, 143; 4 Robinson, 103; 5 McConnell, 100; 6 Hutchinson, 96.

British 125GP Championship, round 10 (15 laps, 31.875 miles/51.300km)
1 Robbie Stewart (Honda), 22m 38.629s, 84.46mph/135.92km/h.
2 Michael Wilcox (Honda); 3 Luke Jones (Honda); 4 Matthew Hoyle (Honda); 5 Anthony Rogers (Honda); 6 Lee Costello (Honda); 7 Alec Wright (Honda); 8 Deane Brown (Honda); 9 Rob Guiver (Honda); 10 James Ford (Honda); 11 Stewart Finlay (Honda); 12 Jay Lewis (Honda); 13 Sam Neate (Honda); 14 Martin Glossop (Honda); 15 Ashley Beech (Honda).
Fastest lap: Stewart, 1m 26.613s, 88.32mph/142.14km/h (record).
Championship points: 1 Jones, 188; 2 Coghlan, 148; 3 Wilcox, 113; 4 Stewart, 109; 5 Beech, 106; 6 Coates, 96.

CADWELL PARK CIRCUIT, 27 August 2007. 2.180-mile/3.508km circuit.
Bennetts British Superbike Championship, rounds 21 and 22 (2 x 18 laps, 39.240 miles/63.144km)
Race 1
1 Leon Haslam (Ducati), 26m 21.047s, 89.34mph/143.78km/h.
2 Ryuichi Kiyonari (Honda); 3 Tom Sykes (Honda); 4 Shane Byrne (Honda); 5 Cal Crutchlow (Suzuki); 6 Tommy Hill (Yamaha); 7 Gregorio Lavilla (Ducati); 8 Chris Walker (Suzuki); 9 James Haydon (Kawasaki); 10 Scott Smart (Kawasaki); 11 Michael Rutter (Kawasaki); 12 Chris Martin (Honda); 13 Steve Plater (Yamaha); 14 Dean Thomas (Suzuki); 15 Tristan Palmer (Honda).
Fastest lap: Leon Camier (Honda), 1m 26.911s, 90.30mph/145.32km/h (record).

Race 2
1 Jonathan Rea (Honda), 27m 00.039s, 87.19mph/140.32km/h.
2 Ryuichi Kiyonari (Honda); 3 Gregorio Lavilla (Ducati); 4 Cal Crutchlow (Suzuki); 5 Tom Sykes (Honda); 6 Chris Walker (Suzuki); 7 Tommy Hill (Yamaha); 8 James Haydon (Kawasaki); 9 Steve Plater (Yamaha); 10 Michael Rutter (Kawasaki); 11 Chris Martin (Honda); 12 Scott Smart (Kawasaki); 13 Tristan Palmer (Honda); 14 James Buckingham (Honda); 15 Tom Tunstall (Honda).
Fastest lap: Leon Haslam (Ducati), 1m 26.654s, 90.56mph/145.74km/h (record).
Championship points: 1 Kiyonari, 388; 2 Rea, 347; 3 Haslam, 313; 4 Lavilla, 294; 5 Byrne, 257; 6 Sykes, 230.

Maxxis British Supersport Championship, round 11 (16 laps, 34.880 miles/56.128km)
1 Michael Laverty (Suzuki), 24m 28.062s, 85.53mph/137.65km/h.
2 Billy McConnell (Yamaha); 3 Tom Grant (Yamaha); 4 John McGuinness (Honda); 5 Martin Jessopp (Ducati); 6 Dennis Hobbs (Honda); 7 Joe Dickinson (Honda); 8 Jamie Robinson (Honda); 9 Aaron Walker (Honda); 10 Sam Owens (Honda); 11 Paul Young (Triumph); 12 Ben Wilson (Suzuki); 13 James Westmoreland (Honda); 14 Jack Kennedy (Honda); 15 James Hillier (Kawasaki).
Fastest lap: Laverty, 1m 30.962s, 86.27mph/138.8km/h.
Championship points: 1 Laverty, 190; 2 Hobbs, 153; 3 Lowry, 149; 4 McConnell, 120; 5 Robinson, 111; 6 McGuinness, 104.

British 125GP Championship, round 11 (13 laps, 28.340 miles/45.604km)
1 Robbie Stewart (Honda), 20m 44.172s, 82.00mph/131.97km/h.
2 Ashley Beech (Honda); 3 Luke Jones (Honda); 4 Anthony Rogers (Honda); 5 Kev Coghlan (Honda); 6 Matthew Hoyle (Honda); 7 Deane Brown (Honda); 8 Rob Guiver (Honda); 9 Tom Hayward (Honda); 10 Stewart Finlay (Honda); 11 Sam Neate (Honda); 12 Joe Akroyd (Honda); 13 Jenny Tinmouth (Honda); 14 Connor Behan (Honda); 15 Rhys Moller (Honda).
Fastest lap: Beech, 1m 34.153s, 83.35mph/134.14km/h.
Championship points: 1 Jones, 204; 2 Coghlan, 159; 3 Stewart, 134; 4 Beech, 126; 5 Wilcox, 113; 6 Coates, 96.

DONINGTON PARK GRAND PRIX CIRCUIT, 23 September 2007. 2.500-mile/4.023km circuit.
Bennetts British Superbike Championship, rounds 23 and 24 (2 x 20 laps, 50.000 miles/80.460km)
Race 1
1 Leon Haslam (Ducati), 30m 37.871s, 97.94mph/157.62km/h.
2 Tom Sykes (Honda); 3 Shane Byrne (Honda); 4 Gregorio Lavilla (Ducati); 5 Jonathan Rea (Honda); 6 Chris Walker (Suzuki); 7 Scott Smart (Kawasaki); 8 James Haydon (Kawasaki); 9 Michael Rutter (Kawasaki); 10 Steve Plater (Yamaha); 11 Ian Hutchinson (Honda); 12 Tristan Palmer (Honda); 13 Marty Nutt (Yamaha); 14 Aaron Zanotti (Honda); 15 David Johnson (Honda).
Fastest lap: Ryuichi Kiyonari (Honda), 1m 30.899s, 99.01mph/159.34km/h (record).

Race 2
1 Leon Haslam (Ducati), 30m 35.829s, 98.04mph/157.78km/h.
2 Tom Sykes (Honda); 3 Ryuichi Kiyonari (Honda); 4 Chris Walker (Suzuki); 5 Gregorio Lavilla (Ducati); 6 Shane Byrne (Honda); 7 Jonathan Rea (Honda); 8 Michael Rutter (Kawasaki); 9 Steve Plater (Yamaha); 10 Karl Harris (Honda); 11 Ian Hutchinson (Honda); 12 Aaron Zanotti (Honda); 13 Chris Martin (Honda); 14 Jon Kirkham (Yamaha); 15 Tristan Palmer (Honda).
Fastest lap: Kiyonari, 1m 30.943s, 98.96mph/159.26km/h.
Championship points: 1 Kiyonari, 404; 2 Rea, 367; 3 Haslam, 363; 4 Lavilla, 318; 5 Byrne, 283; 6 Sykes, 270.

Maxxis British Supersport Championship, round 12 (8 laps, 20.000 miles/32.184km)
1 Michael Laverty (Suzuki), 12m 50.920s, 93.39mph/150.30km/h.
2 Ian Lowry (Suzuki); 3 Billy McConnell (Yamaha); 4 John McGuinness (Honda); 5 Aaron Walker (Honda); 6 Sam Owens (Honda); 7 Jamie Robinson (Honda); 8 Joe Dickinson (Honda); 9 James Hillier (Kawasaki); 10 Tom Grant (Yamaha); 11 Craig Fitzpatrick (Yamaha); 12 Steven Neate (Yamaha); 13 Martin Jessopp (Ducati); 14 Daniel Cooper (Honda); 15 Christian Elkin (Honda).
Fastest lap: Lowry, 1m 35.179s, 94.55mph/152.16km/h.
Championship points: 1 Laverty, 215; 2 Lowry, 169; 3 Hobbs, 153; 4 McConnell, 136; 5 Robinson, 120; 6 McGuinness, 117.

British 125 GP Championship, round 12 (15 laps, 37.500 miles/60.345km)
1 Robbie Stewart (Honda), 25m 38.730s, 87.73mph/141.19km/h.
2 Luke Jones (Honda); 3 Louis Rossi (Honda); 4 Ashley Beech (Honda); 5 Valentin Debise (Honda); 6 Anthony Rogers (Honda); 7 Matthew Hoyle (Honda); 8 Lee Costello (Honda); 9 Nikki Coates (Honda); 10 Jamie Mossey (Honda); 11 Tom Hayward (Honda); 12 Sam Neate (Honda); 13 Kev Coghlan (Honda); 14 Alec Wright (Honda); 15 Jenny Tinmouth (Honda).
Fastest lap: Stewart, 1m 41.223s, 88.91mph/143.09km/h.
Championship points: 1 Jones, 224; 2 Coghlan, 162; 3 Stewart, 159; 4 Beech, 139; 5 Wilcox, 113; 6 Coates, 103.

BRANDS HATCH INDY CIRCUIT, 14 October 2007. 1.199-mile/1.929km circuit.
Bennetts British Superbike Championship, rounds 25 and 26
Race 1 (30 laps, 35.970 miles/57.870km)
1 Gregorio Lavilla (Ducati), 23m 35.208s, 91.47mph/147.21km/h.
2 Jonathan Rea (Honda); 3 Ryuichi Kiyonari (Honda); 4 Leon Haslam (Ducati); 5 Cal Crutchlow (Suzuki); 6 Shane Byrne (Honda); 7 Chris Walker (Suzuki); 8 Michael Rutter (Kawasaki); 9 Simon Andrews (Yamaha); 10 Steve Plater (Yamaha); 11 Scott Smart (Kawasaki); 12 Ian Hutchinson (Honda); 13 Marty Nutt (Yamaha); 14 Tristan Palmer (Honda); 15 Tommy Bridewell (Suzuki).
Fastest lap: Lavilla, 45.460s, 94.91mph/152.74km/h (record).

Race 2 (20 laps, 23.980 miles/38.580km)
1 Gregorio Lavilla (Ducati), 15m 22.873s, 93.51mph/150.49km/h.
2 Jonathan Rea (Honda); 3 Cal Crutchlow (Suzuki); 4 Ryuichi Kiyonari (Honda); 5 Leon Haslam (Ducati); 6 Chris Walker (Suzuki); 7 Tom Sykes (Honda); 8 Karl Harris (Honda); 9 James Haydon (Kawasaki); 10 Michael Rutter (Kawasaki); 11 Steve Plater (Yamaha); 12 Scott Smart (Kawasaki); 13 Tommy Hill (Yamaha); 14 Ian Hutchinson (Honda); 15 Tristan Palmer (Honda).
Fastest lap: Lavilla, 45.842s, 94.87mph/152.68km/h.

British Supersport Championship, round 13 (22 laps, 26.378 miles/42.438km)
1 Billy McConnell (Yamaha), 17m 33.977s, 90.06mph/144.94km/h.
2 Dennis Hobbs (Honda); 3 Michael Laverty (Suzuki); 4 Tom Grant (Yamaha); 5 Steve Brogan (Honda); 6 Ian Lowry (Suzuki); 7 Sam Owens (Honda); 8 Jamie Robinson (Honda); 9 James Westmoreland (Honda); 10 Martin Jessopp (Ducati); 11 Daniel Cooper (Honda); 12 Steven Neate (Yamaha); 13 James Webb (Kawasaki); 14 Sam Lowes (Honda); 15 Steve Allan (Yamaha).
Fastest lap: Grant, 47.321s, 91.18mph/146.74km/h.

British 125GP Championship, round 13 (8 laps, 9.592 miles/15.432km)
1 Luke Jones (Honda), 6m 46.057s, 85.01mph/136.81km/h.
2 Robbie Stewart (Honda); **3** Ashley Beech (Honda); **4** Matthew Hoyle (Honda); **5** Tom Hayward (Honda); **6** Nikki Coates (Honda); **7** Lee Costello (Honda); **8** Stewart Finlay (Honda); **9** Deane Brown (Honda); **10** Luke Hinton (Honda); **11** Ross Constable (Honda); **12** Anthony Rogers (Honda); **13** Tim Hastings (Honda); **14** Connor Behan (Honda); **15** Jay Lewis (Honda).
Fastest lap: Stewart, 49.376s, 87.39mph/140.64km/h.

Final British Superbike Championship points

1	Ryuichi Kiyonari	433
2	Jonathan Rea	407
3	Leon Haslam	387
4	Gregorio Lavilla	368
5	Shane Byrne	293
6	Tom Sykes	279

7 Chris Walker, 225; **8** Leon Camier, 199; **9** Cal Crutchlow, 152; **10** Tommy Hill, 138; **11** Karl Harris, 121; **12** Michael Rutter, 118; **13** Scott Smart, 95; **14** Ollie Bridewell, 56; **15** Steve Plater, 51.

Final British Supersport Championship points

1	Michael Laverty	231
2	Ian Lowry	179
3	Dennis Hobbs	173
4	Billy McConnell	161
5	Jamie Robinson	128
6	John McGuinness	117

7 Tom Grant, 103; **8** Ian Hutchinson, 96; **9** James Westmoreland, 69; **10** Stuart Easton, 66; **11** Martin Jessopp, 60; **12** Sam Owens, 58; **13** Paul Young, 56; **14** Aaron Walker, 55; **15** Daniel Cooper, 37.

Final British 125GP Championship points

1	Luke Jones	249
2	Robbie Stewart	179
3	Kev Coghlan	162
4	Ashley Beech	155
5	Nikki Coates	113
6	Michael Wilcox	113

7 Tom Hayward, 92; **8** Lee Costello, 87; **9** Anthony Rogers, 75; **10** Rob Guiver, 73; **11** Matthew Hoyle, 72; **12** Luke Mossey, 52; **13** Stewart Finlay, 46; **14** Alec Wright, 40; **15** Deane Brown, 39.

Supersport World Championship

LOSAIL, Qatar, 24 February 2007. 3.343-mile/5.380km circuit.
Supersport World Championship, round 1 (18 laps, 60.174 miles/96.840km)
1 Kenan Sofuoglu, TUR (Honda), 37m 22.452s, 96.602mph/155.466km/h.
2 Kevin Curtain, AUS (Yamaha); **3** Katsuaki Fujiwara, JPN (Honda); **4** Fabien Foret, FRA (Kawasaki); **5** Pere Riba, SPA (Kawasaki); **6** Robbin Harms, DEN (Honda); **7** Massimo Roccoli, ITA (Yamaha); **8** Gianluca Nannelli, ITA (Ducati); **9** Barry Veneman, NED (Suzuki); **10** Vesa Kallio, FIN (Suzuki); **11** Javier Fores, SPA (Honda); **12** Craig Jones, GBR (Honda); **13** Lorenzo Alfonsi, ITA (Honda); **14** David Salom, SPA (Yamaha); **15** Gianluca Vizziello, ITA (Yamaha).
Fastest lap: Sébastien Charpentier, FRA (Honda), 2m 02.949s, 97.884mph/157.529km/h (record).
Championship points: **1** Sofuoglu, 25; **2** Curtain, 20; **3** Fujiwara, 16; **4** Foret, 13; **5** Riba, 11; **6** Harms, 10.

PHILLIP ISLAND, Australia, 4 March 2007. 2.762-mile/4.445km circuit.
Supersport World Championship, round 2 (21 laps, 58.002 miles/93.345km)
1 Fabien Foret, FRA (Kawasaki), 33m 46.218s, 103.053mph/165.847km/h.
2 Kenan Sofuoglu, TUR (Honda); **3** Broc Parkes, AUS (Yamaha); **4** Sébastien Charpentier, FRA (Honda); **5** Katsuaki Fujiwara, JPN (Honda); **6** Pere Riba, SPA (Kawasaki); **7** Robbin Harms, DEN (Honda); **8** Barry Veneman, NED (Suzuki); **9** Lorenzo Alfonsi, ITA (Honda); **10** Yoann Tiberio, FRA (Honda); **11** Kevin Curtain, AUS (Yamaha); **12** Gregory Leblanc, FRA (Honda); **13** Sébastien Gimbert, FRA (Yamaha); **14** Craig Jones, GBR (Honda); **15** David Salom, SPA (Yamaha).
Fastest lap: Charpentier, 1m 34.976s, 104.692mph/168.485km/h (record).
Championship points: **1** Sofuoglu, 45; **2** Foret, 38; **3** Fujiwara, 27; **4** Curtain, 25; **5** Riba, 21; **6** Harms, 19.

DONINGTON PARK, Great Britain, 1 April 2007. 2.500-mile/4.023km circuit.
Supersport World Championship, round 3 (22 laps, 55.000 miles/88.506km; aggregated result)
1 Kenan Sofuoglu, TUR (Honda), 34m 56.601s, 94.430mph/151.971km/h.
2 Robbin Harms, DEN (Honda); **3** Katsuaki Fujiwara, JPN (Honda); **4** Craig Jones, GBR (Honda); **5** Simone Sanna, ITA (Honda); **6** Davide Giugliano, ITA (Kawasaki); **7** Yoann Tiberio, FRA (Honda); **8** Massimo Roccoli, ITA (Yamaha); **9** David Checa, SPA (Yamaha); **10** Gianluca Nannelli, ITA (Ducati); **11** Sébastien Gimbert, FRA (Yamaha); **12** Gianluca Vizziello, ITA (Yamaha); **13** David Salom, SPA (Yamaha); **14** Barry Veneman, NED (Suzuki); **15** Pere Riba, SPA (Kawasaki).
Fastest lap: Fujiwara, 1m 33.848s, 95.891mph/154.322km/h (record).
Championship points: **1** Sofuoglu, 70; **2** Fujiwara, 43; **3** Harms, 39; **4** Foret, 38; **5** Curtain, 25; **6** Riba, 22.

VALENCIA, Spain, 15 April 2007. 2.489-mile/4.005km circuit.
Supersport World Championship, round 4 (23 laps, 57.247 miles/92.115km)
1 Kenan Sofuoglu, TUR (Honda), 38m 08.523s, 90.039mph/144.903km/h.
2 Andrew Pitt, AUS (Honda); **3** Gianluca Nannelli, ITA (Ducati); **4** Fabien Foret, FRA (Kawasaki); **5** Broc Parkes, AUS (Yamaha); **6** David Salom, SPA (Yamaha); **7** Massimo Roccoli, ITA (Yamaha); **8** Joan Lascorz, SPA (Honda); **9** Vesa Kallio, FIN (Suzuki); **10** Craig Jones, GBR (Honda); **11** Gianluca Vizziello, ITA (Yamaha); **12** Davide Giugliano, ITA (Kawasaki); **13** Lorenzo Alfonsi, ITA (Honda); **14** David Checa, SPA (Yamaha); **15** Sébastien Gimbert, FRA (Yamaha).
Fastest lap: Katsuaki Fujiwara, JPN (Honda), 1m 37.570s, 91.821mph/147.771km/h (record).
Championship points: **1** Sofuoglu, 95; **2** Foret, 51; **3** Fujiwara, 43; **4** Harms, 39; **5** Nannelli, 30; **6** Parkes, 27.

ASSEN, Holland, 29 April 2007. 2.830-mile/4.555km circuit.
Supersport World Championship, round 5 (21 laps, 59.430 miles/95.655km)
1 Kenan Sofuoglu, TUR (Honda), 36m 04.418s, 98.860mph/159.100km/h.
2 Andrew Pitt, AUS (Honda); **3** Fabien Foret, FRA (Kawasaki); **4** Barry Veneman, NED (Suzuki); **5** David Salom, SPA (Yamaha); **6** Sébastien Charpentier, FRA (Honda); **7** David Checa, SPA (Yamaha); **8** Vesa Kallio, FIN (Suzuki); **9** Davide Giugliano, ITA (Kawasaki); **10** Steve Martin, AUS (Yamaha); **11** Lorenzo Alfonsi, ITA (Honda); **12** Pere Riba, SPA (Kawasaki); **13** Simone Sanna, ITA (Honda); **14** Massimo Roccoli, ITA (Yamaha); **15** Arie Vos, NED (Honda).
Fastest lap: Sofuoglu, 1m 42.096s, 99.801mph/160.614km/h (record).
Championship points: **1** Sofuoglu, 120; **2** Foret, 67; **3** Fujiwara, 43; **4** Pitt, 40; **5** Harms, 39; **6** Nannelli, 30.

MONZA, Italy, 13 May 2007. 3.600-mile/5.793km circuit.
Supersport World Championship, round 6 (16 laps, 57.600 miles/92.688km)
1 Kenan Sofuoglu, TUR (Honda), 29m 44.471s, 116.190mph/186.989km/h.
2 Fabien Foret, FRA (Kawasaki); **3** Anthony West, AUS (Yamaha); **4** Gianluca Nannelli, ITA (Ducati); **5** Barry Veneman, NED (Suzuki); **6** Katsuaki Fujiwara, JPN (Honda); **7** Yoann Tiberio, FRA (Honda); **8** Lorenzo Alfonsi, ITA (Honda); **9** David Salom, SPA (Yamaha); **10** Simone Sanna, ITA (Honda); **11** Massimo Roccoli, ITA (Yamaha); **12** Pere Riba, SPA (Kawasaki); **13** Vesa Kallio, FIN (Suzuki); **14** David Checa, SPA (Yamaha); **15** Joan Lascorz, SPA (Honda).
Fastest lap: Sofuoglu, 1m 50.550s, 117.219mph/188.646km/h (record).
Championship points: **1** Sofuoglu, 145; **2** Foret, 87; **3** Fujiwara, 53; **4** Nannelli, 43; **5** Veneman, 41; **6** Pitt, 40.

SILVERSTONE, Great Britain, 27 May 2007. 2.213-mile/3.561km circuit.
Supersport World Championship, round 7 (22 laps, 48.686 miles/78.342km)
1 Anthony West, AUS (Yamaha), 39m 16.245s, 74.375mph/119.695km/h.
2 Robbin Harms, DEN (Honda); **3** Katsuaki Fujiwara, JPN (Honda); **4** Fabien Foret, FRA (Kawasaki); **5** Gianluca Vizziello, ITA (Yamaha); **6** Matthieu Lagrive, FRA (Honda); **7** Javier Fores, SPA (Honda); **8** Lorenzo Alfonsi, ITA (Honda); **9** Julien Enjolras, FRA (Yamaha); **10** Barry Veneman, NED (Suzuki); **11** Miguel Praia, POR (Honda); **12** Sébastien Gimbert, FRA (Yamaha); **13** Jesco Günther, GER (Honda); **14** Gregory Leblanc, FRA (Honda); **15** Joan Lascorz, SPA (Honda).
Fastest lap: West, 1m 44.188s, 76.455mph/123.043km/h.
Championship points: **1** Sofuoglu, 145; **2** Foret, 100; **3** Fujiwara, 69; **4** Harms, 59; **5** Veneman, 47; **6** Nannelli, 43.

MISANO, Italy, 17 June 2007. 2.597-mile/4.180km circuit.
Supersport World Championship, round 8 (22 laps, 57.134 miles/91.960km; aggregated result)
1 Anthony West, AUS (Yamaha), 36m 47.866s, 93.171mph/149.944km/h.
2 Broc Parkes, AUS (Yamaha); **3** Kenan Sofuoglu, TUR (Honda); **4** Massimo Roccoli, ITA (Yamaha); **5** Robbin Harms, DEN (Honda); **6** Simone Sanna, ITA (Honda); **7** Javier Fores, SPA (Honda); **8** Katsuaki Fujiwara, JPN (Honda); **9** Gianluca Vizziello, ITA (Yamaha); **10** Sébastien Charpentier, FRA (Honda); **11** Yoann Tiberio, FRA (Honda); **12** Matthieu Lagrive, FRA (Honda); **13** Barry Veneman, NED (Suzuki); **14** Sébastien Gimbert, FRA (Yamaha); **15** Gilles Boccolini, ITA (Kawasaki).
Fastest lap: West, 1m 39.109s, 94.345mph/151.833km/h (record, new track).
Championship points: **1** Sofuoglu, 161; **2** Foret, 100; **3** Fujiwara, 77; **4** Harms, 70; **5** West, 66; **6** Veneman, 50.

BRNO, Czech Republic, 22 July 2007. 3.357-mile/5.403km circuit.
Supersport World Championship, round 9 (18 laps, 60.426 miles/97.254km)
1 Kenan Sofuoglu, TUR (Honda), 38m 09.132s, 95.036mph/152.946km/h.
2 Craig Jones, GBR (Honda); **3** Fabien Foret, FRA (Kawasaki); **4** Massimo Roccoli, ITA (Yamaha); **5** Joshua Brookes, AUS (Honda); **6** Katsuaki Fujiwara, JPN (Honda); **7** David Checa, SPA (Yamaha); **8** Sébastien Charpentier, FRA (Honda); **9** Sébastien Gimbert, FRA (Yamaha); **10** Barry Veneman, NED (Suzuki); **11** Vesa Kallio, FIN (Suzuki); **12** Jason O'Halloran, AUS (Yamaha); **13** Broc Parkes, AUS (Yamaha); **14** Lorenzo Alfonsi, ITA (Honda); **15** Gianluca Nannelli, ITA (Ducati).
Fastest lap: Sofuoglu, 2m 06.089s, 95.854mph/154.262km/h (record).
Championship points: **1** Sofuoglu, 186; **2** Foret, 116; **3** Fujiwara, 87; **4** Harms, 70; **5** West, 66; **6** Roccoli, 59.

BRANDS HATCH, Great Britain, 5 August 2007. 2.301-mile/3.703km circuit.
Supersport World Championship, round 10 (23 laps, 52.923 miles/85.169km)
1 Broc Parkes, AUS (Yamaha), 34m 34.688s, 91.804mph/147.745km/h.
2 Kenan Sofuoglu, TUR (Honda); **3** Massimo Roccoli, ITA (Yamaha); **4** Robbin Harms, DEN (Honda); **5** Tommy Hill, GBR (Yamaha); **6** Fabien Foret, FRA (Kawasaki); **7** Lorenzo Alfonsi, ITA (Honda); **8** Barry Veneman, NED (Suzuki); **9** Pere Riba, SPA (Kawasaki); **10** Matthieu Lagrive, FRA (Honda); **11** Gianluca Vizziello, ITA (Yamaha); **12** Joan Lascorz, SPA (Honda); **13** Sébastien Gimbert, FRA (Yamaha); **14** Gregory Leblanc, FRA (Honda); **15** Mauro Sanchini, ITA (Honda).
Fastest lap: Parkes, 1m 29.021s, 93.024mph/149.708km/h (record).
Championship points: **1** Sofuoglu, 206; **2** Foret, 126; **3** Fujiwara, 87; **4** Harms, 83; **5** Parkes, 75; **6** Roccoli, 75.

LAUSITZ, Germany, 9 September 2007. 2.650-mile/4.265km circuit.
Supersport World Championship, round 11 (23 laps, 60.950 miles/98.095km)
1 Broc Parkes, AUS (Yamaha), 39m 25.235s, 92.774mph/149.305km/h.
2 Kenan Sofuoglu, TUR (Honda); 3 Matthieu Lagrive, FRA (Honda); **4** Craig Jones, GBR (Honda); **5** Tommy Hill, GBR (Yamaha); **6** David Checa, SPA (Yamaha); **7** Massimo Roccoli, ITA (Yamaha); **8** Joan Lascorz, SPA (Honda); **9** Sébastien Charpentier, FRA (Honda); **10** Barry Veneman, NED (Suzuki); **11** Gianluca Nannelli, ITA (Ducati); **12** Sébastien Gimbert, FRA (Yamaha); **13** Gianluca Vizziello, ITA (Yamaha); **14** Simone Sanna, ITA (Honda); **15** Stefan Nebel, GER (Kawasaki).
Fastest lap: Sofuoglu, 1m 41.946s, 93.584mph/150.609km/h (record).
Championship points: **1** Sofuoglu, 226; **2** Foret, 126; **3** Parkes, 100; **4** Fujiwara, 87; **5** Roccoli, 84; **6** Harms, 83.

VALLELUNGA, Italy, 30 September 2007. 2.554-mile/4.110km circuit.
Supersport World Championship, round 12 (17 laps, 43.418 miles/69.870km)
1 Kenan Sofuoglu, TUR (Honda), 28m 42.956s, 90.713mph/145.989km/h.
2 Craig Jones, GBR (Honda); **3** Joan Lascorz, SPA (Honda); **4** Broc Parkes, AUS (Yamaha); **5** Gianluca Vizziello, ITA (Yamaha); **6** Matthieu Lagrive, FRA (Honda); **7** Arne Tode, GER (Honda); **8** Simone Sanna, ITA (Honda); **9** Sébastien Charpentier, FRA (Honda); **10** Katsuaki Fujiwara, JPN (Honda); **11** Graeme Gowland, GBR (Honda); **12** Vesa Kallio, FIN (Suzuki); **13** Sébastien Gimbert, FRA (Yamaha); **14** Fabien Foret, FRA (Kawasaki); **15** David Checa, SPA (Yamaha).
Fastest lap: Sofuoglu, 1m 40.231s, 91.726mph/147.619km/h (record, new track).
Championship points: **1** Sofuoglu, 251; **2** Foret, 128; **3** Parkes, 113; **4** Fujiwara, 93; **5** Roccoli, 84; **6** Harms, 83.

MAGNY COURS, France, 7 October 2007. 2.741-mile/4.411km circuit.
Supersport World Championship, round 13 (22 laps, 60.302 miles/97.042km)
1 Kenan Sofuoglu, TUR (Honda), 37m 55.892s, 95.381mph/153.501km/h.
2 Broc Parkes, AUS (Yamaha); **3** Craig Jones, GBR (Honda); **4** Gianluca Vizziello, ITA (Yamaha); **5** Tommy Hill, GBR (Yamaha); **6** David Checa, SPA (Yamaha); **7** Joshua Brookes, AUS (Honda); **8** Katsuaki Fujiwara, JPN (Honda); **9** Gregory Leblanc, FRA (Honda); **10** Massimo Roccoli, ITA (Yamaha); **11** Sébastien Charpentier, FRA (Yamaha); **12** Arne Tode, GER (Honda); **13** Simone Sanna, ITA (Honda); **14** Kenny Foray, FRA (Honda); **15** David Perret, FRA (Kawasaki).
Fastest lap: Sofuoglu, 1m 42.740s, 96.040mph/154.561km/h (record).

Final World Championship points

1	Kenan Sofuoglu, TUR	276
2	Broc Parkes, AUS	133
3	Fabien Foret, FRA	128
4	Katsuaki Fujiwara, JPN	101
5	Craig Jones, GBR	94
6	Massimo Roccoli, ITA	90

7 Robbin Harms, DEN, 83; **8** Barry Veneman, NED, 70; **9** Anthony West, AUS, 66; **10** Gianluca Vizziello, ITA, 60; **11** Sébastien Charpentier, FRA, 51; **12** David Checa, SPA, 50; **13** Gianluca Nannelli, ITA, 49; **14** Matthieu Lagrive, FRA, 46; **15** Lorenzo Alfonsi, ITA, 45.